The Antigospel

The Perversion of
Christ's Grace Gospel

Edward Hendrie

"I marvel that ye are so soon removed from him that called you into the grace of Christ unto another gospel: Which is not another; but there be some that trouble you, and would pervert the gospel of Christ. But though we, or an angel from heaven, preach any other gospel unto you than that which we have preached unto you, let him be accursed. As we said before, so say I now again, If any man preach any other gospel unto you than that ye have received, let him be accursed." Galatians 1:6-9.

GREAT MOUNTAIN PUBLISHING

Fifth Edition
Copyright © 2005-2011 by Edward Hendrie
All Rights Reserved

ISBN-13: 978-0-9832627-4-9   (paperback)
ISBN-10: 0983262748   (paperback)
ISBN-13: 978-09832627-5-6   (ePUB)
ISBN-10: 0983262756   (ePUB)

Other books by Edward Hendrie:

Antichrist Conspiracy
9/11-Enemies Foreign and Domestic
Solving the Mystery of BABYLON THE GREAT
Bloody Zion
What Shall I Do to Inherit Eternal Life?

Available at: www.antichristconspiracy.com, www.lulu.com, www.911enemies.com, www.mysterybabylonthegreat.net, www.antigospel.com, and www.amazon.com.

Edward Hendrie rests on the authority of the Holy Bible alone for doctrine. He considers the Holy Bible to be the inspired and inerrant word of God. Favorable citation by Edward Hendrie to an authority outside the Holy Bible on a particular issue should not be interpreted to mean that he agrees with all of the doctrines and beliefs of the cited authority.

All Scripture references are to the Authorized (King James) Version of the Holy Bible, unless otherwise indicated.

"Finally, my brethren, be strong in the Lord, and in the power of his might. Put on the whole armour of God, that ye may be able to stand against the wiles of the devil. For we wrestle not against flesh and blood, but against principalities, against powers, against the rulers of the darkness of this world, against spiritual wickedness in high places." Ephesians 6:10-12.

Table of Contents

i

Introduction

Most people who attend their church services each week are not hearing the gospel. They are hearing an anti-gospel.

The English word "anti" is a preposition derived from the same word in Greek.[1] It means "against, opposite, contrary, or in place of."[2] The antichrist is against Christ, and at the same time he seeks to replace Christ. He also seeks to replace the gospel of Christ with a contrary gospel, an anti-gospel.

The word gospel literally means God spell (God's word). In order to recognize and guard against the influence of the false gospel, it is important for the reader to be like the noble Bereans and check everything that is said against God's word found in the Holy Bible. *See* Acts 17:10-11.

The devil is a very subtle liar who opposes God and his gospel. *See* Genesis 3:1; John 8:44. That old serpent has stealthily introduced his deceptive anti-gospel into the pulpits of churches around the world. He has very craftily mixed the leaven of the Pharisees and Sadducees into the gospel and ruined the whole loaf. Matthew 16:6-12. The resulting false gospel is premised on the idea that all men are freed from the bondage to sin and therefore have the ability to choose of their own free will whether or not to believe in Jesus.

This is not a dispute over a fine distinction that is only of interest to theologians. This issue goes to the heart of the gospel. It goes to the heart of salvation. It goes to the heart of who Jesus is. The bible states that man is spiritually dead and must be born again by the power of God. Ephesians 2:1-6; John 3:3-8. God has elected certain to be saved by his grace through faith in Jesus Christ. Ephesians 1:3-9; 2:8-10. He imbues his elect with the faith needed to believe in Jesus. Romans 3:21-26; John 1:12-13.

The devil's false gospel reverses the order of things. Under the false gospel preached in most churches, Jesus does not choose his elect for salvation; instead, all men have a free will to choose Jesus. Instead of God choosing man, man chooses God. This mythology is not supported by the bible. It is at the heart of a devilish conspiracy against God and man. The free will anti-gospel denies the sovereignty of God and blasphemously makes God out to be a liar. The free will gospel is a heathen gospel that has a god, but that god is not the God of the bible.

The calling of the true Jesus is effectual; all who are chosen for salvation will believe in him. John 6:37-40. The free will gospel has a false Jesus who only offers the possibility of salvation, with no assurance. The scriptures warn about such a false Jesus. 2 Corinthians 11:4. The free will gospel denies the total depravity of man and the sovereign election of God.

The true gospel has a Jesus who loves only his children and saves them for eternity in heaven. The devilish anti-gospel has a false Jesus who loves everyone in the world, but this false Jesus casts most of those whom he loves in hell, to suffer in torments for eternity in a lake of fire. The true Jesus makes it clear in Matthew 7 that he never loved those who are sent to hell. "I never knew you: depart from me, ye that work iniquity." Matthew 7:23. *See also* Romans 9:21-23. The true God of the bible saves those whom he has elected for salvation and he condemns those whom he has elected for condemnation. *See* Romans 9.

The false Jesus of the anti-gospel looks on helplessly while the sinner who is spiritually dead in trespasses and sin decides whether to believe in him. The true Jesus preordained and chose his elect to believe in him before the foundation of the world. Ephesians 1:4-5. The false Jesus is an impotent Jesus, who must yield to the desires of men; if men decide after they are saved that they would rather reject Jesus and take their chances with being thrown into hell, they can forfeit their salvation. The false Jesus is powerless to stop them. The true Jesus is Lord of Lords and King of Kings, who is able to preserve his elect and will lose none of those whom he has chosen for salvation. John 10:27-29.

1   Paul Warns About the Anti-Gospel

The anti-gospel was manifested by false teachers during the lives of the apostles. Paul warned in the book of Acts that grievous spiritual wolves would enter in among the Christian believers and pervert the gospel. Paul made clear that the true gospel that he preached was "received of the Lord Jesus"and is in fact the **"gospel of the grace of God."** Paul explicitly stated that the true gospel is based upon God's sovereign grace, he even refers to the gospel as **"the word of his grace."** For Paul to clearly label the gospel as "gospel of the grace of God" and describe it as the "word of his grace" indicates that God's grace is the fundamental feature of the gospel. The false gospel about which Paul was warning must necessarily be founded upon something other than God's sovereign grace.

> But none of these things move me, neither count I my life dear unto myself, so that I might finish my course with joy, and the ministry, which I have received of the Lord Jesus, to testify the **gospel of the grace of God**. And now, behold, I know that ye all, among whom I have gone preaching the kingdom of God, shall see my face no more. Wherefore I take you to

record this day, that I *am* pure from the blood of all
men. For I have not shunned to declare unto you all
the counsel of God. Take heed therefore unto
yourselves, and to all the flock, over the which the
Holy Ghost hath made you overseers, to feed the
church of God, which he hath purchased with his
own blood. **For I know this, that after my
departing shall grievous wolves enter in among
you, not sparing the flock. Also of your own selves
shall men arise, speaking perverse things, to draw
away disciples after them**. Therefore watch, and
remember, that by the space of three years I ceased
not to warn every one night and day with tears. And
now, brethren, I commend you to God, and to the
word of his grace, which is able to build you up, and
to give you an inheritance among all them which are
sanctified. (Acts 20:24-32 AV)

What was the nature of the corruption of the gospel that Paul
warned about in Acts? In his letter to the Galatians, Paul explained
more explicitly the nature of the false gospel that would be preached
by the minions of Satan. Paul wrote to the Galatians regarding his
concern for those who would be so soon removed from the gospel of
the grace of Christ and follow after "another gospel." The context of
his letter suggests the nature of this new and different anti-gospel.

Paul, an apostle, (**not of men, neither by man, but
by Jesus Christ, and God the Father**, who raised
him from the dead;) . . . **I marvel that ye are so
soon removed from him that called you into the
grace of Christ unto another gospel**: Which is not
another; but there be some that trouble you, and
would pervert the gospel of Christ. But though we,
or an angel from heaven, preach any other gospel
unto you than that which we have preached unto you,
let him be accursed. As we said before, so say I now
again, If any *man* preach any other gospel unto you
than that ye have received, let him be accursed. **For**

do I now persuade men, or God? or do I seek to
please men? for if I yet pleased men, I should not be
the servant of Christ. But I certify you, brethren, that
**the gospel which was preached of me is not after
man.** For I neither received it of man, neither was I
taught *it*, but by the revelation of Jesus Christ.
(Galatians 1:1, 6-12 AV)

Paul starts out by stating emphatically that he was an apostle
not of or by men but by Jesus Christ and God the Father. He sets the
tone at the outset by stating a foundational principle of Christianity,
the sovereign grace of God, in order to distinguish it from the
theology of the false gospel being followed by the Galatians. The
context of Paul's admonition indicates the nature of the false gospel
to which the Galatians were following. Notice that they were being
removed from the **"grace of Christ"** to another gospel. That other
gospel would be something other than the grace of Christ. Satan,
who is the great adversary of God, can be expected to have
theological doctrines which are contrary to the theology of God. The
opposite of the sovereign grace of Christ would be the free will of
man.

Paul states that if any man preach any other gospel then the
one that they have received from him let him be accursed. Paul then
asks a rhetorical question: **"For do I now persuade men, or God?"**
That question is a clear reference to the nature of the accursed false
gospel. The false gospel involves the persuasion of the free will of
man. Paul's rhetorical question gives us another clue as to the nature
of the false gospel; the false gospel involves the persuasion of God.
That is, in the false gospel, man by his free will chooses to be saved
and thus persuades God to save him. Under the anti-gospel, instead
of God sovereignly choosing his elect, the sinner persuades God to
save him.

Paul makes clear that the gospel that he preached was **"not
after man."** What does he mean by the term "not after man?" He
means that the gospel of Christ is not a gospel which is based on the
free will of man.

In the next sentence he makes it clear that the gospel of Christ that he preaches is a gospel which he received by "revelation of Jesus Christ." Just as the gospel was received by revelation of Jesus Christ, so also is the salvation facilitated by revelation, and that revelation comes from Jesus Christ, not man. Paul states clearly in verses 3 and 4 that Jesus came to deliver us from our sins, not according to our will, but rather "according to the will of God and our Father."

> Grace *be* to you and peace from God the Father, and *from* our Lord Jesus Christ, Who gave himself for our sins, that he might deliver us from this present evil world, **according to the will of God and our Father**: (Galatians 1:3-4 AV)

The Grace of God is the very heart of the gospel of Jesus Christ. Anyone who preaches anything else is under a curse. In the midst of explaining that the true gospel is based upon the grace of God, Paul emphasized by repeating it twice that any man who preaches any other gospel is under a curse from God.

> But though we, or an angel from heaven, preach any other gospel unto you than that which we have preached unto you, **let him be accursed**. As we said before, so say I now again, If any man preach any other gospel unto you than that ye have received, **let him be accursed**. (Galatians 1:8-9 AV)

2 Satanic Conspiracy

The anti-gospel is a dethroning of God and enthroning of man. The anti-grace of that false gospel strips God of his sovereignty. Man is made the sovereign master of his destiny, with God merely a hopeful observer. The anti-gospel rejects the sovereign grace of God in his election of those for salvation. This injection of the Roman Catholic free will theological poison into nominal "Christian" denominations is the result of a satanic conspiracy. This strategy will give rise to an ecumenical movement that will ultimately result in the nominal "Christian" denominations falling under the yoke of the Vatican.

As we have seen, the free will anti-gospel took root soon after Jesus founded his New Testament church. That anti-gospel has been labeled by theologians as Pelagianism, after a fifth century A.D. theologian named Pelagius.[3] Pelagius preached that man was completely free to do good or evil and that God's grace only facilitated what man would choose in his own free will.[4] Pelagius further taught that man had a free will and could choose his own salvation. Pelagius, in order to remain consistent with his free will view, also taught that man could choose to fall away and lose his salvation by his own free choice.[5] Pelagianism was seen by the Christian community as a false gospel and so it never really took hold.

5

Less than a century later, a form of Pelagianism rose from the ashes; it was known as Semi-Pelagianism.[6] Under semi-Pelagianism, man is not free from the bondage of sin and therefore cannot choose to be good. However, man still has the ability of his own free will to believe in Jesus. Man makes the first move toward God in faith and then cooperates with God thereafter, but man must maintain his faith through the exercise of his free will. Semi-Pelagianism allows men to freely choose to reject God's salvation even after they have previously taken hold of it.

Under Semi-Pelagianism, man has fallen and his will is hindered by sin, but not totally so. According to Semi-Pelagians, man is not spiritually dead, but only spiritually sick. Semi-Pelagians taught that man could utilize his faith to cooperate with God in facilitating his own salvation. Semi-Pelagians accepted that God was sovereign, but at the same time they promoted the inconsistent view that man had free will in order to choose whether to be saved. Semi-Pelagianism became the generally accepted doctrine of the Roman Catholic Church. The Catholic Church codified this semi-Pelagian anti-gospel, with accompanying curses, at the Council of Trent (circa 1547).

If anyone saith that, since Adam's sin, the free will of man is lost and extinguished; or that it is a thing with only a name, yea, a name without reality, a figment, in fine, introduced into the Church by Satan; let him be anathema. COUNCIL OF TRENT, SESSION VI, DECREE ON JUSTIFICATION, Canon V, January 13, 1547.

If anyone saith that man's free will, moved and excited by God, by assenting to God exciting and calling, no wise cooperates towards disposing and preparing itself for obtaining the grace of justification; that it cannot refuse its consent, if it would, but that, as something inanimate, it does nothing whatever and is merely passive; let him be anathema. COUNCIL OF TRENT, SESSION IV,

DECREE ON JUSTIFICATION, Canon IV, January 13, 1547.

If anyone saith that by faith alone the impious is justified; in such wise as to mean that nothing else is required to cooperate in order to the obtaining the grace of justification, and that is not in any way necessary that he be prepared and disposed by the movement of his own will; let him be anathema. COUNCIL OF TRENT, SESSION VI, DECREE ON JUSTIFICATION, Canon IX, January 13, 1547.

Semi-Pelagianism was promoted by a Jesuit priest named Luis de Molina. Molina taught the semi-Pelagian view that God predestined believers to salvation but at the same time man had a free will to choose to be saved. This doctrine became popularly known as Molinism.[7]

Michael Bunker reveals some of the characters behind the infection of the Protestant churches with the Roman Catholic false gospel of free will:

Here is where our mystery gets increasingly interesting. Back in Amsterdam there was a movement of "counter-reformation" begun supposedly by a rich merchant named Dirck Coornhert. Coornhert was a Dutch humanist who was enamored with the teachings of the Catholic humanist Erasmus and a Spanish Jesuit monk named Luis de Molina. Coornhert disdained the reformation teachings on Grace, and sought to confront them wherever he found them. Coornhert had read with growing affections the teachings of de Molina regarding Free Will and Predestination. The Jesuits had hit on a brilliant way of dismantling the debate, they would preach that BOTH were true, and that a good God who was truly sovereign surely might have given his creations a freedom of the will in order to

allow them to choose to be saved. Luis de Molina
was creating a doctrine that would eventually be
called Media Scientia or "Middle-Knowledge".
Eventually this heresy would be called Molinism. In
an article on Luis de Molina entitled, Contending for
the Faith, Rev. Bernard Woudenberg said of de
Molina, "Being a Romanist, he was forced to honor
the theology of Thomas Aquinas with its acceptance
of divine sovereignty, but at the same time, as a
Jesuit, he was committed to defending the papacy
against the growing influences of Calvinism. And so
de Molina set forth to steer between these by
proposing his original and highly influential concept
of the media scientia, or 'middle- knowledge.' In this
he proposed that 'between God's knowledge of the
cause and effect relations which He had implanted in
the universe, and that of divine freedom whereby He
remains free at any time to do what He wills, there is
an area of middle-knowledge which God provides for
man in which man is granted freedom to do whatever
he chooses without outside necessity or
predetermination of any kind.'" The Hegelian
dialectic was in full force. The Catholic lie on
justification had been countered by the true doctrine
of Salvation by Grace through faith, so an evil
"compromise" was now offered to the reformed
churches, and by deceit and subterfuge, the
compromise would eventually become the
predominant teachings in all the churches of the
world.[8]

The Roman Catholic church knew that Protestant Christians
would never adopt Molinism if it were known to have sprung from a
Jesuit priest, so they decided to use a front man in order to introduce
this anti-gospel into the Protestant churches. They used a man named
Jacobus Arminius (1560-1609), who was an admirer of Molina, to
popularize the free will doctrine of Molina among Protestants.

Bunker explains how Molinism was recast as Arminianism:

Back in Geneva, Theodore Beza at this time had reason to suspect that his student Jacobus Arminius was not what he proposed to be. Questions were being asked about comments that Arminius was making to fellow students, and there were still questions about his support from the rich, aristocratic merchants of Holland. Apparently Arminius was able to lie well enough to get past Beza's questioning, a skill that would come in handy years later when he would be looking for a teaching job in Amsterdam. Beza then asked Arminius to answer and refute the teachings of Dirck Coornhert. Although Arminius completed the task, he later claimed to be convinced by Coornhert's arguments, and he became ardently opposed to the teachings of the reformers. In 1586, Arminius was released from Geneva, but instead of heading back to Amsterdam where he was under contract to the City to labor in order to pay back his tuition, he headed to Rome for a "vacation".

Generally, most Calvinists believe that it was during this time in Rome that Arminius was recruited by the Jesuits to their point of view. That allegation cannot be proven, and I believe that there is enough other evidence that Arminius was compromised long before his pilgrimage to Rome. By this time, he had become a private student of the writings of de Molina, and in 1588, the same year in which Arminius was ordained a minister (by the endorsement of Beza), de Molina published his treatise on the will entitled A Reconciliation of Free Choice with the Gifts of Grace, Divine Foreknowledge, Providence, Predestination and Reprobation. What the Jesuits were loathe to admit, was that Molinism was nothing more than a rebirth of the ancient Pelagianism heresy, although it actually more easily likened to "Semi-Pelagianism" which contends that man cannot be saved apart from God's grace; however, fallen man must cooperate and assent to God's grace before he will be saved. The Jesuits recognized that the Protestants would never embrace the teachings of a Catholic Spanish monk, so they capitalized on the growing and open debates taking place within Protestantism. Molinism would be recast as Arminianism, and eventually, it would take over the ecclesiastical world. A famous quote from de Molina eerily fortells of the Jesuit lie that proceeds from the mouths of "evangelical" leaders today: "all human beings are endowed with equal and sufficient divine grace without distinction as to their individual merits, and that salvation depends on the sinner's willingness to receive grace". The Catholics say of Molinism: "Molinism is an influential system within Catholic theology for reconciling human free choice with God's grace, providence, foreknowledge and predestination. Originating within the Society of Jesus in the late sixteenth and early seventeenth centuries, it encountered stiff opposition from Bezian Thomists and from the self-styled Augustinian disciples of Michael Baius and Cornelius Jansen." - Alfred J. Freddoso, Catholic Professor at Notre Dame

Upon returning to Amsterdam in 1590, Arminius married the daughter of one of Holland's wealthiest aristocrats. To see how far Jacobus had fallen from his original reformed ideals, we note that in 1591, he was hired by his wealthy benefactors to draw up a church order that would subordinate the church to a place of dependence and obedience to the state. That particular belief is now the most prevalent abuse of both Christians and the scriptures taught in "churches" today. The policy of abusing Romans 13 for the purposes of enslaving Christians to tyrannical

civil magistrates had found a hero in Jacobus
Arminius. The Catholic church, even today, admires
Arminius. Here is what it says about him in the
Catholic Encyclopedia: "A leader was sure to rise
from the Calvinistic ranks who should point out the
baneful corollaries of the Genevan creed, and be
listened to. Such a leader was Jacobus Arminius
(Jakob Hermanzoon), professor at the University of
Leyden." -- Catholic Encyclopedia.[9]

Some Arminians object to characterizing Arminianism as
semi-Pelagianism.[10] They claim that Arminian theology, unlike semi-
Pelagianism, acknowledges that man is fallen and cannot be good or
believe in Jesus. However, that acknowledgment is rendered moot,
by the Arminian doctrine of "prevenient" grace. Arminians claim
that God gave a "prevenient" grace to all men that frees their will and
enables them to choose whether to believe in Jesus.

Under Arminianism, those who choose to believe in Jesus
can also of their free will choose to reject Jesus and lose the salvation
that they had previously grasped. The slight difference of
"prevenient grace" under Arminianism is a distinction without a
difference from semi-Pelagianism. Despite the objections from
Arminians, Arminianism is essentially dressed up semi-Pelagianism.

As a result of the successful efforts of Arminius and other
Jesuit agents, Molinism has since become popularized not as
Molinism but as Arminianism.[11] Many view Arminianism as an
orthodox Christian view of Scripture, when in fact it is a corruption
of the gospel that has been injected into the Protestant denominations
by Jacobus Arminius. Arminianism is simply repackaged Roman
Catholic, semi-Pelagian doctrine.[12]

Augustus Toplady, the author of the famous hymn *Rock of
Ages*, concluded that Jacobus Arminius was a secret agent of the
Jesuits. Arminius' purpose was to infect the Christian church with
the heathen Catholic doctrine of free will. Toplady wrote:

The Jesuits were moulded into a regular body,
towards the middle of the sixteenth century: toward
the close of the same century, Arminius began to
infest the Protestant churches. It needs therefore no
great penetration, to discern from what source he
drew his poison. His journey to Rome (though
Monsicur Bayle affects to make light of the
inferences which were at that very time deduced
from it) was not for nothing. If, however, any are
disposed to believe, that Arminius imbibed his
doctrines from the Socinians in Poland, with whom,
it is certain, he was on terms of intimate friendship, I
have no objection to splitting the difference: he
might import some of his tenets from the Racovian
brethren, and yet be indebted, for others, to the
disciples of Loyola.[13]

Toplady's conclusion was not just based upon circumstantial
inference. The Jesuits themselves have revealed that Arminius was
their secret agent sent to poison the doctrine of the Protestant
churches. William Laud, the Archbishop of Canterbury, was working
secretly with the Jesuits to infect the Church of England (Anglican
Church) with Roman Catholic doctrine, including Arminianism. In
1638 Laud ordered the exclusive use of a "papistical" liturgy upon
the Church of Scotland. It became known as "Laud's Liturgy." Laud
was eventually found out, and in 1645 he was beheaded for treason
against England. Toplady explains one of the papers found among
Laud's effects after his death:

When archbishop Laud's papers were examined, a
letter was found among them, thus endorsed with that
prelate's own hand: "March, 1628. A Jesuit's Letter,
sent to the Rector at Bruxels, about the ensuing
Parliament." The design of this letter was to give the
Superior of the Jesuits, then resident at Brussels, an
account of the posture of civil and ecclesiastical
affairs in England; an extract from it I shall here
subjoin: "Father Rector, let not the damp of

astonishment seize upon your ardent and zealous
soul, in apprehending the sodaine and unexpected
calling of a Parliament. We have now many strings to
our bow. We have planted that soveraigne drugge
Arminianisme, which we hope will purge the
Protestants from their heresie; and it flourisheth and
beares fruit in due season. For the better prevention
of the Puritanes, the Arminians have already locked
up the Duke's (of Buckingham) eares; and we have
those of our owne religion, which stand continually
at the Duke's chamber, to see who goes in and out:
we cannot be too circumspect and carefull in this
regard. I am, at this time, transported with joy, to see
how happily all instruments and means, as well great
as lesser, co-operate unto our purposes. But, to return
unto the maine fabricke:--OUR FOUNDATION IS
ARMINIANISME. The Arminians and projectors, as
it appears in the premises, affect mutation. This we
second and enforce by probable arguments."[14]

That letter found among Lauds belongings is proof, from a
high Jesuit agent reporting to his superior at Brussels, that the very
foundation of the effort to bring Protestant England back into the
Catholic fold was to infect the Church of England with Catholic
doctrine, and that the contagion of that infection was Arminianism.
The writer proudly proclaimed virtual victory over Protestant
England through the spiritual germ of Arminianism. **"We have
planted that soveraigne drugge Arminianisme, which we hope
will purge the Protestants from their heresie; and it flourisheth
and beares fruit in due season."**[15]

Arminianism springs from Rome and it draws all who adhere
to it back to Rome. Toplady explains the significance of the
documents found among Laud's belongings and the effect that the
Catholic Arminian attack had on the Church of England:

The "Sovereign drug, Arminianism," which said the
Jesuit, "we (i.e. we Papists) have planted" in

England, did indeed bid fair "to purge our Protestant Church effectually. How merrily Popery and Arminianism, at that time, danced hand in hand, may be learned from Tindal: "The churches were adorned with paintings, images, altar-pieces, & etc. and, instead of communion tables, altars were set up, and bowings to them and the sacramental elements enjoined. The predestinarian doctrines were forbid, not only to be preached, but to be printed; and the Arminian sense of the Articles was encouraged and propagated." The Jesuit, therefore, did not exult without cause. The "sovereign drug," so lately "planted," did indeed take deep root downward, and bring forth fruit upward, under the cherishing auspices of Charles and Laud. Heylyn, too, acknowledges that the state of things was truly described by another Jesuit of that age, who wrote: "Protestantism waxeth weary of itself. The doctrine (by the Arminians, who then sat at the helm) is altered in many things, for which their progenitors forsook the Church of Rome: as limbus patrum; prayer for the dead, and possibility of keeping God's commandments; and the accounting of Calvinism to be heresy at least, if not treason."[16]

August Toplady reveals how Arminius himself acknowledged that his free will Semi-Pelagianism was completely in line with the Roman Catholic doctrine, and the Catholic Church considered predestination by the sovereign will of God as the arch-heresy against those Catholic doctrines. It is interesting that Arminius explains how the liberal branch of the Lutheran Church and the Anabaptists in his day were infected with the Semi-Pelagian heresy that undermined the grace of God; they were of one mind with Rome in their opposition against the gospel of God's grace. The Arminian free will tradition is still endemic in most Lutheran and Baptist churches today.

Certain it is, that Arminius himself was sensible, how

greatly the doctrine of predestination widens the
distance between Protestantism and Popery. "There
is no point of doctrines (says he) which the Papists,
the Anabaptists, and the (new) Lutherans more
fiercely oppose, nor by means of which they heap
more discredit on the reformed churches, and bring
the reformed system itself into more odium; for they
(i.e. the Papists, & etc.) assert, that no fouler
blasphemy against God can be thought or expressed,
than is contained in the doctrine of predestination."[17]
For which reason, he advises the reformed world to
discard predestination from their creed, in order that
they may live on more brotherly terms with the
Papists, the Anabaptists, and such like.[18]

3 The Five Points of Arminianism

Arminians continually try to discredit the biblical doctrine of grace by giving it a pejorative label, to make it seem as though it is a man-made doctrinal contrivance. The label they commonly use is Calvinism. John Calvin lived in the 16th century, and although he acknowledged the doctrine of God's grace, he never broke it down and expressed it as the so-called five points of Calvinism attributed to him. The five points of Calvinism did not surface until after Calvin and Arminius were both dead. It was the followers of Jacobus Arminius that came up with five points of Arminianism and then labeled the Christian objection to those five points the five points of Calvinism.

After Arminius' death (1609), his supporters, led by Simon Episcopius issued a remonstrance in 1610. The remonstrance contained five articles summarizing their divergence from the fundamental aspects of accepted Christian orthodoxy. After issuing the remonstrance, Aminius' followers became known as "The Remonstrants."

The five articles of the Arminian Remonstrance are: Article 1: God's election was conditioned on the free will choice of man; Article 2: Jesus atoned for the sins of everyone in the world, both saved and unsaved; Article 3: While man is depraved, God provides a special (prevenient) grace to all men that partially awakens them from their depravity so that they can make a free will choice whether to believe in Jesus; Article 4: Man can resist the grace of God; Article 5: God assists one who is saved in resisting the temptations of the devil, but a person can by the exercise of his free will reject God and lose his salvation.[19]

The five articles of the Arminian Remonstrance were the focus of the Synod of Dordtrecht (a/k/a Synod of Dordt) in the Netherlands. The synod responded to the remonstrance in 1619 with The Canons of Dordt, wherein the Dutch Reformed Church rejected the teachings of Arminius.[20]

The so-called five points of Calvinism were actually developed from the Cannons of the Synod of Dordtrecht in response to the Arminian Remonstrants and not from John Calvin, who had been long dead before the Synod of Dordtrecht met.[21] The Arminians had to find a way to get out from under the cloud of heresy after their theology was refuted by an official synod of the Dutch Reformed Church. The Arminians came up with the idea of creating a straw man in John Calvin. Rather than argue that the theological dispute was Arminianism vs. the Synod of Dordt (or more accurately Arminianism vs. Christianity), the Arminians re-labeled the conflict as Arminianism vs. Calvinism. Once the Arminians succeeded in re-labeling the dispute, Arminianism could gain the false appearance of being on firmer theological footing.

The Moody Bible Institute, named after Arminian revivalist Dwight L. Moody, publishes the *Moody Handbook of Theology*. The Moody handbook is typical of the inaccuracies in the historical record regarding Arminianism. The *Moody Handbook of Theology* describes Arminianism as being expressed "in the Remonstrance, a document produced in 1610, formally protesting Calvinism in the Netherlands."[22] The mis-impression given by the Moody handbook is that "Calvinism" was identified as such before the Remonstrance was issued. In fact, the label "Calvinism" was not coined until after the Synod of Dordt issued its articles in response to the Arminian

Remonstrance. The Moody handbook also defines Arminianism in its glossary in pertinent part as: "A doctrinal system formed by Jacobus Arminius (1560-1609) as a response to Calvinism in the Netherlands."[23] Again, the handbook is misleading; it gives the false impression that "Calvinism," as such, predated Arminianism, and that Arminianism addressed the doctrines of "Calvinism." In fact, it was the biblical doctrine of the sovereign grace of God that predated Arminianism, and that is to what Arminianism was a response.

Over the years, those who defended the sovereign grace of God ignorantly fell for the ploy of the Arminians by calling themselves "Calvinists." They did not understand that the "Calvinist" title played into the hands of the Arminians, by suggesting that the biblical doctrine of the sovereign grace of God is the brain-child of John Calvin. Claiming to be a follower of Calvin or a follower of Arminius demonstrates a carnality of the mind that should be resisted. "For while one saith, I am of Paul; and another, I am of Apollos; are ye not carnal?" 1 Corinthians 3:4. As Christians, we are to be followers only of Jesus Christ. "For other foundation can no man lay than that is laid, which is Jesus Christ." 1 Corinthians 3:11.

One little known fact is that John Calvin, himself, did not adhere to all five points of what became known as Calvinism. For example, in his 1552 book *Concerning the Eternal Predestination of God* Calvin made a statement that indicates that Calvin did not believe in limited atonement, which is one of the so-called five points of Calvinism. Calvin stated:

> It is also a fact, without controversy, that Christ came
> to atone for the sins of the whole world. . . . we
> conclude that although reconciliation is offered unto
> all men through Him, yet, that the great benefit
> belongs peculiarly to the elect, that they might be
> gathered together and be made together partakers of
> eternal life.[24]

Calvin confirmed his universal atonement position in his

Sermon on Ephesians 5:11-1. Calvin reaffirmed his universal atonement position in his *Sermon CXVI on the Book of Job.* Calvin stated in that sermon that "it is not in us to discern between the righteous and the sinners that go to destruction, but that Jesus Christ has suffered His death and passion as well for them as for us."[25] Calvin likewise stated in his commentary on Romans 5:18:

> He makes this favor common to all, because it is propounded to all, and not because it is in reality extended to all; for though Christ suffered for the sins of the whole world, and is offered through God's benignity indiscriminately to all, yet all do not receive him.[26]

That means that Calvin actually agreed with the Arminian theology of universal atonement as stated in Article 2 of the Arminian Remonstrance. It did not matter to the Arminians that their chosen straw man, John Calvin, did not completely fit the bill in opposing their five points of Arminianism, but they needed someone and so Calvin would have to do. Calvin was adequate enough to step in as a replacement for the biblical opposition to their heathen doctrine. That way they could attack the theological writings of Calvin and not have to address the bible passages that impeach their Arminian theology.

Labeling the Christian response to the Arminian error as Calvinism was a subtle way to give the impression that Arminianism was a theological doctrine on equal footing with another theological doctrine they labeled Calvinism. Thus, the people could be sold the bill of goods that Arminianism is a theological doctrine, the adherents of which are opposed by Calvinists, rather than what it really is: an attack on biblical Christianity. By use of the label Calvinism, the Arminians could reduce the stature of the biblical objection to Arminianism and thus lower the defenses of the common people to the danger of the spiritual contagion.

Once the Arminians labeled the gospel of grace "Calvinism" they could begin their attack on it, not by attacking the bible, but by attacking the character of John Calvin. All men are sinners, and when the devil can ascribe a biblical doctrine to a man, it is a simple matter of destroying the credibility of the man to tarnish the truth of that doctrine. That strategy is still in use today. For example, David Cloud, founder of *Way of Life Literature* and publisher of the *Fundamental Baptist Information Service,*[27] uses that strategy when discussing the theological soundness of the sovereignty of God in salvation. Cloud begins by attacking the grace gospel by describing it as a Calvinism. Cloud states: "Calvinism is a theology that was developed by John Calvin (1509-64) in the sixteenth century . . . every standard point of TULIP theology can be found in Calvin's *Institutes.*" Once Cloud attributes the gospel of God's sovereign grace to Calvin, he then rips into Calvin, destroying Calvin's credibility, which serves to undermine the doctrine of God's sovereign grace.

> Calvin was vicious toward his enemies, acting more like a devouring wolf than a harmless sheep. Historian William Jones observed that "that most hateful feature of popery adhered to Calvin through life, the spirit of persecution." Note how he described his theological opponents: "...all that filth and villainy...mad dogs who vomit their filth against the majesty of God and want to pervert all religion. Must they be spared?" (Oct. 16, 1555). Calvin hated the Anabaptists, though they were miles closer to the Scriptural pattern for the New Testament church than he was. He called them "henchmen of Satan." Four men who disagreed with Calvin on who should be admitted to the Lord's Supper were beheaded, quartered, and their body parts hung in strategic locations in Geneva as a warning to others. He burned Michael Servetus (for rejecting infant baptism and for denying Christ's deity). Calvin wrote about Servetus, "One should not be content with simply killing such people, but should burn them cruelly."[28]

The implication of Cloud's attack on Calvin is clear. Stay clear of the doctrine of God's sovereign grace, because the author of that theology, John Calvin, was a "devouring wolf" who "had a "spirit of persecution" that drove him to "hate Anabaptists," whom he called "henchmen of Satan." If that is not bad enough, Calvin had men "beheaded," "quartered," and "burned" for disagreeing with him. Once Cloud establishes the devilish character of Calvin, he begins his argument against Calvinism. It is not surprising to find that he claims that Calvinism is not biblically based but rather that "Calvinism interprets scripture by theology rather than by context."[29]

Cloud deceptively analyzes the issues under headings that draw the battle lines as "The Bible vs. The Calvinist Doctrine." "THE BIBLE VS. THE CALVINIST DOCTRINE THAT FAITH IS A WORK . . . THE BIBLE VS. THE CALVINIST DOCTRINE THAT THE NEW BIRTH PRECEDES FAITH . . . THE BIBLE VS. THE CALVINIST DOCTRINE OF THE TOTAL DEPRAVITY OF MAN . . . THE BIBLE VS. THE CALVINIST DOCTRINE OF IRRESISTIBLE GRACE . . . THE BIBLE VS. THE CALVINIST DOCTRINE OF LIMITED ATONEMENT."[30] (all capital letters in original).

Notice Cloud claims that Calvinists believe that "faith is a work." That is absolutely false. Opponents of Arminianism believe that the Arminian doctrine of salvation by the free will of man has at its core a theology of salvation by works. Opponents of Arminianism do not believe that faith is a work.

The following excerpt is found on BibleBelievers.net, which is a popular website with thousands of unique visitors each month. BibleBelievers.net describes itself as "Independent, Fundamental, Evangelical, Born-Again Christians Using Only the AV1611 (KJV)." The excerpt posted by BibleBelievers.net is from a position paper by an organization known as the "Fundamental Baptist World-Wide Mission." The position paper is representative of the Arminian approach in many Baptist churches. It is an example of the subtle methods used by the devil to undermine the grace of biblical Christianity by undermining the man (Calvin) whom the Arminians put in place of Christ to represent the gospel of God's sovereign grace.

> As for John Calvin, he was not a Baptist. He was a Reformer. He was not Christian in his attitude and behavior. He was a tyrant who cast those who disagreed with him into prison. In 1553, Michael Servetus, a Spaniard, a scholar, a physician, a scientist of originality, and a man who was deeply religious and devoted to Christ, vigorously opposed Calvin on the doctrines of predestination and infant baptism.[31]

The Fundamental Baptist World-Wide Mission then explains how Servetus was unmercifully burned at the stake, allegedly at the insistence of John Calvin. The conclusion is that if you believe the gospel of grace you are a Calvinist and a follower of a brutal tyrant who burns people at the stake. The Fundamental Baptist World-Wide Mission position paper notes in a parenthetical: "while Servetus is to be commended for opposing predestination and infant baptism, some resources note that he also taught against the essential Christian doctrine of the Trinity which is heresy."[32] Notice how the Baptist mission organization lump infant baptism (advocated by Calvin), which is unbiblical with predestination, which is clearly biblical. By doing that they link in the mind of the reader that since infant baptism advocated by Calvin is unbiblical so too must be predestination advocated by Calvin.

Arminians must attack Calvin in order to avoid appearing to attack the bible, which is their real target. The bible states clearly: "Having **predestinated** us unto the adoption of children by Jesus Christ to himself, **according to the good pleasure of his will."** Ephesians 1:5. If that is not convincing enough, Ephesians 1:11 states unequivocally: "In whom also we have obtained an inheritance, **being predestinated according to the purpose of him who worketh all things after the counsel of his own will."** Ephesians 1:11. Romans, chapter 8 further affirms the doctrine of predestination:

> **For whom he did foreknow, he also did
> predestinate** to be conformed to the image of his
> Son, that he might be the firstborn among many
> brethren. Moreover **whom he did predestinate**,
> them he also called: and whom he called, them he
> also justified: and whom he justified, them he also
> glorified. Romans 8:29-30.

How does the Baptist mission organization address those
passages? What follows is the deceptive treatment of those passages
by the Baptist organization:

> The word predestination is found in only two books
> of the Bible, Romans 8:29-30 and Ephesians 1:5,11.
> In both texts predestination speaks not of people
> being lost or saved, but rather of position or privilege
> to be shared in the future by those who are already
> saved.[33]

The deception is subtle. The Fundamental Baptist World-
Wide Mission correctly states that the passages address position or
privilege, but then states that the passages do not speak about people
being lost or saved, as though somehow God predestined the
privileges of those saved but he did not predestine their salvation
itself. The very idea is unsupportable by any passage in the bible.
Certainly, each passage addresses the blessings of salvation, but they
also address the predestination of those who were chosen for
salvation by the sovereign will of God. The writer tries to dismiss
the passages as inapplicable to the discussion, when in fact they
address directly the issue and should end the discussion.

Romans 8:29-30 expressly states the progressive steps to
salvation that begin with the foreknowledge of God: "whom he did
foreknow, he also did predestinate . . . whom he did predestinate,
them he also called: and whom he called, them he also justified: and
whom he justified, them he also glorified." Clearly, that passage
addresses the progression from foreknowledge to predestination to
calling to justification to glorification of those chosen by God for

salvation. There is simply no other biblical interpretation, but that those who are saved are predestined for salvation. Ephesians 1:5 states clearly: that he "predestinated us unto the adoption of children." The adoption by God as his children is by definition salvation. To suggest otherwise is simply wrong.

The only way around those passages is to ignore the passages by deceptively saying they do not apply and put John Calvin in their place and attack him. The Baptist mission position paper goes on the attack and labels its discourse: "The Heresy of John Calvin." As is typical for Arminians, the writings of John Calvin are cited by Arminians in place of the bible to represent the sovereign grace of the gospel of Christ. By attacking their straw man, John Calvin, Arminians feel that they are absolved from having to cite to the bible passages that support the sovereign grace of God. As we have seen, if there are any bible passages inconvenient to the Arminian agenda, Arminians simply dismiss them as inapplicable. They then cherry pick other bible passages taken out of context and twisted to support their Arminian theology. The Arminians juxtapose their context free bible passages interpreted to mean what they do not actually say against the writings of John Calvin. The subtle deception is accomplished.

Michael Bunker explains some of the historical details leading up to the development of the so-called five points of Calvinism and the spread of the Arminian error in churches throughout the world:

> In the late 1590's Jacobus Arminius was back in
> Amsterdam, teaching his Pelagian/Molinist lies.
> Enough questions had been brought forth concerning
> his anti-Grace teachings, that a strict Calvinist by the
> name of Franciscus Gomarus was called upon to
> interview Arminius to test his orthodoxy. Arminius
> was applying for a professorship in Theology at the
> University of Leyden, and the occasion of his job
> interview would allow his belief system also to be
> tested. Apparently, Arminius had either become so

skilled a liar or his skills in evasion and escape had
become so attuned by this point, that he passed the
test with flying colors. The question of why Beza and
Gomarus, both strict Grace and Election adherents,
had both approved of Arminius is unclear, but both
were likely blinded by their belief in honor and
integrity amongst theologians. During a time when
men were willing to die for their faith, the thought
that someone would patently lie about his beliefs in
order to receive promotions and to avoid detection
would have been far from the minds of these two
reformers. But lying and deceit were well within the
oath and charter of the Jesuits. We will see that these
traits are also widely accepted by the intellectual
heirs of Jacobus Arminius.

Arminius died in 1609, long before the upheavals
caused by his teachings would erupt in full force. In
1610, the disciples of Arminius signed a
"Remonstrance" or a petition to the government for
protection of their Arminian views. In their
Remonstrance, the Arminians put forth their theology
finally for the entire world to see. It consisted of five
main points:

1. Conditional election. The Remonstrants held to the
Molinist view of Middle-Knowledge. Election was
conditional on both God's foreknowledge, and the
free will of humans.

2. Universal atonement. The Remonstrants held to
the Jesuit/Molinist view on the atonement, as pushed
by the Catholics in the Council of Trent. The
redemptive blood of Jesus Christ was available to all
mankind, and God had not applied or given this
atonement to any specific "elect".

3. Total depravity. The Remonstrants held on to the

view of original sin, but believed that since humans were HUMANS, and not sticks or plants, there was enough human left in them to enable them to believe on Christ, or reject Him. In effect, humans were not TOTALLY depraved.

4. Sufficient but resistible grace. The Remonstrants believed that Grace was sufficient to save, but that this Grace could be resisted by man. Thereby man could thwart the will of God (which evidently was to save ALL men) by refusing to be saved.

5. Uncertainty about the perseverance of the saints. The Remonstrants believed that a truly born-again believer could cast off that Grace by certain behavior and subsequently go to Hell.

I will tell you that what you have just read is the common teaching of the Protestant churches throughout the world, with very few exceptions.

I will also tell you that these beliefs, commonly called "Arminian", are cogent, logical and ultimately WRONG. I say that they are cogent and logical in order to tell you that the only thing WORSE than the Arminian viewpoint is any viewpoint that attempts to COMPROMISE between these points and the Doctrines of Grace as taught in the Bible. Challenges to the Doctrines of Grace are usually predicated by the attempt to label them as "Calvinism", although Calvin AND Arminius were gone by the time this Remonstrance was published. What the enemies of Grace term as "Calvinism" or now the more hated "Hyper-Calvinism" was actually just the Gospel response to the Remonstrance of 1610! It is as if a man named Gomer created a new doctrine called GOMERISM, in which he proposed that we all evolved slowly from dirt particles on the eyelids of

gnats. If another man named Goober published a
biblical challenge to this stupid doctrine, it is as if
folks ran about for another 400 years preaching
against Gooberism (or worse, Hyper-Gooberism) as a
contrivance of that heretic Goober!

In 1611, the true preachers of the Gospel answered
with the Contra-Remonstrance of 1611. Robert
Godfrey writes, "It it surely ironic that through the
centuries there has been so much talk of the 'five
points of Calvinism' when in fact Calvinists did not
originate a discussion of five points. Indeed
Calvinism has never been summarized in five points.
Calvinism has only offered five responses to the five
errors of Arminianism."

The Jesuits were not done with their work. Although
they had planted the seeds of their papal tares in the
Lord's ground, they had not yet seen their crop come
to fruition. In the 1700's, the doctrine of Arminianism
would be fully embraced and rapidly distributed by
John Wesley, the founder of Methodism. Wesley
wrote a defense of Arminianism entitled, "What is an
Arminian". The folly of Arminianism was also
challenged, and rightly so, by that great Christian
thinker Jonathan Edwards, who published his treatise
"Sinners in the Hands of an Angry God" in 1741, a
sermon that profoundly trounced the foolishness of
Arminian doctrine. Edwards became president of
Princeton in 1758, but "mysteriously" died of a
smallpox vaccine within weeks (see the oath of the
Jesuit above).[34]

Michael Bunker explains the bitter harvest manifested in the
churches today from the Arminian contagion and what is at stake by
that corruption of the gospel of grace.

Loyola's plan has come to fruition. The Jesuit

doctrines of anti-Grace have become the dominant
teaching of the churches of the world. The Woman
that Rides the Beast, that mother of Harlots, has seen
her offspring grow up into maturity. The Whore
churches that dot every street corner have the stench
of their mother.

Those people who are NOT brain-addled and
stupefied in the sugar-water Harlot Churches are
busy decrying the evil of the coming New World
Order, while in ignorance they embrace the very
doctrines of Antichrist.

It is the Ultimate Conspiracy, and if it were possible,
it would deceive even the very elect. Do Catholics go
to heaven? You better find out, because odds are you
are one.[35]

Keith Drury is an Arminian theologian who teaches courses
in practical ministry at Indiana Wesleyan University. Drury confirms
Bunker's assessment. Drury honestly reveals the dangers of the
Arminian theology. Drury explains that Arminianism is a very
attractive philosophy for the unsaved world, and it often leads to
humanism. Humanism is a theology where the God of the bible does
not exist and man instead is his own god. It is the foundational
philosophy for communism.

Drury's admissions are yet more evidence that Arminian
churches are full of unsaved "tares," who worship a different Jesus
from the true Jesus in the bible. The unsaved develop a taste for the
deadly spiritual poison of Arminianism and feel quite comfortable
with the Arminian message. A true Christian may find himself in an
Arminian church for a time, but he will begin to feel spiritually ill
from the Arminian anti-gospel poison and eventually leave that
church in search of the eternal medicine found in the true gospel.
"And a stranger will they not follow, but will flee from him: for they
know not the voice of strangers." John 10:5. The sheep of Christ will
leave the stranger who preaches the false anti-gospel of Arminianism

and seek out the doctrine of Christ. "My sheep hear my voice, and I know them, and they follow me." John 10:27. This constant purging from the Arminian churches of the true wheat leaves behind in those churches the unsaved tares sowed by the enemy. *See* Matthew 13:24-30.

Notice that in the excerpt from Drury's article below that Drury describes the struggle as being between two opposing theological camps: Calvinism vs. Arminianism. That makes it easy to sway the reader by the "logic" of Arminianism. The unsaved world views the simplicity of the true gospel as "foolishness." The Arminians use their "logic" against their straw-man, Calvinism. That way the Arminians can attack "foolish" Calvinism, instead of being seen as attacking the "foolish" gospel. "For the preaching of the cross is to them that perish foolishness; but unto us which are saved it is the power of God." 1 Corinthians 1:18. Keith Drury explains:

> There is little doubt about it: Arminianism has triumphed in the pew, if not in the seminary. The average Christian is a practicing Arminian, even if he claims to be a Calvinist in theory. "Practical" modern church members are increasingly rejecting traditional "five-point Calvinism." While Arminianism has been a "minority view" for decades, today there is a major drift toward Arminianism in most Calvinist churches.
>
> I spent several years as a determined five-pointer as a young man before changing my mind to accept Arminianism. I made the switch purposefully and with quite a bit of painful study as a student at Princeton Seminary. But many Calvinists today are making the switch for purely pragmatic reasons. They have not become convinced the Bible really teaches the Arminian approach. Frankly, Arminianism is simply more palatable to a secular culture. It "fits in" to the mind-set of the people in their pews. Like it or not, the secular mind is naturally Arminian in its outlook. I've discovered this

repeatedly myself by administering a theological questionnaire to secular students in an adult education program. These "unchurched Harrys" invariably register Arminian theologically.

Face it, Arminianism is simply more logical. It makes sense to the person on the street. And today's church is scrambling to make sense to unbelievers. We want to sound sensible, logical, rational, enlightened, fair. Arminianism is so much more appealing to worldly people.

* * *

I admit that I am a committed Arminian. Of course I welcome the host of new "practical Arminians" joining ranks with my theological tradition. I think this approach fits better with the Bible, reason, tradition, and experience. But I must be honest. There are some real hazards over here in the Arminian ocean—especially for Calvinistic churches. You can sink your theological ship here. As a local "pilot," I'd suggest you keep your eyes open wide for submerged rocks!

We Arminians tend to put too much emphasis on man and his decisions, and not enough on God and the gospel. Sometimes we are tempted to act as if God is helpless without us and our work. We lean toward pragmatism and are constantly looking for "what works best" as if methodology were more important than the message. Since we believe that all men can be saved, we tend to assume that if they aren't saved, we have not packaged the invitation (or the message) right. We especially love management, leadership, programs, marketing, and research data. We tend to focus more on the "potential convert" than on the eternal gospel. Arminianism easily leans

toward a NIKE mentality—"Just do it." We are
somewhat less inclined to pray in order to move God
to "do it" (see Divine-Human Synergism in
Ministry).

And, as has always been true, Arminianism can be
taken to the extreme of humanism. Calvinists have a
sovereign God and an inactive man. Humanists have
a sovereign man and an inactive God. Arminians lean
toward the humanist end of this continuum and thus
are always in danger of becoming humanists (see
Humanism in Scripture and Culture: Recovering a
Balance).

So if you are a former Calvinist who has drifted into
Arminianism with little thought and for mostly
pragmatic reasons, be careful as you navigate in this
territory. You probably knew the dangers of your
former theology, especially of "hyper-Calvinism."
But you may not be aware of the dangers over here.

* * *

If you are recently coming from the Calvinistic end,
be careful not to pass right by the middle ground and
run off to extreme Arminianism: man-centered
humanism.[36]

4 The Jesuit Oath

I t is difficult for the ordinary person to grasp the
nefariousness of the Jesuit order and its secret
machinations in planting and nurturing Arminianism
without some knowledge of the Jesuit oath. The following is
information obtained from Professor Arthur Noble regarding the
blasphemous and sinister oath of induction into the Order of the
Society of Jesus (The Jesuit Order).

[The following is the text of the Jesuit Extreme Oath
of Induction as recorded in the Journals of the 62nd
Congress, 3rd Session, of the United States
Congressional Record (House Calendar No. 397,
Report No. 1523, 15 February, 1913, pp. 3215-3216),
from which it was subsequently torn out. The Oath is
also quoted by Charles Didier in his book
Subterranean Rome (New York, 1843), translated
from the French original. Dr. Alberto Rivera, who
escaped from the Jesuit Order in 1967, confirms that
the induction ceremony and the text of the Jesuit
Oath which he took were identical to what we have
cited below. – A. N.][37]

When a Jesuit of the minor rank is to be elevated to

command, he is conducted into the Chapel of the Convent of the Order, where there are only three others present, the principal or Superior standing in front of the altar. On either side stands a monk, one of whom holds a banner of yellow and white, which are the Papal colours, and the other a black banner with a dagger and red cross above a skull and crossbones, with the word INRI, and below them the words IUSTUM NECAR REGES IMPIUS. The meaning of which is: It is just to exterminate or annihilate impious or heretical Kings, Governments, or Rulers.

Upon the floor is a red cross at which the postulant or candidate kneels. The Superior hands him a small black crucifix, which he takes in his left hand and presses to his heart, and the Superior at the same time presents to him a dagger, which he grasps by the blade and holds the point against his heart, the Superior still holding it by the hilt, and thus addresses the postulant:[38]

(The Superior speaks:)

My son, heretofore you have been taught to act the dissembler: among Roman Catholics to be a Roman Catholic, and to be a spy even among your own brethren; to believe no man, to trust no man. Among the Reformers, to be a Reformer; among the Huguenots, to be a Huguenot; among the Calvinists, to be a Calvinist; among other Protestants, generally to be a Protestant; and obtaining their confidence, to seek even to preach from their pulpits, and to denounce with all the vehemence in your nature our Holy Religion and the Pope; and even to descend so low as to become a Jew among Jews, that you might be enabled to gather together all information for the benefit of your Order as a faithful soldier of the

Pope. You have been taught to plant insidiously the seeds of jealousy and hatred between communities, provinces, states that were at peace, and to incite them to deeds of blood, involving them in war with each other, and to create revolutions and civil wars in countries that were independent and prosperous, cultivating the arts and the sciences and enjoying the blessings of peace; to take sides with the combatants and to act secretly with your brother Jesuit, who might be engaged on the other side, but openly opposed to that with which you might be connected, only that the Church might be the gainer in the end, in the conditions fixed in the treaties for peace and that the end justifies the means. You have been taught your duty as a spy, to gather all statistics, facts and information in your power from every source; to ingratiate yourself into the confidence of the family circle of Protestants and heretics of every class and character, as well as that of the merchant, the banker, the lawyer, among the schools and universities, in parliaments and legislatures, and the judiciaries and councils of state, and to be all things to all men, for the Pope's sake, whose servants we are unto death. You have received all your instructions heretofore as a novice, a neophyte, and have served as co-adjurer, confessor and priest, but you have not yet been invested with all that is necessary to command in the Army of Loyola in the service of the Pope. You must serve the proper time as the instrument and executioner as directed by your superiors; for none can command here who has not consecrated his labours with the blood of the heretic; for "without the shedding of blood no man can be saved". Therefore, to fit yourself for your work and make your own salvation sure, you will, in addition to your former oath of obedience to your order and allegiance to the Pope, repeat after me:

(Text of the Oath:)

I_____ , now in the presence of
Almighty God, the blessed Virgin Mary, the blessed
St. John the Baptist, the Holy Apostles, St. Peter and
St. Paul, and all the saints, sacred host of Heaven,
and to you, my Ghostly Father, the superior general
of the Society of Jesus, founded by St. Ignatius
Loyola, in the pontification of Paul the Third, and
continued to the present, do by the womb of the
Virgin, the matrix of God, and the rod of Jesus
Christ, declare and swear that His Holiness, the
Pope, is Christ's Vice-Regent and is the true and only
head of the Catholic or Universal Church throughout
the earth; and that by the virtue of the keys of
binding and loosing given to His Holiness by my
Saviour, Jesus Christ, he hath power to depose
heretical Kings, Princes, States, Commonwealths,
and Governments, and they may be safely destroyed.
Therefore to the utmost of my power I will defend
this doctrine and His Holiness's right and custom
against all usurpers of the heretical or Protestant
authority whatever, especially the Lutheran Church
of Germany, Holland, Denmark, Sweden and
Norway, and the now pretended authority and
Churches of England and Scotland, and the branches
of same now established in Ireland and on the
continent of America and elsewhere and all adherents
in regard that they may be usurped and heretical,
opposing the sacred Mother Church of Rome. I do
now denounce and disown any allegiance as due to
any heretical king, prince or State, named Protestant
or Liberal, or obedience to any of their laws,
magistrates or officers. I do further declare the
doctrine of the Churches of England and Scotland of
the Calvinists, Huguenots, and others of the name of
Protestants or Masons to be damnable, and they
themselves to be damned who will not forsake the

same. I do further declare that I will help, assist, and advise all or any of His Holiness's agents, in any place where I should be, in Switzerland, Germany, Holland, Ireland or America, or in any other kingdom or territory I shall come to, and do my utmost to extirpate the heretical Protestant or Masonic doctrines and to destroy all their pretended powers, legal or otherwise. I do further promise and declare that, notwithstanding, I am dispensed with to assume any religion heretical for the propagation of the Mother Church's interest; to keep secret and private all her agents' counsels from time to time, as they entrust me, and not to divulge, directly or indirectly, by word, writing or circumstances whatever; but to execute all that should be proposed, given in charge, or discovered unto me by you, my Ghostly Father, or any of this sacred order. I do further promise and declare that I will have no opinion or will of my own or any mental reservation whatever, even as a corpse or cadaver (perinde ac cadaver), but will unhesitatingly obey each and every command that I may receive from my superiors in the militia of the Pope and of Jesus Christ. That I will go to any part of the world whithersoever I may be sent, to the frozen regions north, jungles of India, to the centres of civilisation of Europe, or to the wild haunts of the barbarous savages of America without murmuring or repining, and will be submissive in all things, whatsoever is communicated to me. I do further promise and declare that I will, when opportunity presents, make and wage relentless war, secretly and openly, against all heretics, Protestants and Masons, as I am directed to do, to extirpate them from the face of the whole earth; and that I will spare neither age, sex nor condition, and that will hang, burn, waste, boil, flay, strangle, and bury alive these infamous heretics; rip up the stomachs and wombs of their women, and crush their infants' heads against the

walls in order to annihilate their execrable race. That
when the same cannot be done openly I will secretly
use the poisonous cup, the strangulation cord, the
steel of the poniard, or the leaden bullet, regardless
of the honour, rank, dignity or authority of the
persons, whatever may be their condition in life,
either public or private, as I at any time may be
directed so to do by any agents of the Pope or
Superior of the Brotherhood of the Holy Father of the
Society of Jesus. In confirmation of which I hereby
dedicate my life, soul, and all corporal powers, and
with the dagger which I now receive I will subscribe
my name written in my blood in testimony thereof;
and should I prove false, or weaken in my
determination, may my brethren and fellow soldiers
of the militia of the Pope cut off my hands and feet
and my throat from ear to ear, my belly be opened
and sulphur burned therein with all the punishment
that can be inflicted upon me on earth, and my soul
shall be tortured by demons in eternal hell forever.
That I will in voting always vote for a Knight of
Columbus in preference to a Protestant, especially a
Mason, and that I will leave my party so to do; that if
two Catholics are on the ticket I will satisfy myself
which is the better supporter of Mother Church and
vote accordingly. That I will not deal with or employ
a Protestant if in my power to deal with or employ a
Catholic. That I will place Catholic girls in Protestant
families that a weekly report may be made of the
inner movements of the heretics. That I will provide
myself with arms and ammunition that I may be in
readiness when the word is passed, or I am
commanded to defend the Church either as an
individual or with the militia of the Pope. All of
which I,_____, do swear by the blessed
Trinity and blessed sacrament which I am now to
receive to perform and on part to keep this my oath.
In testimony hereof, I take this most holy and blessed

sacrament of the Eucharist and witness the same further with my name written with the point of this dagger dipped in my own blood and seal in the face of this holy sacrament.

(He receives the wafer from the Superior and writes his name with the point of his dagger dipped in his own blood taken from over his heart.)

(Superior speaks:)

You will now rise to your feet and I will instruct you in the Catechism necessary to make yourself known to any member of the Society of Jesus belonging to this rank. In the first place, you, as a Brother Jesuit, will with another mutually make the ordinary sign of the cross as any ordinary Roman Catholic would; then one crosses his wrists, the palms of his hands open, and the other in answer crosses his feet, one above the other; the first points with forefinger of the right hand to the centre of the palm of the left, the other with the forefinger of the left hand points to the centre of the palm of the right; the first then with his right hand makes a circle around his head, touching it; the other then with the forefinger of his left hand touches the left side of his body just below his heart; the first then with his right hand draws it across the throat of the other, and the latter then with a dagger down the stomach and abdomen of the first. The first then says Iustum; and the other answers Necar; the first Reges; the other answers Impious. The first will then present a small piece of paper folded in a peculiar manner, four times, which the other will cut longitudinally and on opening the name Jesu will be found written upon the head and arms of a cross three times. You will then give and receive with him the following questions and answers:

From whither do you come? Answer: The Holy faith.

Whom do you serve? Answer: The Holy Father at Rome, the Pope, and the Roman Catholic Church Universal throughout the world.

Who commands you? Answer: The Successor of St. Ignatius Loyola, the founder of the Society of Jesus or the Soldiers of Jesus Christ.

Who received you? Answer: A venerable man in white hair.

How? Answer: With a naked dagger, I kneeling upon the cross beneath the banners of the Pope and of our sacred order.

Did you take an oath? Answer: I did, to destroy heretics and their governments and rulers, and to spare neither age, nor sex, nor condition; to be as a corpse without any opinion or will of my own, but to implicitly obey my Superiors in all things without hesitation or murmuring.

Will you do that? Answer: I will.

How do you travel? Answer: In the bark of Peter the fisherman.

Whither do you travel? Answer: To the four quarters of the globe.

For what purpose? Answer: To obey the orders of my General and Superiors and execute the will of the Pope and faithfully fulfil the conditions of my oaths.

Go ye, then, into all the world and take possession of all lands in the name of the Pope. He who will not

accept him as the Vicar of Jesus and his Vice-Regent
on earth, let him be accursed and exterminated.[39]

The Jesuits have carried out their sinister oath with
effectiveness throughout the world. Because of their seditious
activities they have been expelled from over 70 countries. For
example, the Jesuits were expelled from Russia (1820), Belgium,
Portugal (1834), the Italian states (1859), Spain (three times-1820,
1835, and 1868), Germany (1872), Guatemala (1872), Mexico
(1873), Brazil (1874), Equador (1875), Colombia (1875), Costa Rica
(1884), and France (twice-1880 and 1901).[40] They caused the Swiss
Civil war in 1847; as a result they were banished from Switzerland in
1848.[41] Up until the year 2000, the Swiss Constitution (article 51)
forbade the Jesuits from engaging in any cultural or educational
activity in Switzerland.[42] In the year 2000 Switzerland ratified a new
constitution, in which article 51 was removed. The Jesuit subversion
has continued to modern times, causing the Jesuits to be expelled
from Haiti in 1964 and Burma in 1966.[43]

Let us look at recent Catholic writings regarding the infection
of the Church of England with Catholic doctrine. The following
passage is from a Roman Catholic encyclopedic website, *New
Advent*. The passage addresses the influences that changed the
Anglican Church forms of worship and doctrine to more closely align
with the Roman Catholic Church. Note how the passage glorifies the
fidelity of the Anglican bishops (among whom is listed Laud) to the
Catholic theology.

> A third influence which made itself felt upon
> Anglicanism, and one more vital and more
> penetrating and progressive than the other two, has
> been that of Catholicism, whether as reflected in
> Catholic antiquity or as beheld in the actual Catholic
> and Roman Church. The effect of this influence may
> be traced in what has been called the historic High
> Church party. A number of Anglican bishops and
> divines in the seventeenth and eighteenth centuries,
> while bitterly opposed to Rome, and loyally

Protestant, stood above the prevailing low level of
churchmanship, and put forward higher and
philocatholic views, in the matters of Church
authority, belief, and worship. Although
comparatively few in number, and vehemently
assailed by their fellow churchmen, they were
destined to serve as a point d'appui for a subsequent
development. Such writers as Bishop Andrews (d.
1626), Bishop Overall (d. 1644), Bishop Montague
(d. 1641), Archbishop Laud (d. 1644), Archbishop
Bramhall (d. 1663), Dr. Thorndike (d. 1672), Bishop
Ken (d. 1711), Dr Waterland (d. 1740), may be
regarded as representative of this section.[44]

Notice the method used by Satan. The Protestant clerics
publicly opposed Rome, but worked to bring their churches under the
yoke of Rome by adopting the Roman theology. Archbishop of
Canterbury Laud was so favored by Rome for his service that he was
twice offered by the Pope to be made a Cardinal in the Catholic
Church, yet he portrayed himself as an ardent foe of Rome.

5 Preventing Grace

The bible makes it clear that man is dead in trespasses and sin. "And you hath he quickened, who were dead in trespasses and sins." Ephesians 2:1. A man who is spiritually dead cannot make himself spiritually alive again; that is a rebirth that only God can accomplish. Even Arminius had to acknowledge that truth.

Arminius and his Romish accomplices had to come up with a way to work around that obvious scriptural impediment to a free will gospel doctrine. What they did was package their graceless free will doctrine in a package labeled "grace." If the package is appealing enough, then the victims will not notice the spiritual poison inside.

In order to deceive people into accepting his poisonous doctrine of free will, Arminius came up with the myth of "prevenient grace." According to Arminius man was corrupted by original sin, but God provided a prevenient grace to all men.[45] This fictional prevenient grace is supposed to free the will of all men and enable them to cooperate with God and believe in Jesus Christ. According to Arminius, by virtue of the prevenient grace of God all men have the free will to either believe in Jesus or reject him. Kenneth Jones, an Arminian theologian, explains: "The prevenient grace of God's convicting Spirit simply lifts the sinner up to the point where the choice is possible."[46]

The prevenient grace doctrine is biblically impossible. The bible states that "there is none that seeketh after God." Romans 3:11. To address man's depraved condition, God, by his grace, gives those he has chosen for salvation the faith of Jesus. Romans 3:21-26. It is only those whom God has elected for salvation who are the object of his grace. John 17:9-12. Once God gives his elect the faith to believe in Jesus, his elect will certainly believe in Jesus. John 6:39. The faith of God's elect is not left to the chance free will decisions of men. John 1:13. The claim by Arminians that all men are given a prevenient grace that frees their will to choose to believe in God is an unbiblical invention of corrupt haters of the sovereign God.

Mark Herzer explains how prevenient grace is a necessary construct for the Arminians in order to keep the free will theory intact and at the same time acknowledge the fall of man. The prevenient grace construct is a way to explain how man can have a free will after the fall. The problem with the prevenient grace myth is that it saves no one. Under the Arminian model, salvation requires an act of man's free will, aside from any influence by God other than his act of initially freeing the will through prevenient grace.

> Their doctrine of prevenient grace is ultimately
> rooted in their insistence upon the absolute
> non-negotiable of their theology, namely, man must
> be free enough to accept or reject. They wish to be
> debtors to Free Will and we to Sovereign Grace.
> They argue that since prevenient grace came before
> our choice, therefore their theology is one of grace.
> But then again, this sort of argument was advanced
> by the Papists. It is true that this universal prevenient
> grace came before our choice; but it affected no one
> efficaciously. It led none to salvation. The
> efficacious act came from man who could accept or
> reject the prevenient grace. Man's choice is the sine
> qua non of their theology and not God's sovereign
> irresistible grace. We, on the other hand, declare, "Of

Him are ye in Christ Jesus!"[47]

Arminians had to come up with a theory to explain how man, who the bible states clearly is spiritually dead and enslaved to sin from the fall, could have a free will to believe in Jesus. It was out of this theological necessity that the myth of prevenient grace was born.

Prevenient grace is a myth that cannot pass biblical muster, but it nonetheless is part and parcel of the Arminian theology. Indeed, Arminianism cannot stand without it. Arminian theologian John Miley avoids using the term "prevenient grace," although in order to maintain his Arminian construct, he must adhere to the universal partial grace inherent in the prevenient grace concept. Miley calls prevenient grace "a helping grace."

> Man is fallen and corrupt in his nature, and therein morally helpless; but man is also redeemed and the recipient of a helping grace in Christ whereby he is invested with capabilities for a moral probation. He has the power of meeting the terms of an actual salvation. All men have this power. It is none the less real or sufficient because of its gracious source. Salvation is thus the privilege of every man, whatever his religious dispensation.[48]

Arminius defined the mythical prevenient grace given to all men as a "preventing or preceding grace." Arminius stated: "No man believes in Christ except he has been previously disposed and prepared, by **preventing or preceding grace**, to receive life eternal."[49] In witchcraft words and symbols often have two meanings. There is one meaning for the general public and a hidden meaning for the initiated. Prevenient grace literally means "preventing grace." The word "prevent" has two meanings; prevent means to stop in advance something from happening, but it also means to come before. In the context of Arminius' writings, he intended for the public to understand that he meant by prevenient grace a grace that prepares the souls of all men for faith by freeing their wills to believe.

The hidden meaning behind prevenient grace is that of "stopping grace." The reprobate mind of Arminius thinks that man can do the impossible, limit and stop the Grace of God. According to Arminius, prevenient grace gives men the free will not only to believe in Christ but also to choose to reject Christ. According to Arminius, men are given power to resist the calling of God. Therefore, under this so called prevenient grace, men can actually thwart the will of God by rejecting God's decision to save them. Prevenient grace is a grace in name only. It is actually a mythical concept that ineffectually attempts to frustrate God's will to save a sinner. Prevenient grace is an anti-grace springing from an anti-gospel. There is not a single scriptural authority that supports the prevenient grace deception. In fact, as documented in this book, the theme of the bible weighs against Arminius' so called prevenient grace.

One of the denominations following the Arminian doctrine of free will through prevenient grace is the Methodist (Wesleyan) Church. The Methodist Church was founded by John Wesley, who was an ardent Arminian. Augustus Toplady had this to say about John Wesley: "I believe him to be the most rancourous hater of the gospel system that ever appeared in England." Toplady further said that Wesley "is still as dead to the feelings of shame as he is blind to the doctrines of God." Paragraph 8 of *The Constitution Of The North American General Conference* of the Wesleyan (Methodist) Church states:

We believe that man's creation in the image of God included ability to choose between right and wrong. Thus man was made morally responsible for his choices. But since the fall of Adam, man is unable in his own strength to do the right. This is due to original sin, which is not simply the following of Adam's example, but rather the corruption of the nature of every man, and is reproduced naturally in Adam's descendants. Because of it, man is very far gone from original righteousness, and of his own nature is continually inclined to evil. He cannot of himself even call upon God or exercise faith for salvation. **But through Jesus Christ the prevenient grace of God makes possible what man in himself cannot do. It is bestowed freely upon all men, enabling all who will to turn and be saved.**[50] (emphasis added)

The subtlety of the Arminian gospel is found in the use of the word **"all."** The prevenient grace of Arminius is granted to "all." Clearly the bible supports the doctrine that God imbues those chosen for salvation the ability to believe in him. However, that faith is a gift only given to his elect; it is not given to all men.

God seeks men, men do not seek God. **"So then *it is* not of him that willeth, nor of him that runneth, but of God that sheweth mercy."** (Romans 9:16 AV) From the beginning of Jesus' ministry he made it clear that he was Lord, and he chose his disciples, they did not choose him. "Ye have not chosen me, but I have chosen you, and ordained you, that ye should go and bring forth fruit, and *that* your fruit should remain: that whatsoever ye shall ask of the Father in my name, he may give it you." (John 15:16 AV)

God has not changed his methods. Today, Jesus, the sovereign Lord of Heaven, chooses his elect for salvation. By choosing those who will be saved, he also necessarily chooses those who will be lost. **"The LORD hath made all things for himself: yea, even the wicked for the day of evil."** Proverbs 16:4.

God exercises his will in all matters; God is sovereign. Man is impotent to impede the will of God. **"And all the inhabitants of the earth are reputed as nothing: and He doeth according to His will in the army of heaven, and among the inhabitants of the earth: and who can stay His hand, or say unto Him, What doest Thou?"** Daniel 4:35.

How could Arminius say that all men have a free will to believe in Jesus when the bible states clearly that salvation comes not by the will of man, but totally of God? "But as many as received him, to them gave he power to become the sons of God, *even* to them that believe on his name: **Which were born, not of blood, nor of the will of the flesh, nor of the will of man, but of God.**" (John 1:12-13 AV)

The universalism of the Arminian anti-gospel has an attraction to the masses, because it is all-inclusive. Under the Arminian anti-gospel, all men have the ability to believe in Jesus, and anyone by their free will can do so. That is not the way of God under the true gospel. Under the gospel of Jesus, salvation is exclusive to those whom God has chosen for salvation. Notice in John 17:9 how Jesus specifically stated that he did not pray for the world; he prayed only for the elect given to him by the father. **"I pray for them: I pray not for the world, but for them which thou hast given me; for they are thine."** (John 17:9 AV)

In John 12:37-40 God reveals that those who do not believe in him don't do so because they do not have the ability to believe in him! Those passages impeach directly the authority of Arminius' prevenient grace, wherein Arminius alleges that all are given the ability to believe in Christ.

> But though he had done so many miracles before
> them, yet they believed not on him: That the saying
> of Esaias the prophet might be fulfilled, which he
> spake, Lord, who hath believed our report? and to
> whom hath the arm of the Lord been revealed?
> **Therefore they could not believe, because that
> Esaias said again, He hath blinded their eyes, and
> hardened their heart; that they should not see
> with *their* eyes, nor understand with *their* heart,
> and be converted, and I should heal them.** (John
> 12:37-40 AV)

God makes it clear in John 12:37-40 that the unsaved will not believe in Jesus because God has blinded their eyes and hardened their hearts to the gospel. The unsaved have been prevented by God from believing. "For the LORD hath poured out upon you the spirit of deep sleep, and hath closed your eyes." (Isaiah 29:10 AV)

Those who do not believe have been spiritually blinded by God. They have not received prevenient grace, which Arminius alleges was showered on all men, and frees their will to believe in Jesus. Unbelievers have instead received a spirit of slumber from God. They do not believe, because they cannot believe. Their will is not free, it is in bondage to sin, and they will reject God because their enslaved will prevents them from any other course.

> What then? Israel hath not obtained that which he seeketh for; **but the election hath obtained it, and the rest were blinded** (According as it is written, **God hath given them the spirit of slumber, eyes that they should not see, and ears that they should not hear**;) unto this day. And David saith, Let their table be made a snare, and a trap, and a stumblingblock, and a recompence unto them: (Romans 11:7-9 AV)

Romans 11:7-9 is yet more biblical authority that directly contradicts the prevenient grace doctrine of Arminius, which supposedly enables all men to freely believe in Jesus. Only the elect of God are given the free gift of faith, and that gift is given solely by the grace of God.

The free will gospel in effect takes away sovereignty from God and puts man in control over eternal life. The Arminian god is not the sovereign God of the bible. The free will gospel is an ear tickler; it sounds good at first blush, but it is an unbiblical myth. Under the Arminian gospel man is primary, and an impotent god is secondary. In fact, their god is a virtual spectator who is holding out the gift of eternal salvation, hoping that some men by their free will choose to accept his gift. This Arminian god is forlornly left holding the bag, while most men exercise their free will and reject his gift of eternal life.

The true gospel, on the other hand, holds that our faith is a gift from God, it does not come from our free will. "For by grace are ye saved through faith; **and that not of yourselves: *it is* the gift of God.**" (Ephesians 2:8 AV) Notice that Ephesians 2:8 says: "and **that not** of yourselves." To what is God referring when he says "that?" It is obvious by the context that he means faith. Clearly grace is from God; that point needs no clarification. The only point that needs clarification is the source of faith; "that" faith is **not** of yourselves, "it [faith] is the gift of God." That passage alone makes free will impossible as the means of salvation.

Ernest Reisinger explains that the free will of man was the principal issue of the reformation:

> When most Christians think of the Reformation, the first thing that comes to their mind is justification by faith alone. There is good reason for that assumption; justification by faith alone was the key doctrine that came out of the Reformation; however, it was not the key issue at the foundation of the Reformation. A careful study of the historical facts will clearly show that the issue of man's will was at the heart of the theological difference between Martin Luther and the Roman Catholic Church.[51]

The Roman Catholic anti-gospel has made new inroads since the reformation. Arminianism has been promoted by "Christian" luminaries all over the world including but not limited to John Wesley and Charles Finney of yesteryear to today's Billy Graham, Dave Hunt, Chuck Colson, Chuck Swindol, Chuck Smith, and Hank Hanegraff.

This Arminian gospel has today permeated most of the nominal "Christian" churches. That anti-gospel is a direct attack on the sovereignty of God. Under the Arminian gospel, man is sovereign. The Arminian preachers speak of Jesus, but he is more an ornament to their theology. B.B. Warfield once observed of the Arminian theology of Charles Finney: "God might be eliminated from it entirely without essentially changing its character."[52]

Arminianism is a continuation of the seduction begun in the garden of Eden, where the serpent deceived Adam and Eve into eating of the fruit that would give them knowledge of good and evil. He told them "ye shall be as gods." Genesis 3:5.

A person seeking Christ is brought to the point where he cries out for help from God "Lord, I believe; help thou mine unbelief." Mark 9:24. However, a seeker exposed to the Arminian anti-gospel does not cry out for help from God, because he is convinced by the Arminian preacher that he does not need God to help him with his unbelief, it is all up to him and his own free will. He will be told that Jesus will not interfere with his free will decision.

The Arminian anti-gospel actually prevents true repentance from sin and turning toward God. Instead the seeker is told to look not to God for help with his unbelief, but rather that he has the power of his own free will to believe. Oh, they are told to believe in Jesus, but their belief is not in the Jesus of the Bible. In order to believe in the Jesus of the bible, a person must have the faith of the Jesus of the bible, not the faith of their free will. "But the scripture hath concluded all under sin, that the promise by **faith of Jesus** Christ might be **given to them that believe**." (Galatians 3:22 AV)

Often a seeker is counseled by an Arminian pastor, who advises the seeker to recite a form statement. He is then told he is born again. However, there is no spiritual rebirth. The person is a counterfeit Christian who has a worldly belief in Jesus. That is not unlike the belief that even the devils have. James 2:19. That type of belief is not a saving faith. The counterfeit Christian goes through the motions of being a Christian, but his is just one of the many tares added to the wheat in the church. Tares look just like the wheat, but their end is quite different. Jesus explained this very phenomenon to his disciples in Mark 13.

> Another parable put he forth unto them, saying, The
> kingdom of heaven is likened unto a man which
> sowed good seed in his field: But while men slept,

his enemy came and sowed tares among the wheat,
and went his way. But when the blade was sprung up,
and brought forth fruit, then appeared the tares also.
So the servants of the householder came and said
unto him, Sir, didst not thou sow good seed in thy
field? from whence then hath it tares? He said unto
them, An enemy hath done this. The servants said
unto him, Wilt thou then that we go and gather them
up? But he said, Nay; lest while ye gather up the
tares, ye root up also the wheat with them. Let both
grow together until the harvest: and in the time of
harvest I will say to the reapers, Gather ye together
first the tares, and bind them in bundles to burn them:
but gather the wheat into my barn. . . . Then Jesus
sent the multitude away, and went into the house:
and his disciples came unto him, saying, Declare
unto us the parable of the tares of the field. He
answered and said unto them, He that soweth the
good seed is the Son of man; The field is the world;
the good seed are the children of the kingdom; but
the tares are the children of the wicked *one*; The
enemy that sowed them is the devil; the harvest is the
end of the world; and the reapers are the angels. As
therefore the tares are gathered and burned in the
fire; so shall it be in the end of this world. The Son
of man shall send forth his angels, and they shall
gather out of his kingdom all things that offend, and
them which do iniquity; And shall cast them into a
furnace of fire: there shall be wailing and gnashing of
teeth. Then shall the righteous shine forth as the sun
in the kingdom of their Father. Who hath ears to
hear, let him hear. (Matthew 13:24-30, 36-42 AV)

One might think that there must be some passage in the bible
that supports the idea of prevenient grace. No, there is no such bible
passage. In order to suggest that there is biblical authority, the
Arminians use the satanic trick of quoting bible verses out of context.
Virtually any false doctrine can be supported by biblical text taken

out of context, even to the extent of trying to prove that "there is no
God." Indeed, Psalm 14:1 states: "There is no God." It is an accurate
quote, but it has been taken out of context. When we see the passage
in context, we see that the quoted clause has quite a different
meaning. The entire passage reads: "The fool hath said in his heart,
There is no God. They are corrupt, they have done abominable
works, there is none that doeth good." Psalm 14:1. The context we
see gives quite a different meaning than is intended by our
hypothetical atheist. As we explore the Arminian scriptural
authority, we will see that in a series of verses they have wrongly
divided God's word from its context to give a meaning contrary to
God's intended meaning.

The Arminian strategy (of taking bible passages out of
context to make the case for prevenient grace) is illustrated by Dr.
Jack Graham's effort. Jack Graham (no relation to Billy Graham) is
the pastor of Prestonwood Baptist Church in Dallas, Texas.
Prestonwood is a mega-church with over 28,0000 members. It is the
17th largest church in the United States.[53] According to the church
website "Dr. Graham has served two terms as president of the
Southern Baptist Convention, the largest American Protestant
denomination, with 16 million members and as president of the SBC
Pastor's Conference."[54] Graham also has a large and successful radio
and television broadcast ministry called PowerPoint Ministries.
Although Graham did not use the term prevenient grace, that is what
he meant when he said the following:

> Somebody says but wait a minute, wait a minute,
> wait a minute, doesn't God have to give us even the
> faith to believe? You will hear this often. Because we
> are so dead and depraved in sin God has to give us
> even the faith to believe. He has to regenerate us
> before we can even believe in Him. Now thats a little
> backwards, isn't it?... But that is the way this logic--
> or illogic--goes. God has to regenerate you before
> you can ever say, I receive Christ. No the Bible says
> believe on the Lord Jesus Christ and you will be
> saved. You say but doesn't God have to give us faith

to be saved. Didn't you say salvation is of the Lord?
Absolutely. Even our faith comes from God. And
guess what? Romans 12:3 says that God has given to
every man, to all men a measure of faith. Every
person has been given by God this faculty this
opportunity to believe.[55]

Notice Graham cites to Romans 12:3. Typical of Arminian
preachers, he takes the passage out of context. He states that Romans
12:3 supports the prevenient faith concept whereby God gives every
person the ability to believe in Jesus. Graham has wrongly divided
the word of God. When one reads Romans 12:3 in context, it is clear
that the passage is not saying that every man in the entire world is
given the ability to believe in Jesus. The passage is referring only to
the saved members of the church.

When Romans 12:3 is read in context it is evident that Paul is
addressing the "brethren" in Christ and explaining that grace is given
in a different way to every member of the body of Christ. Some
have, by God's grace, the gift of prophecy, others have the gift of
ministry, yet others the gift of teaching, etc., and each are to be done
"according to the proportion of faith."

So when Paul says in Romans 12:3 that God through his
grace gave to every man a measure of faith, he means that God gave
the various spiritual gifts in accordance with the differing proportions
of faith for each saved member of the church body. The differing
proportions of faith are determined by the sovereign grace of God.
Every member of the church body has faith and is saved. But not
every member has the same measure of faith or spiritual calling in the
church. When Paul said "every man" has been dealt a measure of
faith, it was in the context of a message to his "brethren" in the
church. The "every man" was a reference to "every man" in the
church.

I beseech you therefore, **brethren**, by the mercies of
God, that ye present your bodies a living sacrifice,
holy, acceptable unto God, which is your reasonable

service. And be not conformed to this world: but be
ye transformed by the renewing of your mind, that ye
may prove what is that good, and acceptable, and
perfect, will of God. For I say, through the grace
given unto me, **to every man that is among you**, not
to think of himself more highly than he ought to
think; but to think soberly, **according as God hath
dealt to every man the measure of faith**. For as we
have many members in one body, and all members
have not the same office: So we, being many, are one
body in Christ, and every one members one of
another. Having then gifts differing according to the
grace that is given to us, whether prophecy, let us
prophesy **according to the proportion of faith**; Or
ministry, let us wait on our ministering: or he that
teacheth, on teaching; Or he that exhorteth, on
exhortation: he that giveth, let him do it with
simplicity; he that ruleth, with diligence; he that
sheweth mercy, with cheerfulness. (Romans 12:1-8
AV)

Prevenient grace is a man-made artifice constructed to fill a
theological hole in the Arminian free will mythology. There is a
complete lack of biblical support for the prevenient grace construct; it
is based entirely on the imaginations of huckster theologians. John
Hendryx points out the lack of biblical support for Arminianism:

[T]he Bible never teaches in a clear and open manner
the concept of prevenient grace. . . . Arminians
awkwardly force this on the Scripture in order to
hold their system together. This alone should lead us
to reject it. Unaided reason should NEVER be the
foundation of our theological insights, especially one
of such critical importance.[56]

Prevenient grace is a concept that is so difficult to reconcile
with the bible that its proponents must come up with sometimes
discombobulated explanations for it. One example of this is found in

Tome Gender's book, *The Narrow Road: How Does God Save Sinners?*. Gender states:

> Prevenient grace will lead to genuine faith in Christ unless it is finally resisted by the sinner. In this way, it makes faith possible, without making it necessary. It preserves the basis on which God sovereignly chooses to deal with human beings for salvation- by their free choices.[57]

First, Gender states that prevenient grace will lead to faith unless it is resisted. So, right off the bat we have a battle of wills. God wills the sinner to be saved, but the sinner has veto power over God's will. Second, Gender states that faith is made possible, but it is not necessary. Gender's theology has jumped off the biblical tracks. Faith is in fact necessary for salvation. Romans 3:28.

Gender gives an explanation of prevenient grace wherein he tries to work in some biblical words as camouflage for his unbiblical Arminian theology. However, he uses the words in a way that strips them of their true meaning. His use of the words "sovereign" and "choose" are completely decoupled from their true biblical meanings. Gender states the prevenient grace is the basis for God to "sovereignly choose to deal with human beings for salvation - by their free choices." That makes no sense. How can God "sovereignly choose" men for salvation, if those same men are supposed to be saved by their own "free choices?" The two concepts of man's free choice and God's sovereign choice are mutually exclusive.

The theme of the bible is that God chooses man, man does not (indeed he cannot) choose God. John 1:13; 15:16; Ephesians 2:1. Gender states that God is sovereign, but man makes a free choice as to whether to believe in him. According to Gender, God does not choose his elect for salvation. Instead, God chooses to bestow a prevenient grace whereby the sinner then exercises his (mythical) free will to choose Jesus. Gender uses the term "choose" differently than does God when he stated that he chose us in Jesus before the foundation of the world. Ephesians 1:4. God's elect constitute a generation chosen by God. 1 Peter 2:9. Gender, as do all prevenient grace proponents, reverses the order of events and makes the sinner the one choosing God.

6 The Gospel

In order to understand why the free will doctrine is actually an anti-gospel whose purpose is to supplant and oppose the true gospel we must juxtapose it against the true gospel. Our first order of business is to read God's word for what it says, not for what we would like it to say or what we have been told it says. Let God speak, let us listen. Let us look and see what Jesus states is the means for obtaining eternal life. First, Jesus makes clear that all the law and the prophets are summarized in just two commandments.

> Then one of them, *which was* a lawyer, asked *him a question*, tempting him, and saying, Master, which *is* the great commandment in the law? Jesus said unto him, Thou shalt love the Lord thy God with all thy heart, and with all thy soul, and with all thy mind. This is the first and great commandment. And the second *is* like unto it, Thou shalt love thy neighbour as thyself. **On these two commandments hang all the law and the prophets**. (Matthew 22:35-40 AV)

Second, God states that in order to gain entrance into heaven one must obey and keep all of God's law. **"For whosoever shall keep the whole law, and yet offend in one *point*, he is guilty of**

all." James 2:10. *See also* Matthew 17:17-19.

> **And, behold, a certain lawyer stood up, and**
> **tempted him, saying, Master, what shall I do to**
> **inherit eternal life? He said unto him, What is**
> **written in the law?** how readest thou? And he
> answering said, Thou shalt love the Lord thy God
> with all thy heart, and with all thy soul, and with all
> thy strength, and with all thy mind; and thy
> neighbour as thyself. And he said unto him, Thou
> hast answered right: **this do, and thou shalt live**.
> (Luke 10:25-28 AV)

If we sin by transgressing God's law, we must be punished, for God is just. One cannot enter heaven with any sins, God's wrath is upon all who have sinned. "For this ye know, that no whoremonger, nor unclean person, nor covetous man, who is an idolater, hath any inheritance in the kingdom of Christ and of God. Let no man deceive you with vain words: for because of these things cometh the wrath of God upon the children of disobedience." (Ephesians 5:5-6 AV) All who do not keep every one of God's commands are under a curse. **"For as many as are of the works of the law are under the curse: for it is written, Cursed *is* every one that continueth not in all things which are written in the book of the law to do them."** (Galatians 3:10 AV) The cursed punishment for violating God's law is eternal. *See* John 5:29; Matthew 25:1-46.

> But after thy hardness and impenitent heart treasurest
> up unto thyself wrath against the day of wrath and
> revelation of the righteous judgment of God; Who
> will render to every man according to his deeds: To
> them who by patient continuance in well doing seek
> for glory and honour and immortality, eternal life:
> But **unto them that are contentious, and do not**
> **obey the truth, but obey unrighteousness,**
> **indignation and wrath**. (Romans 2:5-8 AV)

The Son of man shall send forth his angels, and they

shall gather out of his kingdom all things that offend,
and them which do iniquity; And **shall cast them
into a furnace of fire: there shall be wailing and
gnashing of teeth.** Then shall the righteous shine
forth as the sun in the kingdom of their Father. Who
hath ears to hear, let him hear. (Matthew 13:41-43
AV)

And to you who are troubled rest with us, when the
Lord Jesus shall be revealed from heaven with his
mighty angels, In flaming fire **taking vengeance on
them that know not God, and that obey not the
gospel of our Lord Jesus Christ: Who shall be
punished with everlasting destruction** from the
presence of the Lord, and from the glory of his
power; (2 Thessalonians 1:7-9 AV)

God's standard is perfect righteousness. Examine yourself;
have you ever lied, coveted, envied, stolen, idolized, hated, lusted,
gotten drunk, fornicated, been angry with someone without just cause
(Matthew 5:21-22), or called someone a fool? If you have done any
of those things, then the punishment for your sins is to be cast into
the lake of fire and brimstone.

**Know ye not that the unrighteous shall not inherit
the kingdom of God?** Be not deceived: neither
fornicators, nor idolaters, nor adulterers, nor
effeminate, nor abusers of themselves with mankind,
Nor thieves, nor covetous, nor drunkards, nor
revilers, nor extortioners, shall inherit the kingdom of
God. (1 Corinthians 6:9-10 AV)

He that overcometh shall inherit all things; and I will
be his God, and he shall be my son. But **the fearful,
and unbelieving, and the abominable, and
murderers, and whoremongers, and sorcerers,
and idolaters, and all liars, shall have their part in
the lake which burneth with fire and brimstone:**

which is the second death. (Revelation 21:7-8 AV)

Now the works of the flesh are manifest, which are *these*; **Adultery, fornication, uncleanness, lasciviousness, Idolatry, witchcraft, hatred, variance, emulations, wrath, strife, seditions, heresies, Envyings, murders, drunkenness, revellings, and such like**: of the which I tell you before, as I have also told *you* in time past, that **they which do such things shall not inherit the kingdom of God**. (Galatians 5:19-21 AV)

These six *things* doth the LORD hate: yea, seven *are* an abomination unto him: A proud look, a lying tongue, and hands that shed innocent blood, An heart that deviseth wicked imaginations, feet that be swift in running to mischief, A false witness *that* speaketh lies, and he that soweth discord among brethren. (Proverbs 6:16-19 AV)

God's standard for righteousness is so high it even accounts for idle words. "But I say unto you, That **every idle word that men shall speak, they shall give account thereof in the day of judgment**." (Matthew 12:36 AV) God's standard is not a physical standard that only addresses conduct, his standard is a spiritual standard that judges men's hearts. Even if you have not acted upon your evil thoughts, your sin still must be punished. For instance, if you have ever lusted after another, then you have committed adultery in your heart. Matthew 5:28. If you have committed any of the above sins, you are not alone. The fact is that no one is capable of keeping God's law through their own effort; none is righteous, not one single person.

As it is written, **There is none righteous, no, not one: There is none that understandeth, there is none that seeketh after God**. They are all gone out of the way, they are together become unprofitable; **there is none that doeth good, no, not one**. Their

throat *is* an open sepulchre; with their tongues they
have used deceit; the poison of asps *is* under their
lips: Whose mouth *is* full of cursing and bitterness:
Their feet *are* swift to shed blood: Destruction and
misery *are* in their ways: And the way of peace have
they not known: There is no fear of God before their
eyes. Now we know that what things soever the law
saith, it saith to them who are under the law: **that
every mouth may be stopped, and all the world
may become guilty before God**. (Romans 3:10-19
AV)

It being the case, that not one person is righteous, nobody
could ever inherit eternal life by their works. So now we have a
dilemma. All who do not keep the law of God are under a curse.
God requires us to be perfectly righteous and keep the whole law, but
we are incapable of doing so. It would seem that there is no way for
us to be freed from the curse of the law and get into heaven.

God resolved the dilemma by coming to earth and living a
perfect life and then he, being innocent of any sin, allowed himself to
be punished in our place for our sins. "For he hath made him *to be*
sin for us, who knew no sin; that we might be made the righteousness
of God in him." (2 Corinthians 5:21 AV) Jesus was an atoning
sacrifice for our sins; his crucifixion and death was a propitiation for
our sins that satisfied God's requirement that sin be punished. 1 John
4:10.

If you believe in the Lord Jesus Christ, his perfect life will be
imputed to you, and in the eyes of God you are sinless and righteous.
Galatians 3:6-9. You are justified not because you are good, but
because Christ is good and paid the price for your sins. If you
believe in Jesus, his righteousness will be imputed to you. He took
the total punishment for your sin, which was required by God's
perfect justice, so that he could forgive you completely, according to
his perfect mercy. The key is that it is through faith in the work of
Jesus Christ and not by one's own works that one is saved.

But now the righteousness of God without the law is
manifested, being witnessed by the law and the
prophets; Even the righteousness of God *which is* by
faith of Jesus Christ unto all and upon all them that
believe: for there is no difference: For all have
sinned, and come short of the glory of God; Being
justified freely by his grace through the redemption
that is in Christ Jesus: Whom God hath set forth *to
be* a propitiation through faith in his blood, to declare
his righteousness for the remission of sins that are
past, through the forbearance of God; To declare, *I
say*, at this time his righteousness: that he might be
just, and the justifier of him which believeth in Jesus.
Where *is* boasting then? It is excluded. By what law?
of works? Nay: but by the law of faith. **Therefore
we conclude that a man is justified by faith
without the deeds of the law**. (Romans 3:21-28 AV)

What shall we say then that Abraham our father, as
pertaining to the flesh, hath found? For if Abraham
were justified by works, he hath *whereof* to glory;
but not before God. For what saith the scripture?
Abraham believed God, and it was counted unto him
for righteousness. Now to him that worketh is the
reward not reckoned of grace, but of debt. But **to
him that worketh not, but believeth on him that
justifieth the ungodly, his faith is counted for
righteousness**. Even as David also describeth the
blessedness of the man, unto whom God imputeth
righteousness without works, *Saying*, Blessed *are*
they whose iniquities are forgiven, and whose sins
are covered. Blessed *is* the man to whom the Lord
will not impute sin. (Romans 4:1-8 AV)

Jesus has redeemed us from the curse of the law by being
cursed in our stead. He, who knew no sin, was punished for our sins.

But that no man is justified by the law in the sight of

God, *it is* evident: for, The just shall live by faith.
And the law is not of faith: but, The man that doeth
them shall live in them. **Christ hath redeemed us
from the curse of the law, being made a curse for
us: for it is written, Cursed *is* every one that
hangeth on a tree:** That the blessing of Abraham
might come on the Gentiles through Jesus Christ;
that we might receive the promise of the Spirit
through faith. (Galatians 3:11-14 AV)

Why didn't God just forgive all our sins without coming to
earth and sacrificing himself for our sins?   Because God's character
is that he is both perfectly just and perfectly merciful.

And the LORD descended in the cloud, and stood
with him there, and proclaimed the name of the
LORD. And the LORD passed by before him, and
proclaimed, The LORD, The LORD God, merciful
and gracious, longsuffering, and abundant in
goodness and truth, **Keeping mercy for thousands,
forgiving iniquity and transgression and sin, and
that will by no means clear *the guilty*;** visiting the
iniquity of the fathers upon the children, and upon
the children's children, unto the third and to the
fourth *generation.* (Exodus 34:5-7 AV)

God's perfect justice requires complete punishment for sin.
God's perfect mercy requires that he forgive our sins. God must
punish our sin perfectly and at the same time forgive our sin totally.
A seemingly impossible task. Nothing, however, is impossible for
God. God punished himself in our place for our sins on the cross,
according to his perfect justice. Those that believe in Jesus Christ are
then forgiven of all their sins and are cloaked with the perfect
righteousness of Christ.

If God planned all along to come to earth and sacrifice
himself for us and knew we could not keep the law, what then is the
purpose of the law? It is a schoolmaster that was instituted in order

to teach us that we are sinners in need of a savior. Jesus fulfilled the requirements of the law for us, so that through faith in him we can be justified. "Therefore by the deeds of the law there shall no flesh be justified in his sight: for by the law *is* the knowledge of sin." Romans 3:20. Jesus did not do away with the law, he fulfilled the requirements of the law for us. Matthew 5:17-18. Those who try to work their way into heaven have not submitted to the righteousness of God, but have put themselves under the curse of God. True righteousness comes only through faith in the Lord Jesus Christ. Romans 10:3-4; John 14:6.

> Now to Abraham and his seed were the promises made. He saith not, And to seeds, as of many; but as of one, And to thy seed, which is Christ. And this I say, *that* the covenant, that was confirmed before of God in Christ, the law, which was four hundred and thirty years after, cannot disannul, that it should make the promise of none effect. For if the inheritance *be* of the law, *it is* no more of promise: but God gave *it* to Abraham by promise. Wherefore then *serveth* the law? It was added because of transgressions, till the seed should come to whom the promise was made; *and it was* ordained by angels in the hand of a mediator. Now a mediator is not *a mediator* of one, but God is one. *Is* the law then against the promises of God? God forbid: for if there had been a law given which could have given life, verily righteousness should have been by the law. But the scripture hath concluded all under sin, that the promise by faith of Jesus Christ might be given to them that believe. But before faith came, we were kept under the law, shut up unto the faith which should afterwards be revealed. **Wherefore the law was our schoolmaster *to bring us* unto Christ, that we might be justified by faith. But after that faith is come, we are no longer under a schoolmaster. For ye are all the children of God by faith in Christ Jesus.** (Galatians 3:16-26 AV)

It is not by one's own efforts in keeping God's law that one is saved. Rather, it is by God's grace through faith in Jesus Christ that we are born again. "Jesus answered and said unto him, Verily, verily, I say unto thee, Except a man be born again, he cannot see the kingdom of God." (John 3:3 AV) Being born a new spiritual creature, the old creature of the flesh was crucified with Christ on the cross. "Knowing this, that our old man is crucified with *him*, that the body of sin might be destroyed, that henceforth we should not serve sin." (Romans 6:6 AV) We are now in Christ. "Therefore if any man *be* in Christ, *he is* a new creature: old things are passed away; behold, all things are become new." (2 Corinthians 5:17 AV)

We who believe in Jesus are adopted children of God. We were chosen by God for adoption before the world was created. **"According as he hath chosen us in him before the foundation of the world, that we should be holy and without blame before him in love: Having predestinated us unto the adoption of children by Jesus Christ to himself, according to the good pleasure of his will."** (Ephesians 1:4-5 AV)

> Even so we, when we were children, were in bondage under the elements of the world: But when the fulness of the time was come, **God sent forth his Son, made of a woman, made under the law, To redeem them that were under the law, that we might receive the adoption of sons. And because ye are sons, God hath sent forth the Spirit of his Son into your hearts, crying, Abba, Father. Wherefore thou art no more a servant, but a son; and if a son, then an heir of God through Christ.** (Galatians 4:3-7 AV)

We have become a part of the body of Christ. "Now ye are the body of Christ, and members in particular." (1 Corinthians 12:27 AV) We, who believe in Jesus Christ, were predestined to be glorified with Christ. "The Spirit itself beareth witness with our spirit, that **we are the children of God**: And if children, then heirs; heirs of God, and joint-heirs with Christ; if so be that we suffer with *him*, that **we may be also glorified together.**" (Romans 8:16-17 AV) **"For whom he did foreknow, he also did predestinate *to be* conformed to the image of his Son, that he might be the firstborn among many brethren.** Moreover whom he did predestinate, **them he also called: and whom he called, them he also justified: and whom he justified, them he also glorified.**" (Romans 8:29-30 AV)

> For our conversation is in heaven; from whence also we look for the Saviour, the Lord Jesus Christ: **Who shall change our vile body, that it may be fashioned like unto his glorious body**, according to the working whereby he is able even to subdue all things unto himself. (Philippians 3:20-21 AV)

> Behold, what manner of love the Father hath bestowed upon us, that we should be called the **sons of God**: therefore the world knoweth us not, because it knew him not. Beloved, **now are we the sons of God**, and it doth not yet appear what we shall be: but we know that, when he shall appear, **we shall be like him**; for we shall see him as he is. (1 John 3:1-2 AV)

To be glorified with Christ as an adopted son of God is to wonderful a thought to even comprehend. "But as it is written, Eye hath not seen, nor ear heard, neither have entered into the heart of man, the things which God hath prepared for them that love him." (1 Corinthians 2:9 AV)

7 Dead in Trespasses and Sins

What about faith? Some may ask: doesn't a person have to be smart enough, educated enough, good enough, to believe in Jesus? The Holy Bible states that faith is a gift from God. We, who are saved, were at one time dead in sin, but God, through his Holy Spirit, made us alive by his glorious grace. "And you hath he quickened, who were dead in trespasses and sins." Ephesians 2:1. It is not possible for a dead man to do anything, a dead man cannot even have faith, he must be made alive again. Man does not have it in him to come to Jesus; God must draw him.

Arminian preacher David Cloud, however, believes that man is able to come to Christ of his own free will. Cloud is the founder of *Way of Life Literature*, which he describes as a "fundamental Baptist preaching and publishing ministry."[58] Cloud also runs the *Fundamental Baptist information Service*. *Way of Life* Publishes *The Way of Life Encyclopedia of the Bible & Christianity* and *The Advanced Bible Studies Series*. *Way of Life* also publishes *The Fundamental Baptist Digital Library*, which is Composed of approximately 3,500 select books.[59] *Way of Life* has produced bible study materials in over 12 languages. "In 1984, *Way of Life* began publishing O TIMOTHY MAGAZINE, a monthly publication with the aim of urging preachers to stand for the truth and to resist error."[60]   Cloud proudly portrays himself as an expert in Christian doctrine. His website states: "Cloud has spent an average of at least six hours per day in study since his conversion in 1973. He has built a 6,000-volume research library."[61] Let's examine what all of Cloud's study and writing has produced.

Cloud thinks that it is heresy to believe that man is totally unable to come to Christ of his own free will.

> Well, if we are going to take the "dead man" analogy literally, a dead man can't sin either. When the Bible says the sinner is dead in trespasses and sins it means that he is separated from God's divine life because of sin. To take this analogy beyond the actual teaching of the Bible and to give it other meanings, such as to reason that since the sinner is dead in trespasses and sins he must not be able to believe, is to move from truth to heresy.[62]

Cloud explains his view of man's ability to believe in Jesus of his own free will.

> The Bible teaches that man is morally corrupt (Jer. 17:9; Rom. 3:10-18) and dead in trespasses and sins (Eph. 2:1) and spiritually blind (1 Cor. 2:14), but it nowhere teaches that man cannot respond to the gospel. When I have challenged Calvinists to provide me with even one verse that says man is dead in trespasses and sins in SUCH A MANNER that he cannot even believe the gospel, they have never provided such a verse.[63] (emphasis in original)

It is not clear to whom Cloud talked, but his claim of challenging others to prove the total inability of man to come to Christ is probably a myth, since all Cloud needed to do was read his bible during one of his 6 hour study sessions and that truth would have jumped out at him. John 6:44 makes it clear that man is unable to come to Jesus without God the Father drawing him. "No man can come to me, except the Father which hath sent me draw him: and I will raise him up at the last day." *Id.* The bible is clear that salvation is not by the "will of the flesh, nor of the will of man, but of God." John 1:13.

Cloud's blindness to the plain meaning of the words in the bible seems to be endemic among Arminians. For example, Dr. John G. Mitchell ignores the plain meaning of John 6:44 and twists it to conform to his Arminian theology:

> Now please don't take John 6:44 - "No man can come to me, except the Father which hath sent me draw him" - out of its context to stress the sovereignty of God and to deny the free will of man. ... There are some who believe that God is going to save only those He has predestined to save. The have no choice in the matter because He has elected them. The bible doesn't teach that.[64]

The bible expressly teaches the very thing that Dr. Mitchell denies. Notice how Dr. Mitchell left out the operative language in John 6:44: "and I will raise him up at the last day." By ignoring that clause, Mitchell is able to construct a theology whereby God draws everyone in the world. However, with that clause read in context, it is clear to any reader that all who are drawn by the Father will be raised up on the last day. There will be none among the drawn who will be lost. *See* John 6:37-39. To be saved, one must be drawn; all who are drawn will be raised up on the last day. Hence, the Father only draws those whom he has elected for salvation. Read in its entirety and in context, John 6:44 renders the Arminian theology impossible.

Being in the first graduating class from Dallas Theological Seminary in 1927, Dr. Mitchell was among the first of a torrent of Arminian preachers from that institution to spread their error throughout the country and indeed the world. Dr. Mitchell went on to be the founder of Multnomah School of the Bible.

Returning to Cloud, he seems to think that man can be "morally corrupt" and "dead in trespasses and sins" and "spiritually blind" and yet still have the capacity to believe the gospel of his own free will. Sadly, Cloud's Arminian theology is very popular. "Cloud has preached in more than 550 churches in every State of the Union except one and in many foreign countries."[65] Cloud is blind to the meaning of the passages he has cited. The very passages cited by Cloud make the point that "man is dead in trespasses and sins in such a manner that he cannot even believe the gospel."

The entire theme of the bible is that it is because man is dead in trespasses and sins that he cannot believe in Jesus without the intervention of God. Cloud cites Ephesians 2:1, and admits that man is spiritually dead, but he denies the truth of the passage, which is that the spiritual death is an impediment to man believing in Jesus. When reading the verse in context, it is clear that man needs God to make him spiritually alive, so that man can believe in him. The passage clearly refers to the quickening of our spirits by God. Cloud ignores God's quickening and represents the passage as only meaning that man is spiritually dead. He ignores the fact that man is so completely dead that God must intervene to make him spiritually alive. According to Cloud's theology it is unnecessary for God to spiritually quicken his elect, because they can come to Christ on their own.

> **And you hath he quickened, who were dead in trespasses and sins**; Wherein in time past ye walked according to the course of this world, according to the prince of the power of the air, the spirit that now worketh in the children of disobedience: Among whom also we all had our conversation in times past in the lusts of our flesh, fulfilling the desires of the flesh and of the mind; and were by nature the children of wrath, even as others. But God, who is rich in mercy, for his great love wherewith he loved us, **Even when we were dead in sins, hath quickened us together with Christ, (by grace ye are saved**;) And hath raised us up together, and made

us sit together in heavenly places in Christ Jesus:
That in the ages to come he might shew the
exceeding riches of his grace in his kindness toward
us through Christ Jesus. For by grace are ye saved
through faith; and that not of yourselves: it is the gift
of God:" (Ephesians 2:1-8 AV)

Cloud further cites to Romans 3:10-18, but he seems to
suggest that those verses only mean that man is morally corrupt. Man
is certainly morally corrupt, but he is much worse off than that.
Cloud fails to mention that Romans 3:11 states clearly that no one
seeks God. "There is none that understandeth, there is none that
seeketh after God." (Romans 3:11 AV) If none seek after God, then it
must be God that seeks after men. In fact, man is so completely lost
and helpless it was necessary for God to redeem us by being crucified
and then to justify us totally by his grace. "Being justified freely by
his grace through the redemption that is in Christ Jesus:" (Romans
3:24 AV)

Cloud cites 1 Corinthians 2:14, but dismisses it as a proof
that man is unable of his own free will to come to Jesus. Cloud
admits that the verse describes the spiritual blindness of man, but
somehow he does not think that spiritual blindness is an impediment
to belief. The passage is clear proof that spiritual blindness makes
man unable to receive or understand the gospel. "But the natural man
receiveth not the things of the Spirit of God: for they are foolishness
unto him: neither can he know *them*, because they are spiritually
discerned." (1 Corinthians 2:14 AV)

God must give his elect a new spiritual heart to receive and
understand the gospel. In fact, the two preceding passages make a
distinction between the spirit of the world and the Spirit of God. It is
only through the intervention of the Holy Spirit that man can believe
in Jesus. The gift of the Holy Spirit is freely given by God to his
elect.

Now we have received, not the spirit of the world,
but the spirit which is of God; that we might know

the things that are freely given to us of God. Which
things also we speak, not in the words which man's
wisdom teacheth, but which the Holy Ghost teacheth;
comparing spiritual things with spiritual." (1
Corinthians 2:12-13 AV)

Cloud seems to think that God wasted his time giving us his
Holy Spirit; man can believe in Jesus without God having to
intervene to spiritually born him anew. According to Cloud, man is
capable of coming to Jesus through his own free will.

In addition to misrepresenting the scope and import of bible
passages, the preachers of the Arminian gospel take scripture
passages out of context. They wrongfully divide God's word. The
bible admonishes against such ungodly tactics. God states that if you
quote his word, it should be properly done. We are to rightly divide
his word, otherwise it subverts the hearers of his word.

Of these things put *them* in remembrance, charging
them before the Lord that they **strive not about
words to no profit,** *but* **to the subverting of the
hearers.** Study to shew thyself approved unto God,
a workman that needeth not to be ashamed, **rightly
dividing the word of truth**. But shun profane *and*
vain babblings: for they will increase unto more
ungodliness. And their word will eat as doth a
canker: of whom is Hymenaeus and Philetus; (2
Timothy 2:14-17 AV)

An example of this is the practice of the promoters of the
anti-gospel, who quote Philippians 2:12 out of context to give the
appearance that the bible supports their view that man must of his
own free will believe in Jesus and thereafter make certain that they
do not lose their faith.[66] According to their anti-gospel, the faith they
have in Jesus is theirs, and therefore they can choose to reject Christ
at any time and lose their salvation. Such a one must work daily to
maintain his faith and not fall away to damnation.

An example of a theologian wrongly dividing Philippians 2:12 to support the Arminian theology is found in Dan Corner's criticism of Charles Spurgeon's defense of the perseverance of Christians. Corner cites Philippians 2:12 as authority to support his Arminian theology that man can lose his salvation.

Furthermore, as already cited, Spurgeon wrote:

> "It must be a very commendable thing in them [Christians who believe they can *fall from grace*] to be able to get through a day without despair."

But Paul and the other early Christians were not overcome with despair, as Spurgeon suggests should come to rejecters of the *perseverance of the saints* doctrine as they were. Instead, they walked in the fear of God themselves, as they also *worked out their salvation with fear and trembling*:

> "Wherefore, my beloved, as ye have always obeyed, not as in my presence only, but now much more in my absence, **work out your own salvation with fear and trembling**" (Phil. 2:12, KJV). (bold and italics emphasis in Corner's original article)[67]

Philippians 2:12, at first blush, seems to support Corner's Arminian theory that man can lose his salvation. However, Corner has wrongly divided that passage. The next sentence (Philippians 2:13), which explains the meaning of the passage, has been left out. Because the passage has been wrongly divided, it works to subvert the hearers to believe the lie of man's free will, and even salvation by works. When we look at that passage in context we see that the actual meaning is quite different from the Arminian deception.

> Wherefore, my beloved, as ye have always obeyed, not as in my presence only, but now much more in my absence, work out your own salvation with fear and trembling. **For it is God which worketh in you**

both to will and to do of *his* good pleasure.
(Philippians 2:12-13 AV)

Arminians avoid Philipians 2:13 like the plague for obvious reasons. That passage makes clear that it is God that works in the believer to both "will" and "to do" of his (God's) good pleasure. The salvation that is worked out is worked out according to God's good pleasure. Man may think he is acting in accordance with his own will and pleasure, but in fact it is God who is working in the believer to will and to do of God's good pleasure. How does God work in the believer? The Holy Ghost indwells the believer. 1 Corinthians 3:16; 1 John 4:16.

In proverbs 16:1-4 God explains that the preparations of the heart of man is from the Lord. God not only puts the faith in the heart of those who are saved, he also made the unbeliever for the day of destruction according to his good pleasure.

> **The preparations of the heart in man, and the answer of the tongue, *is* from the LORD.** All the ways of a man *are* clean in his own eyes; but the LORD weigheth the spirits. Commit thy works unto the LORD, and thy thoughts shall be established. **The LORD hath made all *things* for himself: yea, even the wicked for the day of evil.** (Proverbs 16:1-4 AV)

8 Chosen Before the Foundation of the World

In order to enter the kingdom of God, a man must be born again. John 3:3. It is not possible to birth oneself, God must do it. **"Of his own will begat he us with the word of truth**, that we should be a kind of firstfruits of his creatures." (James 1:18 AV) Those who are born again, have been chosen by God before the world was even created. "According as he hath **chosen us in him before the foundation of the world,** that we should be holy and without blame before him in love: Having **predestinated** us unto the adoption of children by Jesus Christ to himself, according to the good pleasure of his will." Ephesians 1:4-5.

Those chosen by God for salvation have done nothing to merit that salvation. We were not good, we were simply chosen, because God decided according to his own purpose to choose us. "Who hath saved us, and called us with an holy calling, **not according to our works, but according to his own purpose and grace**, which was given us in Christ Jesus before the world began." 2 Timothy 1:9. "In whom also we have obtained an inheritance, **being predestinated according to the purpose of him who worketh all things after the counsel of his own will."** (Ephesians 1:11 AV) Jesus made clear to his disciples that they did not choose him, he chose them. "Ye have not chosen me, but I have chosen you, and ordained you, that ye should go and bring forth fruit, and that your fruit should remain: that whatsoever ye shall ask of the Father in my name, he may give it you." John 15:16.

Indeed, God states that he knew and loved and ordained Jeremiah to be a prophet before he was even conceived. That is certainly foreknowledge by God, but it is more than foreknowledge; it is God predestinating Jeremiah to be a prophet.

> Before I formed thee in the belly I knew thee; and before thou camest forth out of the womb I sanctified thee, and I ordained thee a prophet unto the nations. Jeremiah 1:5.

Consider the example of Paul. How did God choose him and save him? Did he use gentle persuasion? No, he knocked Paul to the ground, changed his heart, and then commenced giving him commands as to what he must do. Notice what Paul said immediately after being knocked to the ground. "Lord, what wilt thou have me do?" In a split second, Paul went from a persecutor of the church to a member of the church, all according to the will of God, who chose him and changed his heart.

> And as he journeyed, he came near Damascus: and suddenly there shined round about him a light from heaven: And he fell to the earth, and heard a voice saying unto him, Saul, Saul, why persecutest thou me? And he said, Who art thou, Lord? And the Lord said, I am Jesus whom thou persecutest: *it is* hard for thee to kick against the pricks. And he trembling and astonished said, Lord, what wilt thou have me to do? And the Lord *said* unto him, Arise, and go into the city, and it shall be told thee what thou must do. (Acts 9:3-6 AV)

How did he select his apostles? He commanded them to follow him, and they dropped what they were doing and followed him. They immediately obeyed his command to follow him, without hesitation or question. That is the supernatural power of God at work.

> And Jesus, walking by the sea of Galilee, saw two
> brethren, Simon called Peter, and Andrew his
> brother, casting a net into the sea: for they were
> fishers. And **he saith unto them, Follow me, and I
> will make you fishers of men. And they
> straightway left** *their* **nets, and followed him**. And
> going on from thence, he saw other two brethren,
> James *the son* of Zebedee, and John his brother, in a
> ship with Zebedee their father, mending their nets;
> and **he called them. And they immediately left the
> ship and their father, and followed him.** (Matthew
> 4:18-22 AV)

Some may ask: "doesn't man have a free will to choose to believe or not believe in Jesus?" The answer is that man has a will, but it is not free. Man is enslaved by sin and death. Sinful man wishes to rule in his own life; his every impulse is in rebellion against God. Indeed, man cannot freely believe in God. God must transform man by the rebirth wrought by the Holy Spirit.

The reality is that man's will is enslaved to sin. Man will not serve God nor seek God, because man is spiritually dead. "As it is written, **There is none righteous, no, not one: There is none that understandeth, there is none that seeketh after God.**" (Romans 3:10-11 AV)

Jesus came to set us free. "If the Son therefore shall make you free, ye shall be free indeed." (John 8:36 AV) He gives his elect a new spiritual birth and they are set free from sin and death to serve the Lord. By his grace we are spiritually born again. Once born again, our old flesh driven existence comes to an end, and we are led by the spirit, which up to that time was dead, but now is alive. A Christian becomes a new creation, set free from sin to serve the living God.

Knowing this, that **our old man is crucified with**
***him*, that the body of sin might be destroyed, that**
henceforth we should not serve sin. For he that is
dead is freed from sin. Now if we be dead with
Christ, we believe that we shall also live with him:
Knowing that Christ being raised from the dead dieth
no more; death hath no more dominion over him.
For in that he died, he died unto sin once: but in that
he liveth, he liveth unto God. Likewise **reckon ye**
also yourselves to be dead indeed unto sin, but
alive unto God through Jesus Christ our Lord."
(Romans 6:6-11 AV)

A Christian is justified by God. God does the choosing, not
man. James 1:18. God does not love us because we first loved him.
"We love him, because he first loved us." (1 John 4:19 AV) It is an
act of his Grace toward us that frees us from the bondage of sin. Once
we are freed from the bondage of sin we can bear the fruit of
righteousness. "But now being **made free from sin**, and become
servants to God, ye have your fruit unto holiness, and the end
everlasting life." (Romans 6:22 AV) *See also,* Romans 5:16-19; 7:1-
8:17. However, it is all a work of God, by his grace. **"For all have**
sinned, and come short of the glory of God; Being justified freely
by his grace through the redemption that is in Christ Jesus."
(Romans 3:23-24 AV)

Chapter 6 of John makes clear that salvation is all of God.
God "giveth" eternal life to his chosen through faith in his son, Jesus.

Then Jesus said unto them, Verily, verily, I say unto
you, Moses gave you not that bread from heaven; but
my Father **giveth** you the true bread from heaven.
For the bread of God is he which cometh down from
heaven, and **giveth life** unto the world. Then said
they unto him, Lord, evermore give us this bread.
And Jesus said unto them, **I am the bread of life: he**
that cometh to me shall never hunger; and he that
believeth on me shall never thirst. (John 6:32-35

AV)

Jack Graham is typical of many Arminian pastors. Jack
Graham (no relation to Billy Graham) is the pastor of the mega-
church, Prestonwood Baptist Church in Dallas, Texas.[68] Graham
pejoratively describes the irresistible grace of God as forceful and
coercive, as though God graciously transforming man for salvation is
a bad thing:

> Some teach that God's grace is irresistible. In other
> words, that you have no choice in the matter of
> whether you receive Christ or reject Christ. That
> once the grace of God appears to you it attacks you,
> and forces you and coerces you to believe. You
> couldn't say 'No,' if you wanted to. Because God's
> grace is irresistible.[69]

Jack Graham engages in the usual sophistry of Arminian
pastors; he mischaracterizes God's grace by ascribing to God a
despotic character. Graham believes the myth that man has a free
will. He believes that man can thwart the will of God. Graham
disregards the very theme of the bible that man's will is enslaved to
sin as a result of the fall. Because Graham does not believe what
God has said in the bible about man, he thinks that God's gracious
gift of eternal life is a despotic act. Graham states: "God does not
impose His will upon us. Lest God would be a despot a dictator. God
has given us in Christ the opportunity and the awesome responsibility
to either reject the gospel or receive the gospel."[70]

Jack Graham thinks that God is a despot for changing our
sinful rebellious character to believe in Jesus, an act that would
otherwise be impossible but for God's intervention. Graham hates
the true gospel of grace and blasphemes God for his act of mercy in
saving his elect. Graham prefers his graceless god who offers a
mythical opportunity at salvation.

It is impossible for man to actually obtain salvation under
Graham's theology, because his theology has a mythical prevenient

grace that is supposed to free the will of all men, who then must exercise their mythical free will to choose to believe (or not) in an impotent Jesus. The Jesus that Graham preaches does not exist. Graham's Jesus is a false Jesus, and his gospel is a false gospel. If a man believes that his faith is generated from his own free will, which does not in fact exist, and he exercises that faith to believe in an impotent Jesus, who does not in fact exist, that would mean that he has a salvation that does not in fact exist. Paul warned about just such a false gospel and false Jesus. 2 Corinthians 11:4.

9   Ordained by God to Believe Not

Jesus states that his chosen are drawn by the Father to him. John 6:44. Some, such as David Cloud, who labels himself as a "fundamental Baptist," believe that everyone is drawn to Jesus by the Father, but not everyone who is drawn believes in Jesus.[71] Cloud states on his *Way of Life* website: "while it is true that no man can come to Christ except that he be drawn by God, it is equally true that all men are being drawn and that those who are rejected are those who reject the truth and do not believe."[72] Cloud believes that, of those who are drawn, the only ones who are saved are those who, of their own free will, believe in Jesus.[73]

The problem with Cloud's argument is that it contradicts the express words of Jesus. In John 6:44, Jesus states clearly that no man can come to him unless the Father draws him and Jesus will raise up those who are drawn to him on the last day. All who are drawn by the Father to Jesus will believe in him and be saved. The drawing by God is effectual. Once one is drawn to Jesus, he will believe in Jesus and be raised by Jesus on the last day. "No man can come to me, except the Father which hath sent me draw him: and I will raise him up at the last day." (John 6:44 AV)

What does it mean to be drawn to Jesus? Jesus explains what it means in John 6:45. To be drawn to Jesus by the Father means that

God opens one's ears to hear and learn from the Father and believe in Jesus. "It is written in the prophets, And they shall be all taught of God. **Every man therefore that hath heard, and hath learned of the Father, cometh unto me.**" John 6:45. Notice that it is not just some, but "every" man who hears and learns from the Father comes to Jesus. The faith to believe in Jesus comes from God. Faith in Jesus is a gift from God; it is not the exercise of the free will of man. Those who come to Jesus do so in faith, and Jesus states that "He that believeth on me hath everlasting life." John 6:47. It is clear, "no man" can come to Jesus unless the Father draws him, and "every man" that is drawn to Jesus will come to him and believe in him.

Those who do not believe in Jesus and are not saved do not believe because the Father has not drawn them to Jesus. "No man" can come to Jesus unless the Father gives him the faith to come to Jesus. In John 6:63-66, Jesus stated to those who "believed not" in him that they did not believe in him because the Father had not given them the faith to believe in him. The message of John 6 and the entire gospel is clear. Salvation is by the will of God and not by the will of man. *See* John 1:12-13. In John 6 many of the supposed disciples went back and walked no more with Jesus. They walked away from Jesus not because they were saved and lost their salvation, but as Jesus explained, because the faith to believe in him was not given to them by his Father.

> It is the spirit that quickeneth; the flesh profiteth nothing: the words that I speak unto you, *they* are spirit, and *they* are life. But there are some of you that believe not. For Jesus knew from the beginning who they were that believed not, and who should betray him. And he said, **Therefore said I unto you, that no man can come unto me, except it were given unto him of my Father.** From that time many of his disciples went back, and walked no more with him. (John 6:63-66 AV)

The point is driven home in John 6 that salvation is by God's sovereign grace and that faith, which is the means of salvation, is a gift of God. In John 6:70-71, Jesus stated that one of the twelve he had "chosen" was a devil, referring to Judas. Judas did not lose his salvation; he was never saved to begin with, because he was not chosen for salvation. Jesus chose him for the purpose that Judas would betray him. Eleven were chosen for salvation and one (Judas) was chosen for damnation.

> **Jesus answered them, Have not I chosen you twelve, and one of you is a devil?** He spake of Judas Iscariot *the son* of Simon: for he it was that should betray him, being one of the twelve. (John 6:70-71 AV)

Jesus lost none of those whom he had chosen for salvation. God preserves all who are chosen for salvation. Judas was preordained to be lost in order to fulfill the prophecy in scripture.

> While I was with them in the world, I kept them in thy name: **those that thou gavest me I have kept, and none of them is lost**, but the son of perdition; that the scripture might be fulfilled. (John 17:12 AV)

Judas was chosen for damnation before the foundation of the world according to the will of God, just as the other apostles were chosen for salvation before the foundation of the world according to the will of God. *See* Ephesians 1:4-5.

Jesus expressly told the Jews who confronted him in Jerusalem that they do not believe in him because they were not chosen to be of his flock.

> But ye believe not, because ye are not of my sheep, as I said unto you. My sheep hear my voice, and I know them, and they follow me: And I give unto them eternal life; and they shall never perish, neither shall any man pluck them out of my hand. (John 10:26-28 AV)

Notice that Jesus did not say that they if you were smart enough you could believe of your own free will. Instead he put it right in their faces that they did not believe, and indeed would never believe because they were not of his sheep. He said that to them after they asked him if he was the Christ. "Then came the Jews round about him, and said unto him, How long dost thou make us to doubt? If thou be the Christ, tell us plainly. Jesus answered them, I told you, and ye believed not: the works that I do in my Father's name, they bear witness of me." John 10:24-25.

Faith is not only the means of salvation, it is the fruit of the spirit that is proof that God has elected the person for salvation. Man does not elect God by believing in Jesus, rather God elects man and gives him the faith to believe in Jesus. All who do not believe in Jesus were not elected by God for salvation. John Hendryx explains:

[W]e should take notice that Jesus tells us many times in Scripture why some do not believe. "You do not believe because you are not my sheep" (John 10). The order here is of great importance. Jesus does not say, "You are not my sheep because you do not believe," thereby making belief a condition of becoming a sheep. Rather, he says the exact opposite, "You do not believe because you are not my sheep." To believe therefore, far from being a condition, is the sign (or fruit) that one is already a sheep. So too, Jesus speaking to some of the Jews said, "Whoever is of God hears the words of God. The reason why you do not hear them is that you are not of God." The nature of the person determines the choice he makes. And who exactly is "of God"? Jesus answers clearly in his prayer to the Father in John 17: 9 when he says, "I am praying for them. I am not praying for the world but for those whom you have given me, for they are yours." The Father has set apart certain persons for Himself and, in His prayer here, Jesus is seen to only pray for them, while simultaneously excluding others who were not "given" to Him.[74]

Kevin Bauder explains that "Arminians see God's
foreknowledge as His foresight. God looks ahead through the
corridors of time and sees what free people will choose. For
Arminians, divine foreknowledge is essentially reactive."[75]
Arminians would argue that Jesus knew by looking through time who
would believe in him, and he knew by doing so those Jews in John
10:24-25 would not believe in him. The problem with that
explanation is that it is directly contrary to what God states in his
Holy Bible. The Arminians have a hard time getting around John
12:39-41 where Jesus stated:

> Therefore **they could not believe,** because that
> Esaias said again, **He hath blinded their eyes, and
> hardened their heart; that they should not see
> with their eyes, nor understand with their heart,
> and be converted, and I should heal them.** These
> things said Esaias, when he saw his glory, and spake
> of him. (John 12:39-41 AV)

God has purposely blinded the eyes and hardened the hearts
of many to the gospel to prevent their conversion. Notice that Jesus
stated that these things were prophesied by Isaiah. Clearly, God is
not simply looking through the corridors of time and seeing whether
men of their own free will would believe; God has determined
beforehand who would believe and who would not believe. Isaiah
6:9-10, which was fulfilled in John 12:39-41, shows that God planned
in advance that certain people would not believe in Jesus:

> And he said, Go, and tell this people, Hear ye indeed,
> but understand not; and see ye indeed, but perceive
> not. Make the heart of this people fat, and make their
> ears heavy, and shut their eyes; lest they see with
> their eyes, and hear with their ears, and understand
> with their heart, and convert, and be healed. Isaiah
> 6:9-10.

In Romans 11:7-8 God makes the point once again that those
who do not believe cannot believe because they were not elected to

believe.

> What then? Israel hath not obtained that which he
> seeketh for; **but the election hath obtained it, and
> the rest were blinded.** (According as it is written,
> God hath given them the spirit of slumber, eyes that
> they should not see, and ears that they should not
> hear;) unto this day. Romans 11:7-8.

This is more than God merely omnisciently predicting who would not believe in him and thus be condemned; God is omnipotently determining who they would be ahead of time. God predestined those who would believe and those who would not believe; he "predestinated us unto the adoption of children by Jesus Christ." Ephesians 1:5. *See also* Ephesians 1:11; Romans 8:29-30. He chose those who would believe in Jesus before the foundation of the world. "According as he hath **chosen us in him before the foundation of the world,** that we should be holy and without blame before him in love." Ephesians 1:4. Concomitantly, God chose those destined for destruction before the foundation of the world. Proverbs 16:1-4.

Arminians cannot ignore the plain language in the bible that God predestined his elect for salvation and therefore also predestined the unelected for damnation. Arminians conjured an argument to get around those bible passages. Arminians simply redefined the word "predestinate." Arminians claim that "predestinate" when referring to God's election of those to be saved is limited to mean only that God knows those who will exercise their free will and believe in Jesus. The Arminian interpretation is that "God in his divine foresight, looked down through the corridors of time and saw all of those who would choose salvation in Jesus Christ. Having this divine knowledge, He then ratified men's votes of confidence in His ability to save them."[76]

Romans 8:29-30 completely eviscerates the Arminian theology.

For whom he did foreknow, he also did predestinate
to be conformed to the image of his Son, that he
might be the firstborn among many brethren.
Moreover whom he did predestinate, them he also
called: and whom he called, them he also justified:
and whom he justified, them he also glorified.
Romans 8:29-30.

Best selling Arminian author Dave Hunt dodges Romans
8:29-30 by dismissing the connection of predestination to salvation.
His position is that "in the Bible predestination/election is never unto
salvation."[77]

David Bennett explains his Arminian view of Romans 8:29-
30, that predestinate does not actually mean predestined. According
to Bennett predestinate means only that God affirms the free will
decision of those who choose Jesus. Bennett, as with all Arminians,
wants God to butt out of man's free will decision. In order to strip
God of his sovereignty, he must strip "predestinate" of its meaning.
He claims "predestinate or any form of the word does not even
remotely hint as God predetermining who would have eternal life."[78]
Predestinate is a word that invalidates the Arminian religion, and so
Arminians must redefine the word to remove it as an impediment to
their free will theology. Bennett states:

> Those that God *predestined* means He predestined
> for Glory those who would accept him. ... Romans
> 8:29-30 tells us what the promise is if we believe and
> accept His invitation, as do many other verses in the
> Scriptures. Never does *election* or *predestination*
> refer to salvation, but always and only to particular
> benefits which is Christlikeness. *Predestination....*
> *simply means that God has predetermined that those*
> *who respond affirmatively to His call...will be*
> *justified...and furthermore will be glorified. All this*
> *is 'according to His purpose'...* Herschel H. Hobbs,
> *Fundamentals of our Faith*, (Nashville: Broadman,
> 1960), 94-99. ... It should be clear then that the word

predestinate or any form of the word does not even
remotely hint as God predetermining who would
have eternal life with Him or suffer eternal
damnation because He willed it just because He
could. Predestination clearly refers to God's plan for
salvation of those who freely accept God's gift.[79]
(italics in original)

John Wesley had yet a different Arminian explanation.
Wesley claimed that since God knows everything at any moment, he
knows nothing ahead of time, and therefore he does not foreknow or
predestinate anything. Wesley stated:

The sum of all is this: the almighty, all-wise God
sees and knows, from everlasting to everlasting, all
that is, that was, and that is to come, through one
eternal now. With him nothing is either past or
future, but all things equally present. He has,
therefore, if we speak according to the truth of
things, **no foreknowledge, no afterknowledge.**[80]

The problem with Wesley's interpretation is that God himself
in Romans 8:29-30 says that he does exactly what Wesley claimed
God does not do. God makes it clear that he foreknows and
predestinates his elect. Wesley is making up a different gospel out of
whole cloth.

Wesley compounded his error by making the following
incredible allegation:

Yet when he speaks to us, knowing whereof we are
made, knowing the scantiness of our understanding,
he lets himself down to our capacity, and speaks of
himself after the manner of men. Thus, in
condescension to our weakness, he speaks of his own
purpose, counsel, plan, foreknowledge. Not that God
has any need of counsel, of purpose, or of planning
his work beforehand. Far be it from us to impute

these to the Most High; to measure him by ourselves!
It is merely in compassion to us that he speaks thus
of himself, as foreknowing the things in heaven or
earth, and as predestinating or fore-ordaining them.
But can we possibly imagine that these expressions
are to be taken literally?"[81]

In essence, Wesley claims that God thinks we are too stupid
to understand what he is really doing, and so he tells us a fib in
Romans 8:29-30 about foreknowing and predestinating men. Wesley
is calling God a liar. The brilliant John Wesley, however, was able to
see through God's purported prevarication and understand the
supposed truth that is the diametric opposite of the lies that Wesley
alleges God tells in the bible.

Wesley's Arminian god is a liar who says he foreknows and
predestinates, but actually does neither. The true God of the bible,
however, does not lie.

God is not a man, that he should lie; neither the son
of man, that he should repent: hath he said, and shall
he not do it? or hath he spoken, and shall he not
make it good?" (Numbers 23:19 AV)

Wesley was a false teacher "who changed the truth into a
lie." Romans 1:25. Despite Wesley's claims to the contrary, God is
not lying to us when he says he foreknows and predestinates his elect.
God means what he says. "Hath he spoken, and shall he not make it
good?" Numbers 23:19.

Many Arminians are not satisfied with Wesley's or Bennett's
approaches and use a different strategy to get around Romans 8:29-
30. They theorize that "predestinate" in Romans 8:29-30 is not in
reference to the certain election of individuals, but rather to the
election of a group of people. B. J. Oropeza, Ph.D., Associate
Professor in Biblical Studies in the School of Theology at Azusa
Pacific University claims that "the predestination and election of
Christians in Romans 8:29-30 may rest on Paul's assumption that

election to final perseverance refers to the election of a community rather than individuals as such."[82]

Despite the clear statement in Romans 8:29-30 that God predestinates individuals to heaven, Arminian author and pastor Andrew Telford contradicts the bible and states that "God never predestinated an individual to Heaven, and God never predestinated an individual to Hell; for God neither predestinates individuals to Heaven nor to Hell."[83]　Telford believes that "God is not here [in Ephesians 1:4-5] deciding the destination of individuals as individuals, but is telling us that before the foundation of the world He had decided the destination of the Church the corporate group."[84]

The Arminian interpretation is that God predestinates a group of persons to potentially be saved, but that the members of that group maintain their free will to choose or reject God. The Arminians claim that God only foreknows the individuals who will be saved, but he does not predestinate their individual salvation. Their individual salvation is up to their free will decision.

The Arminian argument is easily exposed as sophistry. The exact same people who are foreknown by God for salvation in Romans 8:29 are "**also**" predestinated for salvation. The "**whom**" he foreknew are the same "**whom**" he "**also**" predestinated. The word "also" links together "foreknow" and "predestinate" and applies both actions to "whom." It means that in addition to foreknowing his elect, God "**also**" predestinated his elect "to be conformed to the image if his Son." There is no way to separate the persons who are foreknown from the persons who are predestinated to salvation; they are the same persons.

Notice also in Romans 8:29-30 that it is "**he**" (God) alone who 1) foreknows, 2) predestinates, 3) calls, 4) justifies, and 5) glorifies "them." There is no reference to anything done by the free will of the "them" "whom" God foreknows, predestinates, calls, justifies, and glorifies. From foreknowing to predestining to calling to justifying to glorifying, "**he**" (God) does it all. The pronoun "**he**" is repeated in reference to God nine times in Romans 8:29-30. There is no way in the passage to shoehorn man's mythical free will to believe. There is no room in the passage to squeeze in the Arminian claim that God predestinated a group made up of saved and unsaved persons, all of whom have only the potential to be saved, and that God only foreknew (but did not predestinate) the persons in that group who would exercise their free will to believe in Jesus and be saved.

The Arminians have interpreted "predestinate" in Romans 8:29-30 in such a way as to render it meaningless surplusage. Even though the passage states clearly that God predestinated his elect, the Arminians redefine predestinate such that God only knows ahead of time those who will choose of their own free will to believe in him. The Arminian predestination goes hand in hand with their prevenient grace mythology. In order for Arminians to be consistent, every person in the world who is predestinated (which is redefined by Arminians to mean only known about by their god ahead of time) is first given prevenient grace to believe in Jesus. However, not all who receive the prevenient grace believe in Jesus; most who receive prevenient grace reject Jesus and end up in hell. The prevenient grace is a (largely ineffective) mythical grace; in like manner, the Arminian predestination is a mythical predestination (being only foreknowledge). They Arminian theology is a mess, with words stripped of meaning, grace stripped of its effectiveness, and a god stripped of his power.

The Arminian theology requires redefinition of bible terms in order to maintain their mythology that God is powerless to determine or effectuate salvation. The Arminians deceptively redefine "predestinate" in the same way that they reduce God's grace to only a prevenient grace. Prevenient grace is not really grace, Arminian predestination is not really predestination, and the Arminian god is not really God.

The Arminian god is an impotent liar; his ministers call people from "the grace of Christ unto another gospel." Galatians 1:6. Because they pervert the gospel by replacing the grace of Christ with the free will of man, they are under a curse from God.

> I marvel that ye are so soon **removed from him
> that called you into the grace of Christ unto
> another gospel**: Which is not another; but there be
> some that trouble you, and would **pervert the gospel
> of Christ**. But though we, or an angel from heaven,
> preach any other gospel unto you than that which we
> have preached unto you, **let him be accursed**. As we
> said before, so say I now again, If any man preach
> any other gospel unto you than that ye have received,
> **let him be accursed**. (Galatians 1:6-9 AV)

Brian Schwertley explains further the error of the Arminian view of predestination:

> Virtually all modern evangelicals and
> fundamentalists emphatically reject the biblical
> doctrine of unconditional election. They teach that
> election is based not solely upon God's choice or
> good pleasure but upon God's foreknowledge of
> man's exercise of faith. In other words, before God
> created the world, He looked down the corridors of
> time and observed all those who exercised faith in
> Christ and then chose them. Arminians, broadly
> speaking, hold that election is based upon God's
> foreknowledge of who will actively co-operate with
> God in the saving of his own soul.
>
> The view that God only chooses those who first elect
> Him by making a decision for Christ is based on
> Romans 8:29: "For whom He foreknew, He also
> predestined to be conformed to the image of His Son,
> that He might be the firstborn among many
> brethren." The Arminian or semi-Pelagian
> understands the word foreknow simply to mean an
> intellectual knowledge of something before it
> happens. Thus they argue that God knew beforehand
> who would believe and repent and then elected them.
> There are a number of reasons why the Arminian

understanding of Romans 8:29 is unscriptural and impossible.

The first reason that the Arminian understanding of Romans 8:29 is unscriptural is the fact that "foreknow" in this passage does not simply mean to know an event before it happens. Paul uses "foreknow" in the Old Testament Hebraistic sense of to love beforehand. John Murray writes: "Although the term 'foreknow' is used seldom in the New Testament, it is altogether indefensible to ignore the meaning so frequently given to the word 'know' in the usage of Scripture; 'foreknow' merely adds the thought of 'beforehand' to the word 'know.' Many times in Scripture 'know' has a pregnant meaning which goes beyond that of mere cognition. It is used in a sense practically synonymous with 'love,' to set regard upon, to know with peculiar interest, delight, affection, and action (cf. Gen. 18:19; Exod. 2:25; Psalm 1:6; 144:3; Jer. 1:5; Amos 3:2; Hosea 13:5; Matt. 7:23; 1 Cor. 8:3; Gal. 4:9; 2 Tim. 2:19; 1 John 3:1). . . . It means 'whom he set regard upon' or 'whom he knew from eternity with distinguishing affection and delight' and is virtually equivalent to 'whom he foreloved.'" God's electing love originates from Himself and not out of a foreseen faith or repentance. Therefore, when the Bible discusses election, it always grounds it in God and not sinful, depraved humanity. Election is "according to His good pleasure" (Eph. 1:9). It is "after the counsel of His own will" (Eph. 1:11).[85]

Probably the most devastating to the Arminian argument is the context of Romans 8:29. Arminians claim that God's love is passive; that God sits back and waits upon the exercise of the free will of man. However, in the very next verse we read that God's love is active: "Moreover whom he did predestinate, them he also called: and whom he called, them he also justified: and whom he justified, them he also glorified." Romans 8:30.

Schwertley explains how the Arminian interpretation of
Romans 8:29 that God only knew ahead of time what men would do
of their own free will turns the biblical doctrine of the fall of man on
its head:

> The Arminian interpretation of Romans 8:29 would
> place a blatant contradiction within Scripture. It
> would contradict the biblical teaching with regard to
> man's state after the fall. The Bible teaches that
> unsaved, unregenerate men hate both Christ and the
> truth (Jn. 3:19-21). Unregenerate fallen man: dwells
> in darkness (Jn. 1:4-5); is dead spiritually (Eph.
> 2:1-5); has a heart of stone which is unable to
> respond to divine truth (Ezek. 11:19); is helpless
> (Ezek. 16:4-6); is unable to repent (Jer. 13:23); is
> enslaved to Satan (Ac. 26:17-18); and is unable to
> see or comprehend divine truth (1 Cor. 2:14).
> Unconditional election is the logical corollary to total
> depravity. Thus Jesus Christ taught: "No one can
> come to Me unless the Father who sent Me draws
> him.... No one can come to Me unless it has been
> granted to him by My Father" (Jn.. 6:44, 65). An
> unregenerate man can no more choose Christ as
> Savior than can a rotting corpse.

> Since the Bible teaches that the fall has rendered man
> incapable of believing in Christ and repenting, the
> idea that God looked through time and chose those
> who first chose him is absurd and impossible. That is
> why the Bible teaches that faith and repentance are
> gifts from God (cf. Jn. 3:3-8; 6:44-45, 65; Eph. 2:8;
> Phil. 1:29; 2 Pet. 1:2). "For unless God by sovereign,
> operative grace had turned our enmity to love and
> our disbelief to faith we would never yield the
> response of faith and love." Furthermore, the biblical
> passages which teach unconditional election are clear

and abundant.[86]

The Arminian god is stripped of his omnipotence and only
retains a remnant of his omniscience. Some Arminians even strip
their god of his omniscience. Dr. Michael Scott Horton explains how
Arminian theologian, Dr. Clark Pinnock, who was Professor Emeritus
of Systematic Theology at McMaster Divinity College, stripped the
mythical Arminian god of his omniscience:

> Once he became an Arminian, Dr. Pinnock notes, "I
> soon realized something would have to be done about
> the received doctrine of God." God is no longer
> timeless, changeless, or even all-knowing. After all,
> "decisions not yet made do not exist anywhere to be
> known even by God."[87]

The God of the bible foreknows who will believe in him,
because he has predestined that they believe in him. The God of the
bible is both omniscient and omnipotent; he does according to his
will and pleasure. God foreknows those who will believe in him,
indeed, he foreknows all things. God also brings to pass the
foreordained salvation of his elect and all events, according to his
purpose and will.

> I am God, and there is none else; I am God, and there
> is none like me, Declaring the end from the
> beginning, and from ancient times the things that are
> not yet done, saying, My counsel shall stand, and **I
> will do all my pleasure.** Calling a ravenous bird
> from the east, the man that executeth my counsel
> from a far country: yea, **I have spoken it, I will also
> bring it to pass; I have purposed it, I will also do
> it.** Isaiah 46:9-11.

Not all Arminians would go as far as Pinnock and say that
God is not omniscient. It seems that the standard Arminian view is
that God retains his omniscience; but they limit God to omniscience,
by improperly interpreting Romans 8:29 to mean that God only

foresees but does not effectuate the faith of his elect. The true God of the bible, however, is omniscient and therefore knows everything, but he is also omnipotent, and the gospel message is that God exercises his omnipotence to supply the faith for those who he foreknows will believe in him. Hence, God predestinates his elect for salvation. John Murray, who was an instructor in Systematic Theology at Princeton Theological Seminary and helped found the Westminster Theological Seminary, explains that God foresees those who will believe in him and supplies the faith for the foreseen belief.

> Even if it were granted that 'foreknew' means foresight of faith, the biblical doctrine of sovereign election is not thereby eliminated or disproven. For it is certainly true that God foresees faith; he foresees all that comes to pass. The question would then simply be: whence proceeds this faith which God foresees? And the only biblical answer is that the faith which God foresees is the faith he himself creates (cf. John 3:3-8; 6:44;45,65; Eph. 2:8; Phil. 1:29; II Pet. 1:2). Hence his eternal foresight of faith is preconditioned by his decree to generate this faith in those whom he foresees as believing, and we are thrown back upon the differentiation which proceeds from God's own eternal and sovereign election to faith and its consequents.[88]

Brian Schwertley explains how the Arminian free will gospel is truly an unbiblical anti-gospel that evidences a hatred by Arminians for the sovereignty of God. Instead of God electing man for salvation, the Arminians have man electing God. It is devilishly backwards.

> It is truly sad that so many who profess the name of Christ hate the doctrine of unconditional election, for it is the heart of biblical religion and a God-glorifying doctrine. What is more fundamental to biblical truth than the fact that salvation is a gift from God? "For by grace you have been saved

through faith, and that not of yourselves; it is the gift
of God, not of works, lest anyone should boast. For
we are His workmanship, created in Christ Jesus for
good works, which God prepared beforehand that we
should walk in them" (Eph. 2:8-10). Those who hate
the doctrine in reality hate God's sovereign grace.
They would ignore the doctrine if they could, but
since it is taught so clearly and often in the New
Testament, they have no choice but to attempt to
explain it away. Their main attempt—the idea that
election is based on a foreseen faith—turns election
into its very opposite: God does not elect man, but
rather man elects God. Furthermore, predestination
in such a scheme is really a postdestination. The
Arminian viewpoint is unbiblical and illogical for it
makes the eternal counsel and choice of God
contingent upon the choice of men who are
spiritually dead and unable to choose Christ (apart
from regeneration) and who do not even exist yet!
The Arminian scheme has temporal events
controlling and conditioning the eternal, unchanging
will of God. In other words, the clay has control over
the potter. The Arminian, by taking election out of
God's hands and placing it in the hands of depraved
man, has destroyed salvation by grace alone and
replaced it with a humanistic synergism. Christ
testified against such Scripture twisting when He
said to His disciples: "You have not chosen me, but I
have chosen you" (Jn. 15:16). Arminianism is
unscriptural, irrational, and takes the glory due to
God alone and bestows it upon sinful man.[89]

The passages that most assuredly put to rest the theory that
God did not choose us for salvation but only knew by looking
through the corridors of time who would choose him are found at
Romans 9:9-13. In those passages God makes the point that he chose
Jacob over Esau before they were ever born and before they had
"done any good or evil." God chose Jacob before either of them

made any decisions to do anything. God makes it perfectly clear that he did not choose Jacob based upon his foreknowledge of what Jacob would do or what he would will or what he would believe. God states unequivocally in verse 12, that the reason he chose Jacob was so "that the purpose of God according to election might stand, not of works, but of him that calleth." God elected Jacob, period. God did not consider anything that he knew Jacob would do or will to do in deciding to choose him over Esau. In Romans 9:16 God drives the point home that salvation is **"not of him that willeth."**

The Arminians contradict God and claim that salvation is in fact of him that willeth. They claim that God knows who they are who will believe in Jesus, and God just affirms the decision of the believer. That is pure sophistry. Nothing can be clearer in the bible but that God predestinates some for salvation without regard to any merit on their part.

The passages in Romans 9 impeach those that claim that man chooses salvation of his own free will and that God only knows in advance who will choose him. Limiting God to only knowing the future is contrary to God's whole purpose, which is to call and to elect and to show mercy, according to his sovereign will. God gives spiritual life to the spiritually dead, according to his will. "The Son quickeneth whom he will." John 5:21. God does not merely know who will believe in him, he determines who will believe in him. God makes that determination, independent of the will of man. It is not of the "will of the flesh, nor of the will of man, but of God." John 1:13.

10 Not Willing that Any Should Perish

The unbiblical doctrine that God is willing that all should be saved, and that it is only man's free will that thwarts God's desires, has crept into many ostensibly Protestant churches. These corrupted churches point to part of 2 Peter 3:9 taken out of context as authority for their doctrine. In fact, this single passage is so key to the Arminian theology that it is the motto of the *Society of Evangelical Arminians*.[90] Figure 2 shows their seal, containing the statement: **"Not Willing That Any Should Perish"**, which is a clause taken out of context from 2 Peter 3:9.

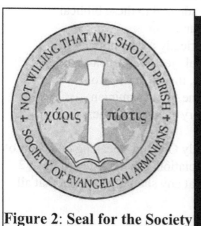

Figure 2: Seal for the Society of Evangelical Arminians

The Arminians have hijacked the gospel and all of the terms that have traditionally been used in the Christian community to describe orthodox biblical Christianity. An organization calling itself the *Society of Evangelical Arminians* makes no historical sense. While almost all Arminians consider themselves evangelicals, they deny the foundational biblical doctrines that are at the core of what it historically meant to be an evangelical. Dr. Michael Scott Horton, who is the J. Gresham Machen Professor of Systematic Theology and Apologetics, in his article *Evangelical Arminians, Option or Oxymoron?*, explains that it is an oxymoron for an Arminian to be described as an evangelical.

> [T]he evangelicals who faced this challenge of
> Arminianism universally regarded it as a heretical
> departure from the Christian faith. One simply could
> not deny total depravity, unconditional election,
> justification by grace alone through faith alone
> because of Christ alone, and continue to call himself
> or herself an evangelical. There were many
> Christians who were not evangelicals, but to be an
> evangelical meant that one adhered to these biblical
> convictions. ... Today one can be an
> evangelical-which has historically meant holding to
> total depravity, unconditional election, justification
> by grace through faith alone, the sufficiency of
> scripture-and at the same time be an Arminian,
> denying or distorting this very evangelical message.[91]

Franklin Graham, son of Billy Graham, speaking on behalf of the Billy Graham Evangelistic Association, stated: "According to 2 Peter 3:9, the Lord is 'not willing that any should perish but that all should come to repentance.'"[92]

At first glance it would appear that 2 Peter 3:9 supports what Graham has said. Closer examination of that passage reveals that the passage does not in fact support that false Arminian doctrine promoted by Graham. Notice the missing passage. "The Lord is [...] not willing that any should perish, but that all should come to repentance." 2 Peter 3:9.

Those who try to force the square peg of scripture into the round hole of their false doctrine must shave off parts of the bible in order to get it to fit. In this case, Graham, as is the practice with all Arminians, shaved that portion of the passage which limits its application to those who are already chosen for salvation. What God means in that passage is that God is not willing that any who have been chosen for salvation should perish, but that all those who are saved should come to repentance. Read the entire passage in context and you will see that God is **"longsuffering to us-ward."** God is not willing that "us" should perish and that "us" should come to repentance.

> The Lord is not slack concerning his promise, as some men count slackness; **but is longsuffering to us-ward**, not willing that any should perish, but that all should come to repentance. 2 Peter 3:9.

Who are the "us" in 2 Peter 3:9? Simply read the first paragraph of the letter and we see that Peter is writing to "them that have obtained like precious faith with us." "Simon Peter, a servant and an apostle of Jesus Christ, **to them that have obtained like precious faith with us** through the righteousness of God and our Saviour Jesus Christ:" (2 Peter 1:1 AV)

One can see that in 2 Peter 3:9, Peter was stating that God was not willing that any who believe in Jesus should perish. God's will is always done, and his will cannot be thwarted by man's will. If God has foreordained one to salvation, no one can stay his hand. "And all the inhabitants of the earth are reputed as nothing: and he doeth according to his will in the army of heaven, and among the inhabitants of the earth: and none can stay his hand, or say unto him, What doest thou?" (Daniel 4:35 AV)

11 Salvation Hath Appeared to All Men

Many anti-gospel preachers who advocate the free will of a person to believe in Jesus cite Titus 2:11. "For the grace of God that bringeth salvation hath appeared to all men." They argue that Titus 2:11 indicates that God has bestowed his grace on all men and it is up to them to accept the free gift of salvation.[93] That is, all men are given the grace for potential salvation, and they of their own free will must choose to accept that free gift of salvation. For example, David Stewart states:

> "[F]or Calvinists and Hyper-Calvinists to teach that God is 'selective' in choosing who will or won't be saved is certainly NOT Biblical. Titus 2:11 clearly teaches, 'For the grace of God that bringeth salvation hath appeared to all men.' Did you read that...ALL men?"[94]

The epistle to Titus does not support Stewart's Arminian position. Verse 11 is not referring to every man in the world. If one reads all of chapter 2, up to verse 11, one will see that it discusses "aged men . . . aged women . . . young women . . . young men . . . servants . . . masters." Titus 2:1-10. If one puts them all together, one sees that the "all men" referred to in verse 11 are the "all men" discussed in the previous ten verses; that is, all kinds of men in the world: aged, young, servants, and masters.

"All men" does not mean every single man in the world; rather, it means every type of man in the world. God bestows his grace on men according to his will, not according to whether they are men, women, young, old, servants, or masters, and certainly not according to their will! God saves people according to his grace guided by the pleasure of his will. "God is no respecter of persons." Acts 10:34. It does not matter what station a man occupies or in what nation he resides.

The scripture is clear that God's calling is effectual. All those who are chosen for salvation will in fact believe in Jesus and be saved. Those who do not believe in Jesus were ordained by God not to believe. God's election is in accordance with the pleasure of his will and not according to the station of the man.

12 Born Not of the Will of Man

Another passage taken out of context by those who would like to reduce God to a passive participant in the salvation of men is John 1:12. "But as many as received him, to them gave he power to become the sons of God, even to them that believe on his name:"

The following was written by "Reverend" D.A. Waite who has the impressive credentials of both a Th.D. and a Ph. D. He cites John 1:12 and alleges that it refutes the biblical doctrine of limited atonement and also by implication the biblical doctrine of total depravity.

> A. THE TERMS OF JOHN 1:12 REFUTE "LIMITED ATONEMENT "
>
> "But as many as received Him, to them gave He power to become the sons of God, even to them THAT BELIEVE ON HIS NAME."
>
> 1. The Goal Of John 1:12
>
> The "goal" spoken of in this verse is the "power to become the sons God." This is another way of saying

to be "saved" or to have "eternal life." This is the net result if the requirements in the verse are fulfilled by the individual.

2. The Partakers In That Goal In John 1:12

The verse is quite clear that those who partake in this goal of becoming "the sons of God " by being born again and regenerated by the Holy Spirit through faith, are (1) "as many as received Him" [Christ] and/or (2) "to them that BELIEVE on His Name" [Christ's]. These two synonymous expressions of "receiving" and "believing on His Name" are the only qualifications needed for becoming a "son" or "child" of God. Any others who do NOT meet one or the other of these two qualifications (actually they are the same, but spoken in slightly different words), cannot be the "sons of God" and cannot be saved.

3. The Refutation of "LIMITED ATONEMENT" In John 1:12

There is not a hint in this verse that this INVITATION to sinners to become saints is LIMITED only "to the elect" or that we are to restrict the INVITATION artificially by theological words. We are to preach that "as many" sinners who would "receive" Christ as Savior and "to them that BELIEVE" on His name" whoever they might be- would be guaranteed by God to "become" a "son" or "child" of God! We can make this UNIVERSAL offer, because Jesus Christ died for the SINS OF THE WHOLE WORLD--barring none! They have to "receive" Him and "believe on His Name" to be saved, and to partake of Christ's benefits on their behalf. Not receiving of Him--No benefits!![95] (emphasis in original).

Dr. Waite is very slyly deceiving the reader by isolating John 1:12 from its context. He has wrongly divided God's word and tried to construct an argument by ignoring the whole counsel of God. Those, like Dr. Waite, who would elevate the will of man over the will of God argue that John 1:12 means that a person must be willing to receive that free gift of God by believing in Jesus. Dr. Waite expressly rejects the notion that God has chosen his elect, who will then believe in him.

Dr. Waite argues that Jesus died for the sins of every person in the whole world, and therefore every person in the whole world can be saved, if only they would of their own free will believe in Jesus. Under Dr. Waite's interpretation of John 1:12, it is man who chooses God and not God who chooses man. According to Waite's false doctrine, God is passively offering salvation as a gift, but man must receive that gift of his own free will in order to be saved. John 1:12, however, does not say any such thing. John 1:12 simply explains that those who receive Jesus, meaning those who believe in Jesus, will be saved and become adopted sons of God.

When the John 1:12 is read in context we see that the very next passage (verse 13) explains the source of that saving faith through which one is born again. "But as many as received him, to them gave he power to become the sons of God, *even* to them that believe on his name: **Which were born, not of blood, nor of the will of the flesh, nor of the will of man, but of God.**" (John 1:12-13 AV) John 1:13 makes it crystal clear that we are saved by the will of God alone, and not by our own will.

Why didn't Dr. Waite quote verse 13 or even try to explain it? Because, it completely refutes his Arminian construct that all men of their own free will can believe in Jesus. Dr. Waite portrays himself as an bible expert (Th.D., Ph. D.). In fact, he is head of *The Bible For Today, Inc.*, which has an available resource library of over 2,600 articles. With his expertise in the bible, we can assume that he is not ignorant of verse 13. Obviously, he is purposely trying to mislead the reader as to what God means in John 1:12, by taking it out of its context. That is typical of Arminian theologians.

Dr. Waite repeats his strategy of quoting passages out of context as a way to conceal the gospel of grace in his treatment of Matthew 11:28.

> When [in Matthew 11:28] our Savior extended these gracious words, "come unto Me, ALL YE that labour and are heavy laden," I believe that this was an UNLIMITED invitation to an UNLIMITED group of people. This invitation extended, thus, to the ENTIRE WORLD of mankind who would be born . . . His invitation was backed up by his UNLIMITED PROVISION for "REST" in His "UNLIMITED ATONEMENT" at the Cross for the sins of the entire world![96] (emphasis in original).

When, however, Matthew 11:28 is read in context, it is clear from the preceding verse (verse 27) that it is only those whomsoever the Son will reveal the Father who are heavy laden and will come to Jesus.

> All things are delivered unto me of my Father: and no man knoweth the Son, but the Father; **neither knoweth any man the Father, save the Son, and he to whomsoever the Son will reveal him.** Come unto me, all ye that labour and are heavy laden, and I will give you rest. (Matthew 11:27-28 AV)

Dr. Waite continues with his Arminian strategy of hide the grace by citing Hebrews 2:9 out of context. Dr. Waite states:

> The verse [Hebrews 2:9] clearly teaches that Jesus Christ, in His incarnation, at the Cross of Calvary, "should taste death FOR EVERY MAN." . . . this is another clear and plain verse which teaches Christ's "UNLIMITED ATONEMENT" for everyone, barring none![97] (emphasis in original)

Waite's argument is that Jesus died for everyone in the world and therefore everyone in the world has a chance at salvation if they would only believe in Jesus of their own free will. Waite seems ignorant of the fact that the Epistle to the Hebrews was written by Paul to Jews. Paul was explaining the superiority of Jesus and his New Testament over the Old Testament types, which only foreshadowed the coming of Christ. In writing to the Jews, Paul wanted the Jews to understand that Christ died for both Jews and Gentiles. That is why he said that he "should taste death for every man." Paul meant every kind of man, not just the Jews, but also the Gentiles. Hebrews 9:15 reveals that it is only those Jews and Gentiles who are called by God who are saved.

> And for this cause he is the mediator of the new testament, that by means of death, for the redemption of the transgressions *that were* under the first testament, **they which are called might receive the promise of eternal inheritance**." (Hebrews 9:15 AV)

The gospel is that no one can come to Jesus without the calling of the Father. John 6:44,65. God's calling is effectual; all who are called will be saved. John 6:37-39. There is no middle group, as suggested by Waite's theology, that is made up of those whom God called, but are damned to hell, because they decided of their own free will to reject the calling of God.

Furthermore, Waite conceals the fact that only four verses later God explains who are among the "every man" that he referenced in verse 9. God states that Jesus' crucifixion was a way of "bringing many sons unto glory" and those sons are the "children which God hath given me."

> But we see Jesus, who was made a little lower than the angels for the suffering of death, crowned with glory and honour; **that he by the grace of God should taste death for every man**. For it became him, for whom *are* all things, and by whom *are* all things, in bringing many sons unto glory, to make the

captain of their salvation perfect through sufferings.
For both he that sanctifieth and they who are
sanctified *are* all of one: for which cause he is not
ashamed to call them brethren, Saying, I will declare
thy name unto my brethren, in the midst of the
church will I sing praise unto thee. And again, I will
put my trust in him. **And again, Behold I and the
children which God hath given me.** (Hebrews 2:9-
13 AV)

The passage in context proves that Jesus died only for his
elect, who were given to him by God the Father. Jesus died on the
cross to sanctify his children and Jesus and his children "are all of
one." Hebrews 2:9-13 states that Jesus suffered and died to sanctify
his children and make them perfect. If, as claimed by Waite, Jesus's
sanctified children includes everyone in the entire world, that would
mean that God sends to hell most of his sanctified children.

Verse 13 impeaches Waite's claim, by identifying the "every
man" for whom Jesus "tasted death" in verse 9 as being only the
"children which God hath given me." Who are the children that God
hath given to Jesus? The whole counsel of God, which Waite
eschews, states that Jesus' children are only those whom the Father
draws to the Son, and no others. *See* John 6:37, 39, 44, 65.

Before salvation, we are dead in trespasses and sin such that
Jesus must supply the faith for our salvation. That's right, he is not
only the object of our faith, but he is also the source of our faith.
Everything for our salvation is supplied by and through Christ. **Our
faith in Christ is the faith of Christ**. *See e.g.*, Romans 3:22;
Galatians 3:22; Revelation 14:12.

Knowing that a man is not justified by the works of
the law, but by the **faith of Jesus Christ**, even we
have believed in Jesus Christ, that we might be
justified by the **faith of Christ**, and not by the works
of the law: for by the works of the law shall no flesh
be justified. (Galatians 2:16 AV)

And be found in him, not having mine own
righteousness, which is of the law, but that which is
through the **faith of Christ**, the righteousness which
is of God by faith. (Philippians 3:9 AV)

Arminianism is a false gospel that was born of Rome. Read
one of the many curses the Roman Catholic Church rains down upon
those who believe the true gospel: "If anyone saith that the grace of
justification is only attained to by those who are predestined unto
life; but that all others who are called are called indeed, but bought
receive not grace, as being, by the divine power, predestined unto
evil; let him be anathema."[98]

The Bible is in direct contradiction to the free will doctrines
of the Catholic Church. If God chooses some for salvation, that
means that those not chosen for salvation are in turn chosen for
damnation. "Jesus answered them, Have not I chosen you twelve,
and one of you is a devil?" John 6:70.

Many Arminians use Revelation 3:20 as a proof text that it is
up to the sinner to make the choice and decide to follow Christ.[99]
"Behold, I stand at the door, and knock: **if any man hear my voice**,
and open the door, I will come in to him, and will sup with him, and
he with me." Revelation 3:20. Michael Boling explains the common
Arminian interpretation of that passage:

> The Holy Spirit is seen in Arminianism as the one
> who effectually initiates the offer of salvation
> described by Christ in Revelation 3:20, "Here I am! I
> stand at the door and knock. If anyone hears my
> voice and opens the door, I will come in and eat with
> him, and he with me." Arminianism states that
> mankind is unencumbered by the weight of sin.
> Additionally, it is believed that man has not lost their
> freedom and ability to respond to God's call and is
> not in need of total regeneration prior to accepting
> salvation.[100]

Arminians claim that God is helplessly knocking at the door of the believer's heart in the hope that he will open the door and believe in him. That is not at all what that passage means. If the Lord wills that the person hear his voice, the person will open the door. The opening of the door is according to God's will, not man's will. Man is impotent against the will of God. Only a few verses earlier, John, the inspired writer of Revelation, states that the Lord is "he that openeth, and no man shutteth; and shutteth, and no man openeth." Revelation 3:7.

Revelation 3:20 states that "if any man hear my voice, and open the door." It does not say, as some would suppose: "if any man *decides to* hear my voice and *chooses of his own free will* to open the door." It is clear that any man who hears Christ's calling and responds to it, Christ will come to him. It does not say that it is the free will decision of the person to hear. It is a statement of fact that those who are chosen by God will hear. It is not a statement of condition that the hearer of God's voice must now decide of his own free will whether to allow Jesus in. Jesus made this point to Pilate when he said: **"Every one that is of the truth heareth my voice."** John 18:37. Those who hear God's calling will respond, because they were chosen by God to respond. The calling of Christ is effectual. God is not a helpless and impotent being, who must rely on the free will "decisions" of men.

Jesus states time and again throughout the Bible: "If any man have ears to hear, let him hear." Mark 4:23. What does he mean by that? In Matthew 13:9-17 Jesus explains that he speaks in parables because not all who hear his words will understand. Those who are chosen by him will hear his voice and understand with their hearts and be converted. The parables are spiritual and can only be understood by those whom God has chosen for salvation. Revelation 3:20 is completely explained in Matthew 13:9-17. Those who are chosen by God will hear his voice and open the door, those that are not chosen will not hear his voice, because they cannot hear his voice. In fact, Jesus explained that he used parables not only to reveal the gospel to those chosen for salvation, but also to hide the gospel from those chosen for destruction.

Who hath ears to hear, let him hear. And the
disciples came, and said unto him, Why speakest
thou unto them in parables? He answered and said
unto them, **Because it is given unto you to know
the mysteries of the kingdom of heaven, but to
them it is not given.** For whosoever hath, to him
shall be given, and he shall have more abundance:
but whosoever hath not, from him shall be taken
away even that he hath. Therefore speak I to them in
parables: because they seeing see not; and **hearing
they hear not**, neither do they understand. And in
them is fulfilled the prophecy of Esaias, which saith,
**By hearing ye shall hear, and shall not
understand**; and seeing ye shall see, and shall not
perceive: For this people's heart is waxed gross, and
their **ears are dull of hearing**, and their eyes they
have closed; **lest at any time they should see with**
their **eyes, and hear with** *their* **ears, and should
understand with** *their* **heart, and should be
converted, and I should heal them. But blessed**
are **your eyes, for they see: and your ears, for they
hear.** For verily I say unto you, That many prophets
and righteous *men* have desired to see *those things*
which ye see, and have not seen *them*; and to hear
those things which ye hear, and have not heard *them*.
(Matthew 13:9-17 AV)

And when he was alone, they that were about him
with the twelve asked of him the parable. And he
said unto them, Unto you it is given to know the
mystery of the kingdom of God: but unto them that
are without, all *these* things are done in parables:
That seeing they may see, and not perceive; and
hearing they may hear, and not understand; lest at
any time they should be converted, and *their* sins
should be forgiven them. (Mark 4:10-12 AV)

The unsaved will not believe in Christ because they cannot

believe in him. Only the chosen sheep, who have been born again from heaven, can believe in the good shepherd. **"But ye believe not, because ye are not of my sheep."**(John 10:26 AV)

The Old Testament is an example; it is an allegorical pattern of the spiritual reality that is God's kingdom. *See* Galatians 4:22-26; Hebrews 8:5. God hardened Pharaoh's heart which is an example of how he hardens the hearts of unbelievers. "For the scripture saith unto Pharaoh, Even for this same purpose have I raised thee up, that I might shew my power in thee, and that my name might be declared throughout all the earth. **Therefore hath he mercy on whom he will *have mercy*, and whom he will he hardeneth**." Romans 9:17-18.

Those who do not believe in Jesus cannot believe, because God has blinded their eyes and stopped their ears, just as he hardened Pharaoh's heart. Only the elect of God are saved. "What then? Israel hath not obtained that which he seeketh for; but **the election hath obtained it, and the rest were blinded (According as it is written, God hath given them the spirit of slumber, eyes that they should not see, and ears that they should not hear;)** unto this day." (Romans 11:7-8 AV)

Looking back at Pharaoh, we see that Pharaoh had no choice in the matter. God was in complete control. God hardened Pharaoh's heart so that he would not let the children of Israel go. God also hardened the heart of Pharaoh's servants.

And when Pharaoh saw that the rain and the hail and the thunders were ceased, he sinned yet more, and hardened his heart, he and his servants. And the heart of Pharaoh was hardened, neither would he let the children of Israel go; as the LORD had spoken by Moses. And the LORD said unto Moses, Go in unto Pharaoh: for **I have hardened his heart, and the heart of his servants**, that I might shew these my signs before him: (Exodus 9:34-10:1 AV)

David Cloud, who fashions himself as a fundamentalist Baptist bible scholar, who states that he has spent hours each day over the past 38 years studying the bible and has preached in hundreds of churches throughout the world,[101] takes up the Arminian banner and tries to explain away God's hardening of Pharaoh's heart.

> As for Pharaoh, the Bible says that he rejected God's Word in Exodus 5:2 before God hardened his heart in Exodus 7:3. "Pharaoh said, Who is the LORD, that I should obey his voice to let Israel go? I know not the LORD, neither will I let Israel go" (Ex. 5:2). Also the Bible twice says that Pharaoh hardened his own heart. "But when Pharaoh saw that there was respite, he hardened his heart, and hearkened not unto them; as the LORD had said" (Ex. 8:15). See also Exodus 9:34. This is not a case of sovereign reprobation. The Scripture teaches that it is always God's will for men to serve Him, but when they reject Him He rejects them and judges them and makes examples of them.[102]

The problem with Cloud's Arminian analysis is that he overlooked a key passage (Exodus 4:21) that clearly states that it was God who planned ahead of time to harden Pharaoh's heart. If Cloud is the bible expert that he claims to be, that would mean that his failure to mention Exodus 4:21 was purposeful. It seems he has avoided Exodus 4:21, because it impeaches his Arminian theology.

God told Moses before he even returned to Egypt that he would harden Pharaoh's heart against the children of Israel so that Pharaoh would not let them go. "And the LORD said unto Moses, When thou goest to return into Egypt, see that thou do all those wonders before Pharaoh, which I have put in thine hand: **but I will harden his heart, that he shall not let the people go.**" (Exodus 4:21 AV)

Cloud puts every bible passage through his Arminian prism. He ignores the meaning of the plain words and instead constructs a meaning that is the very opposite of the passages themselves. For example, Cloud claims that the bible is clear that God did not create Pharaoh for the purpose of hardening his heart.

> These sinners [in 2 Thessalonians 2:10-12] will be damned but not because they are not sovereignly elected and not because they are sovereignly reprobate but because of their personal decision in regard to the truth. Words could not be plainer. God did make an example of Pharaoh and God did harden his heart for this purpose, but to go beyond what the Bible says and to claim that God chose to create Pharaoh for the purpose of reprobating him is a great error and is to malign the name of the loving God.[103]

Cloud asserts that to claim that God created Pharaoh for the purpose of reprobating him is a great error and maligns God. It may malign his Arminian god, but it does not malign the God of the bible. The God of the bible states unequivocally that he raised up Pharaoh for the purpose of hardening his heart, smiting him with pestilence, and then killing him.

> For now I will stretch out my hand, that I may smite thee and thy people with pestilence; and thou shalt be cut off from the earth. And in very deed for this cause have I raised thee up, for to shew in thee my power; and that my name may be declared throughout all the earth. Exodus 9:15-16; *See also* Romans 9:16.

Cloud does not think much of the God of the bible. The God of the bible did the very thing to which Cloud objects. Cloud seems to think that God is unrighteous to raise up Pharaoh for the purpose of hardening his heart and then destroying him. God has this to say to Cloud:

> What shall we say then? *Is there* unrighteousness with God? God forbid. For he saith to Moses, I will

have mercy on whom I will have mercy, and I will have compassion on whom I will have compassion. So then *it is* not of him that willeth, nor of him that runneth, but of God that sheweth mercy. For the scripture saith unto Pharaoh, Even for this same purpose have I raised thee up, that I might shew my power in thee, and that my name might be declared throughout all the earth. Therefore hath he mercy on whom he will *have mercy*, and whom he will he hardeneth. Thou wilt say then unto me, Why doth he yet find fault? For who hath resisted his will? Nay but, O man, who art thou that repliest against God? Shall the thing formed say to him that formed *it*, Why hast thou made me thus? Hath not the potter power over the clay, of the same lump to make one vessel unto honour, and another unto dishonour? *What* if God, willing to shew *his* wrath, and to make his power known, endured with much longsuffering the vessels of wrath fitted to destruction: And that he might make known the riches of his glory on the vessels of mercy, which he had afore prepared unto glory. (Romans 9:14-23 AV)

The unsaved cannot believe in Jesus because God has hardened their hearts and blinded their eyes.

Therefore they could not believe, because that Esaias said again, He hath blinded their eyes, and hardened their heart; that they should not see with *their* eyes, nor understand with *their* heart, and be converted, and I should heal them. (John 12:39-40 AV)

Jesus rejoiced that the truth of the gospel was revealed to the saved and hidden from the unsaved, according to God's will.

In that hour Jesus rejoiced in spirit, and said, I thank thee, O Father, Lord of heaven and earth, that **thou hast hid these things from the wise and prudent,**

and hast revealed them unto babes: even so, Father; for so it seemed good in thy sight. (Luke 10:21 AV)

It is a lie that God loves everybody. The Bible makes clear that most will be cast into an eternal lake of fire, where there will be weeping and gnashing of teeth. Matthew 22:13. "Enter ye in at the strait gate: for wide *is* the gate, and broad *is* the way, that leadeth to destruction, and many there be which go in thereat: Because strait *is* the gate, and narrow *is* the way, which leadeth unto life, and few there be that find it." (Matthew 7:13-14 AV) "For many are called, but few *are* chosen." (Matthew 22:14 AV) If God loves everybody, then casting most into hell is an perverse way of showing his love.

God does the choosing; he has already chosen who will be saved and who will be cast into the eternal lake of fire. He made his selection before the world was created. God will have mercy on whom he will have mercy, and he will have compassion on whom he will have compassion. "It is not of him that willeth, nor of him that runneth, but of God that sheweth mercy." Romans 9:16. Those who are chosen for eternal destruction are not loved by God; God hates them.

(For *the children* being not yet born, neither having done any good or evil, that the purpose of God according to election might stand, not of works, but of him that calleth;) It was said unto her, The elder shall serve the younger. As it is written, **Jacob have I loved, but Esau have I hated.** (Romans 9:11-13 AV)

God has made all things for a purpose, and one of his purposes in creating some is to reserve them for eternal punishment.

The LORD hath made all *things* for himself: yea, even the wicked for the day of evil. (Proverbs 16:4 AV)

The Lord knoweth how to deliver the godly out of temptations, and **to reserve the unjust unto the day of judgment to be punished**: (2 Peter 2:9 AV)

That the wicked is reserved to the day of destruction? they shall be brought forth to the day of wrath. (Job 21:30 AV)

13 Falling Away

Another of the favorite passages for Arminians to read out of context is Hebrews 6:4-6. That passage reads:

> For *it is* impossible for those who were once enlightened, and have tasted of the heavenly gift, and were made partakers of the Holy Ghost, And have tasted the good word of God, and the powers of the world to come, If they shall fall away, to renew them again unto repentance; seeing they crucify to themselves the Son of God afresh, and put *him* to an open shame. Hebrews 6:4-6.

Jim McGuiggan tries to explain Hebrews 6 as meaning that a person who is saved has the power to reject God and lose his salvation.

> It's true that faith is a gracious work of God in us (Philippians 1:29, Romans 10:17, Acts 18:27 and elsewhere) but God doesn't inject it into us and by its very nature it doesn't exist unless it has our free and vital ongoing consent and commitment. The graciousness of the gift doesn't render us incapable of despising it and throwing it away from us. . . . [T]this

relationship has the free consent of our hearts and minds. We aren't zombies or automata. We are friends of God in Jesus Christ. And we can turn from him (2 Peter 2:20-22) and refuse to abide in him (John 15:5-6). To do that is to reject God and the relationship is ended. To say that we're powerless to reject God and the relationship is to ignore the meaning of "reconciliation" and "friendship" with God.[104]

The argument by the Arminians is that Hebrews 6:4-6 contemplates one who once was saved but has fallen away from the grace of God by the power of his own free will. Such an interpretation is directly contrary to the expressed promises of Christ. **"All that the Father giveth me shall come to me; and him that cometh to me I will in no wise cast out."** (John 6:37 AV)

All who are chosen by the Father for salvation will be saved. John chapter 6 precludes the possibility of falling away from salvation, the falling away referred to in Hebrews chapter 6 is the falling away from the church, not salvation. There are those like Judas who appear for a time to be part of the church but in the end they make manifest that they are enemies of the gospel. "They went out from us, but they were not of us; for if they had been of us, they would no doubt have continued with us: but they went out, that they might be made manifest that they were not all of us." (1 John 2:19 AV) Judas and others like him went out, not because they were saved and lost their salvation, but rather because from the beginning "they were not of us." That is they were pretenders to salvation; they were unsaved tares congregating among the saved wheat. Matthew 13:27-43.

Those who do not believe in Christ are lost because they have not been chosen by God for salvation. Those who are chosen for salvation cannot lose their salvation. John 10:26-30. There is simply no such thing as a person losing his salvation.

But ye believe not, because ye are not of my sheep,

**as I said unto you. My sheep hear my voice, and I
know them, and they follow me: And I give unto
them eternal life; and they shall never perish,
neither shall any *man* pluck them out of my hand.
My Father, which gave *them* me, is greater than
all; and no *man* is able to pluck *them* out of my
Father's hand. I and *my* Father are one.** (John
10:26-30 AV)

There are only two possibilities in the gospel. First, those
who are lost cannot believe because God has not chosen them to
believe. The other possibility is the flip side of the first, those who
are chosen to believe will in fact believe, and they cannot ever lose
their faith, "no man is able to pluck them out of my Father's hand."
There is no category for persons to be first saved and then for them to
overrule God's choice by the power of their free will and "unsave"
themselves. Such an occurrence is an impossibility. The only way to
build such a theology is to ignore the clear message of the gospel.

Furthermore, when we read Hebrews 6:4-6 in context, we can
see that it refers to persons who were never saved to begin with. That
is evident when one reads the very next passage. That passage refers
to the difference between the earth that drinks in the rain and brings
forth fine herbs, and the parched earth that only tastes of the rain and
brings forth thorns and briers. That passage makes a distinction
between the saved who drink in the word of God and the unsaved
who have only tasted the word of God.

For *it is* impossible for those who were once
enlightened, and have tasted of the heavenly gift, and
were made partakers of the Holy Ghost, And have
tasted the good word of God, and the powers of the
world to come, If they shall fall away, to renew them
again unto repentance; seeing they crucify to
themselves the Son of God afresh, and put *him* to an
open shame. **For the earth which drinketh in the
rain that cometh oft upon it, and bringeth forth
herbs meet for them by whom it is dressed,**

**receiveth blessing from God: But that which
beareth thorns and briers** *is* **rejected, and** *is* **nigh
unto cursing; whose end** *is* **to be burned.** (Hebrews
6:4-8 AV)

Partaking of the Holy Ghost for the lost soul in Hebrews
chapter 6 does not mean a total submersion by the Holy Ghost, which
the bible refers to as a baptism of the Holy Ghost. The change in one
who is saved goes far beyond the enlightenment attributed to the lost
soul in Hebrews chapter 6. The saved person is born again. He
becomes a new spiritual creation of God. "Jesus answered and said
unto him, Verily, verily, I say unto thee, Except a man be born again,
he cannot see the kingdom of God." (John 3:3 AV) The saved person
is born again through the baptism of the Holy Ghost. "Then
remembered I the word of the Lord, how that he said, John indeed
baptized with water; but **ye shall be baptized with the Holy Ghost."**
(Acts 11:16 AV)

The baptism of the Holy Ghost is not merely a taste of the
spiritual waters. Indeed, the baptism of the Holy Ghost is the total
submergence such that God's elect are completely cleansed of their
sin in God's sight and are spiritually resurrected with Christ as new
creations. "Buried with him in baptism, wherein also ye are risen
with *him* through the faith of the operation of God, who hath raised
him from the dead. And you, being dead in your sins and the
uncircumcision of your flesh, hath he quickened together with him,
having forgiven you all trespasses;" (Colossians 2:12-13 AV)

The word of God is referred to as that spiritual water that
cleanses Christ's church from sin. One who is saved does not just
taste God's word. He drinks it in; indeed, he immerses himself in
God's word and is washed clean thereby. God's church is cleansed
by his word which is the spiritual water of salvation. "That he might
sanctify and cleanse it with the **washing of water by the word,** That
he might present it to himself a glorious church, not having spot, or
wrinkle, or any such thing; but that it should be holy and without
blemish." (Ephesians 5:26-27 AV)

Notice how Jesus in John 15 analogizes himself to a vine, with God the Father being the husbandman. In that passage a saved person does not merely taste of the heavenly gift and the word of God; the elect of God "abides" as a branch in the vine of God. That is the only way that a person can bring forth the spiritual fruit evidencing salvation. All who do not abide in Jesus are cast from the vine and burned. They are as the thorns and briers referred to in Hebrews 6:8 "whose end *is* to be burned."

> I am the true vine, and my Father is the husbandman.
> Every branch in me that beareth not fruit he taketh
> away: and every *branch* that beareth fruit, he purgeth
> it, that it may bring forth more fruit. Now ye are
> clean through the word which I have spoken unto
> you. Abide in me, and I in you. As the branch cannot
> bear fruit of itself, except it abide in the vine; no
> more can ye, except ye abide in me. I am the vine, ye
> *are* the branches: He that abideth in me, and I in him,
> the same bringeth forth much fruit: for **without me
> ye can do nothing. If a man abide not in me, he is
> cast forth as a branch, and is withered; and men
> gather them, and cast *them* into the fire, and they
> are burned.** If ye abide in me, and my words abide
> in you, ye shall ask what ye will, and it shall be done
> unto you. Herein is my Father glorified, that ye bear
> much fruit; so shall ye be my disciples." (John 15:1-8
> AV)

The Armininan might say "ah, but you still have not presented proof that the decision to abide in the vine of God is not a decision born of the free will of man." In fact, we read in the beginning of this chapter how Jim McGuiggan cited John 15:5-6 to support his argument that man has the power of his own free will to throw away his salvation. When the entire passage in John chapter 15 is read in context, the sovereign grace of God in the election and preservation of the saints becomes clear. In John 15:16-18 Jesus explains the meaning of the metaphor of the vine and branches. Those who are saved are chosen by him. Jesus explicitly states that one does not choose him, rather Jesus does the choosing. He has chosen his elect branches out of the world and ordained them to bear spiritual fruit.

> **Ye have not chosen me, but I have chosen you, and ordained you, that ye should go and bring forth fruit, and *that* your fruit should remain:** that whatsoever ye shall ask of the Father in my name, he may give it you. These things I command you, that ye love one another. If the world hate you, ye know that it hated me before *it hated* you. If ye were of the world, the world would love his own: but because ye are not of the world, but **I have chosen you out of the world**, therefore the world hateth you. (John 15:16-19 AV)

In John 15:4-5, Jesus also states that the branches chosen by him can do nothing aside from him. He chooses the branches and they bear fruit because he has purposed that they continue to abide in him. **"for without me ye can do nothing."** (John 15:5 AV) That statement alone impeaches the false notion that man is a free agent in deciding and keeping his salvation. It is not the branches through their free will that support the root, it is the root that supports the branches, and that root is Christ. "Boast not against the branches. But if thou boast, **thou bearest not the root, but the root thee."** (Romans 11:18 AV) Jesus chooses and nourishes the branches, and without him they can do nothing, period.

Notice what God says in 1st Peter. "Being born again, not of corruptible seed, but of incorruptible, by the word of God, which liveth and abideth for ever. For all flesh *is* as grass, and all the glory of man as the flower of grass. The grass withereth, and the flower thereof falleth away:" (1 Peter 1:23-24 AV) We see God using a simile of the earth and the plants springing from the earth. A saved Christian is born again from the incorruptible seed of the Holy Spirit. All flesh, however, is as grass. Those who have not been reborn and made new spiritual creations remain in the flesh and are like the grass that withers and falls away. The unsaved grass in 1 Peter chapter 1, as the unsaved briers and thorns in Hebrews chapter 6, are good only to be burned.

Read also what Jesus says in Matthew chapter 13 about the unsaved tares that were sown among the wheat. The tares are the "children of the wicked one" who were sown by the devil. At the end of the world the angels will gather the tares and burn them in the fires of hell, where there will be weeping and gnashing of teeth for eternity. Matthew 13:36-43. The wheat are the children of the kingdom who are born of the good seed of Jesus; they will shine forth as the sun in the kingdom of God.

At the end of the parable of the wheat and the tares in Matthew 13, Jesus repeats "who hath ears to hear, let him hear." Matthew 13:43. Jesus is indicating that the truths he is revealing can only be understood and accepted by those to whom he has given spiritual ears with which to understand.

Those in Hebrews chapter 6 who only taste the word of God are like the tares in Matthew chapter 13; they are left dry and bring forth spiritual thorns and briers. The thorns and briers are symbolic of their spiritual condition. They are the spiritual weeds in God's kingdom, to be pulled up and burned in the fires of hell. When we read the passages that immediately follow the metaphor of the dry ground that brings forth briers and thorns in Hebrews chapter 6, we read that the good soil that drinks in the rain and brings forth abundant fruit are those who "inherit the promises."

> But, beloved, we are persuaded better things of you, and **things that accompany salvation**, though we thus speak. For God *is* not unrighteous to forget your work and labour of love, which ye have shewed toward his name, in that ye have ministered to the saints, and do minister. And we desire that every one of you do shew the same diligence to the full assurance of hope unto the end: That ye be not slothful, but followers of them who through faith and patience **inherit the promises.** For when God made

promise to Abraham, because he could swear by no greater, he sware by himself. (Hebrews 6:9-13 AV)

In Hebrews chapter 6, God explains that the referenced promises are the promises made by God to Abraham. Hebrews 6:13. The promises were according to the sovereign election of God. That is the whole point of the gospel. It all comes back to the election of God according to his sovereign grace.

> That is, **They which are the children of the flesh, these *are* not the children of God: but the children of the promise are counted for the seed.** For this *is* the word of promise, At this time will I come, and Sara shall have a son. And not only *this*; but when Rebecca also had conceived by one, *even* by our father Isaac; (For *the children* being not yet born, neither having done any good or evil, **that the purpose of God according to election might stand, not of works, but of him that calleth**;) (Romans 9:8-11 AV)

Romans 9 clearly states that God's spiritual seed are the object of God's promise and are chosen by God. It is not the children of the flesh that are the children of God (whether by fleshly heredity or fleshly will). Indeed all flesh is as grass to be burned. God's election is according to his sovereign will and purpose, wherein his elect brings forth the fruit of salvation. The heirs of the promise made to Abraham are chosen by God, not by man. The promise was made by God, and it is God who fulfills that promise in Christ. "And if ye *be* Christ's, then are ye Abraham's seed, and heirs according to the promise." (Galatians 3:29 AV)

Once saved, a believer is sealed for eternity by the Holy Spirit. "In whom ye also *trusted*, after that ye heard the word of truth, the gospel of your salvation: in whom also after that ye believed, ye were sealed with that holy Spirit of promise," (Ephesians 1:13 AV) No one is able to break God's seal.

14 How Often Would I Have
Gathered Thy Children

A rminians are fond of quoting Matthew 23:37 out of context from corrupt bible versions, alleging that the passage supports their argument that man's free will can thwart the will of God. For example, Norman Geisler quotes the NIV version of Matthew 23:37 in support of his Arminian theology in his popular book, *Chosen But Free.*[105] Dr. Norman Geisler (Ph.D., Loyola University) is president of Southern Evangelical Seminary and author or coauthor of over fifty books including Baker's Encyclopedia of Apologetics. After quoting the NIV version of Matthew 23:37, Geisler stated: "In short, it is God's ultimate and sovereign will that we have free will even to resist His will that everyone be saved."[106] Wow! One can only marvel at such Arminian nonsense.

Chad Meister, who is an Arminian theologian and an assistant professor of philosophy at Bethel College quotes the NIV bible version of Matthew 23:37 and identifies it as one of the prime passages that supports the Arminian theology that man has free will and can use it to resist the sovereign will of God. Meister states:

[T]he Bible strongly affirms human free will (the ability to initiate a moral decision either for or against any given option). Jesus laments over His city in Matthew 23:37: "O Jerusalem, Jerusalem, you who kill the prophets and stone those sent to you, how often I have longed to gather your children together, as a hen gathers her chicks under her wings, *but you were not willing*!" (NIV, emphasis added). [107]

The NIV passage quoted by Geisler and Meister is wrong. God did not state "but you were not willing." God actually stated "ye would not." The actual passage in God's word, which is found in the Authorized (King James) Version (AV) of the bible:

> O Jerusalem, Jerusalem, thou that killest the prophets, and stonest them which are sent unto thee, how often would I have gathered thy children together, even as a hen gathereth her chickens under her wings, and ye would not! (Matthew 23:37 AV)

There is an eternity of difference between "but you were not willing" in the NIV and "ye would not" in the AV. God was not saying that Jerusalem was able to thwart the will of God through the exercise of their will, as alleged by Geisler and Meister. Rather, God was stating "would I have gathered thy children" but "ye would not" gather thy children. God rejected the earthly Jerusalem and instead uses his church to "gather" his "children." The earthly Jerusalem of which Jesus spoke was adverse to God, and that is why it did not gather its children to God. "He that is not with me is against me: and he that gathereth not with me scattereth." Luke 11:23.

The misuse of Matthew 23:37 is yet another example where the Arminians have taken a bible passage out of context and misinterpreted it to say something contrary to God's gospel. Before Jesus made the statement in Matthew 23:37, Jesus was teaching through parables in the temple at Jerusalem. *See* Matthew 21:23. Jesus made the comment in Matthew 23:37 after reciting several parables and upbraiding the scribes and Pharisees who sat in Moses' seat in Jerusalem. Jesus told a wedding parable against the scribes and Pharisees. That wedding parable explains the meaning of

Matthew 23:37. Jesus stated:

> And Jesus answered and spake unto them again by
> parables, and said, The kingdom of heaven is like
> unto a certain king, which made a marriage for his
> son, And sent forth his servants **to call them that
> were bidden to the wedding**: and they would not
> come. Again, he sent forth other servants, saying,
> Tell them which are bidden, Behold, I have prepared
> my dinner: my oxen and my fatlings are killed, and
> all things are ready: come unto the marriage. But
> they made light of it, and went their ways, one to his
> farm, another to his merchandise: And the remnant
> took his servants, and entreated them spitefully, and
> slew them. But when the king heard thereof, he was
> wroth: and he sent forth his armies, and destroyed
> those murderers, and burned up their city. Then saith
> he to his servants, The wedding is ready, but they
> which were bidden were not worthy. Go ye therefore
> into the highways, and as many as ye shall find, bid
> to the marriage. So those servants went out into the
> highways, and **gathered together all as many as
> they found**, both bad and good: **and the wedding
> was furnished with guests**. And when the king came
> in to see the guests, he saw there a man which had
> not on a wedding garment: And he saith unto him,
> Friend, how camest thou in hither not having a
> wedding garment? And he was speechless. Then said
> the king to the servants, Bind him hand and foot, and
> take him away, and cast him into outer darkness,
> there shall be weeping and gnashing of teeth. **For
> many are called, but few are chosen.** Matthew
> 22:1-14.

Jesus was speaking of the Jewish religious leaders, who ruled
from Jerusalem. They had rejected God and set up their own religion
contrary to God's commands. "Making the word of God of none
effect through your tradition, which ye have delivered: and many

such like things do ye." (Mark 7:13 AV) Jesus was explaining in
Matthew 22 that God had rejected them.

Notice that in Matthew 22:3 when the king first sent an
invitation to the wedding, they were "bidden to the wedding," but
nobody responded. They did not respond because they did not have
the ability to respond. No man can come to Jesus unless the father
draw him. John 6:44. Later, the king told his servants to "go ye
therefore into the highways, and as many as ye shall find, bid to the
marriage." Matthew 22:9. The king's servants then did something
that was not done during the earlier invitation. In addition to bidding
the guests to the wedding, the servants "gathered together all as many
as they found." Matthew 22:10. No one came to the first invitation,
and it was necessary for the king to affirmatively "gather" people to
the wedding.

Once the king's servants gathered the guests, "the wedding
was furnished with guests." Matthew 22:10. The king furnished the
wedding with guests by gathering them, just as God furnishes heaven
with his elect by gathering them. "And he shall send his angels with
a great sound of a trumpet, and they shall **gather** together his elect
from the four winds, from one end of heaven to the other." (Matthew
24:31 AV)

The king's first invitation was not enough to convince his
guests to come to the wedding.   Just as the wedding required the
king's servants to "gather" guests, so also salvation requires God to
draw his elect. The wedding parable in Matthew 22 was punctuated
with Jesus' statement: "For many are called, but few are chosen." It
was the chosen who were "gathered" and brought to the wedding.
The reference by Jesus in Matthew 23:37 to Jerusalem was to earthly
Jerusalem. The true holy city of Jerusalem is made up of the saints
who have faith in Jesus, not fleshly Jews. "And I John saw the holy
city, **new Jerusalem**, coming down from God out of heaven,
prepared as a **bride** adorned for her husband." Revelation 21:2.

The man that came to the wedding without wedding clothes
in Matthew 22 was not chosen among those that were "gathered."

He, of his own free will, decided to try to enter, but he was not among those that were "gathered," and so did not have the proper wedding garment. All those that seek to come into the kingdom of heaven must have on the wedding garment of the perfect righteousness of Christ. They must have their robes washed in the blood of God's lamb, who is Jesus. Revelation 7:14. No one can get into heaven through their own righteousness; those seeking entrance into heaven must have the righteousness of Christ (the wedding garment).

> Let us be glad and rejoice, and give honour to him:
> for the marriage of the Lamb is come, and his wife
> hath made herself ready. **And to her was granted
> that she should be arrayed in fine linen, clean and
> white: for the fine linen is the righteousness of
> saints.**" Revelation 19:7-8. *See also* Revelation 3:5;
> Romans 4, 9:30-31; Galatians 3:26-29.

Jesus followed the parable in Matthew 12 with a direct attack on the Pharisees and scribes:

> But woe unto you, scribes and Pharisees, hypocrites!
> for **ye shut up the kingdom of heaven against men:
> for ye neither go in yourselves, neither suffer ye
> them that are entering to go in.** Woe unto you,
> scribes and Pharisees, hypocrites! for ye devour
> widows' houses, and for a pretence make long prayer:
> therefore ye shall receive the greater damnation. Woe
> unto you, scribes and Pharisees, hypocrites! for ye
> compass sea and land to make one proselyte, and
> when he is made, ye make him twofold more the
> child of hell than yourselves. Woe unto you, ye blind
> guides, which say, Whosoever shall swear by the
> temple, it is nothing; but whosoever shall swear by
> the gold of the temple, he is a debtor! Ye fools and
> blind: for whether is greater, the gold, or the temple
> that sanctifieth the gold? And, Whosoever shall
> swear by the altar, it is nothing; but whosoever

sweareth by the gift that is upon it, he is guilty. Ye fools and blind: for whether is greater, the gift, or the altar that sanctifieth the gift? Whoso therefore shall swear by the altar, sweareth by it, and by all things thereon. And whoso shall swear by the temple, sweareth by it, and by him that dwelleth therein. And he that shall swear by heaven, sweareth by the throne of God, and by him that sitteth thereon. Woe unto you, scribes and Pharisees, hypocrites! for ye pay tithe of mint and anise and cummin, and have omitted the weightier matters of the law, judgment, mercy, and faith: these ought ye to have done, and not to leave the other undone. Ye blind guides, which strain at a gnat, and swallow a camel. Woe unto you, scribes and Pharisees, hypocrites! for ye make clean the outside of the cup and of the platter, but within they are full of extortion and excess. Thou blind Pharisee, cleanse first that which is within the cup and platter, that the outside of them may be clean also. Woe unto you, scribes and Pharisees, hypocrites! for ye are like unto whited sepulchres, which indeed appear beautiful outward, but are within full of dead men's bones, and of all uncleanness. Even so ye also outwardly appear righteous unto men, but within ye are full of hypocrisy and iniquity. Woe unto you, scribes and Pharisees, hypocrites! because ye build the tombs of the prophets, and garnish the sepulchres of the righteous, And say, If we had been in the days of our fathers, we would not have been partakers with them in the blood of the prophets. Wherefore ye be witnesses unto yourselves, that ye are the children of them which killed the prophets. Fill ye up then the measure of your fathers. **Ye serpents, ye generation of vipers, how can ye escape the damnation of hell?** Wherefore, behold, I send unto you prophets, and wise men, and scribes: and some of them ye shall kill and crucify; and some of them shall ye scourge in your synagogues, and persecute them from city to city: That upon you may come all the righteous blood shed upon the earth, from the blood of righteous Abel unto the blood of Zacharias son of Barachias, whom ye slew between the temple and the altar. Verily I say unto you, All these things shall come upon this generation. **O Jerusalem, Jerusalem, thou that killest the prophets, and stonest them which are sent unto thee, how often would I have gathered thy children together, even as a hen gathereth her chickens under her wings, and ye would not!** Behold, your house is left unto you desolate. For I say unto you, Ye shall not see me henceforth, till ye shall say, Blessed is he that cometh in the name of the Lord. Matthew 23:13-39.

When Jesus said "O Jerusalem" he was referring to the religious leaders against which he pronounced "woe" after "woe" in the preceding verses. Jesus was stating that they killed the prophets whom God had sent to them, which had the effect (according to God's will) of shutting "up the kingdom of heaven against men." Matthew 23:13. Jesus then told the Pharisees and scribes that they and their followers are damned to hell.

One must read Matthew 23:37 in context and distinguish between "Jerusalem" and the "children." It was the Jews (referred to as "children") who were under the care of Jerusalem (the Pharisees and scribes, who sat in Moses' seat of authority). Notice, that it was "Jerusalem" who "would not" gather its children under its wings. The children of Jerusalem were not gathered by God, because nobody can come to God unless he draws them to him. John 6:44. They were not drawn. They were given an invitation by the prophets, but the religious leaders killed and stoned the prophets. As the parable of the wedding explains, they were not chosen among those "gathered" for the wedding. "For many are called, but few are chosen." Matthew 22:14.

Notice that God used the same word to describe what he did

not do in Jerusalem in Matthew 23:37 and what he did do in the
parable of the kings wedding in Matthew 22:1-14. In the parable of
the king's wedding the king's servants "gathered" the guests for the
wedding. In Matthew 23:37, however, God did not "gather" the
children of Jerusalem, because the religious leaders "would not"
gather them by obeying God's word. Arminians contend that the
religious leaders had the ability to accept God's invitation. However,
the passage says no such thing. The passage simply states the fact
that they "would not"gather their children. The religious leaders, like
the first guests who were invited to the wedding, "took his servants,
and entreated them spitefully, and slew them." Matthew 22:6. What
happens to those that are not gathered? God gathers his elect, and
the rest are thrown in an eternal fire. God "will throughly purge his
floor, and gather his wheat into the garner; but he will burn up the
chaff with unquenchable fire." (Matthew 3:12 AV)

The Jews tried to establish their own righteousness as a
means to salvation. They refused to submit to God in repentance and
faith.

> For they being ignorant of God's righteousness, and
> going about to establish their own righteousness,
> have not submitted themselves unto the righteousness
> of God. For Christ is the end of the law for
> righteousness to every one that believeth. Romans
> 10:3

The Jews erected a religion, whereby salvation was by good
works. God, however, saves his elect by his grace alone. "And if by
grace, then is it no more of works." Romans 11:6. God planned that
the Jews would fail in their effort to establish their own
righteousness. God planned on the Jews not responding to his
invitation to salvation by faith. God was making an example of them
to show us the futility of man's efforts to gain salvation by good
works. *See* 1 Corinthians 10:11.

God elected men for salvation, both among the gentiles and
among the Jews. "For there is no difference between the Jew and the

Greek: for the same Lord over all is rich unto all that call upon him. For whosoever shall call upon the name of the Lord shall be saved." Romans 10:11-12. The Jews, on the other hand, have constructed a religion where they claim a unique blessing and status that is distinct and superior to gentiles.

God has revealed that those whom God elected for salvation are not even seeking him. God makes himself manifest to them. That means that salvation is entirely the work of God, by his grace. He elects those for salvation who are not even of their own will seeking salvation. In fact, God explains that "there is none that seeketh after God." Romans 11. God draws his elect and makes them seek him. Without God's drawing, no man would come to God. John 6:44, 64-65. All who are drawn by God will come to him. John 6:39. The Jews of Jerusalem to whom he referred in Matthew 23:37 were not among those whom God drew. God stretched out his hand to them, but their very nature was to reject God, just as Jesus explained in the wedding parable in Matthew 22.

> But Esaias is very bold, and saith, **I was found of them that sought me not; I was made manifest unto them that asked not after me. But to Israel he saith, All day long I have stretched forth my hands unto a disobedient and gainsaying people**. Romans 10:20-21.

God had blinded the Jews of Jerusalem to whom he spoke in Matthew 23:37. He gave the Jews a spirit of slumber so that they could not respond to his invitation. Those whom the king in Matthew 22 ultimately gathered to the wedding were chosen to come to the wedding, whereas those who rejected his first invitation were foreordained to reject the invitation. God elects some for salvation and the others are sent to an eternal lake of fire.

> What then? Israel hath not obtained that which he seeketh for; but the election hath obtained it, and the rest were blinded. (According as it is written, God hath given them the spirit of slumber, eyes that they

should not see, and ears that they should not hear;)
unto this day. And David saith, Let their table be
made a snare, and a trap, and a stumblingblock, and a
recompence unto them: Let their eyes be darkened,
that they may not see, and bow down their back
alway. Romans 11:7-10.

The children of the worldly Jerusalem are the children of the
flesh; they are not the children of God. Romans 9:8. Jesus stated
emphatically in Matthew 23:38: "Behold, your house is left unto you
desolate." The house of Jerusalem includes the children of that
house. The children of God are the elect children of the spirit, who
look for a heavenly Jerusalem. "And he carried me away in the spirit
to a great and high mountain, and shewed me that great city, the holy
Jerusalem, descending out of heaven from God." Revelation 21:10.

The earthly Jerusalem is in bondage to sin. The children of
the heavenly Jerusalem are the children of promise, who were elected
by God for salvation. Romans 9:11. The Arminian view that
somehow the fleshly children of Jerusalem could have been saved if
only they were willing is not supported by scripture. In Galatians 4
God makes it clear that the earthly Jerusalem and her children are in
bondage to sin, whereas it is the heavenly Jerusalem that is freed
from sin and is elected by God to inherit the kingdom of heaven.

For it is written, that Abraham had two sons, the one
by a bondmaid, the other by a freewoman. But he
who was of **the bondwoman was born after the
flesh**; but **he of the freewoman was by promise.**
Which things are an allegory: for these are the two
covenants; the one from the mount Sinai, which
gendereth to bondage, which is Agar. For this Agar is
mount Sinai in Arabia, and answereth to **Jerusalem
which now is, and is in bondage with her children.
But Jerusalem which is above is free, which is the
mother of us all.** For it is written, Rejoice, thou
barren that bearest not; break forth and cry, thou that
travailest not: for the desolate hath many more

children than she which hath an husband. **Now we, brethren, as Isaac was, are the children of promise.** But as then he that was born after the flesh persecuted him that was born after the Spirit, even so it is now. Nevertheless what saith the scripture? Cast out the bondwoman and her son: for the son of the bondwoman shall not be heir with the son of the freewoman. **So then, brethren, we are not children of the bondwoman, but of the free.** Galatians 4:23-31.

The children of the heavenly Jerusalem are children of God because they are the children of promise. Their status as children is not based upon anything that they have done. Romans 9:11. The earthly Jerusalem was not elected by God for salvation. The Jerusalem of God is a heavenly city. "But ye are come unto mount Sion, and unto the city of the living God, the heavenly Jerusalem, and to an innumerable company of angels." Hebrews 12:22. Those elected by God will be children in the heavenly Jerusalem.

Him that overcometh will I make a pillar in the temple of my God, and he shall go no more out: and I will write upon him the name of my God, and **the name of the city of my God, which is new Jerusalem, which cometh down out of heaven from my God**: and I will write upon him my new name. Revelation 3:12.

The children who are chosen by God certainly come to him, just as Jesus explained in his parable of the wedding feast in Matthew 22:1-14. It is God who does both the calling and the choosing. "For many are called, but few are chosen." Matthew 22:14. The children of God are elected by God to be children of God. "For the children being not yet born, neither having done any good or evil, that the purpose of God according to election might stand, not of works, but of him that calleth." Romans 9:11.

It was "Jerusalem" who "would not" gather its children by

following God's word. The children of Jerusalem would not come to God, because the religious leadership had bewitched them into following the traditions of men, rather than seeking after the righteousness of God. *See* Mark 7:13. Jesus called them children of hell. Matthew 23:15. The spiritual children of the promise, whom God gathers, come with the wedding garment of the righteousness of Jesus Christ provided for them by God. Revelation 21:2. God's children are chosen by the grace of God through faith in Jesus Christ. The children of the flesh are rejected by God and their house is left unto them desolate. Matthew 23:38.

15 Ye Do Always Resist the Holy Ghost

nother passage taken out of context to support the Arminian theology is Acts 7:51. The claim of the Arminians is that because Stephen said the Jews resisted the Holy Ghost, that allegedly means that man can resist the will of God to save his elect. Again, the Arminians hide the important context, which is that Stephen chastised the Jews who "always resist the Holy Ghost" by killing both the prophets and Christ. Arminian theologian Chad Meister states:

> [T]he Bible strongly affirms human free will (the ability to initiate a moral decision either for or against any given option). ... In Acts 7:51, Stephen chastises the Jewish council for resisting God: "You stiff-necked people, with uncircumcised hearts and ears! You are just like your fathers: You always resist the Holy Spirit!" (NIV, emphasis added).[108]

Dr. Richard P. Bucher, a Lutheran theologian, quotes Acts 7:51 in support of his claim that man can veto God's election of a person for salvation:

> Calvinism correctly teaches that we are saved by grace

alone. Their notion of a sovereign God, however,
incorrectly leads them to confess that God's grace can not
be resisted or rejected. According to Scripture, people can
and do resist and reject God's gracious offer of salvation. ...
[C]onsider the words of Stephen to the Sanhedrin, "You
stiff-necked people, with uncircumcised hearts and ears!
You are just like your fathers: You always resist the Holy
Spirit!" (Acts 7:51). Sadly, even though God wants all to be
saved, though Christ died for all, and though he extends his
grace to all, many have and will reject the offer.[109]

When Acts 7:51 is read in context, we get a different meaning
from that alleged by Meister and Bucher.

Ye stiffnecked and uncircumcised in heart and ears, ye do
always resist the Holy Ghost: as your fathers did, so do ye.
**Which of the prophets have not your fathers
persecuted? and they have slain them which shewed
before of the coming of the Just One; of whom ye have
been now the betrayers and murderers: Who have
received the law by the disposition of angels, and have
not kept it.** Acts 7:51-53.

The passage read in context reveals that it only addresses how
the Jews had persecuted and killed the prophets and murdered Jesus
Christ. That is what Stephen meant by resisting the Holy Ghost. He
was not suggesting that the men had the ability to resist the will of
God to save those whom God had elected for salvation. Stephen was
defining both their fathers' conduct in killing the prophets and their
conduct in crucifying Christ as resisting the Holy Ghost. The Jews
were stiffnecked and uncircumcised in the heart, which means that
they were unregenerate.

For he is not a Jew, which is one outwardly; neither is that
circumcision, which is outward in the flesh: But he is a
Jew, which is one inwardly; and **circumcision is that of
the heart, in the spirit**, and not in the letter; whose praise
is not of men, but of God. Romans 2:28-29.

The Jews being addressed by Stephen were no different from all other unregenerate persons. All men, by their fallen nature, resist the Holy Ghost. Romans 3:10-18. The Jews to whom Stephen was speaking, resisted the Holy Ghost by crucifying Christ, just as their fathers had killed the prophets. That does not mean, however, that man can thwart the will of God in saving his elect. *See* Romans 9:11; John 1:12-13; 6:39-40. The crucifixion of Christ was planned by God and executed according to his foreordained plan. Acts 2:22-24; 4:24-28 . Similarly, the persecution and murder of the prophets was according to God's sovereign will.

The heart of all sinners must be circumcised (born again) by God to be saved. John 3:3. All whom God chooses are born again, and the new birth is solely by the power of God. John 1:13. The sovereign God, if he so chose, could overcome any person's resistance to the Holy Ghost, just as he did with the great persecutor of the church, Saul, who later became the Apostle Paul. Acts 9. The passage at Acts 7:51 does not support the claim that man can successfully resist the will of God to save those sinners he has elected for salvation. God's "will be done in earth, as it is in heaven." Matthew 6:10.

16 Only Two Types of Religions in the World

There are only two types of religion in the entire world. They are diametrically opposed to each other, as though separated by a great gulf. On the one side of that gulf are the many varieties of the religion of free will. The free will religions require an adherent to exercise his free will to gain the blessings of God. Such religions are premised upon the adherent either working to gain the blessings of their god or working to keep the blessings of their god.

On the other side of the great gulf is the one and only religion of the free grace of God, found in the Holy Bible. The religion of God's grace boldly proclaims that the sovereign God planned salvation for helpless sinners and that he also furnishes them with the ability and the desire to receive it. John Reisinger explains the commonality of the many varieties of the free will (i.e., works oriented) religion:

> There are basically only two religions in the world. One says, "If you will do such and such, God will graciously bestow His blessing upon you." The thousand and one varieties of this religion differ only on what the "such and such" is that you must be willing to do. One variety says

bathe in a sacred river, another bids you kiss the sacred
rock located in the holy city, still another says be baptized
or some similar rite, and in distinctly evangelical circles
this religion emphasizes, "If you will open your heart, then
God . . ."

Notice carefully the three key words IF YOU WILL.

(1) God's forgiveness is possible IF . . .
(2) God's forgiveness is possible if YOU . . .
(3) God's forgiveness is possible if you WILL . . .

The ultimate success or failure of this religion is
determined solely by the will of man. Everything depends
on an "if," and on "you," and on "your willingness" to do
your part. Redemption is always conditional since it
depends on man's cooperation for success. The great work
of salvation is not actually accomplished until God can find
someone who is willing to "cooperate with Him." Our
forefathers called this "if you will" system the "religion of
works." It was also called "Arminianism" and
"semi-Pelagianism" since these were the men who
originally caused division in the church by introducing this
error of free will. Regardless of the name attached to it by
friend or foe, the distinguishing marks are always the same
— the IF, the YOU, and YOUR WILL are the decisive
factors that make the plan of salvation work. This religion
offers a wonderful plan of salvation that is able to do
mighty things if you will only let it. The God of this free
will religion can only desire and offer to save sinners. He is
helpless to secure, by His own power, what He longs to do.
The goal of redemption cannot be reached unless man, of
his own free will, chooses to permit God to accomplish His
purposes.[110]

Alexander Pringle explains that Arminianism is in direct
opposition to the sovereignty of God and plays to man's corrupt
nature.

Of all the devices formed by Satan, and employed to sully
the glory of divine truth, that which is now commonly
called ARMINIANISM, is the most ancient, the most
dangerous, and the most successful. Since the fall of man, it
has existed in the world, in every age and in every country.
It may be called the religion of our fallen nature; and will
never want friends and advocates on earth, so long as the
spirit of error and the corrupt heart are permitted to exert
their wicked influence. It is a system of principles, stated in
direct opposition to the sovereignty of God, displayed in the
distribution of his favours among men; and is utterly
eversive of the whole plan of grace revealed in the gospel.
It proclaims open war against the essential prerogative of
Deity—his absolute right of determining the final state of
rational beings, considered as guilty and fallen; and makes
the divine purpose entirely dependent on the creature's will.
The great God is impiously dethroned, that the vile idol of
free will may be exalted in his room. The proud usurper,
being seated on the throne, dares to arraign at his bar every
thing human and divine; and presumes to judge, approve, or
condemn every article of the divine testimony, and every
piece of divine conduct, as they appear right or wrong to
the corrupt heart—the depraved will.

This is a system founded in ignorance, supported by pride,
fraught with atheism, and will end in delusion. But it is well
calculated to gain general consent among all who were
never thoroughly convinced of the evil of sin, nor felt the
burden of guilt pressing their consciences; nor have seen
the purity of the divine law, their own lost and helpless
state, and the absolute necessity of Christ's righteousness
for justification and eternal life. The carnal heart is
naturally proud, and regards, with fond attention, whatever
tends to flatter its vanity and self-importance. Such is the
palpable tendency of the Arminianism scheme. It gently
whispers us in the ear, that, even in a fallen state, we retain
both the will and the power of doing what is good and
acceptable to God:—that Christ's death is accepted by God

as an universal atonement for the sins of all men; in order
that every one may, if he will, save himself by his own free
will, and good works:—that, in the exercise of our natural
powers, we may arrive at perfection even in the present life,
&c. These, and the like unscriptural tenets, are so much
adapted to the legal bias of the corrupt heart, that we need
not wonder at the favourable reception they have met with
in every period of the church.

***

Arminianism, of all others, is the most prevalent; and may
be styled the vulgar error. It comes soliciting our
acceptance with all the false charms of a harlot, decked out
in such captivating colours, as too well suit the vitiated and
depraved taste of corrupt nature. It finds an advocate in
every man's bosom. Its cause is pleaded by all the strength
and subtlety of carnal reason.[111]

Arminians are fond of citing John 6:40 out of context to
demonstrate that it is God's will to save everyone in the entire world,
if only they would cooperate with God and exercise their free will to
believe in Jesus. John 6:40 states:

And this is the will of him that sent me, that every one
which seeth the Son, and believeth on him, may have
everlasting life: and I will raise him up at the last day. John
6:40.

Part and parcel of the free will Arminian gospel is that man can
choose to reject God's offer of salvation, and should he choose to
accept salvation he can later change his mind and lose his salvation.
Arminian theologian Daniel Whedon, in his commentary on John
6:40, presents the standard Arminian interpretation of that verse:

So long as he [the believer] performs the condition, so long
is he heir of the salvation. When he ceases to be a believer
he loses all claim to the divine promise, and all interest in

eternal life. That he has once believed no longer secures him heaven, any more than the fact that he has once disbelieved secures eternal death.[112]

The entire passage taken in context does not even come close to what Whedon claims. In fact, the entire sixth chapter of John read in context says the contrary of Whedon's interpretation.

God has provided a built in parallelism that explains the gospel message. One example is found in the two verses at John 6:39 and 6:40. We see that both verses begin and end with the same teachings. The idea that God seeks to explain is framed at the beginning and the end by the same idea. First, Jesus explains in both verses that what he is going to say is the will of God. We know that God's will is done on earth as it is in heaven, and no one can stay God's hand. Daniel 4:35; Luke 11:2.

Next, Jesus states in verse 39 that he will lose none of all the Father has given him. The parallel verse is found in verse 40 where Jesus states that everyone that believes on him may have everlasting life. Jesus is explaining in verses 39 and 40 that all who believe in him will have everlasting life, and all those who believe in him are those whom the father has given him, and he will lose none of them. That means that the only persons who believe in Jesus are those whom that Father has given him and elected for salvation. The final parallel clauses in verses 39 and 40 make clear that all of God's elect, who are those who believe in him, will be raised up at the last day.

John 6:39, Clause 1	John 6:40, Clause 1
And this is the Father's will which hath sent me,	And this is the will of him that sent me,

John 6:39, Clause 2	John 6:40, Clause 2
that of all which he hath given me I should lose nothing,	**that every one which seeth the Son, and believeth on him, may have everlasting life:**

John 6:39, Clause 3	John 6:40, Clause 3
but should raise it up again at the last day.	and I will raise him up at the last day.

The same persons in verses 39 and 40 are raised up the last day according to the will of God the Father. That group is "all" whom the Father has given to Jesus and none will be lost (verse 39). "All" of those given to Jesus will believe in him unto eternal life (verse 40). Jesus makes clear that none can come to him unless the Father draws him and gives him the faith to believe in Jesus. John 6:44, 65. That means that it is only the exclusive group who are elected by God for salvation who believe in Jesus and are saved; all others are unable to believe in Jesus and are lost. The saving of his elect and the damning of the lost are both done according to the will of God.

Salvation is not taken from God; it is given by God to those whom he has chosen for salvation. To make that point even clearer Jesus states in John 6:36-40 that God the Father has given Jesus those chosen for salvation and that "all" those that are chosen by God the Father "shall" come to Jesus. Furthermore, Jesus assures that he will lose none of those whom God the Father has given him; he will in no wise cast them out, they shall "all" be saved. Christians do not work to earn salvation; their salvation is assured by Jesus:

But I said unto you, That ye also have seen me, and believe
not. **All that the Father giveth me shall come to me; and
him that cometh to me I will in no wise cast out.** For I
came down from heaven, not to do mine own will, but the
will of him that sent me. And this is the Father's will
which hath sent me, that **of all which he hath given me I
should lose nothing,** but should raise it up again at the last
day. And this is the will of him that sent me, that every one
which seeth the Son, and believeth on him, may have
everlasting life: and I will raise him up at the last day. (John
6:36-40 AV)

"All" "shall"come to Jesus that are chosen by God. Once they
are chosen they will not ever lose their salvation. In addition, the
only way that one can come to believe in Jesus is if he is drawn to
Jesus by God the Father.

**No man can come to me, except the Father which hath
sent me draw him: and I will raise him up at the last
day.** It is written in the prophets, And they shall be all
taught of God. **Every man therefore that hath heard, and
hath learned of the Father, cometh unto me.** Not that
any man hath seen the Father, save he which is of God, he
hath seen the Father. Verily, verily, I say unto you, He that
believeth on me hath everlasting life. (John 6:44-47 AV)

John chapter 6 must be read in the context of the entire bible.
The theme of the bible is that regeneration precedes saving faith. It is
the work of God to put his law in the heart of his elect. It is God who
gives his elect saving faith.

Not according to the covenant that I made with their fathers
in the day *that* I took them by the hand to bring them out of
the land of Egypt; which my covenant they brake, although
I was an husband unto them, saith the LORD: But this *shall
be* the covenant that I will make with the house of Israel;
After those days, saith the LORD, **I will put my law in
their inward parts, and write it in their hearts; and will**

be their God, and they shall be my people. **And they shall teach no more every man his neighbour, and every man his brother, saying, Know the LORD: for they shall all know me, from the least of them unto the greatest of them, saith the LORD: for I will forgive their iniquity, and I will remember their sin no more.** (Jeremiah 31:32-34 AV)

That prophecy in Jeremiah was fulfilled and explained in chapter 8 of Hebrews:

For this *is* the covenant that I will make with the house of Israel after those days, saith the Lord; **I will put my laws into their mind, and write them in their hearts: and I will be to them a God, and they shall be to me a people: And they shall not teach every man his neighbour, and every man his brother, saying, Know the Lord: for all shall know me, from the least to the greatest. For I will be merciful to their unrighteousness, and their sins and their iniquities will I remember no more.** (Hebrews 8:10-12 AV)

In 1 John chapter two God explains that due to the anointing of the Holy Spirit, God's elect do not need to be taught by any man. God can teach his elect all truth through his word as guided by the Holy Spirit.

But the anointing which ye have received of him abideth in you, and ye need not that any man teach you: but as the same anointing teacheth you of all things, and is truth, and is no lie, and even as it hath taught you, ye shall abide in him. (1 John 2:27 AV)

That is a fulfillment of the prophecy in Isaiah. All of God's children will be taught "of" the LORD.

And all thy children *shall be* taught of the LORD; and great *shall be* the peace of thy children. In righteousness shalt

thou be established: thou shalt be far from oppression; for
thou shalt not fear: and from terror; for it shall not come
near thee. (Isaiah 54:13-14 AV)

To be taught of the LORD means to be both taught about him
and by him. That is explained by Jesus in chapter 6 of John. Where
Jesus explains that it is a fulfilment of God's plan, which was
prophesied in Isaiah 54:13-14, that those who have both heard and
learned of the Father will come to him.

It is written in the prophets, And they shall be all taught of
God. Every man therefore that hath heard, and hath learned
of the Father, cometh unto me. (John 6:45 AV)

John 6:45 follows directly after Jesus stated "No man can come
to me, except the Father which hath sent me draw him: and I will
raise him up at the last day." John 6:44. It is the Father who is doing
the drawing and the teaching. The Father's teaching is both effectual
and necessary. Jesus explained the necessity of the Father's drawing
in the same discourse: "no man can come unto me, except it were
given unto him of my Father." John 6:65. He further explained the
effectiveness of the Father's drawing: "All that the Father giveth me
shall come to me; and him that cometh to me I will in no wise cast
out." John 6:37. Jesus explains that salvation is all of God.

There is no assurance of salvation for the Arminians.[113] In
order for the Arminian free will theology to be consistent, man must
be able to lose his salvation.[114] If man can choose to be saved, he
must also be able to change his mind and choose not to be saved.
The tenuous nature of salvation under the Arminian anti-gospel
inexorably requires the adherent to be on constant guard to keep his
salvation. His salvation under the Arminian theology is dependant
upon his free will choice. If he should change his mind, he would
lose his salvation. Such a theology necessitates salvation by works.

Under the true gospel, God saves his elect by God's grace
through faith in Jesus Christ. Good works are the evidence of faith.
Hebrews 11:1-40. Faith without works is dead. James 2:14-20.

Good works are done as a consequence of salvation; they do not earn salvation. God has done all the work for you. If you believe in Jesus, then you can please God with your good works, which he has foreordained for you to do. "For we are his workmanship, created in Christ Jesus unto good works, which God hath before ordained that we should walk in them." (Ephesians 2:10 AV)

   A salvation based upon works requires its adherents to be righteous enough to earn their salvation. That was the religion of Babylon, which was adopted by the Pharisees and inculcated into the Roman Catholic Church. Arminianism requires salvation by works in order for the Arminian philosophy to make sense. If man can lose his salvation by the exercise of his free will, then he needs also to ensure that he is righteous enough not to do something that will cause him to lose his salvation. Essentially, the Arminian must be actually righteous. No matter how you cut it, requiring actual righteousness for salvation is salvation by works. R.C. Sproul explains how the word "faith" used by Arminians is just a word that conceals a system of works that is based upon salvation by the righteous acts of the will:

   All the Arminian wants and intends to assert is that man has
   the ability to exercise the instrumental cause of faith
   without first being regenerated. This position clearly
   negates sola gratia, but not necessarily sola fide. Then why
   say that Arminianism "in effect" makes faith a meritorious
   work? Because the good response people make to the
   gospel becomes the ultimate determining factor in
   salvation. I often ask my Arminian friends why they are
   Christians and other people are not. They say it is because
   they believe in Christ while others do not. Then I inquire
   why they believe and others do not? "Is it because you are
   more righteous than the person who abides in unbelief?"
   They are quick to say no. "Is it because you are more
   intelligent?" Again the reply is negative. They say that God
   is gracious enough to offer salvation to all who believe and
   that one cannot be saved without that grace. But this grace
   is cooperative grace. Man in his fallen state must reach out
   and grasp this grace by an act of the will, which is free to

accept or reject this grace. Some exercise the will rightly
(or righteously), while others do not. When pressed on this
point, the Arminian finds it difficult to escape the
conclusion that ultimately his salvation rests on some
righteous act of the will he has performed. He has "in
effect" merited the merit of Christ, which differs only
slightly from the view of Rome.[115]

The Arminian theology denies the power of God to save and
impute his righteousness to his elect. Instead, they seek actual
righteousness, which is at the heart of Arminianism. God warned his
elect to stay away from those who have a form of godliness, but
denying the true righteousness that can only come from the power of
God. "Having a form of godliness, but denying the power thereof:
from such turn away." (2 Timothy 3:5 AV)

Most Arminians will deny that their theology requires actual
righteousness. However, there is simply no getting around actual
righteousness as a requirement under Arminianism, since their
theology allows that man has a free will to both obtain and lose his
salvation. Once salvation is centered on the free will decision of the
believer, and his salvation is dependent on his continued
"faithfulness," it necessarily follows that his "faithfulness" depends
on his actual righteousness, rather than the imputed righteousness of
Christ. To deny these facts about Arminianism plunges Arminianism
into a confused jumble of sophistry, with words that are stripped of
their true meaning.

It is no surprise, therefore, to find that there is a branch of
Arminians who admit that Arminianism requires that man must be
actually righteous to be saved. Their admission is a denial of that
which is clearly set forth in the bible. The scriptures are clear that it
is not necessary for the believer to be *de facto* righteous (in fact
righteous) to be saved. Instead, Jesus imputes his righteousness to
the believer, who is consequently made *de jure* righteous (legally
righteous). 2 Corinthians 5:21. Christians are justified by the Lord
Jesus Christ, and by virtue of having been made legally righteous, we
have peace with God. Romans 5:1.

Some Arminians admit that their theology makes it necessary for God to "impart" actual righteousness to the believer. Arminians replace the biblical doctrine of imputed righteousness, which is a forensic (legal) act of God, with the doctrine of imparted righteousness, which is an actual righteousness of the believer. Requiring actual righteousness for salvation is nothing less than salvation by works.

For example, Jim McGuiggan is adamant that salvation is not a legal transaction, but rather requires actual righteousness, whereby man can lose his salvation if he does not keep on the straight and narrow of his own free will. "Salvation is an aspect of our relationship with God and our relationship with God is not, I repeat, it is not a legal decision!"[116] Once it is decided that salvation is not legal, but instead involves imparted actual righteousness, that religion will necessarily require works of the "believers" to maintain their status as "believers."

Mark Herzer describes this doctrine of imparted righteousness as "unbiblical and not protestant or evangelical. It is nothing less than the Romish notion of infused righteousness."[117] The Roman Catholic mythology of infused righteousness is the foundation of their adding works to faith as the means of salvation. If one is infused with actual righteousness, then you must necessarily do good works in accordance with the infused actual righteousness. Herzer calls the Arminian theology of imparted righteousness "Roman Catholicism in Protestant garb."[118]

Christians trust in the righteousness of Christ being imputed to them, whereas Arminians trust in the impartation of Christ's righteousness, which thus makes them holy and righteous in fact. The difference between imputed righteous contained in the gospel and the Arminian imparted righteousness is explained by John Mark Hicks:

> This is no mere semantical difference. It is a fundamental disagreement concerning the ground of grace itself. It is the difference between being clothed in Christ's perfect

righteousness and being clothed in our own partial
righteousness voluntaristically . . . imputed to us. It is the
difference between righteousness being wholly derived
from Christ's work or righteousness partially derived from
our own faith.[119]

H. Orton Whiley's three volume work titled *Christian Theology*
is described by Herzer as probably the most influential and
representative work on Arminianism theology. In that treatise,
Whiley blasphemes the biblical doctrine of imputed righteousness,
saying that it is not only erroneous, but dangerous.

The subtlety of a doctrine which holds that man can be
instantaneously sanctified by an imputed standing, but not
actually sanctified by an impartation of righteousness and
true holiness, makes the error more dangerous.[120]

Herzer points out that in defending their imparted, actual
righteousness theology, Arminians "frequently remark that we will
not see God unless we are entirely holy."[121] That sounds very much
like the Roman Catholic theology of faith plus works.

This Arminian doctrine that one can attain actual righteousness
is the very error of the Jews. Arminians have a zeal for God, just as
did the Jews, but it is not according to knowledge. Arminians try to
establish their own righteousness, rather than rest in the imputed
righteousness of Christ.

For I bear them record that they have a zeal of God, but not
according to knowledge. For they being ignorant of God's
righteousness, and going about to establish their own
righteousness, have not submitted themselves unto the
righteousness of God. For Christ is the end of the law for
righteousness to every one that believeth. Romans 10:2-4.

The error of the Arminian impartation of actual righteousness is
apparent when one considers the fact that the atonement of Christ
was a legal exchange. That means that the sins of the elect were

imputed to Christ, and the righteousness of Christ was imputed to God's elect. 2 Corinthians 5:18-21. If, as required by the Arminian theology, there is an actual exchange (and not a forensic exchange), that would mean that the sinner becomes actually righteous, and it would also mean that Christ became actually sinful. That is blasphemy!

A pardon excuses a person from the penalty for a crime. However, the person pardoned is not absolved of the guilt. God does more than just pardon believers, he justifies them. When a person is justified for an alleged wicked act, it means more than a pardon. Justification is a declaration that the person is absolved not only of the punishment, but also of the guilt. The person justified is not subject to the punishment for the wicked act, and, in addition, he is not guilty. When the bible declares that one is justified though, it does not mean that the person is imparted with actual righteousness of his own, because the person is in fact guilty of the sin. Rather, justification through Christ means that God imputes the righteousness of Christ to the believer, and thus God views the person as not guilty of the sin. It is a legal, spiritual exchange, the believer's sins are imputed to Christ, who paid the penalty for them, and Christ's righteousness is imputed to the believer.

For man to declare someone justified for wickedness is an abomination to the Lord. "He that justifieth the wicked, and he that condemneth the just, even they both are abomination to the LORD." Proverbs 17:15. Justification in Proverbs 17:15 is similar to the justification provided for by God, in the sense that it is a declaration of justification and not an impartation of actual righteousness. It is the epitome of evil for man to justify the wicked by declaring them not guilty for their wickedness. That is because a declaration by man that the wicked is justified is by definition an injustice. Even if the sinner were to be punished for his wickedness, he cannot be justified, because is still guilty of the wicked act. Being punished does not justify the act and render him not guilty.

While it is the epitome of unrighteousness for man to justify the wicked, it is the epitome of righteousness for God to do that same thing. That is because God justifies the wicked through the atonement of his Holy Son, Jesus Christ. If God were to punish the sinner directly, the sinner would be punished, but he could never be justified, because the guilt for the sin would remain. The only way to justify the sinner is by having Jesus trade places with the sinner. There was a perfect legal exchange at the cross, which facilitated justification. The righteousness of Jesus is imputed to the sinner, and the sins of the sinner are imputed to Jesus.

Without the imputation of the righteousness of Christ to the sinner, justification of the sinner would be an abomination. That is why Jesus had to atone for the sins of his elect. It is only through the grace of God by faith in Jesus Christ that man can be justified. The sacrifice of Jesus facilitated the justification of the wicked, because God only sees the righteousness of Christ when he sees a believer. The believer is thus justified in God's eyes. The believer only needs to believe in Jesus. His faith in Jesus will justify him before God. Notice in the parallel passages below that justification is by grace and also by faith. Faith and grace go hand in hand, which indicates that faith is provided by God, through his sovereign grace.

Being **justified freely by his grace** through the redemption that is in Christ Jesus: Romans 3:24

Therefore being **justified by faith**, we have peace with God through our Lord Jesus Christ. Romans 5:1.

That being **justified by his grace**, we should be made heirs according to the hope of eternal life. Titus 3:7.

17 The Command to Preach the Gospel

In view of the sovereignty of God in the salvation of his elect, what is a Christian's duty regarding the preaching of the gospel? Jesus made it clear in Mark 16:15 that a Christian is to preach the gospel. "And he said unto them, Go ye into all the world, and preach the gospel to every creature." (Mark 16:15 AV)

Jesus also made it clear in his very next statement in Mark 16:16 that there would be those who believe and those who would not believe. "He that believeth and is baptized shall be saved; but he that believeth not shall be damned." Mark 16:16. The responsibility of a Christian is to preach the gospel; it is the responsibility, indeed the very promise of God, to choose those whom he has elected by giving them spiritual ears to hear. God draws his chosen and saves them. He does so by means of the preaching of the gospel. "Faith cometh by hearing, and hearing by the word of God." Ephesians 1:1-2:22.

In Romans 10:9-11:10 God explains how he uses his living word to give spiritual life to his elect. The free will religionists, however, selectively take certain passages out of context and deceptively misrepresent those passages. They often quote out of context Romans 10:9, which states: "That if thou shalt confess with thy

157

mouth the Lord Jesus, and shalt believe in thine heart that God hath raised him from the dead, thou shalt be saved." The Arminian preachers misrepresent that passage to mean that salvation is a decision springing from the free will of man. They theorize, without scriptural support, that every man in the entire world is given a prevenient grace from God that frees their dead souls from the enslavement to sin only to the extent that they can choose whether to believe in Jesus. The Arminians do not believe there is a particular election of God, nor do they believe that God effectually draws his elect, despite clear biblical authority. John 6:44; 1 Peter 2:9; 2 Thessalonians 2:13.

Arminians misrepresent Romans 10:11 and 10:13 to mean that salvation is a free will decision independent of the sovereign election of God. Romans 10:11 states: "For the scripture saith, Whosoever believeth on him shall not be ashamed." Romans 10:13 states: "For whosoever shall call upon the name of the Lord shall be saved." The Arminian preachers seek to exile God from any active role in the process of salvation. To them, Jesus did what he could at the cross, gave them a little doble of grace to free their wills to choose, now it is completely up to man to decide his own fate.

Now let us read those passages (Romans 10:9, 10:11, and 10:13) in context and see how Arminians have taken those passages out of context to misrepresent their true meaning. Those passages read in context in fact explain that one cannot be saved unless one believes in Jesus. One cannot believe unless one hears the gospel. One cannot hear the gospel unless God sends someone to preach the gospel and God opens the hearer's spiritual ears to hear the gospel. Those who do not believe do not believe because God has not chosen them for salvation: **"God hath given them the spirit of slumber, eyes that they should not see, and ears that they should not hear; unto this day."** Romans 11:8. Those who are saved are saved according to God's election by his sovereign grace. **"Even so then at this present time also there is a remnant according to the election of grace. And if by grace, then *is it* no more of works: otherwise grace is no more grace."** Romans 11:5.

That if thou shalt confess with thy mouth the Lord Jesus, and shalt believe in thine heart that God hath raised him from the dead, thou shalt be saved. For with the heart man believeth unto righteousness; and with the mouth confession is made unto salvation. For the scripture saith, Whosoever believeth on him shall not be ashamed. For there is no difference between the Jew and the Greek: for the same Lord over all is rich unto all that call upon him. For whosoever shall call upon the name of the Lord shall be saved. **How then shall they call on him in whom they have not believed? and how shall they believe in him of whom they have not heard? and how shall they hear without a preacher? And how shall they preach, except they be sent? as it is written, How beautiful are the feet of them that preach the gospel of peace, and bring glad tidings of good things! But they have not all obeyed the gospel. For Esaias saith, Lord, who hath believed our report? So then faith** *cometh* **by hearing, and hearing by the word of God.** But I say, Have they not heard? Yes verily, their sound went into all the earth, and their words unto the ends of the world. But I say, Did not Israel know? First Moses saith, I will provoke you to jealousy by *them that are* no people, *and* by a foolish nation I will anger you. But Esaias is very bold, and saith, I was found of them that sought me not; I was made manifest unto them that asked not after me. But to Israel he saith, All day long I have stretched forth my hands unto a disobedient and gainsaying people. I say then, Hath God cast away his people? God forbid. For I also am an Israelite, of the seed of Abraham, *of* the tribe of Benjamin. God hath not cast away his people which he foreknew. Wot ye not what the scripture saith of Elias? how he maketh intercession to God against Israel, saying, Lord, they have killed thy prophets, and digged down thine altars; and I am left alone, and they seek my life. But what saith the answer of God unto him? I have reserved to myself seven thousand men, who have not bowed the knee to *the image of* Baal. **Even so then at this present time also there is a remnant according to the**

election of grace. And if by grace, then *is it* no more of works: otherwise grace is no more grace. But if *it be* of works, then is it no more grace: otherwise work is no more work. What then? Israel hath not obtained that which he seeketh for; but the election hath obtained it, and the rest were blinded (According as it is written, God hath given them the spirit of slumber, eyes that they should not see, and ears that they should not hear;) unto this day. And David saith, Let their table be made a snare, and a trap, and a stumblingblock, and a recompence unto them: Let their eyes be darkened, that they may not see, and bow down their back alway. (Romans 10:9-11:10 AV)

What is even more telling is that just one chapter earlier in Romans chapter 9 God clearly states that man's enslaved will is irrelevant to salvation. Salvation is completely an act of mercy by God. **"It is not of him that willeth, nor of him that runneth, but of God that sheweth mercy."** Romans 9:16. Salvation is completely within the sovereign choice of God. He chooses some for salvation and others for damnation. He mercifully softens the heart of those whom he has chosen for salvation so that they can respond to the gospel call, and he hardens the heart of those whom he has damned so that they will not respond to the gospel. **"Therefore hath he mercy on whom he will have mercy, and whom he will he hardeneth."** Romans 9:18.

Jesus uses the parable of the sower in Luke 8:4-17 to further illustrate his sovereign grace. In the parable he explains that the seed (the word of God) is sown and only those whose hearts are honest and good hear the gospel and bring forth the fruit of salvation. Notice that Jesus gives a hint at what it means to have an honest and good heart. At the end of the parable he cried: "He that hath ears to hear, let him hear." Luke 8:8. What did Jesus mean by that? He explained to his disciples: "Unto you it is given to know the mysteries of the kingdom of God: but to others in parables; that seeing they might not see, and hearing they might not understand." Luke 8:10. Those who are not saved are not saved because they have

not been given spiritual ears to hear the gospel. God has stopped
their ears to the truth of the gospel. Jesus made clear that one
purpose of the parables is to conceal the spiritual truths of the gospel
from those who have been chosen for damnation. God is the one that
makes a heart honest and good and able to hear and believe the
gospel. God is the husbandman who tills the soil of men's hearts and
makes it soft to receive the gospel. The gospel is the means of
bringing the hearer to a knowledge of Jesus Christ. Salvation is
through faith in Jesus Christ by the grace of God.

> And when much people were gathered together, and were
> come to him out of every city, he spake by a parable: A
> sower went out to sow his seed: and as he sowed, some fell
> by the way side; and it was trodden down, and the fowls of
> the air devoured it. And some fell upon a rock; and as soon
> as it was sprung up, it withered away, because it lacked
> moisture. And some fell among thorns; and the thorns
> sprang up with it, and choked it. And other fell on good
> ground, and sprang up, and bare fruit an hundredfold. And
> when he had said these things, he cried, He that hath ears to
> hear, let him hear. And his disciples asked him, saying,
> What might this parable be? **And he said, Unto you it is
> given to know the mysteries of the kingdom of God: but
> to others in parables; that seeing they might not see, and
> hearing they might not understand.** Now the parable is
> this: The seed is the word of God. Those by the way side
> are they that hear; then cometh the devil, and taketh away
> the word out of their hearts, lest they should believe and be
> saved. They on the rock *are they*, which, when they hear,
> receive the word with joy; and these have no root, which
> for a while believe, and in time of temptation fall away.
> And that which fell among thorns are they, which, when
> they have heard, go forth, and are choked with cares and
> riches and pleasures of *this* life, and bring no fruit to
> perfection. But that on the good ground are they, which in
> an honest and good heart, having heard the word, keep *it*,
> and bring forth fruit with patience. No man, when he hath
> lighted a candle, covereth it with a vessel, or putteth *it*

under a bed; but setteth *it* on a candlestick, that they which
enter in may see the light. For nothing is secret, that shall
not be made manifest; neither *any thing* hid, that shall not
be known and come abroad. (Luke 8:4-17 AV)

It is not for a man of his own free will to choose. Election is
completely within the province of God. It is not for man to determine
who is chosen by God. It is our responsibility, indeed our duty, to
preach the gospel and allow that spiritual seed of God's word to find
the soil prepared by God for salvation.

God causes those whom he has chosen for salvation to come in
faith to him. **"Blessed is the man whom thou choosest, and
causest to approach unto thee**, that he may dwell in thy courts: we
shall be satisfied with the goodness of thy house, even of thy holy
temple." Psalms 65:4. God uses his gospel as his means of drawing
his elect. In Acts chapter 2 Peter explained the ministry and
crucifixion of Jesus Christ. In that passage we see how God uses his
gospel to call those whom he has chosen for salvation. The free will
promoters often quote Acts 2:21 out of context to deceive their
followers that salvation is entirely a free will decision of man. That
passage states: "And it shall come to pass, *that* whosoever shall call
on the name of the Lord shall be saved." (Acts 2:21 AV) When read
in context, however, we find out that it is only those God has chosen
for salvation who will understand the gospel and call on the name of
the Lord and be saved.

In Acts chapter 2, when the people heard the gospel preached by
Peter they "were pricked in their heart" and asked "what shall we
do?" Peter told them to repent and be baptized. What is revealing is
what Peter said next about those who would receive the gift of the
Holy Ghost. It was only those whom God had chosen for salvation
that would receive the promise of salvation. God called them to
salvation by the preaching of the gospel. The entire passage in
context explains that the promise of salvation is only for those whom
God shall call to salvation.

Therefore let all the house of Israel know assuredly, that

God hath made that same Jesus, whom ye have crucified,
both Lord and Christ. **Now when they heard** *this,* **they
were pricked in their heart, and said unto Peter and to
the rest of the apostles, Men** *and* **brethren, what shall
we do?** Then Peter said unto them, Repent, and be baptized
every one of you in the name of Jesus Christ for the
remission of sins, and ye shall receive the gift of the Holy
Ghost. **For the promise is unto you, and to your
children, and to all that are afar off,** *even* **as many as the
Lord our God shall call.** (Acts 2:36-39 AV)

It is clear that it is the Lord who adds to the church those whom
he has decided should be saved. Salvation is all of God, who chooses
those who will believe in him. Men are powerless to believe in Jesus
without the sovereign election of God giving them a spiritual rebirth,
whereby they are imbued with spiritual eyes to see and ears to hear.

And they, continuing daily with one accord in the temple,
and breaking bread from house to house, did eat their meat
with gladness and singleness of heart, Praising God, and
having favour with all the people. **And the Lord added to
the church daily such as should be saved.** (Acts 2:46-47
AV)

"Jesus Christ the same yesterday, and to day, and for ever."
Hebrews 13:8. God is sovereign, and as always, will continue to
exercise his sovereignty in electing his chosen. **"For thou art an
holy people unto the LORD thy God: the LORD thy God hath
chosen thee to be a special people unto himself, above all people
that are upon the face of the earth."** Deuteronomy 7:6. God has
chosen his church, which is spiritual Israel. *See* Galatians 3:28-29,
6:16.

The false gospel of free will on the other hand creates a very
different result from the true gospel of election by grace. Jesus
explained the result of a false gospel in his parable of the tares and
wheat. The tares look just like the wheat in outward appearance, but
they are unfruitful children of the devil sown in the midst of the

children of God. At the end of the world they are gathered and
thrown into the eternal lake of fire. Matthew 13:24-43.

The free will gospel has the effect of filling the churches with
the unsaved tares of the world. These unsaved tares have changed
the very nature of the "church," so called, as it is represented in the
world. The theology these ersatz churches has degenerated to the
point that a false Jesus has been constructed, who has been reduced
to a helpless sap wringing his hands in heaven hoping that someone
will exercise their free will and accept his gift of salvation.

Within these ersatz churches are found the wheat chosen by God
intermixed with the tares planted by the devil. The wheat are usually
miserable and unfulfilled in such dead churches, but they do not
know the cause of their misery until God sends someone to reveal to
them the delusion of the false gospel under which they have been
laboring. Ultimately, the saved wheat move on, and the Arminian
preacher is glad to see them go, because they are usually the ones
who question the biblical authority of what is being preached. John
Reisinger explains the result of the false gospel of the mythical free
will of man:

> The most drastic error in free will religion lies at the very
> heart of its message. At the point where a helpless sinner
> needs God's help and power the most, the sinner is
> deliberately and dogmatically pointed away from God and
> told to look to himself. Arminianism tells men that God will
> not, yea, He cannot, do any more than He has already done.
> Read C. H. Spurgeon's article, *'Should We Preach Total
> Depravity?'*, on page 7, and see how he emphasized the
> need to "throw sinners down in utter helplessness." Free
> will informs the sinner that he is not helpless at the
> beginning of conversion; in fact this error boldly declares
> that it is only the sinner's power that can do the job at this
> point. God waits for the man to furnish the power–the *will*
> power. The poor sinner is told, "God has done all He can
> do, it is now all up to you." Instead of throwing sinners
> down, this is exalting them. Instead of forcing them to look

up to God in utter helplessness to find grace and strength, free will throws God down in helplessness and exalts man as the only one with the ability to win the day!

Thank God His great salvation is not merely a possibility based on an *if you will ... then God can ...*, but it is based on a certainty. It is an absolute certainty because God ...!

Must the sinner be willing to come to Christ before he can be saved? Of course he must, but that is not the question. Is man able to make himself willing to come? Absolutely not. Is God's whole scheme of grace to fail because of the inability and stubbornness of man? No, my friend, the Bible assures us that the God of grace is also the God *of power*. "Thy people shall be willing in the day of thy power..." (Ps. 110:3) in a sure promise! Were those who believed the gospel in Acts 13:48 willing to be saved? Did Lydia in Acts 16:14 willingly open her heart to Christ as Paul preached to her? Were the men in Acts chapter two willing to seek mercy? The answer is obvious, of course they were willing–in all three cases. The real question is this: "Who and what made them willing?" Read each instance and see if it was the power of free will or the power of sovereign grace. The real question is this: "How can a dead sinner with a carnal mind actively opposed to God and righteousness be so changed as to be willing and sincerely desirous of being saved unto holiness?" Exactly how God accomplishes this grand and glorious "mystery" (John 3:8) is beyond me, but I know He does it, and I also know it is *ALL His doing.*[122]

Reisinger mentions Lydia in Acts 16:14. Read what God did with Lydia. He opened her heart so that she was able to pay attention and understand what Paul was preaching. Without God's intervention, Lydia would not have been able to receive the gospel into her heart. "And a certain woman named Lydia, a seller of purple, of the city of Thyatira, which worshipped God, heard *us*: **whose heart the Lord opened**, that she attended unto the things which were spoken of Paul." (Acts 16:14 AV)

God could have chosen not to open the heart of all that heard Paul that day. That is the same with the preaching of the gospel today. Many who see the excitement of the change manifested in true believers wish to be part of the new experience, but as with the seed sown among thorns or on stony ground, the cares of the world or persecution causes the seed to die. *See* Mark 4:2-20. The seed of faith does not die because the hearers were once saved and had fallen away, but because the faith was not the true faith wrought by God, but was the counterfeit faith that is born of man's enslaved will. Such were never chosen by God to begin with.

There is a true faith from God and a counterfeit faith from man. Read Mark 9:24: "And straightway the father of the child cried out, and said with tears, Lord, **I believe; help thou mine unbelief.**" The man believed, but it was not the belief from God, and so he said to Jesus: "help thou mine unbelief." Jesus said the following when the man first ran up to him to explain the plight of his son possessed by an evil spirit: "He answereth him, and saith, **O faithless generation**, how long shall I be with you? how long shall I suffer you? bring him unto me." (Mark 9:19 AV) Jesus had at the outset identified the man as being part of a faithless generation. God is revealing in this passage that the man's belief was at that moment really the unbelief born out of his faithless will. True faith comes from God.

God does the choosing, not man. **"Ye have not chosen me, but I have chosen you, and ordained you, that ye should go and bring forth fruit, and *that* your fruit should remain:** that whatsoever ye shall ask of the Father in my name, he may give it you." (John 15:16 AV) That fruit of the believer is brought forth through the spreading of the seed of God's word. As explained by Paul in 1 Corinthians 3:5-7, believers are ministers of God who plant the seeds of the gospel. However, it is up to God to give the increase. It is not the sower of the seed that gets the glory, it is God who "giveth the increase," who gets the glory.

Who then is Paul, and who *is* Apollos, but ministers by

whom ye believed, even as the Lord gave to every man? **I
have planted, Apollos watered; but God gave the
increase.** So then neither is he that planteth any thing,
neither he that watereth; but God that giveth the
increase.** (1 Corinthians 3:5-7 AV)

God works through the believers in his church to spread the
word. "For we are labourers together with God: ye are God's
husbandry, *ye are* God's building." (1 Corinthians 3:9 AV) Each new
believer becomes a new spiritual creation of God, for whom God as
the husbandman prunes and cares so that the believer brings forth
more spiritual fruit.

I am the true vine, and my Father is the husbandman. Every
branch in me that beareth not fruit he taketh away: and
every *branch* that beareth fruit, he purgeth it, that it may
bring forth more fruit. Now ye are clean through the word
which I have spoken unto you. Abide in me, and I in you.
As the branch cannot bear fruit of itself, except it abide in
the vine; no more can ye, except ye abide in me. I am the
vine, ye *are* the branches: He that abideth in me, and I in
him, the same bringeth forth much fruit: for **without me ye
can do nothing**. (John 15:1-5 AV)

Notice what Jesus makes clear in John 15:5: **"without me ye
can do nothing."** Hebrews 12:2 confirms what Jesus said in John
15:5, and pretty well precludes any source for our faith other than
Jesus: "Looking unto **Jesus the author and finisher of *our* faith**;
who for the joy that was set before him endured the cross, despising
the shame, and is set down at the right hand of the throne of God."
(Hebrews 12:2 AV)

If Jesus is the author of our faith, then that precludes man from
being the author through his free will decision. An author is "one
that originates or creates."[123] There is no mention in the bible of
there being any coauthors of our faith, it is Jesus alone who is the
author of our faith. He originates and creates faith in the believer.
Jesus is also the finisher of our faith, that is, he completes and

perfects our faith. So there is no room for anyone to say that God
only makes an offer of salvation, and that we must accept that offer
of our own free will. That is to contradict God's word and say that
man is the finisher of his own faith. The bible makes it clear that
Jesus is the finisher of our faith. Jesus must first set our will free
from the bondage of sin. Our faith in Jesus is both authored and
finished by Jesus. Our will is enslaved to sin, and we can only
believe in Jesus if Jesus frees us from that bondage and imparts the
faith in us, making us new creations by the Spirit of God.

Read what Jesus said in John chapter 8. He states that whoever
commits sin is a servant of sin. The only way for our will to be freed
from that servitude to sin is though him. He came to set his chosen
free from that bondage of sin.

> Jesus answered them, Verily, verily, I say unto you,
> Whosoever committeth sin is the servant of sin. And the
> servant abideth not in the house for ever: *but* the Son
> abideth ever. If the Son therefore shall make you free, ye
> shall be free indeed. (John 8:34-36 AV)

The truth of the gospel comes by revelation. Only after God has
opened the heart of the enslaved sinner can he truly have a free will
to believe in him. "And ye shall know the truth, and the truth shall
make you free." (John 8:32 AV) Jesus has freed the will of his
chosen from the bondage of sin and the rudiments of the world.
"Stand fast therefore in the liberty wherewith Christ hath made us
free, and be not entangled again with the yoke of bondage."
(Galatians 5:1 AV)

Sinful man thinks his will is free, because he does what he
wants. Man does not perceive that his desire to do what he wants (his
will) is enslaved to sin. In Ephesians chapter 2 God reveals that
man's sinful flesh tempts him to sin because that is man's nature.
God must quicken the dead spirit of man and make it alive to Christ,
so that he can break loose from the bondage of sin, thus giving him
the power and will to believe in and obey God.

**And you *hath he quickened*, who were dead in trespasses
and sins; Wherein in time past ye walked according to
the course of this world, according to the prince of the
power of the air, the spirit that now worketh in the
children of disobedience: Among whom also we all had
our conversation in times past in the lusts of our flesh,
fulfilling the desires of the flesh and of the mind; and
were by nature the children of wrath, even as others.
But God, who is rich in mercy, for his great love
wherewith he loved us, Even when we were dead in
sins, hath quickened us together with Christ, (by grace
ye are saved;)** (Ephesians 2:1-5 AV)

Man by his nature desires to rebel against God. In Romans
chapter six, God reveals that once one is saved, he goes from a bond
servant to sin to a free man. God must change man's nature in order
to set his will free from its bondage to sin. Once a man's will is set
free by God, he can then believe in Jesus and become a servant of
righteousness. God bestows upon his chosen the truly free gift of
eternal life.

Know ye not, that to whom ye yield yourselves servants to
obey, his servants ye are to whom ye obey; whether of sin
unto death, or of obedience unto righteousness? But God
be thanked, that ye were the servants of sin, but ye have
obeyed from the heart that form of doctrine which was
delivered you. **Being then made free from sin, ye became
the servants of righteousness.** I speak after the manner of
men because of the infirmity of your flesh: for as ye have
yielded your members servants to uncleanness and to
iniquity unto iniquity; even so now yield your members
servants to righteousness unto holiness. **For when ye were
the servants of sin, ye were free from righteousness.**
What fruit had ye then in those things whereof ye are now
ashamed? for the end of those things *is* death. **But now
being made free from sin, and become servants to God,
ye have your fruit unto holiness, and the end everlasting
life.** For the wages of sin *is* death; but the gift of God *is*

eternal life through Jesus Christ our Lord. (Romans 6:16-23 AV)

The chosen of Jesus have a glorious liberty. **"Because the creature itself also shall be delivered from the bondage of corruption into the glorious liberty of the children of God."** (Romans 8:21 AV) If Jesus has set you free from the bondage of sin and death, you are truly free. **"If the Son therefore shall make you free, ye shall be free indeed."** (John 8:36 AV)

Man is not born in the flesh with a free will. Man's will is enslaved to sin. In order for a man to be set free from that bondage to sin, he must be spiritually born again by Jesus. John 3:3. Once a man is born of the Spirit of God, his will is then freed to turn from his bondage to sin toward Christ in faith. Our faith is truly a gift from God. Ephesians 2:8. That gift of faith is bestowed only upon those to whom God has predestined to receive it according to **God's will**, not according to the mythical free will of man. **"Having predestinated us unto the adoption of children by Jesus Christ to himself, <u>according to the good pleasure of his will</u>."** (Ephesians 1:5 AV)

18 No Flesh Should Glory in His Presence

You won't hear sovereign election of God preached in the Catholic Church or even most nominal "Christian" churches. Why? Because there is no profit in it. If God does it all, then who needs the sacraments, and why give money to the church for Masses, etc. If God gets the glory, there is no glory left for the "reverend." In fact, taking the title reverend is an attempt by pastors to take God's glory. "Reverend" is used only once in all of the Holy Scriptures and it is used to describe the name of the Lord God Almighty.

> He sent redemption unto his people: he hath commanded
> his covenant for ever: **holy and reverend *is* his name**.
> (Psalms 111:9 AV)

God's name is holy and reverend. What man can claim to be reverend? Reverend means to be worthy of respect mingled with fear and awe, to be venerated.[124] The veneration of persons is a heathen custom that is foreign to Christianity.

> But Jesus called them *to him*, and saith unto them, Ye know
> that they which are accounted to rule over the Gentiles

171

exercise lordship over them; and **their great ones exercise
authority upon them. But so shall it not be among you:
but whosoever will be great among you, shall be your
minister**: And whosoever of you will be the chiefest, shall
be servant of all. For even the Son of man came not to be
ministered unto, but to minister, and to give his life a
ransom for many. (Mark 10:42-45 AV)

All men are sinners, none is righteous. Our salvation is a gift
from God. No man can boast in his salvation or place in God's
Kingdom, because they did not do anything to earn it. No man
should be reverend in God's church.

That **no flesh should glory in his presence**. But of him are
ye in Christ Jesus, who of God is made unto us wisdom,
and righteousness, and sanctification, and redemption:
That, according as it is written, **He that glorieth, let him
glory in the Lord.** (1 Corinthians 1:29-31 AV)

But **he that glorieth, let him glory in the Lord**. For not
he that commendeth himself is approved, but whom the
Lord commendeth. (2 Corinthians 10:17-18 AV)

God will not share his glory with anyone! In the following
passage he first states that his name is the LORD (the same name that
is holy and reverend) and then emphatically states that he will not
give his glory to another.

I *am* the LORD: that *is* my name: and my glory will I
not give to another, neither my praise to graven images.
(Isaiah 42:8 AV)

Many so-called "reverends" love to take credit for saving souls.
They are often heard to give a number of how many people were
saved at such-and-such a revival or ceremony. How do they know
the number of people who were saved? They wrongly think that
because the person walks to the front of the church and recites a
formula of words that is some seal of salvation.

Even the language used by many in the Christian community reveals their mistaken view of salvation as being based upon free will. It is often asked: "when did you get saved?" It is telling that the subject of the question is not Jesus, but rather the person who "got saved." A person doesn't "get saved" as though going to the store to "get milk." The question should be "when did Jesus save you?"

The Lord Jesus Christ reaches down from heaven and saves the individual. We receive salvation from Jesus, who gives it to us; we don't go and get it. Language like "getting saved" suggests that we have some active role in our salvation. In fact, Jesus is the "author and finisher of our faith." Hebrews 12:2. That means that Jesus is the originator of our faith and he sees the faith to its culmination, which is salvation. There is no room between author and finisher for the free will of man. Man is not the co-author of his faith. Jesus alone authors the faith of a believer. Faith is truly and completely a gift from God. Ephesians 2:8.

God draws us to him and brings us to the point where we submit to him and are born again. John 6:34-47. Jesus is deserving of all glory and honor for our salvation; to claim that we had some part through our supposed free will decision robs God of his glory and honor. *See* Isaiah 42:8; 1 Timothy 1:17; Revelation 4:11.

John Hendryx explains how the Arminian free will gospel takes the glory from God and gives it to man:

Arminian synergists assert that prevenient grace resolves the problem of human boasting since God initiates with grace. But in reality this sleight of hand does not resolve the problem at all and only begs the question. For if God gives this prevenient grace to everybody, we must ask: why do some respond positively to Christ and not others? What makes them to differ? Jesus Christ or something else? The problem of boasting is not removed, for if God gives grace to everybody and only some believe, then the heart that believes still thinks that it made the wiser decision by improving on grace while others did not. The person affirming prevenient grace still must ultimately attribute his repenting and believing to his own wisdom, prudence, sound judgment, or good sense. So in the Arminian belief system, they are not willing to confront the obvious question of why some believe and not others? The only answer I have ever heard to this question in all my years debating this was "because some believed". But, this avoids the question, because I did not ask them what they did, but why they did it? And the "why" seems to be a question that Jesus goes out of his way to answer. (John 8:46-47 & John 10:26).[125]

19 Does the Sovereign Holy God Create Evil?

God is all powerful. He rules and controls all things in heaven and on the earth. For example, God told Nebuchadnezzar, King of Babylon, who was the most powerful ruler in the world at the time, that he would take his kingdom from him for seven years and then restore him to power; God then proceeded to do that very thing. For seven years Nebuchudnezzar was made to eat grass like the beasts of the field; his hair grew long and became matted like feathers, and his nails grew to be like an eagle's claws. After seven years, God restored Nebachadnezzar to his former greatness. After Nebuchadnezzar was restored to power, he said this about God:

> And all the inhabitants of the earth *are* reputed as nothing: and he doeth according to his will in the army of heaven, and *among* the inhabitants of the earth: and none can stay his hand, or say unto him, What doest thou? (Daniel 4:35 AV)

Indeed, God is sovereign over heaven and all the earth and does whatever he desires:

> For I know that the LORD is great, and that our Lord is

above all gods. Whatsoever the LORD pleased, that did he in heaven, and in earth, in the seas, and all deep places. Psalms 135:5-6.

Arminians, however, do not believe that God exercises his sovereignty. They believe that God rolled the dice with Adam and Eve, and was hoping that they would remain obedient, but they disappointed God. Eric Landstrom explains the Arminian position:

> Thus with God's predestinating all things the problem of evil arises for the Calvinist as a logical problem . . . In the Calvinist scheme Adam was the means that God used to kill mankind, to cause all of creation to fall, to create endless suffering, to foster bitterness and hatred and vitriol and shame. In the Calvinist scheme God did this. . . . In contrast to the difficulties that Calvinism faces, Arminianism doesn't have the same difficulty with the problem of evil because Arminians believe that grace is resistible.[126]

Chapter one of Ephesians refutes the Arminian position and confirms that God predestinated the fall, since he chose his elect from the fallen "before the foundation of the world" Ephesians 1:4. The Arminians simply cannot accept that God is completely sovereign. They use man's wisdom to argue against God's word. They argue that God could not have predestined Adam and Eve to fall because to do such a thing would mean that God predestined evil. God, however, states that he is sovereign, and in his sovereignty he creates evil:

I form the light, and create darkness: I make peace, and create evil: I the LORD do all these things. Isaiah 45:7.

Chad Meister, who is an Arminian theologian and an assistant professor of philosophy at Bethel College, opines that God could not be the author of evil, because in Meister's mind that would mean that God himself is evil. In order to get around this perceived Arminian conundrum, Meister states that evil is explained not by God creating evil but rather by man of his own free will, apart from the sovereign will of God, choosing to commit evil acts.

> If God is the predetermining cause of all events, and people
> thus are simply acting out His divine program, then God
> turns out to be the author of evil. The problem here is that
> there is no qualitative difference between being the author
> of evil and being evil. ... The central issue in this dialogue
> is straightforward: how do we account for evil in a universe
> that God created? Either God is the author of evil or He is
> not. To say God is the author of evil is unbiblical and
> horrifying. If He is not the author of evil, however, then
> where did it come from? The only reasonable answer we
> are left with is "free will."[127]

The holy scriptures testify that God creates evil. *See, e.g.,* Isaiah
45:7. Meister blasphemes God by opining that if God causes evil, that
necessarily makes God evil. To call God evil is the same as calling
God an evil spirit, since "God is a Spirit." John 4:24. Jesus warned
against calling God an evil spirit. "But he that shall blaspheme
against the Holy Ghost hath never forgiveness, but is in danger of
eternal damnation: Because they said, He hath an unclean spirit."
(Mark 3:29-30 AV)

Meister is not alone among Arminians in his characterization of
the sovereign God of the bible as evil. William W. Birch, who states
that he is known as "The Arminian," has a bachelor's degree in
Christian and Biblical Studies, and is presently in the Master of
Divinity program at Southeastern Baptist Theological Seminary and
plans to enter a Ph.D. program elsewhere upon graduating.[128] "The
Arminian," William W. Birch, states:

> [Dr. Roger] Olson has publicly stated that at times, from
> certain comments which Calvinists make about God, he
> finds distinguishing between God and Satan rather difficult.
> In Olson's defense, when some Calvinists attribute
> authorship of sin to God, as does R.C. Sproul, Jr., then I
> side with Olson.[129]

Who is Dr. Roger Olson with whom Birch agreed? Dr. Roger Olson (Ph.D., Religious Studies, Rice University) is professor of theology at George W. Truett Theological Seminary of Baylor University. Dr. Olson describes himself as "a Christian theologian of the evangelical Baptist persuasion. I am also a proud Arminian!"[130] Any theologian who is a Christian should know that "pride goeth before destruction." Proverbs 16:18. Nonetheless, Dr. Olson is a highly esteemed theologian in the Arminian community. He is the author of many books, including *The Story of Christian Theology* (winner of the Gold Medallion Award from the Evangelical Christian Publishers Association[131]), *The Mosaic of Christian Belief,* and *The Westminster Handbook to Evangelical Theology.*

The bible refutes Birch's, Olson's and Meister's blasphemous Arminian theology. God's word states that God is perfectly holy, and at the same time God creates evil. Isaiah 6:3; 45:7. "For of him, and through him, and to him, are all things: to whom be glory for ever. Amen." Romans 11:36. All things includes good things and evil things.[132]

Arminians will not have the sovereign God reign over them. Arminians are like the citizens in the parable in Luke 19. "But his citizens hated him, and sent a message after him, saying, We will not have this man to reign over us." (Luke 19:14 AV) For example, Arminian theologian, Dr. Roger Olson, in his book, *Against Calvinism*, stated that he would not worship the sovereign God depicted by Calvinists (and indeed the bible) because he considers such a God a "moral monster." Dr. Olson stated:

> One day, at the end of a class session on Calvinism's doctrine of God's sovereignty, a student asked me a question I had put off considering. He asked: "If it was revealed to you in a way you couldn't question or deny that the true God actually is as Calvinism says and rules as Calvinism affirms, would you still worship him?" I knew the only possible answer without a moment's thought, even though I knew it would shock many people. I said no, that I would not because I could not. Such a God would be a

moral monster.[133]

Jesus describes the end of those who will not submit to his reign: "But those mine enemies, which would not that I should reign over them, bring hither, and slay them before me." (Luke 19:27 AV)

God states that he creates evil, however, that does not mean, as alleged by Meister, that God is evil. God is perfectly righteous. "The LORD *is* righteous in all his ways, and holy in all his works." (Psalms 145:17 AV) God is perfect in his ways, he is perfect in his judgment, he is perfect in his justice, and he is perfect in his righteousness. God is holy. "Holy, holy, holy, is the LORD of hosts: the whole earth is full of his glory." Isaiah 6:3. There is not one spot of iniquity in God.

> Because I will publish the name of the LORD: ascribe ye
> greatness unto our God. *He is* the Rock, his work *is* perfect:
> for all his ways *are* judgment: a God of truth and without
> iniquity, just and right *is* he. (Deuteronomy 32:3-4 AV)

God is so pure that he can not even look upon iniquity, which is why it was necessary for Jesus to die on the cross to wash all of our sins away. Without the sacrifice of Jesus, with his righteousness imputed to his elect, no one could ever enter heaven.

> Thou art of purer eyes than to behold evil, and canst not
> look on iniquity: wherefore lookest thou upon them that
> deal treacherously, and holdest thy tongue when the wicked
> devoureth the man that is more righteous than he?
> (Habakkuk 1:13 AV)

E. Calvin Beisner, associate professor of historical theology and social ethics at Knox Theological Seminary, explains the historical Christian view of a perfect God, who nonetheless creates evil creatures and indeed evil itself in order to bring about righteous ends.

> They [Luther, Calvin, the Westminster Divines] argue that
> although it would not have been logically impossible for

180

God to create only moral creatures that would never sin, He in fact created a moral world with creatures whose evil He foreordained for His own good purposes—to display His justice in punishing some (Prov. 16:4) and His grace in redeeming and pardoning others (Eph. 1:5–6; 2:7).

Does this mean God justifies His means by His ends? Yes. Is that wicked? No. An end-justifies-the-means ethic is fallacious and therefore wicked for finite men (who can neither control nor know all the results of their choices), but it is perfectly fitting for the infinite God (who both controls and knows all the results of His choices)–and, after all, God being supreme need not justify His choices to anyone.[134]

Beisner quotes Romans 9:15-21, to drive home the point that God acts according to his perfect will with his creation. God is not to be questioned or resisted. God's judgments are perfect.

I will have mercy on whom I will have mercy, and I will have compassion on whom I will have compassion. So then it is not of him that willeth, nor of him that runneth, but of God that sheweth mercy. For the scripture saith unto Pharaoh, Even for this same purpose have I raised thee up, that I might shew my power in thee, and that my name might be declared throughout all the earth. Therefore hath he mercy on whom he will have mercy, and whom he will he hardeneth. Thou wilt say then unto me, Why doth he yet find fault? For who hath resisted his will? Nay but, O man, who art thou that repliest against God? Shall the thing formed say to him that formed it, Why hast thou made me thus? Hath not the potter power over the clay, of the same lump to make one vessel unto honour, and another unto dishonour? Romans 9:15-21.

While God creates evil, he does it for a purpose. He never does it to tempt someone to sin.

Let no man say when he is tempted, I am tempted of God:

for God cannot be tempted with evil, neither tempteth he
any man: But every man is tempted, when he is drawn away
of his own lust, and enticed. Then when lust hath
conceived, it bringeth forth sin: and sin, when it is finished,
bringeth forth death. (James 1:13-15 AV)

The evil that God creates, spoken of in Isaiah 45:7, is defined in
the passage through parallelism. God states "I form the light and
create darkness." We see that God has juxtaposed light with its
opposite, which is darkness. We see God's creation of darkness in
Genesis.

In the beginning God created the heaven and the earth. And
the earth was without form, and void; and darkness *was*
upon the face of the deep. And the Spirit of God moved
upon the face of the waters. And God said, Let there be
light: and there was light. And God saw the light, that *it*
was good: and God divided the light from the darkness.
(Genesis 1:1-4 AV)

The earth was without form and "darkness" was upon the face of
the deep immediately upon its creation. Notice what God does next.
He creates light, which is the very opposite of darkness. God states
that the light was good. He did not, however, say the darkness was
good.

God created darkness, which is something which is no part of
God. Indeed, 1 John 1:5 states: "God is light, and in him is no
darkness at all." (1 John 1:5 AV) Yet, God uses darkness as his secret
place. "He made darkness his secret place; his pavilion round about
him *were* dark waters *and* thick clouds of the skies." (Psalms 18:11
AV) God creates darkness and uses darkness, but there is no darkness
in God.

Why is that important? Because God creates something
(darkness) which is not at all a characteristic of God. In the same
way that God creates darkness, he also creates evil; just as there is no
darkness in God, so also there is no evil in God. Jesus created all

things. Colossians 1:6. Jesus is: "The mighty God, The everlasting
Father, The Prince of Peace." Isaiah 9:6. God calling himself the
Prince of Peace indicates that peace is part of God's very character.
In Isaiah 45:7 God states "I make peace, and create evil." He parallels
that with his statement that "I form the light, and create darkness." In
that same way that God is light and has no darkness in him and
creates both light and darkness, God is the Prince of Peace and has no
evil in him and creates both peace and evil.

Do we have examples of God creating evil? In fact, the entire
book of Job is an illustration of God creating evil against Job. At the
end of the book of Job God explains that all Job's brothers, sisters,
and friends came to comfort Job **"over all the evil that the LORD
had brought upon him."** Job 42:11.

How did it all start with Job? It began when God removed his
protection from Job and gave Satan power to take from Job all that he
had.

> Then Satan answered the LORD, and said, Doth Job fear
> God for nought? Hast not thou made an hedge about him,
> and about his house, and about all that he hath on every
> side? thou hast blessed the work of his hands, and his
> substance is increased in the land. But put forth thine hand
> now, and touch all that he hath, and he will curse thee to
> thy face. And the LORD said unto Satan, Behold, all that he
> hath *is* in thy power; only upon himself put not forth thine
> hand. So Satan went forth from the presence of the LORD.
> (Job 1:9-12 AV)

Satan then used his power over evil men to drive them to kill
Job's servants, and steal his camels, asses, and oxen. Fire came down
from heaven and consumed Job's other servants and his sheep. A
great wind collapsed the house of Job's eldest son and it killed all of
Job's ten children. Who created the great wind, the fire from heaven,
and who created the wasters and destroyers of Job's children,
servants, and cattle? God, of course. "I have created the waster to
destroy." (Isaiah 54:16 AV)

When Job did not curse God, Satan was disappointed and told God that if he allowed him to strike at Job's physical health, Job would curse him. God gave Satan permission to strike at Job's health short of killing him.

> And Satan answered the LORD, and said, Skin for skin, yea, all that a man hath will he give for his life. But put forth thine hand now, and touch his bone and his flesh, and he will curse thee to thy face. And the LORD said unto Satan, Behold, he *is* in thine hand; but save his life. So went Satan forth from the presence of the LORD, and smote Job with sore boils from the sole of his foot unto his crown. (Job 2:4-7 AV)

Job was struck head to foot with painful boils. In the end, God healed Job and restored Job to riches beyond that with which he started, including blessing him with seven more sons and three daughters. Job 42:12-13. God knows the end from the beginning and he had a perfect purpose in bringing evil upon Job. "And we know that all things work together for good to them that love God, to them who are the called according to *his* purpose." (Romans 8:28 AV)

Job is just one example of God using Satan to accomplish God's ends. There are other bible passages which reveal that God uses evil spirits according to his divine will and purpose.

> **Then God sent an evil spirit** between Abimelech and the men of Shechem; and the men of Shechem dealt treacherously with Abimelech: (Judges 9:23 AV)

> But the Spirit of the LORD departed from Saul, and **an evil spirit from the LORD** troubled him. (1 Samuel 16:14 AV)

God has blinded the eyes and hardened the heart of the lost (John 12:39-40) and given them a spirit of slumber (Romans 11:8) so that they will not see with their eyes or understand with their hearts and be converted. Paul reveals in his second letter to the Corinthians that God uses Satan himself, whom he describes as the "god of this world," as the blinder of the lost.

> But if our gospel be hid, it is hid to them that are lost: In whom **the god of this world hath blinded the minds of them which believe not**, lest the light of the glorious gospel of Christ, who is the image of God, should shine unto them. (2 Corinthians 4:3-4 AV)

God used Satan to guide Judas to betray Jesus. In Luke 22:3 Satan entered into Judas, who then conspired with the chief priests to crucify Jesus. Again, when Jesus told John that the person to whom he would give a sop was the person who would betray him, Jesus gave the sop to Judas. Immediately, Satan once again entered Judas, and Jesus told Judas, who was now possessed by Satan, to go quickly and betray him. Jesus Christ was giving Satan his marching orders.

> **And after the sop Satan entered into him. Then said Jesus unto him, That thou doest, do quickly.** (John 13:27 AV)

Lest one think that the crucifixion was out of Jesus' control, read what happened in John 18 when Judas came with the chief priests, the pharisees and the band of soldiers to arrest Jesus. Jesus put them all on their backs. He did that to demonstrate to us that he was in complete control of the situation and could have stopped his arrest and crucifixion at any time if he so wished. However, God predestinated Jesus' arrest and crucifixion, and it happened exactly as God planned it.

> Judas then, having received a band of men and officers from the chief priests and Pharisees, cometh thither with lanterns and torches and weapons. Jesus therefore, knowing all things that should come upon him, went forth, and said unto them, Whom seek ye? They answered him, Jesus of Nazareth. Jesus saith unto them, I am he. And Judas also, which betrayed him, stood with them. **As soon then as he had said unto them, I am he, they went backward, and fell to the ground.** (John 18:3-6 AV)

While God sends evil spirits, that does not mean that God himself is evil. God is holy and perfectly righteous. God is so holy that day and night, without rest, four beasts proclaim in heaven: "Holy, holy, holy, Lord God Almighty, which was, and is, and is to come." Revelations 4:8. The Psalmist further explains: "Gracious is the LORD, and righteous; yea, our God is merciful." Psalms 116:5. It is blasphemy to say, as some Arminians say, that in order for God to create evil, God himself must be evil. *See* Mark 3:29-30; Matthew 12:32.

The crucifixion of Jesus Christ is the prime instance of God creating evil that ultimately works together for the good of them who love God. God placed his hand on Herod, Pontius Pilate, the Jews, and the Romans and moved them to commit the evil act of crucifying an innocent man, Jesus Christ.

> Ye men of Israel, hear these words; Jesus of Nazareth, a man approved of God among you by miracles and wonders and signs, which God did by him in the midst of you, as ye yourselves also know: Him, **being delivered by the determinate counsel and foreknowledge of God, ye have taken, and by wicked hands have crucified and slain**: Whom God hath raised up, having loosed the pains of death: because it was not possible that he should be holden of it. Acts 2:22-24.

> And when they heard that, they lifted up their voice to God with one accord, and said, Lord, thou art God, which hast made heaven, and earth, and the sea, and all that in them is: Who by the mouth of thy servant David hast said, Why did the heathen rage, and the people imagine vain things? The kings of the earth stood up, and the rulers were gathered together against the Lord, and against his Christ. For of a truth against thy holy child Jesus, whom thou hast anointed, both **Herod, and Pontius Pilate, with the Gentiles, and the people of Israel, were gathered together, For to do whatsoever thy hand and thy counsel determined before to be done.** (Acts 4:24-28 AV)

Pilate tried to tell Jesus he had complete freedom to crucify him or set him free. Jesus contradicts him and tells him that Pilate could have no power over him to do either unless God in heaven granted him the power. God was in complete control of the situation. The crucifixion of Christ was done according as God willed and preordained it to be done.

Then saith Pilate unto him, Speakest thou not unto me? knowest thou not that I have power to crucify thee, and have power to release thee? Jesus answered, **Thou couldest have no power at all against me, except it were given thee from above**: therefore he that delivered me unto thee hath the greater sin. (John 19:10-11 AV)

Indeed, God is sovereign and he brings about all things both good and evil. The bible contains example after example of God's goodness and severity. Romans 11:22:

Shall a trumpet be blown in the city, and the people not be afraid? **shall there be <u>evil</u> in a city, and the LORD hath not done <i>it</i>?** (Amos 3:6 AV)

"Who <i>is</i> he <i>that</i> saith, and it cometh to pass, <i>when</i> the Lord commandeth <i>it</i> not? **Out of the mouth of the most High proceedeth not <u>evil</u> and good?**" (Lamentations 3:37-38 AV)

Now therefore go to, speak to the men of Judah, and to the inhabitants of Jerusalem, saying, Thus saith the LORD; Behold, **I frame <u>evil</u> against you**, and devise a device against you: return ye now every one from his evil way, and make your ways and your doings good. (Jeremiah 18:11 AV)

Thus saith the LORD, Behold, **I will raise up <u>evil</u> against thee** out of thine own house, and I will take thy wives before thine eyes, and give <i>them</i> unto thy neighbour, and he shall lie with thy wives in the sight of this sun. (2 Samuel

12:11 AV)

And Absalom and all the men of Israel said, The counsel of Hushai the Archite *is* better than the counsel of Ahithophel. For the LORD had appointed to defeat the good counsel of Ahithophel, **to the intent that the LORD might bring evil upon Absalom**. (2 Samuel 17:14 AV)

And I *am* this day weak, though anointed king; and these men the sons of Zeruiah *be* too hard for me: **the LORD shall reward the doer of evil according to his wickedness**. (2 Samuel 3:39 AV)

Thus saith the LORD, Behold, **I will bring evil upon this place, and upon the inhabitants thereof,** *even* all the curses that are written in the book which they have read before the king of Judah: Because they have forsaken me, and have burned incense unto other gods, that they might provoke me to anger with all the works of their hands; therefore my wrath shall be poured out upon this place, and shall not be quenched. (2 Chronicles 34:24-25 AV)

20 He That Was Dead Came Forth

Jesus' miracle of raising Lazarus from the dead illustrates the grace of God, and completely refutes the Arminian theology. Jesus loved Lazarus and could have saved Lazarus from dying in the first place, but Jesus tarried for two days, rather than acting to prevent his death. John 11:5-6. Jesus allowed Lazarus to die and, when he knew that Lazarus died, he told his disciples "I am glad for your sakes that I was not there, to the intent ye may believe; nevertheless let us go unto him." John 11:15. We see in that passage the sovereignty of God. Jesus stated that he was glad that he was not there to prevent Lazarus' death, which he could have done. Jesus allowed Lazarus to die in order to further his purpose of demonstrating his power and grace.

Jesus' purpose of letting Lazarus die was so that his disciples would believe in him. As Jesus approached Martha and Mary's house, Martha ran to meet Jesus and exclaimed that if he had been there Lazarus would not have died. "Jesus saith unto her, Thy brother shall rise again." John 11:23. Martha responds by saying that she understands that "he shall rise again in the resurrection at the last day." John 11:24. Jesus, however, was talking about raising Lazarus then and there. He was not talking about the resurrection on the last day. Jesus does not plainly tell Martha that he is going to raise Lazarus from the dead. Instead, Jesus draws a parallel between

what he is about to do in raising Lazarus and the spiritual life he
gives to all who believe in him.

> Jesus said unto her, I am the resurrection, and the life: he
> that believeth in me, though he were dead, yet shall he live:
> And whosoever liveth and believeth in me shall never die.
> Believest thou this? John 11:25-26.

Jesus is explaining to Martha his point in allowing Lazarus to
die. He was drawing a direct correlation between the resurrection of
Lazarus and the spiritual rebirth of those who believe in him. Jesus'
purpose was to illustrate that he was "the resurrection and the life."
He stated that "he that believeth in me, though he were dead, yet shall
he live." Jesus was making the point that man is spiritually dead and
it is by the grace of God that man believes in him and thus is made
spiritually alive. Faith is the means of spiritual resurrection; Jesus is
the source of that faith.

Just as Lazarus was physically dead and was physically raised
by the power of Jesus, so also are sinners spiritually dead and must
be spiritually raised by power of Jesus. Their spiritual resurrection is
by the power and grace of Jesus, just as the physical resurrection of
Lazarus came by the power and grace of Jesus. Spiritual resurrection
comes by God's grace to those who are completely dead in trespasses
and sin and incapable of believing in Jesus. Just as Lazarus was dead
in the grave and incapable of his own power to raise himself, so also
are sinners spiritually dead to God and incapable of spiritually raising
themselves from their death in sin and trespasses. God must give
them eternal life.

We can see the great love that God has for his elect. Here God
Almighty weeps over the death of Lazarus.

> When Jesus therefore saw her weeping, and the Jews also
> weeping which came with her, he groaned in the spirit, and
> was troubled. And said, Where have ye laid him? They
> said unto him, Lord, come and see. Jesus wept. Then said
> the Jews, Behold how he loved him! John 11:33-36.

Now when Jesus came to Lazarus' tomb, Lazarus had no free will, indeed, he had no will at all, he was dead. Jesus had to make him alive first. Jesus commanded him to rise, and Lazarus did what Jesus commanded. Lazarus did not have the ability to resist the will of Jesus, just as his elect do not have the free will to resist his calling. Just as Jesus made Lazarus alive, he in like manner makes his elect spiritually alive.

> And when he thus had spoken, he cried with a loud voice, Lazarus, come forth. And he that was dead came forth, bound hand and foot with graveclothes: and his face was bound about with a napkin. Jesus saith unto them, Loose him, and let him go. John 11:33-34.

Jesus planned to have Lazarus die so that he could raise him from the dead. He did it to illustrate that Jesus is the resurrection, and the life: he that believes in Jesus, though he were dead, yet shall he live. John 11:25-26. The whole point of allowing Lazarus to die was to illustrate the truth that eternal life is completely by the grace of God. Jesus loved Lazarus and raised him from the dead by his power and grace. Jesus did for Lazarus what Lazarus was incapable of doing for himself. Jesus does the same for his elect, who are in like manner incapable of believing to eternal life without being made spiritually alive by the sovereign grace of God.

One point that is often missed in the passage is that "Jesus loved Martha, and her sister, and Lazarus." John 11:5. Jesus raised Lazarus from the dead because he loved him, just as he raises his elect from spiritual death because he loves them.

The fraud of the free will anti-gospel becomes apparent when it is held up to the light of the true gospel. It is only those who have been chosen by God that can believe in Jesus. Notice what happened in Acts when the gospel was preached to the Gentiles; only those who were preordained by God for eternal life believed. "And when the

Gentiles heard this, they were glad, and glorified the word of the
Lord: and **as many as were ordained to eternal life believed**."
(Acts 13:48 AV)

　　Those who do not believe in Jesus, do not believe because they
cannot believe. "[T]he natural man receiveth not the things of the
Spirit of God: for they are foolishness unto him: neither can he know
them, because they are spiritually discerned." (1 Corinthians 2:14
AV) It is Christ who dwells in the believer that quickens him from
death to life eternal. Without that Holy Spirit it is impossible to
believe in Jesus. Those chosen by God for salvation cannot lose
their salvation. *See* John 10:26-30.

> For they that are after the flesh do mind the things of the
> flesh; but they that are after the Spirit the things of the
> Spirit. For to be carnally minded *is* death; but to be
> spiritually minded *is* life and peace. Because the carnal
> mind *is* enmity against God: for it is not subject to the law
> of God, neither indeed can be. So then they that are in the
> flesh cannot please God. But ye are not in the flesh, but in
> the Spirit, if so be that the Spirit of God dwell in you. Now
> if any man have not the Spirit of Christ, he is none of his.
> And if Christ *be* in you, the body *is* dead because of sin; but
> the Spirit *is* life because of righteousness. **But if the Spirit
> of him that raised up Jesus from the dead dwell in you,
> he that raised up Christ from the dead shall also
> quicken your mortal bodies by his Spirit that dwelleth
> in you.** (Romans 8:5-11 AV)

God makes one a Christian. God must change your heart. As
Jesus said, a man must be born again. John 3:3. No man is born of
himself. One must be born of God. Salvation is not by the will of
man. "Which were born, not of blood, nor of the will of the flesh, nor
of the will of man, but of God." John 1:13. God must draw you.
"No man can come to me, except the Father which hath sent me draw
him: and I will raise him up at the last day." John 6:44. Unless God
draws a man, he will have no desire to be a Christian.

Man by nature is spiritually dead. God must quicken you, that is, make you spiritually alive. Ephesians 2:1-10. You then become a new spiritual creation through God's Holy Spirit.

There is no way that a man would accept those things written in the Holy Bible unless God has first opened his heart to the spiritual truths in the Bible. If one accepts that Jesus Christ is Lord God, the creator of the universe who reigns from heaven, he should submit completely to his authority. Ask the Lord in prayer to help you and he will. "And straightway the father of the child cried out, and said with tears, Lord, I believe; help thou mine unbelief." Mark 9:24.

Understand this simple truth, that if you ask Jesus to save you, he will. You will not, indeed you cannot, unless God draws you and gives you the ability to do so. He will then give you the gift of the Holy Spirit. Pray to Jesus for salvation.

And he said unto them, Which of you shall have a friend, and shall go unto him at midnight, and say unto him, Friend, lend me three loaves; For a friend of mine in his journey is come to me, and I have nothing to set before him? And he from within shall answer and say, Trouble me not: the door is now shut, and my children are with me in bed; I cannot rise and give thee. I say unto you, Though he will not rise and give him, because he is his friend, yet because of his importunity he will rise and give him as many as he needeth. And I say unto you, **Ask, and it shall be given you; seek, and ye shall find; knock, and it shall be opened unto you. For every one that asketh receiveth; and he that seeketh findeth; and to him that knocketh it shall be opened.** If a son shall ask bread of any of you that is a father, will he give him a stone? or if he ask a fish, will he for a fish give him a serpent? Or if he shall ask an egg, will he offer him a scorpion? If ye then, being evil, know how to give good gifts unto your children: how much more shall your heavenly Father give the Holy Spirit to them that ask him? (Luke 11:5-13 AV)

Those that ascribe to the free will mythology will cite the above passage as authority for their position that the source of faith is the will of man. However, that passage says nothing of the source of the faith, the passage simply explains the result of faith.

Faith comes from God, it is a gift; he will shower you with his merciful grace if you ask him. You must humble yourself before almighty God and ask for his mercy and grace. The only way that you can come to Christ is if he draws you and causes you to ask him to save you. John 6:44. **"Blessed is the man whom thou choosest, and causest to approach unto thee,** that he may dwell in thy courts: we shall be satisfied with the goodness of thy house, *even* of thy holy temple." (Psalms 65:4 AV)

21 The Judas Gospel

The false gospel of salvation by the free will of man separates the method of salvation (faith) from the source of that salvation (God). Under the true gospel of Jesus Christ, saving faith is not from man; it is a spiritual gift from God. The gift of faith is bestowed upon the believer according to the will and good pleasure of God. Salvation is totally by the grace of God, not the will of man. "But as many as received him, to them gave he power to become the sons of God, even to them that believe on his name: Which were born, not of blood, nor of the will of the flesh, nor of the will of man, but of God." (John 1:12-13 AV)

The key difference between the gospel and the free will anti-gospel is the object of the glory for salvation. God is deserving of glory, and he will not share his glory with anyone or anything. *See* Luke 2:14; Isaiah 42:8.

Satan, however, seeks to take God's glory from him. Isaiah 14:14. His anti-gospel attempts to do just that. Salvation is by the grace of God. Ephesians 2:8. God chose certain for salvation before the foundation of the world. Ephesians 1:4. In order to be born again and thus be saved from the eternal punishment for sin, one must believe in Jesus Christ. Romans 3:28. The crux of the issue is the source of that faith. The anti-gospel of Satan contends that the source of that faith is man; that man has the free will to choose to believe in God. The gospel of Jesus Christ, however, unequivocally states that God is the source of the faith. John 1:13.

The free will anti-gospel is actually a Judas gospel. The anti-gospel is a gospel of, by, and for men, whereby everything is contingent on the will of man. Under the anti-gospel, God is no longer the sovereign potentate of the universe; man has veto power over God and can overrule God's plan for salvation. According to the anti-gospel, if Judas had not of his own free will chosen to betray Jesus, then Jesus would not have been crucified and atoned for our sins.

Under the anti-gospel our salvation was contingent on the free will choice of Judas. Not only is the anti-gospel a Judas gospel, but if it were true, then Satan would share in the glory with Judas for our salvation. The free will gospel assumes that Satan and man are free agents unhindered by a sovereign God. Read Luke 22:3-4 and you will see that Satan entered into Judas and inspired him to betray Jesus. Satan and Judas acted in concert to betray Jesus.

Then entered Satan into Judas surnamed Iscariot, being of the number of the twelve. And he went his way, and communed with the chief priests and captains, how he might betray him unto them. (Luke 22:3-4 AV)

Free will assumes a will unhindered by God. The anti-gospel has God rolling the dice and hoping that Judas would betray Jesus. Under that devilish doctrine, the crucifixion of Christ was one big gamble that paid off for God and man.

The true gospel, however, tells a different story. Judas betrayed Jesus as prophesied by God hundreds of years earlier. Jesus stated, while praying to God the Father: "While I was with them in the world, I kept them in thy name: those that thou gavest me I have kept, and **none of them is lost, but the son of perdition; that the scripture might be fulfilled.**" (John 17:12 AV)

The betrayal of Jesus by Judas was planned by God. In Jeremiah we read a prophecy written approximately 600 years before the betrayal of Jesus by Judas: "Yea, mine own familiar friend, in whom I trusted, which did eat of my bread, hath lifted up *his* heel against me." (Psalms 41:9 AV) Jesus, referring to the prophecy in Jeremiah, told the apostles: "I speak not of you all: I know whom I have chosen: but that the scripture may be fulfilled, He that eateth bread with me hath lifted up his heel against me." (John 13:18 AV)

Jesus knew Judas would betray him: "For he knew who should betray him; therefore said he, Ye are not all clean." (John 13:11 AV) Judas had no more a free will in the matter than a pencil has a free will to write. Judas, like the pencil, was an instrument completely under God's control.

God did not leave our salvation to the chance that Judas might not betray Jesus. God is love. 1 John 4:8. It would be the very antithesis of love to leave our salvation to chance. God is not a gambler.

Judas was preordained by God to betray Jesus. Judas had no choice in the matter. God predicted what Judas would do hundreds of years before he did it and then predicted it to his apostles moments before it happened. Jesus then personally gave Judas orders to hurry up and betray him. Judas could not resist the will of God.

> Jesus answered, He it is, to whom I shall give a sop, when I have dipped *it*. And when he had dipped the sop, he gave *it* to Judas Iscariot, *the son* of Simon. And after the sop Satan entered into him. Then said Jesus unto him, That thou doest, do quickly. (John 13:26-27 AV)

Not only did Judas not have a free will to choose whether to betray Jesus, but every single act of Herod, Pontius Pilate, the Jews, and the Romans was preordained and orchestrated by the sovereign God of Heaven. "For of a truth against thy holy child Jesus, whom thou hast anointed, both Herod, and Pontius Pilate, with the Gentiles, and the people of Israel, were gathered together, **For to do**

whatsoever thy hand and thy counsel determined before to be done." (Acts 4:27-28 AV) In fact, God orders the steps of all men and controls their very tongue. "The preparations of the heart in man, and the answer of the tongue are from the Lord." Prov. 16:1.

Many religious charlatans cannot let go of the godhood of man and so they attempt to explain away clear scriptural passages by denying the meaning of the plain language. Arminian free will theologians create an unbiblical theology whereby their mythical god is stripped of his omnipotence and only retains a semblance of omniscience. After all, if they are going to conjure up a god, they are going to make sure that he does not have the power to meddle in their affairs. Read the following reprobate analysis of the plain language in Acts 4:27-28 from the Christian Apologetics and Research Ministry:

> There is no logical reason to claim that if God knows what choices we are going to make that it means we are not free. It still means that the free choices we will make are free -- they are just known ahead of time by God. If we choose something different, then that choice will have been eternally known by God. Furthermore, this knowledge by God does not alter our nature in that it does not change what we are, free to make choices. God's knowledge is necessarily complete and exhaustive because that is His nature to know all things. In fact, since He has eternally known what all our free choices will be, He has ordained history to come to the conclusion that He wishes including and incorporating our choices into His divine plan: "For truly in this city there were gathered together against Thy holy servant Jesus, whom Thou didst anoint, both Herod and Pontius Pilate, along with the Gentiles and the peoples of Israel, to do whatever Thy hand and Thy purpose predestined to occur," (Acts 4:27-28).[135]

Notice the final passage (Acts 4:27-28) in the above quote impeaches the premise that we have a free will. Yet the writer cites the passage as though it supports his thesis. The writer ignores the

plain language in the passage that states that God determined before
hand that Herod, Pontius Pilate, the gentiles, and the Jews were to
condemn Jesus.

The Arminian writer makes the absurd claim that God did not
predestine the crucifixion of Jesus as the passage says he did. The
writer, instead, claims that God only knew Jesus would be crucified
and adopted the free will choices of Herod, Pontius Pilate, the
Gentiles, and the Jews as his plan. The Arminians have God simply
adopting the plans of men, even though God states he determined
before hand that Jesus would be crucified. The Arminians ignore the
plain meaning of God's words.

The Arminian "experts" don't think much of God's word. It is
typical for them to use corrupted versions of the bible. In their
corrupt bible passage (Acts 4:27-28) cited above, Jesus goes from
being the "holy child Jesus" (who is the sovereign creator of the
universe, Colossians 1:16) to being "Thy holy servant Jesus." While
Jesus is referred to as God's servant in Matthew 12:18, God was
identifying him in Acts chapter 4 in the Authorized (King James)
Version as his child.

By changing the passage from child to servant, Jesus' status as
God's holy child, "the only begotten Son of God." (John 3:18) is lost.
The point that they crucified God's holy child Jesus, who is the only
begotten Son of God, is obscured in the corrupt bible passage. While
Jesus was certainly a holy servant of God, he was much more; he was
God himself in human flesh. *See* John 1:1-3, 14. God wanted that
point made in Acts chapter 4, but the Arminian outlaw wordsmiths
decided that they know better than God, and so they overruled God
and changed the passage.

Changing the passage to refer to Jesus as a servant fits rather
nicely with the Arminian free will theology, whereby their Jesus is
simply a servant, who dares not intervene in their affairs, except
when called upon to grant their every desire, like some heathen genie,
whenever they decide of their own free will to "pray" for health and
wealth. The Arminian god is reduced to a cosmic errand boy to be

bossed around by his sovereign masters on earth.

Notice further that the puny Arminian god must comport his plans to the free will of men by "incorporating our choices into His divine plan." They state that "since He has eternally known what all our free choices will be, He has ordained history to come to the conclusion that He wishes." That is ridiculous double talk.

If their god is limited to only knowing what man will do, but has no influence over man or history, then history concludes as man wishes, not as their god wishes. That is not a divine plan, that is an earthly plan of sinful men. According to that free will theology, it is man that is calling the shots and the mythical Arminian god simply incorporates the free choices of men into what they call "his divine plan." Their god truly does not have a plan, so it is misleading to call it "his divine plan." In essence, it is sinful man that is in control, and their god is a helpless bystander, who like a heathen fortune teller can foresee what will happen, but has no power to control events.

The Arminian view is that their god has a type of omniscience. Even if the Arminians acknowledge their god's omnipotence, it makes no difference, because they argue that he chooses not to exercise his omnipotence; he simply adopts the free will choices of men.

Many of the Arminian theologians, in order to be consistent within their Arminian construct, have come out and flat denied even the omniscience of their Arminian god. How could they do otherwise? If Arminianism is followed to its logical conclusion, the Arminian god indeed cannot be omniscient. That is because it is required by the Arminian theology that man is a free agent of choice and is outside the guidance of their Arminian god. Consequently, their god must not truly know what a man exercising his free will is going to do next.

Mark Herzer spent years studying the leading Arminian theologians. During his years of study, he amassed a huge library of their works. Herzer made some surprising discoveries as he studied

the Arminian theology. One discovery was that some of the principal
Arminian authorities hold that their Arminian god is not omniscient;
that he does not actually know who will choose to believe in Jesus.
They are essentially free will "theists."

> They, the Arminians who are Freewill Theists, are not
> willing to concede that God knows all things, at least not in
> the traditional sense. For example, Clark Pinnock argues
> that "omniscience need not mean exhaustive foreknowledge
> of all future events. If that were its meaning, the future
> would be fixed and determined, as is the past."[136] For them,
> the idea of foreknowledge "requires only that we define the
> scope of foreknowledge with care. In some respects the
> future is knowable, in others it is not. God knows a great
> deal about what will happen. He knows everything that will
> ever happen as the direct result of factors that already exist.
> He knows infallibly the content of his own future actions,
> to the extent that they are not related to human choices. All
> that God does not know is the content of future free
> decisions, and this is because decisions are not there to
> know until they occur."[137] The problem with Rice's
> seemingly harmless formulation is that the whole future, as
> envisioned by this explanation, is filled with nothing but
> numerous human decisions. In order for God to know even
> two seconds into the future, God must know the decisions
> of the first second which He is not permitted to know (or, as
> they argue, He chose not to know). If He does not know it,
> then how can He know His own future actions when they
> are dependent upon the free acts of man? Thus God in fact
> does not know the future at all because He does not know
> our decisions nor His responses to them. Rice is even more
> adamant in another book: "Not even God knows the future
> in all its details. Some parts remain indefinite until they
> actually occur, and so they can't be known in advance."[138]
> This sort of formulation is gaining ground among some
> evangelicals.[139]

This would quite naturally lead to the notion of "divine

learning." Namely, God must learn as the future unfolds. May it never be said that He infallibly knows all things. In fact, without much shame, they virtually concede in some measure that God is surprised. "God is not startled and is never struck dumb as the future unfolds, but an element of surprise embraces the divine knowledge just as it does ours even when we think our predictive powers are at their height. Were you a god, would you not find it dull to fix the future irrevocably from eternity?"[140] That last question typifies and exposes their theological tendency, namely, God created in the image of man. In response, I ask, "What does it matter if I should be bored? How does my own boredom determine the nature of God's knowledge? And in what real sense do we have any predictive powers? Isn't God's predictive power the sheer evidence of His majestic divinity?" Yet Rice's assumption admits this central thesis: God is merely a superhuman being.

John Sanders's thesis is more subtle but also just as destructive. He argues that the nature of the relationship necessitates risks and therefore God's providence is a risk of a sort. He states that God is "amazingly creative" and enters into a risk relationship with human beings. "In the God-human relationship God sometimes decides alone what will happen; at other times God modifies his plans in order to accommodate the choices, actions and desires of his creatures."[141] God, in effect, reacts to our decisions and actions. But that is Sanders's point: God takes risks. He further explains that when God created the world, He had a "great chance of success and little possibility of failure while concomitantly having a ... high amount of risk in the sense that it matters deeply to God how things go."[142] He says that sin was possible, but not plausible because God took a risk. Sanders is aware that our sensibilities would be "shocked" with this sort of formulation. But a God of risk taking (unaware of what the future infallibly holds) is for Sanders the most relational picture of God. In essence, his view could be summed up by these words: "But God sovereignly decides not to control each and every event, and some things go contrary to what God intends and may not turn out completely as God desires. Hence, God takes risks in creating this sort of world."[143]

The Arminian god is like some comic book super-hero; he is "super-duper" powerful and can do some really cool things, but he is neither omnipotent nor omniscient. The Arminian super-hero god is like a river boat gambler. According to the Arminians their god took a calculated risk with his creation and the gamble has, so far, paid off.

Furthermore, these reprobate experts maintain that God does not mean what he is saying in his Holy Bible. They implicitly allege that God is deceiving us when he states clearly and unequivocally in Acts 4:27-28 that he gathered together Herod, Pontius Pilate, the Gentiles, and Israel together to crucify Jesus. Free will theologians falsely claim that God only knew what sinful men were going to do regarding the crucifixion of Christ, and that God did not have a hand in those events at all. These charlatans make the true God out to be a liar in order to prop up their mythical god, who has no power to intervene in the affairs of men, because they believe that man has a sovereign free will.

God does what he pleases in heaven and on earth. **"Whatsoever the LORD pleased, *that* did he in heaven, and in earth, in the seas, and all deep places."** (Psalms 135:6 AV)

God revealed to David that he not only watched David's every step, he also compassed him about, laid his hand upon him, led him by the hand, and indeed held David in his right hand. There is no doubt that God does the same for all of his elect.

<<To the chief Musician, A Psalm of David.>> O LORD, thou hast searched me, and known *me*. Thou knowest my downsitting and mine uprising, thou understandest my thought afar off. Thou compassest my path and my lying down, and art acquainted *with* all my ways. For *there is* not

a word in my tongue, *but*, lo, O LORD, thou knowest it altogether. **Thou hast beset me behind and before, and laid thine hand upon me.** *Such* knowledge *is* too wonderful for me; it is high, I cannot *attain* unto it. Whither shall I go from thy spirit? or whither shall I flee from thy presence? If I ascend up into heaven, thou *art* there: if I make my bed in hell, behold, thou *art there*. *If* I take the wings of the morning, *and* dwell in the uttermost parts of the sea; **Even there shall thy hand lead me, and thy right hand shall hold me.** (Psalms 139:1-10 AV)

God states that even the heart of the king is under the control of Lord's will. "The king's heart *is* in the hand of the LORD, *as* the rivers of water: he turneth it whithersoever he will." (Proverbs 21:1 AV) Most men do not understand that their steps are not under their own direction. "O LORD, I know that the way of man is not in himself: it is not in man that walketh to direct his steps." Jeremiah 10:23. Who directs the steps of men? God gives us the answer: "Man's goings are of the LORD; how can a man then understand his own way?" Proverbs 20:24.

In 1 Samuel, chapter 9, God gives an example of how God determines the very steps of men without them even understanding that it is God who is guiding them. In 1 Samuel 9, Saul and his servant are searching far and wide for Kish's (Saul's father's) lost asses. Saul was not able to find the asses and decided to return to his father. Saul's servant, however, suggested that they visit Samuel the prophet in a nearby city to ask his advice. Neither Saul nor his servant had ever met Samuel before. In fact, the servant had only heard of Samuel's reputation and referred to him not as Samuel, but as "a man of God." Saul agrees to seek out the prophet. *See* 1 Samuel 9:5-10. Saul and his servant were able to find Samuel. From Saul's and his servant's perspectives, it seemed to them that they were making free and independent decisions. However when we read further in 1 Samuel 9, we find that it was God who had guided Saul to seek out Samuel. God had told Samuel the day before Saul and his servant ever decided to seek out Samuel that he would "send" Saul to him.

> Now the LORD had told Samuel in his ear a day before Saul came, saying, To morrow about this time I will send thee a man out of the land of Benjamin, and thou shalt anoint him to be captain over my people Israel, that he may save my people out of the hand of the Philistines: for I have looked upon my people, because their cry is come unto me. And when Samuel saw Saul, the LORD said unto him, Behold the man whom I spake to thee of! this same shall reign over my people. 1 Samuel 9:15-17.

God is not a passive observer of his elect. He preserves his elect for ever. "The LORD shall preserve thy going out and thy coming in from this time forth, and even for evermore." (Psalms 121:8 AV)

22 John 3:16

rminians always take John 3:16 out of context and subtly
twist it to mean what it does not say. John 3:16 states
that "God so loved the world, that he gave his only
begotten Son, that whosoever believeth in him should not perish, but
have everlasting life." *Id.* Clearly the passage is talking about God's
love for the world. That is a given. The Arminian free will
advocates, however, subtly deceive their followers by misinterpreting
the words "so loved" to mean "loved everyone in the world so
much."[144]

The Arminians argue that God has a great love for the world and
everyone it. Dr. Jack Graham, pastor of the mega-church
Prestonwood Baptist Church, for example, states that John 3:16
means that God loves everyone. He stated: "I can stand up here and
say to you: God loves you, every person."[145] Graham elaborated: "It
[John 3:16] doesn't say that God so loved the elect or God so loved
his chosen ones, or God so loved part of the world. But God so loved
the world. And you know, we better be careful about adding [to] and
subtracting from the Bible and playing little theological games with
truth."[146] Graham continues with: "Why don't we just believe the
Bible and take God's Word as it is? God loves every person. That's
what the Bible teaches."[147]

The highly esteemed bible scholar, Dr. D.A. Waite of *The Bible for Today, Inc.*, agrees with Graham. Waite states:

> "That WHOSOEVER BELIEVETH IN HIM should not
> perish, but have everlasting life" shows that the OFFER of
> God's great love is for ANYONE who believes in the Lord
> Jesus as Savior. "WHOSOEVER BELIEVETH" does not
> restrict God 's offer of salvation to some LIMITED group,
> but to EVERYONE in this wide world![148] (emphasis in
> original).

The context gives us a clue as to the meaning of "world." In
John 3:1 Nicodemus, who approached Jesus at night, is introduced as
"a man of the Pharisees" and "a ruler of the Jews." In verse 10, Jesus
called Nicodemus "a master of Israel." Jesus' point in saying that
God so loved "the world" was to tell Nicodemus that God's plan for
salvation is not limited to Jews. God's love extends beyond the Jews
to "the world." Jesus does not mean he loves every single person in
the world; he means his love is not limited to Jews only, but that his
love is for all of his elect in the world without distinction to whether
a person is a Jew or a Gentile.

John 3:14-15 is a parallel passage to John 3:16. Jesus draws a
parallel between Moses lifting up the serpent in the wilderness to
save the Jews from the bites of the fiery serpents and how God so
loved the world, made up of both Jews and Gentiles, that he gave his
only begotten Son by lifting him up on the cross "that whosoever
believeth in him should not perish, but have eternal life." John 3:15.

It was God who sent the fiery serpents among the Jews to bite
them in the wilderness. *See* Numbers 21:6. When the people went to
Moses and asked him to pray to God for help from the serpents.
Moses did so, and God instructed Moses to raise a fiery serpent on a
pole "that every one that is bitten, when he looketh upon it, shall
live." Numbers 21:8. It was God who drove the Jews to look upon
the serpent on the pole by sending the fiery serpents to bite them, just
as it is God who draws his elect in the world (both Jews and Gentiles)
to look to Jesus in faith.

Furthermore, Arminians seem to skip over John 3:8, which makes clear that those who are saved are born of the Holy Spirit, who is completely outside the control of man. Jesus compares the Holy Spirit to the wind; the wind can be heard but no one can determine from where it comes or where it goes. In like manner, people can perceive the effects of the Holy Spirit in the rebirth of the elect, but no one has control over the Holy Spirit. Those in the world who are loved by God are saved through the Holy Spirit by the sovereign "list" (will) of God, not through the mythical will of man. The Holy Spirit goes wherever he listeth (wills). "The wind bloweth where it **listeth**, and thou hearest the sound thereof, but canst not tell whence it cometh, and whither it goeth: so is every one that is born of the Spirit." (John 3:8)

In the John 3:16 passage, the words "so loved" do not mean that God has a great love for everyone in the world, but rather that he has a particular kind of love for a particular people in the world. The context tells us what kind of love God has and for whom he had that love.

The word "world" has a different meaning in different passages. The context sometimes gives a clue as to what God means. For example, in Romans 11:12 the context clearly indicates that God uses "world" to refer to only the Gentiles. In John 13:1 God uses "world" to refer to the earth. In John 15:18-19 God used the word "world" to refer only to the unregenerate in the world, which does not include believers. In 1 John 2:15 God is referring to the material temptations. In 1 John 2:2 and 2 Corinthians 5:19 God refers to only those chosen for salvation out of the world. Those passages will be discussed in more detail in a later chapter.

What did God mean by world in John 3:16? To answer that we must look at the context and the whole counsel of God found in the bible. We read in John 3:3 that Jesus tells Nicodemus that he must be born again to see the kingdom of God. That is a spiritual rebirth that cannot be by the will of man or through the flesh. In fact, God made it clear just two chapters earlier that this new spiritual birth comes to those "[w]hich were born, not of blood, nor of the will of the flesh, nor of the will of man, but of God." (John 1:13 AV)

Jesus was explaining the spiritual rebirth to Nicodemus when he said in John 3:16 that "God so loved the world, that he gave his only begotten Son, that whosoever believeth in him should not perish, but have everlasting life." "God so loved the world" in that context means that God loved the world in this way: "that he gave his only begotten Son, that whosoever believeth in him should not perish, but have everlasting life." The spiritual rebirth is all of God. God "so loved the world" with a special love whereby that he gave his only begotten Son for the salvation of his elect. His elect are then born again of the Spirit unto salvation. God's love is a special sacrificing love for his elect; it is not a general love for all.

Jesus' statement that he "so loved the world" in John 3:16 was made on the heels of his statement in John 3:14-15 that "as Moses lifted up the serpent in the wilderness, even so must the Son of man be lifted up: That whosoever believeth in him should not perish, but have eternal life." The point was that God "so loved the world" in the same way he sent the serpents among the Jews in the wilderness so that they would look to the brass serpent on the pole held by Moses. It was only the Jews who were bitten who looked to the brass serpent held by Moses in order to be saved from death by the snake bites. In that same way, it is only those whom God draws to Jesus who believe in him and are then saved from their sins. God "so loved the world" that he draws his elect to Jesus the same way he used the fiery serpents to bite the Jews thus driving them to look to the serpent held up by Moses. It was only the Jews who had been bitten by the fiery serpents who had any motivation to look to the brass serpent held by Moses; in the same way it is only those drawn by God who have any motivation to believe in Jesus.

God draws his elect to Jesus through hardship and infirmities. That is how God works. He makes his elect weak in the things of the world so that they can become strong in the things of the spirit. Jesus explained that point to Paul when he told him: "My grace is sufficient for thee: for my strength is made perfect in weakness." (2 Corinthians 12:9) God may take that which is important in this world away from his elect in order to draw them to him.

Just as the Jews looked to the brass image of the serpent on the pole to be saved from death brought about by the serpents' bites in Numbers 21:6-9, so also God's elect look to Christ crucified, who was made sin on their behalf to take the punishment of their sin on himself, thus saving them from eternal punishment. "For he hath made him to be sin for us, who knew no sin; that we might be made the righteousness of God in him." (2 Corinthians 5:21) As explained in John 3:14-16, the Jews were saved from physical death by looking to the brass serpent, so also God's elect throughout the whole world (both Jews and Gentiles) are saved from spiritual death by looking to Jesus Christ.

Jesus was explaining not that he loved the whole world and everyone in it, but rather that he loved the world in a particular way. To interpret John 3:16 to mean that Jesus loves everyone in the world makes God speak with a forked tongue. For in John 17:9 we read that Jesus would not pray for the world, but rather only those that his Father had given to him. "I pray for them: **I pray not for the world**, but for them which thou hast given me; for they are thine." (John 17:9 AV) Clearly, Jesus does not love everyone in the world, for he would not even pray for them, he only prayed for his elect. In fact, God states clearly in Romans 9:13: "As it is written, Jacob have I loved, but Esau have I hated." Clearly, God does not love everyone in the world.

The Arminians argue that "whosoever believeth in him" in John 3:16 means that man has a free will choice to believe or not in Jesus. The Arminians seem to rewrite John 3:16 to say that whosoever "of their own free will" believes in Jesus shall be saved. In fact, John 3:16 says no such thing. John 3:16 is a statement of fact, not a statement defining the source of faith. It is a fact that whosoever believes in Jesus will have everlasting life, and that is what Jesus intended to convey in that passage. Salvation is totally God's decision, God's choice, God's work, according to his sovereign mercy; salvation is by faith, which is supplied by God; it is not a free will choice of man. "So then it is not of him that willeth, nor of him that runneth, but of God that sheweth mercy." Romans 9:16.

In John 3:17 Jesus makes clear that "God sent not his Son into the **world** to condemn the **world**; but that the **world** through him might be saved." It is obvious that in light of the entire gospel, the "world" referred to in John 3:17 could not mean everyone in the world, since we know that most will not be saved. *See* Matthew 7:13. God sent his son that the world might be saved. He did not send his son on a futile mission. God sent his son to accomplish salvation for the world. By "world" in John 3:17, God meant those whom Jesus saved. If Jesus was referring only to the saved world and not to everyone in the world in John 3:17, he must also have meant only the saved world in John 3:16.

John makes it even clearer in John 3:18 that the "world" is not everyone in the world, because Jesus states that "[h]e that believeth on him is not condemned: but he that believeth not is condemned already." There are those in the world who would believe on Jesus and those who would not, and it is only to those who would believe on him that he loves. Jesus saves his elect from condemnation; he does not save anyone else. Matthew 25:31-46.

Clearly, God does not love those who are under condemnation, whom he has the ability to save and yet does not save. The true God of the bible saves those whom he has elected for salvation and he condemns those he has elected for condemnation. *See* Romans 9. Those who are saved are chosen for salvation according to the election of God, not man. 1 Peter 1:2. That is what Jesus meant when he said: "Ye have not chosen me, but I have chosen you, and ordained you, that ye should go and bring forth fruit, and that your fruit should remain" John 15:16.

The mythical Arminian god, on the other hand, is powerless to overcome the free will of man and therefore leaves man's salvation up to his fleshly free will. There is no spiritual rebirth from God under the Arminian theology; it is left to the mythical ability of man by his own free will to believe in Jesus. The Arminian god loves everyone but is a helpless spectator to the free will decision of man.

Arminians would object to that characterization of their theology and argue that they believe that God is omnipotent, and he knows the choices that individuals will make, but he still gives individuals the power to ultimately choose (or reject) salvation.

That leaves the Arminians with a theological problem. In John 3:17 Jesus states: "For God sent not his Son into the world to condemn the world; but that the world through him might be saved." The Arminian god cannot be omnipotent, if John 3:17 is to make any sense. That is because the Arminian's believe that "the world" in John 3 includes everyone in the world, and their god sent his son into the world for the purpose of saving everyone in the world. Yet the Arminians acknowledge that most people in the world are not saved. *See* Matthew 7:13. An omnipotent God would accomplish his goal of saving all those whom he has decided to save. The Arminian god cannot be omnipotent, since he has failed to save everyone in the world. According to the Arminian theology, their god is foiled by the superior power of the free will of man.

If one accepts the argument of the Arminians that their god is omnipotent, that creates an untenable theological result. Arminians interpret John 3:16 to mean that their god loves everyone in the world, yet most of the world ends up in an eternal lake of fire. If, as claimed, the Arminian god were truly omnipotent, he could save those whom he loves and prevent their eternal destruction. Yet the omnipotent Arminian god does not lift a finger to save his loved ones, and instead stands idly by while they ignorantly reject his love and are cast into an eternal lake of fire, where there is weeping and gnashing of teeth. Who casts them into the lake of fire? Revelations tells us that it is God Almighty, Jesus Christ, at the white throne judgement. Revelation 20:11-15.

So the Arminian god is omnipotent and can save his loved ones, but does not do so and instead casts them into an eternal lake of fire. The Arminian omnipotent god has a perverse way to show his love. According to the Arminians, hell is populated with people whom their god loves. Whereas, the true God of the bible casts into hell those whom he never loved.

Since <u>not</u> everyone is saved, the truly omnipotent God must have decided to save some and not others. That is exactly what God states he has done in Romans 9. Therefore, God could not have meant everyone in the world when he states that "the world through him might be saved" in John 3.

God has redeemed only his people. "Blessed be the Lord God of Israel; for he hath visited and redeemed **his people**." Luke 1:68 (emphasis added). Jesus is the good shepherd. He did not give his life for the goats, but he gave his life only for the sheep. "I am the good shepherd: the good shepherd giveth his life for the sheep." John 10:11. The sheep are known in particular by God, and his sheep know him. "I am the good shepherd, and **know my sheep**, and am known of mine." John 10:14 (emphasis added). Jesus did not come to save all people from their sins, he came only to save "his people" from their sins. "And she shall bring forth a son, and thou shalt call his name JESUS: for he shall save **his people** from their sins." Matthew 1:21 (emphasis added).

According to the Arminian mythology God loves everyone in the world, but they theorize that most rebel and refuse his free offer of salvation, thus forfeiting (of their own free will) the gift of salvation. The Arminians have a difficult case, however, when it comes to Judas, who betrayed Jesus. We have already seen how the free will doctrine is contradicted by the prophesied betrayal of Jesus by Judas. Either Judas was preordained to betray Jesus by God or he had a free will choice to betray Jesus. There is no middle ground. Either one believes the gospel of Jesus or the Arminian mythology.

The case of Judas also poses a problem for the myth that God loves everyone. According to the Arminian free will theory, God loved Judas, but Judas of his own free will rebelled and betrayed Jesus. That Arminian interpretation of Judas' betrayal simply cannot be true.

In John 13:18 Jesus states in pertinent part: "I know whom I have chosen: but that the scripture may be fulfilled, He that eateth bread with me hath lifted up his heel against me." (John 13:18 AV)

Notice that Jesus explains that his betrayal is according to scripture prophecy. Where is the prophecy found? It is found at Psalms 41:9. That Psalm states: "Yea, mine own familiar friend, in whom I trusted, which did eat of my bread, hath lifted up his heel against me." (Psalms 41:9 AV) Psalm 41:9 was written approximately 1,000 years before Judas was born. So here we have God prophesying his betrayal at the hands of Judas approximately 1,000 years before he was manifested in the flesh on earth.

Clearly, Judas had no choice in the matter. He was preordained to betray Jesus. God did not love Judas. Jesus called Judas a devil in John 6:70. "Jesus answered them, Have not I chosen you twelve, and one of you is a devil?" (John 6:70 AV) Jesus pronounced a woe against Judas and stated that it would have been better if he were not born. "The Son of man goeth as it is written of him: but woe unto that man by whom the Son of man is betrayed! it had been good for that man if he had not been born. Then Judas, which betrayed him, answered and said, Master, is it I? He said unto him, Thou hast said." (Matthew 26:24-25 AV)

In John 17:12 Jesus called Judas the son of perdition. "While I was with them in the world, I kept them in thy name: those that thou gavest me I have kept, and none of them is lost, but the son of perdition; that the scripture might be fulfilled." (John 17:12 AV) God did not love Judas. He never loved Judas. Judas was a vessel chosen for destruction and God prophesied of Judas' betrayal of Jesus approximately 1,000 years before it happened. Judas was a vessel preordained and fitted for destruction. If Judas was preordained for destruction, as prophesied and fulfilled in the bible, then the Arminian interpretation of John 3:16 that God loves everyone in the world cannot be true. God explains that some are preordained to be saved for glory and others are fitted beforehand for destruction.

Hath not the potter power over the clay, of the same lump to make one vessel unto honour, and another unto dishonour? *What* if God, willing to shew *his* wrath, and to make his power known, endured with much longsuffering the vessels of wrath fitted to destruction: And that he might make known the riches of his glory on the vessels of mercy, which he had afore prepared unto glory. (Romans 9:21-23 AV)

Jesus is clear that he never loved those who will be cast into the lake of fire. "I never knew you: depart from me, ye that work iniquity." Matthew 7:23. God does not say he once loved them; he states clearly that he never knew them. Matthew 7:23 is a real problem for the Arminian claim that God loves everyone in the world, and yet people end up in hell because they exercise their mythical free will turn their back on God's love, and choose of their free will not to believe in Jesus. If Jesus never knew them, how could he have ever held out any chance of salvation for them? The answer is ineluctable; God never held out a chance of salvation for them.

Those chosen for damnation were so chosen before the foundation of the world. God never knew them! "Then shall he say also unto them on the left hand, Depart from me, ye cursed, into everlasting fire, prepared for the devil and his angels." Matthew 25:41. Notice in Matthew 25:41 Jesus calls those who are cast into everlasting fire "cursed." They were never loved by God; they are cast into the lake of fire because they were cursed from the beginning.

The fact that the damned were never loved by God is confirmed by the fact that those chosen for salvation were chosen from the foundation of the world. "Then shall the King say unto them on his right hand, Come, ye blessed of my Father, inherit the kingdom prepared for you from the foundation of the world." Matthew 25:34. If those chosen for salvation were chosen from the foundation of the world, then the cursed ones cast into the lake of fire were also chosen for damnation from the foundation of the world. That means that God could not have loved everyone in the world as the Arminians claim is the case in John 3:16. When God states he never knew those damned to hell, he means literally he "never" "ever" knew them. The God of the bible casts those whom he never knew into hell, he never loved them "ever." His word is clear on that.

When one reads John 3:16-18 in context, the gospel of grace is clear, and what Jesus meant by "world" is also clear. Notice, that in verse 18 Jesus states "he that believeth not is condemned already." Jesus means that the condition of man is that he is already condemned. Man is unable to come to God, and so Jesus came to bring salvation to his elect.

Jesus explains that he was not sent into the world to condemn the world, but to save the world. The world he saved is the same world "God so loved." That world is the world made up of those who believe in him and are therefore "not condemned." John 3:18. The believers are "born again;" they are given a spiritual rebirth that is totally by the grace of God through faith in Jesus Christ. John 3:3.

> For God so loved the **world**, that he gave his only begotten Son, that whosoever believeth in him should not perish, but have everlasting life. For God sent not his Son into the **world** to condemn the **world**; but that the **world** through him might be saved. He that believeth on him is not condemned: but he that believeth not is condemned already, because he hath not believed in the name of the only begotten Son of God. (John 3:16-18 AV)

Look closely at the four uses of the word "world" in John 3:16-18. First, "God so loved the **world**;" second, "God sent not his Son into the **world** to condemn the **world**;" third, he did so "that the **world** through him might be saved."

Notice that the passage ends with God explaining the reason that Jesus was sent into the world: to save the world. God accomplished his goal. The point in John 3:16-18 is that God saved the world that he loved. Who are those that God saves? He tells us in verse 18 that those who believe in Jesus are saved. Those are the people in the "world" that God so loved and that he saved. Those are the people for whom Jesus died.

If, as claimed by the Arminians, the "world" includes everyone in the world, including those who are condemned, then God failed in his goal of giving his only begotten son to save everyone in the world from condemnation.

We know that the Arminian view is wrong, because God is omnipotent. "For with God nothing shall be impossible." Luke 1:37. God accomplishes all he sets out to do. "The LORD of hosts hath sworn, saying, Surely as I have thought, so shall it come to pass; and as I have purposed, so shall it stand." Isaiah 14:24. God can save all whom he decides to save. "In whom also we have obtained an inheritance, being predestinated according to the purpose of him who worketh all things after the counsel of his own will." Ephesians 1:11. God is an omnipotent ruler. "[T]he Lord God omnipotent reigneth." Revelation 19:6.

We know, therefore, that the "world" that God set out to save in John 3:16-18 was in fact saved. That "world" could only be those whom God elected for salvation by his grace through faith in Jesus Christ, and does not include (as claimed by the Arminians) those preordained to be condemned to hell.

Jesus made the point that God can accomplish what is impossible for man; he saves men from the penalty of their sins. When he was asked by his disciples who could be saved, Jesus stated: "With men this is impossible; but with God all things are possible." Matthew 19:26. Notice that Jesus states that salvation is impossible for men. The context of his statement is important. Jesus had just told his disciples that "[i]t is easier for a camel to go through the eye of a needle, than for a rich man to enter into the kingdom of God." Matthew 19:24. His disciples thought that salvation then was impossible and asked him: "Who then can be saved?" Matthew 19:25. Jesus made the point that salvation was impossible for man, but all things, including salvation, are possible for God. This impeaches the Arminian claim that man can choose salvation of his own free will. Jesus states that is impossible; only God can do the impossible of saving his elect.

The instance of the rich man in Matthew 19 completely eviscerates the Arminian position that Jesus died for the everyone in the world and that all are given the ability to believe or not believe as they choose out of their own free will. Jesus is approached by a man who asks Jesus: "Good Master, what good thing shall I do, that I may have eternal life?" Matthew 19:16. Jesus tells him in pertinent part: "there is none good but one, that is, God." Matthew 19:17. Jesus is not denying that he (Jesus) is good, certainly Jesus is good, because he is God; Jesus is pointing out to the man that he (the man) is not good. So why is the man not good? Because the bible tells us that all men are enslaved to sin and are evil. Romans 3:23-24; 7:14-25; Jeremiah 17:9.

What Jesus said next points out to all the futility of man to believe in Jesus without being spiritually reborn by God. Jesus tells the man to keep all of the commandments, and the man claims that he has done that. Jesus then tells him that he must do one last thing: "If thou wilt be perfect, go and sell that thou hast, and give to the poor, and thou shalt have treasure in heaven: and come and follow me." Matthew 19:21. "But when the young man heard that saying, he went away sorrowful: for he had great possessions." Matthew 19:22.

Jesus then explained to his disciples: "It is easier for a camel to go through the eye of a needle, than for a rich man to enter into the kingdom of God." Matthew 19:24. Jesus stated that what is impossible for man is possible for God. Jesus was making the point that it was impossible for the rich to give up his possessions and follow Jesus. To follow Jesus requires that a man be born again. Man cannot do that of their own will because their will is enslaved to sin. The man found it impossible to follow Jesus because he was enslaved to sin.

It is at this point that most preachers, particularly Arminian preachers, opine that the man was not saved, because he lacked faith. The passage, however, says no such thing. It simply states that he went away sorrowful because he had great possessions. When one looks to the whole counsel of God we see that the man was ultimately saved, which was manifested at some time after he spoke with Jesus. Going to the gospel of Mark we read: "Then Jesus beholding him loved him." Mark 10:21. If Jesus loved the rich man, then that means that the man was at some point saved. He may not have been born again with saving faith at the moment Jesus spoke with him, but it certainly came later. If Jesus loves someone, they will be saved. The gospel is clear that all those in the "world" "God so loved" in John 3:16 are saved; in John 3:16, "world" means only those that "God so loved."

The Arminian view, however, is that Jesus just let the rich man go his way into perdition even though Jesus loved him. The Arminians claim that God will not interfere with man's (supposed) free will. But let us look at what the bible says about the love of God. In John 14:13, Jesus states: "Greater love hath no man than this, that a man lay down his life for his friends." Jesus then tells his disciples that they are not his servants, but rather his friends. John 14:14-15. Jesus then makes it clear: "Ye have not chosen me, but I have chosen you." John 14:13. Jesus laid down his life for his friends, whom he loved. All of those for whom Jesus laid down his life were chosen by Jesus; they did not choose him. That means that the "world" that "God so loved" in John 3:16 were saved by the sacrifice of the only begotten son of God, who laid down his life for his friends.

The modern Arminian model of evangelism bears no resemblance to how Jesus evangelized the rich man in Matthew 19. John Cheeseman explains why:

I am convinced that much modern preaching which purports to be evangelical falls short of scriptural teaching and has little in common with the example of the Master Evangelist, the Lord Jesus Christ Himself. How would much modern evangelistic preaching and writing answer the question of the rich young ruler, 'What must I do to inherit life?'? The following answer is probably typical: 'If I am to benefit from Christ's death I must take three simple steps, of which the first two are preliminary, and the third so final that it will make me a Christian: I must believe that I am, in God's sight, a sinner, that is, I must admit my need; I must believe that Christ died for me; I must come to him, and claim my

personal share in what He did for everybody.' Under the
third and final step is explained how the willing sinner must
'open the door of his heart to Christ', the Christ who waits
patiently outside the door until we open it to Him.

It is undeniable that such an answer, or something like it, is
frequently presented today, and those who use this method
probably justify it by claiming that it includes the central
doctrines of the gospel — repentance, faith, conversion,
substitutionary atonement, the sinfulness of man, and so on.
If someone 'takes the step' but later questions the validity
of his conversion, he is assured, 'You took a simple step,
you committed yourself to Jesus Christ, but then God
performed a stupendous miracle. He gave you new life; you
were born again.' The concluding advice is often given:
'Tell somebody today what you have done.' This answer
bears little resemblance to Jesus' reply to the rich young
ruler (Mark 10:17-22).

The following is a summary of some of the basic doctrines
or presuppositions of this modern gospel:

Unregenerate men can repent and believe.

Christ died for the sins of every man individually.

Committing oneself to Christ, or deciding for Him, or
coming to Him, is an act which the sinner can do as he wills
at any time; that is, it is an act of free will.

Although God may be said to have taken the initiative in a
general sense by sending Christ to die to make salvation
possible, in any particular conversion it is the sinner who
takes the initiative by coming to Christ, and it is God who
responds.

Now let us compare these doctrines with the teaching of
scripture:

The unregenerate man cannot believe the gospel, because it is foolishness to him; spiritual truths are spiritually discerned, and he lacks the requisite faculty, being spiritually dead in trespasses and sins (1 Cor. 1:18; 2:14, Eph. 2:1).

It follows that he must be born again (which is the sovereign act of God) before he can repent and believe. Faith in Christ is the gift of God. Thus salvation is wholly of the Lord; He takes the initiative (John 3:3-8, Phil. 1:6, 29, Jon. 2:9, 1 Pet. 1:2).

There is no gospel command in Scripture to believe that Christ died for your sins. No one can have legitimate assurance of this until he has been saved and can make his 'calling and election sure' by wholehearted trust and obedience. Rather, the gospel command is to repent and believe in Christ as the only Saviour, believing his promises and casting oneself on His mercy. We have already seen that Christ died for the elect (or, for those who believe) (John 10:11—16; 15:13—14, Rom. 5:6—11, Eph. 5:25-27, Heb. 9:15).

This modern gospel is presented with no hint that God is sovereign and active in drawing to Himself those whom He has chosen. In Scripture these truths are not hidden lest they should cause offence; they are declared and even emphasized, since God is glorified when man can boast of nothing in himself as the cause of salvation. 'I contribute nothing to my salvation except the sin from which I need to be saved' (Acts 13:48, Matt. 11:25—30, John 6:63—65; 15:16, Rom. 9:14—24).

It is implied that Christ's death merely made salvation possible for all, the salvation becoming actual only on the condition of belief. But the Scriptures without exception speak of Christ's death as actually effective in itself, because of its substitutionary nature, to redeem, reconcile, ransom and save to the uttermost (Rom. 5:10, 2 Cor. 5:21, Eph. 2:13, 1 Thess. 5:9, 10, Heb. 10:10, 1 Pet. 1:18-20, 1 John 4:10, Rev. 1:5).[149]

The helplessness of man of his own unregenerate will to believe in Jesus without first being born again by the sovereign election of God is revealed by Jesus in John 10. Jesus states: **"I am the good shepherd: the good shepherd giveth his life for the sheep."** John 10:11. The Jews later approached Jesus at Jerusalem and asked him if he is the Christ, to which Jesus states:

> I told you, and ye believed not: the works that I do in my Father's name, they bear witness of me. **But ye believe not, because ye are not of my sheep,** as I said unto you. My sheep hear my voice, and I know them, and they follow me: And I give unto them eternal life; and they shall never perish, neither shall any man pluck them out of my hand. My Father, which gave them me, is greater than all; and no man is able to pluck them out of my Father's hand. I and my Father are one.

Jesus is stating how his sheep are elected by him through faith. Notice that Jesus did not say they are not his sheep because they don't believe, he instead states that they don't believe because they are not his sheep. Such passages, found throughout the bible, impeach the Arminian theology. Jesus is the good shepherd who gives his life for his sheep. Those who do not believe that he is the Christ are not his sheep. Jesus did not lay his life down for those who do not believe in him. In John 15:19, Jesus makes the point that he chose those who would believe in him "out of the world." Jesus' sheep do not choose him, Jesus chooses his sheep. John 14:13. The great love Jesus had of laying down his life for his friends is limited to only those who are his sheep, his chosen. Those passages put an end to the Arminian nonsense that John 3:16 means that Jesus died for the everyone in the "world," both saved and unsaved.

God did the impossible of saving the "world," as he expressly stated he would in John 3:16-18. The "world" God saved is made up only of those whom God elected by his sovereign and omnipotent grace to believe in Jesus.

The single passage of the bible that best sheds light on what is meant by John 3:16 is found in 1 John 4:9-10.

> In this was manifested the love of God toward us, because that God sent his only begotten Son into the world, that we might live through him. Herein is love, not that we loved God, but that he loved us, and sent his Son to be the propitiation for our sins. (1 John 4:9-10 AV)

In that passage we see that John is pointing out that God manifested his love "for us" by sending Jesus "to be the propitiation for our sins." A propitiatory sacrifice is a sacrifice that appeases and satisfies God's need to justly punish sin. Obviously, Jesus was only a propitiation for the sins of those whom he chose for salvation.

If, as claimed by the Arminians, Jesus died for everyone in the world, God would be sending people to hell for sins for which Jesus already satisfied God. Under the Arminian view, where Jesus died for all of the sins of everyone in the world, the sacrifice of Jesus on the cross was largely ineffective. God was not satisfied by the sacrifice of the Arminian Jesus. Which means that the Arminian Jesus' sacrifice on the cross was not a propitiation. That simply cannot be! The propitiation by Jesus' sacrifice is the whole point of the gospel! The Arminian gospel is the different gospel that Paul warned us about. 2 Corinthians 11:4; Galatians 1:6.

Another point made in 1 John 4:9-10 is "Herein is love, not that we loved God, but that he loved us." It was God who loved us, and sent Jesus as a propitiation for our sins. Man is incapable of his own free will to love God. It was necessary for God to send Jesus to save his elect. Man's condition is that he does not love God, he sent Jesus not to condemn the world, the world was already condemned. God "so loved" the world that he sent Jesus to save the world, by sacrificing himself on the cross. The "world" God "so loved" was saved by the sacrifice of his only begotten son who was a propitiation only for those whom he had chosen for salvation.

The God of the bible has an unconditional love for his children; whereas the Arminian god has a conditional love for his children. The love of the Arminian god is conditioned on the free will faith of the Arminian believer. The Arminian god is a treacherous god, who the Arminians claim loves everyone in the world, but in the end he casts most of his loved ones into a lake of fire to be tormented for all eternity.

The God of the bible has an unconditional love for his children. God provides the faith for those whom he has chosen for salvation, because they are powerless in themselves to have faith. Jon Hendryx explains:

> God's love is unconditional for those He intends to adopt as His children. He does not make us meet a condition (faith) before He will love us, as the Arminian affirms. Rather, He meets the condition for us in Christ by doing for us what we are unable to do for ourselves, that is, giving us everything we need for salvation, including a new heart to believe. (Ezek 36:26).[150]

23 Propitiation for the Sins of the Whole World

any Arminians cite the verse at 1 John 2:2 as authority for the proposition that Jesus died for all the sinners in the world.[151] "And he is the propitiation for our sins: and not for ours only, but also for the sins of the whole world." (1 John 2:2 AV) At first blush, it would seem that 1 John 2:2 supports the Arminian view. The reason the passage seems to support their position is that they have isolated that passage from the whole counsel of God. The Arminians have wrongly divided the passage from the whole gospel and given it a meaning that was not intended by God. People who do not search the scripture, as did the noble Bereans, will be easily deceived by the Arminian sophistry. *See* Acts 17:10-11.

Bible passages taken out of context may seem to be all encompassing, but when the passage is read in context, it becomes clear that God has a more limited application only to the subject under discussion. For example, in 1 Corinthians 3:5, God stated that "every man" is given belief. Obviously, the every man is not every man in the whole world, but rather every man elected to believe.

Who then is Paul, and who is Apollos, but ministers by whom ye believed, even **as the Lord gave to every man**? I

have planted, Apollos watered; but God gave the increase.
So then neither is he that planteth any thing, neither he that
watereth; but God that giveth the increase. 1 Corinthians
3:5-7.

Another point made by God in the passage, which is the
consistent theme throughout the bible, is that God gives the increase.
Paul and Apollos were simply ministers of the gospel. It is God that
saves. He gives the belief to every man elected for salvation. The
church is God's building constructed according to the election of his
grace. 1 Corinthians 3:9-10.

If one reads 1 John 2:2 in view of the entire gospel, it becomes
clear that the "world" in that passage does not mean everyone in the
world. The word "world" has a different meaning in different
passages, based upon the context of the passage. That topic was
touched upon in the previous chapter, but it bears repeating and some
elaboration.

Different contexts give rise to different meanings for "world."
For example, in Romans 11:12 the context clearly indicates that God
uses "world" to refer to only the Gentiles: "Now if the fall of them
be the riches of the world, and the diminishing of them the riches of
the Gentiles; how much more their fulness?" (Romans 11:12 AV)

In other passages God uses "world" to refer to the earth: "Now
before the feast of the passover, when Jesus knew that his hour was
come that he should depart out of this world unto the Father, having
loved his own which were in the world, he loved them unto the end."
(John 13:1 AV)

In John 15:18-19 God used the word "world" to refer only to the
unregenerate in the world, which does not include believers:

If the **world** hate you, ye know that it hated me before it
hated you. If ye were of the **world**, the **world** would love
his own: but because ye are not of the **world**, but I have
chosen you out of the **world**, therefore the **world** hateth

you. (John 15:18-19 AV)

Notice that in John 15 Jesus states that he chose his disciples out of the "world" and that the "world" hates them, because the "world" hates Jesus. The most illuminating point for our present topic is that Jesus states that his chosen "are not of the world." That means that the "world" in John 15 does not include believers. It is a very different "world" from the "world" in 1 John 2:2. If the believers are "not of the world" that means that there is a world that is made up of only the lost who hate Jesus and are damned to hell. Clearly that is not the "whole world" for whom Jesus is a propitiation for sins in 1 John 2:22. In order to be saved, a person must have faith that Jesus' atoning blood will save him; one who hates Jesus is not such a person.

We see also in 1 John 5:19 that God is not referring to believers: "And we know that we are of God, and the whole world lieth in wickedness." 1 John 5:19. In 1 John 2:15 God is referring to the material temptations of the world: "Love not the world, neither the things that are in the world. If any man love the world, the love of the Father is not in him." 1 John 2:15.

God had a different world in mind in 1 John 2:15, where he admonishes his followers to "love not the world," from the world he had in mind when he stated in John 3:16: "For God so loved the world, that he gave his only begotten Son, that whosoever believeth in him should not perish, but have everlasting life." Obviously, God would not "so love" the same "world" that he tells his disciples to "love not." They are different worlds.

Who is a part of this world in John 3:16? That world is only one that God "so loved." Who is in that world? We must look at the whole counsel of God. The answer is found in 2 Corinthians 5:19, where God explains the special people of his world: "To wit, that God was in Christ, reconciling the **world** unto himself, **not imputing their trespasses unto them**; and hath committed unto us the word of reconciliation." (2 Corinthians 5:19 AV)

Obviously, 2 Corinthians 5:19 does not refer to the entire world. The theme of the bible is that there are those who will be condemned and those that will be saved from condemnation. Revelation 20:10-15. God will not save the everyone in the world. Matthew 25:31-46. Additionally, God is not going to send people into hell to burn in a lake of fire for eternity after promising in 2 Corinthians 5:19 that he would not impute their trespasses to them.

In fact, God has stated that he would completely forgive and even forget the sins of his elect. "For I will be merciful to their unrighteousness, and their sins and their iniquities will I remember no more." (Hebrews 8:12 AV) Though the sins be crimson red God will so cleanse the sinner that they shall be white as snow. Isaiah 1:18. So, we know that those in the "world" to which God referred in 2 Corinthians 5:19 are those he has saved from damnation. Christ has reconciled God to them and no sins will be imputed to them.

There you have it. In 2 Corinthians 5:19, God explains that the world God "so loved" in John 3:16 is that world that he has reconciled unto himself and will not impute to them their trespasses. How did God reconcile the world "he so loved?" The answer brings us right back to 1 John 2:2. "And he is the propitiation for our sins: and not for ours only, but also for the sins of the whole world." (1 John 2:2 AV) Dr. D.A. Waite, however, interprets 2 Corinthians 5:19 to mean that Jesus reconciled to himself "every single man, woman, and child who has ever been born or who ever will be born in the future."

> The OBJECT of God's "RECONCILING" work in this verse is "THE WORLD." It is the same OBJECT as God's "LOVE" in John 3:16, "For God so LOVED THE WORLD...." It is NOT the world, merely of "the ELECT," but it is the "world" which includes every single man, woman, and child who has ever been born or who ever will be born in the future. . . . "Here is something that I did through My Son's Work at the Cross of Calvary which had an effect on the WHOLE, ENTIRE WORLD of mankind, barring NONE!!" The plain meaning of this verse is that in

some sense, God "RECONCILED" the entire WORLD unto
Himself in Christ. This does NOT mean, however, that all
the "WORLD" is thereby "SAVED." It merely means that
the PROVISION at Calvary was for ALL![152] (emphasis in
original).

Waite's Arminian interpretation of 2 Corinthians 5:19 simply
does not make biblical sense, because if Christ reconciled every
person in the entire world, on what basis does he punish most people
for eternity in hell? According to Waite, those sent to hell are not
sent there for their sins, because according to Waite, those were
atoned by Christ on the cross. According to Waite "the ONLY sin
that will 'condemn' a sinner, is the sin of 'NOT BELIEVING'"[153]
(emphasis in original).

Waite voices a popular Arminian view, that is also promoted by
best selling Arminian author Dave Hunt:

As a result of Christ's death having paid the full penalty, no
one will spend eternity in the lake of fire because of his
sins; they will be there for rejecting Christ and the salvation
He obtained and freely offers to all.[154]

The problem with the mythology of Hunt and Waite is that the
bible states clearly that people are sent to hell for "all" of their sins,
not just the sin of unbelief. Men will be judged according to the
"things" (plural) done in the body, not just the singular sin of
unbelief. Just nine verses earlier, in chapter 5 of Corinthians, Paul
makes that very point, a point that Hunt and Waite have missed.

For we must all appear before the judgment seat of Christ;
that every one may receive the things done in his body,
according to that he hath done, whether it be good or bad.
(2 Corinthians 5:10 AV)

If one is saved, his sins have been washed in the blood of the
lamb of God; he will therefore appear before God without spot,
wrinkle, or blemish. Ephesians 5:27. God will only see the perfect

righteousness of Christ, when he sees the believer. The believer's name is in the book of life. Whereas, the unsaved will be judged according to their "works" (plural). The bible is clear the men will be judged according to their many sins and it says nothing about men being judged according to the single sin of unbelief as claimed by Waite and other Arminians.

And I saw the dead, small and great, stand before God; and the books were opened: and another book was opened, which is the book of life: and the dead were judged out of those things which were written in the books, according to their works. (Revelation 20:12 AV)

Dr. Waite's Arminian theology cannot bear the weight of God's word. Jesus states clearly in Matthew 25:41-46 that the lost are judged according to their many individual sins. Those who are damned to hell gave no meat, gave no drink, did not cloth the naked, etc. Jesus did not atone for their sins, which means that Jesus did not reconcile the entire world to God by atoning for the sins of everyone in the world. He only reconciled the elect to God by atoning only for the sins of those he chose for salvation.

Then shall he say also unto them on the left hand, Depart from me, ye cursed, into everlasting fire, prepared for the devil and his angels: For I was an hungred, and ye gave me no meat: I was thirsty, and ye gave me no drink: I was a stranger, and ye took me not in: naked, and ye clothed me not: sick, and in prison, and ye visited me not. Then shall they also answer him, saying, Lord, when saw we thee an hungred, or athirst, or a stranger, or naked, or sick, or in prison, and did not minister unto thee? Then shall he answer them, saying, Verily I say unto you, Inasmuch as ye did *it* not to one of the least of these, ye did *it* not to me. And these shall go away into everlasting punishment: but the righteous into life eternal." (Matthew 25:41-46 AV)

In 1 John 2:2 we have Jesus described as the "propitiation" for the "whole world." The "whole world" in 1 John 2:2 is the same world God "so loved" in John 3:16 and that he reconciled to himself in 2 Corinthians 5:19. How can we be so sure? The answer is found in the context. The world in 1 John 2:2 is the world for which Jesus "is the propitiation."

What does propitiation mean? It means to atone in order to appease and to gain favor or goodwill. If Jesus was an atoning sacrifice to satisfy God, that sacrifice is all sufficient. Jesus does not partially save, he saves his elect to the "uttermost." Hebrews 7:25. Therefore, the "world" for which Jesus was the propitiation must all be saved and their sins completely forgiven through faith in his shed blood. Colossians 1:14. All sins committed by his elect are remitted by the grace of God through faith in the blood of Jesus.

> For all have sinned, and come short of the glory of God; Being justified freely by his grace through the **redemption** that is in Christ Jesus: Whom God hath set forth to be a **propitiation** through faith in his blood, to declare his righteousness for the remission of sins that are past, through the forbearance of God. (Romans 3:24-25 AV)

Jesus was a propitiation only for those he elected for salvation. If the "world" in 1 John 2:22 meant everyone in the world, both saved and damned, then God would be throwing people into hell for eternal punishment, for sins for which he has already been appeased. The Arminian god is a liar. The true God stated that once he is appeased "[T]heir sins and iniquities will I remember no more." (Hebrews 10:17 AV)

The Arminian god, however, is a heathen god, who goes back on his word and remembers the sins he promised to forget. The Arminian god then throws the sinner into hell for sins for which the Arminians claim Jesus died as a propitiation. The propitiatory sacrifice of Jesus is ineffective under the Arminian universal atonement gospel. Dr. D.A. Waite offers a typical Arminian interpretation of 1 John 2:2.

In layman's language, "PROPITIATION" simply means that

God was "SATISFIED" with the work on Calvary's Cross
of His Son, the Lord Jesus Christ! This clear teaching of the
verse of Scripture now under consideration extends God's
"SATISFACTION" in His Son's death not only to the
BELIEVERS, but also to the UNBELIEVERS who may
NEVER receive salvation by personal and individual faith
in Christ. This includes the "WHOLE WORLD." In other
words, God is satisfied that His Son has ACTUALLY, and
REALLY, and LITERALLY PAID for the SINS OF THE
WHOLE WORLD by His SACRIFICE on the Cross. This
does NOT, however, automatically insure the "WHOLE
WORLD" of receiving His forgiveness, pardon, and
everlasting life! It merely means that the PENALTY HAS
BEEN PAID, and now, the sinner need only "receive" and
"believe" (John 1:12) on the Lord Jesus Christ in heart-felt
"faith" (Acts 16:30-31) because, in a very real and literal
sense, as the songwriter has written, "JESUS PAID IT
ALL"!![155] (emphasis in original).

The clear implication of Dr. Waite's Arminian theology is that
the Arminian god unnecessarily punishes men in eternal hell. The
punishment is unnecessary, because Christ's crucifixion truly
satisfied God. Waite even acknowledges that fact. Waite has
artificially carved out a sin that condemns people to hell (the sin of
unbelief) but that is impossible under the Arminian unlimited
atonement, because Waite acknowledges that Christ atoned for all the
sins of everyone, which necessarily includes the sin of unbelief.
Waite is so wedded to his free will theology, he is oblivious to the
fact that he has constructed a false god who literally punishes people
for no reason. That is not the God of the bible.

The holy God of the bible keeps his word and saves to the
uttermost so that we appear to him without blemish or wrinkle.
Ephesians 5:27. If God is appeased for sin, committed by a person,
through the propitiation of Christ, he would not then punish that same
person. God was appeased by the crucifixion of Jesus for the whole
"world" in 1 John 2:2. The "world" in 1 John 2:2 is made up of only
those elected for salvation by God.

The gospel makes it impossible that the "world" in 1 John 2:2 includes anyone that is not saved. Jesus was the lamb of God who came to take sin of the world away. From whom did he succeed in taking sins away? From his elect in the "world." That is what John the Baptist meant when he said upon seeing Jesus: **"Behold the Lamb of God, which taketh away the sin of the world."** (John 1:29 AV) Jesus came to take away the sin of the world. Which "world" did John have in mind? Clearly, he did <u>not</u> have in mind the world ordained for damnation.

If God had in mind everyone in the world in John 1:29, then God failed, because most people in that "world" die in their sin. *See* Matthew 7:13-14. He did not take away the sins from the unsaved part of the world, for we know that they are cast into hell to be punished for their sins.

Jesus was the sacrificial lamb who died to take away the sin of the "world." John 1:29 was referring to the sin of the "world" who are elected by God for salvation. Marc Carpenter explains how clearly unbiblical is the Arminian interpretation that the "world" in John 1:29 means everyone in the entire world:

> Universal atonement advocates use John 1:29 to try to prove that their "christ" took away the sins of everyone without exception. Yet they also say that there are some who are burning in hell. Were the sins of those who are burning in hell taken away by the blood of their "christ"? If so, why are they burning in hell? It is because their "christ" actually accomplished NOTHING on the cross. There are people burning in hell for sins that were not pardoned or taken away. Their god is a liar when he says that this "christ" took away the sins of everyone without exception. The blood of their "christ" is of no effect in and of itself. And they blaspheme the true Jesus Christ by using His Name in their damnable heresy, claiming that the true Jesus Christ of the Bible paid the sin debt for everyone without exception.[156]

The Arminians' interpretation of John 1:29 is that Jesus failed in his mission to remit sins, since his sacrifice on the cross was ineffective for most. According to the Arminian view hell is populated with people for whom Jesus died. God has made it clear, however, that where there is remission of sin there is no more offering for sin needed. "Now where remission of these is, there is no more offering for sin." (Hebrews 10:18 AV) How can any of those for whom Jesus died ever be in hell, paying a price for sin for which there has already been atonement? It is impossible.

Jesus came for the purpose of taking away our sins. 1 John 3:5. "For this is my blood of the new testament, which is shed for many for the remission of sins." (Matthew 26:28 AV)   "[H]e appeared to put away sin by the sacrifice of himself." (Hebrews 9:26 AV) The Arminian theology that Jesus died for the whole world, saved and unsaved, means that they do not believe that Jesus succeeded in his mission of remitting sin.

Arminians treat John 12:47 similar to their treatment of 1 John 2:2. Arminians claim that the "world" in John 12:47 means everyone in the world.[157] In fact, when John 12:47 is read in context it is clear that the "world" Jesus describes is limited to only those who believe in Jesus. In John 12:47, Jesus stated that he came "to save the world." The context, however, indicates that there are those who would not believe in him. Obviously, "the world" Jesus came to save does not include everyone in the world; "the world" he came to save is made up only of those in the world chosen for salvation.

> I am come a light into the world, that whosoever believeth on me should not abide in darkness. And if any man hear my words, and believe not, I judge him not: for **I came not to judge the world, but to save the world**. He that rejecteth me, and receiveth not my words, hath one that judgeth him: the word that I have spoken, the same shall judge him in the last day. John 12:46-48.

If the "world" in John 12 means every person in the world, Jesus failed in his mission to save that "world." The bible, however, makes it clear that Jesus succeeded in his mission to save the world. Jesus succeeded in saving those whom he has chosen for salvation. Salvation is only for the elect of Jesus by his grace through the faith in his redeeming blood. "In whom we have redemption through his blood, the forgiveness of sins, according to the riches of his grace;" (Ephesians 1:7 AV)

Jesus' sacrifice on the cross was effective in cleansing those he elected for salvation. "[T]he blood of Jesus Christ his Son cleanseth us from all sin." (1 John 1:7 AV) He paid the price for their sin on the cross and redeemed them, so they no longer have to pay the price for that sin. Galatians 3:13.

The blood of Jesus satisfied God, and therefore all those for whom Jesus sacrificed himself are saved from the wrath of God. "Much more then, being now justified by his blood, we shall be saved from wrath through him." (Romans 5:9 AV) The sacrifice of Jesus on the cross was the purchase price to redeem us from the consequences of sin. 1 Corinthians 6:20. "Verily, verily, I say unto you, He that heareth my word, and believeth on him that sent me, hath everlasting life, and shall not come into condemnation; but is passed from death unto life." (John 5:24 AV)

Jesus washes his elect with his blood; his shed blood was effective; it was not simply, as claimed by the Arminians, a conditional sacrifice that only made it possible for salvation if man of his own free will decides to believe. "And from Jesus Christ, who is the faithful witness, and the first begotten of the dead, and the prince of the kings of the earth. Unto him that loved us, and washed us from our sins in his own blood." (Revelation 1:5 AV) **"As far as the east is from the west, *so* far hath he removed our transgressions from us."** Psalms 103:10-12.

The blood of Jesus satisfied God, and therefore all those for whom Jesus sacrificed himself are saved from the wrath of God. "Much more then, being now justified by his blood, we shall be saved from wrath through him." (Romans 5:9 AV) His sacrifice was prophesied; the effectiveness of his sacrifice was also prophesied.

His sacrifice healed us from our sins. "But he was wounded for our transgressions, he was bruised for our iniquities: the chastisement of our peace was upon him; and with his stripes we are healed." (Isaiah 53:5 AV) It is unbiblical to suggest, as the Arminians do, that Jesus died as a propitiation for all, because under that Arminian universal atonement fiction, Jesus' sacrifice is ineffective for most people. God, however, was "satisfied" by the sacrifice of Jesus, who bore all of our iniquities on the cross.

> He shall see of the travail of his soul, and **shall be satisfied**: by his knowledge shall my righteous servant justify many; for he shall bear their iniquities. Isaiah 53:11 (emphasis added).

The scripture states that Jesus' promised propitiation was effective. He healed believers from their sin by taking them upon himself on the cross, just as prophesied in Isaiah: "Who his own self bare our sins in his own body on the tree, that we, being dead to sins, should live unto righteousness: by whose stripes ye were healed." (1 Peter 2:24 AV) Every sin that is forgiven by God has been paid for by Jesus on the cross. Every sin that has not been forgiven, was not paid for by Jesus on the cross. Jesus only atoned for those whom God elected for salvation by his grace through faith in Jesus' atoning blood.

Jesus was <u>not</u> a substitutionary sacrifice for <u>everyone</u> in the world; he was a substitionary sacrifice <u>only</u> for those <u>chosen</u> by God for salvation. **"Who gave himself for <u>us</u>, that he might redeem <u>us</u> from all iniquity**, and **purify unto himself a peculiar people**, zealous of good works." (Titus 2:14 AV) Jesus' elect are a peculiar people whom Jesus has redeemed from **"all iniquity."** If Jesus **"gave himself"** to redeem his elect from **"all iniquity"** how could the Arminians claim that most of those for whom Jesus died will end up in hell for their iniquity? The Arminian theology is simply wrong. The Arminian theology is directly contrary to the gospel message of he atoning sacrifice of Jesus, which redeems only his elect from all sin and the penalty for that sin.

Many seminaries teach the ineffectual atonement of Jesus. These seminaries are putting out hundreds of graduates each year who spread their false doctrine like a plague into churches throughout the world. One of example is that of Dallas Theological Seminary, which is perhaps the largest and most prestigious Protestant seminary in the United States. On July 20, 1977, Dallas Theological Seminary's President, John P Walvoord, wrote a letter to Dr. D.A. Waite, which was intended to be published, wherein he expressly denied the limited atonement of Jesus. Dr. Walvoord stated that the official position of Dallas Theological Seminary is that Jesus atoned for the sins of everyone in the entire world.

> Dr. Walvoord spoke of the Seminary's Doctrinal Statement on this issue: Our DOCTRINAL STATEMENT does not deal with the subject of the five points of Calvinism or use the terminology of LIMITED OR UNLIMITED ATONEMENT. It does, however, indicate that CHRIST DIED FOR THE WHOLE WORLD, and in my thinking, THIS IS NOT IN KEEPING WITH THE DOCTRINE OF LIMITED OR PARTICULAR ATONEMENT as is commonly thought. (op. cit.) . . . Walvoord talked of the present faculty's position on this question: Through the years of its existence, Dallas Seminary's position has been and is that CHRIST DIED FOR ALL in the provisional sense, even though only the elect are saved. Our position on this doctrine, as well as all others stated in our doctrinal statement, HAS NOT CHANGED. Members of our FACULTY under contract to teach for the school year beginning July 1, 1977, SPECIFICALLY HOLD TO UNLIMITED ATONEMENT. (op. cit.).[158] (emphasis in original).

It is sad that the largest Protestant seminary in the United States adamantly adheres to a doctrinal position which stands for the proposition that everyone who is sent to hell is sent there to be punished for sins for which the penalty was already paid by Jesus on the cross.

The substitutionary atonement of Christ puts a hole right through the Arminian theology. Arminians have come up with various explanations in an attempt to hide that theological hole. One method is to ignore the clear biblical authority and claim that Jesus' crucifixion did not pay the penalty for sin at all. Some Arminians claim that Jesus' death on the cross "could not have been to pay the penalty, since no one would then ever go into eternal perdition."[159] This mythology is echoed by Methodist theologian William Burt Pope, who theorized that while Christ died for the whole world, he could not have shed his blood for everyone as a substitutionary sacrifice, otherwise most of his blood was shed in vain.[160]

Not all Arminians buy the argument that Christ did not die on the cross as an atonement for sin. The bible authority establishing Christ's atonement is just too compelling for them. The clear biblical authority, however, puts Arminians in a theological quandary. If Christ died on the cross as an atonement for the sins of everyone in the world, as claimed by Arminians, why are most people cast into hell?

One theologian, Donald Lake, tries to answer that difficult question for Arminians by claiming that people are not cast into hell for their sins. His theory is similar to Waite's and Hunt's. Lake opines that Jesus died as an atonement for the sins of the whole world and therefore everyone, including people cast into hell, are legally sinless. Lake claims that people are damned to hell not based upon their sin but rather their "reaction to what God has done in Christ."[161] Lake states:

> [S]ince Christ has finished his work of redemption upon the cross, the ground of our salvation has completely shifted. What is it that condemns a man? Is it his sins, large or small, numerous or few, that condemns a man and sends him into a Christless eternity? The answer of the New Testament is an absolute No! What condemns a man is not sins. Why? Because Christ's redemptive and atoning work is complete and satisfying. Even man's rejection cannot frustrate the purposes of God. The issue of every man's

salvation turns not upon his sins, but rather upon his
relationship to the Son! Sin may have made the cross
necessary, but the cross has now made sin irrelevant as far
as man's relationship to God is concerned. This is, perhaps,
a little too strong, but the fact is, that man's problem now is
not so much sin or sins, but his reaction to what God has
done in Christ[162]

As with Waite's and Hunt's mythology, Lake's construct makes
no sense. Responding to Christ in unbelief is a sin. Even so, Lake
has his Arminian god throwing sinless people into hell. Mark Herzer
has this reaction to Lake's unbiblical folderol:

If the above quote [from Lake] is true, then it also follows
that one cannot really call anyone a 'sinner' because no sin
can technically be imputed to them. However, unbelief is
sin but didn't Christ die for all sins? Alas, I quibble. Who
am I to say that such inconsistency is laughable? Perhaps
we should shudder instead.[163]

The universal atonement model of the Arminians is impossible
according to scripture, because Jesus's atonement was a
substitutionary atonement. That means that Jesus took the sins of his
elect and his elect received the righteousness of Christ. If Jesus was
an atoning sacrifice for everyone in the world, that means that
everyone in the world would have taken on the righteousness of
Christ. If everyone took on the righteousness of Christ, then in God's
eyes they are legally righteous and would not be punished for their
sins. The Arminian theology of universal atonement populates hell
with those who have the righteousness of Christ

The bible tells us that only those chosen by God for salvation by
the Grace of God through faith in Jesus Christ are given the
righteousness of Christ. All sins for which Jesus was a propitiation
were remitted, and all who have had their sins remitted are declared
righteous in God's eyes. The Arminian universal atonement allows
for only two possibilities: 1) hell is populated entirely with persons
who have the perfect righteousness of Christ, or 2) Jesus's sacrifice

on the cross was ineffective in atoning for sin. The inerrant word of
God does not allow for either possibility.

> For all have sinned, and come short of the glory of God;
> Being justified freely by his grace through the **redemption**
> that is in Christ Jesus: Whom God hath set forth to be a
> **propitiation through faith in his blood, to declare his**
> **righteousness for the remission of sins** that are past,
> through the forbearance of God. (Romans 3:23-25 AV)

All those for whom Jesus died were imputed with Jesus's
righteousness. That was the purpose of Jesus's crucifixion. The
Arminian universal atonement frustrates God's purpose and
condemns to hell most of those who have been imputed with the
righteousness of Jesus.

> And all things are of God, who hath reconciled us to
> himself by Jesus Christ, and hath given to us the ministry of
> reconciliation; To wit, that God was in Christ, reconciling
> the world unto himself, **not imputing their trespasses**
> **unto them**; and hath committed unto us the word of
> reconciliation. Now then we are ambassadors for Christ, as
> though God did beseech *you* by us: we pray you in Christ's
> stead, be ye reconciled to God. **For he hath made him to**
> **be sin for us, who knew no sin; that we might be made**
> **the righteousness of God in him.** (2 Corinthians 5:18-21
> AV)

How do the Arminian theologians address this truth that crushes
their theology? They simply deny the biblical account. The popular
Arminian theologian and bible commentator Adam Clarke denies the
imputation of the righteousness of Christ to the believer.

> To say that Christ's personal righteousness is imputed to
> every true believer, is not scriptural: To say that he has
> fulfilled all righteousness for us, in our stead, if by this is
> meant his fulfilment of all moral duties, is neither scriptural
> nor true? In no part of the Book of God is Christ's

righteousness ever said to be imputed to us for our
justification.[164]

This denial of the imputation of Christ's righteousness to the
believer is well established among Arminian theologians. The
eminent Arminian theologian Richard Watson joins with Clarke in
contradicting the bible on the issue of the imputation of the
righteousness of Christ. Clarke states that Christ's righteousness "as
to be accounted as our own, [has] no warrant in the Word of God."[165]
Arminian theologian A.M. Hills adds his opinion that "there can be
no such thing as a transfer, or imputation, either of guilt or of
righteousness."[166] William Burt Pope, yet another Arminian
theologian, joins the chorus against the biblical imputation of
righteousness by claiming that there is no imputation of our sins to
Christ nor his righteousness to us.

> Is the personal righteousness of Christ Himself reckoned to
> the believer as his own? Assuredly not; any more than the
> personal sin of the sinner was reckoned to be Christ's.
> Moreover, as the Divine Son of God could not have our
> individual sins imputed to Him, so His Divine-human
> obedience was altogether beyond the range of man's
> obedience to the law. There could not be any such personal
> transfer.[167]

Just saying that there is no imputation of righteousness of Christ
to the believer does not make it so. These eminent Arminian
theologians have a problem, because their theology is directly
contrary to what the bible states. *See* 2 Corinthians 5:18-21; Romans
3:23-25. God states that "**the righteousness of God** without the law
is manifested, being witnessed by the law and the prophets; Even **the
righteousness of God** which is by faith of Jesus Christ **unto all and
upon all them that believe**." Romans 3:22. A believer indeed is
crucified with Christ, and Christ and his righteousness live in the
believer. Galatians 2:20. Not only is Christ in us, we are in Christ,
and we are imbued with his righteousness. 1 Corinthians 1:30.

The simplicity of the gospel is just too much for the Arminians;

it is foolishness to them to think that God predestined his elect for salvation by the grace of God through faith in the atoning blood of Jesus Christ. The universal atonement fiction is necessary in order for the Arminian free will fiction to make any sense. While the concepts of universal atonement and free will are logically consistent, they are biblically wrong. The Arminians must take the glory from God and give back to man a fictional free will whereby he may glory in his fictional salvation, whereby he is reborn of his own free will.

> For the preaching of the cross is to them that perish foolishness; but unto us which are saved it is the power of God. For it is written, I will destroy the wisdom of the wise, and will bring to nothing the understanding of the prudent. Where is the wise? where *is* the scribe? where *is* the disputer of this world? hath not God made foolish the wisdom of this world? For after that in the wisdom of God the world by wisdom knew not God, it pleased God by the foolishness of preaching to save them that believe. For the Jews require a sign, and the Greeks seek after wisdom: But we preach Christ crucified, unto the Jews a stumblingblock, and unto the Greeks foolishness; But unto them which are **called**, both Jews and Greeks, Christ the power of God, and the wisdom of God. Because the foolishness of God is wiser than men; and the weakness of God is stronger than men. For ye see your **calling**, brethren, how that not many wise men after the flesh, not many mighty, not many noble, are **called**: But God hath **chosen** the foolish things of the world to confound the wise; and God hath **chosen** the weak things of the world to confound the things which are mighty; And base things of the world, and things which are despised, hath God **chosen**, yea, and things which are not, to bring to nought things that are: That no flesh should glory in his presence. But of him are ye in Christ Jesus, who of God is made unto us wisdom, and righteousness, and sanctification, and redemption: That, according as it is written, He that glorieth, let him glory in the Lord. (1 Corinthians 1:18-31 AV)

24 Denying the Lord that Bought Them

Many Arminians cite 2 Peter 2:1 in support of their claim that Jesus died to atone for the sins of everyone in the world, both the lost and the saved. Let us read that passage in context. 2 Peter 2:1-3 states:

> But there were false prophets also among the people, even as there shall be false teachers among you, who privily shall bring in damnable heresies, even **denying the Lord that bought them**, and bring upon themselves swift destruction. And many shall follow their pernicious ways; by reason of whom the way of truth shall be evil spoken of. And through covetousness shall they with feigned words make merchandise of you: **whose judgment now of a long time lingereth not, and their damnation slumbereth not**. 2 Peter 2:1-3.

Robert Lightner provides an Arminian interpretation of that passage. He claims that the false teachers have had their sins atoned by Jesus, even though they are clearly damned to hell. They are damned to hell because, according to Lightner, the false teachers did not believe in Jesus. Lightner's conclusion is based entirely on his interpretation that the world "bought" means atoned.

[T]here are instances in Scripture where the word "redeem"
or its cognates are used of Christ-rejectors. The best
example of such a usage is found in 2 Peter 2:1 (cf. Gal. 4:4
5). Therefore, since the word "atonement" has come to refer
to the totality of the completed work of Christ, and since
redemption used of both saved and unsaved, we have used
them both when speaking of Christ's work on the cross. It is
readily admitted, of course, that no one benefits from that
purchased redemption until he believes in Christ as his
Redeemer.[168]

Samual Telloyan is yet another Arminian voice interpreting 2
Peter 2:1 as supporting unlimited atonement. His claim is that Jesus
atoned for the sins of both the elect and those who are damned to
perdition.

The false prophets in this verse are unsaved, for they are
headed for destruction. Peter under the Holy Spirit says that
even though they are unsaved Christ died for them. Lenski
stated, "Here we have an adequate answer to Calvin's
limited atonement: The Sovereign, Christ, bought with His
blood not only the elect but also those who go to
perdition."[169]

Lightner and Telloyan's claim that 2 Peter 2:1 is authority for
their unlimited atonement theory is not supported by language in the
passage itself. They claim that "bought" in that passage means that
Christ atoned for the sins of the lost false teachers. Thus, the lost
have the possibility of salvation if they would only exercise their free
will and believe. The problem with that interpretation is that the
passage could not be referring to atonement, since the atonement in
that passage is described as a completed purchase, which means
salvation.

If "bought" in 2 Peter 2:1 means "atonement," that would mean
that the false teachers mentioned in 2 Peter 2:1 were saved by Christ.
That is because verse one makes it clear that the purchase by the Lord
was an accomplished fact, not just a possibility. The Lord did not

make the purchase possible, he accomplished it, he "bought them." If a person purchases something, he is said to have bought it. There is no contingency. It is an accomplished fact. "Bought" in 2 Peter 2:1 is not a potential purchase, it is a completed purchase. "Bought," therefore, could not mean a potential for salvation was ever held out to the false teachers, since "bought" means a completed act. The passage makes it clear that the false teachers are damned to hell, hence "bought" could not mean salvation. Simon Escobedo explains:

> Notice what the text says. These men were "bought" by the Master. These men were not "potentially" bought but were in fact "bought," period! The non-Reformed exegete is inconsistent in using this passage in the form in which Peter wrote it. . . . [Arminians use the following argument:]
>
> "Isn't it possible for me to purchase an ice cream cone each for 10 children and have 5 of them refuse to take one? Does their refusal to accept my "purchase" mean that I never really purchased any ice cream for them at all?"
>
> One can see that the argument was not thought through. The illustration is seriously flawed and only proves my point. What is bought in the above illustration? Ice cream. That is, ice cream is the direct object of the objector's own verb "buy."

* * *

2 Peter 2:1, again states, "denying the Lord who bought them." In other words, in laymen's terms, what is the object of the participle bought? Quite simply, it is "them" i.e. the false teachers. To suggest that He "bought them" but does not "own them" is to betray the simple reading of the text. It is often argued by non-Reformed folk that Reformed adherents "reject" the "plain" meaning of Scripture.

* * *

Notice the illustration does not say that he bought ten children. Such would then parallel Peter's words. Rather, the illustration states that he bought something for 10 children. Peter, however, does not say that they denied the Lord who bought something for them (the implication is redemption) but that they themselves were the objects of the Master's purchase. Could Peter have stated that any more clearly?

* * *

Do we need to add the words "potential," "died," "to purchase" to the text? When we see, "denying the Lord who bought them," do we not simply take it as it is? Whatever else Peter may be saying, what he is not saying is that these were men who were potentially bought and hence did not belong to the Master at all.[170]

The context of "bought" used in 2 Peter 2:1 poses a problem for the Arminian view of that verse, since the language in the verse simply does not support the claim that the false teachers are given the possibility of salvation through the atonement of Christ, which the Arminians claim was not realized by the false teachers due to their unbelief. If "bought" means "atonement," as claimed by the Arminians, that means that the atonement was effective in saving the false teachers. But interpreting "bought" to mean "atone" makes no sense, since verses 3, 12, and 17 of 2 Peter, chapter 2, expressly state that the false teachers are lost.

The only way for Arminians to plausibly explain the passage is to claim that the false teachers are to be saved and then later lose their salvation through their willful unbelief. However, that is not the claim made by Arminians, and there is nothing in the passage to support that view. In fact, verses 3, 12 and 17 of 2 Peter 2 make that interpretation impossible.

It is impossible that the false teachers are to be saved but later lose their salvation, because Peter is actually making a prophecy in verses 3 of 2 Peter, chapter 2, regarding the eventual damnation of the false teachers. Peter refers to the false teachers by stating: "whose judgment now of a long time lingereth, and their damnation slumbereth not."

Peter reaffirms the prophecy of destruction in verse 17 where he states that "the mist of darkness is reserved for ever" for the false teachers. The false teachers had not yet made their entrance onto the stage of history, and yet Peter had already announced that they are damned to hell. Obviously, the false teachers have no chance for salvation.

Jesus did not atone for their sins; the false teachers are preordained for destruction. Indeed, Peter states that they were made by God to be destroyed. How could there be an unlimited atonement available to the false teachers if Peter states clearly that God "made them to be taken and destroyed?" God made the false teachers for the purpose of destroying them in darkness that was reserved them.

> But these, as natural brute beasts, **made to be taken and destroyed**, speak evil of the things that they understand not; and shall utterly perish in their own corruption. . . . These are wells without water, clouds that are carried with a tempest; **to whom the mist of darkness is reserved for ever**. 2 Peter 2:12, 17.

There are passages in the bible where "bought" means redeemed by the blood of Christ. *See, e.g.* 1 Corinthians 6:20. However, that is not the sense that "bought" is used in 2 Peter 2:1. The clue to what is meant by bought in 2 Peter 2:1 is found in the first clause "there were false prophets also among the people." He was referring to the false prophets among the Jews in the Old Testament. We read in Deuteronomy 32:5-6:

> They have corrupted themselves, their spot is not the spot of his children: they are a perverse and crooked generation. Do ye thus requite the LORD, O foolish people and unwise? is **not he thy father that hath bought thee?** hath

he not made thee, and established thee? Deuteronomy 32:5-6.

Peter alluded to Old Testament events that were all too familiar to the early church. Just as there were false prophets among the people of Israel, so also would there be false teachers of the same kind among them. Peter equated the false teachers of the New Testament with the false prophets of the Old Testament.

Wayne Grudem explains the meaning of 2 Peter 2:1 in light of Deuteronomy 32:6:

> 'Is not he your Father who has bought you?'...Peter is drawing an analogy between the past false prophets who arose among the Jews and those who will be false teachers within the churches to which he writes...From the time of the exodus onward, any Jewish person would have considered himself or herself one who was 'bought' by God in the exodus and therefore a person of God's own possession. ...So the text means not that Christ had redeemed these false prophets, but simply that they were rebellious Jewish people (or church attenders in the same position as rebellious Jews) who were rightly owned by God because they had been bought out of the land of Egypt (or their forefathers had), but they were ungrateful to him.[171]

The false teachers in 2 Peter 2:1 are Jews of the same sort as the pernicious false prophets criticized in Deuteronomy 32:5-6. In both cases they denied the Lord who purchased them. Jesus did not atone for their sins, in no sense are the false teachers ever saved, nor is there any possibility for their salvation.

25 Free Will Repentance is Salvation by Works

The key fact that kills Arminianism as a Christian theology is that God calls believers to repentance. "Bring forth therefore fruits meet for repentance:" Matthew 3:8. *See also* Acts 26:20. Indeed, the bible is clear that salvation brings repentance. Repentance is the flip side of faith. Once God moves a person to be born again, he is freed from sin and turns toward God in faith. The turning toward God involves a turning away from the former sin. While faith is not a work, repentance is manifested through works. If faith comes from God, then so does repentance.

> Or despisest thou the riches of his goodness and forbearance and longsuffering; not knowing that **the goodness of God leadeth thee to repentance**? (Romans 2:4 AV)

Repentance, which is the the turning from sin toward God is accomplished by God.

> **Turn us, O God of our salvation**, and cause thine anger toward us to cease. (Psalms 85:4 AV)

Man does not, indeed he cannot, repent of his sin on his own, because his will is enslaved to sin. Repentance is entirely of God. God changes the hearts of his elect and turns them to repent of their sins. "Unto you first God, having raised up his Son Jesus, sent him to bless you, **in turning away every one of you from his iniquities**." (Acts 3:26 AV)

If, as Arminians claim, the turning toward God is a free will decision, that means that the turning away from sin is also a free will decision. That, however, is not what God says. God reveals in the book of Acts that it is God who "grants" repentance.

> When they heard these things, they held their peace, and glorified God, saying, Then hath **God also to the Gentiles granted repentance unto life**. (Acts 11:18 AV)

The fact that repentance comes from God and not from the free will of man was clearly understood by the early church. We see the writer of 2 Timothy expressing God's sovereign rule over the hearts of men; God "gives" repentance.

> And the servant of the Lord must not strive; but be gentle unto all *men*, apt to teach, patient, In meekness instructing those that oppose themselves; **if God peradventure will give them repentance to the acknowledging of the truth**. (2 Timothy 2:24-25 AV)

Without God moving the heart of the penitent, there could never be repentance. It is Jesus that supplies the faith and the repentance.

> Him hath God exalted with his right hand *to be* a Prince and a Saviour, for **to give repentance to Israel**, and forgiveness of sins. (Acts 5:31 AV)

Repentance is manifested by works. If repentance is by the free will of man, that means that those works are born of man's free will. Such a theology constitutes salvation by works.

Read what the book of Acts states about the relationship of

repentance to salvation.

> Therefore let all the house of Israel know assuredly, that
> God hath made that same Jesus, whom ye have crucified,
> both Lord and Christ. Now when they heard *this*, they were
> pricked in their heart, and said unto Peter and to the rest of
> the apostles, Men *and* brethren, what shall we do? Then
> Peter said unto them, **Repent**, and be baptized every one of
> you in the name of Jesus Christ for the remission of sins,
> and ye shall receive the gift of the Holy Ghost. (Acts 2:36-
> 38 AV)

Notice that when the people heard Peter preach the gospel "they
were pricked in their heart." That was God effectually drawing them
to Christ. They then asked Peter "what shall we do?" Peter told
them to "repent, and be baptized." Repentance in the biblical context
means to change one's mind and stop sinning. If the people could
repent of their own free will that would make Peter's command to
repent a command to work their way to salvation.

The gospel, however, states that the spiritual rebirth is entirely
the work of the Holy Spirit. That means that repentance is a fruit of
the Spirit, which is also accomplished by God. It is not a work of the
free will of man at all. The gospel is salvation by grace through faith,
with repentance from sin being the fruit of the true faith of Jesus
Christ. Peter's command to the people to repent and be baptized was
not a command to work toward heaven, because they could not
repent, unless God gave then the faith of Jesus to turn toward him in
faith. Paul told King Agrippa how he preached the gospel to the
Gentiles. Paul stated that Jesus told him:

> But rise, and stand upon thy feet: for I have appeared unto
> thee for this purpose, to make thee a minister and a witness
> both of these things which thou hast seen, and of those
> things in the which I will appear unto thee; Delivering thee
> from the people, and *from* the Gentiles, unto whom now I
> send thee, To open their eyes, *and* to turn *them* from
> darkness to light, and *from* the power of Satan unto God,

that they may receive forgiveness of sins, and inheritance
among them which are sanctified by faith that is in me.
Whereupon, O king Agrippa, I was not disobedient unto the
heavenly vision: But shewed first unto them of Damascus,
and at Jerusalem, and throughout all the coasts of Judaea,
and *then* to the Gentiles, that **they should repent and turn
to God, and do works meet for repentance.**" (Acts 26:16-
20 AV)

Jesus commanded Paul to go to the Gentiles and "open their
eyes, and turn them from darkness to light, and from the power of
Satan unto God, that they may receive forgiveness of sins, and
inheritance among them which are sanctified by faith that is in me."
Paul's mission was to preach the gospel to the Gentiles. What did
Paul tell the Gentiles to do? Paul told the Gentiles to repent of their
sin and "do works meet for repentance." If repentance is a fruit of
the Spirit that is born by the faith of Jesus Christ, then Paul's
admonition was in complete accord with the gospel. If, as claimed by
Arminians, repentance is an act of the free will of man, then Paul was
all wrong in his approach. If repentance is a free will act, then Paul
was preaching a false gospel of works by telling them to "do works
meet for repentance."

Repentance and faith go hand in hand. Without works faith is
dead. That is what James meant when he said: "Even so faith, if it
hath not works, is dead, being alone." (James 2:17 AV) If, as claimed
by the Arminians, faith is from the free will of man, and given that
faith without works is dead, under the Arminian theology salvation is
by the free will works of man. Since under Arminianism man can
lose his salvation, he must be kept on his toes to work, work, work
his way to heaven lest he be found lacking.

A true Christian, on the other hand, will manifest his faith by his
works. The works, however, do not merit salvation. The faith of the
elect is from God and so are their works. The works are prepared by
God ahead of time for his elect to walk in them. Ephesians 2:10.
James explained:

Was not **Abraham** our father **justified by works**, when he had **offered Isaac** his son upon the altar? Seest thou how faith wrought with his works, and by works was faith made perfect? (James 2:21-22 AV)

Notice how James stated that works that are born of repentance are necessary fruits of saving faith. He even cites the very example of Abraham. Repentance is the flip side of faith and is manifested by works. Notice that in Hebrews 11:17 Paul states that Abraham offered up Isaac by "faith," yet James states that Abraham was "justified by works" when he offered Isaac as a sacrifice.

By faith Abraham, when he was tried, **offered up Isaac**: and he that had received the promises offered up his only begotten son," (Hebrews 11:17 AV)

James drives the point home that faith without works is not saving faith. Abraham's faith was perfect faith since it was manifested by his works. **"Seest thou how faith wrought with his** [Abraham's] **works, and by works was faith made perfect?"** (James 2:22 AV)

This same parallelism is seen with Rahab. James states that she was Justified by works (meaning that her faith was true faith that was manifested by works).

Likewise also was not **Rahab** the harlot **justified by works**, when she had received the messengers, and had sent *them* out another way? (James 2:25 AV)

However, that same Rahab was given as an example of faith in the letter to Hebrews.

By faith the harlot **Rahab** perished not with them that believed not, when she had received the spies with peace. (Hebrews 11:31 AV)

We are saved to bear fruit. God has ordained that his elect bear fruit. If you are saved, you will bear fruit, because God has willed it. "Ye have not chosen me, but I have chosen you, and **ordained you, that ye should go and bring forth fruit**, and that your fruit should remain: that whatsoever ye shall ask of the Father in my name, he may give it you." (John 15:16 AV)

That fruit will be manifested in the good works that spring from the new charitable heart God has given those who believe. Faith without works is dead!

> **Even so faith, if it hath not works, is dead**, being alone. Yea, a man may say, Thou hast faith, and I have works: shew me thy faith without thy works, and I will shew thee my faith by my works. Thou believest that there is one God; thou doest well: the devils also believe, and tremble. But wilt thou know, O vain man, **that faith without works is dead**? (James 2:17-20 AV)

God prunes us so that we will bear fruit: "Every branch in me that beareth not fruit he taketh away: and every branch that beareth fruit, he purgeth it, that it may bring forth more fruit." (John 15:2 AV) If a branch does not bear fruit it is good for nothing but destruction.

Jesus stated any fruit comes from him and that without him man can bear no fruit. "I am the vine, ye *are* the branches: He that abideth in me, and I in him, the same bringeth forth much fruit: for **without me ye can do nothing**." (John 15:5 AV)

There can be no faith without repentance, all repentance brings forth fruit. The bible states that all faith and repentance and fruit are from God. They all go together. The Arminian theology has faith and repentance and fruit, but they all come from man. The fruit of faith and repentance is good works. Since the Arminian believer is the source of the good works, Arminianism constitutes salvation by works.

The Arminian model of repentance is explained in the Arminian

Confession of 1621, which was drafted by Simon Episcopius (A/K/A Simon Bisschop), who was a protégé of Jacobus Arminius, and one of the principal Arminian Remonstrants. Arminianism requires that repentance be effectual, sincere, and continual.[172] The Arminian repentance requires the free will exercise of good works. Repentance "must always outwardly exert itself through acts of virtue, as often as there is occasion and can be done."[173]

While Episcopious acknowledges that the righteousness of Christ is imputed to one who believes, he gives that imputed righteousness a very different meaning than is given in the bible. He seems to mean that the righteousness is an imparted actual righteousness rather than a legal imputed righteousness. He states that the righteousness must be manifested in good works and that the good works are the means of justification. He cites to James, who does indeed state that "by works a man in justified, and not by faith only." James 2:24. James' point was made in light of the gospel of grace that faith without works is dead, which means that all who are saved will in fact do good works, which are prepared ahead of time by Christ for his elect to walk in them. Ephesians 2:10. Episcopius takes James 2:24 out of context to mean that man of his own free will can and indeed must do good works to obtain and maintain salvation. Episcopius bobs and weaves between bible verses in order to present the appearance of biblical authority, however, he is concealing the Arminian poison of free will *sub-silentio* in his argument.

According to the Arminian view of repentance, a Christian must continue to repent by doing good works of one's own free will. The Arminian theology is that a person who does not continue repenting and doing good works can lose his salvation. The official Arminian view, as presented in the remonstrance of 1610 is that a man who is saved is "capable, through negligence, of forsaking again the first beginnings of their life in Christ, of again returning to this present evil world, of turning away from the holy doctrine which was delivered them, of losing a good conscience, of becoming devoid of grace,"[174] and hence losing his salvation. Arminians believe that a believer can become an unbeliever through faithlessness that is manifested in persistent, unrepentant sin. There is simply no other way to describe the Arminian free will repentance than salvation by works.

Dr. Michael Scott Horton reveals that John Wesley, in his Minutes of the Methodist Conference, concluded that "his own position was but 'a hair's breadth' from 'salvation by works.'"[175] Dr. Horton informs us:

> Further, the Minutes for the First Annual Methodist Conference affirm that repentance and works must precede faith, if by works one means "obeying God as far as we can." "If a believer willfully sins, he thereby forfeits his pardon." "Are works necessary to continuance of faith? Without doubt, for a man may forfeit the gift of God either by sins of omission or commission."

If it walks like a duck and quacks like a duck, it is a duck. No matter how Arminians claim otherwise, their theology quacks "salvation by works." Dr. Horton explains:

> While Wesleyans insist they affirm justification by faith alone, they define it in the same moral terms rejected by evangelicals ever since the Reformation debate. Lawson himself defines justification as "the first and all-important stage in a renewed manner of life, actually changed for the better in mind and heart, in will and action." Thomas Aquinas could hardly have improved on this definition.[176]

Dan Corner, who is founder and director of *Evangelical Outreach* and author of two popular books in support of Arminianism: *The Believer's Conditional Security* and *The Myth of Eternal Security,* explains how under the Arminian doctrine, man must of his own free will live a righteous life in order to keep from losing his salvation.

> The truth is: man has free will both before and after initial Salvation. A saved person can be deceived, turn to evil and die spiritually. Hence, it is man's responsibility (NOT

God's) under grace to hold on, keep what he has and continue in the faith following the Lord Jesus. Many have failed in that regard over the centuries and consequently got back on the road to hell.[177]

Arminians object to Christians characterizing their theology as being based upon salvation by works. Corner joins the chorus of objections and argues that he does not preach salvation by works. The Arminian objections are disingenuous. Proof of the insincerity of their objections is found in Corner's preaching that not only can a person "get saved" by his own free will, he can lose his salvation by his sin, and then after losing it, get it back again by renewed free will effort. Corner's Arminian theology, which is based upon salvation by continual free will repentance, is clearly an unbiblical salvation by works.

Some of the people who lose their salvation want to find their way back to God, but feel that they may have sinned too much to ever be forgiven. In contrast, the Bible gives us examples of how others have returned to God and have been forgiven again. When a person becomes repentant, turning away from their idols to serve God, they can find forgiveness and salvation.[178]

Corner's articulation of the Arminian principal of conditional security, whereby one falls out of grace and then back again, is the very same principle that is used by the Roman Catholic Church to justify all manner of sin. Catholic penitents continually commit sin of all sort, with the hope that if they lose their salvation through a particularly bad sin, they can get it back again by going to confession and doing penance. The Catholic Church rates the sins, with more serious sins being called mortal sins and the less serious sins being called venial sins. The great fear for all Roman Catholics is to die while outside a state of grace. That fear is how the Roman church keeps their penitents under their complete control and subservience.

The Roman Catholics, like the Arminians, trust in their own righteousness, rather than the righteousness of Christ, for their salvation. They are doing as did the Jews before them: "For they being ignorant of God's righteousness, and going about to establish their own righteousness, have not submitted themselves unto the righteousness of God." (Romans 10:3 AV) A true Christian relies on the righteousness of Christ: "And be found in him, not having mine own righteousness, which is of the law, but that which is through the faith of Christ, the righteousness which is of God by faith:" (Philippians 3:9 AV)

It is no surprise that Arminianism has many aspects in common with Roman doctrine, since Arminianism came directly from Rome. About the only distinction between Arminianism and Catholicism is that the hope for most Catholics is not heaven but rather Purgatory. They believe that they will have an indeterminate sentence in Purgatory after they die.[179] Catholics are taught that they will eventually be released from Purgatory, but only after they have been sufficiently punished for the sins for which they themselves did not do sufficient penance while alive.

The Arminian theology that man must of his own free will hold on to his salvation by his continual repentance and good works is unsupportable by scripture. God orders the steps of all men and controls their very tongue. "The preparations of the heart in man, and the answer of the tongue are from the Lord." Prov. 16:1. In God's sight, the works of those whom he has saved are "perfect." How can a Christian's works be perfect? God made his elect to do good works, which God ordained ahead of time according to his perfect will. Ephesians 2:10. If the works are ordained by God, they are perfect, because he is perfect. When God sees our good works at the judgment seat of Christ, he sees the perfect works of Christ himself.

Now the God of peace, that brought again from the dead our Lord Jesus, that great shepherd of the sheep, through the blood of the everlasting covenant, **Make you perfect in every good work to do his will, working in you that which is wellpleasing in his sight, through Jesus Christ**; to whom *be* glory for ever and ever. Amen. (Hebrews

13:20-21 AV)

There is a repentance that can come by the will of man.
However, that type of repentance does not bring about a change in
the heart, as would be the case with regeneration by the Holy Spirit.
The repentance that is born of free will brings death. Whereas the
godly repentance that is born of the Holy Spirit brings salvation. "For
godly sorrow worketh repentance to salvation not to be repented of:
but the sorrow of the world worketh death." 2 Corinthians 7:10.

The repentance that is wrought by God turns a person away from
sin and toward Jesus. Repentance that is brought by the enslaved will
of man brings only regret. There is no turning toward Jesus in faith.
The scripture gives an example of such repentance by the enslaved
will of man. It is found in Matthew 27:3, which tells of the
repentance of Judas. Judas repented that he he had betrayed Jesus.
His repentance, however, did not come from God, it came from
"himself."

> Then Judas, which had betrayed him, when he saw that he
> was condemned, **repented himself**, and brought again the
> thirty pieces of silver to the chief priests and elders.
> (Matthew 27:3 AV)

What was the result of the repentance by Judas?   "[H]e cast
down the pieces of silver in the temple, and departed, and went and
hanged himself." (Matthew 27:5 AV) The repentance that came from
"himself" and not from the Holy Spirit brought Judas to feel sorry for
himself to the point of suicide. There was no regeneration.

There is no such thing as free will repentance, as claimed by the
Arminian gospel, because man's will is enslaved to sin. The
repentance that comes by the enslaved will of man can never bring
about regeneration to salvation. Only the hand of God can do that.
Judas is an example of one who "repented himself," as advocated by
the Arminian theologians. Judas was condemned to hell. Mark
14:21. Repenting by the enslaved will of man can never bring
salvation.

26 Stripping the Sheep's Clothing Off John Wesley

John Wesley's brand of Arminianism grew to become the Methodist Church. John Wesley has been falsely portrayed as a model of Christian charity by the leadership of the Methodist Church. The great Christian August Toplady, who knew Wesley and his pernicious behavior, gives us a different opinion of Wesley:

> It has also been suggested, that "Mr. Wesley is a very laborious man:" not more laborious, I presume, than a certain active being, who is said to go to and fro in the earth, and walk up and down in it: (Job 1:7 with 1 Peter 5:8) nor yet more laborious, I should imagine, than certain ancient Sectarians, concerning whom it was long ago said, "Woe unto you Scribes, hypocrites; for ye compass sea and land to make one proselyte:" Matthew 23:15.[180]

The facts are that Wesley was a lying plagiarist. Wesley had a practice of misrepresenting the biblical account of predestination. Doug Wilson reveals that Wesley's misrepresentation of the doctrines of the Synod of Dordt could only be described as purposeful deception:

[T]he mistakes in his rendering were not honest mistakes; it seems evident he was making them as a result of and on account of his well-known rebellion against a particular truth contained in the Word of God. He had a great theological enemy, and that enemy was the Bible's teaching on predestination. He was not willing for it to be true, and his enmity was such that it affected his ability to deal with the subject.[181]

Wilson explains further how futile Wesley's effort was in trying to use scripture to support his unsupportable Arminian attack on God's sovereignty:

A sympathetic biographer presents Wesley's encounter with the subject of God's sovereignty in the Biblical text: "In his sermon On Predestination he plunged his head boldly into the lion's mouth, preaching from the most explicit of all the Pauline texts of the subject, Romans viii. 29,30....It might well be thought, if it was not quite severed, his head was not extracted unscathed from the lion's mouth." Stanley Ayling, John Wesley, (Cleveland: William Collins Publishers, Inc. 1979)m p. 276-77. I believe that a sober assessment of Wesley's work on this issue reveals a man, contrary to the spirit of the Bereans (Acts 17:11), who was unwilling for the Bible to teach certain things. And this sort of unwillingness is not consistent with submission to Scripture, which is the foundation of all holy living.[182]

Wilson's research into the life of John Wesley uncovered evidence that Wesley was a well practiced plagiarist.

Wesley's ministry included the time prior to and during the American War for Independence. How to respond to colonial demands was a hot political issue in England, and Wesley waded right into the middle of it. Reversing an earlier position, Wesley came out in strong support of the legitimacy of taxing the colonies. His position was put before the public in an address entitled A Calm Address to

Our American Colonies. The tract caused a sensation in
England (but not in America, where a friend of the
Methodists destroyed all the copies, lest the Methodist
preachers be persecuted). T. Herbert, John Wesley as Editor
and Author (Ann Arbor: University Microfilms
International, 1978), pp. 107-108.

The problem with the pamphlet was that Wesley did not
write substantial portions of it. In the course of
approximately ten pages, Wesley used numerous sections
taken verbatim from Samuel Johnson's Taxation No
Tyranny. In the first edition of Calm Address, Wesley did
not indicate in any way that he had borrowed text from
Johnson -- Wesley represented the work as his own. This
laid him open to the just charge of plagiarism, and those
charges were not long in coming. In a preface to the second
edition, Wesley acknowledged his indebtedness to the other
pamphlet, but this was too late. A plagiarist does not cease
to be a plagiarist because he admits the obvious after he has
been caught.[183]

Plagiarism is a type of larceny, and Wilson rightly calls those
who would protect Wesley from the charge of plagiarism - cowards.

There are many other sections like this. Now, what would
we call this if we did not know the names of the principal
individuals involved? We would identify it by its proper
name -- plagiarism -- and recognize it as a species of theft.
Should we refuse to call it by its proper name because the
reputation of Wesley is such that such charges will only
recoil on those who make them? That has a name too --
cowardice.[184]

The true John Wesley (who is hidden from the Methodist
faithful) was proven not only to be a plagiarist, but also a liar and
slanderer. Augustus Toplady was an ardent preacher of the gospel of
grace who opined that "Arminianism is the grand religious evil of
this age and country."[185] He wrote a book, which was in large part a

translation from Latin of a book by Jerom Zanchius, which exposed Arminianism as a pernicious error. Wesley could not address the points in the book head-on, so he instead used deception. Wilson explains:

> In 1769, a young man named Augustus Toplady ("Rock of Ages") published a book entitled The Doctrine of Absolute Predestination Stated and Asserted. It was a translation "in great measure" from the Latin of Jerom Zanchius.
>
> In a polemical response, John Wesley took the liberty of abridging the book down to tract size, to which he attached the following ending:
>
> The sum of all is this: One in twenty (suppose) of mankind are elected; nineteen in twenty are reprobated. The elect shall be saved, do what they will; the reprobate will be damned, do what they can. Reader believe this, or be damned. Witness my hand,
>
>   A.......T.......
>
> The problem was that Augustus Toplady ("A.T.") had written no such thing. In this paragraph, Wesley was not only guilty of a grossly inaccurate summary of Toplady's thinking, he attempted to represent that inaccurate summary as Toplady's own words. This is evident through the misleading and slanderous use of "witness my hand."[186]

Toplady wrote a public letter to Wesley, to which Wesley did not respond, setting forth Wesley's deception and fraud. Toplady had this to say about the character (or rather lack thereof) of Wesley:

> Though you are neither mentioned, nor alluded to, throughout the whole book, yet it could hardly be imagined that a treatise apparently tending to lay the axe to the root of those pernicious doctrines which, for more than thirty years past, you have endeavoured to palm on your

credulous followers, with all the sophistry of a Jesuit, and the dictatorial authority of a pope, should long pass without some censure from the hand of a restless Arminian, who has so eagerly endeavoured to distinguish himself as the bellwether of his deluded thousands.

***

In almost any other case, a similar forgery would transmit the criminal to Virginia or Maryland, if not to Tyburn. If such an opponent can be deemed an honest man, where shall we find a knave? --What would you think of me, were I infamous enough to abridge any treatise of yours, sprinkle it with interpolations, and conclude it thus: Reader, buy this book, or be damned, Witness my hand, John Wesley?"

***

Much less, if you descend to your customary resource of false quotations, despicable invective, and unsupported dogmatisms, shall I hold myself obliged again to enter the lists with you. An opponent who thinks to add weight to his arguments by scurrility and abuse, resembles the insane person, who rolled himself in mud, in order to make himself fine. I would no more enter into a formal controversy with such a scribbler, than I would contend for the wall with a chimney-sweeper.

***

How miserably have you pillaged even my publication? Books, when sent into the world, are no doubt in some sense public property. Zanchius, if you chose to buy him, was yours to read; and, if you thought yourself equal to the undertaking, was yours to answer: but he was not yours to mangle. Remember how narrowly you escaped a prosecution some years ago, for pirating the Poems of Dr. Young.

I would wish you to keep your hands from literary picking
and stealing. However, if you cannot refrain from this kind
of stealth, you can abstain from murdering what you steal.
You ought not, with Ahab, to kill as well as take
possession: nor, giant like, to strew the area of your den
with the bones of such authors as you have seized and slain.

***

Let me likewise ask you when or where I ever presumed to
ascertain the number of God's elect? Point out the treatise
and the page, wherein I assert that only "One in twenty of
mankind are elected." The book of life is not in your
keeping, nor in mine. The Lord, and the Lord only, knoweth
them that are his. He alone who telleth the number of the
stars, and calleth them all by their names, calleth also his
own sheep by name, and leadeth them out, first from a state
of sin into a state of grace, and then into the state of
glory.[187]

Toplady challenged Wesley to point out where Toplady ever
wrote anywhere at any time that "one in twenty of mankind are
elected" as Wesley alleged in his forgery. Wesley never responded to
Toplady, instead, he responded via a tract titled *The Consequence
Proved* to his own forgery, still pretending that it was written by
Toplady. Incredibly, Wesley introduced his *The Consequence
Proved* tract by stating:

Mr. Toplady, a young, bold man, lately published a
pamphlet, an extract from which was soon after printed,
concluding with these words: —

"The sum of all is this: One in twenty, suppose, of mankind
are elected; nineteen in twenty are reprobated. The elect
shall be saved, do what they will: The reprobate shall be
damned, do what they can."[188]

Wesley knew no shame. He was determined to play out the fraud to the end, even though Toplady had already exposed the writing that Wesley attributed to Toplady as a forgery created by Wesley himself. Wesley could not refute the truth of the sovereignty of God, so he created a straw man and wrote a tract against his own straw man. He sought to both assassinate the character of Toplady and refute the sovereign grace of God in one tract. He failed.

What Wesley accomplished through his subtle attempt to deceive was to expose himself as a minion of that most subtle beast (Genesis 3:1). The devil is the father of lies and so it is no wonder that his minions will also be subtle liars (John 8:44). Toplady was well acquainted with the corrupt doctrine and methods of Wesley, which is why he was so strident in his condemnation of him. Jesus should be our model, who was likewise strident in his condemnation of the chief priests, scribes, and Pharisees. *See, e.g.,* Matthew 23. We are admonished by God to "have no fellowship with the unfruitful works of darkness, but rather reprove them." (Ephesians 5:11 AV) Toplady was being obedient to God when he exposed Wesley as a wolf in sheep's clothing.

Wesley's subtle attack on Toplady did not end with his forgery. Wesley did not fare well in his dispute with Toplady and so he tried a yet more subtle way to undermine the doctrine of grace and assassinate Toplady's character. Wesley wanted to make sure this time that Toplady could not expose him as a preacher of guile, so Wesley waited until he was sure that Toplady was about to die before he initiated his final attack on Toplady. Wesley, like a vulture impatient for death, then struck and perniciously spread a lie that Toplady had recanted and disavowed the grace of God and embraced the Arminian theology. Wesley spoke too soon. While Toplady was indeed on death's door, when Toplady heard of the rumor being spread by the arch-liar Wesley, he dragged himself from his deathbed and publicly affirmed his adherence to the grace gospel and refuted Arminianism. William MacLean explains how the events unfolded:

John Wesley, the great apostle of Arminianism in the following century, manifested the same malicious spirit of persecution against Augustus Toplady, an earnest defender in his day of the doctrines of free and sovereign grace, and author of 'Rock of Ages Cleft for Me.'

When Toplady was thought to be on his death-bed, Wesley industriously circulated a report that Toplady had recanted the principles which it had been the business of his life to advocate. Wesley supposed Toplady to be too near the grave to contradict this foul calumny and write in his own defence. "But to the confusion of his enemies" to quote from Volume I of Toplady's Works "strength was given him to do both." Nor did he ever appear more triumphant than when, almost with his dying breath, he made so honourable and so successful an effort to repel the attacks of calumny and maintain the cause of truth.

On Lord's-day, June 14th, less than two months before his death, he came from Knightsbridge, and after a sermon by his assistant, the Rev. Dr. Illingworth, he ascended the pulpit, to the utter astonishment of his people, and delivered a very short but a very effective discourse from 2 Peter 1:13,14, Yea, I think it meet, as long as I am in this tabernacle, to stir you up by putting you in remembrance; knowing that shortly I must put off this, my tabernacle, even as our Lord Jesus Christ hath shewed me.' When speaking of the abundant peace he experienced, and the joy and consolation of the Holy Ghost, of which for months past he had been a partaker, together with the persuasion that in a few days he must resign his mortal part to corruption, as a prelude to seeing the King in His beauty, the effect produced was such as may, perhaps, be conceived, but certainly cannot at all be described. His closing address was in substance the same with the following paper which was published the week after, and entitled, 'The Rev. Mr. Toplady's Dying Avowal of His Religious Sentiments.'

Concerning Toplady's end we are told,

All his conversations, as he approached nearer and nearer to his decease, seemed more heavenly and happy. He frequently called himself the happiest man in the world. 'O!' (says he) 'how this soul of mine longs to be gone! Like a bird imprisoned in a cage, it longs to take its flight. O that I had wings like a dove, then would I flee away to the realms of bliss and be at rest for ever!' .... Being asked by a friend if he always enjoyed such manifestations, he answered, 'I cannot say there are no intermissions; for, if there were not, my consolations would be more or greater than I could possibly bear; but when they abate they leave such an abiding sense of God's goodness and of the certainty of my being fixed upon the eternal Rock Christ Jesus, that my soul is still filled with peace and joy.'

Within the hour of his death he called his friends and his servant... and said,

It will not be long before God takes me; for no mortal man can live (bursting while he said it into tears of joy) after the glories which God has manifested to my soul.' Soon after this he closed his eyes and found (as Milton finely expresses it)—'A death like sleep, A gentle wafting to immortal life' on Tuesday, August the 11th, 1778, in the 38th year of his age. (pp. 119, 120).

Toplady was not long in his grave when John Wesley publicly asserted that "the account published concerning Mr. Toplady's death was a gross imposition on the public; that he had died in black despair, uttering the most horrible blasphemies, and that none of his friends were permitted to see him." Sir Richard Hill, a friend of Mr. Toplady's, and also the Rev. J. Gawkrodger publicly wrote John Wesley and accused him of vilifying the ashes and traducing the memory of the late Mr. Augustus Toplady," and affirming that "many respectable witnesses could testify that Mr. Toplady departed this life in the full triumph of faith." (Vol.

I, pp. 121-128).

The report continues that a pious dissenting minister
expostulated in a pamphlet with Mr. Wesley on his unjust
assertions in the following words:

Mr. Wesley and his confederates, to whom this letter is
addressed, did not only persecute the late Mr. Toplady
during his life, but even sprinkled his death-bed with
abominable falsehood. It was given out, in most of Mr.
Wesley's societies, both far and near, that the worthy man
had recanted and disowned the doctrines of sovereign
grace, which obliged him, though struggling with death, to
appear in the pulpit emaciated as he was, and openly avow
the doctrines he had preached, as the sole support of his
departing spirit. Wretched must that cause be, which has
need to be supported by such unmanly shifts, and seek for
shelter under such disingenuous subterfuges. O! Mr.
Wesley, answer for this conduct at the bar of the Supreme.
Judge yourself and you shall not be judged. Dare you also
to persuade your followers that Mr. Toplady actually died
in despair! Fie upon sanctified slander! Fie! Fie!

Those who have read the preceding letters (by Sir Richard
Hill and Rev. J. Gawkrodger) astonished as they must have
been at their contents, will yet be more astonished to hear,
that to the loud repeated calls thus given to him to speak for
himself, Mr. Wesley answered not a word. Nor is it too
much to say, that by maintaining a pertinacious silence in
such circumstances, the very vitals of his character were
stabbed by himself. He thus consented to a blot remaining
on his name, among the foulest that ever stained the
reputation of a professed servant of Christ.

Why should Toplady who kept the faith and finished his
course in this world with joy be the target of the shafts of
Wesley's venom?

It is because he refuted on Scriptural grounds the Arminianism of Wesley, and fearlessly stood in defence of the eternal truths of free and sovereign grace.

"By what spirit," writes Toplady: "this gentleman and his deputies are guided in their discussion of controversial subjects, shall appear from a specimen of the horrible aspersions which, in 'The Church Vindicated from Predestination,' they venture to heap on the Almighty Himself. The recital makes one tremble; the perusal must shock every reader who is not steeled to all reverence for the Supreme Being. Wesley and Sallon are not afraid to declare that on the hypothesis of divine decrees, the justice of God is no better than the tyranny of Tiberius. That God Himself is 'little better than Moloch.' 'A cruel, unwise, unjust, arbitrary, a self-willed tyrant.' A being devoid of wisdom, justice, mercy, holiness, and truth.' 'A devil, yea, worse than the devil.' Did the exorbitancies of the ancient ranters, or the impieties of any modern blasphemers, ever come up to this? ... Observe, reader, that these also are the very men who are so abandoned to all sense of shame, as to charge me with blasphemy for asserting with Scripture, that God worketh all things according to the counsel of His own will, and that whatever God wills is right."

"... being predestinated according to the purpose of him who worketh all things after the counsel of his own will" (Ephesians 1:11).[189]

Thus is documented the reprehensible conduct of John Wesley, and it is a testimony to his lack of Christian character. The bad fruit of his life testifies to the falsehood of his Arminian doctrine. Jesus warned us of such liars and their false doctrines: "Beware of false prophets, which come to you in sheep's clothing, but inwardly they are ravening wolves. Ye shall know them by their fruits. Do men gather grapes of thorns, or figs of thistles? Even so every good tree bringeth forth good fruit; but a corrupt tree bringeth forth evil fruit." (Matthew 7:15-17 AV)

27   Rewards for Works

The false Arminian doctrine of faith and repentance coming by the free will of man has given rise to a theology based upon rewards for those good works. It is inevitable that a theology whereby righteousness is attained by the free will of man will necessarily have as part of that theology some way to reward the adherent for a job well done. If there is a reward for a job well done, that also means that there is a loss of reward for a job not so well done. Satan and his minions have used a tried and true method of creating the appearance of biblical authority for their system of rewards. That method is to wrongfully divide a passage in the word of God from its context and then give it a different meaning from that intended by God. In addition, when scripture is read through the clouded lens of free will, bible passages taken out of context can be twisted and falsely portrayed to support a theory of rewards in heaven for good works or losses for failure to do good works.

The theory of the loss of rewards doctrine is that, while a Christian will not lose his salvation, if a Christian sins or has insufficient good works, Christ will withhold rewards that would otherwise be given to him in heaven. Is that theory supported by scripture? No, it is not. The very theme of the bible is that God's glorification of his elect in heaven is not a reward that is earned, it is a free gift. God's elect are sons of God who will be like Jesus in

glory in heaven. 1 John 3:2. "We shall also reign with him." 2
Timothy 2:12. What reward possibly could be added to that?

If we are sons and heirs, what blessing will God hold back from
us? All things will be bequeathed to us as gifts, because God made
us heirs. Titus 3:7; Romans 8:17. Our status as sons of God is the
basis for our salvation. We are not rewarded for what God put in our
heart to do. God only sees the righteous works of Christ that he
performed through us. All the works done by Christians are prepared
ahead of time by Jesus for us to walk in them. Ephesians 2:10.
Taking rewards away from Christians means that God is disinheriting
his children. The loss of rewards theology has God going back on his
word.

This theology of rewards and losses in heaven is similar in
concept to the Catholic doctrine of Purgatory. While Purgatory is
considered to be temporary punishment, the myth of loss for failing
to do good is not considered a punishment by its adherents (at least
that is their claim), but rather only a loss of rewards that would
otherwise be obtained. The loss suffered by the believer is assessed
at the judgment seat of Christ. This Arminian system of rewards is so
subtle that it has spread beyond Arminian churches to infect even
churches that preach sovereign grace.

Randy Alcom, founder of Eternal Perspective Ministries, opines
that Christians will be judged according to their own works, with
rewards bestowed based upon the merits of the works. He claims that
believers will suffer loss if they have not done enough good works.

What we seldom consider is that Scripture plainly tells us
there is a judgment of believers, not simply of our faith but
of our works, that will determine for all eternity certain
aspects of our place or position in heaven. . . . In heaven
there waits for him a great welcoming committee, and a
hearty "Well done." But this is not automatic for
believers—the conditional "if, then" makes it clear that if
we do not do what Peter prescribes, then we will not
receive this rich welcome when we enter heaven.. . . The

receiving of reward from Christ is an unspeakable gain with
eternal implications. The loss of reward is a terrible loss
with equally eternal implications.[190]

The purveyors of this false doctrine wrongly divide 2
Corinthians 5:10 from its context and inject into it a meaning not
supported by God's word. 2 Corinthians 5:10 states:

> For we must all appear before the judgment seat of Christ;
> that every one may receive the things done in his body,
> according to that he hath done, whether it be good or bad.
> (2 Corinthians 5:10 AV)

Randy Alcom explains his view that 2 Corinthians 5:10 means
that God will assess the good and bad things a Christian has done
during his life on earth and use that assessment to assign his position
and rewards in heaven.

> Where we spend eternity, whether heaven or hell, will be
> determined by our faith. Our further station in either place
> will be determined by our works.[191]

The "loss of rewards" theologians are quick to point out that a
Christian will not be punished at the judgment seat of Christ. The
modern theologians subtly twist God's words. They cannot say that
Christians will be punished at the final judgment, because that would
be so clearly contrary to what the bible says. So they must make a
distinction between losing rewards and punishment. They claim that
losing rewards is not really a punishment at all. But they put it in
such terms that the loss of rewards sounds no different from
punishment. For example, Pastor John Hamel describes the mythical
loss of rewards as suffering an eternity of "corruption," "demotion,"
and "shame."

> Every reward at this Judgment will be an earned reward,
> not a gift. . . . Rewards are not given out for salvation.
> They are given out for service. Sincere service. . . . The
> compromisers will be saved – but only by the skin of their

teeth. Eternal life is not lost – only Eternal rewards. What a **shameful, shameful** day for so, so many! What a glorious day for so many more! . . . Will you receive crowns or **corruption**? Will you receive promotion or **demotion**? Praise or **shame**?[192] (emphasis added)

David Cloud's Way of Life website, which advertises itself as a fundamental Baptist information service, is typical of the "loss of rewards" advocates. Cloud denies that there will be punishment for the believer, but the loss of rewards seems very much like a punishment, since the loss of rewards means "all of his effort was expended for nothing."

[T]he judgment seat of Christ is not for punishment but for rewards or loss of rewards. The believer's punishment fell upon Christ! The judgment seat of Christ is like an athlete completing for the Olympics. If he loses the race, he is not punished but he loses the crown that he could have earned, and **all of his effort was expended for nothing.**[193] (emphasis added)

Kenneth Emilio, who received his Masters in Arts in Biblical Studies from Louisiana Baptist University explains that "we need to be careful not to lose our inheritance in Heaven, or to do those things that might lead to a diminished inheritance."[194]

Emilio cites as one of his authorities Dr. Paul N. Benware, who is Professor of Bible and Doctrine at Philadelphia Biblical University. Dr. Benware has also taught at the Moody Bible Institute and at the Los Angeles Baptist College. Dr. Benware is of the view that a saved Christian can lose at least part, and perhaps all, of his inheritance in heaven based upon his sin or lack of good works.[195]

Clearly, a Christian who loses a part of his inheritance has lost something that he would ordinarily inherit. The bible, however, states that all who are children of God get a full inheritance, to the same degree as Christ himself. There can be no diminishment of our inheritance, since we are "joint-heirs with Christ."

The Spirit itself beareth witness with our spirit, that we are the children of God: And if children, then heirs; heirs of God, and joint-heirs with Christ; if so be that we suffer with him, that we may be also glorified together. Romans 8:16-17.

When a testator takes away a portion of an inheritance from an heir, it is to express his dissatisfaction for something the heir has done. Disinheritance is a punishment. There is no amount of sophistry that will change that fact. Punishment of the children of God through disinheritance is not possible according to Romans 8:16-17.

Robert Wilkin, the Executive Director of the Grace Evangelical Society (GES), makes it clear that the loss of rewards is in fact a hellish type of punishment where the sorrow and remorse at the judgment seat of Christ of the "unfaithful" believers (an oxymoron, if there ever was one) will involve "weeping and gnashing of teeth."[196]

Wilkin's view is not a marginal view within the ersatz "Christian" community. For example, the terrible punishment in heaven to the point of "weeping and gnashing of teeth" was a belief espoused by Zane Hodges,[197] who held a master of theology degree from Dallas Theological Seminary. He taught New Testament Greek and Exegesis for 27 years at Dallas Seminary, where he instructed hundreds of seminarians, who later became preachers spreading his poisonous teachings throughout the world. Hodges was also the chairman of the New Testament Department. Hodges was the pastor at Victor Street Bible Chapel for almost 50 years and was founder and president of Kerugma Ministries. Wilkin and Hodges differ from other loss of rewards theologians, in that they opine that punishment will not be for eternity, that perhaps the "weeping and gnashing of teeth" could possibly only be for a few moments.[198] The bible passages that speak of weeping and gnashing of teeth do not describe such pain and suffering happening in heaven; all such passages address the pain and suffering of those who are damned to hell for eternity. Matthew 13:41-42 is just one example.

> The Son of man shall send forth his angels, and they shall
> gather out of his kingdom all things that offend, and them
> which do iniquity; And shall cast them into a furnace of
> fire: **there shall be wailing and gnashing of teeth**
> (Matthew 13:41-42).

Wilkin, Hodges and their ilk are simply wrong. There can be no
weeping and gnashing of teeth for any amount of time in heaven.
The bible states that God will wipe away all tears. There shall be no
sorrow or crying or pain.

> And I heard a great voice out of heaven saying, Behold, the
> tabernacle of God is with men, and he will dwell with them,
> and they shall be his people, and God himself shall be with
> them, and be their God. And **God shall wipe away all**
> **tears from their eyes; and there shall be no more death,**
> **neither sorrow, nor crying, neither shall there be any**
> **more pain**: for the former things are passed away.
> Revelation 21:3-4.

Emilio reveals that the reward system applies to believers based
upon their works through the effort of the believer.

> All believers are saved by grace through faith alone. The
> second aspect pertains to rewards for things done on earth.
> Rewards will vary according to how a believer behaved
> during his lifetime. ... Make a decision to make your lives
> count for eternity NOW. We think the effort will be worth
> it.[199]

Emilio states that the theological reward system is not based
upon salvation by works but rather rewards based upon works. The
effect, however, seems to be the same for the believer under either
the salvation by works or the rewards by works systems. Under the
rewards system, the believer works hard so that he is not denied his
full inheritance. Being denied his full inheritance would be a
punishment, for which he would be subjected to eternal shame,
regret, and remorse. That is directly contrary to the biblical truth of

full inheritance in heaven.

Hampton Keathley, III , Th.M., who is now deceased, advocated the "loss of rewards" doctrine. Keathley claims that a Christian will not be punished, but only suffer loss of rewards. Keathley was a 1966 graduate of Dallas Theological Seminary and a pastor for 28 years. He wrote for the Biblical Studies Foundation and taught New Testament Greek at Moody Bible Institute, Northwest Extension for External Studies in Spokane, Washington. Keathley stated the following in his article titled *The Doctrine of Rewards: The Judgment Seat (Bema) of Christ*:

> [T]hough it is tremendously serious with eternal ramifications, the judgment seat of Christ is not a place and time when the Lord will mete out punishment for sins committed by the child of God. Rather, it is a place where rewards will be given or lost depending on how one has used his or her life for the Lord.[200]

The following quote from Keathley, indicates that he realizes that the loss of rewards doctrine seems to be a works doctrine, which is contrary to the gospel of grace.

> While salvation is a gift, there are rewards given for faithfulness in the Christian life and loss of rewards for unfaithfulness. Rewards become one of the great motives of the Christian's life or should. But we need to understand the nature of these rewards to understand the nature of the motivation. Some people are troubled by the doctrine of rewards because this seems to suggest "merit" instead of "grace," and because, it is pointed out, we should only serve the Lord out of love and for God's glory.[201]

How does Keathley resolve this conflict with the gospel? In order to prop up the loss of rewards artifice, the true gospel of grace must be watered down. Otherwise there would be no basis for withholding rewards from a Christian. The Arminian philosophy of man's sovereignty is seen in Keathley's theology. Keathley, and indeed all loss of rewards theologians, ever so subtly undermine the gospel of grace and the sovereignty of God. In order to have loss of rewards at the judgment seat of Christ, the rewards must be based upon the merits due to man's own efforts, born of his own will, without regard to God's grace.

> Of course we should serve the Lord out of love and for God's glory, and understanding the nature of rewards will help us do that. But the fact still remains that the Bible promises us rewards. God gives us salvation. It is a gift through faith, but He rewards us for good works. God graciously supplies the means by which we may serve Him. Indeed, **He works in us both to will and to do as <u>we</u> volitionally appropriate His grace** (Phil. 2:12-13), **but the decision to serve, and the diligence employed in doing so, are <u>our responsibility and our contribution</u> and God sees this as rewardable.**[202] (emphasis added)

Notice the subtle twist made by Keathley. He seems to preach the gospel of Grace, but then, almost imperceptibly, he drops in the poisonous glorification of man, who merits some reward. Keathley cites Philippians 2:12-13, however, in order to accomplish his twisting of the gospel; he mischaracterizes the meaning of the passage by stating: "He works in us both to will and to do as <u>we</u> volitionally appropriate His grace." On the contrary, Philippians 2:13 actually states: **"For it is God which worketh in you both to will and to do of <u>his</u> good pleasure."** There is a world of difference between willing and doing of "<u>his</u> good pleasure," as stated in the bible, and willing and doing as "<u>we</u> volitionally appropriate his grace," as stated by Keathley. The passage in Philippians makes clear that good works of Christians are the work of God, who works in us "both to will and to do of <u>his</u> good pleasure."

The good works of a Christian are prepared ahead of time by God for us to walk in them. "We are his workmanship, created in Christ Jesus unto good works, which God hath before ordained that we should walk in them." Ephesians 2:10. Once a person is regenerated through the new birth in Christ, he becomes a new

creature, with a new free will. 2 Corinthians 5:17. Jesus has freed
our will from sin. Romans 6:7. With our regenerated will, we are
able to resist the temptation of our flesh and follow our new born
desire to serve God. We are truly free; Jesus accomplished what he
set out to do; he came to set us free from death and sin. John 8:31-
36; Romans 8:1-17.

We still sin, because our flesh will tempt us to sin, but our sin is
contrary to our new born will to serve God. Romans 18:14-25. Once
saved, we desire to submit to Christ and walk according to the
guidance of the Holy Spirit, who is able to overcome the carnal flesh,
which tempts us to sin. "And they that are Christ's have crucified the
flesh with the affections and lusts. If we live in the Spirit, let us also
walk in the Spirit." Galatians 5:24-25. It is the Holy Spirit that
moves the believer to do the will of God through works that are well
pleasing in his sight. "Make you perfect in every good work **to do
his will**, working in you that which is wellpleasing in his sight,
through Jesus Christ; to whom *be* glory for ever and ever. Amen."
Hebrews 13:20-21.

Keathley, however, takes God out of the equation; he has God
stepping back to let us of our own volition do good works, for which
we take responsibility and receive rewards. God's word, however,
explains that the good works of the saints are the result of God's
sovereign will working in us. Philippians 2:13; Hebrews 13:20-21.
Consequently, God cannot withhold rewards for our failure to
perform that which we most certainly will perform, because it is
God's will and pleasure that we do so. God's will is done on earth as
it is in heaven. Matthew 6:10.

There can be no compromise on the grace of the gospel. Under
the gospel, God's grace flows to his elect. There is no merit that
comes from man. Any watering down of the grace of the gospel is no
longer the true gospel. Any amount of works that are accounted as
merits establishes a false hybrid gospel of works. There can be no
mixing of grace and works. **"And if by grace, then *is it* no more of
works: otherwise grace is no more grace. But if *it be* of works,
then is it no more grace: otherwise work is no more work."**

(Romans 11:6 AV)

The "loss of rewards" theologians do not adequately explain the difference between losing rewards that one would ordinarily receive and being punished. Wouldn't suffering loss, remorse, regret, and shame based upon one's conduct be a punishment? Of course it would. However, according to the apostate theologians, the loss of rewards at the judgment seat of Christ is not a punishment. These theologians state that loss of rewards is not a punishment nor is it salvation by works, yet they advise Christians that they should work hard to avoid suffering remorse, regret, and shame in heaven.

This reward theology is an inevitable result of the philosophy that repentance comes from the free will effort of man. The authority for the system of rewards was so skillfully and subtly put in place that it is being spread by preachers who are not theologically Arminian. Dr. John MacArthur is an example of a non-Arminian loss-of-rewards preacher. MacArthur is the pastor of Grace Community Church in Sun Valley, California and president of The Master's College and Seminary. MacArthur has written over 100 books, which have sold millions worldwide. MacArthur believes that those who are saved from their sins will nevertheless lose rewards for what they have done during their lives:

> The judgment seat of Christ then is this: a man goes who has lived believing in Jesus Christ, all of the works which he has done are there in the mind of God. It is then a process of God subtracting the worthless ones from the valuable ones and then rewarding the believer on the basis of the valuable ones that remain. The difference in rewards is only going to come because some believers have understood their priorities and they're going to have a pile of valuable things while other believers, probably most, are going to have a monstrous pile of worthless things. . . . And you know this is the tragedy of so many Christian's lives that they don't live horribly immoral lives; they just live disastrously inconsequential ones. That really if they died there wouldn't be anybody in the world, spiritually

speaking, who would miss them. And everybody's going to
be saved, and everybody's going to have praise of God and
there are crowns for all of us, but believe me there are some
who are going to receive more than others. . . . There's the
promise that awaits, either reward or loss. For some it's
going to be a day of wonderful rewards. . . . But listen,
beloved, I hesitate to say this, but yet I say it because it's in
the word of God. **Some of you are going to be there and
you're going to suffer loss.** You're not going to receive the
full reward that you could have received. Why? Because
you haven't lived the kind of life you should have lived.
You haven't ordered your priorities. . . . **You can forfeit
your crowns by some sin in your life.**[203]

MacArthur acknowledges that the loss is a result of sin. That is
directly contrary to what the bible states. The bible states that Jesus
died to take away all of our sins. John 1:29. MacArthur's theology
sounds very much like a type of Purgatory. The Catholic mythology
of Purgatory is based upon the fiction that if a person dies "in God's
grace and friendship" but before he done enough penance to atone for
his own sins while living, he must go to a place called Purgatory,
where he must "undergo purification, so to achieve the holiness
necessary to enter the joy of heaven."[204] After an indeterminate
sentence in Purgatory, where he is punished for his un-atoned sins,
the person is then allowed entrance into heaven. The difference is
that the mythical Purgatory is a temporary suffering as sins are
purged, while most loss of rewards theologians have the Christian
suffering shame, regret, and remorse for an eternity in heaven.

Arminians will protest that their rewards theology is not a form
of purgatory, however, their claims seem hollow when one considers
implications of what they are saying in their writings. Abraham
Lincoln once asked: "If you call a dog's tail a leg, how many legs
does he have?" Abe answered: "Just four. Calling a tail a leg doesn't
make it one."[205] In like manner, denying that the loss of rewards is a
Protestant form of Purgatory does not mean that the denial is true.
J.D. Faust in his popular book, *The Rod--Will God Spare It?*, states
that when he speaks in terms of losing rewards, he means

punishment. That sure sounds like Purgatory.

> The answer rests in the fact that unworthy, sinful deeds
> merit no reward...Reward will be granted only for
> righteous deeds. ... Reward can be either positive or
> NEGATIVE.[206] (emphasis in original)

Dr. Douglas Stauffer is even clearer in his pronouncement that there will be punishment in heaven for unrighteousness. This heavenly state of punishment sounds very much like purgatory, only with no hope of delivery therefrom. "Dr. [Douglas] Stauffer currently serves as president of Victory Bible Institute and theological Seminary in Millbrook, Alabama; president of Faith Rescue Mission in Montgomery, Alabama; and is on the pastoral staff of Victory Baptist Church. He has thousands of hours teaching experience and ten years serving in pastoral ministries."[207] Dr. Stauffer states that Christians will be punished in heaven for doing wrong, and that there will be those in heaven who are ashamed because of their own unrighteousness.

> Preachers that teach that our loss of rewards is the extent of
> our suffering at the Judgment Seat of Christ are mocking
> God and are deceived by the Devil. ... We are told that there
> will be those in heaven ashamed. ...We are saved by the
> righteousness of Jesus Christ (Philippians 3:9), but
> rewarded based on our own righteousness. That means that
> our standing is determined by the righteousness of Jesus
> Christ, but our state by our own righteousness. Our work is
> related to righteousness. ... Those that claim that Christians
> need only be concerned with a loss of rewards at the
> Judgment Seat of Christ never consider that the Bible
> clearly points out that we will receive for the wrong too. ...
> The Bible clearly teaches that the Judgment Seat of Christ
> for an unfaithful Christian is not just a matter of losing
> rewards. Christians will receive something too. What may
> that be? My purpose is to warn every believer based on my
> knowledge of what the Bible says about the terror of the
> Lord and the fact that God is not mocked.[208]

Dr. Stauffer teaches that some Christians will be "ashamed" for an eternity in heaven as they endure "sufferings" under the "terror of the Lord." That sounds more like hell than heaven. Stauffer "warns" Christians that they should be afraid of the "terror of the Lord." The bible, however, states that Jesus "delivered us from the wrath to come." 1 Thessalonians 1:10. "For God hath not appointed us to wrath, but to obtain salvation." 1 Thessalonians 5:9. Christians should have no fear of judgment; they can come boldly before the Lord.

> Herein is our love made perfect, **that we may have boldness in the day of judgment**: because as he is, so are we in this world. There is no fear in love; but perfect love casteth out fear: because fear hath torment. He that feareth is not made perfect in love." (1 John 4:17-18 AV)

Many loss of rewards theologians argue that their theology does not mean Christians will be punished. They argue that not getting a reward means simply that and no more. However, in the next breath they contradict that limitation and state that the loss of rewards brings shame, remorse, and regret for eternity. That is quite different from what the bible states: "But as it is written, Eye hath not seen, nor ear heard, neither have entered into the heart of man, the things which God hath prepared for them that love him." (1 Corinthians 2:9 AV)

Even the most limited view of loss of rewards is unsupportable by scripture. Read further in 2 Corinthians 5 and one can see clearly that the doctrinal theory of a Christian losing rewards at the judgment seat of Christ is not only unsupportable by the scriptures, it contradicts the promises in the gospel.

> Therefore if any man *be* in Christ, *he is* a new creature: old things are passed away; behold, all things are become new. And all things *are* of God, who hath reconciled us to himself by Jesus Christ, and hath given to us the ministry of reconciliation; To wit, that **God was in Christ, reconciling the world unto himself, not imputing their trespasses unto them**; and hath committed unto us the word of

The Anti-Gospel   283

reconciliation. Now then we are ambassadors for Christ, as though God did beseech *you* by us: we pray *you* in Christ's stead, be ye reconciled to God. For he hath made him *to be* sin for us, who knew no sin; that **we might be made the righteousness of God in him.**" (2 Corinthians 5:17-21 AV)

2 Corinthians 5 makes it clear that Christians are imputed with the righteousness of God! That means that we are perfectly righteous in his sight. Jesus paid the penalty for our sin and gave us his righteousness in place of our sin. All our sin is forgiven.

One might ask, "what if a Christian doesn't sin, instead he just doesn't do good, won't God hold a Christian accountable for his failure to do good?" First, such a state is impossible, since all have sinned. The difference between a Christian and an non-Christian is that the Christian's sins are forgiven. Second, failure to do good is not some in-between category of action between sin and righteousness. Failure to do good, when one knows to do good, is a sin!

Randy Alcorn explains that the judgment of believers is not a judgement for our sins, but judgment of our works. Typical of the Arminian theologians, he then contradicts himself and states that the judgement is in fact for "the commission of sins and the omission of righteous acts we should have done."[209]   According to Alcorn's theology, a believer receives his eternal "due"for his works, whether it is good or bad.

Our sins are totally forgiven when we come to Christ, and we stand justified in him. Nevertheless, Scripture says what it does about our coming judgment. This judgment of believers by Christ is a judgment of our works, not our sins. However, **the commission of sins and the omission of righteous acts we should have done, apparently replaces or prevents the laying up of precious stones on the foundation of Christ. Therefore these sins contribute directly to the believer's "suffering loss." Through this loss of reward the believer is considered to be receiving**

his "due" for his works "whether good or bad." Hence
what we do as believers, both good and bad, will one way
or the other have effects for eternity.[210]

The problem with Alcom's construct is that it is directly
contrary to what the bible states. Alcom's claim that the believer is
judged for his failure to perform righteous acts, is wrong, because the
omission of righteous acts is a sin, and a believer has had all of his
sins (including the omission of righteous acts) forgiven. The key
passage that completely refutes the theory that Christians will suffer
loss in heaven for a lack of good works, is found in James 4:17. In
that passage, God make it clear that it is a sin for those who are given
an opportunity to do good and knowingly do not do it. **"Therefore
to him that knoweth to do good, and doeth it not, to him it is sin."**
(James 4:17 AV)

Violating God's commandments (which is God's law) is a sin.
"Whosoever committeth sin transgresseth also the law: for **sin is the
transgression of the law**. And ye know that he was manifested to
take away our sins; and in him is no sin." (1 John 3:4-5 AV)

The bottom line is that all unrighteousness of whatever sort is a
sin. **"All unrighteousness is sin."** (1John 5:17 AV) Any time we do
not show charity toward another, it is a sin. It is not a suggestion by
God that we love one another, it is a command.

Then one of them, *which was* a lawyer, asked *him a
question*, tempting him, and saying, Master, which *is* the
great commandment in the law? Jesus said unto him, Thou
shalt love the Lord thy God with all thy heart, and with all
thy soul, and with all thy mind. This is the first and great
commandment. And the second *is* like unto it, Thou shalt
love thy neighbour as thyself. **On these two
commandments hang all the law and the prophets**.
(Matthew 22:35-40 AV)

Jesus commanded us to love one another as he has loved us. "A
new commandment I give unto you, That ye love one another; as I

have loved you, that ye also love one another." (John 13:34 AV)
Anytime we fall short of that standard, we are in violation of his
command, which is a sin, because sin is the transgression of God's
law. In fact, God states that "whatsoever is not of faith is sin."
Romans 14:23.

Why is that important? Because if it is a sin not to do good
when it is within a Christians power, a Christian cannot suffer any
loss, because God has forgiven all of the Christian's sins and imputed
the righteousness of Christ to him. 1 John 3:4-5 makes it clear that
Jesus came to "take away our sins." The construct of the loss of
rewards theology simply cannot be true, because the whole scheme is
based upon a distinction between sin and failure to perform righteous
acts. Omitting a righteous act is in fact a sin. Therefore, there can be
no loss of rewards for the failure to do a righteous act, since Jesus
forgives all sin. By God's grace, through faith, we are cleansed from
"all unrighteousness," including our failure to perform righteous
acts.

> If we confess our sins, he is faithful and just to forgive us
> our sins, and to **cleanse us from all unrighteousness**. 1
> John 1:9.

The loss of rewards theologians require good works to avoid
losing rewards. However, God states that by faith in Jesus, his
perfect righteousness is imputed to us <u>without our works</u>. If we are
perfectly righteous, based upon the imputed righteousness of Christ,
on what basis could Christ withhold rewards? There is no basis for
withholding rewards.

> But to him that **<u>worketh not</u>**, but believeth on him that
> justifieth the ungodly, his **<u>faith is counted for
> righteousness</u>**. Even as David also describeth the
> blessedness of the man, unto whom **God imputeth
> righteousness without works**, Saying, Blessed are they
> whose iniquities are forgiven, and whose sins are covered.
> Romans 4:5-7.

When Jesus takes away our sins, they are gone and replaced with the righteousness of Christ. "Even the **righteousness of God** *which is* by faith of Jesus Christ **unto all and upon all them that believe**: for there is **no difference**:" (Romans 3:22 AV) All sins of all Christians are forgiven and are replaced with the righteousness of Christ - "there is no difference!" Romans 3:22. We are justified by the grace of God. "Being **justified** freely by his grace through the redemption that is in Christ Jesus:" (Romans 3:24 AV)

Since we have been justified in his sight, God will not examine what we have done on earth in our physical bodies in order to find whether we have failed to meet his expectations. Anything unacceptable to God is a sin, and all sins committed by Christians are completely blotted out from his memory.

> **And their sins and iniquities will I remember no more.
> Now where remission of these *is, there is* no more
> offering for sin.** (Hebrews 10:17-18 AV)

If God forgets our sin, how then can a believer's sins ever come to account before God at the judgment seat? They cannot; all sins are forgiven <u>and forgotten</u>.

All the sins of Christians are covered by the blood of Jesus. God imputes the righteousness of Christ in place of that sin. If we have the righteousness of Christ, what blessing could God withhold from a Christian? He withholds no blessing from his children.

> Blessed are they whose iniquities are forgiven, and whose sins are covered. **Blessed *is* the man to whom the Lord will not impute sin.** (Romans 4:7-8 AV)

The bible states that our trespasses are not imputed unto us once we believe in Jesus. What does that mean? It means that God will not remember our sins anymore.

> And they shall teach no more every man his neighbour, and every man his brother, saying, Know the LORD: for they

shall all know me, from the least of them unto the greatest of them, saith the LORD: for I will forgive their iniquity, and **I will remember their sin no more.** (Jeremiah 31:34 AV)

God has stated that he will be merciful to our unrighteousness and he will therefore remember our sin no more.

> **For I will be merciful to their unrighteousness, and their sins and their iniquities will I remember no more.** (Hebrews 8:12 AV)

Because the sins are remitted, there is no more offering that can be made for sin. If there is no offering that can be made for sin and the sin is forgotten then the sin is irrelevant to those that are saved when they stand before God at the judgment seat. God has washed us clea; no matter how deep red our sins are, they are white as snow in God's eyes.

> Come now, and let us reason together, saith the LORD: **though your sins be as scarlet, they shall be as white as snow; though they be red like crimson, they shall be as wool.** (Isaiah 1:18 AV)

To suggest that somehow God is going to deal with believers on the basis of the bad things that we have done and remove from us rewards that we would ordinarily receive is contrary to the word of God. He makes clear that he will not reward us according to our iniquities. Our transgressions are removed from us as far as the east is from the west.

> **He hath not dealt with us after our sins; nor rewarded us according to our iniquities.** For as the heaven is high above the earth, *so* great is his mercy toward them that fear him. **As far as the east is from the west, *so* far hath he removed our transgressions from us.** (Psalms 103:10-12 AV)

In fact, when Christians appear before the judgment seat of Christ, we will appear without spot and blameless. "Wherefore, beloved, seeing that ye look for such things, be diligent that ye may be found of him in peace, **without spot, and blameless**." (2 Peter 3:14 AV) If we appear without spot and blameless, that means that God will not hold us accountable for any unrighteousness.

Christians will commit sin, but those sins are not held to their account. Once a person is saved, his attitude toward sin changes. Paul explains in Romans 7:22-8:1 how his flesh tempts him to sin, however, his mind has been changed to delight in the law of God. His ultimate point cannot be missed. That is that while a Christian sins, he faces "no condemnation" from Christ for those sins.

Paul makes another important point that those who are saved from their sins walk after the spirit not after the flesh. It is the spiritual walk that bears fruit that Christ will see at his judgment seat. Christ will not see the sin committed in the flesh, because once a person is in Christ, he will face no condemnation.

> For I delight in the law of God after the inward man: But I see another law in my members, warring against the law of my mind, and bringing me into captivity to the law of sin which is in my members. O wretched man that I am! who shall deliver me from the body of this death? I thank God through Jesus Christ our Lord. So then with the mind I myself serve the law of God; but with the flesh the law of sin. **There is therefore now no condemnation to them which are in Christ Jesus, who walk not after the flesh, but after the Spirit.** Romans 7:22-8:1.

God himself changes our minds through repentance so that we turn from dead works to serving the living God. Our hearts are created anew to live in obedience to his will, to love our neighbor as he has loved us.

All that are called to the service of Christ will receive the promise of eternal life, which is our inheritance as children of God.

We do good works, not to attain the inheritance, but rather because God has changed our hearts to desire to serve him. Our inheritance in heaven is not based upon what we do, bu rather who we are, children of God.

> How much more shall the blood of Christ, who through the eternal Spirit offered himself without spot to God, **purge your conscience from dead works to serve the living God**? And for this cause he is the mediator of the new testament, that by means of death, for the redemption of the transgressions *that were* under the first testament, **they which are called might receive the promise of eternal inheritance**. (Hebrews 9:14-15 AV)

God does what he pleases in heaven and on earth. Psalms 135:6. God not only watched David's every step, he also compassed him about, laid his hand upon him, lead him by the hand, and indeed held David in his right hand. Psalms 139:5, 10. There is no doubt that God does the same for all of his elect. "The LORD shall preserve thy going out and thy coming in from this time forth, and even for evermore." (Psalms 121:8 AV) Indeed, God numbers the steps of every man, be he either elect or lost. "Man's goings are of the LORD; how can a man then understand his own way?" (Proverbs 20:24 AV) Even the heart of the king is under the control of the Lord's will. Proverbs 21:1.

All those that are saved will bear the fruit of good works and that is all that God will see of the believer on judgment day. "Herein is my Father glorified, that ye bear much fruit; so shall ye be my disciples." (John 15:8 AV) There are not two judgments, there is one judgment where both the saved (sheep) and unsaved (goats) both appear before God's judgment seat.

> When the Son of man shall come in his glory, and all the holy angels with him, then shall he sit upon the throne of his glory: And before him shall be gathered all nations: and he shall separate them one from another, as a shepherd divideth *his* sheep from the goats: And he shall set the

sheep on his right hand, but the goats on the left. Then
shall the King say unto them on his right hand, Come, ye
blessed of my Father, **inherit the kingdom prepared for
you from the foundation of the world**: For I was an
hungred, and ye gave me meat: I was thirsty, and ye gave
me drink: I was a stranger, and ye took me in: Naked, and
ye clothed me: I was sick, and ye visited me: I was in
prison, and ye came unto me. Then shall the righteous
answer him, saying, Lord, when saw we thee an hungred,
and fed *thee*? or thirsty, and gave *thee* drink? When saw we
thee a stranger, and took *thee* in? or naked, and clothed
thee? Or when saw we thee sick, or in prison, and came
unto thee? And the King shall answer and say unto them,
**Verily I say unto you, Inasmuch as ye have done *it* unto
one of the least of these my brethren, ye have done *it*
unto me.** Then shall he say also unto them on the left hand,
Depart from me, ye cursed, into everlasting fire, prepared
for the devil and his angels: For I was an hungred, and ye
gave me no meat: I was thirsty, and ye gave me no drink: I
was a stranger, and ye took me not in: naked, and ye
clothed me not: sick, and in prison, and ye visited me not.
Then shall they also answer him, saying, Lord, when saw
we thee an hungred, or athirst, or a stranger, or naked, or
sick, or in prison, and did not minister unto thee? Then
shall he answer them, saying, Verily I say unto you,
**Inasmuch as ye did *it* not to one of the least of these, ye
did *it* not to me.** And these shall go away into everlasting
punishment: but the righteous into life eternal. (Matthew
25:31-46 AV)

Christians who appear before the throne of Christ, will find it to
be a throne of mercy, not judgment. "Let us therefore come boldly
unto **the throne of grace**, that we may obtain mercy, and find grace
to help in time of need." (Hebrews 4:16 AV) How can the judgment
seat of Christ be a throne of grace, if God will judge all (saved and
unsaved) according to their works, and the bible makes it clear that
we cannot be saved by works? The answer is found in the bible. In
Ephesians 2 God states that Christians are saved by his grace through

faith in Jesus Christ and are pre-ordained to walk in good works. We are spiritual creations of God for the purpose of walking in good works. Those good works are prepared by God in advance for us to perform.

> For by grace are ye saved through faith; and that not of yourselves: *it is* the gift of God: Not of works, lest any man should boast. For we are his workmanship, **created in Christ Jesus unto good works, which God hath before ordained that we should walk in them.** (Ephesians 2:8-10 AV)

If his will is that we will do good works, then we will do good works; his will is done on earth just as his will is done in heaven. "Thy kingdom come. **Thy will be done in earth, as** *it is* **in heaven.**" (Matthew 6:10 AV) God acts in accordance with his will and no one can stay the hand of God!

> And all the inhabitants of the earth *are* reputed as nothing: and **he doeth according to his will** in the army of heaven, **and** *among* **the inhabitants of the earth: and none can stay his hand**, or say unto him, What doest thou? (Daniel 4:35 AV)

Notice in Matthew 25:31-46 on judgment day, Jesus sees only the good works of the sheep (saved Christians) and he sees only the bad works of the goats (unsaved heathen). Why is that? Because aside from Jesus no man can do any good. "Even so every good tree bringeth forth good fruit; but a corrupt tree bringeth forth evil fruit. **A good tree cannot bring forth evil fruit, neither** *can* **a corrupt tree bring forth good fruit.** Every tree that bringeth not forth good fruit is hewn down, and cast into the fire." (Matthew 7:17-19 AV)

Only those who are in Jesus will have any good works on judgment day. Without Jesus a person can do no good works by God's standard. "I am the vine, ye *are* the branches: **He that abideth in me, and I in him, the same bringeth forth much fruit: for without me ye can do nothing.**" (John 15:5 AV) All those who are saved will bear fruit. The very idea that his children will not bear fruit contradicts the word of God. Just as without Christ no man can bear fruit, so also with Christ no man can be fruitless.

In 1 Corinthians 15:10, Paul confirms that without Christ he cannot bring forth fruit from his labor. His labor bore abundant fruit not by his own merit, but rather by God's grace.

But by the grace of God I am what I am: and his grace which was bestowed upon me was not in vain; but I laboured more abundantly than they all: **yet not I, but the grace of God which was with me.** (1 Corinthians 15:10 AV)

What are the fruits of salvation bestowed upon us by Christ? They include faith, virtue, knowledge, temperance, patience, godliness, brotherly kindness, and charity.

And beside this, giving all diligence, add to your faith virtue; and to virtue knowledge; And to knowledge temperance; and to temperance patience; and to patience godliness; And to godliness brotherly kindness; and to brotherly kindness charity. For if these things be in you, and abound, they make *you that ye shall* neither *be* barren nor unfruitful in the knowledge of our Lord Jesus Christ. (2 Peter 1:5-8 AV)

In Matthew 25 Jesus tells his sheep "inherit the kingdom prepared for you from the foundation of the world." He has made all Christians to inherit his kingdom. We are God's children and his heirs. "And hath made us kings and priests unto God and his Father; to him *be* glory and dominion for ever and ever. Amen." (Re 1:6 AV) What blessing is he going to withhold from his children? "But as it is written, Eye hath not seen, nor ear heard, neither have entered into the heart of man, the things which God hath prepared for them that love him." (1Co 2:9 AV)

Notice also in Revelation 20 the great and small stand before

God and there are "books"that are opened. One of the books is the
book of life. The dead are judged according to what was in the
books. Only those that are not found in the book of life were cast
into the lake of fire. Just as in Matthew 25 all are judged according
to their works.

> And I saw a great white throne, and him that sat on it, from
> whose face the earth and the heaven fled away; and there
> was found no place for them. And I saw the dead, small and
> great, stand before God; **and the books were opened: and
> another book was opened, which is *the book* of life: and
> the dead were judged out of those things which were
> written in the books**, according to their works. And the sea
> gave up the dead which were in it; and death and hell
> delivered up the dead which were in them: and they were
> judged every man according to their works. And death and
> hell were cast into the lake of fire. This is the second death.
> And **whosoever was not found written in the book of life
> was cast into the lake of fire.** (Re 20:11-15 AV)

Only those that are saved have done any good works, and they
are the only ones found in the book of life. "And there shall in no
wise enter into it any thing that defileth, neither *whatsoever* worketh
abomination, or *maketh* a lie: but **they which are written in the
Lamb's book of life.**" (Re 21:27 AV)

So we see from Matthew 25 that in 2 Corinthians 5:10 when all
appear at the judgment seat of Christ, those who receive according to
the good they have done are saved Christians (sheep on his right
hand) and those who receive the bad are unsaved heathen (goats on
his left hand). "For we must all appear before the judgment seat of
Christ; that every one may receive the things *done* in *his* body,
according to that he hath done, whether *it be* good or bad." (2
Corinthians 5:10 AV)

Without Jesus Christ, a person is unsaved and can do no good:
"I am the vine, ye *are* the branches: He that abideth in me, and I in
him, the same bringeth forth much fruit: for **without me ye can do**

nothing." (John 15:5 AV) All the supposed good and righteous
works of the heathen are worthless to the Lord. "But we are all as an
unclean *thing*, and **all our righteousnesses** *are* **as filthy rags**; and
we all do fade as a leaf; and our iniquities, like the wind, have taken
us away." (Isaiah 64:6 AV)

With Jesus Christ, a Christian bears much fruit and God sees no
bad in him and forgets all his sins: "**For I will be merciful to their
unrighteousness, and their sins and their iniquities will I
remember no more**." (Hebrews 8:12 AV)

There is no "in between" where God sees the good and bad of
Christians and the good and bad of the unbelieving heathen. It is all
or nothing with God. One is either perfectly holy in his kingdom by
the imputed righteousness of Christ or he is evil according to man's
fallen nature. With regard to the unregenerate man, God's view is:
"They are all gone out of the way, they are together become
unprofitable; **there is none that doeth good, no, not one**." (Romans
3:12 AV) However, the believer is "justified:" "For all have sinned,
and come short of the glory of God; **Being justified freely by his
grace** through the redemption that is in Christ Jesus:" (Romans 3:23-
24 AV)

Works are a manifestation of our salvation they do not earn
salvation nor any rewards. Any Christian who relies on rewards in
heaven for his works on earth has abandoned God's grace and instead
is looking for God to pay a debt instead of relying on the mercy of
God. "Now to him that worketh is the **reward** **not reckoned of
grace, but of debt**. But to him that **worketh not, but believeth** on
him that justifieth the ungodly, his **faith is counted for
righteousness**." (Romans 4:4-5 AV)

Romans 4:4-5 is clear. There can be no mixing of grace and
reward. There can be no grace if there is a reward. If reward is not
of grace, what is it? Quite simply, It is an unbiblical system of merits
based upon a debt owed by God to a believer for his works. J.D.
Faust, an Arminian theologian, explains that those who receive
rewards will get great blessing and gain, while those who do not

receive rewards will "experience real and eternal loss."

> All sinful deeds, thoughts, and motives will be consumed
> instantaneously as works of the flesh which are unworthy of
> reward. Some Christians will stand empty-handed, without
> excuse, having had much of their work and service rendered
> unworthy of reward. They will experience a real and eternal
> loss of reward, but they themselves shall be saved, yet so as
> through fire.[211]

When Jesus saved us, he made us to be zealous to do good
works. "Who gave himself for us, that he might redeem us from all
iniquity, and purify unto himself a peculiar people, **zealous of good
works**." (Titus 2:14 AV) God makes Christians zealous to do good
works. Good works flow from the zeal given to us by Christ. Good
works are not to earn salvation or rewards in heaven. They are the
fruits of salvation ordained by God. Read Titus 3:4-8 and you will
see clearly that we are saved not according to our works of
righteousness but rather according to God's mercy. Read verse 8,
where Paul explains that Christians should be careful to do good
works. Why? Not to gain rewards in heaven, but rather because they
are "good and profitable unto men."

> But after that the kindness and love of God our Saviour
> toward man appeared, **Not by works of righteousness
> which we have done, but according to his mercy he
> saved us**, by the washing of regeneration, and renewing of
> the Holy Ghost; Which he shed on us abundantly through
> Jesus Christ our Saviour; That being justified by his grace,
> we should be made heirs according to the hope of eternal
> life. *This is* a faithful saying, and these things **I will that
> thou affirm constantly, that they which have believed in
> God might be careful to maintain good works. These
> things are good and profitable unto men.** (Titus 3:4-8
> AV)

The very idea of a second class Christian in heavenly glory is
not supported anywhere in scripture. In simplest terms: good = sheep

and bad = goats. There is no middle category. There is heaven and there is hell. There is no category of person who walks around sad in heaven because he did not get all of the crowns he could have had, but failed to achieve because he didn't quite meet some standard of godliness.

Despite the above passages that clearly prove that loss of rewards for Christians at the judgment seat of Christ cannot be true, theologians (so called) persist in arguing that in fact there will be loss of rewards for Christians. For example, Hampton Keathley, III , Th.M., in reference to the Christians standing before the Judgment seat of Christ, stated: "[W]e need to be ever mindful that God's Word clearly teaches there are specific and very serious consequences, both temporal and eternal, for sin or disobedience."[212]

What are the eternal consequences according to Keathly? He claims: "The believer will forfeit rewards which he could have received, but he will not be punished in the judicial sense of 'paying' for his sins."[213]   Keathly's argument is pure sophistry. It makes absolutely no sense to claim that forfeiting eternal rewards is not a punishment. The loss of rewards doctrine is unbiblical nonsense, which is evidenced in Keathly's writings. Keathly states that the bible suggests there will be shame for the believer at the judgment seat of Christ. The only passages that support such a claim are those that are wrongly divided from their context, and then misinterpreted contrary to the scores of passages that refute that claim. Keathly explains his theology of heavenly shame:

> The Bible suggests that there will be shame at the judgment seat of Christ to a greater or lesser degree, depending on the measure of unfaithfulness of each individual believer. Therefore it should be each believer's impelling desire to be well-pleasing to the Lord in all things. Although Christians apparently will reflect on this earthly life with some regret, they will also realize what is ahead for them in the heavenly life. This latter realization will be the source of boundless joy.[214]

Keathly states that there will be unavoidable remorse, regret, and shame for the Christian at the judgment seat of Christ. That position is so completely without biblical support, he is forced to admit in the next sentence that the New Testament does not support that view. However, Keathly continues with this hogwash by contradicting what he states is revealed in the bible:

> The elements of remorse, regret, and shame cannot be avoided in an examination of the judgment seat of Christ. But this sorrow must be somewhat relative because even for the finest of Christians there will be some things worthy of unceasing remorse in the light of God's unapproachable holiness. This would mean that the finest of Christians could be sorrowful throughout eternity. However, this is not the picture that the New Testament gives of heaven. The overwhelming emotion is joyfulness and gratefulness. Although there is undeniably some measure of remorse or regret, this is not the overriding emotion to be experienced throughout the eternal state.[215]

Not satisfied with the complete confusion he has wrought, Keathly continues his onslaught on the gospel by comparing the judgment seat of Christ to a commencement ceremony. He is quick to point out that he does not want to overdo the "sorrow aspect" of the judgment seat of Christ, because he admits that would make heaven into hell (which is precisely the problem with his theology). However, he is equally quick to remind his readers that faithfulness of one's own efforts is the basis of rewards, and the failure of our own efforts will be the source of eternal sorrow.

> The judgment seat of Christ might be compared to a commencement ceremony. At graduation there is some measure of disappointment and remorse that one did not do better and work harder. However, at such an event the overwhelming emotion is joy, not remorse. The graduates do not leave the auditorium weeping because they did not earn better grades. Rather, they are thankful that they have been graduated, and they are grateful for what they did

achieve. To overdo the sorrow aspect of the judgment seat
of Christ is to make heaven hell. To underdo the sorrow
aspect is to make faithfulness inconsequential.[216]

Keathly does not want to "underdo" the "sorrow aspect" of what
Christians will feel in heaven. He has one insurmountable obstacle in
this, and that is God. God has not only underdone the sorrow aspect,
he has removed all sorrow from Christians in heaven. God states in
Revelation 21:4 that there will be no more sorrow or pain or tears for
Christians in heaven. God states that the former things have passed
away. If God states that the former things have passed away, who is
Keathly to contradict God and allege that the former things will
always be before the Christian, who will then suffer loss and feel
sorrow, remorse, regret, and shame? In Revelation 21:5, God has
promised to make all things new. "And he that sat upon the throne
said, **Behold, I make all things new**. And he said unto me, Write:
for these words are true and faithful." (Revelation 21:5 AV) I believe
God and his promises, because his words are "true and faithful;" I,
therefore, reject the false loss of rewards doctrine.

Where is Keathly's writing on the loss of rewards found? It is
found on a website at www.bible.org. Why is that significant?
Because those that run www.bible.org have tampered with the very
word of God. They have created their own bible version called the
New English Translation (NET). In Revelation 20:12 the small and
great stand before God, who is seated on a great white throne. In the
Authorized (King James) Version of the Bible we read: "And I saw
the dead, small and great, **stand before God**; and the books were
opened: and another book was opened, which is *the book* of life: and
the dead were judged out of those things which were written in the
books, according to their works." (Revelation 20:12 AV) However,
in the NET, and other corrupted versions of the bible, Satan
accomplishes his ultimate goal of taking God from his throne; in
those new versions all mention of God sitting on the throne is
deleted. The small and great are simply standing before "the throne."

Oh how Satan is subtle. He creates a mythology that Christians
suffer loss of rewards before the Judgment seat of Christ. He then

creates a bible version where Christ is removed from that judgment seat. And who do you think it is that is the real accuser of the saints? It is not God, as the loss of rewards purveyors would have you believe; it is the devil himself. How convenient for the devilish NET translation that God is removed from the throne. The removal of God from the throne in the NET makes room for Satan to take the mythical Arminian judgment throne and accuse the saints. It fits nicely with his loss of rewards mythology where the blessings and joy of salvation are turned into sorrow and shame. The same Satan who stands before God accusing Christians day and night, is the source of the loss of rewards heresy.

> And I heard a loud voice saying in heaven, Now is come salvation, and strength, and the kingdom of our God, and the power of his Christ: for **the accuser of our brethren is cast down, which accused them before our God day and night**." (Revelation 12:10 AV)

God has made the point in the Holy Bible that **every word** of God is important. "And Jesus answered him, saying, It is written, That man shall not live by bread alone, **but by every word of God**." (Luke 4:4 AV) Incidentally, the doctrine of Luke 4:4 is missing in the NET and other new bible versions. The NET leaves out the last clause and simply states: "It is written, 'Man does not live by bread alone.'" (Luke 4:4 NET) The NET and other new versions leave the reader in ignorance as to what it is other than bread by which man lives.

"**Every** word of God *is* pure" (Proverbs 30:5) and important, but the NET translators don't want that to be known because they have changed God's words and are pawning their counterfeit bible as the real thing.

God takes the misuse of his name very seriously, but it is even more serious to tamper with God's word.

God's name is so exalted that one should not even say his name unless one is talking about him or praying to him.

> Thou shalt not take the name of the LORD thy God in vain;
> for the LORD will not hold him guiltless that taketh his
> name in vain. (Exodus 20:7 AV)

God's name is so precious that the biblical penalty for
blaspheming his name is death.

> And he that blasphemeth the name of the LORD, he shall
> surely be put to death, *and* all the congregation shall
> certainly stone him: as well the stranger, as he that is born
> in the land, when he blasphemeth the name *of the LORD*,
> shall be put to death. (Leviticus 24:16 AV)

The NET publishers should take note that God holds his word in
even higher esteem than his name.

> **[T]hou hast magnified thy word above all thy name**.
> (Psalms 138:2 AV)

God has warned us not to tamper with his Holy word.

> Ye shall not add unto the word which I command you,
> neither shall ye diminish *ought* from it, that ye may keep
> the commandments of the LORD your God which I
> command you. (Deuteronomy 4:2 AV)

> What thing soever I command you, observe to do it: thou
> shalt not add thereto, nor diminish from it. (Deuteronomy
> 12:32 AV)

> Every word of God *is* pure: he *is* a shield unto them that put
> their trust in him. Add thou not unto his words, lest he
> reprove thee, and thou be found a liar. (Proverbs 30:5-6
> AV)

If the penalty for blaspheming God's name is death, what do you
suppose the penalty for altering God's word would be? The Bible

tells us that it is eternal damnation in hell.

> For I testify unto every man that heareth the words of the
> prophecy of this book, If any man shall add unto these
> things, God shall add unto him the plagues that are written
> in this book: And if any man shall take away from the
> words of the book of this prophecy, God shall take away his
> part out of the book of life, and out of the holy city, and
> *from* the things which are written in this book. (Revelation
> 22:18-19 AV)

The writers and promoters of the NET should reflect on what
God has said in the above passage; their eternal souls are at stake.
They seem comfortable with promoting the idea that Christians can
lose their rewards at the judgment seat of Christ. The loss of rewards
for Christians is a myth. It is not a myth, however, that tampering
with God's word brings with it an eternal curse from God.

This loss of rewards heresy is contrary to the gospel of God's
grace. In the parable of the penny paid to workers, Jesus made it
clear that our heavenly blessings are not based upon what we do, but
rather on God's perfect grace.

> For the kingdom of heaven is like unto a man *that is* an
> householder, which went out early in the morning to hire
> labourers into his vineyard. And when he had agreed with
> the labourers for a penny a day, he sent them into his
> vineyard. And he went out about the third hour, and saw
> others standing idle in the marketplace, And said unto
> them; Go ye also into the vineyard, and whatsoever is right
> I will give you. And they went their way. Again he went out
> about the sixth and ninth hour, and did likewise. And about
> the eleventh hour he went out, and found others standing
> idle, and saith unto them, Why stand ye here all the day
> idle? They say unto him, Because no man hath hired us. He
> saith unto them, Go ye also into the vineyard; and
> whatsoever is right, *that* shall ye receive. So when even was
> come, the lord of the vineyard saith unto his steward, Call

the labourers, and give them *their* hire, beginning from the
last unto the first. And when they came that *were hired*
about the eleventh hour, they received every man a penny.
But when the first came, they supposed that they should
have received more; and they likewise received every man a
penny. And when they had received *it*, they murmured
against the goodman of the house, Saying, These last have
wrought *but* one hour, and thou hast made them equal unto
us, which have borne the burden and heat of the day. But he
answered one of them, and said, Friend, I do thee no wrong:
didst not thou agree with me for a penny? Take *that* thine
is, and go thy way: I will give unto this last, even as unto
thee. **Is it not lawful for me to do what I will with mine
own? Is thine eye evil, because I am good?** So the last
shall be first, and the first last: for many be called, but few
chosen. (Matthew 20:1-16 AV)

In heaven, believers will have the imputed righteousness of
Christ and all that goes with it. "Beloved, now are we the sons of
God, and it doth not yet appear what we shall be: but we know that,
when he shall appear, **we shall be like him**; for we shall see him as
he is." (1 John 3:2 AV) To suggest that somehow a saved Christian
will have less glory than is promised in the bible, because he did not
have enough good works, calls into question the promise that "we
shall be like him."

What does it mean to be like Christ? All saved Christians are
one with Christ. "For both he that sanctifieth and they who are
sanctified *are* **all of one**: for which cause he is not ashamed to call
them brethren," (Hebrews 2:11 AV) Jesus made that point in John
14:20, where he said: "At that day ye shall know that I *am* in my
Father, and ye in me, and I in you." (John 14:20 AV) The prayers of
Jesus are always answered by the Father. He prayed to the Father the
following prayer:

**That they all may be one; as thou, Father, *art* in me, and
I in thee, that they also may be one in us**: that the world
may believe that thou hast sent me. **And the glory which**

thou gavest me I have given them; that they may be one, even as we are one: I in them, and thou in me, that they may be made perfect in one; and that the world may know that thou hast sent me, and **hast loved them, as thou hast loved me.** (John 17:21-23 AV)

You see that all Christians are one with Christ. He is in us and we are in him. In John 17, Jesus states that the glory that the Father has given him he has given to those who believe in him. We are one with Jesus in glory. That means that when we go to heaven we will have the very glory of Jesus Christ.

How then can any Christian forfeit blessings at the judgment seat of Christ? It is impossible. Jesus himself states in John 17, that we will be "**made perfect in one**." What is the one with whom Christians are made perfect? Christians are made perfect in one with God!

What does it mean to be perfect? Open a dictionary and read the definition. Perfect means to conform absolutely to the definition or description of the ideal type; to be excellent or complete beyond practical or theoretical improvement; to be entirely without any flaws, defects or shortcomings; to be correct in every detail; to be pure and unmixed. (http://dictionary.reference.com/browse/perfect)

A Christian who is in heaven and in glory cannot lack anything by having blessings taken away, because God has stated that Christians will be "perfect!" That is, we will be complete, beyond any improvement, without any flaws and not having any shortcomings.

To claim that a Christian must work to establish his perfection in heaven is to attempt to do that which God has admonished against. "Are ye so foolish? having begun in the Spirit, are ye now made perfect by the flesh?" (Galatians 3:3 AV) God, in Colossians 1, explains that Christians are saved to be presented "perfect **in** Christ Jesus." We are not perfected by works, we are perfected by our being one "in" Jesus. The works that are done by Christians, are in fact orchestrated by Jesus. The labors of Christians are "according to his working."

> To whom God would make known what *is* the riches of the glory of this mystery among the Gentiles; which is Christ in you, the hope of glory: Whom we preach, warning every man, and teaching every man in all wisdom; that we may present every man **perfect in Christ Jesus**: Whereunto I also labour, striving **according to his working, which worketh in me mightily**. (Colossians 1:27-29 AV)

Christians are part of the spiritual assembly in heaven made up of those who have been made perfect by Christ.

> But ye are come unto mount Sion, and unto the city of the living God, the heavenly Jerusalem, and to an innumerable company of angels, To the general assembly and church of the firstborn, which are written in heaven, and to God the Judge of all, and to the **spirits of just men made perfect**, (Hebrews 12:22-23 AV)

If we are made perfect in one with God and share in his glory, what is there lacking? The answer is nothing. Jesus states emphatically in his prayer that God has loved us as he has loved Jesus. We share in the same love, blessing and glory with Jesus when we enter heaven. We know this because Jesus tells us in John 17:22. This is the very same glory that Christ had with the Father before he was manifest in the flesh on earth. "And now, O Father, glorify thou me with thine own self with the glory which I had with thee before the world was." (John 17:5 AV)

We are not partially saved, we are saved to the uttermost, that is completely. "Wherefore he is able also to **save them to the uttermost** that come unto God by him, seeing he ever liveth to make intercession for them." (Heb 7:25 AV) Uttermost salvation means that we are completely saved to the greatest extent possible. Being saved to the uttermost means that there is no blessing that we will lack and there will be no loss of rewards due to our unrighteousness.

We need not work to add to what is already perfect. We are saved perfectly by the one offering of Jesus Christ. "For by one offering he hath perfected for ever them that are sanctified." (Hebrews 10:14 AV) To attempt to add to his one offering is to doubt the sufficiency of his offering, and his promise that we are completely and perfectly saved.

Notice how in Revelation 21 God gives of the water of life "freely" and those that overcome the world inherit "all things." God give to us "freely" and we will inherit "all things," not some things.

And he said unto me, It is done. I am Alpha and Omega, the beginning and the end. **I will give unto him that is athirst of the fountain of the water of life freely. He that overcometh shall inherit all things**; and I will be his God, and he shall be my son. But the fearful, and unbelieving, and the abominable, and murderers, and whoremongers, and sorcerers, and idolaters, and all liars, shall have their part in the lake which burneth with fire and brimstone: which is the second death. (Re 21:6-8 AV)

In 1 Peter 1 God states that our perfect inheritance in heaven is "incorruptible." If God says our inheritance is incorruptible, who is man to contradict him and say "oh yes it is, it can be corrupted by your failure to do good works"? We cannot by our own misdeeds in the flesh corrupt our rewards in heaven. Our inheritance is not based upon the merits of what we have done, but rather on the perfect righteousness of Jesus imputed to us, and so we cannot lose our eternal gifts. We did nothing to earn them and therefore we can do nothing to lose them.

Blessed *be* the God and Father of our Lord Jesus Christ, which according to his abundant mercy hath begotten us again unto a lively hope by the resurrection of Jesus Christ from the dead, To an **inheritance incorruptible, and undefiled**, and that fadeth not away, reserved in heaven for you," (1Peter 1:3-4 AV)

Christians will receive a crown of glory that will never fade away at the judgment seat of Christ.. "And when the chief Shepherd shall appear, ye shall receive a crown of glory that fadeth not away." (1Peter 5:4 AV) The reason a Christian's inheritance is incorruptible and cannot fade away is that Christians are in Christ and Christ is in them. We are one with Christ and are partakers of the divine nature of Christ. "Whereby are given unto us exceeding great and precious promises: that by these ye might be partakers of the divine nature, having escaped the corruption that is in the world through lust." (2Peter 1:4 AV)

Some cite 1 Corinthians 3:12-15 in an effort to support the unbiblical view that one will lose blessings at the judgment seat of Christ. 1 Corinthians 3:12-15 states:

Now if any man build upon this foundation gold, silver, precious stones, wood, hay, stubble; Every man's work shall be made manifest: for the day shall declare it, because it shall be revealed by fire; and the fire shall try every man's work of what sort it is. If any man's work abide which he hath built thereupon, he shall receive a reward. If any man's work shall be burned, he shall suffer loss: but he himself shall be saved; yet so as by fire. (1 Corinthians 3:12-15 AV)

H.A. Ironside (1876-1951), was for 18 years the pastor of the Moody Memorial Church in Chicago and authored more than 60 books and pamphlets. He presents the popular misinterpretation of the passage at 1 Corinthians 3:12-15:

But even though all one's work should be burned up, the Spirit of God tells us the believer himself shall be saved, yet so as by fire. But who that knows the saving grace of God and appreciates the love of Christ would wish thus to stand before Him? It is for Him we should labor. His glory should ever be before us, and then when we receive our rewards at His hand, it will be because of the delight which He Himself has found in our service.[217]

Lee Roberson, D.D., pastor of Highland Park Baptist Church for over 40 years, agrees with Ironside. In his book titled *Some Golden Daybreak,* Roberson interprets 1 Corinthians 3:12-15 to mean that Christians will stand before God at the judgment seat of Christ, with some Christians losing rewards and suffering shame for their works.

> "If any man's work shall be burned, he shall suffer loss: but he himself shall be saved; yet so as by fire." You will remember that we said only saved people stand at this judgment; therefore, we cannot lose our souls, for we are standing there in resurrection and translated bodies. We will not lose Heaven at the judgment seat, but we can lose our reward. ... Yes, we must stand before the judgment seat of Christ. Will you be happy, proud, and rejoicing as you look into the face of the Saviour, or will you bow your head in shame?[218]

James Melton takes Ironside's interpretation of 1 Corinthians 3:12-15 a step further. Melton claims that Christians will receive rewards based upon their personal good works. Melton claims that those saints without sufficient good works will receive "trash" from God.

> A fine companion passage for this is I Corinthians 3:11-15 ... Godly Christian service produces TREASURE in Heaven for the Christian. At the Judgment Seat of Christ, we (Christians) will receive our rewards. ... Most people are only concerned with going to Heaven or Hell, if even that, but the Bible instructs us to be concerned about our REWARDS. My eternal RESIDENCE was settled when I trusted Jesus Christ as my Saviour, but my eternal REWARDS are only settled when I deny myself and serve God in the Spirit. ... According to I Corinthians 3:11-15, the Judgment Seat of Christ will reveal gold, silver and precious stones for some Christians, but wood, hay, and stubble for others. Some will have treasures, while others will have trash. What will YOU have when you stand before your Lord?[219] (emphasis in original).

Dr. Douglas Stauffer takes 1 Corinthians 3:12-15 even further than Melton and seems to accomplish the desire of the devil, sending Christians to hell, for Stauffer presents a rather hellish version of heaven awaiting Christians. Stauffer states that "those that claim that Christians need only be concerned with a loss of rewards at the Judgment Seat of Christ never consider that the Bible clearly points out that we will receive for the wrong too."[220] Stauffer claims that Christians will not just lose rewards in heaven for their unrighteousness, but will also be subjected to punishment, "shame," and even "condemnation."[221] Stauffer states that Christians will be punished for their sins in heaven: "Because of the preachers' understanding of the terror of the Lord, we should be warning Christians to live for God. God is not mocked. We are not 'getting away with our sin' down here."[222]

To suggest that somehow God will hold his elect to account for some failure to do good is completely impeached by the scriptures. In Romans, chapter 8, we read that all those whom God foreknew he predestinated and called and justified and glorified. Romans 8:29-30. With what glory does he glorify his elect? God glorifies them by conforming them to the very image of his Son. Romans 8:29. If his elect are in the image of Jesus Christ, how can there be any loss of rewards? It is impossible. Indeed, immediately after Paul explains in Romans, chapter 8, that God's elect are chosen to be glorified, he asks the rhetorical questions:

> What shall we then say to these things? If God be for us, who can be against us? He that spared not his own Son, but delivered him up for us all, how shall he not with him also freely give us all things? Who shall lay any thing to the charge of God's elect? It is God that justifieth. Who is he that condemneth? It is Christ that died, yea rather, that is risen again, who is even at the right hand of God, who also maketh intercession for us. Romans 8:31-34.

Indeed, "who shall lay any thing to the charge of God's elect?" The answer is no one; for they will be conformed to the image of the Son of God, Jesus Christ himself, who is the "firstborn among many brethren." Romans 8:29.

1 Corinthians 3:12-15 does not support the proposition that the believer loses eternal blessings. If we read the passage in context we see that it addresses the building of the temple of God, which is made up of believers. The verse following the verse on works being burned up states: **"Know ye not that ye are the temple of God**, and *that* the Spirit of God dwelleth in you?"** (1 Corinthians 3:16 AV) The verses that lead into the description of gold, silver, precious stones, wood, hay stubble state: "According to the grace of God which is given unto me, as a wise masterbuilder, I have laid the foundation, and another buildeth thereon. But let every man take heed how he buildeth thereupon. For other foundation can no man lay than that is laid, which is Jesus Christ." (1 Corinthians 3:10-11 AV)

The entire passage in 1 Corinthians 3 is a metaphor that addresses the building of the temple of believers - the church of Christ. The loss suffered in 1 Corinthians 3 is by the person who preaches the gospel to those who seemed to be saved but turn out to be pretenders, who flee the faith when exposed to the fires of persecution.

The fire of persecution reveals the resilience of the building material used to build the church. The gold, silver, and precious stones are Christians who will survive the fire of persecution, whereas the wood, hay, and stubble are nominal false-Christians who will be consumed by the fires of persecution and disappear from the church. The preacher suffers loss of the wood, hay, and stubble he brought into the church, but he does not lose his own salvation. The preacher himself is saved, and he will persevere during the fires of persecution.

In Hebrews 3, God states that Jesus is worthy of more glory than Moses, just as the builder of the house is worthy of more glory than the house itself. He is equating Jesus as the builder with the house, being Moses. God then states that Christ is the son over his house and that we Christians are his house, just as Moses is his house. The house, like the temple in 1 Corinthians 3, is an allegory for Christ's

church of believers. Where Christ, who is the chief corner stone, is
the builder of that house, made up of believers. We are one with
Christ, his "holy brethren."

> Wherefore, **holy brethren**, partakers of the heavenly
> calling, consider the Apostle and High Priest of our
> profession, Christ Jesus; Who was faithful to him that
> appointed him, as also Moses *was faithful* in all his house.
> For this *man* was counted worthy of more glory than
> Moses, inasmuch as he **who hath builded the house hath
> more honour than the house**. For every house is builded
> by some *man*; but **he that built all things *is* God**. And
> Moses verily *was* faithful in all his house, as a servant, for a
> testimony of those things which were to be spoken after;
> But **Christ as a son over his own house; whose house are
> we**, if we hold fast the confidence and the rejoicing of the
> hope firm unto the end. (Hebrews 3:1-6 AV)

1 Corinthians 3 states that the "day" declares the works of men
and it is revealed by fire. What is the day to which God refers? It is
a reference to the open revelation in this temporal world. Jesus
explained in John 9: "I must work the works of him that sent me,
while it is day: the night cometh, when no man can work." (John 9:4
AV) Notice that Jesus was talking about working the works of God in
present tense "while it is day." He meant right then and there on
earth. The day to which he was referring was the opportunity to put
faith, love, and hope into action then and there. He set the example
for all Christians by being perfectly righteous while it was day. We
are his "children of the day."

> But ye, brethren, are not in darkness, that that day should
> overtake you as a thief. Ye are all the children of light, and
> the **children of the day**: we are not of the night, nor of
> darkness. Therefore let us not sleep, as do others; but let us
> watch and be sober. For they that sleep sleep in the night;
> and they that be drunken are drunken in the night. But let
> us, who are **of the day**, be sober, putting on the breastplate
> of faith and love; and for an helmet, the hope of salvation."

(1 Thessalonians 5:4-8 AV)

What does 1 Corinthians 3:13 mean when it says that works will be revealed by fire? John the Baptist explained in Matthew 3:

> I indeed baptize you with water unto repentance: but he that cometh after me is mightier than I, whose shoes I am not worthy to bear: **he shall baptize you with the Holy Ghost, and *with* fire**: Whose fan *is* in his hand, **and he will throughly purge his floor, and gather his wheat into the garner; but he will burn up the chaff with unquenchable fire.** (Matthew 3:11-12 AV)

John the Baptist stated that Jesus would baptize "with the Holy Ghost, and *with* fire." So the fire that is referred to in 1 Corinthians 3:13 must be a baptism of fire. What does that mean? 1 Peter 4:12-19 helps explain what this baptism of fire means.

> Beloved, think it not strange concerning **the fiery trial which is to try you**, as though some strange thing happened unto you: But rejoice, inasmuch as **ye are partakers of Christ's sufferings**; that, when his glory shall be revealed, ye may be glad also with exceeding joy. If ye be reproached for the name of Christ, happy *are ye*; for the spirit of glory and of God resteth upon you: on their part he is evil spoken of, but on your part he is glorified. But let none of you suffer as a murderer, or *as* a thief, or *as* an evildoer, or as a busybody in other men's matters. Yet if *any man suffer* as a Christian, let him not be ashamed; but let him glorify God on this behalf. **For the time *is come* that judgment must begin at the house of God: and if *it* first *begin* at us, what shall the end *be* of them that obey not the gospel of God?** And if the righteous scarcely be saved, where shall the ungodly and the sinner appear? Wherefore **let them that suffer according to the will of God commit the keeping of their souls *to him* in well doing, as unto a faithful Creator**. (1 Peter 4:12-19 AV)

Notice that the baptism of fire is a fiery trial of persecution of Christians. 1 Peter 4:12-19 makes it clear that this persecution is a "judgment" that begins at the "house of God." Christians suffer according to the "will of God." Jesus himself refers to the baptism by fire in Luke 12:50. This reference to another baptism is obviously not a reference to a baptism of water, but rather a baptism of fire, his crucifixion.

Jesus first states that he has come to send fire on the earth and then refers to his baptism of fire (crucifixion), which will be the catalyst for the subsequent persecutions of his church. "**I am come to send fire on the earth**; and what will I, if it be already kindled? But **I have a baptism to be baptized with**; and how am I straitened till it be accomplished!" (Luke 12:49-50 AV) In fact Jesus tells James and John, the sons of Zebedee that they will in fact be baptized with the baptism with which Jesus would be baptized.

> They said unto him, Grant unto us that we may sit, one on thy right hand, and the other on thy left hand, in thy glory. But Jesus said unto them, Ye know not what ye ask: can ye drink of the cup that I drink of? and be baptized with the baptism that I am baptized with? And they said unto him, We can. And Jesus said unto them, **Ye shall indeed drink of the cup that I drink of; and with the baptism that I am baptized withal shall ye be baptized**: But to sit on my right hand and on my left hand is not mine to give; but *it shall be given to them* for whom it is prepared." (Mark 10:37-40 AV)

We are partakers of the sufferings of Christ. Why must we endure the fiery trials of suffering? He stated that we would be persecuted for our faith in him. Jesus explained in John 15:

> I am the true vine, and my Father is the husbandman. **Every branch in me that beareth not fruit he taketh away: and every *branch* that beareth fruit, he purgeth it, that it may bring forth more fruit.** Now ye are clean through the word which I have spoken unto you. Abide in me, and I in

you. As the branch cannot bear fruit of itself, except it abide in the vine; no more can ye, except ye abide in me. I am the vine, ye *are* the branches: He that abideth in me, and I in him, the same bringeth forth much fruit: for without me ye can do nothing. **If a man abide not in me, he is cast forth as a branch, and is withered; and men gather them, and cast *them* into the fire, and they are burned.** If ye abide in me, and my words abide in you, ye shall ask what ye will, and it shall be done unto you. Herein is my Father glorified, that ye bear much fruit; so shall ye be my disciples. As the Father hath loved me, so have I loved you: continue ye in my love. If ye keep my commandments, ye shall abide in my love; even as I have kept my Father's commandments, and abide in his love. These things have I spoken unto you, that my joy might remain in you, and *that* your joy might be full. This is my commandment, That ye love one another, as I have loved you. Greater love hath no man than this, that a man lay down his life for his friends. Ye are my friends, if ye do whatsoever I command you. Henceforth I call you not servants; for the servant knoweth not what his lord doeth: but I have called you friends; for all things that I have heard of my Father I have made known unto you. **Ye have not chosen me, but I have chosen you, and ordained you, that ye should go and bring forth fruit, and *that* your fruit should remain: that whatsoever ye shall ask of the Father in my name, he may give it you.** These things I command you, that ye love one another. If the world hate you, ye know that it hated me before *it hated* you. If ye were of the world, the world would love his own: but because ye are not of the world, but I have chosen you out of the world, therefore the world hateth you. Remember the word that I said unto you, **The servant is not greater than his lord. If they have persecuted me, they will also persecute you**; if they have kept my saying, they will keep yours also. But all these things will they do unto you for my name's sake, because they know not him that sent me." (John 15:1-21 AV)

Jesus purges the branches through suffering so that they will bear fruit. However there are those branches that bear no fruit. They are the branches that wither under the fire of Christian trials. Jesus explains this point in the parable of the sower:

> Hear ye therefore the parable of the sower. When any one heareth the word of the kingdom, and understandeth *it* not, then cometh the wicked *one*, and catcheth away that which was sown in his heart. This is he which received seed by the way side. But he that received the seed into stony places, the same is he that heareth the word, and anon with joy receiveth it; Yet hath he not root in himself, but dureth for a while: **for when tribulation or persecution ariseth because of the word, by and by he is offended**. He also that received seed among the thorns is he that heareth the word; and the care of this world, and the deceitfulness of riches, choke the word, and he becometh unfruitful. But he that received seed into the good ground is he that heareth the word, and understandeth *it*; which also beareth fruit, and bringeth forth, some an hundredfold, some sixty, some thirty." (Matthew 13:18-23 AV)

The apostle Paul saw this very thing happen, and he named names:

> **This thou knowest, that all they which are in Asia be turned away from me**; of whom are Phygellus and Hermogenes. The Lord give mercy unto the house of Onesiphorus; for he oft refreshed me, and was not ashamed of my chain: But, when he was in Rome, he sought me out very diligently, and found *me*. The Lord grant unto him that he may find mercy of the Lord in that day: and in how many things he ministered unto me at Ephesus, thou knowest very well. (2 Timothy 1:15-18 AV)

Did Paul suffer loss? Yes, the three years he spent in Asia being beaten and falsely accused resulted in all turning away from him. Not only were Phygellus and Hermogenes losses to him, but also

Demas. "For **Demas hath forsaken me**, having loved this present
world, and is departed unto Thessalonica; Crescens to Galatia, Titus
unto Dalmatia." (2 Timothy 4:10 AV) Demas was earlier described
by Paul as his fellow laborer in Christ. "Marcus, Aristarchus,
Demas, Lucas, **my fellowlabourers**." (Philemon 1:24 AV) Paul's
loss was according to God's will. Paul explains earlier in 2 Timothy:

> Be not thou therefore ashamed of the testimony of our
> Lord, nor of me his prisoner: but **be thou partaker of the**
> **afflictions of the gospel according to the power of God;**
> **Who hath saved us, and called** *us* **with an holy calling,**
> **not according to our works, but according to his own**
> **purpose and grace, which was given us in Christ Jesus**
> **before the world began,** (2 Timothy 1:8-9 AV)

The persecution and loss that Paul suffered was according to the
will of God, who purposed it before the world was created. Paul
made the important point that he was called to a holy calling of
spreading the gospel not according to his works but according to
God's "own purpose and grace."

Some people seem to have lost sight of the fact that not all
references to rewards and losses in the bible are references to eternal
rewards and losses. Some of the rewards and losses are rewards and
losses during our temporal life on earth. For example: "But thou,
when thou prayest, enter into thy closet, and when thou hast shut thy
door, pray to thy Father which is in secret; and thy Father which
seeth in secret shall **reward thee openly**." (Matthew 6:6 AV) The
open reward is a clear reference to a reward during our temporal
existence on earth.

We saw how Paul suffered loss. However, what does Paul say is
his reward? In 1 Corinthians 9 he tells us what is his reward. First, he
states that he has no reason to Glory. Second, he states that his
reward is preaching the gospel without charge. He states that the
preaching of the gospel without charge is its own reward!

> **For though I preach the gospel, I have nothing to glory of**: for necessity is laid upon me; yea, woe is unto me, if I preach not the gospel! **For if I do this thing willingly, I have a reward**: but if against my will, a dispensation *of the gospel* is committed unto me. **What is my reward then?** *Verily* **that, when I preach the gospel, I may make the gospel of Christ without charge, that I abuse not my power in the gospel. For though I be free from all** *men*, **yet have I made myself servant unto all, that I might gain the more.**" (1 Corinthians 9:16-19 AV)

How could the preaching itself be a reward? Because it is Christ who determines the increase. Whether someone comes to the knowledge of Christ is not up to Paul, it is up to Christ. Therefore, the only thing of which Paul can make certain is that he preaches faithfully the word of God. If he preaches the word faithfully and accurately then the preaching will bear fruit.

However, as Jesus pointed out in the parable of the sower in Matthew 13, not all who seem to follow Christ have the true faith of Christ. Christ is not only the object of our faith he is the very source of our faith. We are dead in trespasses and sin such that Jesus must supply the faith for our salvation. "And you *hath he quickened*, who were dead in trespasses and sins;" (Ephesians 2:1 AV) Everything for our salvation is supplied by and through Christ. **Our faith in Christ is the faith of Christ**. *See e.g.*, Romans 3:22; Galatians 3:22; Revelation 14:12.

> Knowing that a man is not justified by the works of the law, but by the **faith of Jesus Christ**, even we have believed in Jesus Christ, that we might be justified by the **faith of Christ**, and not by the works of the law: for by the works of the law shall no flesh be justified. (Galatians 2:16 AV)

Our salvation is all of Christ. Jesus is the **"author and finisher of our faith."** Hebrews 12:2. That means he originates, creates, and establishes our faith. He does not then leave us to our own devices. Jesus then preserves us in him forever. Our salvation is truly by his grace through faith, it is none of our own, it is all of Christ.

> **But God, who is rich in mercy, for his great love
> wherewith he loved us, Even when we were dead in sins,
> hath quickened us together with Christ, (by grace ye are
> saved;)** And hath raised *us* up together, and made *us* sit
> together in heavenly *places* in Christ Jesus: That in the ages
> to come he might shew the exceeding riches of his grace in
> *his* kindness toward us through Christ Jesus. **For by grace
> are ye saved through faith; and that not of yourselves:** *it
> is* **the gift of God:** Not of works, lest any man should boast.
> For we are his workmanship, created in Christ Jesus unto
> good works, which God hath before ordained that we
> should walk in them. (Ephesians 2:4-10 AV) (emphasis
> added)

Our calling by Christ is not according to any merit or works we
have done. "Who hath saved us, and called *us* with an holy calling,
**not according to our works, but according to his own purpose
and grace**, which was given us in Christ Jesus before the world
began," (2 Timothy 1:9 AV) As with our salvation, so also our very
calling is not based upon some merits through works we have done
on earth. Our calling to preach the gospel is according to his purpose
and grace. In fact, Paul states clearly in 2 Timothy that we all receive
a crown of righteousness. How then can some lose any of their
heavenly blessings if we all receive a crown of righteousness that is
from Christ? "Henceforth there is laid up for me a **crown of
righteousness**, which the Lord, the righteous judge, shall give me at
that day: **and not to me only, but unto all them also that love his
appearing.**" (2 Timothy 4:8 AV)

Let us take a closer look at 1 Corinthians 3 in context. We see
that the topic is the church. Early in the chapter Paul makes the point
that the laborers in preaching the gospel and building the church are
laborers with God! Not only that, the laborers are also the plants
upon which God is husbanding. That is, the members of the church
(gold, silver, precious stones) are also working to add more gold,
silver, precious stones. "We are of God: he that knoweth God

heareth us; he that is not of God heareth not us. Hereby know we the spirit of truth, and the spirit of error." (1John 4:6 AV) However, without Christ the workers can do nothing and so Christ is right alongside them guiding the work. Christians are laboring with God, and Jesus is the good shepherd, shepherding us along.

As explained in Ephesians 2, whatever good we do is preordained by God. We have no reason to boast and there is no eternal reward for any of our good works because our salvation is not by works but by the grace of God. Even our very faith is from God. That is why Paul stated that he had nothing to glory about. "For though I preach the gospel, I have nothing to glory of: for necessity is laid upon me; yea, woe is unto me, if I preach not the gospel!" 1 Corinthians 9:16. Jesus drove home the point when he stated: "So likewise ye, when ye shall have done all those things which are commanded you, say, We are unprofitable servants: we have done that which was our duty to do." (Luke 17:10 AV)

Consequently, if persons come to the knowledge of Christ and are saved due to the preaching of the gospel, that is due to the work of Christ. There is not some added blessing to be received by the preacher in heaven because the gospel they preached was effectual. The glory for saving the soul goes to God and God alone. "So then neither is he that planteth any thing, neither he that watereth; but God that giveth the increase." (1 Corinthians 3:7 AV)

Our blessing in heaven is not based upon some debt owed to us for works done on earth. Our blessing in heaven is based completely on the mercy and grace of God. Read again what God states: "For by grace are ye saved through faith; and that not of yourselves: ***it is the gift of God: Not of works***, lest any man should boast." (Ephesians 2:8-9 AV)

The topic of 1 Corinthians 3 is the church, and the foundation of the church is Christ. The issue in 1 Corinthians 3 is whether the spiritual building being built is made up of true Christians. The wood, hay, and stubble seems to be those who fall away during the fiery trials Peter mentioned in 1 Peter 4.

The preachers of the Gospel will suffer loss of the pretended members of the church who fall away (wood, hay, and stubble), but the preachers themselves will be saved. However, they will go through the same fiery trials that caused the false Christians to fall away, but the true Christians will remain as gold, silver, precious stones. The passage makes clear that fire will try every man's work. What work is that? It is the body of the church, the foundation of which is Christ. The product of the work of preaching the gospel will be gold, silver, and precious stones (true Christians) and wood, hay, and stubble (false Christians).

The true Christians will persevere through the fiery trials of the persecutions suffered by Christians, however, the counterfeit Christians will wilt under the heat and fall away. The loss mentioned in 1 Corinthians 3 has nothing to do with loss of eternal blessings in heaven, it is the loss of the false brethren (the wood, hay, stubble).

I have planted, Apollos watered; but God gave the increase. So then **neither is he that planteth any thing, neither he that watereth; but God that giveth the increase. Now he that planteth and he that watereth <u>are one</u>:** and every man shall receive his own reward **<u>according to his own labour</u>**. For **<u>we are labourers together with God: ye are God's husbandry, *ye are* God's building.</u>** According to the grace of God which is given unto me, as a wise masterbuilder, I have laid the foundation, and another buildeth thereon. But let every man take heed how he buildeth thereupon. For **other foundation can no man lay than that is laid, which is Jesus Christ.** Now if any man build upon this foundation gold, silver, precious stones, wood, hay, stubble; Every man's work shall be made manifest: for the day shall declare it, because **it shall be revealed by fire**; and the **<u>fire shall try every man's work</u>** of what sort it is. If any man's work abide which he hath built thereupon, he shall receive a reward. If any man's work shall be burned, he shall suffer loss: but **<u>he himself shall be saved; yet so as by fire. Know ye not that ye are the temple of God</u>**, and *that* the Spirit of God dwelleth in you? If any man defile the temple of God, him shall God destroy; for **the temple of God is holy, which *temple* ye are**. Let no man deceive himself. If any man among you seemeth to be wise in this world, let him become a fool, that he may be wise. For the wisdom of this world is foolishness with God. For it is written, He taketh the wise in their own craftiness. And again, The Lord knoweth the thoughts of the wise, that they are vain. **Therefore let no man glory in men. For all things are yours; Whether Paul, or Apollos, or Cephas, or the world, or life, or death, or things present, or things to come; all are yours; And ye are Christ's; and Christ *is* God's.** (1 Corinthians 3:6-23 AV)

1 Corinthians 3:6-23 clearly refers to the temple of the Lord. The wood, hay, and stubble are those who do not truly belong as part of the temple, whereas the gold, silver, and precious stones are the true Christians who make up the body of Christ. All Christians corporately are the temple of the Lord. **"Ye also, as lively stones**, are built up a spiritual house, an holy priesthood, to offer up spiritual sacrifices, acceptable to God by Jesus Christ." (1Peter 2:5 AV)

The fiery trials suffered by Christians ultimately end with glory at the judgment seat of Christ. "That the **trial of your faith**, being much more precious than of gold that perisheth, though it be **tried with fire**, might be found unto praise and honour and glory at the appearing of Jesus Christ:" (1Peter 1:7 AV)

Now therefore ye are no more strangers and foreigners, but fellowcitizens with the saints, and of the household of God; And are built upon the foundation of the apostles and prophets, Jesus Christ himself being the chief corner *stone*; In whom all the building fitly framed together groweth unto **an holy temple in the Lord: In whom ye also are builded together for an habitation of God through the Spirit.** (Ephesians 2:19-22 AV)

The wood, hay, and stubble do not weather the fiery trials and persecutions and are burned up. This brings us right back to Matthew 3:11-12, where John the Baptist makes clear that the baptism of fire will be the way in which God will separate his wheat from the chaff. The persecutions suffered for Christ are the means by which God separates the wheat from the chaff. The chaff shall be gathered and burned up with unquenchable fire, while the wheat will be gathered and preserved in his garner.

> I indeed baptize you with water unto repentance: but he that cometh after me is mightier than I, whose shoes I am not worthy to bear: **he shall baptize you with the Holy Ghost, and *with* fire**: Whose fan *is* in his hand, **and he will throughly purge his floor, and gather his wheat into the garner; but he will burn up the chaff with unquenchable fire.** (Matthew 3:11-12 AV)

Why would God allow persecution to come to his own chosen children? Because his strength is made perfect through our weakness. Paul explains in 2 Corinthians 12:7-10:

> And lest I should be exalted above measure through the abundance of the revelations, there was given to me a thorn in the flesh, the messenger of Satan to buffet me, lest I should be exalted above measure. For this thing I besought the Lord thrice, that it might depart from me. And he said unto me, My grace is sufficient for thee: for **my strength is made perfect in weakness**. Most gladly therefore will I rather glory in my infirmities, that the power of Christ may rest upon me. Therefore I take pleasure in infirmities, in reproaches, in necessities, in persecutions, in distresses for Christ's sake: for when I am weak, then am I strong." (2 Corinthians 12:7-10 AV)

Those who would follow Christ and live the gospel will suffer persecution, just as did Paul. "Persecutions, afflictions, which came unto me at Antioch, at Iconium, at Lystra; what persecutions I endured: but out of *them* all the Lord delivered me. Yea, and **all that will live godly in Christ Jesus shall suffer persecution.**" (2

Timothy 3:11-12 AV) We must rely totally on Christ for our strength
and to deliver us if it is his will. We are children of God and heirs of
his glory. The sufferings of this world do not compare to the glory
that will be revealed in us.

> And if children, then heirs; heirs of God, and joint–heirs
> with Christ; if so be that we suffer with *him*, that we may be
> also glorified together. For I reckon that the sufferings of
> this present time *are* not worthy *to be compared* with the
> glory which shall be revealed in us. (Romans 8:17-18 AV)

We look forward, beyond our sufferings, to the perfection that
God has awaiting us in eternal glory. Since we will be "perfect" in
heavenly glory, we will not lack any rewards, because being perfect
by definition means we will be completely pure, correct in every
detail, and entirely without any shortcomings. This is done, not by
our works, but rather by God imputing the perfection of Christ to us.

> Whom resist stedfast in the faith, knowing that the same
> afflictions are accomplished in your brethren that are in the
> world. **But the God of all grace, who hath called us unto
> his eternal glory by Christ Jesus, after that ye have
> suffered a while, make you perfect, stablish, strengthen,
> settle *you*.** 1 Peter 5:9-10.

28 Calvary Chapel

A rminianism is tucked into the doctrinal statements of many churches seemingly without much thought to how it contradicts other parts of their statement of faith. For example, the very popular Calvary Chapel, which has churches spread throughout the United States and the world, has the following doctrinal statement authorized by Chuck Smith, the church's founder, on the official Calvary Chapel website:

> We believe that all are sinners (Romans 3:23) and unable by human performance to earn, deserve, or merit salvation (Titus 3:5). We believe that the wages of sin is death (Romans 6:23), and that apart from God's grace, no one can be saved (Ephesians 2:8-9). We believe that none are righteous, or capable of doing good (Romans 3:10-12), and that apart from the conviction and regeneration of the Holy Spirit, none can be saved (John 1:12-13; 16:8-11; I Peter 1:23-25). Mankind is clearly fallen and lost in sin.[223]

So far, so good. That doctrinal statement is biblically sound. However, later in the statement of faith, the doctrine takes a turn and completely redefines grace and the sovereignty of God. God becomes helpless and impotent in the face of the will of man. The god of Calvary Chapel is an errand boy delivering an invitation,

323

which can be accepted or rejected.

> However, the Bible also teaches that **an invitation (or call)
> is given to all, but that only a few will accept it.** ... We
> believe that God's grace is not the result of human effort or
> worthiness (Romans 3:24-28; 11:6), but is the response of
> God's mercy and love to those who will believe in His Son
> (Ephesians 2:4-10). Grace gives to us what we do not
> deserve nor can earn by our performance (Romans 11:6).
> **We believe that God's grace and mercy can be resisted
> by us.**[224] (emphasis added)

The Calvary Chapel statement of faith states: "apart from the
conviction and regeneration of the Holy Spirit, none can be saved
(John 1:12-13; 16:8-11; I Peter 1:23-25). Mankind is clearly fallen
and lost in sin."[225] That is an accurate biblical statement. However,
the Calvary Chapel statement of faith also states that an invitation (or
call) is given to "all," and that calling can be resisted by us. Their
doctrinal statement makes clear that man is completely fallen and
incapable of accepting the invitation to faith without the conviction
and regeneration of the Holy Spirit. In man's fallen condition he is
incapable of accepting any offer of salvation from God. Man cannot
regenerate himself from his fallen condition. The regeneration must
be done by the Holy Spirit. According to Calvary Chapel all men are
called. In order to call "all" men, "all" men must be regenerated by
the Holy Spirit in order to have the ability to accept the offer of
salvation.

Although Calvary Chapel does not use the term "prevenient
grace," their doctrine leads to the same conclusion. The Calvary
Chapel doctrine leads to the inexorable conclusion that once all men
are regenerated by the calling of their mythical god, man can thwart
the impotent efforts of their god to save those whom he has called.
They know that most are lost, therefore, their god's calling is mostly
ineffectual. Their god is clearly not the sovereign God of the Holy
Bible. Their god is the mythical god of Arminian free will.

Chuck Smith has explained his compromised gospel in *Calvary*

Chapel Distinctives, an official publication on the Calvary Chapel website, as follows: "An important characteristic of Calvary Chapel Fellowships is our desire not to divide God's people over non-essential issues."[226] Take a guess at what Calvary Chapel thinks is a "non-essential" doctrine. Calvary Chapel thinks that the very heart of the gospel is a non-essential! For example, Brian Brodersen, the Assistant Pastor of Calvary Chapel at Costa Mesa, California, stated:

> And then there's the issue of eternal security, or losing your salvation. And this is another aspect of the Calvinistic / Arminian dispute. And there are some Christians who believe that you can lose your salvation, and some Christians that believe you can never lose your salvation. But you know what? It's a **non-essential.** But yet there are times when we can get that sort of attitude. It's like, "Oh well, that guy over there, he believes in eternal security. What's he doing here? We don't believe that." Or "That guy over there, he believes that you can lose your salvation. The guy's probably not even saved. Come on." It happens, because we're human, because we're sinful, because at times we don't endeavor.[227] (emphasis added)

Chuck Smith states: "We don't believe that because you are a saint you will necessarily persevere, but that you need to persevere because you're a saint. Jesus said, 'If ye continue in my word, then are ye my disciples indeed.'"[228] (John 8:31).

Incredibly, Smith states that a saint (one set aside by God for salvation) must persevere to be saved, but that not all saints will persevere. He is essentially saying that a saint must of his own effort continue to persevere, and if he doesn't, he will lose the gift of salvation. That is, the Calvary Chapel god will damn some of his saints to an eternal lake of fire. In essence their god has done all he can do, and it is up to the saved to hold on tight to their salvation or lose it. Smith believes that one who is saved can decide to forfeit his salvation; the Arminian god is powerless to prevent it. That is not the sovereign God of the bible.

The Calvary Chapel salvation, in essence, is a salvation by works. That works salvation is subtly concealed beneath their twisted doctrine of perseverance. Under their Arminian theology, works are called perseverance. Under Smith's Arminian gospel, perseverance is not part and parcel of salvation, as is taught in the bible; it is instead a condition of salvation that must be fulfilled by the will of man. All Arminian churches contain this works salvation doctrine, although they never admit it. They are able to twist the biblical doctrine of perseverance into the unbiblical doctrine of salvation by the willing effort of the believer. The believer must persevere by his own will or lose his salvation. This works salvation is so subtle and so well concealed behind the redefined doctrine of perseverance that few perceive the salvation conditioned upon works, but that is exactly what it is.

Smith adds to this blasphemy by quoting from John 8:31, in order to give his devilish doctrine the patina of biblical authority. John 8:31 in no way supports his position. In quoting from John 8:31, Chuck Smith left out the first clause in that passage. The entire passage reads: "Then said Jesus to those Jews which believed on him, If ye continue in my word, *then* are ye my disciples indeed" (John 8:31 AV) That passage means that those who continue in God's word are his true disciples. It does not mean that those who do not continue in his word were once saved and forfeited that salvation of their own free will. Such an interpretation would contradict the very theme of the gospel: that all who are called to believe in God shall be saved; and all who do not believe in God, will not be saved, because they were not chosen by God for salvation. It is impossible for a saint to lose his salvation. The same God who wrote John 8:31 also wrote John 10:26-30 and John 6:38-40:

> For I came down from heaven, not to do mine own will, but the will of him that sent me. And this is the Father's will which hath sent me, that **of all which he hath given me I should lose nothing, but should raise it up again at the last day.** And this is the will of him that sent me, that every one which seeth the Son, and believeth on him, may have everlasting life: and I will raise him up at the last day.

(John 6:38-40 AV)

But ye believe not, because ye are not of my sheep, as I said unto you. My sheep hear my voice, and I know them, and they follow me: And I give unto them eternal life; and **they shall never perish,** neither shall any *man* pluck them out of my hand. My Father, which gave *them* me, is greater than all; and **no *man* is able to pluck *them* out of my Father's hand.** I and *my* Father are one. (John 10:26-30 AV)

When God states that "no *man* is able to pluck *them* out of my Father's hand" he means "no man!" Included in that category are the very saints chosen by God for salvation. They cannot lose their salvation because they are unable to lose their salvation. Those who perish, do so because they are not Jesus' sheep, not because they were once Jesus' sheep and decided to overrule God and become lost. Jesus' sheep will never perish.

Why would Chuck Smith adopt a doctrine which is so clearly contrary to the doctrine of the bible? The answer is money! He admits in *Calvary Chapel Distinctives*: "When you take hard stands on these non-foundational issues, you'll just **empty your church** of all of those who have Methodist, Nazarene, and other Arminian-influenced backgrounds. Why would you want to do that?"[229] (emphasis added)

In order as to not offend anyone, Smith has adopted a free will doctrine that appeals to the largest possible audience. Why? Not because it is supported by the bible. He admits that he does that to draw in the largest possible number of people. He admits he compromises on doctrine in order to draw a large audience. Smith has determined that he is going to have a church with a theology that is attractive to those who are traveling on the broad way to destruction. The bible tells us that "many there be which go in thereat." Matthew 7:13-14.

How successful has Smith been at packing his church? Calvary

Chapel of Costa Mesa, California, where he is senior pastor, is a
mega-church with a membership of approximately 20,000 people.[230]
According to a 2003 article in *Forbes* magazine, Calvary Chapel,
Costa Mesa is the third largest non-Catholic church in the United
States.[231] In addition, he has a regular radio program, "The Word for
Today," which includes edited messages from Smith's sermons at
Calvary Chapel, Costa Mesa.. The television version of *The Word
for Today* is seen nationwide on the blasphemous Trinity
Broadcasting Network.

Calvary Chapel also owns and operates their radio station
(KWVE). Calvary Chapel has a Bible College offering an Associate's
Degree in Theology, and a Bachelor's degree in Biblical Studies.
They own a 47-acre campus in Murietta Hot Springs, California.
They also own a castle in Austria. In addition, Calvary Chapel
ministries include: Calvary Chapel Music, Calvary Chapel Satellite
Network International, Calvary Chapel Conference Center, Calvary
Chapel Christian Camp, Maranatha Christian Academy, and Calvary
Chapel High School. There are over 850 affiliated Calvary Chapels
all over the globe, including approximately 700 in the United States.
Some of the affiliated Calvary Chapels in the United States are mega-
churches in their own right with memberships of more than 5,000
people.[232] *Forbes* magazine lists Calvary Chapel of Fort Lauderdale,
Florida, an affiliate of Calvary Chapel, as the ninth largest non-
Catholic church in the United States, with an average attendance of
17,000.[233]

Calvary Chapel is quite obviously a big and profitable business.
What would happen if he started preaching the narrow way found in
the gospel? If God is sovereign, and salvation is all accomplished by
God, there is no need for the many ministries offered by Calvary
Chapel to ensure that the saints do not lose their salvation. Smith
tries to convince people that he is not compromising on the
"essentials" of the Gospel. Rick Meisel of *Biblical Discernment
Ministries* answers Smith's unbiblical claim:

> The Scriptures do not teach that any portion of the Word of
> God contains doctrines that are "less essential." Our Lord

and Savior left no room for doubt on this subject: "It is written, Man shall not live by bread alone, but by **every word that proceedeth out of the mouth of God"** (Matt. 4:4). . . . In fact, why run so as to win (1 Corinthians 9:24)? If you have the "essentials" down, it's no big deal if you get deceived into other areas. What kind of a warning is Colossians 2:8 then anyway? So what if you're taken in by empty deceit! You have your essentials! Eat and drink (theologically speaking), for tomorrow we all go to heaven! WHAT A LIE! One cannot categorize Bible doctrine as very essential, not so very essential, less essential, non-essential, or whatever other type of human ranking system. Differences in "Importance," yes, but there are no doctrines that are more or less essential than others. **The Bible does not divide doctrine into essential and non-essential. Paul labored to preach the whole counsel of God** (Acts 20:27). Modern evangelicalism claims that certain doctrines are "essential" and others are "non-essential," and that Christian unity revolves strictly around the essentials, while the non-essentials have no meaning in regard to fellowship. But the Bible nowhere says that doctrine can be so divided. "The faith once delivered unto the saints" (Jude 3) describes that body of truth delivered to us by the Lord's Apostles through the inspiration of the Holy Spirit. **The entire body of truth is to be contended for.** Timothy was to allow NO OTHER DOCTRINE to be taught (1 Timothy 1:3). There is no hint here that some Bible doctrine is essential and other doctrine is not.[234] (emphasis added)

What happens to the doctrine of a church when it can throw out the very sovereignty of God and claim that God's sovereignty is non-essential? It brings that church within the ecumenical fold of the Roman Catholic Church. It preaches a different god, a different Jesus, a different gospel; it preaches an anti-gospel. "He that is not with me is against me; and he that gathereth not with me scattereth abroad." Matthew 12:30. If, dear reader, you think that is an exaggeration, read and weep over what Chuck Smith has to say on the matter in his 1993 book, *Answers For Today*:

> We should realize that we're all part of the Body of Christ
> and that there aren't any real divisions in the Body. We're
> all one. What a glorious day when we discover that God
> loves the Baptists! -- And the Presbyterians, and the
> Methodists, and the Catholics. We're all His and we all
> belong to Him. We see the whole Body of Christ, and we
> begin to strive together rather than striving against one
> another"[235]

In Chuck Smith's reprobate mind, he believes that the Catholic
Church is just one of the many Christian denominations in the body
of Christ. Later in this book we will see that the Roman Catholic
church is the church of the antichrist. It is no wonder that it is also
the source of the anti-gospel.

29 "Christian" Rock and Roll

In 1971, Chuck Smith founded "Maranatha! Music", which was a pioneering company in producing "Christian" rock and roll music. Chuck Smith and "Maranatha! Music" were in the forefront of the Jesus people fad (otherwise known as "Jesus freaks"). Under the management of Smith, "Maranatha! Music" produced worldly rock and roll music with ostensible Christian lyrics. "Maranatha! Music" was allegedly sold by Chuck Smith in 1988 to his nephew, Chuck Fromm.

Smith has gotten back into the "Christian" rock and roll music scene through Calvary Chapel Music. Calvary Chapel Music is managed by Holland Davis, who is the musical director at Calvary Chapel, Costa Mesa, and was former marketing director at "Maranatha! Music." Davis apparently still has a close working relationship with "Maranatha! Music," because a recent CD by the group *Smithfield*, titled *Song that Died Away*, although distributed by Calvary Chapel Music, lists Davis as the producer with a parenthetical after his name indicating "Marahatha! Music and Vineyard Music."[236] Chuck Smith is listed as the executive producer on that CD. Apparently, there is a close managerial working relationship between Calvary Chapel Music and "Maranatha! Music."

One of the many groups Calvary Chapel Music produces and promotes is *The Surfaris*,[237] who are famous for the million selling rock and roll tune, "Wipe Out," which they are quite proud to still play today.[238] In fact, *The Surfaris'* most recent CD from Calvary Chapel Music is titled: "Wipe Out" and has a rendition of the original song on the CD.

The "Christian" songs that are produced by Calvary Chapel Music have an unmistakable Arminian slant. For example, Calvary Chapel Music has a song book titled *Worship Life: Anchored Deep.* The website for Calvary Chapel Music has excerpts from three songs out of that songbook. One of the songs is titled *Be Free to Reign.* Not surprisingly, the song exudes an Arminian philosophy where God is invited by the singer to be free to reign in his life:

> Lord of Heaven and of Earth
> Come and reign in my heart
> Lord of life and King I serve
> I invite you to be free
> To reign in every part of me[239]

That song is typical of the Arminian free will mind. The Arminian god is a god who minds his own business until a person invites him to be free to reign in his life. Their god depends on the permission of the believer before he can reign in his life. The reign of their god, and the freedom of their god, are dependent on the sovereignty of man.

One doesn't grant the true God freedom and then invite him to reign in your life. The true God reigns in our lives because he is God; he doesn't need our permission. Read what the bible says about the true God:

> And all the inhabitants of the earth are reputed as nothing: and he doeth according to his will in the army of heaven, and among the inhabitants of the earth: and none can stay his hand, or say unto him, What doest thou? Daniel 4:35

Putting Christian words to rock and roll music creates a spiritual poison for the soul. It is the music that is the real danger. Almost all rock and roll music has a rapid back beat. That rapid drum beat is one of the things that makes rock and roll songs so evil. The music actually causes stress on the body creating what secular scientists call neurotic response.[240] Witches call the response to the music a spell. That neurosis (or spell) is manifested when people impulsively move their bodies to the beat of the music. One never sees such conduct at a classical music concert. However, at a rock and roll concert one often sees large crowds lost in a neurotic frenzy. This magical neurotic spell is a manifestation of the influence of devils over the listeners.

Once a person is placed under this spell, the listener becomes susceptible to temptations of the flesh and to being influenced by the worldly lyrics that have double meanings. Although the lyrics, at first glance, may have only one meaning when read on paper, the fleshly music suggests to the listener an interpretation that plays to the lust of the flesh and the pride of life.

Even ostensibly Christian lyrics can be interpreted differently when put to discordant rock and roll music. When the words are put to music the performer can place emphasis on one part of a phrase in order to influence the listener to interpret the words according to that emphasis. If the music is guttural rock and roll music seemingly innocent words will take on a whole new meaning. The real message is in the music, and sometimes the message is subliminal. Terry Watkins explains:

> The song "Stairway to Heaven" by the group Led Zeppelin is the most popular song in rock history. One line of the song, says, "you know sometimes **WORDS HAVE TWO MEANINGS**." They should know — the song is drenched in satanic backmasking! One part when played forward, says: *"Yes, there are two paths you can go by, but in the long run there's still time to change the road you're on."* But when played backwards, you clearly hear: *"IT'S MY SWEET SATAN . . . Oh I will sing because I live with*

Satan." Jimmy Page of Led Zeppelin is a devout follower
of Satanist Aliester Crowley. Page went so far as purchase
Crowley's old mansion. Let there be no doubt who
Zeppelin's master is - on their song "Houses of the Holy",
they sing, **"Let the music be YOUR MASTER/** Will you
heed the master's call/ Oh, Satan . . ."[241]

The meanings of words can be influenced even by voice
inflection. For example, the phrase "that was real smart" has a literal
meaning that is clear to the reader. However, if the statement is
voiced by a person in a sarcastic manner, the meaning is completely
changed to mean the opposite of the actual words. Much of
communication between people is through the tone and inflection of
the voice.

Another example would be if person is asked "do you mind if I
borrow your pen?" A typical response of a person giving permission
to use his pen might be: "sure." The literal meaning of the word
used by the respondent indicates that the respondent does in fact
mind if the person borrows his pen; the words deny the requestor
permission to borrow his pen. However, both the respondent and the
requestor understand that the respondent is actually giving
permission to borrow his pen. The inflection in the voice of the
respondent carries the real message, while the literal meaning of the
word is ignored. Voice inflection, in a very real sense, can override
the literal meaning of words.

That same phenomenon happens to a much greater degree when
"Christian" words are put to rock and roll music. Many people think
that if a song has Christian words that makes it Christian music. That
is wrong. The real message is carried by the music, not by the words.

The words do not give meaning to the music, rather it is the
music that gives meaning to the words. Fleshly, lustful, prideful
music will give a fleshly, lustful, prideful meaning to the words being
sung. Even bible passages in "Christian" rock and roll can be twisted
to mean something completely different from the meaning intended
by God. The words may seem uplifting, but the music is downward,

earthly, prideful. Consequently the message does not praise God, but rather subliminally encourages sin under the guise of Christian music. In fact, it is common for the words to a rock and roll song to be drowned out by the music, making the words almost unintelligible. The unintelligible words can be interpreted by the listener to say whatever the music subliminally suggests. That is because the real message is in the music, and its hypnotic rhythm.

People should understand the evil nature of rock and roll music, by whatever label under which it is concealed. Whether it is called Christian rock, contemporary Christian music, or Christian rap, there is a sinful message that is carried by the music itself. Rock and roll music is an incantation that casts an evil magic spell. Any music that does not lift the spirit, will instead lower the soul to follow the dictates of sinful flesh. That is why misbehavior is a common occurrence at rock and roll concerts, yet such conduct is never heard of at classical music concerts.

Read what Michael Jackson had to say during a February 10, 1993, live interview with Oprah Winfrey about the effect of rock and roll music on his behavior. The worldwide broadcast was purportedly his first live interview up to that time:

Oprah Winfrey: I have to ask you this; so many mothers in my audience have said to please ask you this question. Why do you always grab your crotch?

Michael Jackson: (Giggle) Why do I grab my crotch?

Oprah Winfrey: You've got a thing with your crotch going on there.

Michael Jackson: **I think it happens subliminally**. When you're dancing, you know you are just interpreting the music and the sounds and the accompaniment if there's a driving base, if there's a cello, if there's a string, you become the emotion of what that sound is, so if I'm doing a movement and I go bam and I grab myself; it's... **it's the music that compels me to do it**; it's not saying that I'm dying to grab down there and it's not in a great place; **you don't think about it; it just happens; sometimes I'll look back at the footage and I go ... and I go did I do that; so I'm a slave to the rhythm, yeah, okay.**[242] (emphasis added)

Notice what Jackson revealed. He opined that the influence of the music over him was subliminal. He had concluded that he was being influenced at an unconscious level to engage in the indecent conduct of grabbing his crotch. He stated that he was not even aware he was doing it, and was sometimes surprised when he saw the film footage later of his lascivious actions.

Jackson attributed the subliminal control of his movements to the "music!" It was not the words, it was the music that took him over, and caused him to unconsciously grab his privates. He stated that he was a "slave to the rhythm." That rhythm drove him to lewdly grab his crotch.

The rock and roll rhythm is an evil rhythm that causes people to do things they would not ordinarily do. Whether you call it "Christian" rock and roll or "secular" rock and roll, it is still rock and roll, and the subliminal influence over the flesh by the evil rhythm is present in both.

One artist promoted by Calvary Chapel Music is *Santos*. Chuck Smith himself offers narration between songs on their most recent CD titled *Santos: Deep and Rich*. The following description appears on the Calvary Chapel Music website describing *Santos*: "Santos tours nationally and has shared stages with The Charlie Daniels Band, The Outlaws, Pure Prairie League, Atlanta Rhythm Section, Moby Grape, Judas Priest, and the Marshall Tucker Band."[243] They proudly state that they have appeared and shared stages with music bands that pander to the flesh, including "Judas Priest!"[244] "Can two walk together, except they be agreed?" Amos 3:3.

Judas Priest is a heavy metal, Satanic rock and roll band. Read a sampling of some of the song titles by Judas Priest; they will give you some idea of the Satanic roots of the band: *Hell Is Home, Burn In Hell, Saints In Hell, Race With The Devil, Genocide, Eat Me Alive, Devil's Child, Touch Of Evil, Deal With The Devil, Devil Digger, Hell Patrol, Demonizer, Hellrider, Blood Stained, Turbo Lover, Screaming For Vengeance, Bloodsuckers, Breaking The Law, Killing Machine, Brain Dead, Decapitate, Metal Gods, Judas Rising,* and *Metal Messiah.*[245]

Terry Watkins explains the influence *Judas Priest* has over young minds with music that is literally a magic spell that possesses its listeners with a devil that drives them to commit suicide; this is the band with whom Calvary Chapel Music's *Santos* was proud to share a stage:

> In December, 1985, eighteen-year-old Raymond Belknap and James Vance after listening to Judas Priest sing "Beyond the Realms of Death", climbed out the bedroom window and went to a nearby church playground. There Belknap put a sawed-off shotgun to his head, pulled the trigger and literally blew his head off. As Belknap lay dead on the playground, Vance took his turn. He said, "There was just tons of blood. It was like the gun had grease on it. There was so much blood I could barely handle it, and I reloaded it and then, you know, it was my turn, and I readied myself. I was thinking about all that there was to live for, so much of your life is right before your eyes, and it was like I DIDN'T HAVE ANY CONTROL . . . MY BODY WAS COMPELLED to do it and I went ahead and shot."
>
> Vance survived the gunshot wound, but slipped into a coma in November, 1988, and died a few days later.
>
> The bereaved parents brought legal action against Judas Priest. The lawsuit stated, "The suggestive lyrics combined with the continuous beat and rhythmic non-changing intonation of the music combined to induce, encourage, aid,

abet and mesmerize the plaintiff into believing the answer to life was death."

According to expert witnesses who analyzed the Judas Priest album, both subliminal messages and backmasking were found. They found the subliminal message "Do it" at least six times. Attorney Kenneth McKenna said, "They just literally obeyed the commands of the music, and the lyrics . . ."[246]

How can an alleged Christian music group of any kind agree to share a stage with a notorious Satanic rock and roll band? John Todd may have an answer to that question.

John Todd (Collins) was a former member of the Illumnati Collins family. The Illuminati is a Satanic society that has within it many layers within layers of secrecy. It operates on a need to know basis. Todd was deeply involved in the dark world of witchcraft. He stated that he personally delivered four million dollars to Chuck Smith in order to enable Smith to start "Maranatha! Music."[247] Todd stated that the money he gave Smith was a partial payment toward a total of eight million dollars of which he was aware was given to Smith by the Illuminati. Todd stated that Smith knew that money was from the Satanic Illuminati. On October 5, 1978, Chuck Smith issued a written denial of the allegations made by Todd. In the course of his denial, Smith made a very odd statement. He stated:

I believe that it is time that the truth be established, and John Todd be declared for what he is--an absolute liar in league with Satan and going around doing a damning work within the church, seeking to divide the body rather than bring it together. If it were not for the scripture concerning going to law with a brother, I would have sued John Todd long ago for liable [sic] and slander; because I do obey the scriptures and seek to obey them, I have not filed this suit against him but the statements that he makes are totally false.[248]

Chuck Smith is a pastor of one of the largest churches in the
United States. At the time he wrote that letter he had been a pastor
for approximately 10 years. Presumably, he knows what the bible
says about suing. He had, no doubt, read the relevant passage
regarding lawsuits against Christian brethren. The pertinent passage
is found at 1 Corinthians 6:1-10. The passage states:

> Dare any of you, having a matter against another, go to law
> before the unjust, and not before the saints? Do ye not
> know that the saints shall judge the world? and if the world
> shall be judged by you, are ye unworthy to judge the
> smallest matters? Know ye not that we shall judge angels?
> how much more things that pertain to this life? If then ye
> have judgments of things pertaining to this life, set them to
> judge who are least esteemed in the church. I speak to your
> shame. Is it so, that there is not a wise man among you? no,
> not one that shall be able to judge between his brethren?
> **But brother goeth to law with brother, and that before
> the unbelievers.** Now therefore there is utterly a fault
> among you, because ye go to law one with another. Why do
> ye not rather take wrong? why do ye not rather *suffer
> yourselves to* be defrauded? Nay, ye do wrong, and defraud,
> and that *your* brethren. **Know ye not that the unrighteous
> shall not inherit the kingdom of God?** Be not deceived:
> neither fornicators, nor idolaters, nor adulterers, nor
> effeminate, nor abusers of themselves with mankind, Nor
> thieves, nor covetous, nor drunkards, nor revilers, nor
> extortioners, shall inherit the kingdom of God. (1
> Corinthians 6:1-10 AV)

That passage admonishes against a Christian suing his Christian
brother. However, Smith made clear in his letter that he considers
Todd "an absolute liar in league with Satan and going around doing a
damning work within the church, seeking to divide the body rather
than bring it together."

Smith further stated in his letter: "John Todd is an unmitigated
liar, a deceiver, a divider within the body of Christ, and needs to be

exposed." He repeats in another section of his letter that "The man is an absolute liar and anybody is insane who listens to him or gives any credence to what he has to say." Smith clearly does not consider Todd a Christian brother.

Smith stated that he did not sue Todd out of obedience to scripture. As we have seen in the relevant bible passage, there is no impediment to a Christian suing a non-Christian. Smith already knew that when he wrote his letter. As a pastor, he is purportedly an expert in the bible, and what it means.

So, if Smith does not believe that Todd is his Christian brother, there is no biblical impediment to suing Todd. That means that Smith was not telling the truth about his reason for not suing Todd, which calls into question Smith's credibility regarding the rest of his denial.

Smith considers Todd a minion of Satan sent to divide the church, and he needs to be exposed. One would think that best way to expose Todd would be to put him on the stand in a court of law and subject him to cross examination under oath. Smith knows, however, that legal action cuts both ways, and that may be the real reason Smith did not sue Todd. In a lawsuit, Smith could also be called to the stand and be subjected to cross examination under oath.

In addition, under the rules of discovery in a slander suit, where the allegation is that a person made a false statement about the plaintiff's source of finances, Todd would be able to get copies of all of Smith's financial records, including relevant underlying documents. Witnesses who have knowledge of Smith's business practices could be subpoenaed and deposed.

Smith's refusal to sue Todd is even more unusual when it is considered in face of the following challenge made by Smith in the same letter:

> If he could do so, I would be happy to give him $50,000, which I don't have, but I would obligate myself to it and would be willing to do so for any kind of evidence that he

could produce to show that his statement has even one shred of truth to it. It is a total fabrication and a complete lie.[249]

If Smith is so sure of himself that he was willing to obligate himself to pay $50,000, that he allegedly did not even have, if Todd could come up with one shred of evidence to prove Todd's claim, why was he so reticent to sue?

Smith challenged Todd to come up with evidence that he knew Todd did not have. Smith knew that if such evidence existed, the evidence will be found in records of which only he has custody. The way to prove his innocence would be to have those records subjected to public scrutiny in a lawsuit. Smith himself stated that "he would have sued John Todd long ago for liable [sic] and slander" if he were not constrained by an alleged biblical prohibition. We now know there is no such biblical prohibition.

In addressing Todd's claim to have delivered $8 million to Smith, Smith said in his letter that he is not wealthy. He stated:

> I am not a wealthy man under any standards. I have always believed in living a very simple life, and I receive a smaller salary than does a brick layer. I do not own any apartment complexes. I do not own any apartments or condominiums. I own the house that I am living in, or rather the savings and loan company owns the house I am living in. I drive a Chevrolet car that was sold to me at dealer's cost because the dealer is a member of Calvary Chapel. I have never driven fancy cars; I do not believe in driving fancy cars. I have always driven used cars up until the dealer offering me a new car at his cost.[250]

That statement should not be read in a vacuum. Smith's nephew, Chuck Fromm, who was at the time President of "Maranatha! Records" also wrote a letter (dated October 3, 1978) defending Smith. Fromm stated:

> Maranatha! Music is a non-profit organization grossing

approximately 1.1 million dollars annually. It was started in connection with Calvary Chapel of Costa Mesa in 1971 (incorporated as a separate organization in 1972) with a loan from Pastor Chuck Smith of under $3000. That money was used to produce the first Maranatha! Music album, which sold over 200,000 copies. The money from those sales furthered the ministry and was the source for funds to produce more albums. Today, fifty per cent of our sales are from our Praise albums.[251]

At the time both the letter by Fromm and the letter by Smith were written, Chuck Smith owned "Maranatha! Music." Whether the corporation is for profit or non profit is of importance primarily for tax reasons. Calling a company "non profit" is actually a misnomer. Non profit organizations are permitted to, and often do, make profits. When the income is retained by a company it becomes retained earnings, which is an asset that belongs to the owner. "Maranatha! Music" had assets and income, both of which belonged to Chuck Smith. According to Fromm, "Maranatha! Music" was a profit generating company that had an annual gross income of 1.1 million dollars. Any profit after expenses belonged to Chuck Smith. Yet, Chuck Smith claimed that "I am not a wealthy man under any standards." Anyone who owns a company that has an annual gross income of 1.1 million dollars would be considered a wealthy man under any standard. Once again, Smith's statements do not hold up to scrutiny. Why would Smith claim poverty, when in fact he is quite wealthy?

I noted an anomaly in Fromm's letter. Fromm claimed that "Maranatha! Music" sold 200,000 copies of their first album. However, David de Sabatino, in his *History of the Jesus Movement*, states that the first two albums from "Maranatha! Music" sold a combined total of 25,000.[252] That is quite a discrepancy! Are Fromm's sales figures accurate? If they are not, why would Fromm inflate the sales figures?

Fromm's letter was written in October 1978. Fromm stated that "Marahatha! Music," which was founded in 1971, grossed 1.1 million dollars per year. It seems that they were making that amount from the very first year. Fromm stated that the first 1971 album sold 200,000 copies. Assuming a wholesale price of $5 per album, that would mean gross income of $1 million on the first album alone. Multiply $1.1 million per year over the 8 years between 1971 and 1978 and we arrive at 8.8 million dollars. Coincidently, John Todd alleged that he gave Chuck Smith 4 million dollars, which he said was the second payment of a total of 8 million dollars from the Illuminati. Did Fromm inflate the sales figures for the album sales in order to use those fictional numbers to provide a documented explanation for the millions of dollars in "Maranatha! Music" assets that actually came from the Illuminati?

Even Fromm's statement of "Maranatha! Music" grossing $1.1 million per year is impeached by Chuck Smith, who stated in his October 1978 letter:

> Even to the present date, Maranatha Music has not done a total of $8 million in business, and this also can be easily verified and confirmed, and any reputable person is welcome to look at the books of both Calvary Chapel and Maranatha Music in order to prove the statements that I make are correct.[253]

Smith denies that "Maranatha Music" had done a total of $8 million in business. However Fromm's statement indicates that "Maranatha! Music" grossed more than $8 million, as of 1978. It seems that Smith and Fromm cannot get their stories or figures straight.

It is intriguing that Smith offers to allow a reputable person to look at their books. However, that seems more bluster than anything else. He knows that his books are not self-authenticating. In fact, the books are simply documentary conclusions. If he will only allow an examiner to look at the final numbers, the examiner will inevitably have to agree with the numbers in the books. The important figures are the figures on documents that underlie the conclusory numbers (which are many times self serving) found in the final "books." The books are of little help in addressing this issue, unless the person examining the books can also ask questions of employees and Smith himself in order to get an explanation, verify the numbers, and examine the evidence that underlies those numbers. It is doubtful that is the kind of examination Smith had in mind.

Fromm stated in his letter that "Maranatha! Music" "was started in connection with Calvary Chapel of Costa Mesa in 1971 (incorporated as a separate organization in 1972) with a loan from Pastor Chuck Smith of under $3000."[254] Keep in mind that Fromm is addressing a specific allegation about the source and amount of funding for "Maranatha! Music." Fromm was the President of "Maranatha! Music," and he had available at his fingertips all of the records for "Maranatha! Music." Yet the best he could do was estimate that the loan from Chuck Smith was "under $3,000."

Chuck Smith for his part, seems not to be able to keep the figure straight. In his October 5, 1978 letter he states that: "Maranatha Music was actually started with my own personal investment of $3,000.00."[255] Yet, three years later, in the Fall of 1981, Smith stated in his church bulletin that:

> We saw the necessity of helping to support the musicians in their ministry by making records. So with $3,500 and a four-track tape recorder, we made the first Maranatha album, a sampler of all the groups called *Maranatha 1*.[256]

Within 3 years the figure went from $3,000 to $3,500. One would think that a person who is just scraping by, as Smith claimed, on "a smaller salary than does a brick layer"[257] would know to the penny how much money he used to start a company. Unless, of course, the story is just fiction, and he could not remember the figure he had made up in the early version of the story.

Notice that when it came to explaining in the church bulletin how Smith started "Maranatha! Music," he did not mention the source of the $3,500. Furthermore, it is unclear under his version of events how he was able to sock away $3,500 on the allegedly modest salary that was less than the salary of a brick layer. Another oddity of his story is that for a pastor on a modest income he seemed to be rather irresponsible with his money. It is the height of irresponsibility to wager a large amount of money (those were 1978 dollars), especially for a poor pastor, on a very risky venture of producing an album for a bunch of hippies. His story just does not pass the smell test.

Why would the Illuminati give money to a "Christian" music producer? He who pays the piper calls the tune. The music that Smith was tasked to produce was Satanic music, labeled and marketed as Christian music. The Illuminati realized what was at stake when Todd went public with his allegation, and so they used every tool at their disposal to destroy Todd's credibility. They orchestrated false rape charges against him. Fritz Springmeier, who has done extensive research on the Illuminati, is convinced that Todd is who he claims to be and that his testimony is true.[258] Jack Chick, a Christian publisher, also understood the power of the Illuminati being brought down on Todd, and that the charges that have been leveled against Todd are false. Chick has continued to publish several comics based upon the information supplied to him by Todd.[259]

We need not rely on Springmeier and Chick to vouch for the accuracy of the information supplied by Todd. The truth is self evident. The sour fruit of Christian Rock, otherwise known as "Jesus Rock," has resulted in dead churches imbedded with a worldly Arminian anti-gospel.

To this day the Calvary Chapel website has many references to Christian Rock and Roll. The youth ministry links on the Calvary Chapel Santa Rosa, website has a link for HM Magazine that describes it as: "Christian Rock, Hardcore, Alternative and everything in between."[260] "Christian rock and roll" is an oxymoron. The term "Christian rock and roll" is the equivalent of "Christian witchcraft." If someone were to try to inject witchcraft into the churches, the flock would recognize the threat immediately. However, the subtlety of rock and roll music was the ideal method for Satan to place nominal Christians under his influence and ruin their testimony. Rock and roll music is from the devil and placing a "Christian" label on it does not make it righteous.

Terry Watkins gives a brief history of rock and roll and its infiltration into the churches through the Christian rock and roll phenomenon started by Chuck Smith:

> In the early 1950's, Cleveland disc jockey Allan Freed revolutionized the music world. Borrowing a ghetto term for sexual fornication, he coined the term "ROCK N ROLL". The Encyclopaedia Britannica Yearbook for 1956 described rock'n roll as, "insistent savagery deliberately competing with the artistic ideals of the jungle." The Christian community cried against this "tool of Satan." But in the 70's, a sinister hand began planting a small, but deadly seed. And the walls began to crumble. And like a raging hurricane, rock began desecrating the sacred music of the church. In they came; Bill Gaither, the Imperials, Dallas Holmes, Randy Stonehill, Keith Greene, and others. Today, rock music is a common companion of the church. And as you'll soon read, the rebellion, the sexual theme, the blasphemy, the occult influence, are found "lurking under the cover" of Christian rock.[261]

* * *

Rock star David Bowie said, "Rock has always been THE DEVIL'S MUSIC." (Rolling Stone, Feb. 12, 1976, p. 83)

Secular rock bad girl Lita Ford, said, "Listen, rock'n roll AIN'T CHURCH. It's nasty business. You gotta be nasty too. If you're goody, goody, you can't sing or play it. . ." (Los Angeles Times, August 7, 1988)

Even secular Time magazine, (March 11, 1985 p.60) in an article about Contemporary Christian Music titled the article, "New Lyrics for the DEVIL'S MUSIC".

The band that started the "Christian Rock" era was a band named

Love Song.[262] The band got its start in Christian Rock by playing at Chuck Smith's Calvary Chapel in Costa Mesa, California. The first two songs recorded by *Love Song* were released in a 1971 album, which also contained songs from other Christian Rock bands. The album was titled *The Everlastin' Livin' Jesus Concert*, and it was the first album produced by "Maranatha! Music."[263]

Today, *Love Song* describes themselves as: "Using a mixture of folk, rock, pop, and country."[264] A sampling of just one of their songs "Don't You Know" reveals the nature of their music. The description of the song is given as: "A 'Beatle-ish' exercise, with Beach Boy overtones."[265]

When one listens to the sampling of the song available on the internet, it becomes clear that the description of the song is accurate. The song is a rock and roll song that sounds very much like a Beatles tune. That is not surprising since as a website devoted to the "Jesus Movement" and *Love Song* states: "Many called them [Love Song] the Christian 'Beatles.'"[266] The song *Don't You Know* has the rapid back beat that is so characteristic of rock and roll songs. Such music is more an incantation, that casts a magic spell, than it is music. Any music that does not lift the spirit, will instead lower the soul to follow the dictates of sinful flesh.

The following is an excerpt of the history of *Love Song*. Notice how their music had to be cleaned up to remove overt "New Age ideas" in order to make the music more acceptable to perform in front of Christian audiences. New Age is simply a term to describe repackaged heathen pantheism.

"New Age" is an antichrist religious philosophy, based upon a belief in man's free will. The New Age adherents are responsible to work their way (typically through Hindu style meditation) ultimately to reach nirvana, otherwise blasphemously known as "Christ consciousness." If they do not succeed in this lifetime, they believe they will be reincarnated again and again in a seemingly endless procession of manifestations until they reach their mythical goal.

The first album was comprised of a combination of songs
that had been written before and after we [Love Song] had
become Christians. We had already written a number of
songs when we first came to Chuck Smith at Calvary Chapel
to "audition". Most of these songs were remarkably
scriptural, although a few "New Age" ideas had crept into
the lyrics. With just a little tweaking, the lyrics were cleaned
up from a biblical standpoint, and the songs became
acceptable to perform in front of Christian audiences.[267]

The first songs originally contained New Age ideas that had to be
given a little "tweaking" to make them acceptable to Christian
audiences! If songs have New Age ideas in them, that makes them
New Age songs. It is unclear exactly what was done to "tweak" or
"clean up" the New Age songs. Those words suggest minor
alterations. The minor alterations were for the purpose of making the
songs "acceptable to perform in front of Christian audiences."

As we have already seen, the words are incidental to the music.
There is no indication that there was any change in the music of the
New Age pagan songs. Furthermore, the standard for Christian music
should not be whether the music can be made minimally acceptable to
nominal Christians. The standard should be whether the music gives
glory and praise to God.

Read how "Christian" rock and roll affects the way one thinks.
Below is a statement from Erick Nelson, who "was one of the many
artists to come out of Calvary Chapel during the Jesus movement. His
name graced many Maranatha! Music recordings of that time and he
was a member of several Jesus bands including Selah and Good
News, in addition to later having a solo career."[268]

Then Love Song came up and played. The visual
presentation of the group was always impressive. **First, they
all had fairly long hair and beards, which was a definite
plus. They weren't boys, but men. You knew they had
been around - had tried drugs, alternative life styles,
religions, ... all of which gave them instant credibility.**[269]

Nelson was impressed that the members of *Love Song* had long hair; he viewed that as a plus. "Doth not even nature itself teach you, that, if a man have long hair, it is a shame unto him?" 1 Corinthians 11:14. Nelson thought that the fact that they had led a life of drugs, alternative lifestyles, and religions gave them instant credibility. How can any amount of sin give a Christian, or anyone for that matter, credibility? Sin brings shame, not credibility.

Even if Nelson intended (which intent is certainly not clear) to express the idea that they formerly, but no longer, led such a life of sin, his judgment of their credibility based on past sins is unbiblical. "They are of the world: therefore speak they of the world, and the world heareth them.." 1 John 4:5. "Denying ungodliness and worldly lusts, we should live soberly, righteously, and godly, in this present world." Titus 2:12. God makes it clear that a Christian should not revel in the sin and temptations of the world; a Christian should resist the devil and his worldly temptations. If one is to be a friend of the world, he will be an enemy of God.

> Ye adulterers and adulteresses, know ye not that **the friendship of the world is enmity with God? whosoever therefore will be a friend of the world is the enemy of God.** Do ye think that the scripture saith in vain, The spirit that dwelleth in us lusteth to envy? But he giveth more grace. Wherefore he saith, God resisteth the proud, but giveth grace unto the humble. Submit yourselves therefore to God. **Resist the devil, and he will flee from you. Draw nigh to God, and he will draw nigh to you. Cleanse *your* hands, *ye* sinners; and purify *your* hearts, *ye* double minded.** Be afflicted, and mourn, and weep: let your laughter be turned to mourning, and *your* joy to heaviness. (James 4:4-9 AV)

What is revealing is that Nelson explains that *Love Song* was a band that had music that sounded like secular music, but was about Jesus.

The overwhelming impression of Love Song was not that

they were another "religious" group, or "gospel" group. Like others at the time, I had originally thought that there was one thing called "religious" music, and another thing called "secular music". **Love Song did something that sounded like secular music, but was about Jesus. Their kind of music, to me, was not just a hip, contemporary version of "gospel music." That's exactly what it was not. It was part of a growing trend in popular music.**[270]

What Nelson does not understand is that there is no such thing as secular music! All music communicates with the spirit of man. When he says that it sounded like secular music, he really means that it sounded like heathen music. All pagan music is Satanic.

Another thing that Nelson does not understand is that pagan music does not become Christian music because it is about Jesus. Pagan music remains heathen music, whether it is about Jesus or not. All pagan music about Jesus either blasphemes Jesus or creates a different Jesus, who is not the omnipotent sovereign of the universe.

Notice how Nelson and Christian rockers have a form of godliness, but they deny the power of God. God predicted such would arise. Such an "anything goes" attitude is a manifestation of the Arminian gospel, in which the power of God to save by the will of his good pleasure is denied. They use Christian language, but they deny the real power of the gospel: the power of God to impart spiritual rebirth upon his elect. God commands us to turn away from such proud and blasphemous lovers of pleasure.

This know also, that in the last days perilous times shall come. For men shall be lovers of their own selves, covetous, boasters, proud, blasphemers, disobedient to parents, unthankful, unholy, Without natural affection, trucebreakers, false accusers, incontinent, fierce, despisers of those that are good, Traitors, heady, highminded, lovers of pleasures more than lovers of God; **Having a form of godliness, but denying the power thereof: from such turn away.** (2 Timothy 3:1-5 AV)

Love Song is known as the "Christian" Beatles. While some of their songs sound like Beatles songs, it is not clear that the group understands the implications of being called the "Christian" Beatles.

The press officer for the Beatles, Derek Taylor, said, "They're COMPLETELY ANTI-CHRIST. I mean, I am anti-Christ as well, but they're so anti-Christ they shock me which isn't an easy thing." (Saturday Evening Post, Aug. 8, 1964).

Paul McCartney said, "We probably seem to be anti-religious. . . none of us believes in God." (Hit Parader, Jan 1970, p.15)

John Lennon, in his book, A Spaniard in the Works, portrays Jesus Christ as, "Jesus El Pifico, a garlic-eating, stinking little yellow, greasy fascist bastard catholic spaniard." (A Spaniard in the Works, p.14).

Lennon also made that infamous statement, "Christianity will go, it will vanish and shrink. I needn't argue about that. I'm right and will be proved right. . . .We're more popular than Jesus now." (San Francisco Chronicle, April 13, 1966, p.26)

Ray Coleman quotes John Lennon as saying, "I've sold my soul to the DEVIL." (Coleman, Ray, Lennon p.256)[271]

Donald Phau further explains the depths of the Beatles Satanic roots by exposing their admiration for Aliester Crowley, who was an infamous Satanist, whose debauchery earned him the moniker: "The Beast:"

The cover of Sgt. Pepper's showed the Beatles with a background of, according to Ringo Starr, people "we like and admire" (Hit Parade, Oct. 1976, p.14). Paul McCartney said of Sgt. Pepper's cover, ". . . we were going to have photos on the wall of all our HEROS . . ." (Musician,

Special Collectors Edition, - Beatles and Rolling Stones, 1988, p.12)

One of the Beatle's heros included on the cover of Sgt. Pepper's was — the infamous Aliester Crowley! Most people, especially in 1967, did not even know who Crowley was — but the Beatles certainly did.[272]

* * *

Aliester Crowley is, without a doubt, the main spiritual "teacher" of rock music. Crowley's mission in life was to destroy Jesus Christ and Christianity, while exalting sex perversion, drugs, magick and Satan.

Aliester Crowley spews his hatred of Jesus Christ in The World's Tragedy: "I do not wish to argue that the doctrines of Jesus, they and they alone, have degraded the world to its present condition. I take it that Christianity is not only the cause but the symptom of slavery." (Aleister Crowley, The World's Tragedy, p. XXXIX)

"That religion they call Christianity; the devil they honor they call God. I accept these definitions, as a poet must do, if he is to be at all intelligible to his age, and it is their God and their religion that I HATE and will DESTROY." (Aleister Crowley, The World's Tragedy, p. XXXI)

In the introduction of The World's Tragedy, Israel Regardie says:

"This long, almost epic poem is one of the most bitter and vicious diatribes against Christianity that I have ever read."

Crowley's most famous teaching, "Do what thou wilt shalt be the whole of the law" became the "mantra" of the 60's revolution of drugs, sexual perversion and anti-Christianity. "Do your own thing" — "If it feels good do it".[273]

* * *

"The whole Beatle idea was to do what you want, right? To
take your own responsibility, do what you want and try not
to harm other people, right? DO WHAT THOU WILT, as
long as it doesn't hurt somebody. . ." ("The Playboy
Interviews with John Lennon & Yoko Ono", by David Sheff
& G. Barry Golson, p. 61)[274]

Notice that the mantra of the disciples of Aliester Crowley in the
rock and roll culture is to "do what thou wilt." To Satanists, that is
the "whole of the law." To them, free will is unfettered by God.
Satanists and rock and roll "artists" are the ultimate Arminians. It is
no wonder that "Christian" rock and roll sprang from an Arminian
church. The Arminian free will philosophy fits rather comfortably
with the rock and roll culture. Because of the disrepute of Christian
Rock and the desire to distance its association in the minds of
Christians from secular rock and roll, the Christian Rock industry
changed its name to Contemporary Christian Music (CCM). The
label changed, but the spiritual poison remains the same.

30 The Hidden Hand of the Illuminati

C huck Smith has slipped up and revealed a part of his character that would shock his followers. In the process he revealed his Zionist plans. Smith and his "ministry"are part of a conspiracy for Zionist conquest of Palestine. Smith's Zionist plans parallel the plans of the Illuminati, which is revealing in light of John Todd's allegations of Illuminati funding for Smith. An investigative team from *The Executive Intelligence Review* discovered a group called the "American Jerusalem Temple Foundation," which was an early source of "massive amounts of money from American-based Darbyite Christian fundamentalists"[275] that were poured into "Jerusalem operations, aimed, ultimately, at blowing up the Muslim holy sites at the Temple Mount, and building the Third Temple."[276]

In the middle of this planned bloodfest we find Chuck Smith, pastor of Calvary Chapel. *The Executive Intelligence Review* discovered the following:

> At the core of the Gnostic "dispensational premillennarianism," advocated by Nineteenth-Century Anglican clergyman John Nelson Darby, is the belief that the extermination of the Jews, in a final battle of Armageddon, brought on by the rebuilding of Solomon's

Temple, is the Biblical precondition for the second coming of the Messiah and the Rapture. **Pastor Chuck Smith, Dolphin's mentor at the Calvary Baptist Church, when asked by EIR whether he had any compunctions about unleashing a holy war that would lead to the possible extermination of millions of Jews and Muslims, replied, "Frankly, no, because it is all part of Biblical prophesy."[277]**

Smith was also full of praise for the Jewish zealots of the Temple Mount Faithful, and their founder, Goldfoot: "Do you want a real radical?" he asked. "Try Stanley Goldfoot. He's a wonder. His plan for the Temple Mount is to take sticks of dynamite and some M-16s and blow the Dome of the Rock and Al-Aqsa Mosques and just lay claim to the site."[278]

Who is Stanley Goldfoot, upon whom Chuck Smith heaps such praise? He is a psychopathic mass murderer and internationally recognized terrorist! He has admitted he helped plan the 1946 dynamite bombing of the King David Hotel that killed approximately 100 Christian, Jewish, and Muslim civilians.[279] Goldfoot has also admitted that he planned and directed the execution of the United Nations mediator, Count Folke Bernadotte, in Jerusalem, in the Fall of 1948.[280]

Chuck Smith is so impressed with Goldfoot that he invited that killer to lecture in his Calvary Chapel![281] Smith has also financed Goldfoot's Zionist activities! The Hebrew University of Jerusalem explains:

Chuck Smith, a noted minister and evangelist whose Calvary Chapel in Costa Mesa, California, has been one of the largest and most dynamic Charismatic churches in America, invited Goldfoot to lecture in his church, and his followers helped to finance Goldfoot's activity.[282]

Smith secured financial support for exploration of the exact site of the Temple. An associate of Smith, Lambert Dolphin, a California physicist and archeologist and leader of the "Science and Archeology Team," took it upon himself to explore the Temple Mount. An ardent premillennialist who believed that the building of the Temple was essential to the realization of messianic hopes.[283]

Can we regard Chuck Smith as a true minister of the gospel when he praises and financially supports a terrorist killer? Why would he do such a thing? Because both he and Goldfoot are Zionists, who want to bring Palestine under the complete control of Israel. One of the key goals of the Zionist Illuminati is to rule the world. Jewish control of Palestine is one step toward that Zionist goal. Let us explore just who are the Illuminati.

The "Illuminati" are a secret organization purportedly founded by a trained Jesuit named Adam Weishaupt in 1776.[284] As I will explain, it was not a coincidence that the Illuminati arose just three years after Pope Clement XIV's suppression of the Jesuits in 1773. Weishaupt was a Jew and a professor of canon law at Ingolstadt University, which was a Jesuit University and the center of the Jesuit counter-reformation.[285]

Alberto Rivera, a former Jesuit priest, stated that the occult Illuminati organization was not founded by Weishaupt, as many believe, but in fact was established long before Weishaupt. The Illuminati is in fact a reincarnation of the ancient *Alumbrados*, whose one time leader was Ignatius of Loyola, the founder of the Jesuits.[286] The Alumbrados and indeed the Illuminati trace their history back to the pharisees.[287]

Benjamin Disraeli was a Jew and a former Prime Minister of England; he revealed that the first Jesuits were Jews.[288] Ignatius of Loyola's secretary, Polanco, was of Jewish descent and was the only person present at Loyola's deathbed. Ignatius Loyola himself was a crypto-Jew of the Occult Cabala. A crypto-Jew is a Jew who converts to another religion and outwardly embraces the new religion, while secretly maintaining Jewish practices. James Lainez, who succeeded

Loyola as the second Jesuit General, was also of Jewish descent. The third Jesuit General was a Belgian Jew named Eberhard Mercurian.

Jews were attracted to the Jesuit order and joined in large numbers.[289] Some of the most influential Jesuits in history, such as Francisco Ribera (1537-1591) and Emanuel Lacunza (1731-1801), were Jews. Many of the Jesuit doctrines are similar to those found in the Babylonian Talmud.

The Illuminati was reconstituted by Lorenzo Ricco, the Jesuit General, in 1776, who used his disciple, Adam Weishaupt, as the front man for the organization (which was really not new at all).[290] The Jesuits, having just been suppressed by the pope in 1773, found it necessary to reemerge under the occult banner of the Illuminati, which was an alliance between the Jesuits and the very powerful Ashkenazi Jewish Banking House of Rothschild.

The purpose of the Illuminati initially was to avenge the papal suppression of the Jesuits by rooting out all religion and overturning the governments of the world, bringing them under a single world government, controlled of course by the Illuminati, under the authority of their god. That world government is commonly referred to by the Illuminati as the "New World Order." The god of the Illuminati is Satan.[291]

Adam Wieshaupt died in 1830 at the age of 82. Giuseppe Mazzini, who was an Italian revolutionary, then became the leader of the Illuminati. He held this position from 1834 until his death in 1872.

Michael Bunker reveals in his book *Swarms of Locusts* that Mazzini was a Roman Catholic Jesuit priest.[292] Bunker's book uncovers the Jesuit corruption of "Protestant Christianity," by injecting into it the poisonous Roman Catholic "free will" doctrine of Molinism, (commonly referred to as Arminianism.). Molinism was so named after Luis de Molina, who was a Jesuit priest.

Giuseppe Mazzini founded a group of revolutionaries formed for

the purpose of freeing Italy from the control of monarchy and the
Pope. Mazzini succeeded and Mazzini is today celebrated as an Italian
patriot. Mazzini's syndicate supported their efforts by robbing banks,
looting, kidnaping for ransom, and running a protection racket where
business were torched if protection money was not paid. As the
terror spread from the actions of Mazzini's gang, the word spread that
"Mazzini autorizza furti, incendi e attentati." In English it means
"Mazzini authorizes theft, arson, and kidnaping." It was
shortened to an acronym: "Mafia."[293]

On August 15, 1871, while Giuseppe Mazzini was the head of
the Illuminati in Europe, he wrote a letter to Albert Pike, who was
then the Sovereign Grand Commander of the Ancient and Accepted
Scottish Rite of Freemasonry of the Southern Jurisdiction U.S.A.
Pike succeeded to that Masonic position from Isaac Long, a Jew, who
in 1801, brought a statue of Baphomet (Satan) to Charleston, South
Carolina, where he helped established the Ancient and Accepted
Scottish Rite.[294]

In his letter to Pike, Mazzini gives the details for a plan for world
conquest, through three world wars. The first war would destroy
Czarist Russia and place that vast territory under the control of the
Illuminati. The second war would be caused by the differences
between the Political Zionists and the German Nationalists. This
would lead to the expansion of Russian Communist power and the
creation of a state of Israel in Palestine. The third war would be
caused by the conflict between the predicted State of Israel and the
Arab Muslims.[295]

In 1754 the first 25 degrees of the Scottish Rite of Freemasonry
were written by the Jesuits in the College of Jesuits of Clermont in
Paris.[296] The crypto-Jewish Jesuits inculcated Freemasonry with the
heathen occultism of the Kabbalah. Albert Pike explains this secret to
Masonry in the doctrinal bible of freemasonry, *Morals and Dogma*:
**"Masonry is a search for Light. That leads us directly back, as
you see, to the Kabalah."**[297]

The pagan Roman Catholic Church has been infiltrated by the

Talmudic Jews, primarily, but not exclusively, through the Jesuit order. Notice the similarities between the imperious whorish woman in Ezekiel 16:14-40, which is apostate Israel, and the Roman Catholic harlot of Revelation 17. They are one and the same. The crypto-Jewish Jesuits of the Roman Catholic Church are modern day Pharisees. Read *Solving the Mystery of Babylon the Great* for more detailed study on the Jewish origins of the Roman Catholic Church.

Albert Pike, the theological pontiff of Masonry, wrote that "[i]t is certain that its true pronunciation is not represented by the word Jehovah; and therefore that *that* is not the true name of Diety, nor the Ineffable Word."[298] God's word, however, states clearly that JEHOVAH is God's name. "That men may know that thou, whose name alone *is* JEHOVAH, *art* the most high over all the earth." (Psalms 83:18 AV)

If the Masons do not recognize JEHOVAH as God, who is their god? The god of the Masons is Lucifer, which was Satan's name before he rebelled against God and was cast out of heaven. Albert Pike said that "[t]he doctrine of Satanism is heresy; and the true and pure philosophic religion is the belief in Lucifer, the equal of Adonay; but Lucifer, God of Light and God of Good is struggling for humanity against Adonay, the God of Darkness and Evil."[299] Adonay is the Old Testament Hebrew word for God. Pike not only acknowledges that Lucifer is the god of Freemasonry, but he also blasphemes God by calling God "the God of Darkness and Evil."

The secret Illuminati organization was the hidden guiding hand behind the brutal French Revolution, during which 300,000 people were massacred in a godless orgy of violence.[300] Moses Mordecai Marx Levi, alias Karl Marx, was a Satanist and a member of the "League of the Just," which was a branch of the Illuminati.[301] In 1847, Marx was commissioned by the Illuminati to write the *Communist Manifesto*, which is an outline of their plans for world domination.[302]

There was nothing new in the *Communist Manifesto*; it was merely a plagiarization of the plans already espoused by Weishaupt and his disciple Clinton Roosevelt (a distant relative of Franklin Delano Roosevelt).[303] Between 1600 and 1750 the Jesuits controlled over a quarter million ignorant natives of Paraguay in over 30 communes which they called "reductions."[304] The Jesuits were the masters of these poor slaves, whose labors made the Jesuits immensely wealthy. The lessons learned in the "reductions" were memorialized in the communist manifesto.

The Illuminati, being pharisitical Jews, are Zionists to the core. All of their efforts are focused upon their Zionist goal to rule the world.[305] Zionism is not just a homeland for the Jews in Palestine as it is generally believed. It is much more than that. The rule of Palestine is just one step toward world domination.[306]

In order to further their Zionist plans it was necessary to inject their Zionist theology into the churches. This was done through a concerted campaign by agents of the Roman Catholic Church.[307] One of the methods used by the Roman Catholic theologians was to relegate much of the book of Revelation to some future time.[308] In 1590 a Roman Catholic Jesuit priest Francisco Ribera, in his 500 page commentary on the book of Revelation, placed the events of most of the book of Revelation in a period in the future just prior to the end of the world.[309] He claimed that the antichrist would be an individual who would not be manifested until very near the end of the world. He wrote that the antichrist would rebuild Jerusalem, abolish Christianity, deny Christ, persecute the church, and dominate the world for three and half years.[310]

Relegating the appearance of the antichrist to some time in the distant future just before the end of the world had the effect of concealing the true identity of the antichrist, that being the Pope of Rome.[311] The sea change in the position of almost all of the Protestant denominations toward Rome has been the direct result of this heretical interpretation of the bible by agents of the Roman Catholic Church, designed to conceal the Pope's identity as the antichrist.[312]

Another Jesuit, Cardinal Robert Bellarmine, promoted Ribera's teachings.[313] This Catholic interpretation of the book of Revelation did not become accepted in the Protestant denominations until a book titled *The Coming of the Messiah in Glory and Majesty* was published in 1812, 11 years after the death of its author.[314] The author of that book was another Jesuit by the name of Emanuel de Lacunza.

William Kimball in his book *Rapture, A Question of Timing*, reveals that Lacunza wrote the book under the pen name of Rabbi Juan Josaphat Ben Ezra.[315] Kimball attributes the pen name to a motive to conceal his identity, thus taking the heat off of Rome, and making his writings more palatable to the Protestant readers.[316] It is as likely that in fact the pen name was not a pen name at all, but rather Lacunza'a true identity as a Jewish Rabbi. It is possible that Lacunza was a crypto-Jew, who wrote the book under his true identity as a rabbi. One does not suddenly convert to Judaism and then become immediately so versed in that religion that one takes on the title "rabbi." He must have had the learning of a rabbi in order to write a book that contains knowledge of Judaism expected of a rabbi. The book was not published by Lacunza himself, but by someone else eleven years after his death

As with the writings of Ribera, Lacunza developed a futuristic perspective which restricted the prophetic fulfillments in the book of Revelation to the end of the world. He stated that the antichrist and all prophecies concerning the antichrist were yet to happen in the future.[317]

He also taught of a partial resurrection of the saints before the appearance of the antichrist, whom he stated was not a single individual but the body of godless masses left behind on the Earth after the resurrection of the saints.[318] The resurrection would be followed by God's judgements of wrath on the inhabitants of the Earth for an indeterminate period of not less than 45 days.[319]

Lacunza also wrote that during a millennium after the tribulation the Jewish animal sacrifices would be reinstated along with the Eucharist (the Mass) of the Catholic Church.[320] Lacunza has followed after Jewish fables and replaced the commandments of God with the commandments of men. *See* Titus 1:13. "They profess that they know God; but in works they deny *him*, being abominable, and disobedient, and unto every good work reprobate." (Titus 1:16 AV)

James Lainez, who succeeded Loyola as the second Jesuit General, was of Jewish descent. Jews were attracted to the Jesuit order and joined in large numbers.[321] Lacunza was no exception. He was a Jew, which explains why he introduced the eschatological teaching of a return to the Jewish animal sacrifices. That doctrine gives the Jews primacy in God's plan and relegates Christians to a prophetic parenthetical to be supplanted by the Jews during the supposed thousand year earthly reign of Christ. This construct has given rise to "Christian" Zionism, the error of which is exposed in this author's book: *Bloody Zion*.

It is no surprise that Chuck Smith's Calvary Chapel is an ardent supporter of Zionism and has a pretribulation rapture doctrine to match its Zionist philosophy.[322] Smith is following in a long line of Zionists, many of whom have been supported and nurtured by the Jewish Illuminati. Probably the most famous "Christian" Zionist was Cyrus I. Scofield, the author of the iconic Scofield Reference Bible. That so called "bible" was instrumental in popularizing the mythical "pretribulation rapture" doctrine so endemic in churches today.

The Scofield bible was funded and nurtured by World Zionist leaders who saw the Christian churches in America as an obstacle to their plan for the establishment of a Jewish homeland in Palestine. These Zionists initiated a program to infiltrate and change the Christian doctrines of those churches. Two of the tools used to accomplish this goal were Cyrus I. Scofield and a venerable, world respected European book publisher: The Oxford University Press.[323]

The scheme was to alter the Christian gospel and corrupt the church with a pro-Zionist subculture. "Scofield's role was to re-write the King James Version of the Bible by inserting Zionist-friendly notes in the margins, between verses and chapters, and on the bottoms of the pages."[324] In 1909, the Oxford University Press published and implemented a large advertising budget to promote the Scofield

Reference Bible.

The Scofield Reference Bible was a subterfuge designed to create a subculture around a new worship icon, the modern State of Israel. The new state of Israel did not yet exist, but the well-funded Zionists already had it on their drawing boards.[325]

"Since the death of its original author and namesake, The Scofield Reference Bible has gone through several editions. Massive pro-Zionist notes were added to the 1967 edition, and some of Scofield's most significant notes from the original editions were removed where they apparently failed to further Zionist aims fast enough. Yet this edition retains the title, "The New Scofield Reference Bible, Holy Bible, Editor C.I. Scofield."[326] It's anti-Arab, Zionist "Christian" subculture theology has fostered unyielding "Christian" support for the State of Israel and its barbaric subjugation of the native Palestinians.

Who was C.I. Scofield? Scofield was a young con-artist who engaged in a continual pattern of fraud and deception both before and after his alleged 1879 conversion. Scofield was a partner with John J. Ingalls, a Jewish lawyer, in a railroad scam which led to Scofield being sentenced to prison for criminal forgery.[327]

"Upon his release from prison, Scofield deserted his first wife, Leonteen Carry Scofield, and his two daughters, Abigail and Helen, and he took as his mistress a young girl from the St. Louis Flower Mission. He later abandoned her for Helen van Ward, whom he eventually married."[328]

Scofield had developed connections with a subgroup of the Illuminati, known as the Secret Six.[329] He was taken under the wing of Samuel Untermeyer, an ardent Zionist who later became Chairman of the American Jewish Committee and President of the American League of Jewish Patriots.[330] "Untermeyer introduced Scofield to numerous Zionist and socialist leaders, including Samuel Gompers, Fiorello LaGuardia, Abraham Straus, Bernard Baruch and Jacob Schiff."[331] These powerful figures financed Scofield's research trips to Oxford and arranged the publication and distribution of his reference bible. He who pays the piper calls the tune.

In 1892 Scofield fraudulently claimed to have a Doctorate of Divinity and began calling himself "Doctor Scofield."[332] In fact, Scofield did not have a doctorate degree from any Seminary or University or for that matter any degree of any kind from any college. His Scofield Reference Bible was a skillfully promoted heresy that has taken root in many churches today. Scofield's theology called for a supposed plan by God to rebuild the Jewish temple and renew the temple sacrifices. That is exactly what Chuck Smith is trying to bring about through his alliance with terrorists like Stanley Goldfoot.

Hebrews 8:1-10:39 makes explicitly clear that Christ fulfilled the requirements of the law by sacrificing himself once for sins for all time. If the blood of animals were sufficient to satisfy God there would be no need for him to come to the earth and sacrifice himself. "But now hath he obtained a more excellent ministry, by how much also he is the mediator of a better covenant, which was established upon better promises. For if that first *covenant* had been faultless, then should no place have been sought for the second." (Hebrews 8:6-7 AV)

> So Christ was **once offered** to bear the sins of many; and unto them that look for him shall he appear the second time without sin unto salvation. (Hebrews 9:28 AV)

> By the which will we are sanctified through the offering of the body of Jesus Christ **once** *for all*. And every priest standeth daily ministering and offering oftentimes the same sacrifices, which can never take away sins: But this man, after he had **offered one sacrifice for sins for ever**, sat down on the right hand of God; From henceforth expecting till his enemies be made his footstool. For **by one offering he hath perfected for ever them that are sanctified**. (Hebrews 10:10-14 AV)

God would not have us return to the weak and beggarly elements of the Old Testament law. *See* Galatians 4:9-11. To teach such a thing is to blasphemously state that Christ's sacrifice was imperfect and insufficient, and that therefore there is a need to reinstate the animal sacrifices. The Old Testament law was to act as a schoolmaster until the promise of Christ. God would have no reason to reinstate something that was intended to be in place only until he came to offer his own body as a perfect sacrifice. In Christ there is neither Jew nor Gentile, we are all one by faith in Christ. He is not going to divide us once again into Jew and Gentile. His church is his body which cannot be divided. 1 Corinthians 1:13. A kingdom divided against itself cannot stand. Mark 3:24.

> But before faith came, we were kept under the law, shut up unto the faith which should afterwards be revealed. Wherefore the law was our schoolmaster *to bring us* unto Christ, that we might be justified by faith. **But after that faith is come, we are no longer under a schoolmaster**. For ye are all the children of God by faith in Christ Jesus. For as many of you as have been baptized into Christ have put on Christ. **There is neither Jew nor Greek, there is neither bond nor free, there is neither male nor female: for ye are all one in Christ Jesus**. And if ye *be* Christ's, then are ye Abraham's seed, and heirs according to the promise. (Galatians 3:23-29 AV)

The bible makes clear that the old covenant is to vanish, being replaced by the new covenant of faith in Jesus Christ. "In that he saith, A new covenant, he hath made the first old. Now that which decayeth and waxeth old *is* ready to vanish away." (Hebrews 8:13 AV) Why would God reinstate something which he has said would vanish away and in which he has had no pleasure? "In burnt offerings and sacrifices for sin thou hast had no pleasure." (Hebrews 10:6 AV)

The true Jews are those that accept their Messiah, Jesus. The kingdom of God is a spiritual kingdom; it is not a kingdom based on race or tribe. Those who are chosen by God to believe in Jesus Christ are the spiritual Israel of God.

Not as though the word of God hath taken none effect. **For they are not all Israel, which are of Israel**: Neither, because they are the seed of Abraham, *are they* all children: but, In Isaac shall thy seed be called. That is, **They which are the children of the flesh, these are not the children of God: but the children of the promise are counted for the seed**. (Romans 9:6-8 AV)

For he is not a Jew, which is one outwardly; neither *is that* circumcision, which is outward in the flesh: But **he** *is* **a Jew, which is one inwardly; and circumcision is that of the heart, in the spirit, *and* not in the letter; whose praise** *is* **not of men, but of God**. (Romans 2:28-29 AV)

God has not cast away Israel. His Israel is made up of those whom he foreknew before the foundation of the world who would believe in Jesus unto salvation. Therefore, all Israel shall be saved.

God hath not cast away his people which he foreknew. (Romans 11:2 AV) And so **all Israel shall be saved**. (Romans 11:26 AV)

31 Arminian Counterfeit Bibles

"Maranatha! Music," founded by Chuck Smith (allegedly sold in 1988 to Smith's nephew, Chuck Fromm), has branched out to providing NIV (New International Version) bibles. Their website states that "Maranatha! Book Publishing was launched in 1999 as we partnered with Zondervan to create The NIV Worship Bible." Zondervan is owned by Harper Collins, which is the publisher of *The Satanic Bible*.[333] "Can two walk together, except they be agreed?" Amos 3:3.

Rupert Murdoch's company, News Corporation, owns Harper Collins.[334] Murdoch owns the exclusive rights to the NIV.[335] Murdoch has been described as an internationalist and a pornographer.[336] *Time* magazine called Murdoch one of the four most powerful people in the world, and for good reason; he has a media empire that includes Twentieth Century Fox, Fox Television, cable television providers, satellites, and newspapers and television stations throughout America, Europe, and Asia.[337] The pope bestowed upon Murdoch the title of "Knight Commander of St. Gregory" for promoting the interests of the Roman Catholic Church.[338]

Although the "Maranatha! NIV Worship Bible" does not carry the title "Satanic Bible," it is in a very real sense a Satanic Bible! The combined effect of having a corrupted text and then having that text interpreted using dynamic equivalence has been that the NIV has 64,098 fewer words than the King James Bible.[339] That is a 10% loss in the bible. That means that an NIV bible would have 170 fewer pages than a typical 1,700 page King James Bible.[340] Let's read what God thinks about such deletions of his holy words. "And if any man shall take away from the words of the book of this prophecy, God shall take away his part out of the book of life, and out of the holy city, and from the things which are written in this book." Revelation 22:19.

The texts of the new bible versions, such as the NIV, manifest the antichrist agenda of its publishers. In Isaiah there is a passage about Lucifer that refers to him as "Lucifer, son of the morning." In the NIV, the Isaiah passage is changed.

KJV	NIV
How art thou fallen from heaven, O **Lucifer**, son of the morning! *how* art thou cut down to the ground, which didst weaken the nations! For thou hast said in thine heart, I will ascend into heaven, I will exalt my throne above the stars of God: I will sit also upon the mount of the congregation, in the sides of the north: I will ascend above the heights of the clouds; I will be like the most High. Yet thou shalt be brought down to hell, to the sides of the pit. (Isaiah 14:12-15 KJV)	How you have fallen from heaven, O **morning star**, son of the dawn! You have been cast down to the earth, you who once laid low the nations! You said in your heart, "I will ascend to heaven, I will raise my throne above the stars of God: I will sit enthroned on the mount of assembly, in the utmost heights of the sacred mountain. I will ascend above the tops of the clouds; I will make myself like the most High." But you are brought down to the grave, to the depths of the pit. (Isaiah 14:12-15 NIV)

Notice that the NIV has changed the subject of the passage from "Lucifer" to the "morning star." What is the significance of that change? In Revelation 22:16, Jesus calls himself the "morning star." Do you see what Satan has done? Jesus is the "morning star" in the NIV Isaiah passage. Satan has taken a passage that refers to Satan's destruction and has twisted it in the NIV to describe the destruction of Jesus, who is Lord God Almighty.

The authors of the NIV, who are evil minions of the devil, have committed the unpardonable sin by blaspheming the Holy Spirit. A person blasphemes the Holy Spirit when he attributes to God the characteristics of the devil. Mark 3:29-30. After the Pharisees alleged that Jesus cast out devils by the power of Beelzebub, the prince of the devils, Jesus said that all sin will be forgiven except for blaspheming the Holy Ghost. Matthew 12:24-32. The NIV has blasphemed the Holy Ghost by changing Isaiah chapter 14 in the NIV to blasphemously attribute to God the evil characteristics of Lucifer. In their Satanic NIV, Isaiah chapter 14 has been changed to prophesy that it is not Lucifer who will in the end be cast into hell, but rather the "morning star," who is the Lord God Jesus Christ.

The NIV is ever so subtle in its twisting of the scriptures in order to conceal the sovereignty of God and instead put the focus on the decision of man. The simple changing of the word "of" to "in" is all it takes in some passages to hide the gospel of grace. Let's look at some examples:

KJV	NIV
Even the righteousness of God which is by **faith <u>of</u> Jesus** Christ unto all and upon all them that believe. (Romans 3:22 KJV) (emphasis added)	This righteousness is given through **faith <u>in</u> Jesus** Christ to all who believe. (Romans 3:22 NIV) (emphasis added)

Notice that the righteousness of God is "by the faith <u>of</u> Jesus Christ." The passage explains the source of the faith; faith comes from Jesus Christ, hence it is the "faith <u>of</u> Jesus Christ." The NIV conceals the source of the faith and simply states the result of the working of Christ, that the righteousness of God "comes through faith

in Jesus Christ." The passage is supposed to reveal the source of our faith, instead it is changed to reveal the object of our faith.

The reader of the NIV can quite comfortably fit the Arminian gospel into the watered down passage. The innocent Christian sheep using an NIV bible will not have any notice that an Arminian "minister" is preaching a false gospel, because the NIV has concealed the word of God from him. If the Christian uses a KJV Bible, it would be impossible to believe the Arminian gospel, unless the reader ignores the plain language of Romans 3:22. That passage indicates that our faith comes from Jesus. One cannot have faith **in** Jesus without being given the faith **of** Jesus. The Arminian gospel, that states that man is the source of his own faith, is exposed as a lie in Romans 3:22. Satan had to do something, so he decided to alter God's word to hide that truth in his NIV bible.

We see the same thing in the NIV corruption of Galatians 2:20:

KJV	NIV
I am crucified with Christ: nevertheless I live; yet not I, but Christ liveth in me: and the life which I now live in the flesh I live **by the faith of the Son of God**, who loved me, and gave himself for me. (Galatians 2:20 KJV) (emphasis added)	I have been crucified with Christ and I no longer live, but Christ lives in me. The life I live in the body, I live **by faith in the Son of God**, who loved me and gave himself for me. (Galatians 2:20 NIV) (emphasis added)

Next, read Galatians 2:16. The KJV passage indicates that Jesus Christ is both the source of our faith and the object of our faith. There is a clear distinction in the passage between the faith "**of**" Jesus and the faith "**in**" Jesus. The passage reveals that the faith "**of**" Christ is the reason we have faith "**in**" Christ. Our Justification is by the faith "**of**" Christ. We believe "**in**" Jesus, because we have the faith "**of**" Jesus. Jesus is both the object of our faith and the source of our faith. The faith supplied by Jesus is the means of our justification. Jesus has done it all! The passage refers to the source of our faith as being "**of**" Christ in two separate clauses. The editors of the NIV removed both references to the faith "**of**" Christ; they end up repeating faith "**in**" Christ 3 times.

KJV	NIV
Knowing that a man is not justified by the works of the law, but **by the faith of Jesus Christ**, even we have **believed in Jesus** Christ, that we might be **justified by the faith of Christ**, and not by the works of the law: for by the works of the law shall no flesh be justified. (Galatians 2:16 KJV) (emphasis added)	Know that a man is not justified by observing the law, but **by faith in Jesus Christ**. So we, too, have put our **faith in Christ Jesus** that we may be justified by **faith in Christ** and not by observing the law, because by observing the law no one will be justified. (Galatians 2:16 NIV) (emphasis added)

The Galatians 2:16 passage in the NIV excises Christ as the source of our faith. In the NIV it is all up to man; Christ is out of the picture, except as the object of faith. The object of faith in the NIV is a different Jesus from the true Jesus of the gospel; the NIV Jesus is a helpless Arminian Jesus. He is not the source of faith.

People are being deceived into believing another gospel (an anti-gospel) with a different Jesus from the true omnipotent Jesus. Their Jesus is a pathetic helpless Jesus, who is reliant upon the weak and enslaved will of man. "For if he that cometh preacheth **another Jesus**, whom we have not preached, or *if* ye receive another spirit, which ye have not received, or another gospel, which ye have not accepted, ye might well bear with him." (2 Corinthians 11:4 KJV)

> **I marvel that ye are so soon removed from him that called you into the grace of Christ unto another gospel:** Which is not another; but there be some that trouble you, and would pervert the gospel of Christ. **But though we, or an angel from heaven, preach any other gospel unto you than that which we have preached unto you, let him be accursed.** As we said before, so say I now again, **If any**

man **preach any other gospel unto you than that ye have
received, let him be accursed.** (Galatians 1:6-9 KJV)

The NIV removes the grace of Christ and replaces it with a
cursed free will gospel! Every passage which describes the "faith **of** "
Jesus Christ has been changed in the NIV to read "faith **in**" Jesus
Christ, or otherwise obscured by other language. *See, e.g.,* Galatians
3:22, 5:22; Ephesians 3:12; Philippians 3:9; James 2:1, and
Revelation 14:12.

It is clear that the NIV has an Armenian agenda. For example in
Revelation 14:12 we read: "Here is the patience of the saints: here are
they that keep the commandments of God, and **the faith of Jesus.**"
This is changed in the NIV to: "This calls for patient endurance on the
part of the saints who obey God's commandments and **remain
faithful to Jesus.**" Notice how nicely the NIV fits in with the
Arminian view that salvation can be lost, and so one must "remain
faithful to Jesus." The NIV Revelation 14:12 passage completely
obscures the description of faith as "the faith **of** Jesus."

Collossians 2:12 is clear; faith is by the operation of God. The
NIV, however, hides that fact from the reader. According to the NIV,
you are raised with Christ through "your" faith. "The faith **of** the
operation of God" is changed in the NIV to "**your** faith **in** the power
of God."

KJV	NIV
Buried with him in baptism, wherein also **ye are risen with him through the faith of the operation of God**, who hath raised him from the dead. (Colossians 2:12 KJV) (emphasis added)	Having been buried with him in baptism and **raised with him through your faith in the power of God**, who raised him from the dead. (Colossians 2:12 NIV) (emphasis added)

Will Kinney reveals how the NIV, and the other modern bible
versions, dilute the true gospel of grace and promote a devilish

Arminian anti-gospel:

> Much of modern Christianity pictures God as a
> grandfatherly figure wishing so badly that his errant
> creatures would heed his pleadings and decide of their own
> free will to choose to believe and cast their vote for God.
> For those of us who have been granted by our gracious Lord
> to see the great truths of election and sovereign grace, we
> should be greatly concerned to see how many of these truths
> have been diluted in the new bible versions.[341]

* * *

There is a subtle twisting of God's inspired words taking
place in many modern versions in how they are rendering
the phrase "respecteth not persons". This is so subtle, that I
believe most Christians have not noticed it. The change in
meaning produced by versions like the NKJV, NIV, and
NASB unfortunately fits in with so much of modern,
popular theology, that many would actually consider it to be
an improvement over the KJB's reading. It fits the
philosophy of the natural mind of man.

The concept that "God has created all men equal" does not
come from the Holy Bible. God obviously has not created
all men equal, nor does He deal with every single individual
or nation in what seems to us as a fair and impartial manner.
Many have become so influenced in their thinking by the
reasoning of the world, that they cannot discern this obvious
truth.

God has created, formed and made each of us. Yet He has
not given to all equal intelligence, good looks, physical
skills, nor spiritual gifts. "He divideth to every man
severally as He will." Exodus 4:11 tells us "And the LORD
said unto him, Who hath made man's mouth? or who maketh
the dumb, or deaf, or the seeing, or the blind? have not I the
LORD?".

Not all are born in a country which even has the word of God in its culture, or where it would be openly taught and encouraged. Psalm 147:19,20 "He sheweth his word unto Jacob, his statutes and his judgments unto Israel. He hath not dealt so with any nation: and as for his judgments, they have not known them. Praise ye the LORD." Some are born in abject poverty, disease and ignorance, while others are blessed with abundant crops, education and families that care for them. "The rich and poor meet together: the LORD is the maker of them all." Proverbs 22:2.

The phrase "to accept the persons of men" or "to respect persons" does not mean, as the modern versions have translated it, "to show partiality" or "to show favoritism". One of the chief arguments of the Arminian side against the doctrine of election is: "God does not show partiality or favoritism, so election cannot be true." The new bibles are reinforcing this fallacious argument.

Not to show partiality is to treat all men equally; and this God does not do, as His word clearly testifies. Daniel Webster's 1828 dictionary defines "respecter of persons" as a person who regards the external circumstances of others in his judgment, and suffers his opinions to be biased by them. God's dealings with a man are not based on outward appearance, position, rank, wealth or nationality. Rather, His own sovereign purpose and pleasure of His will are the only deciding factors.

We are told in Deuteronomy 7:6-8 "For thou art an holy people unto the LORD thy God: the LORD thy God hath chosen thee to be a special people unto himself, above all people that are upon the face of the earth. The LORD did not set his love upon you, nor choose you, because ye were more in number than any people: for ye were the fewest of all people: But because the LORD loved you". Deuteronomy 10: 14-17 "Behold, the heaven and the heaven of heavens is the LORD'S thy God, the earth also, with all that therein is.

Only the LORD had a delight in thy fathers to love them, and he chose their seed after them, even you above all people, as it is this day." Verse 17 "For the LORD thy God is God of gods, and Lord of lords, a great God, a mighty, and a terrible, which REGARDETH NOT PERSONS, nor taketh reward." Here both election and not regarding persons are used in the same context.

God says He chose only the fathers (Abraham, Isaac and Jacob) and their seed to be His people, and not the others. That He "regardeth not persons" means that He does this, not on the basis of their nationality, nor their good moral character (for they were a stiffnecked and rebellious people), but because it was His good pleasure to do so. . . . [T]he NKJV, NIV and NASB have "shows no partiality". If God chose Israel to be His people, and not the others, is not this showing partiality?

Deut. 14:1,2 "Ye are the children of the LORD your God...and the LORD hath chosen thee to be a peculiar people unto himself, above all the nations that are upon the earth." Why did not God choose the other nations to be his children and to know his laws? Isn't this showing partiality or favoritism?

One verse among the hundreds that have been messed up by the NKJV, NIV and NASB is 2 Samuel 14:14. Here Joab saw that king David's heart was toward his son Absalom. So Joab sends a wise woman to speak to the king. In verse 14 she says: "For we must needs die, and are as water spilt on the ground, which cannot be gathered up again: NEITHER DOTH GOD RESPECT ANY PERSON: yet doth he devise means, that his banished be not expelled from him." In other words, we all must die, whether rich, poor, Jew, Gentile, man or woman, king or servant; God does not look at our social station and on this basis exclude some from death.

* * *

[M]any bibles, including the NKJV, NIV and NASB have
the ridiculous reading of "YET GOD DOES NOT TAKE
AWAY LIFE", instead of "neither doth God respect any
person". This is a lie and a contradiction. In this very book
in chapter 12:15 "the LORD struck the child" of David and
Bathsheeba and it died. In I Sam. 2:6 we are told "The
LORD killeth, and maketh alive: he bringeth down to the
grave, and bringeth up", and in Deuteronomy 32:39 God
says "See now that I, even I, am he, and there is no god with
me: I kill, and I make alive; I wound, and I heal: neither is
there any that can deliver out of my hand."

It is not that the Hebrew will not allow the meaning found in
the KJB, that the NKJV, NIV and NASB have so badly
mistranslated 2 Samuel 14:14. They all likewise have
translated these same words in other places as they stand in
the KJB and others.

This phrase "no respecter of persons" is found six times in
the New Testament, and every time the modern versions
have distorted the true meaning. Romans 2:11, Ephesians
6:9, Colossians 3:25, James 2:1 and 9, and Acts 10:34. In
each case it has to do with not receiving the face, outward
position, nationality or social rank of another. But God does
not treat all people the same, nor are we told to do so either.
We are to withdraw from some, avoid, exclude, reject,
separate from, and not cast our pearls before others. Most
importantly, God Himself chose His elect people in Christ
before the foundation of the world and "of the SAME
LUMP" makes one vessel unto honour and another unto
dishonour - Romans 9:21. This is definitely showing
partiality, but it is not respecting persons.

Romans 2:11 says "For there is no respect of persons with
God.". . . But the NKJV, NASB say "no partiality" and the
NIV says "not show favoritism". The Worldwide English
N.T. says: "God does not love some people more than

others". Yet this very book declares in Romans 9 "For the children being not yet born, neither having done any good or evil, that the purpose of God according to election might stand, not of works but of him that calleth...Jacob have I loved, but Esau have I hated...I will have mercy on whom I will have mercy...So then it is not of him that willeth, nor of him that runneth, but of God that sheweth mercy...Therefore hath he mercy on whom he will have mercy, and whom he will he hardeneth."

Please consider the true meaning of the phrase "no respecter of persons" and contrast it with the modern rendering. I hope you will see that it is not the same at all. Only the KJB contains the whole truth of the counsel of God.[342]

God's word in the English language is found in the Authorized (King James) Version (hereinafter referred to as **AV** for Authorized Version or **KJV** for King James Version). The NIV and all new English translations of the bible are materially different; they are the product of the imaginations of interpreters who have applied their personal prejudices to slant already corrupted texts to comport with their own ideas. They are truly counterfeit bibles, or more accurately - Satanic bibles. If you think that is hyperbole, read on, and you will see that the point will be proven.

God's word is the way to salvation. God would not leave us without the means for our salvation. The following scripture passages testify that God has promised that his word will be preserved forever.

For verily I say unto you, Till heaven and earth pass, one jot or one tittle shall in no wise pass from the law, till all be fulfilled. (Matthew 5:18 AV)

Heaven and earth shall pass away, but my words shall not pass away. (Matthew 24:35 AV)

The words of the LORD *are* pure words: *as* silver tried in a furnace of earth, purified seven times. **Thou shalt keep**

them, O LORD, thou shalt preserve them from this generation for ever. (Psalms 12:6-7 AV)

[T]he word of the Lord endureth for ever. And this is the word which by the gospel is preached unto you. (1 Peter 1:25 AV)

The grass withereth, the flower fadeth: but **the word of our God shall stand for ever.** (Isaiah 40:8 AV)

For ever, O LORD, thy word is settled in heaven. (Psalms 119:89 AV)

Satan knows that the word of God is the way to salvation. Satan also knows that God has promised to preserve his words, and so it would be futile for him to try to destroy God's words. Therefore, instead of trying to destroy God's words, Satan instituted a two prong strategy to keep the Holy Scriptures from the people. The first prong of the strategy was to outlaw the possession and reading of the Holy Bible. When, over the years, that strategy proved ineffective, Satan instituted his second prong, which is to deny that God has preserved his words and offer counterfeit bibles to the world and to deceive people into believing his counterfeits are the closest that they can get to God's genuine word.

The Roman Church knows that if the people are able to read for themselves God's word they will discover that the Catholic traditions and doctrines are not just in addition to the Scriptures, they violate the Scriptures. The Catholic Church has a long history of trying to keep God's word from the people. For example, at the *Council of Terragona* in 1234 A.D. the Roman Catholic Church prohibited anyone from possessing any part of the Old or New Testaments in any of the Romance languages (Portuguese, Spanish, Catalan, Provencal, French, Rhaeto-Romance, Italian, Sardinian, and Romanian). The council ruled that anyone owning a Bible was to turn it over to the local Catholic bishop to be burned. In 1229 at the *Council of Toulouse* (Pope Gregory IX presiding), the Catholic Church prohibited "laymen" from having the Holy Scriptures or translating

them into the "vulgar tongue" (common language of the country). In
1551 the Catholic *Inquisitional Index of Valentia* forbade the Holy
Bible to be translated into Spanish or any other "vernacular." In 1559
the Roman Catholic *Index Librorum Prohibitorum* (Index of
Prohibited Books) required permission from the Catholic Church to
read the Catholic version of the Bible; all Christian Bible versions
were simply prohibited. On September 8, 1713, Pope Clement XI
issued his Dogmatic Constitution, *Unigenitus,* which in part
condemned as error the teaching that all people may read the Sacred
Scripture. On May 5, 1824 Pope Leo XII issued his encyclical *Ubi
Primum* which exhorted the bishops to remind their flocks not to read
the Bible. On May 24, 1829 Pope Pius VIII issued the encyclical
Traditi Humilitati, which exhorted Catholics to check the spread of
Bibles translated into the vernacular, because those Bibles endangered
the "sacred" teachings of the Catholic Church. On May 8, 1844, Pope
Gregory XVI issued his encyclical *Inter Praecipuas* in which he
described Bible societies as plotting against the Catholic faith by
providing Bibles to the common people, whom he referred to as
"infidels." On January 25, 1897, Pope Leo XIII issued his Apostolic
Constitution *Officiorum ac Munerum* which prohibited all versions of
the Bible in the vernacular tongue. The 1918 Catholic Code of
Cannon Law, Index of Prohibited Books, Cannon 1385, § 1 prohibited
publishing any edition of the Holy Scriptures without previous
Catholic "ecclesiastical censorship." The 1983 Catholic Code of
Cannon Law, Cannon 825, § 1 prohibits the publishing of the Sacred
Scriptures without the permission of the Apostolic See or the
Conference of Bishops.

The official doctrines of the Catholic Church prohibiting the
publication, possession, or reading of the Holy Bible, were not a
mere suggestions, they were enforced. For example, on October 6,
1536 at Vilvorde (outside Brussels, Belgium) William Tyndale was
burned at the stake.[343] His crime was that he translated the Holy
Scriptures into English and was making copies available to the people
in violation of the rules of the Roman Catholic Church.[344]

The progenitors of the Catholic Church (pharisaic Jews) were
around in the time of the apostles, wresting the Holy Scriptures from

the people.

> And account that the longsuffering of our Lord *is* salvation;
> even as our beloved brother Paul also according to the
> wisdom given unto him hath written unto you;   As also in
> all *his* epistles, speaking in them of these things; in which
> are some things hard to be understood, **which they that are
> unlearned and unstable wrest, as *they do* also the other
> scriptures, unto their own destruction**. Ye therefore,
> beloved, seeing ye know *these things* before, beware lest ye
> also, being led away with the error of the wicked, fall from
> your own stedfastness. (2 Peter 3:15-17 AV)

With the advent of the printing press (circa 1455) making Bibles
available to the ordinary man, it became obvious to Satan that he
could not keep God's word from the masses, so he instituted the
second prong of his attack on God's word in earnest. He offered
counterfeit bibles. The Holy Scriptures reveal a pattern by Satan from
the beginning to tamper with God's word. God commanded Adam
not to eat from the tree of the knowledge of good and evil.

> And the LORD God commanded the man, saying, **Of every
> tree of the garden thou mayest freely eat: But of the tree
> of the knowledge of good and evil, thou shalt not eat of
> it: for in the day that thou eatest thereof thou shalt
> surely die.** (Genesis 2:16-17 AV)

In *Genesis* 3:1-5 the serpent misquotes God, changing God's
words; he tricks Eve into eating from the tree of knowledge of good
and evil by asking her if God commanded that they not eat of any of
the trees in the garden. When Eve responds, she also misquotes God,
saying that he commanded that they should not touch the fruit, when
God merely prohibited the eating of the fruit. God told Adam that if
he ate from the tree "thou shalt surely die."

Once Satan perceived that Eve was ignorant of God's true words
he felt confident that he could convince Eve to disobey God by subtly
misquoting what God had said. Satan took the warning by God and

added one word. Satan said to Eve: "Ye shall **not** surely die." What
Satan said sounded authoritative. It sounded almost like what God had
said; but that one word corrupted God's word and turned it from the
words of God to the words of Satan. The result of the corruption by
Satan of God's word was the greatest tragedy in history, the fall of
Adam and Eve!

> Now the serpent was more subtil than any beast of the field
> which the LORD God had made. And he said unto the
> woman, Yea, hath God said, **Ye shall not eat of <u>every</u> tree
> of the garden**? And the woman said unto the serpent, We
> may eat of the fruit of the trees of the garden: But of the
> fruit of the tree which *is* in the midst of the garden, God
> hath said, Ye shall not eat of it, **neither shall ye touch it**,
> lest ye die. And the serpent said unto the woman, **Ye shall
> not surely die**: For God doth know that in the day ye eat
> thereof, then your eyes shall be opened, and ye shall be as
> gods, knowing good and evil. (Genesis 3:1-5 AV)

In apparent reference to Satan's corruption of God's word in the
Garden of Eden, Jesus admonished Satan: "That man shall not live by
bread alone, but by **every word** of God." (Luke 4:4 AV) Just as
Satan did in the Garden of Eden, he now tries to confuse people about
what God has said: "Yea, hath God said . . . ." Pediatrician Dr.
Lawrence Dunegan attended a lecture on March 20, 1969 at a
gathering of pediatricians at a meeting of the Pittsburgh Pediatric
Society. The lecturer at that meeting was a Dr. Richard Day (who died
in 1989). At the time of the lecture Dr. Day was Professor of
Pediatrics at Mount Sinai Medical School in New York. Previously,
Dr. Day had served as Medical Director of Planned Parenthood
Federation of America. Dr. Dunegan was well acquainted with Dr.
Day and described him as an insider in the "order." Dr. Dunegan did
not explain what the "order" was, but from the lecture it was clear that
it was a very powerful secret society made up of minions in service to
Satan.

During the lecture Dr. Day revealed many of the satanic plans
that the members of the "order" had agreed upon that would change

the United States from a Christian society to a pagan society. One of
the strategies was to introduce new bible versions. By the time of the
lecture in 1969, that strategy had long previously been implemented.
Dr. Day was indicating that the final success of that strategy was in
sight as henceforth it would be implemented with new vigor. Dr.
Dunegan explains:

> Another area of discussion was Religion. This is an avowed
> atheist speaking. And he [Dr. Day] said, "Religion is not
> necessarily bad. A lot of people seem to need religion, with
> it's mysteries and rituals - so they will have religion. But the
> major religions of today have to be changed because they
> are not compatible with the changes to come. The old
> religions will have to go. Especially Christianity. Once the
> Roman Catholic Church is brought down, the rest of
> Christianity will follow easily. Then a new religion can be
> accepted for use all over the world. It will incorporate
> something from all of the old ones to make it more easy for
> people to accept it, and feel at home in it. Most people won't
> be too concerned with religion. They will realize that they
> don't need it.
>
> In order to accomplish this, the Bible will be changed. It
> will be rewritten to fit the new religion. Gradually, key
> words will be replaced with new words having various
> shades of meaning. Then the meaning attached to the new
> word can be close to the old word - and as time goes on,
> other shades of meaning of that word can be emphasized.
> and then gradually that word replaced with another word." I
> don't know if I'm making that clear. But the idea is that
> everything in Scripture need not be rewritten, just key words
> replaced by other words. And the variability in meaning
> attached to any word can be used as a tool to change the
> entire meaning of Scripture, and therefore make it
> acceptable to this new religion. Most people won't know the
> difference; and this was another one of the times where he
> said, "the few who do notice the difference won't be enough
> to matter."[345]

In accordance with the aforementioned conspiracy, Satan and his minions now offer people a whole assortment of different bible versions, which change and twist God's word. God's word is with us today in the **Authorized (King James) Version** (referred to as **AV or KJV**). All other bible versions are tainted by the hands of Satan and his minions, including the New King James Version (NKJV). "Ye have perverted the words of the living God, of the LORD of hosts our God." Jeremiah 23:36. The corrupted bible versions are essentially Roman Catholic bible versions.[346] Sadly, most of the so called church leaders of today have accepted Satan's counterfeit bibles.

The following is a partial list of the fraudulent bible versions: New International Version (NIV), Contemporary English Version (CEV), New Century Version (NCV), New World Translation (NWT), American Standard Version (ASV), New American Standard Bible (NASB), Revised Version (RV), Revised Standard Version (RSV), New Revised Standard Version (NRSV), Amplified Version (AMP), New King James Version (NKJV), 21st Century King James Version (KJ21), Third Millennium Bible (TMB), Douay-Rheims Version (DRV), Good News for Modern Man (GNB), Today's English Version (TEV), Living Bible (LB), Darby Translation (DBY), Jerusalem Bible (JB), and New Jerusalem Bible (NJB).

The Authorized (King James) Version is an English translation of the Masoretic (traditional) Hebrew Old Testament, whereas the NIV bible versions are taken from an inferior and corrupted mixture of the Septuagint (Greek Old Testament), Samaritan Pentateuch, Dead Sea Scrolls, and a variety of other transcripts. The corrupt Septuagint used today was translated by Origen (185-254 A.D.), who was a unitarian evolutionist.[347] Origen believed in reincarnation and denied the existence of hell.[348]

There are approximately 4,489 Greek New Testament manuscripts known to be extant today.[349] Of these, 170 are papyrus fragments dating from the second to the seventh centuries; there are 212 uncial (capital letter) manuscripts, dating from the fourth to the tenth centuries; there are 2,429 minuscule (small letter) manuscripts, dating from the ninth to the sixteenth centuries; and there are 1,678 lectionaries, which are lesson books for public reading that contain extracts from the New Testament.[350] The vast majority of these manuscripts are in agreement and make up what is known as the *Textus Receptus* (received text).

There has been a recent discovery of a small fragment of the earliest known New Testament manuscript not included in the above tally, which was dated to 66 A.D. and is in agreement with the *Textus Receptus*. The King James New Testament is based upon the Greek *Textus Receptus*, whereas the new translations, including the NIV, are based upon a very few number of corrupt manuscripts including the Roman Catholic Greek texts *Vaticanus* and *Sinaiticus,* and a few other texts, the origins of which are a mystery.

The manuscript *Sinaiticus*, which is often referred to by the first letter of the Hebrew alphabet, *Aleph*, is written in book form (codex) on velum.[351] It contains many spurious books such as the Shepherd of Hermes, the Didache, and the Epistle of Barnabas.[352] *Sinaiticus* was discovered in a waste basket in St. Catherine's monastery on Mount Sinai in February of 1859.[353] *Sinaiticus* is covered with alterations that are systematically spread over every page and were made by at least ten different revisors.[354] The alterations are obvious to anyone who examines the manuscript.[355] Most of the revisions to the text were made in the sixth or seventh century.[356]

The manuscript *Vaticanus*, often referred to by the letter "B,"originated in the Vatican library, hence the name.[357] *Vaticanus* was first revealed in 1841; where the transcript had been prior to that date is unclear.[358] One thing this is clear is that the manuscript omits many portions of scripture which explain vital Christian doctrines. *Vaticanus* omits Genesis 1:1 through Genesis 46:28; Psalms 106 through 138; Matthew 16:2,3; Romans 16:24; the Pauline Epistles; Revelation; and everything in Hebrews after 9:14.[359]

It should not be surprising that the Vatican would produce a manuscript that omits the portion of the book of Hebrews which exposes the Mass as completely ineffectual and deletes Revelation chapter 17, which reveals Rome as the seat of "MYSTERY,

BABYLON THE GREAT, THE MOTHER OF HARLOTS AND
ABOMINATIONS OF THE EARTH." Notice that the two primary
manuscripts used by the new bible versions were found in the care
and custody of the Roman Catholic Church.

The *Vaticanus* and *Sinaiticus* manuscripts, which make up less
than one percent of the existing ancient manuscripts, differ
significantly from the Received Text. *Vaticanus* omits at least 2,877
words; it adds 536 words; it substitutes 935 words; it transposes 2,098
words; and it modifies 1,132 words; making a total of 7,578 verbal
divergences from the Received Text. *Sinaiticus* is an even worse
corruption, having almost 9,000 divergences from the Received
Text.[360]

John Burgon, Dean of Westminster and the preeminent Greek
textual scholar of his time, said the following about the Vaticanus
and Sianaiticus manuscripts.

> The impurity of the text exhibited by these codices is not a
> question of opinion but of fact. . . . In the Gospels alone
> Codex B (Vatican) leaves out words or whole clauses no
> less than 1,491 times. It bears traces of careless
> transcription on every page. Codex Sinaiticus abounds with
> errors of the eye and pen to an extent not indeed
> unparalleled, but happily rather unusual in documents of
> first-rate importance. On many occasions, 10, 20, 30, 40
> words are dropped through very carelessness. Letters and
> words, even whole sentences, are frequently written twice
> over, or begun and immediately cancelled; while that gross
> blunder, whereby a clause is omitted because it happens to
> end in the same words as a clause preceding, occurs no less
> than 115 times in the New Testament.[361]

The Vaticanus and Sinaiticus manuscripts are so clearly corrupt
that Dean Burgon was at a loss to explain textual scholars accepting
them as valid. He concluded that those manuscripts have "established
a tyrannical ascendancy over the imagination of the critics which can
only be fitly spoken of as blind superstition."[362] The following is

Dean Burgon's assessment of the new Greek text, which was
produced largely from the *Vaticanus* and *Sinaiticus* manuscripts, and
which underlies the new bible versions.

> [T]he Greek Text which they have invented proves to be
> hopelessly depraved throughout . . . [I]t was deliberately
> invented . . . [T]he underlying Greek . . . is an entirely new
> thing, is a manufactured article throughout. . . . The new
> Greek text was full of errors from beginning to end. . . .
> Shame on [those] most incompetent men who - finding
> themselves in a evil hour occupied themselves . . . with
> falsifying the inspired Greek Text . . . Who will venture to
> predict the amount of mischief which must follow, if the
> 'New' Greek Text . . . should become used.[363]

The personalities behind the basic text for the NIV have an
occult new age agenda. The compilers and translators of the new
editions aren't just unchristian they are antichristian. The compilers
of the corrupted Greek text used in virtually all of the new bible
versions, including the NIV, were Brooke Foss Westcott and Fenton
John Anthony Hort. They were nominal Protestants, but they were
defacto Roman Catholics. Hort denied the infallibility of the Holy
Scriptures, he did not believe in the existence of Satan, he did not
believe in eternal punishment in Hell, nor did he believe in Christ's
atonement.[364] Hort, however, did believe in Darwin's theory of
evolution, he believed in purgatory, and he also believed in baptismal
regeneration.[365] Hort hated the United States and wished for its
destruction during the civil war, because he was a communist who
hated all things democratic.[366]

Westcott was equally Romish in his beliefs.[367] He, like Hort,
rejected the infallibility of the Holy Scriptures.[368] He viewed the
Genesis account of creation as merely an allegory.[369] He did not
believe the biblical account of the miracles of Jesus.[370] He did,
however, believe in praying for the dead and worshiping Mary.[371]
Politically, Westcott was a devout Socialist.[372]

Westcott and Hort were both necromancers who were members

of an occult club called the "Ghostly Guild."[373] Westcott also
founded another club and named it "Hermes."[374] According to
Luciferian H.P. Blavatsky, Hermes and Satan are one and the same.[375]
Hort viewed evangelical Christians as dangerous, perverted, unsound,
and confused.[376] Westcot and Hort's Greek text was largely based on
the fraudulent Catholic texts *Vaticanus* and *Sinaiticus*.[377]

Assisting Westcott and Hort in their revision was Dr. G. Vance, a
Unitarian, who denied the deity of Christ, the inspiration of the Holy
Scriptures, and the Godhead (Jesus Christ, God the Father, and the
Holy Ghost).[378] Jesuit Roman Catholic Cardinal Carlo Maria
Martini, the prelate of Milan, was the editor of the corrupted Greek
text.[379] Martini believed the occult new age philosophy that man can
become divine.[380] Remember, that is the very lie that Satan used to
deceive Eve into eating the forbidden fruit: "ye shall be as gods."
Genesis 3:5.

In addition, the new bible versions use a method of translation
known as dynamic equivalence, rather than the formal equivalence
used in the Authorized Version (AV), which is also known as the
King James Version (KJV). Formal equivalence is a word for word
translation, whereas dynamic equivalence is a thought for thought
translation. A translator using dynamic equivalence is less a
translator and more an interpreter. Thus, the new versions of bibles
should more accurately be called interpretations, rather than
translations. The dynamic equivalent interpreters of the new bible
versions have often made unfounded assumptions as to the meaning of
particular passages. Rather than translate what God wrote, they have,
with some frequency, twisted passages by injecting their own personal
bias. Some of these interpreters have displayed malicious intent and
caused great mischief.

The Holy Bible is a legal document prepared by God. It contains
the Old and New Testaments of Jesus Christ. A testament is a
memorialization of the will of a testator. It only has legal effect once
the testator has died. The New Testament, in reality, is the last will
and testament of Jesus Christ.

And for this cause he is the mediator of the new testament,
that by means of death, for the redemption of the
transgressions *that were* under the first testament, they
which are called might receive the promise of eternal
inheritance. For where a testament *is*, there must also of
necessity be the death of the testator. **For a testament *is* of
force after men are dead: otherwise it is of no strength at
all while the testator liveth.** (Hebrews 9:15-17 AV)

A testator is free to change the testament and add to it. That is
what Jesus did when he added the New Testament to the Old
Testament. "By so much was Jesus made a surety of a better
testament." (Hebrews 7:22 AV) However, it is only the testator who
is allowed to change or add to a testament. If anyone else adds to or
changes a testament, the changes make the resulting document a
forgery.

When trying to determine the meaning of a last will and
testament, courts always try to interpret what is the will of the
testator. That is why a person's testament is called a will. If a will is
to be translated from one language to another, because the heirs or the
court speak a different language, courts always use formal
equivalence because it is important that the heirs know exactly what
the testator said. In fact, a translator must take an oath to faithfully
translate the will of the testator. It is important not to allow any bias
from a translator to affect what is the meaning of the words used.

If a court allowed dynamic equivalence to be used when
translating a last will and testament then the court would not be
interpreting the will of the testator; the interpretation would have
already been done by the translator of the document when he
interpreted the meaning of each passage. The judge would be stuck
with a document which has been injected with meaning by the
translator. The judge would, in effect, be interpreting the intent of the
testator intermixed with the intent of the translator. The final verdict
regarding the intent of the testator would be corrupted by the bias or
errors of the translator.

In the case of the Holy Bible, it is the New and Old Testaments of God Almighty. They are the most important legal documents ever written. God Almighty is the testator. He wrote both testaments. In addition, he created the languages into which his original testaments would be written. He also created the languages into which those testaments would be translated. Genesis 11:7-9. He has supernaturally controlled the process from beginning to end. **"All scripture *is* given by inspiration of God**, and *is* profitable for doctrine, for reproof, for correction, for instruction in righteousness." (2 Timothy 3:16 AV) In addition, he has promised to supernaturally preserve his testaments. **"[T]he word of the Lord endureth for ever**. And this is the word which by the gospel is preached unto you." (1 Peter 1:25 AV) The heirs of Christ are Christians. "The Spirit itself beareth witness with our spirit, that we are the children of God: And if children, then heirs; heirs of God, and joint-heirs with Christ; if so be that we suffer with *him*, that we may be also glorified together." (Romans 8:16-17 AV)

In order for Christ's heirs to understand his will they must have a faithful translation. If his heirs try to interpret God's will by using a translation that contains not the pure intent of God, but instead the intent of the translator, then they can no longer determine God's will. A will that has been rewritten and corrupted with the thoughts of one other than the testator is considered a forgery and a fraud. So also are the new translations of the bible forgeries and frauds.

Defenders of the new bibles claim that the essential doctrines of the Christian Faith are expressed in the new bibles, even though they have been deleted or changed in many passages. James H. Son, author of *The New Athenians,* likened the logic of that argument to removing a stop sign from a busy street intersection and then justifying the removal because the other traffic signals in the city were left intact. Even though the sign only contained one word, that word is of critical importance to those who arrive at the intersection, just as each word in the Holy Bible is of critical importance to those who are reading it.

God has made the point in the Holy Bible that **every word** of

God is important. "And Jesus answered him, saying, It is written, That man shall not live by bread alone, **but by every word of God**." (Luke 4:4 AV) Incidently, the doctrine of Luke 4:4 is missing in the new bible versions. The NASB, for example leaves out the last clause and simply states: "And Jesus answered him, 'it is written, MAN SHALL NOT LIVE ON BREAD ALONE.'" (Luke 4:4 NASB) The new versions leave the reader in ignorance as to what it is other than bread by which man lives.

> And he humbled thee, and suffered thee to hunger, and fed thee with manna, which thou knewest not, neither did thy fathers know; that he might make thee know that man doth not live by bread only, but **by every *word* that proceedeth out of the mouth of the LORD doth man live**. (Deuteronomy 8:3 AV)

> **Every word of God *is* pure**: he *is* a shield unto them that put their trust in him. (Proverbs 30:5 AV)

Look at the passage in Galatians 3:16, wherein God points out the importance of every one of his words. In that passage God explains the importance of the distinction between the singular word "seed" and the plural word "seeds."

> Now to Abraham and his **seed** were the promises made. **He saith not, And to seeds**, as of many; but as of one, And to thy seed, which is Christ. (Galatians 3:16 AV)

If one looks at the AV passages that refer to the promises made to Abraham, one sees that in fact God refers to Abraham's "seed," singular. In the NIV, however, the passages that prophesy the blessings that were to flow from Abraham's seed, Jesus Christ, are changed and obscured. If one were to try to find the passages referred to in Galatians 3:16 in the NIV one would not be able to do so, because the NIV does not use the word chosen by God but has substituted words chosen by man as inspired by Satan.

AV	NIV
And in thy **seed** shall all the nations of the earth be blessed; because thou hast obeyed my voice. (Genesis 22:18 AV)	[A]nd through your **offspring** all nations on earth will be blessed, because you have obeyed me. (Genesis 22:18 NIV)

AV	NIV
And I will establish my covenant between me and thee and thy **seed** after thee in their generations for an everlasting covenant, to be a God unto thee, and to thy **seed** after thee. (Genesis 17:7 AV)	I will establish my covenant as an everlasting covenant between me and you and your **descendants** after you for the generations to come, to be your God and the God of your **descendants** after you. (Genesis 17:7 NIV)

It is important for God's heirs to know who they are. His heirs are those who have the faith of Abraham, not those that have the flesh of Abraham.

Even as Abraham believed God, and it was accounted to him for righteousness. Know ye therefore that they which are of faith, the same are the children of Abraham. And the scripture, foreseeing that God would justify the heathen through faith, preached before the gospel unto Abraham, *saying*, In thee shall all nations be blessed. **So then they which be of faith are blessed with faithful Abraham.** (Galatians 3:6-9 AV)

This point is understood by the passage in Galatians 3:16 that explains what is meant by the precise word "seed" used in the Old Testament. **"And if ye *be* Christ's, then are ye Abraham's seed, and heirs according to the promise."** (Galatians 3:29 AV)

Without the precise word "seed" the meaning of the will of God can be misinterpreted to support false doctrines like the pretribulation rapture fraud, which makes Christ's church a mere parenthesis in history. Under the pretribulation rapture corruption, fleshly Israel is to inherit the promises of God, contrary to God's express intent that it is those who are chosen and justified by his sovereign grace who are his heirs and not those who are born of the flesh of Abraham. **"That being justified by his grace, we should be made heirs according to the hope of eternal life."** (Titus 3:7 AV)

> Not as though the word of God hath taken none effect. For they *are* not all Israel, which are of Israel: Neither, because they are the seed of Abraham, *are they* all children: but, In Isaac shall thy seed be called. That is, **They which are the children of the flesh, these *are* not the children of God: but the children of the promise are counted for the seed."** (Romans 9:6-8 AV)

That is one example of a false doctrine that is supported by the change of just one word. There are other false doctrines that have sprung from other corrupt changes to God's word in the new bible versions.

There are many other passages where the doctrines of God have been completely reversed. In the KJV (AV) the ways of the wicked are always "grievous." Psalms 10:4-5. The devil cannot have that, so Psalms 10:4-5 in his NKJV states the ways of the wicked are always "prospering." The wicked "were forgotten" in Ecclesiastes 8:10 of God's word in the KJV, but in the NIV Ecclesiastes 8:10 passage the wicked "receive praise."

The Zionist disciples of Satan were able to change their bibles to make Israel a "spreading vine" in the NIV and even a "luxuriant vine" in the NASB in Hosea 10:1. God, however, states that "Israel is an empty vine" in his KJV Holy Bible at Hosea 10:1. God states that "the words of a talebearer are as wounds." Proverbs 26:22. However, the NIV change agents contradict God by saying in Proverbs 26:22 of their NIV that "the words of a gossip are like choice morsels." In Proverbs 25:23 God states that "the north wind driveth away rain." The NASB, however, states in their Proverbs 25:23 that "the north wind brings forth rain." These are just a few of the many doctrinal changes. The new bible versions are truly different bibles with a different gospel.

The promoters of the new bible versions claim that they are merely updating the archaic English in the King James Bible. They are being disingenuous. The Holy Bible is a legal document. The English of the King James Bible is not archaic, it is precise. The precise language used has eternal importance. Thee, thou, thy, and thine are singular pronouns. Thou is the subjective second person singular, thee is the objective second person singular, and thy and thine are possessive second person singular. Ye is a subjective second person plural pronoun. In the King James text the precision of the language puts the reader in the midst of the narrative. The reader is able to tell whether the person is the object of the action or the subject causing the action. The reader can also tell if the subject or object is a group or an individual. The new versions use either the pronouns "you" or "your" for all of the narratives and the reader is not able to know anything about the setting of the narrative. All one need do is read Galatians 3:16 to know that singularity and plurality are important to God.

The writers of the Authorized (King James)Version (AV or KJV) did not use the more precise pronouns for the reason that their use was the customary language of the 16th century; they purposely used those words because they wanted to accurately and faithfully translate God's word into English. To prove the point, all one need do is read the dedicatory at the beginning of the Holy Bible (AV); the dedicatory was written at the completion of the AV Holy Bible in 1611 A.D., not once was thee, thou, thy, thine, or ye used in the dedicatory.

What happens to a church whose pastor preaches and teaches from the NIV? The pastor is able to draw large crowds of those who are itching to hear that they are sovereign, that they can choose to believe, that it is up to them. The Southeast Christian Church of Louisville, Kentucky, with an average attendance of 17,863,[381] offers one example of that phenomenon. The Southeast Christian Church is the sixth largest non-Catholic church in the United States.[382] The church website and the pastor's sermons are rife with NIV passages.[383] The pastor, Bob Russell, offers his version of the gospel as follows:

> **You are free to choose** to trust Christ for your salvation or trust yourself.
>
> **God grants you the freedom** to either trust in Him and be rescued or not believe and be separated from Him. **He doesn't violate free will.**
>
> **God wants to rescue you, but not to kidnap you against your will.**
>
> **He invites you to follow Him to safety, but He does not coerce you to do so.**
>
> **You must choose to believe of your own free will** (Heb 11:6).
>
> But make a decision, don't try to mix and match religion - either believe in Christ or reject Him.[384] (emphasis added)

The pastor assures his flock that they are sovereign. He blasphemes God, by rejecting the grace of God and calling it "coercion" and "kidnaping." The god he preaches would not dare invade their free will. The flock is comforted in that they are in complete control over their salvation. Having control over their salvation, they can keep the mythical NIV god out of their business. If man wants to humble himself before the NIV god, that is fine, but it is man's choice. The god of his imagination has no say in the matter.

32 The Devil's Advocates

Arminian free will preaching results in a pathetic, formulaic, mythical salvation, where the counterfeit believer chants some words and is then proclaimed "born again." An example of that is found on the website of the Southwest Radio Church Ministries. Sadly, that ministry has a page titled "How You Can Be Born Again!"[385] On that page are found a series of bulleted quotations from the bible which end with the following two bulleted statements:

> The Prayer: Lord Jesus Christ, be merciful to me a sinner. I do now receive you as my personal Lord and Saviour.
>
> **The Result: If you sincerely prayed the above prayer, you are now born again!** (John 3:3)[386]

Notice, that being born again is completely up to the free will choice of man; according to that theology a man who is dead in trespasses and sin can make himself spiritually alive and give birth to himself. How sad that people actually believe such unbiblical nonsense. The bible makes it clear that man is spiritually dead in trespasses and sin, and it is God (not man) who raises him to spiritual life. "And **you hath he quickened**, who were dead in trespasses and sins." (Ephesians 2:1 AV)

The free will gospel contains all sorts of similarly ridiculous formulas and stratagems that play to the sinful need for man to be in complete control over their lives and salvation. Of course, once they have their free will "salvation," the church must have a whole slew of ministries to make sure that the members do not slip up and lose their "salvation." The Arminian churches get quite large and wealthy, while the poor deluded members work themselves into a frenzy to keep hold on their tenuous salvation.

Since the god of Arminian free will is helpless against the fictional sovereign will of man, Arminians ultimately come around to the conclusion that their helpless pathetic god cannot be the only means of salvation. Once the Arminian preacher strips their god of his sovereignty and omnipotence, sovereign man can find his own alternative channel to salvation other than through that impotent god.

It seems to be an ineluctable result of the Arminian philosophy that the deluded adherents gravitate toward an ecumenical religious doctrine. God has clearly stated that all who are not with him, are against him. "He that is not with me is against me; and he that gathereth not with me scattereth abroad." Matthew 12:30. To accept the validity of non-Christian religions is to be against Christ, which is antichrist.

An example of this antichrist view is Joel Osteen. He is the pastor of the 30,000 member Lakewood Church in Houston, Texas.[387] Forbes magazine did a study of the phenomenon of the growing number of huge churches and their enormous wealth, titled *Megachurches, Megabusinesses*. Forbes listed Lakewood Church as the largest (non-Catholic) congregation in the United States.[388]

The fine print in the Forbes article notes that Catholic Churches were excluded from the study. If the Catholic church was included in the Forbes study of church wealth, it would no doubt dominate the article. The Lakewood Church congregation in Houston is insignificant when compared to the Archdiocese of Galveston/Houston, which has over one million Catholics divided among 150 parishes.[389] The Roman Catholic Church is the mother of all Arminian free will churches. The size of the Catholic Church is a testament to the fact that its message is for those on the broad way to destruction.

Forbes is all too happy to examine the wealth of churches that are ostensibly Protestant. They would not dare expose the wealth and influence of the Catholic Church, which is only rivaled by central banks. Of course, there is always the obstacle of the infamous secrecy of the Catholic church, when it comes to any effort to explore its wealth. Forbes decided to pick the small fruit on the lowest branches rather than go through the extra effort of trying to gather information on the larger Catholic fruit higher up in the money tree.

Lakewood Church recently purchased the Compaq Center; that huge 16,000 seat indoor arena was the former home of the Houston Rockets. As impressive as that arena is, it pales next to the plans of the Catholic Church diocese of Santo Amaro, Brazil, which has designs on building a church with a seating capacity of 100,000.[390]

Lakewood Church spent an additional $95 million renovating the Compaq Center. Lakewood Church can well afford it. Their 2004 revenues were reported by the *New York Times* to be $55 million. That is all in addition to Osteen's sell out appearances throughout the country at huge arenas where tickets are listed at $10 apiece. Some tickets, however, sell on ebay for up to $100.[391] It is contrary to Christian principles for a preacher to charge people a fee to hear the gospel. That should be the first clue to the discerning Christian that Osteen is not preaching the gospel of Jesus Christ.

On Osteen's website, he has the following statement:

Jesus declared in John 14; I am the way, the truth and the life. No one comes to the Father but by me. I believe that Jesus Christ alone is the only way to salvation. However, it wasn't until I had the opportunity to review the transcript of the interview that I realize I had not clearly stated that having a personal relationship with Jesus is the only way to heaven. **It's about the individual's choice to follow**

Him.[392] (emphasis added)

Clearly Osteen is of the opinion that each person has a free choice to follow Jesus. What is revealing about his statement is the context. He is trying to explain why he did not confess that Jesus Christ was the only way to salvation, when he appeared on a nationally televised broadcast of *The Larry King Show*. His attitude is shared by many Arminian preachers. Below is a blow by blow examination by Terry Watkins of the self-destruction of Osteen on *The Larry King Show*:

> The first very alarming portrait of Osteen's heart (Matthew 12:34) deals with the most important subject in the Bible—salvation is only through the redemptive blood of the Lord Jesus Christ at Calvary. Nothing is more important. Nothing is more evident in the scriptures. The following scriptures (among many) loudly and boldly proclaim Jesus Christ as the ONE and ONLY way of salvation, without any room for misinterpretation or misunderstanding. The Bible makes this crystal-clear. Other doctrines may have opportunity for argument, but not this one.
>
> John 14:6
> Jesus saith unto him, I am the way, the truth, and the life: no man cometh unto the Father, but by me.
>
> Acts 4:12
> Neither is there salvation in any other: for there is none other name under heaven given among men, whereby we must be saved.
>
> John 3:36
> He that believeth on the Son hath everlasting life: and he that believeth not the Son shall not see life; but the wrath of God abideth on him.
>
> 1 Timothy 2:5-6
> For there is one God, and one mediator between God and

men, the man Christ Jesus; Who gave himself a ransom for all, to be testified in due time.

On Larry King Live, the following very disturbing conversation occurred with Larry King and Joel Osteen:

KING: What if you're Jewish or Muslim, you don't accept Christ at all?

OSTEEN: You know, I'm very careful about saying who would and wouldn't go to heaven. I don't know ...

At this point, even Larry King appears surprised by Osteen's answer. Then Larry tosses Osteen a "soft-ball" to explain his previous answer. And again Osteen openly denies that Jesus Christ is the ONLY way of salvation.

KING: If you believe you have to believe in Christ? They're wrong, aren't they?

OSTEEN: Well, I don't know if I believe they're wrong. I believe here's what the Bible teaches and from the Christian faith this is what I believe. But I just think that only God will judge a person's heart. I spent a lot of time in India with my father. I don't know all about their religion. But I know they love God. And I don't know. I've seen their sincerity. So I don't know. I know for me, and what the Bible teaches, I want to have a relationship with Jesus.

Again Osteen denies the redemptive work of the Lord Jesus Christ. Notice, he praises the pagan, false-religion of India as "I know they love God." Unbelievable.

I'm sure some reading this are thinking, "Well, maybe Larry caught Joel Osteen flat footed. Maybe Osteen wasn't prepared." If Osteen only had been given another chance to testify of the redemptive work of the Lord Jesus Christ, he'd get it straightened out.

Osteen did get another chance.

After Larry King opened the phone lines, a concerned Christian asks Joel to clarify his previous statement (which we just viewed). Again Osteen could easily clear this up.

CALLER: Hello, Larry. You're the best, and thank you, Joe -- Joel -- for your positive messages and your book. I'm wondering, though, why you side-stepped Larry's earlier question about how we get to heaven? The Bible clearly tells us that Jesus is the way, the truth and the light and the only way to the father is through him. That's not really a message of condemnation but of truth.

OSTEEN: Yes, I would agree with her. I believe that. . .

KING: So then a Jew is not going to heaven?

OSTEEN: No. Here's my thing, Larry, is I can't judge somebody's heart. You know? Only God can look at somebody's heart, and so -- I don't know. To me, it's not my business to say, you know, this one is or this one isn't. I just say, here's what the Bible teaches and I'm going to put my faith in Christ. And I just I think it's wrong when you go around saying, you're saying you're not going, you're not going, you're not going, because it's not exactly my way. I'm just...

KING: But you believe your way.

OSTEEN: I believe my way. I believe my way with all my heart.

KING: But for someone who doesn't share it is wrong, isn't he?

OSTEEN: Well, yes. Well, I don't know if I look at it like that. I would present my way, but I'm just going to let God be the judge of that. I don't know. I don't know.

KING: So you make no judgment on anyone?

OSTEEN: No. But I...

And here Larry really tosses Joel a soft-ball. How about a
God-defying atheist? And again, Osteen will not confess
that Jesus Christ is the ONLY way of salvation.

KING: What about atheists?

OSTEEN: You know what, I'm going to let someone --
I'm going to let God be the judge of who goes to heaven and
hell. I just -- again, I present the truth, and I say it every
week. You know, I believe it's a relationship with Jesus. But
you know what? I'm not going to go around telling
everybody else if they don't want to believe that that's going
to be their choice. God's got to look at your own heart. God's
got to look at your heart, and only God knows that.

Friend, the Bible is clear. There is one, and only one way
out of an eternal hell and that is the blood of the Lord Jesus
Christ. Not simply "a relationship with Jesus Christ." Judas
Iscariot had a "relationship" with Jesus Christ, walking and
talking with the Lord, and even "kissing" the Lord (Luke
22:47), but Judas went to hell (Acts 1:25). Revelation 2:15
reads, "And from Jesus Christ, who is the faithful witness,
and the first begotten of the dead, and the prince of the kings
of the earth. Unto him that loved us, and washed us from our
sins in his own blood."

What can wash away my sins – NOTHING BUT THE
BLOOD OF JESUS!

The teaching professed by Osteen that ". . . God's got to
look at your heart. . ." for salvation is wrong. It is grossly
wrong. It is deadly wrong. God has already "looked at you

heart." In Jeremiah 17:9, the Lord says, "The heart is
deceitful above all things, and desperately wicked: who can
know it?" Proverbs 28:26, says, "He that trusteth in his own
heart is a fool. . ." The Lord Jesus says, in Matthew 15 "But
those things which proceed out of the mouth come forth
from the heart; and they defile the man. For out of the heart
proceed evil thoughts, murders, adulteries, fornications,
thefts, false witness, blasphemies:"[393]

Osteen's pathetic performance on The Larry King Show revealed
Osteen for the religious huckster that he is. His equivocation on the
issue on the sole redemptive salvation of the Lord Jesus Christ sent
shock waves among many of Osteen's followers. The furor made it
necessary for Osteen to issue an apology on his web site, stating:

Dear Friend,

Many of you have called, written or e-mailed regarding my
recent appearance on Larry King Live. I appreciate your
comments and value your words of correction and
encouragement.

It was never my desire or intention to leave any doubt as to
what I believe and Whom I serve. I believe with all my
heart that it is only through Christ that we have hope in
eternal life. I regret and sincerely apologize that I was
unclear on the very thing in which I have dedicated my life.

Jesus declared in John 14; I am the way, the truth and the
life. No one comes to the Father but by me. I believe that
Jesus Christ alone is the only way to salvation. However, it
wasn't until I had the opportunity to review the transcript of
the interview that I realize I had not clearly stated that
having a personal relationship with Jesus is the only way to
heaven. It's about the individual's choice to follow Him.

God has given me a platform to present the Gospel to a very
diverse audience. In my desire not to alienate the people

that Jesus came to save, I did not clearly communicate the convictions that I hold so precious.

I will use this as a learning experience and believe that God will ultimately use it for my good and His glory. I am comforted by the fact that He sees my heart and knows my intentions. I am so thankful that I have friends, like you, who are willing to share their concerns with me.

Thank you again to those who have written. I hope that you accept my deepest apology and see it in your heart to extend to me grace and forgiveness.

As always, I covet your prayers and I am believing for God's best in your life,

Joel Osteen - Pastor Lakewood Church[394]

Osteen is being disingenuous in his letter of apology when he states "I believe with all my heart that it is only through Christ that we have hope in eternal life." If he truly believed that he would have said so on *The Larry King Show.*

Osteen, however, in his desperation to appease his constituency revealed the reason he equivocated on the gospel. He stated in his letter of apology: **"God has given me a platform to present the Gospel to a very diverse audience. In my desire not to alienate the people that Jesus came to save, I did not clearly communicate the convictions that I hold so precious."**[395]

He is cut from the same cloth as Chuck Smith. Neither of them want to alienate their audiences. Both Osteen and Smith understand the gospel, they just choose to alter it so that they can tickle the ears of the lost.

They have done the math; there is a larger audience who will come to their churches to hear their anti-gospel than there is who will come to their church to hear the true gospel. So they have decided to gear their message to the many who are traveling the road to destruction. Their message keeps them coming to church, but it also keeps them oblivious to their fate. The Arminian religious hucksters conceal the true gospel of the grace of God in order not to alienate those who have not been given spiritual ears to hear it.

> Enter ye in at the strait gate: for **wide *is* the gate, and broad *is* the way, that leadeth to destruction, and many there be which go in thereat:** Because strait *is* the gate, and narrow *is* the way, which leadeth unto life, and few there be that find it. Beware of false prophets, which come to you in sheep's clothing, but inwardly they are ravening wolves. (Matthew 7:13-15 AV)

Osteen, Smith, and the other Arminians are keen mathematicians. If the way to destruction is broad, why not fill your church with as many of those people as possible. After all, if a pastor preached the true gospel the church would tend to be rather small, because narrow is the way to salvation and few find it. Those who are on the broad way to destruction would reject the true gospel. But they will stick around to hear a free will anti-gospel. They love to hear how they are in control, and how they have a free will to choose.

The potential for a mega-church is much greater if the preachers preached an antichrist gospel that tickled the ears of the many predestined for destruction. Of course, in return for telling the audience how they have power over God, such preachers expect the audience to empty their wallets into theirs.

That is not to suggest that all those who attend Joel Osteen's Lakewood Church or Chuck Smith's Calvary Chapel are not saved. It simply means that the message of those preachers is designed to keep the lost coming back and to avoid the true gospel so that they are not alienated by the sovereignty of God. There will be a steady stream of true Christians attending those churches, but after a time, they will see through the false message and stop attending. That is no great loss in the eyes of Osteen and Smith. In fact they see true Christians as thorns in their sides, because they tend to ask the tough questions.

For every true Christian trouble-maker who stops attending their churches, there are many more heathen who will take their place. The heathen are much easier to keep in line, because after all, under the Arminian gospel they are told that they must watch their P's and Q's or they might lose their salvation.

Jesus foresaw that there would be true Christians who might get caught in the wide net cast by such false preachers. In the very next verse after explaining that broad is the way that leads to destruction, Jesus warned those chosen for salvation of false preachers who would corrupt the gospel. Jesus knew that there would be false teachers who would alter the gospel to appeal to the large crowd of hopelessly lost people. He explains that the end of those false preachers would be eternal damnation!

> **Beware of false prophets, which come to you in sheep's clothing, but inwardly they are ravening wolves.** Ye shall know them by their fruits. Do men gather grapes of thorns, or figs of thistles? Even so every good tree bringeth forth good fruit; but a corrupt tree bringeth forth evil fruit. A good tree cannot bring forth evil fruit, neither *can* a corrupt tree bring forth good fruit. Every tree that bringeth not forth good fruit is hewn down, and cast into the fire. Wherefore by their fruits ye shall know them. Not every one that saith unto me, Lord, Lord, shall enter into the kingdom of heaven; but he that doeth the will of my Father which is in heaven. **Many will say to me in that day, Lord, Lord, have we not prophesied in thy name? and in thy name have cast out devils? and in thy name done many wonderful works? And then will I profess unto them, I never knew you: depart from me, ye that work iniquity.** (Matthew 7:15-23 AV)

Jesus gives Christians a way to identify the false prophets. Jesus said that by the fruits of the false prophets you will know them. Jesus explains in Luke 6:43-46 that the fruits are not only their sinful works, but also the words that come out of the abundance of their heart. If you compare the preaching of Arminian preachers with the word of

God you will find that they preach the evil fruit of destruction. They preach against Christ; they preach an evil anti-gospel.

> For a good tree bringeth not forth corrupt fruit; neither doth a corrupt tree bring forth good fruit. For every tree is known by his own fruit. For of thorns men do not gather figs, nor of a bramble bush gather they grapes. A good man out of the good treasure of his heart bringeth forth that which is good; and an evil man out of the evil treasure of his heart bringeth forth that which is evil: for of the abundance of the heart his mouth speaketh. And why call ye me, Lord, Lord, and do not the things which I say? (Luke 6:43-46 AV)

Further evidence of the irreverent treatment of the scriptures by Arminian preachers is found in the statements of Billy Graham. To Billy Graham, salvation becomes a formula to be exercised through the free will of man. Graham is presumptuous enough to write a book titled *How to be Born Again*.[396] He thinks man can birth himself again. If man can obtain salvation by the power of his own will, that makes God a passive observer to the extraordinary powers of man. The consequence of that theology goes beyond merely making Jesus a passive observer. Ultimately Jesus becomes unnecessary. As with Osteen, Billy Graham views the gospel of Jesus Christ as unnecessary for salvation.

Below is an interview Graham had with Robert Schuller:

Schuller: Tell me, what do you think is the future of Christianity?

Graham: Well, Christianity and being a true believer - you know, I think there's the Body of Christ. This comes from all the Christian groups around the world, outside the Christian groups. I think everybody that loves Christ, or knows Christ, whether they're conscious of it or not, they're members of the Body of Christ. And I don't think that we're going to see a great sweeping revival that will turn the whole world to

Christ at any time. I think James answered that, the Apostle
James in the first council in Jerusalem, when he said that
God's purpose for this age is to call out a people for his
name. And that's what God is doing today - he's calling
people out of the world for his name, whether they come
from the Muslim world, or the Buddhist world, or the
Christian world or the non-believing world, they are
members of the Body of Christ because they've been called
by God. They may not even know the name of Jesus, but
they know in their hearts that they need something that they
don't have, and they turn to the only light that they have, and
I think that they are saved and that they're going to be with
us in heaven.

Schuller: What, what I hear you saying is that it's possible
for Jesus Christ to come into human hearts and soul and life,
even if they've been born in darkness and have never had
exposure to the Bible. Is that a correct interpretation of what
you're saying?

Graham: Yes it is, because I believe that. I've met people in
various parts of the world in tribal situations, that they have
never seen a Bible or heard about a Bible, and never heard
of Jesus, but they've believed in their hearts that there was a
God, and they've tried to live a life that was quite apart from
the surrounding community in which they lived.

Schuller: I'm so thrilled to hear you say this. There's a
wideness in God's mercy.

Graham: There is. There definitely is.[397]

Under Billy Graham's unbiblical devilish theology, the word of
God is irrelevant. He preaches that people may not even know the
name of Jesus or hear the gospel, but they can be saved and go to
heaven nonetheless. Contrary to Billy Graham, the bible states: **"So
then faith cometh by hearing, and hearing by the word of God."**
Romans 10:17. Before one can believe in Jesus, he must have heard

the gospel of Jesus. The bible states: "And this is his commandment,
That we should believe on the name of his Son Jesus Christ." 1 John
3:23. It is not a suggestion of God, it is a commandment that one
believes on the name of Jesus.

Graham believes that Muslims, Buddhists, or even atheists are
part of the body of Christ. Jesus, however, states: **"Jesus saith unto
him, I am the way, the truth, and the life: no man cometh unto the
Father, but by me."** John 14:6. The only way to heaven is by the
grace of God through faith in Jesus Christ. All adherents to any other
religion in the world are damned to hell. Who are you going to
believe, Billy Graham or the Holy Bible?

In a 1978 McCall's Magazine interview Graham stated: "I used to
think that pagans in far-off countries were lost -- were going to hell --
if they did not have the Gospel of Jesus Christ preached to them. I no
longer believe that ... I believe there are other ways of recognizing the
existence of God -- through nature, for instance -- and plenty of other
opportunities, therefore, of saying yes to God."

Graham's devilish theology parallels the Catholic doctrine,
which is: "Those who, through no fault of their own, do not know the
Gospel of Christ or his church, but who nevertheless seek God with a
sincere heart and, moved by grace, try in their actions to do his will as
they know it through the dictates of their conscience, those too may
achieve eternal salvation."[398]

The above quote seems to contradict the traditional view of the
Catholic Church, which is that the pope is the vicar of Christ on earth,
and all are lost who do not submit to his authority. However, a close
reading of the official Catholic Catechism reveals that Catholic
doctrine is a direct attack solely on biblical Christianity. The
following quote is from § 846 of the 1994 Catechism of the Catholic
Church.

Basing itself on Scripture and tradition, the Council teaches
that the Church, a Pilgrim now on earth, is necessary for
salvation: the one Christ is the mediator and the way of

salvation; he is present to us in his body which is the
Church. He himself explicitly asserted the necessity of faith
and Baptism, and thereby affirmed at the same time the
necessity of the Church which men enter through Baptism as
through a door. **Hence they could not be saved who,
knowing that the Catholic Church was founded as
necessary by God through Christ, would refuse either to
enter it or to remain in it.**[399]

One would think by reading that passage that the Catholic
Church is saying that non-Catholics are lost. However, it is actually a
condemnation of biblical Christianity. That is because it is Christians
who are the group who would knowingly refuse to enter the Catholic
Church and it is those who are born again who would refuse to remain
in it. One might ask: "What about Muslims?" According to the
official teachings of the Catholic Church Muslims go to heaven even
though they are outside the Catholic Church.

The Church's relationship with the Muslims. "The plan of
salvation also includes those who acknowledge the Creator,
in the first place amongst whom are the Muslims; these
profess to hold the faith of Abraham, and together with us
they adore the one, merciful God, mankind's judge on the
last day." CATECHISM OF THE CATHOLIC CHURCH §
841 (1994).

What about Jews? According to the official teachings of the
Catholic Church Jews go to heaven even though they are outside the
Catholic Church, and even though all Jews have rejected Christ.
Once a Jew is saved he becomes a Christian; he is no longer a Jew.
According to the Catholic Church, however, no conversion is
necessary because the Jews have a "sonship" based upon an
"irrevocable" calling of God in the Old Testament. According to the
Catholic doctrine, faith in Jesus is not necessary for the salvation of
Jews.

The relationship of the Church with the Jewish People.
When she delves into her own mystery, the Church, the

People of God in the New Covenant, discovers her link with
the Jewish People, "the first to hear the Word of God." The
Jewish faith, unlike other non-Christian religions, is already
a response to God's revelation in the Old Covenant. **To the
Jews "belong the sonship, the glory**, the covenants, the
giving of the law, the worship, and the promises; to them
belong the patriarchs, and of their race, according to the
flesh, is the Christ," **"for the gifts and the call of God are
irrevocable."** CATECHISM OF THE CATHOLIC
CHURCH § 839 (1994) (footnotes omitted, emphasis
added).

In fact, the official teaching of the Catholic Church is that "Israel
is the priestly people of God, called by the name of the LORD, and
the first to hear the word of God, the people of elder brethren in the
faith of Abraham."[400] The Catholic Church officially views Jews as
elder brethren of the faith of Abraham. That is nonsense. The faith of
Abraham signifies saving faith in Jesus Christ. According to the
Catholic Church, however, Jews are saved without faith in Jesus
Christ.

What about the other pagan religions? Believe it or not,
members of heathen religions are considered by the Catholic church
to be among the saved of the world. The official Catholic doctrine is
that a heathen who does not believe in Jesus is included in God's plan
for salvation, because according to § 843 of the CATECHISM OF
THE CATHOLIC CHURCH God "wants all men to be saved."

The Church's bond with non-Christian religions is in the
first place the common origin and end of the human race:
All nations form but one community. This is so because all
stem from the one stock which God created to people the
entire earth, and also because **all share a common destiny,
namely God. His providence, evident goodness, and
saving designs extend to all** against the day when the elect
are gathered together in the holy city. CATECHISM OF
THE CATHOLIC CHURCH § 842 (1994) (footnote
omitted, emphasis added).

The Catholic plan for salvation sounds pretty inclusive. Who isn't part of the Catholic plan for salvation? The answer is found in § 846 of the CATECHISM OF THE CATHOLIC CHURCH. It states: "Hence they could not be saved who, knowing that the Catholic Church was founded as necessary by God through Christ, would refuse either to enter it or to remain in it."[401]

Remember, Catholic doctrine has a plan for salvation for Jews, Muslims, and other heathen religions that does not require conversion to Catholicism. However there is no plan for salvation for those who refuse to enter or remain in the Catholic Church who are not either a Muslim, a Jew, or some other heathen?

There is only one group left out of the Catholic plan for salvation: Christians. The Catechism of the Catholic Church is a theological attack on the Christian Church. The official Catholic doctrine is that all Christians who refuse to convert to Catholicism or who leave the Catholic Church are damned to hell. All the talk by the Catholic Church calling Protestants "separated brethren" is a diabolical deception. Their official doctrine is that Protestant Christians are unsaved and headed for hell.

Billy Graham has stated: "I find that my beliefs are essentially the same as those of orthodox Roman Catholics"[402] Billy Graham is one of the many fellow travelers in the devilish Catholic doctrine. Graham's Arminian gospel brings him back to the Roman Catholic fountain, from which sprang his free will theology.

In 1980, Billy Graham called Pope John Paul II the greatest spiritual leader of the modern world.[403] Graham usually has Catholics on the platform during his "gospel" crusades and has a regular practice of giving the decision cards that are handed in during the crusade to the area Catholic bishop for follow up by Catholic priests.[404] In a September 21, 1957 interview with the *San Francisco News*, Graham said, "Anyone who makes a decision at our meetings is seen later and referred to a local clergyman, Protestant, Catholic, or Jewish."

Billy Graham admittedly referred Jews right back to local Jewish rabbis when those Jews answered his altar call at his crusades. These Jews were seeking Christ, yet Graham diverts them away from Christ. What is not known by most, but is known by Graham, is that Judaism is an antichrist religion, wherein the hierarchy has an abiding hatred toward Christ and Christians. Billy Graham is an agent of the devil, and he was doing Satan's bidding when he sent the unwitting Jewish sheep right back to the arms of their rabbis, who are spiritual wolves.

The orthodox Jews do not follow the Old Testament. They have replaced God's laws with their traditions. Those traditions were oral traditions at the time of Christ. Jesus criticized the Pharisees for replacing God's word with their religious traditions. "Making the word of God of none effect through your tradition, which ye have delivered: and many such like things do ye." (Mark 7:13 AV)

The Jews later memorialized their traditions in the Talmud and the Kabbalah. The Talmud and the Kabbalah today span numerous volumes. The Talmud and Kabbalah supersede, nullify and ultimately replace the Old Testament in traditional Judaism.[405] According to the Talmud, Christians are allied with hell,[406] and Jesus is not only cursed,[407] he is described as being tormented in boiling hot semen.[408] The Talmud, however, gives immunity to rabbis from ever going to hell.[409]

Judaism is a religion of hate. The hatred of Christians and all gentiles of all races runs through the warp and woof of Judaism. The most revered rabbis (*gedolim*) view gentiles as garbage. For example, Rabbi Shneur Zalman, the esteemed founder of *Chabad-Lubavitch*, taught that the difference between Jew and gentile is not merely religious or racial, but that the souls of Jews and gentiles are completely different in kind. "Gentile souls are of completely different and inferior order. They are totally evil, with no redeeming qualities whatsoever . . . Indeed they themselves are refuse. . . . All Jews are innately good, all gentiles are innately evil."[410]

Jesus explained that those who hate him also hate God the Father. The Jews hate Jesus and therefore they also hate the Father.

The Jews reject Jesus, and therefore their god is not the Father. That leaves only Satan as their god. Do not be surprised by the unrelenting hatred of Jews toward Christians; Jesus clearly warned us that Christians would be hated by the Jews.

> If the world hate you, ye know that it hated me before *it hated* you. If ye were of the world, the world would love his own: but because ye are not of the world, but I have chosen you out of the world, therefore the world hateth you. Remember the word that I said unto you, The servant is not greater than his lord. **If they have persecuted me, they will also persecute you**; if they have kept my saying, they will keep yours also. But all these things will they do unto you for my name's sake, because they know not him that sent me. If I had not come and spoken unto them, they had not had sin: but now they have no cloke for their sin. **He that hateth me hateth my Father also.** If I had not done among them the works which none other man did, they had not had sin: but now have they both seen and hated both me and my Father. But *this cometh to pass*, that the word might be fulfilled that is written in their law, They hated me without a cause." (John 15:18-25 AV)

While the Jews hate all gentiles, they have a particular hatred reserved just for Christians. The hatred by Jews against Christians is so intense that Jews are taught to utter a curse when passing a Christian Church, calling on their heathen god (Hashem) to "destroy this house of the proud."[411]

"The twelfth invocation (formerly the nineteenth) of the *Amidah* (the central prayer of Judaism recited three times daily) is the *birkat ha-minim*, the curse on Christians."[412] The Talmud (*Sanhedrin Folio 90a*) provides that those who read the New Testament ("uncanonical books") have no portion in the world to come.[413] However, according to that same tractate, all Jews ("Israel") are guaranteed a portion in the world to come.[414] Elizabeth Dilling explains: "The 'religious' Orthodox Jew recites the 'Eighteen Benedictions,' or 'Shemoneh Esreh,' three times week days, four times on holidays and Sabbaths,

the 7th and 12th of which curse the Christians and non-Jews to hell
and perdition. Thus, the 'good Orthodox Jew' gives us Christians 6
cursings on ordinary days, 8 on 'specials.'"[415]

Not only did Billy Graham send Jews seeking salvation back to
the hellish religion of Judaism, he also sent Catholics seeking Christ
back to the antichrist Catholic church. In Billy Graham's 1994
Crusades in Minneapolis and Cleveland 6,000 respondents at each
crusade were referred to the Catholic Church. In Graham's September
1996 Charlotte, North Carolina crusade 1,700 respondents were
referred back to the Catholic Church.[416]

How can Billy Graham be so chummy with the Catholic
hierarchy when their official doctrine is that all Protestant Christians
are hell bound? Graham has even praised the Satanic and
blasphemous Catholic Mass. "This past week I preached in the great
Catholic cathedral a funeral sermon for a close friend of mine who
was a Catholic, and they had several Bishops and Archbishops to
participate. And as I sat there going through the funeral Mass, that
was a very beautiful thing, and certainly straight and clear in the
gospel. There was a wonderful little priest that would tell me when to
stand and when to kneel and what to do."[417] God states: "Can two
walk together, except they be agreed?" (Amos 3:3 AV) Graham walks
hand in hand with the false teachers of the Roman Church.

Billy Graham has even accepted the Catholic doctrine of infant
baptism. In 1961, he stated: "I do believe that something happens at
the baptism of an infant, particularly if the parents are Christians and
teach their children Christian truths from childhood. We cannot fully
understand the mysteries of God, but I believe a miracle can happen in
these children so that they are regenerated, that is, made Christians
through infant baptism. If you want to call that baptismal
regeneration, that's all right with me."[418]

There is not a single passage in the Bible that teaches baptismal
regeneration of infants. That is not just unscriptural, it is
antiscriptural. God states: "For by grace are ye saved through faith;
and that not of yourselves: *it is* the gift of God: Not of works, lest any

man should boast." (Ephesians 2:8-9 AV)

All this apostasy of Graham is quite understandable when one considers that Graham is a Freemason.[419]   Indeed, he is likely a 33rd degree Mason. Former 33rd degree Mason, Jim Shaw, has revealed that Billy Graham attended Shaw's 33rd degree induction ceremony. Only other 33rd degree Masons are permitted to attend such ceremonies.

One might ask what is wrong with being a Freemason? Albert Pike, the theological pontiff of Masonry wrote that Lucifer is the god of Freemasonry and that Freemasons look to Lucifer (which means light bearer) to give them light in their struggle against the God of the bible, whom Pike blasphemously calls "the God of Darkness and Evil."[420]

To this day Graham has refused to personally answer the many inquiries whether he is a Freemason. He has left it to his subordinates to deny his membership in Freemasonry for him. His membership in Freemasonry is one reason why Billy Graham has never spoken out against Freemasonry, when God's word states that he should do just that. "And have no fellowship with the unfruitful works of darkness, but rather reprove them." (Ephesians 5:11 AV).

Another famous Arminian free will preacher is Jerry Falwell.[421] During the heyday of the Moral Majority, a conservative organization that he headed, Falwell stated that Catholics made up the largest constituency in the organization.[422] At that time, Moral Majority had 500,000 active contributors and a mailing list of six million people.

It has been estimated that approximately 30% of the organization was Catholic. In his January 1985 *Moral Majority Report*, Falwell called the Pope and Billy Graham great moral and religious leaders. In 1988, Falwell mailed a letter to bookstores advertising a film about John Paul II. Falwell talked in glowing praise of the pope; he stated that the pope provides a shining light for the people of our generation.[423] Falwell knows the Scriptures too well, for anyone to attribute such statements to ignorance.

The Arminian Gospel appeals to the large masses of people who are following the broad way to destruction. As we have seen, the Arminian gospel strips God of his sovereignty. The Arminian gospel leads ultimately to the deification of man. If you think that is an exaggeration, lets look at the theology of one of the largest churches in the United States.

According to the September 17, 2003, edition of Forbes magazine, the second largest (non-Catholic) church in the United States, with an average attendance of 23,093, is World Changers in College Park, Georgia.[424] It should come as no surprise that it is an Arminian church. According to Business Week magazine World Changers is a worldwide "ministry" with houses of worship in Atlanta, New York, Australia, Europe, Nigeria, South Africa, and Britain. The "ministry" has an annual income of $70 million.[425]

The pastor of World Changers is Creflo Dollar, who has two Rolls Royces and travels in a Gulfstream-3 private jet.[426] Creflo Dollar has followed the logic of the Arminian gospel to its inexorable conclusion; he preaches that man is a god:

All right! I'm going to say something, you are gods on this earth. And it's about time we start operating like gods instead of a bunch of mere powerless humans.[427]

Creflo Dollar does not think that man is in any way inferior to God Almighty; he preaches that man is equal to God Almighty:

I have equality with God, that's my way of thinking. Now somebody says, "Well, it's hard to think that way," Well, keep saying it, "I have equality with God" talk yourself into it! You've talked yourself into other things![428]

God, however, has a different view of things: **"I *am* God, and *there is* none else; *I am* God, and *there is* none like me."** (Isaiah 46:9 AV) **"I *am* the LORD, and *there is* none else, *there is* no God beside me."** (Isaiah 45:5 AV) How can man be equal with God, if God himself says that he is the only God, there is no God beside him?

Sounds like Creflo Dollar is in a little disagreement with God. If one disagrees with God, who wins the argument?

Creflo Dollar will sometimes lead his congregation in a chant: "Say it again, I'm just like God!"[429] That is the level of degeneration that results from an Arminian theology.

T.D. Jakes described Creflo Dollar as "one of God's finest."[430] It is not a surprise that Jakes would say that about Dollar, since T.D. Jakes is another Arminian preacher, who believes that people have "failed to appreciate their divinity."[431]

In 2001, T.D. Jakes was pictured on the front cover of Time magazine with a huge caption asking: "Is this Man the Next Billy Graham?" The world loves Arminian preachers. "Ye adulterers and adulteresses, know ye not that **the friendship of the world is enmity with God? whosoever therefore will be a friend of the world is the enemy of God.**" (James 4:4 AV)

The following is the text of a "sermon" tape from Creflo Dollar played approvingly by T.D. Jakes on his May 24, 2004, show. It contains a philosophy to which both of them ascribe:

Quit going before God like a bunch of spiritual sissies and go before God with the covenant on your mind, quit whining before God and go before God like you know your rights. All right, I am going to do something here that it's going to start a revival or a riot. I'm going to say something, now watch this you will be able to identity a covenant person by how they act. **[He gets on one knee looking down]** Watch this we are all too familiar with this, I bow down on my bended knee, "Dear kind and heavenly Father I know that I'm not worth nothing Lord. I know I'm just a filthy rag. I know I ought to go to hell, but Lord if you could just stop by a little while; everything is going to be all right. Ummm, Lord I need you to stop by just a little while I know I ain't no good, Jesus. But if you could stop by everything will be all right. Please Jesus Oh stop by. Please

Ah Please! Please! Jesus, Oh Lord, I Know I Don't
Deserve it Jesus, Please, Please. For Christ sake we pray.
Amen and thank God." **That is a guy that doesn't
understand his covenant. This is a guy that's got to beg
God because he doesn't understand his covenant. A
covenant person will go before God like this [Standing
up looking up at God], "Father in the name of Jesus I
am the righteousness of God. I have a blood bought
right** to have healing in my body; I have a blood right to
have a sound mind. I have a blood bought right. I have a
blood bought right to get answers to my prayers and when I
am in trouble. I have a blood bought right to come before
your throne and to ask you for help in a time of trouble.
Now according to John 16:33, you said whatever I pray in
the name of Jesus it shall be given unto me. You said in
Mark 11:24 if I believe I receive it, then I shall have it.
Therefore, I pray it and say in the name of Jesus and I
believe that I receive it in Jesus name, Amen and good
night."[432]

T.D. Jakes and Creflo Dollar preach a different gospel from the
gospel found in the word of God. Read Christ's view of the repentant
sinner in Luke 18:9-14 and compare it to Creflo Dollars' rendition.
You will notice that Creflo Dollar completely reverses the lesson of
the parable. According to Creflo Dollar, the prideful Pharisee was
justified and the man who humbled himself before God was a sap who
should not have received anything. According to God, however,
"every one that exalteth himself shall be abased; and he that humbleth
himself shall be exalted." Luke 18:14. Choose ye this day whom you
will follow, Jesus or Creflo Dollar.

And he spake this parable unto certain which trusted in
themselves that they were righteous, and despised others:
Two men went up into the temple to pray; the one a
Pharisee, and the other a publican. The Pharisee stood and
prayed thus with himself, God, I thank thee, that I am not as
other men *are*, extortioners, unjust, adulterers, or even as
this publican. I fast twice in the week, I give tithes of all

that I possess. And the publican, standing afar off, would not lift up so much as *his* eyes unto heaven, but smote upon his breast, saying, God be merciful to me a sinner. **I tell you, this man went down to his house justified rather than the other: for every one that exalteth himself shall be abased; and he that humbleth himself shall be exalted.** (Luke 18:9-14 AV)

All discerning Christians understand that the Pope of Rome is antichrist. However, all Arminian roads lead to Rome. Recall that Arminius was an agent of Rome; his free will contagion was spread by secret agents of Rome into the Protestant churches. The ultimate goal of Rome in spreading the Arminian error is to change the theology of the Protestant churches to more closely align with the Roman model. That makes it easier for Rome to accomplish its ecumenical goal of bringing the Protestant churches back under the authority of the pope of Rome.

The free will gospel is an antichrist gospel, so it is not surprising to read that an Arminian preacher like T.D. Jakes praises the pope as a "dedicated and courageous messenger of God." The following is an official statement from T.D. Jakes issued upon the death of Pope John Paul II:

> The Catholic Church and the entire community of faith have suffered a great loss of a great leader. His holiness, John Paul II was truly a dedicated and courageous messenger of God. His legacy will be a model that all of us should follow. His Holiness was not only a leader of the church, but also a leader of the world. His life was an example everyone can learn from. His mission to spread the Good News of faith throughout the world, and his dedication to human rights was an inspiration.
> Bishop T. D. Jakes
> Founder and Senior Pastor
> The Potter's House of Dallas, Inc.[433]

T.D. Jakes' Church, The Potter's House in Dallas, Texas, is the

fourth largest non-Catholic church in the United States, with an
average attendance of 18,500, according to the September 17, 2003,
issue of Forbes Magazine.[434]

T.D. Jakes was an invited speaker at the Willow Creek
Leadership Summit 2004.[435] Willow Creek Community Church, with
an average attendance of 17,115, is the seventh largest non-Catholic
church in the United States,[436] and (you guessed it) the senior pastor
Bill Hybels preaches a free will Arminian gospel.[437] Are we starting
to see a pattern? It seems the largest churches in the United States,
indeed the world, are Arminian churches. The message is geared to
tickle the ears of the lost and appease them. They are flocking in
droves to be assured that they have free will, that they are sovereign,
indeed, that they are gods.

Kenneth Copeland another Arminian preacher, who often has
Creflo Dollar on his television show, also preaches the godhood of
man. Copeland teaches: "God's reason for creating Adam was His
desire to reproduce Himself. I mean a reproduction of Himself, and in
the Garden of Eden He did just that. He was not a little like God. He
was not almost like God. He was not subordinate to God even. ...
Adam is as much like God as you could get, just the same as Jesus. ...
Adam, in the Garden of Eden, was God manifested in the flesh."[438]
God, however, states that there was not any God before him, nor shall
there be any God after him. That pretty much covers forever, because
God always was and always will be.

> Ye *are* my witnesses, saith the LORD, and my servant
> whom I have chosen: that ye may know and believe me, and
> understand that **I am he: before me there was no God
> formed, neither shall there be after me. I, even I, am the
> LORD; and beside me there is no saviour.** (Isaiah 43:10-
> 11 AV)

Note that God states that "beside me there is no saviour."
Kenneth Copeland and like minded Arminian preachers think that
man can be his own savior. Under Copeland's theology man should
pray to himself. Copeland preaches: "Pray to yourself, because I'm in

your self and you're in My self. We are one Spirit, saith the Lord."[439]

Why would Copeland make such a clearly unbiblical statement? Because, as with all Arminians, he believes that God is powerless. Although Copeland puts man equal to God, what he really has done is supplant God in a spiritual *coup d'etat.* In the end, according to Copeland and all Arminians, man is actually over God in power and authority. God cannot act unless man invites him to act. God is helplessly looking on, waiting for the free will of man to invite him to act. The Arminian view is that man is in complete control. God is nothing but a servant for the whims of man. Copeland explains:

God had no avenue of lasting faith or moving in the earth. He had to have covenant with somebody. . . . He had to be invited in, in other words, or He couldn't come. God is on the outside looking in. In order to have any say so in the earth, He's gonna have to be in agreement with a man here.[440]

"I am" is the unique name given by God as a title identifying himself in the Old and New Testaments. It shows that Jesus is the God of both the Old and New Testaments. "Jesus said unto them, Verily, verily, I say unto you, Before Abraham was, **I am.** Then took they up stones to cast at him: but Jesus hid himself, and went out of the temple, going through the midst of them, and so passed by." (John 8:58-59 AV) "And God said unto Moses, **I AM THAT I AM**: and he said, Thus shalt thou say unto the children of Israel, **I AM** hath sent me unto you." (Exodus 3:14 AV)

Copeland knows no end in his Arminian blasphemy. Since Copeland has stripped God of his sovereignty, he figures he might as well take the name of God for his own. Unbelievably, Copeland has no problem taking the very title of God ("I Am"). Read this and weep about what Copeland has said: "I say this with all respect so that it don't upset you too bad, but I say it anyway. **When I read in the Bible where he [Jesus] says, 'I Am,' I just smile and say, 'Yes, I Am, too!'**"[441]

Just when you thought it could not get any worse, Copeland calls the God of the universe a failure. His Arminian mind thinks that all the evil things that have happened did so outside the sovereign will of God. That is because he does not believe God is sovereign. Copeland's Arminian theology leads him to conclude that God is a failure. Copeland stated: "I was shocked when I found out who the biggest failure in the Bible actually is....The biggest one is God....I mean, He lost His top-ranking, most anointed angel; the first man He ever created; the first woman He ever created; the whole earth and all the Fullness therein; a third of the angels, at least--that's a big loss, man. . ."[442]

33 Phony Arminian Evangelism

A rminians claim that preaching the sovereignty of God (they call it Calvinism) kills evangelism. Arminians say things like "[n]othing kills evangelism like Calvinism. Why witness if everything has already been decided?"[443] Arminians further claim that "Calvinism 'kills' churches because it neglects evangelism by teaching that salvation is only for those whom God 'elects,' not for everyone."[444] Both claims are demonstrably false.

Arminian Baptist churches are proud to circulate a tract called the *The Trail of Blood* by J.M. Carroll, which purports to show how the Baptist churches of today are in the trail of blood leading back to the original churches founded by the apostles. More than 2.5 million booklets of *The Trail of Blood* have been sold. Clarence Walker has written an introduction to *The Trail of Blood*, wherein he lists the "Marks of the New Testament Church."[445] Walker lists one of the marks of a New Testament church as:

> Its work--getting folks saved, baptizing them (with a baptism that meets all the requirements of God's Word), teaching them ("to observe all things whatsoever I have commanded you"). (Matt. 28:16-20)[446]

Notice the Arminian influence in Walker's introduction. Walker states that the work of the church is to get folks saved. Walker is

wrong. It is not the work of the church to get folks saved. It is the
work of the Lord Jesus Christ to save. The work of the church is to
spread the gospel of Jesus Christ. We are saved by the grace of God
alone through faith in Jesus Christ alone. "For by grace are ye saved
through faith; and that not of yourselves: it is the gift of God."
(Ephesians 2:8 AV)

Faith can only come by hearing the gospel of Jesus Christ. "Faith
cometh by hearing, and hearing by the word of God." Ephesians
1:1-2:22. That is where the church comes in. "Go ye into the all the
world, and preach the gospel to every creature." Mark 16:15. The
mission of the church is to spread the gospel of Jesus Christ; it is
through faith in Jesus that those who hear the gospel are saved. "He
that believeth and is baptized shall be saved; but he that believeth not
shall be damned." Mark 16:16. The church is to preach the gospel of
Jesus Christ. The key then is to accurately preach the gospel. That is
to preach God's word. We must be accurate in what is preached and
not preach a false gospel. The false gospel cannot save anyone; only
the true gospel of Jesus Christ is able to save.

It is Jesus who "gets" people saved, not the church. We must
preach not just the faith in Jesus but also the faith **of** Jesus. Jesus is
the author and finish of our faith; which means he creates the faith
and brings it to its conclusion. "Looking unto Jesus the author and
finisher of our faith. (Hebrews 12:2 AV) It is the Holy Spirit that
quickens those that are dead in sin so that they can believe in Jesus.
"And you hath he quickened, who were dead in trespasses and sins."
Ephesians 2:1.

It is Jesus who brings forth the fruit of salvation from his holy
gospel. "Of his own will begat he us with the word of truth, that we
should be a kind of firstfruits of his creatures." (James 1:18 AV) Jesus
saved us and called us with a holy calling unto salvation according to
his purpose and grace. "Who hath saved us, and called us with an holy
calling, not according to our works, but according to his own purpose
and grace, which was given us in Christ Jesus before the world
began." 2 Timothy 1:9.

The introduction to the *Trail of Blood* by Clarence Walker is evidence of the Arminian theology within most Baptist churches. The body of the text in J.M. Carroll's *The Trail of Blood* further evidences the Arminian theology. Carroll states:

> This religion of Christ to be individual, personal, and purely voluntary or through persuasion. No physical or governmental compulsion. A matter of distinct individual and personal choice. "Choose you" is the scriptural injunction. It could be neither accepted nor rejected nor lived by proxy nor under compulsion.[447]

Carroll and the Arminian Baptists are correct in resisting the force of government or any ecclesiastical organization over their freedom of conscience. All people should be able to freely practice their religion without government interference. Carroll and the Arminian Baptists, however, have fallen for the trick of the devil. The devil will take a righteous stance and push it beyond biblical bounds in order to create an unbiblical theology. It is like giving a person a boost to get on a horse and then pushing the person past the saddle so that he falls to the ground on the other side. The Baptists resist government interference in their faith, which is commendable. It seems, however, that they also reject the spiritual interference of God in their faith, which is damnable.

The Arminian Baptists do not view man's will as being enslaved to sin and therefore do not perceive the need for God to intervene and free the will of man. The Arminian Baptists have taken their stance on liberty a step too far. They resist the wrongful interference by the temporal government in their freedom of conscience to follow Jesus, and they also resist the righteous grace doctrine of the bible, whereby God interferes with man's will to free him from sin, so that he is able to believe in Jesus. The Arminian Baptists want total freedom from both the government and from God. Carroll is correct that no ecclesiastical organization or government should compel adherence by force to any doctrine. He is wrong, however, that Christianity is "through persuasion." Paul makes it clear in Galatians chapter one that salvation is not through persuasion but rather by the sovereign grace of God.

Arminian Baptists think that it is their job to make the hard sell and persuade a person to "get saved." That is not the proper function of the church. The church is to spread the love of the gospel and let that seed germinate in the heart as God wills. It is truly Jesus who saves, and no one else. All glory goes to Jesus Christ. Jesus had this to say to the Pharisees who were doing the same thing that the Arminian Baptists are doing today:

> Woe unto you, scribes and Pharisees, hypocrites! for ye compass sea and land to make one proselyte, and when he is made, ye make him twofold more the child of hell than yourselves. Matthew 23:15.

While most Baptist churches are Arminian, there are a minority of Baptist churches that have eschewed the Arminian theology and have embraced the gospel of the sovereign grace of God.[448] These grace gospel Baptists are commonly called "Reformed Baptists." Presently, only 10 percent of Southern Baptists are Reformed Baptists.[449] Why are there so few Baptist churches that embrace the gospel of grace? "Because strait is the gate, and narrow is the way, which leadeth unto life, and few there be that find it." Matthew 7:14.

The Reformed Baptists have suffered persecution at the hands of the Arminian Baptist churches. Arminianism is a child of the Vatican and so it is not surprising that the child will act as the parent and persecute the true church. The children of the flesh will persecute the children of the Spirit. Galatians 4:29. One example of this persecution is the intimidation of the Reformed Baptists by the Florida Baptist Convention.

> Some Baptists in this state say the Florida Baptist Convention is intimidating and demonizing churches that believe in Calvinism -- and doing it with the churches' own money. Convention executive director John Sullivan last week sent recordings of sermons by Sullivan's former pastor Jerry Vines to every church in the state, apparently at

convention expense, that identify Calvinism as a threat to Baptist life.

* * *

"This much is clear: The mailing of Dr. Vines' sermon on Calvinism is a clear indication that the executive director of the Florida Baptist Convention has an agenda to demonize the ministers and churches in our state who believe what the founders of the Southern Baptist Convention believed regarding the grace of God in salvation," wrote Ascol, pastor of Grace Baptist Church in Cape Coral and executive director of Founders Ministries, which promotes Calvinist or Reformed theology.[450]

The Arminian churches, whether Baptist, Methodist, or other denomination, have a style of evangelism which is contrary to the method used by Jesus. Jesus is the model we should follow in our evangelistic efforts. However, Jesus' method of evangelism would never pass muster in an Arminian church. In Luke 18:1-7, Jesus presents a parable of the persistent widow, where the point Jesus made is that God avenges only his "elect." Jesus next presents a parable that is a significant contrast to the Arminian model of evangelism.

And he spake this parable unto certain which trusted in themselves that they were righteous, and despised others: Two men went up into the temple to pray; the one a Pharisee, and the other a publican. The Pharisee stood and prayed thus with himself, God, I thank thee, that I am not as other men are, extortioners, unjust, adulterers, or even as this publican. I fast twice in the week, I give tithes of all that I possess. And the publican, standing afar off, would not lift up so much as his eyes unto heaven, but smote upon his breast, saying, God be merciful to me a sinner. I tell you, this man went down to his house justified rather than the other: for every one that exalteth himself shall be abased; and he that humbleth himself shall be exalted. (Luke 18:9-

14 AV)

Jesus spoke the parable to "certain which trusted in themselves."
Arminians trust in their own free will, that is trusting "in themselves."
Jesus is addressing the parable to the self-righteous mind. Notice
which of the two men was justified. It was the man who was
convicted of his sinfulness and asked God to be merciful to him. The
sinful publican did not of his own free will believe in God, he was
broken by God and pleaded with God to save him from his sins. That
is quite different from the Arminian preaching of the gospel, where
man is smart enough and good enough to overcome his slavery to sin
to believe in Jesus. Recall that in a previous chapter it was explained
how Arminian preacher Creflo Dollar contradicts Jesus, Dollar states:

> Quit going before God like a bunch of spiritual sissies and
> go before God with the covenant on your mind, quit whining
> before God and go before God like you know your rights. . .
> . This [repentant sinner] is a guy that's got to beg God
> because he doesn't understand his covenant. . . . A covenant
> person will go before God like this [Standing up looking up
> at God], "Father in the name of Jesus I am the
> righteousness of God."

The Arminian mode of evangelism assumes that man is smart
enough of his own free will to believe in Jesus. That is not that
dissimilar from the prideful Pharisee in Luke 18. In Luke 18, when a
rich ruler approaches him, Jesus exposes the lie of the Arminian free
will nonsense.

> And a certain ruler asked him, saying, Good Master, what
> shall I do to inherit eternal life? And Jesus said unto him,
> Why callest thou me good? none is good, save one, that is,
> God. Thou knowest the commandments, Do not commit
> adultery, Do not kill, Do not steal, Do not bear false witness,
> Honour thy father and thy mother. And he said, All these
> have I kept from my youth up. Now when Jesus heard these
> things, he said unto him, Yet lackest thou one thing: sell all
> that thou hast, and distribute unto the poor, and thou shalt

have treasure in heaven: and come, follow me. And when he heard this, he was very sorrowful: for he was very rich. And when Jesus saw that he was very sorrowful, he said, How hardly shall they that have riches enter into the kingdom of God! For it is easier for a camel to go through a needle's eye, than for a rich man to enter into the kingdom of God. And they that heard it said, Who then can be saved? And he said, The things which are impossible with men are possible with God. (Luke 18:18-27 AV)

The first point Jesus made with the rich ruler was that no one is good. Only God is good. His point is that all men are evil. Then Jesus confronts that man with his evil nature and tells him that in order to have eternal life he must have perfect righteousness. The man claims to be perfectly righteous, but Jesus exposes the falsehood of his claim by telling him that in order to be perfect he must sell all his goods and give the proceeds to the poor and then come and follow him. The key to what took place is when Jesus made the point that it is impossible for a rich man to enter the kingdom of heaven. He then explains that what is impossible for man is possible with God. Jesus teaches that man of his own efforts cannot possibly be good enough or smart enough to gain eternal life. God must make it possible. It is all of God.

Notice that Jesus did not tell the rich ruler that he must believe in him. Jesus instead gave a series of tasks that put the man in a position of realizing that salvation is impossible without the intervention of God. That is the point Jesus was trying to get across. God must work in the sinner to convict him of sin so that he asks God for mercy, just as the publican did in the earlier parable. God changes the heart of the sinner (as he did with the publican) to repent of his sin and turn toward God and ask for mercy. The point he was making with the rich ruler was that a sinner must give up all that is important to him in this world to follow Jesus. That requires a supernatural transformation of the soul. It requires that God entirely change the person so that he become a new creation; he is spiritually born again.

Let us now compare Jesus's method of evangelism with the

Arminian model of evangelism. We will see that the Arminian model
is not transformational. The Arminian method, instead, creates large
churches full of unsaved cosmetic Christians. The Arminian
evangelism is ineffective in saving souls. Bill Bright's ministry,
Campus Crusade for Christ, is typical of Arminian evangelism.

Bright's Campus Crusade for Christ ministry has concocted
tracts that are titled "The Four Spiritual Laws." The tracts have been
translated into almost every known language in the world and
circulated by the millions. This standard formulaic model in the
Campus Crusade for Christ style of evangelism is endemic in the
Arminian churches. The Four Spiritual Laws tracts start out by
introducing the concept of spiritual laws thusly: "Just as there are
physical laws that govern the physical universe, so are there spiritual
laws that govern your relationship with God." The tract then
introduces the first spiritual law:

Law 1

God loves you and offers a wonderful plan for your life.

God's Love
"God so loved the world that He gave His one and only Son,
that whoever believes in Him shall not perish but have
eternal life" (John 3:16, NIV).

God's Plan
[Christ speaking] "I came that they might have life, and
might have it abundantly" [that it might be full and
meaningful] (John 10:10).[451]

The Arminian model of evangelism starts off with a false
premise. The Arminian model of evangelism is premised on the fact
that God loves everyone. As we have seen that is not true. God loves
only his elect. The false premise of the Arminian evangelism does not
convict man of his sin by explaining that his condition is hopeless and
requires the intervention of the omnipotent God to save the sinner as
Jesus did in Luke 18. Instead, the Arminians state that God loves

everyone, there is no need for repentance, no broken heart, no sense of the impossibility of salvation.

Instead, the Arminians tell the sinner that God has a wonderful plan for them, all they have to do is bridge the gap that separates them from God by believing in a mythical Jesus who loves everyone.

Notice that the Campus Crusade for Christ uses the blasphemous New International Version of the Bible. In John 3:16 in the NIV it states that "God gave his one and only Son," whereas the correct Authorized King James Version (AV or KJV) states in John 3:16 that "God gave his only begotten Son." Jesus is the only "begotten" Son of God. Jesus is not the "one and only Son of God." All those who believe in Jesus become adopted children of God. God, therefore, has many children.

Of course, the Arminians want to hide the fact that we are God's adopted children, because we were predestined to that adoption, and the Arminians hate our predestination as children of God.

> According as he hath chosen us in him before the foundation
> of the world, that we should be holy and without blame
> before him in love: Having predestinated us unto the
> adoption of children by Jesus Christ to himself, according to
> the good pleasure of his will (Ephesians 1:4-5 AV)

The First Spiritual Law of Campus Crusade for Christ is followed by the next 3 Spiritual Laws. Law 2: "Man is sinful and separated from God. Therefore, he cannot know and experience God's love and plan for his life."[452] Law 3: "Jesus Christ is God's only provision for man's sin. Through Him you can know and experience God's love and plan for your life."[453] Law 4: "We must individually receive Jesus Christ as Savior and Lord; then we can know and experience God's love and plan for our lives."[454] The tract elaborates under Law 4 that "[w]e receive Jesus Christ by faith, as an act of the will."[455]

According to the Arminian Four Spiritual Laws, God has a plan

to save everyone; it is up to each person to allow God to work his plan
by exercising the his own free will to believe in a mythical Jesus who
will not interfere with the sinner's sovereign will over God's plan.
According to the Arminian mythology, God's plan is contingent on
the sinner allowing Jesus into his life. According to the Arminian
view, Jesus ended his efforts in salvation on the cross; it is all up to
the penitent on his own volition to believe in Jesus. The Arminian
Jesus is a passive Jesus, who waits patiently for the sinner to believe
in him.

Arminianism is a false gospel. Arminianism creates false
Christians who believe in a mythical, impotent Jesus, who is not able
to save anyone. The false Christians spend their lives working
feverishly to keep hold on their tenuous, false salvation, because they
are haunted by the prospect of losing their false faith and falling away
from their false Jesus. Arminianism is the very antithesis of the grace
found in the true gospel. Arminian evangelism is ineffective
evangelism, because the Arminian gospel has a counterfeit Jesus who
offers a counterfeit salvation.

Bill Bright, the founder of Campus Crusade for Christ, is now
dead. He revealed his allegiance to Rome by endorsing an ecumenical
agreement with the Catholic Church called *Evangelicals and
Catholics Together* (ECT).[456]   By endorsing that agreement, Bright
signified his agreement with the Roman Catholic theology. It is no
wonder that he would endorse an ecumenical agreement with Rome,
since the progenitor of Arminianism was Jacob Arminius, who was a
secret agent of Rome. As revealed in a previous chapter, the free will
contagion of Arminianism was spread into the Protestant churches for
the ultimate goal of changing the theology of the Protestant churches
to more closely align with the Roman model, so that the Protestant
churches could be brought under the authority of the pope of Rome.

There were many Protestant signatories to the ecumenical ECT,
including some who are viewed as "Calvinists." That is one reason
why a Christian should eschew such worldly labels like "Calvinist."
A Christian should never announce himself as a "Calvinist." Doing
so would cause people to lump him in with the "Calvinists" who have

strange unchristian ideas. One Calvinist with strange unchristian ideas is J.I. Packer. He was one of the signatories to the ECT manifesto. Packer is considered a conservative "Calvinist;" nonetheless, he signed the ECT, because, like the Arminian Billy Graham, Packer believes that Roman Catholics can be saved "Christians" even while they remain adherents to the blasphemous witchcraft of Roman Catholicism.[457] It seems that the devil has planted his tares in both the "Arminian" and the "Calvinist" camps.

Arminians argue that Paul and Silas evangelized in Acts 16:31 by simply telling the Jailer "believe on the Lord Jesus Christ, and thou shall be saved."[458] That is typical of Arminian preachers to quote that passage out of context.[459] When the Jailer of Paul and Silas found that the doors of the jail were opened and Paul and Silas were freed from their bands, the jailer fell down before Paul and Silas "And brought them out, and said, Sirs, what must I do to be saved? And they said, Believe on the Lord Jesus Christ, and thou shalt be saved, and thy house. And they spake unto him the word of the Lord, and to all that were in his house." Acts 16:30-32.

Notice the critical verse that is almost always skipped over. Verse 32 states that "they spake unto him the word of the Lord, and to all that were in his house." Paul and Silas did not end with the simple phrase "believe on the Lord Jesus Christ, and thou shalt be saved." They proceeded to teach the jailer the word of God. The point that is often missed is that they told him the essence of the gospel, telling the jailer and his household about Jesus.

Chapter 2 of the book of Acts illustrates effective evangelism. Peter begins by explaining that all who call on the name of the Lord shall be saved. He then explains what it takes to call on the name of the Lord. He begins by telling the people that Jesus was crucified by the "determinate counsel and foreknowledge of God." Acts 2:23. He puts the sovereignty of God right up front. He explains that Jesus fulfilled the prophecies of the coming Christ as determined by the preordained plan of God. Acts 2:24-36. He explains that Jesus is Christ, Lord God Almighty, who has risen from the dead and sits at the right hand of God the Father. What happened after Peter preached the sovereign grace of God? "**Now, when they heard this, they were pricked in their heart**, and said unto Peter and to the rest of the apostles, Men and brethren, what shall we do?" Acts 2:37.

How did Peter respond to their question? He did not give them some four step system, he did not have them recite some form statement. He told them to "**repent**, and be baptized every one of you in the name of Jesus Christ for the remission of sins, and ye shall receive the gift of the Holy Ghost." Acts 2:38. That is what Peter meant when he said at the beginning of his discourse that "whosoever shall call on the name of the Lord shall be saved." Acts 2:21. The person must repent of their sin and turn in faith to Jesus. That is impossible for people to do that on their own, because their will is enslaved to sin.

Peter gave them an impossible task; just as Jesus gave the rich man an impossible task in Luke 18:18-27. Only those who are elected by God for salvation can repent. Peter did not mince words; he told them flat out that it is only those whom God had called to salvation who would or even could repent. "For the promise is unto you, and to your children, and to all that are afar off, even **as many as the LORD our God shall call**." Acts 2:39. The outcome of Peter's evangelism was that **"the Lord added to the church daily such as should be saved."** Acts 2:47. Salvation is completely in God's hands; he added to the church only those whom he decided "should be saved." *Id.* Effective evangelism is to preach the sovereign grace of God. Ineffective evangelism is to lie to people and tell them that God loves everyone, that Jesus has done all he can on the cross, and it is all up to them to believe in Jesus of their own free will.

A person cannot simply believe in any old Jesus to be saved. The Jesus who saves is found in the bible. Jesus is not just a word that can be used as a talismanic incantation, as is often done by TV evangelists (virtually all of whom are Arminian). The Arminian Jesus, who is found nowhere in the bible, only presents a possibility of salvation, without any assurance. That phony Arminian Jesus cannot save a sinner.

The Jesus who truly saves is the Jesus who is found in the word of God. The Jesus of God's word is the only potentate (1 Timothy 6:15), who is the omnipotent, sovereign, King of kings and Lord of lords (Revelation 17:14), creator of heaven and earth (Colossians 1:16), who died on the cross as a propitiation for the sins of his elect (Romans 3:25), whom he predestined for salvation (Ephesians 1:5) by his grace through faith (Ephesians 2:8) that he provides for them (Hebrews 12:2).

34 Evangelicals and Catholics Together

Where does all the Arminian theology lead? Right back to Rome. The Arminian gospel is a seduction designed to lead all back into the arms of Rome. Rome uses its Arminian spiritual offspring to seduce the ignorant back into its clutches. The Roman Catholic Church has been losing members, particularly in South America. In order to reverse this trend Roman Catholic pressed its undercover agents (both Arminians and so-called Calvinists) in the ranks of Protestant denominations to stem the tide of losses from its religion by convincing former Catholics to return to the spiritual bondage of the Catholic church.

One artifice recently used by the Roman Catholic Church/State and its Arminian agents is an agreement by highly respected leaders among Protestants with representatives of the Roman Catholic Church. This group met and hammered out a seductive agreement, which was announced in May 1994. The agreement was titled *Evangelicals and Catholics Together* (Hereinafter referred to as ECT).[460]

The foundational principle of the entire document is that both Roman Catholicism and Christianity are religions of equivalent merit, and the doctrines in both should be accorded equal legitimacy under the common label "Christian."

As is evident in the two thousand year history of the church, and in our contemporary experience, there are different ways of being Christian, and some of these ways are distinctively marked by communal patterns of worship, piety, and catechesis. That we are all to be one does not mean that we are all to be identical in our way of following the one Christ. Such distinctive patterns of discipleship, it should be noted, are amply evident within the communion of the Catholic Church as well as within the many worlds of Evangelical Protestantism.[461]

In fact, as will be proven later in this book, Roman Catholicism is distinctly heathen and virulently antichristian. That is the fly in the ointment. There is a world of difference between the gospel of Jesus Christ and the gospel of Rome. Rome and its Arminian agents think that Rome's pagan liturgy is as valid as the Christian gospel.

Three observations are in order in connection with proselytizing. First, as much as we might believe one community is more fully in accord with the Gospel than another, we as Evangelicals and Catholics affirm that opportunity and means for growth in Christian discipleship are available in our several communities.[462]

Rome does not want the gospel of Christ preached. If it is, they lose members. So the ECT agreement discourages spreading the gospel among the lost within the "Christian" [read Catholic] community. They consider such proselytizing improper interference with the "communal allegiance" of members of the Roman Catholic Church. They feel that Christians must assiduously respect the spiritual chains with which Rome has bound its members.

Second, the decision of the committed Christian with respect to his communal allegiance and participation must be assiduously respected.[463]

One of the rather disturbing parts of the agreement was a condemnation of proselytizing. To Proselytize means to convert.

Conversion to Christianity is a result of the working of God through faith which is made possible by evangelism. That is, in the context of the Christian faith, a proselyte is one who has been converted to Christ by the preaching of the gospel. The document views successful evangelism as a bad thing. All successful efforts to spread the gospel are viewed as "sheep stealing." Since any time a person is educated about the gospel, Rome loses adherents, it is no wonder that they want such activity stopped.

The agreement states that evangelizing is acceptable as long as one leaves the sheep in the church in which they were found. Under the ECT, it is okay to evangelize as long as the persons evangelized are left in spiritual chains. In essence, they approve of ineffective evangelization. The problem for them is that there is no such thing as ineffective evangelization when the true gospel of Jesus Christ is preached. Preaching of the true gospel of Jesus Christ will bear spiritual fruit.

The ECT wants what is impossible for a true Christian. They want a watered down gospel that sends the poor confused newly evangelized soul back to pagan Rome. Where would such a gospel be found? It will be found among Arminian free will preachers. They view the Satanic Roman Catholic Church as just "another Christian community." The document actually states:

> Third, in view of the large number of non- Christians in the world and the enormous challenge of our common evangelistic task, it is neither theologically legitimate nor a prudent use of resources for one Christian community to proselytize among active adherents of another Christian community.[464]

Who were the signatories to the abominable ECT agreement? Below is a list of the guilty parties who signed the document; both the nominal, or rather ersatz, evangelicals and Catholic luminaries. On the Protestant side, the list is made up of both nominal Arminians (e.g. Bill Bright) and nominal Calvinists (e.g. J.I. Packer). Regardless of the purported theological stance of any individual signatory (be they Arminian or Calvinist), the document pushes a decidedly Arminian agenda. Putting their imprimatur on the Arminian ECT exposes the Protestants as Arminian accomplices of Rome. The document is a manifestation of the very goal of Arminianism, which is to bring the Protestant churches back into the Vatican fold.

PARTICIPANTS:
Mr. Charles Colson, Prison Fellowship
Dr. Kent Hill, Eastern Nazarene College
Dr. Richard Land, Christian Life Commission of the Southern Baptist Convention,
Dr. Larry Lewis, Home Mission Board of the Southern Baptist Convention
Dr. Jesse Miranda, Assemblies of God
Mr. Brian O'Connell, World Evangelical Fellowship
Mr. Herbert Schlossberg, Fieldstead Foundation
Mr. George Weigel, Ethics and Public Policy Center
Dr. John White, Geneva College and the National Association of Evangelicals
Fr. Richard John Neuhaus, Institute on Religion and Public Life
Msgr. William Murphy, Chancellor of the Archdiocese of Boston
Archbishop Francis Stafford, Archdiocese of Denver
Fr. Juan Diaz-Vilar, S.J.Catholic Hispanic Ministries
Fr. Avery Dulles, S.J.Fordham University
Bishop Francis George, OMI Diocese of Yakima (Washington)

ENDORSED BY:
Dr. Bill Bright, Campus Crusade for Christ Professor
Dr. James J. I. Packer, Regent College (British Columbia)
The Rev. Pat Robertson, Regent University
Dr. John Rodgers, Trinity Episcopal School for Ministry
Dr. William Abraham, Perkins School of Theology
Dr. Elizabeth Achtemeier, Union Theological Seminary (Virginia)
Mr. William Bentley Ball, Harrisburg, Pennsylvania
Mr. Keith Fournier, American Center for Law and Justice
Bishop William Frey, Trinity Episcopal School for Ministry
Professor Mary Ann Glendon, Harvard Law School
Dr. Os Guinness, Trinity Forum

Dr. Nathan Hatch, University of Notre Dame
Dr. James Hitchcock, St. Louis University
Professor Peter Kreeft, Boston College
Fr. Matthew Lamb, Boston College
Mr. Ralph Martin, Renewal Ministries,
Dr. Richard Mouw, Fuller Theological Seminary
Dr. Mark Noll, Wheaton College
Mr. Michael Novak, American Enterprise Institute
John Cardinal O'Connor, Archdiocese of New York
Dr. Thomas Oden, Drew University
Bishop Carlos A. Sevilla, S.J., Archiocese of San Francisco
Robert Destro, Catholic University of America
Fr. Augustine DiNoia, O.P., Dominican House of Studies
Fr. Joseph P. Fitzpatrick, S.J. Fordham University

John MacArthur, pastor of Grace Community Church in Sun Valley, California, has steadfastly maintained that the signers of the ECT should recant their agreement to the ECT, because the bottom line, he says, is that Roman Catholicism is "another religion."[465]

Because of objections from the Christian community, in December 1994 Bill Bright, the founder of Campus Crusade for Christ, found it necessary to issue a statement explaining his reasons for signing the ETC. His statement was not a defense of the gospel, but rather was a defense of Roman Catholicism. Bright stated:

> To non-Christians and the non-believing world who know nothing about Christianity and who may think Protestants and Catholics worship a different God, this affirmation should be a testimony to the Lordship of Christ and the truth of His Word. Catholics do not have a cultic understanding of God. They know Him as Father, Son and Holy Spirit as revealed in Holy Scriptures, with Jesus the Second Person of the triune Godhead, at one with and equal to the Father, who died for our sins, and who has given us His Holy Spirit.[466]

Notice how he states that only those who are not Christians

would suggest that Protestants and Catholics worship a different God. In fact, it is only a Christian who would understand that fact. However, he is suggesting that to believe such a thing puts one in the non-Christian camp.

Bright then explains how Catholics believe in the same God as Protestants. Bill Bright is engaging is a purposeful deception. He knows that statement is not true. Proof of his deception is found in the immediately following paragraphs in his statement:

> **While there was agreement only on the above four doctrinal areas, there was acknowledged disagreement on ten specific issues, issues that have traditionally separated evangelicals and Catholics. These include the purpose of the Lord's Supper, devotion to Mary, and eight others. Believe me, I am well aware of the sharp doctrinal differences with many points of Roman Catholic theology and some of their historic pronouncements.** Please understand that there was no compromise on these matters. The biblical principles upon which I have committed my life, and that guide Campus Crusade for Christ and all that we do, have not changed one bit and, by God's grace, never will.[467]

> **I am also aware that many Roman Catholics, while they may use the phrase, may attach a different meaning to "justification by faith" than what Martin Luther had in mind and what most of us believe.** (Unfortunately, so do many Protestants.) However, in spite of official Roman Catholic doctrine which may not have changed, many Catholics, including theologians, have begun to take a more biblical view on this subject.[468]

Bill Bright acknowledged that the Roman Catholic Church has a different theology regarding "the purpose of the Lord's Supper, devotion to Mary" and eight other unspecified areas. He later admits that Catholics believe in a different means of justification. In fact, he states that when Catholics use the term "justification by faith" they do

not mean the same thing as Christians. He is basically listing some of
the cultic beliefs of the Roman Catholic Church, after stating that
"Catholics do not have a cultic understanding of God."[469] Bright is a
double minded man.

Bright further stated: "I believe this [ECT] agreement will help
open doors to them [meaning Catholics] for the gospel. I have already
received feedback from the field that such is the case."[470] That
statement is contradicted by Richard Bennett, who has stated that the
ECT and the similar ecumenical agreement called *The Gift of
Salvation* have been used by the Catholic Church to undermine
Christian evangelism and lure former Catholics back to the paganism
of Rome. They are then subjected to the endless mumbo jumbo of
Catholic ritualism that sears the conscience and deadens the heart to
any further enlightenment from the gospel of Jesus Christ.

35 Catholic Necromancy

How can Bill Bright possibly state that Catholics and Christians worship that same God, when the Catholics have a different means of justification, they have a physical god made of bread and wine, and that Catholic god shares his godhood with a goddess Catholics call Mary?

Mary is just one among a pantheon of "saints" to whom Catholics pray. The Catholic definition of a saint is quite different from the biblical definition. All who are Christians are also saints. However, Catholics, in direct contravention to the commands of God, pray to dead people whom they call "saints."

> The holy council . . . orders all bishops and others who have the official charge of teaching. . . to instruct . . . the faithful that the **saints**, reigning together with Christ, **pray to God for men** and women; **that it is good and useful to invoke them humbly and to have recourse to their prayers, to their help and assistance, in order to obtain favours from God** through his Son our lord Jesus Christ, who alone is our Redeemer and Saviour. Those who deny that the saints enjoying eternal happiness in heaven **are to be invoked**, or who claim that saints do not pray for human beings or that **calling upon them to pray for each of us** is

idolatry or is opposed to the word of God and is prejudicial to the honour of Jesus Christ, the one Mediator between God and humankind; or who say that it is foolish to **make supplication orally or mentally to those who are reigning in heaven**; all those entertain impious thoughts. *THE GENERAL COUNCIL OF TRENT, TWENTY FIFTH SESSION, DECREE ON THE INVOCATION, THE VENERATION AND THE RELICS OF SAINTS AND ON SACRED IMAGES*, 1560.

[The saints'] . . . intercession is their most exalted service to God's plan. **We can and should ask them to intercede for us and for the whole world.** *CATECHISM OF THE CATHOLIC CHURCH*, § 2683, 1994.

Why would one pray to the saints? God won't listen to their counsel, because he doesn't need counsel. Ephesians 1:11. God puts no trust in his saints.

Behold, **he putteth no trust in his saints**; yea, the heavens are not clean in his sight. (Job 15:15 AV)

Keep in mind that the saints referred to above are those that have died. God has expressly commanded that we not attempt to communicate with the dead. To communicate with the dead is a sin called **necromancy**.

There shall not be found among you *any one* that maketh his son or his daughter to pass through the fire, *or* that useth divination, *or* an observer of times, or an enchanter, or a witch, Or a charmer, or a consulter with familiar spirits, or a wizard, or a **necromancer**.   **For all that do these things *are* an abomination unto the LORD**: and because of these abominations the LORD thy God doth drive them out from before thee. (Deuteronomy 18:10-12 AV)

There is only one mediator between man and God to whom we should pray, and that is Jesus Christ.

For *there is* one God, and one mediator between God and men, the man Christ Jesus; (1 Timothy 2:5 AV)

36 Catholic goddess Worship

ary, the mother of Jesus, is at the apex in the pantheon
of Roman Catholic saints. In fact, Mary is considered a
goddess in the Catholic Church. The Roman Catholic
Church has a different gospel, with a different Jesus than that which is
found in the Bible. *See* 2 Corinthians 11:4. Their different gospel has
different doctrines and a different Mary from the Mary in the Bible.
In the Bible, Mary is the handmaid of the Lord. *See* Luke 1:38. The
Roman Catholic Church Mary, however, is an imperious queen of
heaven, who rules over all things.

The Catholic Mary (as distinguished from the biblical Mary) is a
heathen goddess, who in 1950 was "infallibly" declared by Pope Pius
XII to have been assumed body and soul into heaven and crowned
"Queen over all things."

> Finally the Immaculate Virgin, preserved free from all stain
> of original sin, when the course of her earthly life was
> finished, was taken up body and soul into heavenly glory,
> and exalted by the Lord as **Queen over all things**, so that
> she might be the more fully conformed to her Son, the Lord
> of lords and conqueror of sin and death. Pope Pius XII --
> *Munificentissimus Deus,* 1950.

The problem with that "infallible" pronouncement of the pope is that it is impossible for Mary to be "queen over all things." The Bible states unequivocally that Jesus Christ "is the blessed and **only Potentate**, the Lord of lords and King of kings." 1 Timothy 6:15. A potentate is a sovereign monarch.[471] Jesus Christ is the "only Potentate." Only means only! There is not room in heaven for another Potentate. Mary, therefore, cannot be "queen over all things." Jesus is the **"only Potentate"** over all things!

The Christian God is sovereign; whereas the Catholic god shares his throne with "Mary" the queen of heaven. The Catholic church teaches that salvation comes through both Mary and Jesus. According to Catholic doctrine, by her obedience Mary is the cause of salvation.

> With her whole heart, unhindered by sin, she embraced the **salvific** will of God and consecrated herself totally as a handmaid of the Lord to the person and work of her Son, under whom and with whom, by the grace of the Almighty, **she served in the mystery of the redemption**. Justly, therefore, do the holy Fathers consider Mary not merely as a passive instrument on the hands of God, but as **freely co-operating in the salvation of humankind** by her faith and obedience. As St. Irenaeus says; **'through her obedience she became cause of salvation both for herself and for the whole human race.'** THE SECOND VATICAN COUNCIL, 1964 (emphasis added).[472]

Mary is not the cause of our salvation; Jesus and Jesus alone is the cause of our salvation. He is the only way to salvation, there is no other name under all of heaven that can be invoked for our salvation. **"Salvation is of the LORD."** Jonah 2:9.

> Be it known unto you all, and to all the people of Israel, that by the name of **Jesus Christ of Nazareth**, whom ye crucified, whom God raised from the dead, *even* by him doth this man stand here before you whole. This is the stone which was set at nought of you builders, which is become the head of the corner. **Neither is there salvation in any**

other: for there is none other name under heaven given among men, whereby we must be saved. (Acts 4:10-12 AV)

According to the Romish church, not only is Mary a co-redeemer with Christ, but she is an advocate before God for those who pray to her.

Her assumption into heaven does not mean that she has laid aside her salvific role; **she continues to obtain by her constant intercession the graces we need for eternal salvation.** . . . That is why the Blessed Virgin is invoked in the Church under the titles of **Advocate, Auxiliatrix, Helper, Mediatrix**. THE SECOND VATICAN COUNCIL, 1964 (emphasis added).[473]

Notice that Mary has the status of a Mediatrix between God and man. She also has the role of advocate before God on behalf of sinners. Finally she is a helper to sinners. Who does the Holy Bible say is the mediator, advocate, and helper? Jesus is our mediator, advocate, and helper!

For *there is* **one God, and one mediator** between God and men, the man **Christ Jesus**; (1 Timothy 2:5 AV)

And to **Jesus the mediator of the new covenant**, and to the blood of sprinkling, that speaketh better things than *that of* Abel. (Hebrews 12:24 AV)

My little children, these things write I unto you, that ye sin not. And if any man sin, **we have an advocate with the Father, Jesus Christ** the righteous: (1 John 2:1 AV)

So that we may boldly say, **The Lord *is* my helper**, and I will not fear what man shall do unto me. (Hebrews 13:6 AV)

Its bad enough that the Catholic church encourages its members to pray to Mary and the saints, but the manner of the prayers adds insult to injury. The Catholic rosary, for example, requires a Catholic to say 53 "Hail Marys."[474] "Hail Mary" is a prayer to Mary which was developed by the Catholic church and is often repeated during Catholic ceremonies, such as the saying of a rosary.[475] Jesus admonished his disciples not to pray in the manner of the heathen, who repeat prayers over and over again.

> But **when ye pray, use not vain repetitions**, as the heathen *do*: for they think that they shall be heard for their much speaking. Be not ye therefore like unto them: for your Father knoweth what things ye have need of, before ye ask him. (Matthew 6:7-8 AV)

Satan is using his Catholic Church and its doctrine of Mariolatry, to attempt a futile spiritual *coup d'etat* to supplant Jesus and enthrone its Mary as the "Queen of Heaven." The Catholic Church is dedicated to the worship and service of "Mary," the queen of heaven. Jesus is ancillary and almost incidental to the worship of the Catholic queen of heaven.

For example, the coin commemorating the pontificate of John Paul II has on the front has a declaration that he is the Pontifex Maximus. "On the reverse side is his papal heraldic shield. The large letter M on the shield stands for Mary, the mother of God. The words at the bottom 'TOTUS TUUS' are transposed and excerpted from a latin prayer composed by Saint Louis-Marie Grignion de Montfort: *tuus totus ego sum, et omnia mea tua sunt, O Virgo super omnia benedicta*, which in English reads 'I belong to you entirely, and all that I possess is yours, Virgin blessed above all.'"[476] The pope dedicates his fealty not to Jesus but to "Mary," the Catholic "Queen of Heaven."

In 1978, on the feast day of the Immaculate Conception, Pope John Paul II dedicated and entrusted the Roman Catholic Church and all its property not to their Catholic version of Jesus, but rather to their Catholic version of Mary:

The Pope, at the beginning of his episcopal service in St.
Peter's Chair in Rome, wishes to entrust the Church
particularly to her in whom there was accomplished the
stupendous and complete victory of good over evil, of love
over hatred, of grace over sin; to her of whom Paul VI said
that she is ' the beginning of the better world;' to the Blessed
Virgin. He entrusts to her himself, as the servant of servants,
and all those whom he serves, all those who serve with him.
**He entrusts to her the Roman Church, as token and
principle of all the churches in the world, in their
universal unity. He entrusts it to her and offers it to her
as her property.** Insegnamenti Giovanni Paolo II (1978),
Vatican City: Libreria Editrice Vaticana, 313.[477]

The Catholic Church has a series of ritualistic mysteries that are
recited after each of 15 Catholic "stations of the cross." These
"mysteries" are said while counting beads that are called the rosary.
The primary focus of the Catholic Rosary is not Jesus, it is Mary.
Mary's roles in Christ's birth, death, and resurrection are highlighted,
exaggerated, and in some instances fabricated in 12 of the 15
"mysteries." In fact, the formal title of the Rosary is: **"The Roses of
Prayer for the Queen of Heaven."**[478]

The prayers to Mary in the Rosary outnumber the supposed
prayers to God by roughly 10 to 1. After each mystery is recited,
Catholics say one "Our Father" prayer followed by ten "Hail Mary"
prayers. They blaspheme God by praying to their Mary goddess and
prove themselves heathen by repeating the blasphemous prayers over
and over again in violation of Jesus' command in Matthew 6:7.

It is notable that the rosary said in honor of the queen of heaven
has stations of the cross called "mysteries." There is a woman
mentioned in the Bible whose very name is "mystery."

And the woman was arrayed in purple and scarlet colour,
and decked with gold and precious stones and pearls, having
a golden cup in her hand full of abominations and filthiness
of her fornication: And upon her forehead *was* a name

written, **MYSTERY**, BABYLON THE GREAT, THE
MOTHER OF HARLOTS AND ABOMINATIONS OF
THE EARTH. (Revelation 17:4-5 AV)

Later, when the Bible speaks of the destruction of the "mystery"
harlot, the harlot says in her heart that she sits as a **"queen."**

> Reward her even as she rewarded you, and double unto her
> double according to her works: in the cup which she hath
> filled fill to her double. How much she hath glorified
> herself, and lived deliciously, so much torment and sorrow
> give her: **for she saith in her heart, I sit a queen**, and am
> no widow, and shall see no sorrow. Therefore shall her
> plagues come in one day, death, and mourning, and famine;
> and she shall be utterly burned with fire: for strong *is* the
> Lord God who judgeth her. (Revelation 18:6-8 AV)

God reveals the mystery of the woman. God identifies the
woman as a great city. "And the woman which thou sawest is that
great city, which reigneth over the kings of the earth." (Revelation
17:18 AV)   God also reveals the mystery of the woman.

> **I will tell thee the mystery of the woman**, and of the beast
> that carrieth her, which hath the seven heads and ten horns.
> The beast that thou sawest was, and is not; and shall ascend
> out of the bottomless pit, and go into perdition: and they that
> dwell on the earth shall wonder, whose names were not
> written in the book of life from the foundation of the world,
> when they behold the beast that was, and is not, and yet is.
> And here *is* the mind which hath wisdom. **The seven heads
> are seven mountains, on which the woman sitteth**.
> (Revelation 17:7-9 AV)

So we know that the mystery harlot is a great city that sits on
seven mountains. There is only one city that matches that description
and that is Rome. Rome is famous for the seven mountains upon
which it sits. The mountains are the Capitoline, the Quirinal, the
Viminal, the Esquiline, the Caelian, the Avenue, and the Palatine.[479]

The Catholic Encyclopedia states that **"[i]t is within Rome, called the city of seven hills, that the entire Vatican State is now confined."**[480]

The glorification of the queen of heaven is in a sense a glorification by proxy of the Roman Catholic Church. That is why the Catholic hierarchy refers to their organization as "Mother Church."[481] It is true that the Catholic Church is a mother, **"THE MOTHER OF HARLOTS AND ABOMINATIONS OF THE EARTH."** (Revelation 17:4-5 AV)

That mother of harlots "saith in her heart, I sit a **queen**." Revelation 18:7. There is a spiritual parallel between the wicked harlot queen in the book of Revelation and Mary the queen of heaven glorified by the Catholic Church. The harlot of Revelation and Mary the queen of heaven both draw men from Jesus Christ, who "is the blessed and only Potentate, the Lord of lords and King of kings." 1 Timothy 6:15.

One of the "mysteries" recited during the Catholic rosary is called "the Fifth Glorious Mystery - The Coronation." In that mystery it is claimed by the Catholic Church that "**Mary is the Queen of Heaven**."

Mary had served Jesus all her life. She had loved and served God with her whole heart and soul. She had never committed the slightest sin. So in heaven she was to have her reward. Body and soul, Mary entered heaven. Her Son, Jesus, met her and took her in His grateful arms. The heavenly Father said, "This is My dear devoted daughter." The Divine Son said, "This is My dear faithful Mother." The Holy Spirit said, "This is my sweet, pure bride." And the saints and angels all cried, **"This is our Queen!"** So Jesus, the King of Kings, seated her on her throne. On her head He placed a glorious crown of stars. But Mary looked down to see her children on earth. For now she could help her sons and daughters to reach heaven. **Mary is the Queen of Heaven**. But she is our loving Mother who protects us with her power.[482]

One of the final prayers of the Rosary is a prayer to the Catholic goddess "Mary" called "**Hail Holy Queen**."

> **Hail, holy Queen**, Mother of Mercy! our life, our sweetness, and our hope! To thee do we cry, poor banished children of Eve; to thee so we send up our sighs, mourning and weeping in this valley, of tears. Turn, then, most gracious Advocate, thine eyes of mercy toward us; and after this our exile show unto us the blessed fruit of thy womb, Jesus; O clement, O loving, O sweet Virgin Mary.[483]

The Catholics also have other prayers not said during the rosary to their goddess, the Queen of Heaven:

> **Queen of heaven**, rejoice. Alleluia. The Son whom you were privileged to bear, Alleluia, has risen as he said, Alleluia. Pray to God for us, Alleluia. Rejoice and be glad, Virgin Mary, Alleluia. For the Lord has truly risen, Alleluia. O God, it was by the Resurrection of your Son, our Lord Jesus Christ, that you brought joy to the world. Grant that through the intercession of the Virgin Mary, his Mother, we may attain the joy of eternal life. Through Christ, our Lord. Amen.[484]

The Catholic "Mary" (queen of heaven) is viewed by the Roman Catholic Church as "the **restorer of the world that was lost, and the dispenser of all benefits** . . . the **most powerful mediator (*mediatrix*) and advocate (*conciliatrix*) for the whole world** . . . **above all others in sanctity and in union with Christ** . . . **the primary minister in the distribution of the divine graces**,"[485] "the **beloved daughter of the Father and Temple of the Holy Spirit**,"[486] "the **mother of all the living**,"[487] "the **new Eve**,"[488] "**Mother of the Church**,"[489] "the '**Mother of Mercy**,' the **All Holy One**."[490] She supposedly "**surpasses all creatures, both in heaven and on earth**,"[491] conquered death and was ". . . raised body and soul to the glory of heaven, to **shine refulgent as Queen** at the right hand of her

454   Edward Hendrie

Son, the immortal King of ages."[492]

> [I]ndeed, she is clearly the **mother of the members of Christ since she has by her charity joined in bringing about the birth of believers in the Church** who are members of its head. Wherefore she is hailed as preeminent and as a wholly unique member of the Church, and as its type and outstanding model in faith and charity. The Catholic Church taught by the Holy Spirit, honours her with filial affection and **devotion as a most beloved mother.** THE SECOND VATICAN COUNCIL, 1964 (emphasis added).[493]

What does God think of this Catholic goddess, Mary?

> Thou shalt worship the Lord thy God, and him **only** shalt thou serve. (Luke 4:8 AV)

> Thou shalt have **no other gods** before me. . . . Thou shalt not bow down thyself to them nor serve them: for I the LORD thy God *am* a jealous God.. (Exodus 20:3-5 AV)

Where did the Catholic Church come up with the idea of May being the queen of heaven? The Judaizers who established the Catholic church brought with them their Judaic/Babylonian worship of the queen of heaven.[494] The Catholic goddess Mary is the "queen of heaven" in the Kabbalah, to whom the Jews have been making cake and drink offerings since the time of Jeremiah. "The children gather wood, and the fathers kindle the fire, and the women knead their dough, to make cakes to the **queen of heaven**, and to pour out drink offerings unto other gods, that they may provoke me to anger." Jeremiah 7:18.

Orthodox Jews today still worship the queen of heaven who is called Shekinah or the Sabbath Queen.[495] Daniel Matt in his book *Zohar, The Book of Enlightenment* reveals that the Sabbath Queen and Shekinah are one and the same.[496] In the Kabbalah the Jewish queen of heaven is also known as Matronita, who commands the hosts of

heaven on behalf of Israel against its enemies.[497]   Athol Bloomer
(writing under the *nom de plume* Aharon Yosef) reveals that
"Matronita in this section of Zohar is called the Shekhinah. The
concepts of Shekhinah and Matronita are both symbolized by the
Moon."[498]   Michael Hoffman explains that the "[w]orship of the
Shekinah in the form of the moon goddess is a formal rite in Orthodox
Judaism."[499]

The Catholic church teaches that their queen of heaven, Mary,
was immaculately conceived, and that she was born and lived without
sin.

> [T]he most Blessed Virgin Mary was, from the first moment
> of her conception, by a singular grace and privilege of
> almighty God in view of the merits of Christ Jesus the
> Saviour of the human race, preserved immune from all stain
> of original sin.   POPE PIUS IX, PAPAL BULL
> *INEFFABILIS DEUS*, 8 December 1854.[500]

If Mary was immaculately conceived and was free of sin, why
was it necessary for her to bring a sacrifice to the temple? She did so
because she was a sinner who was bringing an offering for her sin.
Mary herself knew she was a sinner in need of a Saviour.

> And Mary said, My soul doth magnify the Lord, And my
> spirit hath rejoiced in **God my Saviour**. (Luke 1:46-47 AV)

> And when the days of her purification according to the law
> of Moses were accomplished, they brought him to
> Jerusalem, to present *him* to the Lord; (As it is written in
> the law of the Lord, Every male that openeth the womb shall
> be called holy to the Lord;) **And to offer a sacrifice
> according to that which is said in the law of the Lord, A
> pair of turtledoves, or two young pigeons**. (Luke 2:22-24
> AV)

> And when the days of her purifying are fulfilled, for a son,
> or for a daughter, she shall bring a lamb of the first year for

a burnt offering, and a young pigeon, or a turtledove, for a
sin offering, unto the door of the tabernacle of the
congregation, unto the priest: **Who shall offer it before the
LORD, and make an atonement for her**; and she shall be
cleansed from the issue of her blood. This *is* the law for her
that hath born a male or a female. **And if she be not able to
bring a lamb, then she shall bring two turtles, or two
young pigeons; the one for the burnt offering, and the
other for a sin offering: and the priest shall make an
atonement for her, and she shall be clean**. (Leviticus
12:6-8 AV)

The Holy Bible makes it unequivocally clear that nobody is
without sin. Not Mary, not anyone! The only perfect man who ever
walked the earth was the Lord Jesus Christ.

As it is written, **There is none righteous, no, not one:
There is none that understandeth, there is none that
seeketh after God. They are all gone out of the way, they
are together become unprofitable; there is none that
doeth good, no, not one**. Their throat *is* an open sepulchre;
with their tongues they have used deceit; the poison of asps
is under their lips: Whose mouth *is* full of cursing and
bitterness: Their feet *are* swift to shed blood: Destruction
and misery *are* in their ways: And the way of peace have
they not known: There is no fear of God before their eyes.
(Romans 3:10-18 AV)

For all have sinned, and come short of the glory of God;
(Romans 3:23 AV)

37 Catholic Idolatry

Not only does the Catholic Church instruct its members to pray to Mary and the other saints, but it also instructs them to venerate graven images of Jesus, Mary, and the saints. The official doctrine of the Catholic church encourages the sin of idolatry.

Basing itself on the mystery of the incarnate Word, the seventh ecumenical council at Nicaea justified against the iconoclasts the **veneration of icons** - of Christ, but also of the mother of God, the angels, and all the saints. By becoming incarnate, the Son of God introduced a new economy of images. CATECHISM OF THE CATHOLIC CHURCH, § 2131, 1994.

What does God think about this veneration of graven images? The following are the first two of the Ten Commandments.

And God spake all these words, saying, I *am* the LORD thy God, which have brought thee out of the land of Egypt, out of the house of bondage. **Thou shalt have no other gods before me. Thou shalt not make unto thee any graven image, or any likeness *of any thing* that *is* in heaven above, or that *is* in the earth beneath, or that *is* in the**

**water under the earth: Thou shalt not bow down thyself
to them, nor serve them**: for I the LORD thy God *am* a
jealous God, visiting the iniquity of the fathers upon the
children unto the third and fourth *generation* of them that
hate me; And shewing mercy unto thousands of them that
love me, and keep my commandments. (Exodus 20:1-6 AV)

The Roman church teaches that by coming to earth as a man
Christ instituted a new era of images. Why then would God command
Christians time and again to keep away from idols?

Little children, **keep yourselves from idols**. Amen. (1
John 5:21 AV)

But that we write unto them, that they **abstain from
pollutions of idols**, and *from* fornication, and *from* things
strangled, and *from* blood. (Acts 15:20 AV)

Wherefore, my dearly beloved, **flee from idolatry**. (1
Corinthians 10:14 AV)

And **what agreement hath the temple of God with idols**?
for ye are the temple of the living God; as God hath said, I
will dwell in them, and walk in *them*; and I will be their
God, and they shall be my people. (2 Corinthians 6:16 AV)

Now the works of the flesh are manifest, which are *these*;
Adultery, fornication, uncleanness, lasciviousness,
Idolatry, witchcraft, hatred, variance, emulations, wrath,
strife, seditions, heresies, (Galatians 5:19-20 AV)

Despite the heathen idolatry practiced by the Catholic church,
Bill Bright thinks that the "Catholics do not have a cultic
understanding of God," but that Catholics and Christians worship the
same God. Bill Bright admitted in his December 1994 ECT letter that
Catholics and Christians have a different view of the purpose of the
Lord's supper.

In fact, the Catholic doctrine of the Lord's supper is further evidence that proves that the Roman Catholic religion is decidedly pagan and Satanic, with a different god than the Christian God of the bible. The Catholic Lord's supper is a misnomer. It is not a celebration of the Lord's supper, but is an idolatrous Mass where Christ is blasphemously humiliated and re-crucified in effigy.

During the Catholic Mass a piece of bread is actually worshiped as a god. The Catholic Mass is a part and parcel of the institutionalized idolatry of the Roman church.

There is a doctrine in the Catholic church called transubstantiation, under which the Roman church teaches that during Mass a piece of bread (the host) and some wine are both transformed into Jesus. It is the official teaching of the church that the host and wine both become the body, blood, soul, and divinity of the Lord God Jesus Christ. The church teaches that the appearance of bread and wine remain, but that they have actually been transubstantiated into God.

In the most blessed sacrament of the Eucharist 'the body and blood, together with the soul and divinity, of our Lord Jesus Christ and, therefore, *the whole Christ is truly, really, and substantially* contained.' CATECHISM OF THE CATHOLIC CHURCH, § 1374, 1994 (italics in original, bold emphasis added).

It sounds incredible, but the Catholic Church is actually saying, in no uncertain terms, that Jesus Christ himself, God Almighty, is present during the Catholic Mass in the outward form of bread and wine.

By the consecration the transubstantiation of the bread and wine into the Body and Blood of Christ is brought about. Under the consecrated species of bread and wine **Christ himself, living and glorious, is present in a true, real, and substantial manner: his Body and his Blood, with his soul and his divinity.** CATECHISM OF THE CATHOLIC

CHURCH, § 1413, 1994 (emphasis added).

> **Here the pastor should explain that in this Sacrament
> are contained not only the true body of Christ and all the
> constituents of a true body, such as bones and sinews,
> but also Christ whole and entire.** He should point out
> that the word *Christ* designates the God-man, that is to
> say, one Person in whom are united the divine and
> human natures; that the Holy Eucharist, therefore,
> contains both, and humanity whole and entire, consisting
> of the soul, all the parts of the body and the blood, all of
> which must be believed to be in this Sacrament. **In
> heaven the whole humanity is united to the Divinity in
> one hypostasis, or Person; hence it would be impious, to
> suppose that the body of Christ, which is contained in
> the Sacrament, is separated from His Divinity.** THE
> CATECHISM OF THE COUNCIL OF TRENT (emphasis
> added).[501]

Amazing as it may seem, the Catholic doctrine is that during
communion Catholics are actually eating God Almighty when they
consume the Eucharistic host. "If anyone say that Christ, given in the
Eucharist, is eaten spiritually only, and not also sacramentally and
really, let him be anathema." COUNCIL OF TRENT, ON THE
MOST HOLY SACRAMENT OF THE EUCHARIST, Canon VIII.

The Catholic doctrine of transubstantiation is pure and simple
witchcraft. The Catholic church teaches that the bread and wine is to
be worshiped with the same veneration that one would feel if one
were worshiping God. In fact, the Romish church teaches that the
consecrated bread and wine are the most holy sacrament of the church
because they are God and are to be worshiped as God.

> [I]n the modern Roman Rite the public worship of the
> Eucharist is envisaged as a normal part of the liturgical life
> of diocesan, parish and religious communities.[502]

With a delicate and jealous attention the Church has

regulated Eucharistic worship to its minutest details. . . . [E]verything is important, significant, and divine when there is a question of the Real Presence of Jesus Christ.[503]

Wherefore, there is no room left to doubt that all the faithful of Christ may, according to the custom ever received in the Catholic Church, **render in veneration the worship of *latria*, which is due to the true God, to this most holy Sacrament**. For not therefore is it the less to be adored on this account, that it was instituted by Christ the Lord in order to be present therein, of Whom the Eternal Father, when introducing Him into the world, says: 'and let all the angels of God adore Him;'Whom the Magi falling down, adored; Who, in fine, as the Scripture testifies, was adored by the Apostles in Galilee. *THE COUNCIL OF TRENT, DECREE CONCERNING THE MOST HOLY SACRAMENT OF THE EUCHARIST, On the Cult and Veneration to be Shown to This Most Holy Sacrament,* October 11, 1554.

Worship of the Eucharist. In the liturgy of the Mass we express our faith in the **real presence of Christ under the species of bread and wine** by, among other ways, **genuflecting or bowing deeply as a sign of adoration** of the Lord. The Catholic Church has always offered and still offers to the sacrament of the Eucharist the cult of **adoration**, not only during Mass, but also outside of it, reserving the consecrated hosts with the utmost care, exposing them to the **solemn veneration** of the faithful, and carrying them in procession." *CATECHISM OF THE CATHOLIC CHURCH,* § 1378, 1994 (italics in original, bold type added).

The Catholic Church teaches that wine and bread have been turned into the body and blood of Christ, and that when one is consuming the bread and wine it is only the form of bread and wine, it is actually the body, blood, soul, and divinity of Christ.

The Catholic Church teaches that the wine is actually Christ's blood but only appears to be wine, and the bread is actually Christ's flesh but only appears to be bread. The Catholic doctrine of transubstantiation is a sin.

In the following passages God has made it clear that people are to abstain from drinking *any manner* of blood. Presumably, any manner of blood means any manner of blood, including transubstantiated blood.

> Moreover ye shall **eat no manner of blood, *whether it be of fowl or of beast, in any of your dwellings*.** Whatsoever soul *it be* that eateth any manner of blood, even that soul shall be cut off from his people. (Leviticus 7:26-27 AV)

> And whatsoever man *there be* of the house of Israel, or of the strangers that sojourn among you, that eateth **any manner of blood; I will even set my face against that soul that eateth blood**, and will cut him off from among his people. (Leviticus 17:10 AV)

> **[A]bstain from meats offered to idols, and from blood**, and from things strangled, and from fornication: from which if ye keep yourselves, ye shall do well. Fare ye well. (Acts 15:29 AV)

The Catholic church quotes the following passage, purporting it to support its claim that during the Catholic Mass bread is turned into God.

> And he took bread, and gave thanks, and brake *it*, and gave unto them, saying, This is my body which is given for you: **this do in remembrance of me.** (Luke 22:19 AV)

That passage does not support the proposition that bread is thereafter to be turned into God. Before Christ came to earth, God required ceremonial sacrifices from the Jews. Those sacrifices were done in order to bring to mind the coming messiah. The Jews looked forward to Christ, the sacrificial lamb of God. The Old Testament sacrifices themselves did not atone for the sins. Jesus was the atonement. Salvation from sins came then, as now, by the grace of God through faith in God and his Messiah, Jesus. The memorial instituted by Christ during the last supper was for us to look back to the sacrifice of Christ, just as the Jews used to look forward toward Christ's coming. We are to do it in remembrance of him and his sacrifice for us. It was never intended to be a ceremony of witchcraft, where the bread and wine are turned into a god, and then that god was to be eaten and drunk.

38 The Gift of Salvation Manifesto

The controversy over the ECT became so heated that on January 19, 1995, four of the ersatz Protestant signers of the document (Bill Bright, Chuck Colson, Kent Hill, and J. I. Packer) found it necessary to issue a joint statement allegedly affirming that their endorsement of the ECT did "not imply acceptance of Roman Catholic doctrinal distinctive or endorsement of the Roman Catholic church system."[504]

After failing to convince anyone on the merits of the ECT, Bill Bright tried to conceal his involvement in the document. John Robbins revealed that: "In 1996, Bill Bright had his lawyers write letters to The Trinity Foundation, threatening litigation for mentioning on the cover of *Justification by Faith Alone* that Bright was a signer of 'Evangelicals and Catholics Together.'"[505] It is truly amazing that Bill Bright went from trying to justify the ECT to threatening to sue anyone who revealed his involvement in it. A reprobate mind is a terrible thing to behold.

What is most interesting is that none of the Catholic signers of the document were met with similar controversy, and none of them had to explain how their endorsement of the ECT undermined Roman Catholic doctrine or was an acceptance of Protestant Christian beliefs. Why is that? Because there was no compromise of Catholic doctrine in the ECT. The ECT is a clever seduction by the Roman Catholic church to undermine the missionary and gospel work of the true Christian church. True Christians understand that the Catholic church is not Christian and the light of Christianity can have no fellowship with the heathen darkness of Rome. **"Be ye not unequally yoked together with unbelievers: for what fellowship hath righteousness with unrighteousness? and what communion hath light with darkness?"** (2 Corinthians 6:14 AV)

The charlatan religious luminaries were not content with the ECT of May 1994. They came out in 1997 with yet another abomination, titled *The Gift of Salvation*.[506] John Robbins explains the Arminian character of *The Gift of Salvation*:

> The 1997 manifesto from the Cassidy-Colson-Neuhaus Group begins by quoting John 3:16-17, a passage, it is safe to say, that no signatory understands, for they quote it to support their Arminian-Universalist view that Christ died for every man. They do not understand even the rudiments of the Gospel: Christ died for his people, his friends, his sheep, his church, his elect; and that Christ's death actually and completely achieved their salvation. Christ's death did not merely make salvation possible, as the ersatz-evangelicals teach; Christ's death actually saved His people. That is . . . the Gospel.[507]

Below is a list of the guilty who signed that affront to God; they had the audacity to give it the title: *The Gift of Salvation*:

[ERSATZ] EVANGELICAL PROTESTANT

Dr. Gerald L. Bray, Beeson Divinity School
Dr. Bill Bright, Campus Crusade for Christ
Dr. Harold O. J. Brown, Trinity Evangelical Divinity School
Mr. Charles Colson, Prison Fellowship
Bishop William C. Frey, Episcopal Church
Dr. Timothy George, Beeson Divinity School
Dr. Os Guinness, Trinity Forum

Dr. Kent R. Hill, Eastern Nazarene College
Rev. Max Lucado, Oak Hills Church of Christ, San Antonio, TX
Dr. T. M. Moore, Chesapeake Theological Seminary
Dr. Richard Mouw, Fuller Theological Seminary
Dr. Mark A. Noll, Wheaton College
Mr. Brian F. O'Connell, Interdev
Dr. Thomas Oden, Drew University
Dr. James J. I. Packer, Regent College, British Columbia
Dr. Timothy R. Phillips, Wheaton College
Dr. John Rodgers, Trinity Episcopal School for Ministry
Dr. Robert A. Seiple, World Vision U.S.
Dr. John Woodbridge, Trinity Evangelical Divinity School

ROMAN CATHOLICS

Father James J. Buckley, Loyola College in Maryland
Father J. A. Di Noia, O.P., Dominican House of Studies
Father Avery Dulles, S.J., Fordham University
Mr. Keith Fournier, Catholic Alliance
Father Thomas Guarino, Seton Hall University
Dr. Peter Kreeft, Boston College
Father Matthew L. Lamb, Boston College
Father Eugene LaVerdiere, S.S.S., Emmanuel
Father Francis Martin, John Paul II Institute for Studies on Marriage and Family
Mr. Ralph Martin, Renewal Ministries
Father Richard John Neuhaus, Religion and Public Life
Mr. Michael Novak, American Enterprise Institute
Father Edward Oakes, S.J., Regis University
Father Thomas P. Rausch, S.J., Loyola Marymount University
Mr. George Weigel, Ethics and Public Policy Center
Dr. Robert Louis Wilken, University of Virginia

John Robbins continues in his analysis of *The Gift of Salvation* by exposing it as based upon a bankrupt theology that contradicts both the love and sovereignty of God:

In paragraph 4, the Group unequivocally asserts its

universalist position on salvation, and they do it by cleverly misquoting Scripture: "God the Creator is also God the Redeemer, offering salvation to the world. 'God desires all to be saved and come to a knowledge of the truth.' (1 Timothy 2:4)." If one reads the context of the quotation, it is clear that Paul wrote that God desires the salvation of all His people, the sheep of His pasture, not of the goats, who are condemned to everlasting punishment. If God desires the salvation of all men without exception, as the Cassidy-Colson-Neuhaus Group asserts, then His desires are clearly frustrated, and He is not God. In fact, Roman/Arminian theology requires us to say that Hell is populated with people whom God loves. The Arminian-Universalist view contradicts both the love and the sovereignty of God, and removes all grounds of confidence in God.[508]

According to the Catholics joined by their crypto-Catholic brethren who signed *The Gift of Salvation,* Jesus is a superfluous curiosity, who is not really necessary for salvation. John Robbins explains:

[T]he doctrine of creative justification, by regarding Christ as, at best, superfluous, focuses on the sinner, not on Jesus Christ. The sinner - the man - is central; the work of Christ is unnecessary. Oh, the life and death of Christ may be useful as a moral example, or as a device to evoke our pity, but because justification is essentially creative, not judicial, Christ's work does not satisfy the justice of the Father, nor legally benefit his church. This is religious subjectivism with a vengeance.[509]

How can these Catholics and crypto-Catholics get away with such heresy? They use the age old deception of the devil; they redefine the words used in the bible. For example the word justification in *The Gift of Salvation* takes on a man centered meaning. To the drafters of *The Gift of Salvation* justification means that man is actually made righteous rather than the biblical definition of the imputed righteousness of Christ. They have replaced a spiritual truth with a carnal lie. This Catholic self righteousness contradicts the biblical truth that "in me (that is, in my flesh,) dwelleth no good thing." (Romans 7:18 AV). Once again, John Robbins explains:

> [T]he word justification itself has taken on a new meaning in another sense: In the mouths of the Cassidy Group, just as in the mouths of Newman, Kung, and Barth, justification means making righteous. It is the Roman doctrine of justification. That is why the Roman Cardinals and Bishops had no problem with this statement about justification. The ersatz-evangelicals were too witless, too stupid, to understand the statement they signed. Is that too cruel? Well, it would be much crueler to say that they understood what they signed and signed it anyway. I am trying to be as charitable as possible.[510]

Richard Bennett was a Catholic Priest for 22 years, but he was saved by the grace of God. He read carefully *The Gift of Salvation* and reveals below how that document subtly supports and maintains the blasphemous Catholic doctrine of justification.

> It is to be held firmly in mind that Evangelicals throughout the centuries have maintained that justification by faith alone is the way in which sinful human beings are made right and just before the all Holy God. [1] Justification itself is a judicial declarative act on the part of God alone by which He declares that only in Christ is a man perfectly just before Himself, who is the morally perfect Being and Holy Judge over all human beings. His judicial declarative act is not made on the basis of anything within a man, but rather it is made solely and wholly upon the righteous life and sacrificial death of Jesus Christ who lived a perfect life and paid the just penalty for sins upon the cross. Historically, Evangelicals have been in agreement with the Apostle Paul, "to him that worketh not, but believeth on him that justifieth the ungodly, his faith is counted for righteousness" (Romans 4:5).

The Anti-Gospel

The Bible teaches the manifestation of God's righteousness, not man's. "But now the righteousness of God without the law is manifested, being witnessed by the law and the prophets" (Romans 3:21). The Gospel good news is the declaration of God that His righteousness is upon believers, i.e., credited to them. "Even the righteousness of God which is by faith of Jesus Christ unto all and upon all them that believe" (Romans 3:22). Only the Lord Christ Jesus is declared to be, and actually is the Righteousness of God. The believer has His righteousness only credited to him. This is the historical position of Evangelicals.

Historically, and conversely, the Roman Catholic Church teaches as dogma that justification is conferred through her sacraments and that it consists of inner righteousness whereby a man, it is stated, becomes just within himself. The Church of Rome condemns the Biblical doctrine of justification by faith alone. This was done at the Council of Trent. Present day dogma of the RCC not only upholds the teaching of the Council of Trent but also declares that such Councils are infallible. The Council of Trent proclaims the following curses:

> If anyone shall say that justifying faith is nothing else than confidence in the divine mercy which remits sins for Christ's sake, or that it is this confidence alone by which we are justified: let him be anathema [cursed].

> If anyone shall say that by the said sacraments of the New Law, grace is not conferred from the work which has been worked [ex opere operato] but that faith alone in the divine promise suffices to obtain grace: let him be anathema.

Rome's reason for such a curse on those who hold to "justification by faith alone" is logical because of what she refuses to concede. For her, justification is not an immediate declaration of God and received by faith alone; rather, she teaches that grace is conferred through the sacraments. Thus she is able to make a place for herself as a necessary means through which inner righteousness is given. She teaches, "Justification has been merited for us by the Passion of Christ. It is granted us through Baptism."[511]

That same teaching stated clearly 450 years ago, that physical mediation through the sacraments is necessary for salvation, is stated emphatically by Rome in the present time: "The Church affirms that for believers the sacraments of the New Covenant are necessary for salvation. . . ." "Justification is conferred in Baptism, the sacrament of faith. It conforms us to the righteousness of God, who makes us inwardly just by the power of his mercy." This is what the Roman Catholics who signed the document state that they believe. It is what the Evangelicals who signed the document should know the Catholics mean when the Catholics affirm in writing that they are "Catholics who are conscientiously faithful to the teaching of the Catholic Church."[512]

In the face of such clarity, both on the part of Scripture and on the part of the RCC, this new ecumenical document claims that now both sides agree on what had been the primary dividing point between Protestants and Roman Catholics for several hundred years. The document states:

"We agree that justification is not earned by any good works or merits of our own; it is entirely God's gift, conferred through the Father's sheer graciousness, out of the love that he bears us in his Son, who suffered on our behalf and rose from the dead for our justification. Jesus was "put to death for our trespasses and raised for our justification" (Romans 4:25). In justification, God, on the basis of Christ's righteousness alone, declares us to be no longer his rebellious enemies but his forgiven friends, and by virtue of his declaration it is so."[513]

This statement teaches traditional Roman Catholic doctrine, for by careful reading one comes to see that what the two pivotal sentences state grammatically is this:

...it [justification] is entirely God's gift, conferred [rather than imputed]...and by virtue of his [Holy God's] declaration it [justification conferred] is so.

To employ the word "conferred" instead of the Biblical word "imputed" is tantamount to putting aside Scriptural authority on the issue of justification. This is precisely because the same Romans Chapter Four that is quoted clearly teaches the concept of imputation or crediting eleven times; and what the RCC means by conferred justification is just as clearly laid out in her dogma (see above). Since medieval times, the RCC has clearly distinguished between the concept of imputation and the concept of God's grace conferred as a quality of the soul. The Roman Catholic signatories, "Catholics who are conscientiously faithful to the teachings of the Catholic Church," know this dogma.[514]

In the Bible, while there is no mention whatsoever of "conferring" justification, the theme of the imputation of the righteousness of God to the believer is constant. Yet through centuries and in the face of Scriptural clarity, the teaching of Rome tenaciously holds to justification conferred rather than imputed, the present document under consideration being a case in point. Part of the perversion by which the Biblical doctrine of justification by faith alone is accomplished in this document is by the use of the RCC terminology, "conferred". It may be Idris Cardinal Cassidy's "very active support throughout the process [of drawing up the document]" [10] which accomplished the accommodation to Catholic terminology. Through that accommodation, the Biblical teaching of the righteousness of God imputed to the believer is subsumed under Rome's traditional concept of inner or infused righteousness. Evangelicals are accustomed to the Biblical word, imputed.

For them to agree to the Roman Catholic word, conferred, signifying the bringing of God's grace into the soul as a quality, is a major compromise.[515]

* * *

This teaching of justification being "conferred" is the same as that of the Pharisees or that of Rome, "For they being ignorant of God's righteousness, and going about to establish their own righteousness, have not submitted themselves unto the righteousness of God" (Romans 10:3). The statements of this document perpetrate the age-old heresy that justifying righteousness is within man, because wittingly or unwittingly, the document teaches the lie of Satan that you can be as God.[516]

John Robbins explains the blasphemous implications of *The Gift of Salvation:*

If Newman's, Kung's, Barth's, Cassidy's, Colson's, and Neuhaus' doctrine of justification were correct, it would not only make sinners actually righteous, it would make Christ actually sinful, for in the same divine act in which the sinner receives the righteousness of Christ, Christ receives the sins of the sinner. The notion that justification is a moral, internal change cuts both ways: The sinner becomes morally righteous, and Christ becomes morally sinful. If justification is a moral transaction, as the Roman State-Church teaches, then Jesus Christ is a sinful man. However, if justification is a legal exchange of the righteousness of Christ for the sin of his people, then there is no theological problem - and no blasphemy. Imputation makes the sinner legally righteous, but not actually righteous; imputation makes Christ legally sinful, and so liable to punishment on behalf of those he represents, but it does not make Christ actually sinful. But if justification is an internal moral change as the Roman State-Church teaches, and if it involves Christ's work at all, then not only does the sinner become actually righteous, but

Christ becomes actually sinful. That is the price one pays for errors in the doctrine of justification: blasphemy.[517]

John Robbins explains that *The Gift of Salvation* is essentially Roman Catholic doctrine very cleverly packaged to deceive unwary Christians.

The doctrine of justification in "The Gift of Salvation," like the doctrine of justification in "Evangelicals and Catholics Together," is the Roman doctrine. The Roman State-Church has yielded nothing in approving this document; that is why the papal representative - Cardinal Cassidy--at the Group's meetings put his stamp of approval on it. But the Roman State-Church has gained a great deal; it has confused and persuaded many non-Catholics; and it has successfully used Charles Colson as a dupe in its plans to achieve a new Roman Empire.[518]

Robbins is being too kind to Colson to call him a "dupe." Such a description suggests that he is being deceived. The evidence, however, indicates that Colson has not been deceived; he is a willing accomplice.

Robbins reveals how *The Gift of Salvation* very stealthfully avoids certain words in order to ensure that Catholic doctrine makes it through unscathed.

In paragraph 8, on faith, "The Gift of Salvation" asserts that "the gift of justification is received through faith." Not through "faith alone," please note. That little word alone is what makes the difference between Christianity and a false gospel at this point. Its absence is one more indication that the doctrine of justification espoused by the Cassidy-Colson-Neuhaus Group is not Christian. The Roman State-Church teaches that justification is also received through baptism, penance, and other rites and sacraments of the Roman State-Church.[519]

Robbins concludes by putting *The Gift of Salvation* in historical context:

Rome realizes what the central theological issue is, and Rome is moving deliberately and effectively to heal the wound inflicted on her in the sixteenth century by the preaching of the Gospel. Rome apparently is finding plenty of eager dupes-useful idiots, Lenin called them-among the ersatz-evangelicals to accomplish its goal.

The twentieth century has been an ecumenical century. Rome has moved as never before to heal its wound, and to incorporate all professors and churches within itself. These conversations, dialogues, and working relationships with non-Roman ecclesiastical organizations are far too numerous to list here; they have ranged from conversations with the Anglicans in Belgium in the 1920s, led by Cardinal Mercier, to continuous ecumenical efforts with the Lutherans, Anglicans, National Council and World Council of Churches, the charismatics and Pentecostals, the Eastern Orthodox Church, and the ersatz-evangelicals. Billy Graham, the most famous Arminian evangelist of the twentieth century, has sought and received the participation of Romanists in his "crusades" since the late 1950s. The Vatican intends to reinstate its monopoly, and many are worshiping the beast.

The existence of groups like the Colson-Neuhaus Group is not new; what it demonstrates, however, is how thoroughly theologically corrupt the ersatz-evangelicals are. Christians have long known that the National Council of Churches, the World Council of Churches, the mainline denominations, and the charismatic movement are anti-Christian; now the Cassidy-Colson-Neuhaus Group is making it clear that ersatz-evangelicalism is fundamentally at one with Romanism. The Synod of Dordt condemned the Arminian theology of the ersatz-evangelicals as a doctrine from the pit of Hell. Except for a scattered remnant, the American heirs of the Reformation have repudiated the faith of their fathers, they have abandoned the Gospel, and they are falling over each other in their eagerness to fawn before the beast. In the beast they see power and influence, success, respectability, fame, and riches - and they want to enjoy the things the beast can provide.[520]

What is most disturbing about *The Gift of Salvation* is that concealed behind the ostensible agreement is a devilish deception. When Christians read the agreement they give the biblical words their unique biblical meaning. However, the signers are accomplices in a deception. In witchcraft, words have one meaning for the outside world and another different meaning for those initiated in the black arts. The true meaning is concealed behind the artifice of ambiguous phrases designed to give the appearance of one meaning, with the actual meaning being concealed from the uninitiated.

John Robbins and Richard Bennett have revealed the subtlety of the deception in a couple of areas. However, the deception goes even deeper. First, we must read what is said at the end of the document:

We must not allow our witness as Christians to be compromised by halfhearted discipleship or needlessly divisive disputes. While we rejoice in the unity we have discovered and are confident of the fundamental truths about the gift of salvation we have affirmed, we recognize that there are necessarily interrelated questions that require further and urgent exploration. Among such questions are these: the meaning of baptismal regeneration, the Eucharist, and sacramental grace; the historic uses of the language of justification as it relates to imputed and transformative righteousness; the normative status of justification in relation to all Christian doctrine; the assertion that while justification is by faith alone, the faith that receives salvation is never alone; diverse understandings of merit, reward, purgatory, and indulgences; Marian devotion and the assistance of the saints in the life of salvation; and the possibility of salvation for those who have not been evangelized.[521]

The Gift of Salvation purports to be a "unity" on "fundamental truths" regarding "salvation." The manifesto states that there are a number of "interrelated questions that require further and urgent exploration." It would seem then that the listed "interrelated questions" are something other than "fundamental truths," because *The Gift of Salvation* is represented as a manifesto that presents to the world an affirmation of the unity between Catholics and Protestants on "the fundamental truths about the gift of salvation."

Let us explore seriatim some of these "interrelated questions" that seem to be viewed by the signers of *The Gift of Salvation* as being non-fundamental and of secondary importance. By the time we have finished dear reader you will be convinced beyond any doubt that these matters are actually fundamental differences and that Roman Catholicism and Christianity are completely different religions. Roman Catholicism is not just un-Christian, it is anti-Christian. The doctrinal issues that separate Christianity and Catholicism reveal the signers of *The Gift of Salvation* as minions of the devil in league with the antichrist.

39 Modern Day Pharisees

W hen reading either the ECT or *The Gift of Salvation*, understand that the Catholic Church has a completely different definition for "the word of God" than do Christians. The Roman Catholic Church calls the combination of their traditions and God's word "the word of god." Satan wants people to consider him God, so he has grafted his words, which he calls tradition, onto the word of God. With this sleight of hand he has deceived people into following his devilish doctrines.

> **Sacred Tradition and Sacred Scripture make up a single sacred deposit of the Word of God.** *CATECHISM OF THE CATHOLIC CHURCH*, § 97, 1994.

> [T]he church, to whom the transmission and interpretation of Revelation is entrusted, **does not derive her certainty about all revealed truths from the holy Scriptures alone. Both Scripture and Tradition must be accepted and honored with equal sentiments of devotion and reverence.** *Id.* at § 82 (emphasis added).

The Catholic Church considers her traditions as "the word of God." What is at root of the traditions of the Roman Catholic Church? It is the Jewish Talmud and Cabala (a/k/a Kabbalah). The

Babylonian/Jewish origins of the Catholic doctrine is authoritatively exposed in *Solving the Mystery of BABYLON THE GREAT.*[522]

Cabala is a Hebrew word, which literally translated means "tradition." Nesta Webster in her classic book *Secret Societies and Subversive Movements* explained how the Jewish theology of the Cabala was introduced into the Roman Catholic Church by Pope Sixtus IV (1471-1484).

> It was likewise from a Florentine Jew, Alemanus or Datylus that Pico della Mirandola, the fifteenth-century mystic, received instructions in the Cabala and imagined that he had discovered in it the doctrines of Christianity. This delighted Pope Sixtus IV, who thereupon ordered Cabalistic writings to be translated into Latin for the use of divinity students.[523]

Jesus criticized the Pharisees for their religious traditions. Those traditions were oral traditions at that time. Later they were memorialized in the many volumes of the Talmud and the Cabala. Jesus called the pharisees hypocrites, who masqueraded as religious men, but who were in reality irreligious frauds.

> Then came to Jesus scribes and Pharisees, which were of Jerusalem, saying, Why do thy disciples transgress the tradition of the elders? for they wash not their hands when they eat bread. But he answered and said unto them, **Why do ye also transgress the commandment of God by your tradition?** For God commanded, saying, Honour thy father and mother: and, He that curseth father or mother, let him die the death. But ye say, Whosoever shall say to *his* father or *his* mother, *It is* a gift, by whatsoever thou mightest be profited by me; And honour not his father or his mother, *he shall be free.* **Thus have ye made the commandment of God of none effect by your tradition.** *Ye* **hypocrites**, well did Esaias prophesy of you, saying, This people draweth nigh unto me with their mouth, and honoureth me with *their* lips; but their heart is far from me. But **in vain they do worship me, teaching** *for* **doctrines the commandments**

of men. (Matthew 15:1-9 AV)

Magic and occult mysticism runs throughout the Cabala. Judith Weill, a professor of Jewish mysticism stated that magic is deeply rooted in Jewish tradition, but the Jews are reticent to acknowledge it and don't even refer to it as magic.[524]

Gershom Scholem, Professor of Kabbalah at Hebrew University in Jerusalem, admitted that the Cabala contains a great deal of black magic and sorcery, which he explained involves invoking the powers of devils to disrupt the natural order of things.[525]

Professor Scholem also stated that there are devils who are in submission to the Talmud; in the Cabala these devils are called *shedim Yehuda'im*.[526] That is why Jesus said to the Jews: **"Ye are of *your* father the devil, and the lusts of your father ye will do."** John 8:44. The bible states clearly that the magic arts are an abomination to the Lord.

There shall not be found among you *any* one that maketh his son or his daughter to pass through the fire, *or* that useth divination, *or* an observer of times, or an enchanter, or a witch, Or a charmer, or a consulter with familiar spirits, or a wizard, or a necromancer. For all that do these things *are* an abomination unto the LORD: and because of these abominations the LORD thy God doth drive them out from before thee. (Deuteronomy 18:10-12 AV)

The Cabala, like the Talmud, graphically blasphemes Jesus. For example, in Zohar III, 282a, the Cabala refers to Jesus as a dog who resides among filth and vermin.[527]

What did Jesus have to say about the religion of the Pharisees? Jesus said they masqueraded as religious men who have the oracles of God, but they were really irreligious, teaching instead the doctrines of men.

Then came to Jesus scribes and Pharisees, which were of

Jerusalem, saying, Why do thy disciples transgress the tradition of the elders? for they wash not their hands when they eat bread. But he answered and said unto them, **Why do ye also transgress the commandment of God by your tradition?** For God commanded, saying, Honour thy father and mother: and, He that curseth father or mother, let him die the death. But ye say, Whosoever shall say to *his* father or *his* mother, *It is* a gift, by whatsoever thou mightest be profited by me; And honour not his father or his mother, *he shall be free.* **Thus have ye made the commandment of God of none effect by your tradition.** *Ye* **hypocrites**, well did Esaias prophesy of you, saying, This people draweth nigh unto me with their mouth, and honoureth me with *their* lips; but their heart is far from me. But **in vain they do worship me, teaching** *for* **doctrines the commandments of men.** (Matthew 15:1-9 AV)

To what traditions was Jesus referring when he upbraided the Pharisees for using them to transgress and replace the laws of God? Can we find out about those traditions today? Yes; the Talmud is a codification of the traditions of the scribes and Pharisees to which Jesus spoke. Michael Rodkinson (M. Levi Frumkin), who wrote the first English translation of the Babylonian Talmud, states the following in his book *The History of the Talmud*:

Is the literature that Jesus was familiar with in his early years yet in existence in the world? Is it possible for us to get at it? To such inquiries the learned class of Jewish rabbis answer by holding up the Talmud . **The Talmud then, is the written form of that which, in the time of Jesus, was called the Traditions of the Elders**, and to which he makes frequent allusions.[528] (emphasis added)

During the time of Christ the Scribes and Pharisees were constantly heckling and challenging Jesus, and it was they who plotted his crucifixion. Read what Jesus had to say to those Jews.

They answered and said unto him, Abraham is our father.

Jesus saith unto them, If ye were Abraham's children, ye
would do the works of Abraham. But now ye seek to kill
me, a man that hath told you the truth, which I have heard of
God: this did not Abraham. Ye do the deeds of your father.
Then said they to him, We be not born of fornication; we
have one Father, *even* God. Jesus said unto them, If God
were your Father, ye would love me: for I proceeded forth
and came from God; neither came I of myself, but he sent
me. Why do ye not understand my speech? *even* because ye
cannot hear my word. **Ye are of *your* father the devil, and
the lusts of your father ye will do.** He was a murderer
from the beginning, and abode not in the truth, because there
is no truth in him. When he speaketh a lie, he speaketh of
his own: for he is a liar, and the father of it. And because I
tell *you* the truth, ye believe me not. Which of you
convinceth me of sin? And if I say the truth, why do ye not
believe me? He that is of God heareth God's words: **ye
therefore hear *them* not, because ye are not of God.** (John
8:39-47 AV)

In Matthew 23 Jesus has even stronger language to describe the
scribes and Pharisees. Jesus called them serpents, vipers, blind
guides, whited sepulchers, and hypocrites who will be damned to hell.

Woe unto you, scribes and Pharisees, hypocrites! for ye pay
tithe of mint and anise and cummin, and have omitted the
weightier *matters* of the law, judgment, mercy, and faith:
these ought ye to have done, and not to leave the other
undone. *Ye* blind guides, which strain at a gnat, and
swallow a camel. Woe unto you, scribes and Pharisees,
hypocrites! for ye make clean the outside of the cup and of
the platter, but within they are full of extortion and excess.
Thou blind Pharisee, cleanse first that *which is* within the
cup and platter, that the outside of them may be clean also.
Woe unto you, scribes and Pharisees, hypocrites! for ye are
like unto whited sepulchres, which indeed appear beautiful
outward, but are within full of dead *men's* bones, and of all
uncleanness. Even so ye also outwardly appear righteous

unto men, but within ye are full of hypocrisy and iniquity.
Woe unto you, scribes and Pharisees, hypocrites! because ye
build the tombs of the prophets, and garnish the sepulchres
of the righteous, And say, If we had been in the days of our
fathers, we would not have been partakers with them in the
blood of the prophets. Wherefore ye be witnesses unto
yourselves, that ye are the children of them which killed the
prophets. Fill ye up then the measure of your fathers. *Ye
serpents, ye* generation of vipers, how can ye escape the
damnation of hell? (Matthew 23:23-33 AV)

Why would Jesus use such strong language against the Pharisees
and scribes? To answer that we should examine some of the
Talmudic traditions that have developed over the years. For starters,
the Talmudic Jews have a hatred for Gentiles. To them Gentiles are
vile animals, who are unclean and have no legal rights.[529]

Citing Folio 114b of the Tractate *Baba Mezi'a* from the
Babylonian Talmud, *The Jewish Encyclopedia,* states that the Talmud
only considers Jews as men; Gentiles are categorized in the Talmud as
barbarians.[530] Elizabeth Dilling, in her book *The Jewish Religion: Its
Influence Today,* explains the racial view adopted by Jews as codified
in their Talmud:

The basic Talmudic doctrine includes more than a "super-
race" complex. It is an "only" race concept. The non-Jew
thus ranks as an animal, has no property rights and no legal
rights under any code whatever. If lies, bribes or kicks are
necessary to get non-Jews under control - that is legitimate.
There is only one "sin," and that is anything which will
frighten non-Jews and thus make it harder for the Jewish
"humans" to get them under control. "Milk the Gentile," is
the Talmudic rule, but don't get caught in such a way as to
jeopardize Jewish interests. Summarized, Talmudism is the
quintessence of distilled hatred and discrimination - without
cause, against non-Jews.[531]

The following passages from the Talmud attest to the Jewish

hatred of Gentiles:

Baba Mezia 114b: Only Jews are men, gentiles ("heathen") are not men.

Baba Bathra 54b: Property of Gentiles is like the desert; whoever gets there first gets it.

Sanhedrin 57a: If a Gentile robs a Jew, he must pay him back. But if a Jew robs a Gentile, the Jew may keep the loot. Likewise, if a Gentile kills a Jew, the Gentile is to be killed. But if a Jew kills a Gentile, there is no death penalty.

Sanhedrin 52b: Adultery forbidden with the neighbor's wife, but is not forbidden with the wife of a heathen (gentile). The implication is that a heathen is not a neighbor.

The Talmud has a permissive attitude toward Pedophilia and sodomy. For example:

Sanhedrin 55b: It is permitted to have sexual intercourse with a girl three years and one day old. See also Yebamoth 57b, 60b; Abodah Zarah 37a.

Sanhedrin 54b: If a man has sex with a boy less than nine years old, he is not guilty of pederasty.

Kethoboth 11b: When a grown-up man has intercourse with a little girl it is nothing, for when the girl is less than three years old it is as if one puts the finger into the eye, tears come to the eye again and again, so does virginity come back to the little girl under three years.

Talmudic Judaism has the most intense hatred for Jesus.[532] While some Jews will deny that the Talmud teaches such things, Benjamin Freedman, a former Talmudic Jew, stated that: "there have never been recorded more vicious and vile libelous blasphemies of Jesus, of Christians and the Christian faith than you will find between the covers of the 63 books of the Talmud which forms the basis of Jewish religious law, as well as being the textbook used in the training of rabbis."[533] For example:

Sanhedrin 106a & b: Mary was a whore; Jesus was an evil man.

Shabbath 104b: Jesus was a magician and a fool. Mary was an adulteress.

Sanhedrin 43a: Jesus was guilty of sorcery and apostasy; he deserved execution. The disciples of Jesus deserve to be killed.

Gittin 57b: Jesus was sent to hell, where he is punished by boiling excrement for mocking the Rabbis.

The Talmud has similar sentiments for Christians. For Example:

Abodah Zarah 17a: Jews should stay away from Christians. Christians are allied with Hell, and Christianity is worse than incest.

Abodah Zarah 17a: Visiting the house of a Christian is the same as visiting the house of a prostitute.

Abodah Zarah 27b: It is forbidden to be healed by a Christian.

Sanhedrin 90a, 100b: Those who read the gospels are doomed to Hell.

Shabbath 116a: The New Testament is blank paper and are to be burned.

The admonition in the Talmud to burn New Testaments is not hyperbole. Orthodox Jews view the statement in Shabbath 116a as a command to burn New Testaments. On May 21, 2008, USA Today reported: "Orthodox Jews set fire to hundreds of copies of the New Testament in the latest act of violence against Christian missionaries in the Holy Land."[534]

When Or Yehuda Deputy Mayor Uzi Aharon heard that hundreds of New Testaments were distributed by Christian missionaries, he took to the roads in a loudspeaker car and drove through the city urging people to turn over the New Testaments to Jewish religious students, who were going door to door to collect them. The New Testaments were then dumped into a pile and set afire in a lot near a synagogue. Aharon said it was a commandment to burn books that urge Jews to convert to Christianity.[535]

Why do the Jews hate Christians so much? It is because the children of the flesh will always hate the children of the spirit. **"But as then he that was born after the flesh persecuted him *that was born* after the Spirit, even so *it is* now."** (Galatians 4:29 AV)

The influence of the Jews through the Jesuits in the Roman Catholic Church has been manifested from the beginning in Catholic doctrine. The Council of Trent was an attack on Christianity with anathema after anathema against Christian doctrine that was orchestrated by the Jesuits. What most do not know is that the Jesuit order is base upon Jewish ideology. The Jesuit priesthood is a crypto-Jewish order.

The founder of the Jesuits, Ignatius Loyola, was a crypto-Jew. A crypto-Jew is a Jew who converts to another religion and outwardly embraces the new religion, while secretly maintaining Jewish practices. James Lainez, the second Jesuit General, was of Jewish descent. The third Jesuit General, Eberhard Mercurian was a Jew. Some of the most influential Jesuits in history were Jews. Many of the Jesuit doctrines are similar to those found in the Babylonian Talmud.

John Torell explains the Jewish origins of the Jesuit order:

The Illuminati order was not invented by Adam Weishaupt, but rather renewed and reformed. The first known Illuminati order (Alumbrado) was founded in 1492 by Spanish Jews, called "Marranos," who were also known as "crypto-Jews." With violent persecution in Spain and Portugal beginning in

1391, hundreds of thousands of Jews had been forced to convert to the faith of the Roman Catholic Church. Publicly they were now Roman Catholics, but secretly they practiced Judaism, including following the Talmud and the Cabala. The Marranos were able to teach their children secretly about Judaism, but in particular the Talmud and the Cabala, and this huge group of Jews has survived to this very day. After 1540 many Marranos opted to flee to England, Holland, France, the Ottoman empire (Turkey), Brazil and other places in South and Central America. The Marranos kept strong family ties and they became very wealthy and influential in the nations where they lived. But as is the custom with all Jewish people, it did not matter in what nation they lived, their loyalty was to themselves and Judaism. [536]

* * *

In 1491 San Ignacio De Loyola was born in the Basque province of Guipuzcoa, Spain. His parents were Marranos and at the time of his birth the family was very wealthy. **As a young man he became a member of the Jewish Illuminati order in Spain. As a cover for his crypto Jewish activities, he became very active as a Roman Catholic.** On May 20, 1521 Ignatius (as he was now called) was wounded in a battle, and became a semi-cripple. Unable to succeed in the military and political arena, he started a quest for holiness and eventually ended up in Paris where he studied for the priesthood. In 1539 he had moved to Rome where he founded the "JESUIT ORDER," which was to become the most vile, bloody and persecuting order in the Roman Catholic Church. In 1540, the current Pope Paul III approved the order. At Loyola's death in 1556 there were more than 1000 members in the Jesuit order, located in a number of nations. [537]

Setting up the Jesuit order, Ignatius Loyola devised an elaborate spy system, so that no one in the order was safe. If there was any opposition, death would come swiftly. The Jesuit order not only became a destructive arm of the Roman Catholic Church; it also developed into a secret intelligence service. **While the Popes relied more and more on the Jesuits, they were unaware that the hard core leadership were Jewish, and that these Jews held membership in the Illuminati order which despised and hated the Roman Catholic Church.**[538]

The control of the Jews over the Vatican, primarily through the influence of the Jesuits, is so complete that Cardinal Joseph Ratzinger (now Pope Benedict XVI), who was at the time the prefect of the Congregation for the Doctrine of the Faith, issued an official doctrine of Catholic faith that accepts the Jewish view that the messiah is yet to come.

There is apparently much double talk in the document, as it accepts the Jewish view of a coming messiah without overtly rejecting Jesus. Some have interpreted the document as denying the redemptive role of Jesus. The Catholic Church long ago denied the redemptive role of Jesus. The Vatican document is contained in a small book titled "The Jewish People and the Holy Scriptures in the Christian Bible." It is no surprise that this Jewish/Catholic doctrine was drafted by a Jesuit named Albert Vanhoye.[539]

The Jewish influence over the Roman Catholic institution and its doctrines is also manifested in *The Document of the Vatican Commission for Religious Relations with Judaism* § 4, which states: **"We propose, in the future, to remove from the Gospel of St. John the term, 'the Jews' where it is used in a negative sense, and to translate it, 'the enemies of Christ.'"**[540]

At a speech at Hebrew University in Jerusalem, Roman Catholic Cardinal Joseph Bernadine stated:

[T]here is need for . . .theological reflection, especially with what many consider to be the problematic New Testament's texts ... Retranslation ... and reinterpretation certainly need

to be included among the goals we pursue in the effort to
eradicate anti-semitism.

[T]he gospel of John ... is generally considered among the
most problematic of all New Testament books in its outlook
towards Jews and Judaism ... this teaching of John about the
Jews, which resulted from the historical conflict between
the church and synagogue in the latter part of the first
century C.E., can no longer be taught as authentic doctrine
or used as catechesis by contemporary Christianity ...
Christians today must see that such teachings ... can no
longer be regarded as definitive teachings in light of our
improved understanding.[541]

In ancient Palestine the Jews worked hand in hand with the
Romans to crucify Christ. Now, the Jews work hand in glove with the
Roman Catholic Church in their effort to rule the world. In
Revelation 17:5 the great harlot that is the Roman Catholic Church
has a name written upon her forehead, MYSTERY, BABYLON THE
GREAT, THE MOTHER OF HARLOTS AND ABOMINATIONS
OF THE EARTH. Notice that she is a mystery but she is labeled
Babylon.

She is called Babylon because she is Babylonian. It is a mystery
because it is a devilish antichrist religion which has come out of
heathen Babylon masquerading as "the" Christian religion. Christian
labels have been applied to Babylonian heathenism to come up with
the mystery religion we know as the Roman Catholic Church. Both
the Talmudic Jews and the Vatican share that common Babylonian
root.

There is a clear parallel between the traditions of the pharisees of
old and those of modern Roman Catholic priestcraft. Recall that to
add tradition to God's word is rebellion against God's command that
nothing be added or taken away from his words. Revelations 22:18-
19. The Holy Bible warns us about those who would attempt to turn
us away from Christ to follow the traditions of men.

Beware lest any man spoil you through philosophy and vain deceit, **after the tradition of men, after the rudiments of the world**, and not after Christ. (Colossians 2:8 AV)

Wherefore if ye be dead with Christ from the rudiments of the world, why, as though living in the world, are ye subject to ordinances, (Touch not; taste not; handle not; Which all are to perish with the using;) after the commandments and doctrines of men? Which things have indeed a shew of wisdom in will worship, and humility, and neglecting of the body; not in any honour to the satisfying of the flesh. (Colossians 2:20-23 AV)

He answered and said unto them, Well hath Esaias prophesied of you hypocrites, as it is written, This people honoureth me with *their* lips, but their heart is far from me. **Howbeit in vain do they worship me, teaching *for* doctrines the commandments of men. For laying aside the commandment of God, ye hold the tradition of men,** *as* the washing of pots and cups: and many other such like things ye do. And he said unto them, Full well **ye reject the commandment of God, that ye may keep your own tradition.** (Mark 7:6-9 AV)

Making the word of God of none effect through your tradition, which ye have delivered: and many such like things do ye. (Mark 7:13 AV)

Jesus said: "I am the bread of life: he that cometh to me shall never hunger; and he that believeth on me shall never thirst." (John 6:35 AV) Very simply, Jesus promised salvation to all who believed on him. Adding any other requirement to faith in Jesus corrupts the gospel, resulting in the bread of death rather than the bread of life.

Jesus warned his disciples to beware of the doctrine of the religious leaders of their time. Jesus compared their doctrine to leaven. Only a little leaven of man made rules works its way through the whole loaf and corrupts God's pure doctrine. The leaven of

today's religious leaders is no different; the leaven of tradition
corrupts God's pure word. Man's tradition has turned the Bread of
Salvation into spiritual poison killing the souls of those who eat of the
corrupted loaf.

> **Then Jesus said unto them, Take heed and beware of the
> leaven of the Pharisees and of the Sadducees**. And they
> reasoned among themselves, saying, *It is* because we have
> taken no bread. *Which* when Jesus perceived, he said unto
> them, O ye of little faith, why reason ye among yourselves,
> because ye have brought no bread? Do ye not yet
> understand, neither remember the five loaves of the five
> thousand, and how many baskets ye took up?   Neither the
> seven loaves of the four thousand, and how many baskets ye
> took up? How is it that ye do not understand that I spake *it*
> not to you concerning bread, that ye should beware of the
> leaven of the Pharisees and of the Sadducees? **Then
> understood they how that he bade *them* not beware of
> the leaven of bread, but of the doctrine of the Pharisees
> and of the Sadducees**. (Matthew 16:6-12 AV)

> **A little leaven leaveneth the whole lump**. (Galatians 5:9
> AV)

God wants us to purge out the leaven of man's tradition.

> Your glorying *is* not good. Know ye not that a little leaven
> leaveneth the whole lump? **Purge out therefore the old
> leaven, that ye may be a new lump, as ye are unleavened.
> For even Christ our passover is sacrificed for us**:
> Therefore let us keep the feast, not with old leaven, neither
> with the leaven of malice and wickedness; but with the
> unleavened *bread* of sincerity and truth. (1 Corinthians 5:6-
> 8 AV)

Man's tradition requires works to earn salvation. Salvation,
however, is by God's Grace through faith alone on the completed
work of Jesus Christ, who paid for all of our sins on the cross. Good

works flow from salvation; good works cannot earn salvation.

> **For by grace are ye saved through faith; and that not of
> yourselves:** *it is* **the gift of God: Not of works, lest any
> man should boast. For we are his workmanship, created
> in Christ Jesus unto good works, which God hath before
> ordained that we should walk in them.** (Ephesians 2:8-10
> AV)

Once a Roman Catholic receives the sacrament of "Holy Orders"
he becomes a Catholic priest, and is thereafter prohibited from getting
married.[542] In addition, during Lent Catholics are forbidden to eat
meat on Friday.[543] God has expressly identified those two practices as
"doctrines of devils."

> Now the Spirit speaketh expressly, that in the latter times
> some shall depart from the faith, giving heed to **seducing
> spirits, and doctrines of devils**; Speaking lies in
> hypocrisy; having their conscience seared with a hot iron;
> **Forbidding to marry,** *and commanding* **to abstain from
> meats**, which God hath created to be received with
> thanksgiving of them which believe and know the truth. For
> every creature of God *is* good, and nothing to be refused, if
> it be received with thanksgiving: For it is sanctified by the
> word of God and prayer. (1 Timothy 4:1-5 AV)

40 The Catholic Sacraments

T he signatories to *The Gift of Salvation* claim "unity" on "fundamental truths" regarding "salvation" with the Roman Catholic Church. They then suggest that the sacraments of the Catholic Church are a secondary issue that can be discussed later. In fact, the sacraments of the Catholic Church strike at the very heart of the gospel and the signatories know that. The very existence of the Catholic sacraments makes it impossible for any true Christian to have any theological agreement with a Catholic.

How can any Christian claim unity with the Catholic Church on the issue of salvation and in the next breath state that the issue of Catholic sacraments can be worked out later, when the Catholic sacraments are the very means of Salvation under Catholic theology? This double talk is evidence of double minded men and an indication that The *Gift of Salvation* and the ECT manifestos are nothing more than subterfuges designed to spiritually seduce the unwary.

The signatories of both the ECT and *The Gift of Salvation* are either deluded and terribly deceived or they are not truly Christians at all. They have exalted themselves as Doctors of Theology or claim great enlightenment and authority within the Christian community. It is fair to hold them to the level of biblical knowledge that they claim to have. Being experts in Christian theology, it could not be claimed that they have simply made a mistake, especially since the specific points of Catholic theology that are contrary to Christian theology have been brought to their attention since the publication of the heathen manifestos. Yet not one of the signatories has retracted his signature. That would suggest that they are not deceived, but rather are accomplices in a spiritual crime against Christ and his true disciples.

Lest, dear reader, you think that is too harsh, let us examine some of the Catholic sacraments. The seven Catholic sacraments are: Baptism, Eucharist, Reconciliation (confession and forgiveness of sins), Confirmation, Marriage, Holy Orders, and Anointing of the Sick (extreme unction, otherwise known as last rites).

41 The Eucharist

The ECT and the later *The Gift of Salvation* manifestos are deceptive traps by the Catholic Church. Proof of that fact is found in the recent official Vatican statement, *Dominus Iesus*, which was written by the Vatican's chief expert on doctrine, Cardinal Josef Ratzinger (now Pope Benedict XVI) in 2000, after the 1994 ECT manifesto and the later 1997 *The Gift of Salvation* manifesto. In *Dominus Iesus*, the Catholic Church states that "ecclesial communities" that do not recognize the Eucharist mystery, (that is that Almighty God is fully present in the form of bread and wine) are not truly churches at all.

> Therefore, there exists a single Church of Christ, which subsists in the Catholic Church, governed by the Successor of Peter and by the Bishops in communion with him. The Churches which, while not existing in perfect communion with the Catholic Church, remain united to her by means of the closest bonds, that is, by apostolic succession and a valid Eucharist, are true particular Churches. . . . On the other hand, the ecclesial **communities which have not preserved the valid Episcopate and the genuine and integral substance of the Eucharistic mystery, are not Churches in the proper sense.** DECLARATION "DOMINUS IESUS" ON THE UNICITY AND SALVIFIC

UNIVERSALITY OF JESUS CHRIST AND THE
CHURCH, Rome, from the Offices of the Congregation for
the Doctrine of the Faith, August 6, 2000 (emphasis added).

What does the Catholic church mean by "the genuine and
integral substance of the Eucharistic mystery?" They mean that
during the ceremonial Mass, the host (bread) and wine are turned into
the body, blood, soul, and divinity of the Lord God Jesus Christ. As
we have seen above in our discussion of the wolf in sheep's clothing,
Bill Bright, the Catholic Church teaches that the appearance of bread
and wine remain, but that they have actually been transubstantiated
into God.

Although we have already looked at the official doctrine of the
Catholic Church regarding transubstantiation, it is so central to what
the Catholic Church is that it merits repeating. The Catechism of the
Catholic Church states: "By the consecration the transubstantiation of
the bread and wine into the Body and Blood of Christ is brought
about. Under the consecrated species of bread and wine Christ
himself, living and glorious, is present in a true, real, and substantial
manner: his Body and his Blood, with his soul and his divinity."[544]

The Catholic church actually believes that the wine and bread are
turned into God Almighty during the Catholic ceremony they call
Mass. They teach that the bread and wine only appear to be bread and
wine, that in actuality they are Jesus Christ. "In the most blessed
sacrament of the Eucharist 'the body and blood, together with the soul
and divinity, of our Lord Jesus Christ and, therefore, *the whole Christ
is truly, really, and substantially* contained.'"[545]

Let me make this crystal clear, the Catholic Church is saying, in
no uncertain terms, that Jesus Christ himself is completely physically
present during the Catholic Mass; he only appears to be bread and
wine. The Catholic Church official doctrine going back to the
Counsel of Trent states: "Here the pastor should explain that in this
Sacrament are contained not only the true body of Christ and all the
constituents of a true body, such as bones and sinews, but also Christ
whole and entire."[546]

Certainly, we know that is a lie. The Catholic god is a myth.
However, that is what the Catholic Church believes. That is the
organization with whom the ersatz Christian leaders have entered into
the ECT and *The Gift of Salvation* compacts. Those leaders certainly
know better. Since the bread and wine is a Catholic god, the Catholic
church actually admonishes its followers to worship the bread and
wine accordingly.

> ***Worship of the Eucharist.*** **In the liturgy of the Mass we
> express our faith in the real presence of Christ under the
> species of bread and wine by, among other ways,
> genuflecting or bowing deeply as a sign of adoration of
> the Lord.** *CATECHISM OF THE CATHOLIC CHURCH*, §
> 1378, 1994 (italics in original, bold type added).

According to *Dominus Iesus*, any church that does not agree with
that pagan idolatry is not truly a Christian church. That is certainly an
odd twist; the heathen Catholic church has the temerity to state the
anyone who does not engage in their unique witchcraft is not a
Christian church.

Those who will argue that *Dominus Iesus* is just an assertion
from one Cardinal in Rome should understand that the Cardinal is
now Pope Benedict XVI. In addition, the purportedly infallible Pope
John Paul II, with sure knowledge of his alleged apostolic authority
confirmed the declaration. "The Sovereign Pontiff John Paul II, at the
Audience of June 16, 2000, granted to the undersigned Cardinal
Prefect of the Congregation for the Doctrine of the Faith, with sure
knowledge and by his apostolic authority, ratified and confirmed this
Declaration, adopted in Plenary Session and ordered its publication."

Mind you, *Dominus Iesus* was issued after the Catholic church
entered into an agreement with the ersatz evangelicals where they
allegedly agreed that they had a common faith. They allowed at the
end of *The Gift of Salvation* that the issue of the Eucharist was an
issue that required "further exploration." Well, Rome explored the
issue alright, and it decided that anyone who does not join in their
heathen idolatry is not truly a Christian church!

Obviously Rome is not going to compromise on the Eucharistic issue. So that leaves the compromise to be by the ersatz Protestant luminaries. They are well practiced at compromising on the gospel and would likely jump at the opportunity to once again sound the retreat from sound doctrine. Stay tuned for the next abomination from these gospel traitors.

42 A Different Jesus

The ersatz Protestant signatories of the ECT and *The Gift of Salvation* have entered into a theological agreement with priests who claim to be Christ. The Roman Catholic priests claim that when consecrating the bread and wine during Mass they are the Lord Jesus Christ. Read this blasphemous official doctrine of the Roman Catholic Church as announced by the authoritative Council of Trent:

> **The priest is also one and the same, Christ the Lord**; for the ministers who offer Sacrifice, consecrate the holy mysteries, **not in their own person, but in that of Christ** . . . and thus **acting in the Person of Christ the Lord**, he changes the substance of the bread and wine into the true substance of His body and blood. *CATECHISM OF THE COUNCIL OF TRENT.*[547]

The Lord Jesus warned us that there would be just such an organization that would preach a different Jesus.

> For if he that cometh preacheth **another Jesus**, whom we have not preached, or if ye receive another spirit, which ye have not received, or another gospel, which ye have not accepted, ye might well bear with him. (2 Corinthians 11:4

AV)

Jesus alerted his disciples to beware of the many who would come in his name, claiming to be Christ. The many Roman Catholic priests who claim to be "acting in the person of Christ the Lord" are a clear and present fulfilment of that prophesy.

> **Jesus answered and said unto them, Take heed that no man deceive you. For many shall come in my name, saying, I am Christ; and shall deceive many**. (Matthew 24:4-5 AV)

Jesus said that he would be visible in the sky when he returns and warned us not to believe those who point to false Christs and say here is Christ or there is Christ. The Catholic Church points to the consecrated host and says "here is Christ" and points to its priests and says "there is Christ."

Jesus prophesied that there would arise false Christs that would perform great signs and wonders that would deceive many. The Catholic church has deceived the world into believing that their priests can perform the great wonder of turning bread and wine into the Lord God Jesus Christ. When Christ returns to Earth it will not be as a piece of bread in the secret chambers of Catholic altars; he will be as plainly visible as lightning.

> **[I]f any man shall say unto you, Lo, here *is* Christ, or there; believe *it* not. For there shall arise false Christs, and false prophets, and shall shew great signs and wonders; insomuch that, if *it were* possible, they shall deceive the very elect. Behold, I have told you before. Wherefore if they shall say unto you, Behold, he is in the desert; go not forth: behold, *he is* in the secret chambers; believe *it* not. For as the lightning cometh out of the east, and shineth even unto the west; so shall also the coming of the Son of man be**. Matthew 24:23-27.

43 Baptismal Regeneration

Catholicism is not Christianity, it would be more appropriate to call it Churchianity. Catholic doctrine is that everything flows from the church, including faith. The Catholic Catechism states: "It is through the church that we receive faith and new life in Christ by Baptism."[548] Dennis Costella explains the error of Rome and the proper understanding of water baptism in the life of a Christian:

> Water baptism has been viewed by true believers as an outward testimony of the inward reality of having already been "born again" by the power of God. The moment the sinner trusts Christ as his Saviour, he is baptized by the Spirit of God into the Body of Christ (1 Cor. 12:12-13). There is no salvation for anyone who is not "in Christ," and this spiritual regeneration takes place the moment the lost sinner receives Christ by faith (John 1:12; 5:24). All who are saved have received this baptism which God administers, not man.
>
> Water baptism, on the other hand, is properly understood to be an ordinance of the Church administered only to those who have already been saved. Baptism by immersion symbolizes what has already been accomplished by God.

The ordinances (Baptism and the Lord's Supper) and "good works" (obedience to the will of God as found in the Word of God) are after the fact of regeneration and the result of saving faith, not a means of saving grace. Salvation cannot be conferred by any church, for the church is but a fellowship of born again believers who have already availed themselves of salvation in the Lord Jesus Christ.[549]

We can see in the bible itself that the baptism that saves us is not the baptism with water, but rather the baptism of the Holy Spirit, through faith in Jesus Christ.

Buried with him in baptism, wherein also ye are risen with him through the faith of the operation of God, who hath raised him from the dead. Colossians 2:12

The baptism with water which only cleanses the filth of our flesh is not the baptism that saves us. Water baptism is only a symbolic ordinance, which signifies what has happened inside of the believer. The baptism that saves us is the rebirth of our spirit that awakens our conscience to desire to do the will of God. *See* Romans 10:9-10; 6:3-4; Hebrews 9:14.

The like figure whereunto *even* baptism doth also now save us (not the putting away of the filth of the flesh, but the answer of a good conscience toward God,) by the resurrection of Jesus Christ: (1 Peter 3:21 AV)

44 Salvation by Works

To require baptism as a condition of salvation is to add works to faith. Works salvation is an outgrowth of the heathen view, discussed above by Richard Bennett, that one who is saved becomes actually righteous. That is contrary to the biblical doctrine of imputed legal righteousness. We do not become actually righteous once saved, rather we have the righteous of Christ imputed to us. The idea that salvation is not a legal act, but is rather a factual transformation, necessarily results in a system of salvation by works. God makes that clear in his gospel that we are not saved by works but by his grace through faith.

> Who hath saved us, and called us with an holy calling, **not according to our works, but according to his own purpose and grace**, which was given us in Christ Jesus before the world began. 2 Timothy 1:9.

The Catholic Church teaches that one must add works to faith in order to merit entry into heaven.[550] Not only that, but they curse anyone who says that faith is not by the will of man.

> If anyone saith that by faith alone the impious is justified; in such wise as to mean that nothing else is required to cooperate in order to the obtaining the grace of justification,

and that is not in any way necessary that he be prepared and disposed by the movement of his own will; let him be anathema. COUNCIL OF TRENT, SESSION VI, DECREE ON JUSTIFICATION, Canon IX, January 13, 1547.

The gospel of Rome is faith by the free will of man. That Arminian free will theology was inserted through the secret agents of Rome into many Protestant churches. The Arminian gospel is essentially a false salvation by works. That is because once a man has determined that he has saved himself, that same man can lose his salvation. His life then becomes an endless series of works to maintain his salvation.

The gospel, however, makes it clear that salvation is by God's Grace through faith alone on the completed work of Jesus Christ, who paid for all of our sins on the cross. Good works flow from salvation, good works cannot earn salvation.

> **For by grace are ye saved through faith; and that not of yourselves: it is the gift of God: Not of works, lest any man should boast. For we are his workmanship, created in Christ Jesus unto good works, which God hath before ordained that we should walk in them.** (Ephesians 2:8-10 AV)

The Catholic church not only contradicts the above doctrine of grace pronounced by God, but curses God for his grace. That is not hyperbole. Read the curse for yourself.

> If anyone say that the justice received is not preserved and also increased before God through good works; but that the said works are merely the fruits and signs of justification obtained, but not a cause of the increase thereof, let him be anathema. COUNCIL OF TRENT, SESSION VI, DECREE ON JUSTIFICATION, Canon XXIV, January 13, 1547.

That is a curse on anyone that says that one is justified solely by the grace of God as pronounced in Ephesians 2:8-10. The "anyone"

referred to in that Catholic curse would certainly include the author of
that doctrine: God himself. The Catholic Church is a church of
blasphemy. Dennis Costella concludes:

> The entire Biblical exegesis of "saving faith" stresses
> absolute reliance upon the finished work of Christ apart
> from the works or supposed merit of man. The faith that
> saves always produces fruit or good works in the life, but
> this is always after the initial miracle of the new birth
> effected by the power of God. Those who insist on
> "believing and... in order to be saved" do not have the
> "saving faith" of which the Bible speaks.[551]

Dennis Costella has quite accurately summarized the very theme
of the bible. If one adds anything to faith in order to be saved, such
faith is not the faith that saves. In fact, such conduct is proof of a lack
of faith, because the person is demonstrating that he does not believe
in the sufficiency of the sacrifice of Christ. The bible makes it clear
that salvation is through faith alone. Righteousness is imputed to the
believer by faith alone, it is not attained by works.

> What shall we say then that Abraham our father, as
> pertaining to the flesh, hath found? For if Abraham were
> justified by works, he hath *whereof* to glory; but not before
> God. For what saith the scripture? Abraham believed God,
> and it was counted unto him for righteousness. Now to him
> that worketh is the reward not reckoned of grace, but of
> debt. But **to him that worketh not, but believeth on him
> that justifieth the ungodly, his faith is counted for
> righteousness**. Even as David also describeth the
> blessedness of the man, unto whom God imputeth
> righteousness without works, *Saying*, Blessed *are* they
> whose iniquities are forgiven, and whose sins are covered.
> Blessed *is* the man to whom the Lord will not impute sin.
> (Romans 4:1-8 AV)

The Catholic church, however, curses all who follow the gospel
Christ and believe his promise of salvation by the grace of God alone.

If anyone saith that the good works of one of that is justified
are in such manner the gifts of God, as they are not also the
good merits of him that is justified; or that the said justified,
by the good works which he performs through the grace of
God and the merit of Jesus Christ, whose living member he
is, does not truly merit increase of grace, eternal life, and the
attainment of that eternal life, – if so be, however, that he
depart in grace, –and also an increase of glory; let him be
anathema. COUNCIL OF TRENT, SESSION VI, DECREE
ON JUSTIFICATION, Canon XXXII, January 13, 1547.

The Catholic Church has placed a hellish, but ineffectual, curse
on anyone who believes the gospel: that we are saved by God's grace,
that Christ paid the whole penalty for sin, and that there is no need for
any works to merit justification. The Catholic Church doesn't just
have different teachings from the Bible, it is the avowed enemy of the
God's word, God's method of salvation, and Christ.

If anyone saith that men are justified, either by the sole
imputation of the justice of Christ or by the sole remission
of sins, to the exclusion of the grace and charity which is
poured forth in their hearts by the Holy Ghost and is
inherent in them; or even that the grace, whereby we are
justified, is only the favor of God ; let him be anathema.
COUNCIL OF TRENT, SESSION VI, DECREE ON
JUSTIFICATION, Canon XI, January 13, 1547.

This issue of salvation by faith alone is not some incidental issue,
it is the very heart of the gospel. The reprobate minds of those who
have signed the ECT and *The Gift of Salvation*, however, think that
this is a matter of secondary importance that can be worked out later.
God, on the other hand, thinks this issue is quite important. In regards
to salvation, faith and works are mutually exclusive.

**And if by grace, then *is it* no more of works: otherwise
grace is no more grace. But if *it be* of works, then is it no
more grace: otherwise work is no more work.** (Romans
11:6 AV)

45 Priests Claim Power to Forgive Sins

Since the Catholic Church claims that the priests are another Christ and another Lord, it should be no surprise that the Catholic Church claims that its priests have the same authority as the Lord to forgive sins. The priests hear confessions from people seeking absolution for their sins. The confessional has been the sight of countless seductions of lonely women by priests.[552]

Indeed bishops and priests, by virtue of the sacrament of Holy Orders, have the power to forgive sins.
CATECHISM OF THE CATHOLIC CHURCH, § 1461, 1994.

Even the Jewish scribes understood that only God has the authority to forgive sins because sin is the violation of God's law. *See e.g.,* Exodus 32:33, Numbers 32:33, Deuteronomy 9:16, Joshua 7:20, 2 Samuel 12:13, Psalm 41:4, Jeremiah 3:25, Jeremiah 50:14, and Luke 15:21.

When Jesus saw their faith, he said unto the sick of the palsy, Son, thy sins be forgiven thee. But there were certain of the scribes sitting there, and reasoning in their hearts, **Why doth this *man* thus speak blasphemies? who can forgive sins but God only?** And immediately when Jesus perceived in his spirit that they so reasoned within themselves, he said unto them, Why reason ye these things in your hearts? Whether is it easier to say to the sick of the palsy, *Thy* sins be forgiven thee; or to say, Arise, and take up thy bed, and walk? But **that ye may know that the Son of man hath power on earth to forgive sins, (he saith to the sick of the palsy,) I say unto thee, Arise, and take up thy bed, and go thy way into thine house**. And immediately he arose, took up the bed, and went forth before them all; insomuch that they were all amazed, and glorified God, saying, We never saw it on this fashion. (Mark 2:5-12 AV)

The priests in the Catholic hierarchy take the title of God the Father, by taking the title "father." Jesus warned against calling a person father in the spiritual sense; that is a title reserved for God alone.

And call no *man* your father upon the earth: for one is your Father, which is in heaven. (Matthew 23:9 AV)

These words spake Jesus, and lifted up his eyes to heaven, and said, **Father**, the hour is come; glorify thy Son, that thy Son also may glorify thee: (John 17:1 AV)

And now, **O Father**, glorify thou me with thine own self with the glory which I had with thee before the world was. (John 17:5 AV)

That they all may be one; as thou, **Father**, *art* in me, and I in thee, that they also may be one in us: that the world may believe that thou hast sent me. (John 17:21 AV)

The Catholic priest claims to be the Lord Jesus and to act as mediator between God and man.

[T]he priest is constituted an interpreter and **mediator between God and man**, which indeed must be regarded as the principal function of the priesthood. *CATECHISM OF THE COUNCIL OF TRENT.*[553]

God says otherwise. There is only one God and only one mediator between God and man, that is Jesus Christ.

> For *there is* **one God, and one mediator** between God and men, the man **Christ Jesus**; (1 Timothy 2:5 AV)

There is only one Christ; however, there are many antichrists. All of the priests, bishops, cardinals, and popes of the Romish church are not Christs, they are antichrists.

> Little children, it is the last time: and as ye have heard that antichrist shall come, **even now are there many antichrists**; whereby we know that it is the last time. (1 John 2:18 AV)

46 The Profitable Myth of Purgatory

The Romish church teaches that the sacrifice of Jesus Christ on the cross did not satisfy God. God requires additional punishment of the believer in order to expiate the sins. This expiation can be done on earth through penance. If, however, the sin is not punished on earth the sin must be punished after death in a place called Purgatory. Purgatory is a place where sins are purportedly purged and after the sins are purged the poor tormented one is then finally granted entrance into heaven.[554]

> All who die in God's grace and friendship, but are imperfectly purified, are indeed assured of their eternal salvation; but after death they undergo purification, so to achieve the holiness necessary to enter the joy of heaven. The church gives the name *Purgatory* to this final purification of the elect, which is entirely different from the punishment of the damned. CATECHISM OF THE CATHOLIC CHURCH, §§ 1030-1031 (1994).

The gospel of Jesus Christ, however, is that our sins are remitted once and for all by the sacrifice of Jesus on the cross. There is no more sacrifice needed for our sins.

By the which will **we are sanctified through the offering**

of the body of Jesus Christ once *for all*. And every priest standeth daily ministering and offering oftentimes the same sacrifices, which can never take away sins: But this man, after he had offered one sacrifice for sins for ever, sat down on the right hand of God; From henceforth expecting till his enemies be made his footstool. For by one offering he hath perfected for ever them that are sanctified. *Whereof* the Holy Ghost also is a witness to us: for after that he had said before, This *is* the covenant that I will make with them after those days, saith the Lord, I will put my laws into their hearts, and in their minds will I write them; **And their sins and iniquities will I remember no more. Now where remission of these *is, there is* no more offering for sin.** (Hebrews 10:10-18 AV)

The Catholic Church contradicts God with their doctrine of Purgatory and in fact curses God for having offered himself once for the remission of all our sins.

If anyone saith that, after the grace of justification has been received, to every penitent sinner the guilt is remitted, and the debt of the eternal punishment is blotted out in such a way that there remains not any debt of temporal punishment to be discharged either in this world, or in the next in Purgatory, before the entrance to the Kingdom of Heaven can be opened (to him); let him be anathema. COUNCIL OF TRENT, SESSION VI, DECREE ON JUSTIFICATION, Canon XXX, January 13, 1547.

Purgatory is a money maker for the Catholic Church. Under that abominable doctrine, people are compelled to give to the Catholic Church in order to pay the penalty for sins purportedly not atoned for by Christ's sacrifice. These alms and penance are not just given for one's own sins but also for the sins of others who have already died as a way of getting them out of Purgatory.

From the beginning the Church has honored the memory of the dead and offered prayers in suffrage for them, above all

the Eucharistic sacrifice, so that thus purified they may
attain the beatific vision of God. The church also commends
almsgiving, indulgences, and works of penance undertaken
on behalf of the dead. CATECHISM OF THE CATHOLIC
CHURCH, § 1032 (1994).

Despite the claims of the Catholic Church that the doctrine of
Purgatory is based on scripture, there is absolutely no authority in the
Bible for such a place as purgatory. In fact, the doctrine of purgatory
is directly contrary to the gospel of Christ. The Gospel is that we are
saved from the wrath of God by the grace of God through faith in
Jesus Christ.

And to wait for his Son from heaven, whom he raised from
the dead, *even* Jesus, which **delivered us from the wrath to
come**. (1 Thessalonians 1:10 AV)

For **God hath not appointed us to wrath**, but to obtain
salvation by our Lord Jesus Christ, (1 Thessalonians 5:9
AV)

Much more then, being now justified by his blood, **we shall
be saved from wrath** through him. (Romans 5:9 AV)

Verily, verily, I say unto you, **He that heareth my word,
and believeth on him that sent me, hath everlasting life,
and shall not come into condemnation; but is passed
from death unto life**. (John 5:24 AV)

There is only Heaven and Hell that awaits those who die. There
is a great gulf between Heaven and Hell. Once a person is in Hell, he
cannot ever enter Heaven.

And it came to pass, that the beggar died, and was carried by
the angels into Abraham's bosom: the rich man also died,
and was buried;   And in hell he lift up his eyes, being in
torments, and seeth Abraham afar off, and Lazarus in his
bosom.   And he cried and said, Father Abraham, have

mercy on me, and send Lazarus, that he may dip the tip of
his finger in water, and cool my tongue; for I am tormented
in this flame. But Abraham said, Son, remember that thou
in thy lifetime receivedst thy good things, and likewise
Lazarus evil things: but now he is comforted, and thou art
tormented.   And beside all this, **between us and you there
is a great gulf fixed: so that they which would pass from
hence to you cannot; neither can they pass to us, that
would come from thence**. (Luke 16:22-26 AV)

Then shall he say also unto them on the left hand, Depart
from me, ye cursed, into **everlasting fire**, prepared for the
devil and his angels . . . And these shall go away into
everlasting punishment: but the righteous into **life eternal**.
(Matthew 25:41, 46 AV)

He that believeth on the Son hath **everlasting life**: and **he
that believeth not the Son shall not see life; but the
wrath of God abideth on him**. (John 3:36 AV)

Verily, verily, I say unto you, He that believeth on me hath
everlasting life. (John 6:47 AV)

But now being made free from sin, and become servants to
God, ye have your fruit unto holiness, and the end
everlasting life. (Romans 6:22 AV)

Since Jesus has atoned for our sins there is nothing more for us to
do. If we believe in Christ, our sins are forgiven and we are justified
before God. God has promised that if we believe he will remember
our sins no more. We are not justified because of what we have done
but because of what Jesus has done for us. God does not want
penance from us, he wants repentance.

Above when he said, Sacrifice and offering and burnt
offerings and *offering* for sin thou wouldest not, neither
hadst pleasure *therein*; which are offered by the law;   Then
said he, Lo, I come to do thy will, O God. He taketh away

the first, that he may establish the second. By the which will **we are sanctified through the offering of the body of Jesus Christ once *for all*.** And every priest standeth daily ministering and offering oftentimes the same sacrifices, which can never take away sins: But this man, after he had offered one sacrifice for sins for ever, sat down on the right hand of God; From henceforth expecting till his enemies be made his footstool. **For by one offering he hath perfected for ever them that are sanctified.** *Whereof* the Holy Ghost also is a witness to us: for after that he had said before, This *is* the covenant that I will make with them after those days, saith the Lord, I will put my laws into their hearts, and in their minds will I write them; **And their sins and iniquities will I remember no more. Now where remission of these *is, there is* no more offering for sin.** (Hebrews 10:8-18 AV)

47 Indulgences

T he Bible teaches that "the love of money is the root of all evil." 1 Timothy 6:10. The Roman church loves money. The Roman Catholic Church is the single richest organization in the world.[555] The wealth of the Catholic Church has been amassed over many centuries. At the time of the Mexican Revolution, the Catholic Church owned between one third to one half of all the land in Mexico.[556]

D. Antonio Gavin was a Catholic priest in Spain in the 1600's. He was forced to flee from Spain during the Spanish Inquisition to the safety of England. There he wrote a book titled *A Master Key to Popery*, which exposed just a small portion of the Vatican wealth. For example, the Cathedral of St. Salvator, in the small city of Zaragoza, contained ten thousand ounces of silver, 84 chalices, 20 of which were made of solid gold. The *custodia* used to carry the Host in procession was five hundred pound weight, solid gold, and set with diamonds, emeralds and other precious stones. The *custodia* was so valuable that several goldsmiths tried but were unable to estimate its value.[557]

Our Lady of the Pillar, another church in Zaragova, had a crown on the image of the Virgin Mary that was twenty five pounds weight and set all over with so many diamonds that no gold could be seen on it. People seeing the crown thought it was made entirely of diamonds. The idol of Mary also had 6 other pure solid gold crowns set with diamonds and emeralds. The image of Mary had 365 necklaces of pearls and diamonds (one for each day of the year), and innumerable crafted roses of diamonds and other precious stones. There were so many diamond roses, in fact, that a different set of roses could adorn the idol each day for three years straight. The graven image had a different skirt for each day of the year; the skirts were embroidered in gold, diamonds, and other precious stones. That was not the only image in the church, another five foot image was made entirely of silver and adorned with precious stones with a diamond studded crown of pure gold.[558]

When the General of the English forces, the "Right Honorable Lord Stanhope," was shown the treasures at the cathedral of St. Salvator he exclaimed that if all the kings of Europe gathered together all of their treasuries they could not buy half of the riches in the cathedral.[559] That was just one cathedral, in one small city in Spain, 300 years ago.

The Vatican wealth continues to compound. Avro Manhattan, the world's foremost authority on Vatican politics, revealed in his book, *The Vatican Billions*, that as of 1983 the Jesuit order of priests had tax free annual income from the United States alone of no less than $250 million.[560] Manhattan determined that the Jesuits held a 51% ownership interest in the Bank of America (which in 1998 merged with Nationsbank to form Bank America), and that they are also major stockholders in companies that have strategic military significance to the U.S., such as Boeing and Lockeed.[561]

Those holdings represent only a portion of the Jesuit wealth. The Jesuit wealth, in turn, is only a small portion of the vast Vatican wealth. There are hundreds of other orders of Catholic priests including 125 orders of monks and 414 orders of nuns operating in the United States.[562] One order of nuns, the Little Sisters of the Poor, have assets valued conservatively in excess of one billion dollars.[563]

"In a statement published in connection with a bond prospectus, the Boston archdiocese listed its assets at Six Hundred and Thirty-five Million ($635,891,004), which is 9.9 times its liabilities. This leaves a net worth of Five Hundred and Seventy-one million dollars ($571,704,953). It is not difficult to discover the truly astonishing wealth of the church, once we add the riches of the twenty-eight archdioceses and 122 dioceses of the U.S.A., some of which are even wealthier than that of Boston."[564] The Catholic Church's wealth just in the United States alone has been conservatively estimated at over $100 billion.[565]

The above figures are as of 1983. No doubt the amounts have increased exponentially since 1983 in view of the fact that the church pays no real estate taxes, income taxes, inheritance taxes, sales taxes, or gift taxes.[566]

The Catholic Church has accumulated such vast wealth that as of 1965 it owned 25 percent of all privately owned real estate in the United States.[567] The Catholic Church is a recipient of hundreds of millions of dollars in federal and state grants for construction of hospitals and other buildings and projects.[568] Nino Lo Bello, former Rome correspondent for *Business Week*, calls the Vatican "the tycoon on the Tiber." His research indicates that the Vatican owns one third of Rome's real estate and is the largest holder of stocks and bonds in the entire world.[569]

The Roman cult, however, is not satisfied with its immense wealth, it wants more. In fact Pope Innocent II claimed ownership of the entire universe as the "TEMPORAL SOVEREIGN OF THE UNIVERSE."[570] Even today the Pope wears a triple crown because he claims to rule as king over Heaven, Hell, and Earth.

Vatican doctrines are set up to extract the most money possible from its flock. This fleecing of the flock started from the beginning and continues today. One of the doctrines used to make the harlot of Rome rich is the doctrine of indulgences. Under Catholic doctrine an indulgence is the removal of the temporal punishment for sins.

The Catholic Church teaches that the sin has been forgiven

through the Catholic sacraments but that a person must be punished
for that sin either on earth or after death for an unspecified time in
purgatory. That punishment, however, can be remitted through an
indulgence granted by the Catholic Church.[571]

An indulgence can be of the entire punishment (plenary
indulgence) or only a part of the punishment (partial indulgence).[572]
A Catholic church member can also obtain an indulgence from the
church on behalf of another person whether the recipient of the
indulgence is living or dead.

> It has likewise defined, that, if those truly penitent have
> departed in the love of God, before they have made
> satisfaction by worthy fruits of penance for sins of
> commission and omission, the souls of these are cleansed
> after death by purgatorial punishments; and so that they may
> be relieved from punishments of this kind, namely, the
> sacrifices of Masses, prayers, and almsgiving, and other
> works of piety, which are customarily performed by the
> faithful for other faithful according to the institutions of the
> Church. COUNCIL OF FLORENCE, 1439.[573]

In the middle ages the Romish church was quite brazen and
would actually sell indulgences outright.[574] The Romish church is still
selling indulgences, it is just not as direct about it as it once was. In
order to get a loved one out of the torments of Purgatory it is
necessary to pay money for Masses.

There are two types of Masses in the Catholic Church, High
Mass and Low Mass. High Masses are more expensive than Low
Masses. "Any priest who celebrates Mass may receive an offering or
'Mass stipend' to apply that Mass for a specific intention. This
approved custom of the Church is regulated by the Code of Canon
Law and provincial and diocesan laws."[575] The Irish have a saying:
high money, High Mass; low money; Low Mass; no money, NO
MASS![576]

The Gospel clearly states that neither salvation nor any gift of

God can be purchased with gold, silver, or anything else. Salvation has already been purchased with the precious blood of Christ.

> **Forasmuch as ye know that ye were not redeemed with corruptible things,** *as* **silver and gold, from your vain conversation** *received* **by tradition from your fathers; But with the precious blood of Christ,** as of a lamb without blemish and without spot: Who verily was foreordained before the foundation of the world, but was manifest in these last times for you, Who by him do believe in God, that raised him up from the dead, and gave him glory; that your faith and hope might be in God. (1 Peter 1:18-21 AV)

> And when Simon saw that through laying on of the apostles' hands the Holy Ghost was given, he offered them money, Saying, Give me also this power, that on whomsoever I lay hands, he may receive the Holy Ghost. But Peter said unto him, **Thy money perish with thee, because thou hast thought that the gift of God may be purchased with money.** (Acts 8:18-20 AV)

48 Light Can Have No Fellowship With Darkness

There can be no theological agreement between true Christians and Catholics. Indeed, God makes it clear that light (Christianity) can have no theological fellowship with darkness (Catholicism).

> Be ye not unequally yoked together with unbelievers: for what fellowship hath righteousness with unrighteousness? and what communion hath light with darkness? (2 Corinthians 6:14 AV)

Yet, the agreement between the Catholic church and the ersatz Evangelicals in *The Gift of Salvation* states that neither of them have abandoned their respective separate beliefs. Yet they contradict that affirmation by stating that they have reached "unity in the Gospel." Those two positions are mutually exclusive and therefore cannot both be true.

> As Evangelicals who thank God for the heritage of the Reformation and affirm with conviction its classic confessions, as Catholics who are conscientiously faithful to the teaching of the Catholic Church, and as disciples together of the Lord Jesus Christ who recognize our debt to

519

our Christian forebears and our obligations to our
contemporaries and those who will come after us, we affirm
our unity in the Gospel that we have here professed. In our
continuing discussions, we seek no unity other than unity in
the truth. Only unity in the truth can be pleasing to the Lord
and Savior whom we together serve, for he is "the way, the
truth, and the life" (John 14:6).[577]

The above statement suggests agreement. If what is said is to be
believed, it would be impossible for these two groups to ever agree.
The traditional view of the Protestant Reformation is that the pope is
the antichrist. The belief that the pope is the antichrist was once a
virtually unanimous belief among Protestant denominations.

In fact, the Westminster Confession of Faith (Church of England)
states: "There is no other Head of the Church but the Lord Jesus
Christ, nor can the Pope of Rome, in any sense, be head thereof, but is
that antichrist, that man of sin, and Son of perdition, that exalteth
himself in the Church against Christ and all that is called God." Other
Protestant confessions of faith identified the pope as the antichrist,
including but not limited to the Morland Confession of 1508 and 1535
(Waldenses) and the Helvetic Confession of 1536 (Switzerland).[578]

The Catholic Church teaches that Peter is the rock upon which
God has built his church, and that the Pope as the bishop of Rome is
Peter's successor as the vicar of Christ.[579] Protestant Christians,
however, understand that headship of the church is reserved to Christ
alone. "[H]e is the head of the body, the church: who is the
beginning, the firstborn from the dead; that in all *things* he might have
the preeminence." (Colossians 1:18 AV)

Christ will not share his glory nor his authority nor his station
with anyone; Christ has preeminence in all things. "For thou shalt
worship no other god: for the LORD, whose name *is* Jealous, is a
jealous God." (Exodus 34:14 AV)

The Old Testament prophecies of the coming Christ indicate that
the cornerstone of the church is to be a heavenly stone (Jesus Christ)

that is cut out without hands, and the church will grow from this stone to become a **great mountain** and fill the earth. *See* Daniel 2:34-45.

This prophesied rock of salvation is Jesus Christ. Romans 9:33. For a man to claim to be the rock of the church is to claim to be Christ, because the Bible makes clear that Christ is the rock, the head of the church. To falsely claim to be Christ, the head of the church, fulfills the prophecies that identify the antichrist.

> Let no man deceive you by any means: for *that day shall not come*, except there come a falling away first, and that man of sin be revealed, the son of perdition; **Who opposeth and exalteth himself above all that is called God, or that is worshipped; so that he as God sitteth in the temple of God, shewing himself that he is God.** (2 Thessalonians 2:3-4 AV)

> And the king shall do according to his will; and **he shall exalt himself, and magnify himself above every god, and shall speak marvellous things against the God of gods**, and shall prosper till the indignation be accomplished: for that that is determined shall be done. Neither shall he regard the God of his fathers, nor the desire of women, nor regard any god: for **he shall magnify himself above all.** (Daniel 11:36-37 AV)

There is only one head of the church; the church is not a monster with two heads. To claim to be the rock of the church is to implicitly deny that Jesus is the rock of the church. To deny that Jesus is the rock is to deny that Jesus is Christ. Denying that Jesus is the Christ is a doctrine specifically identified in 1 John 2:22-23 as a teaching of the antichrist.

> Who is a liar but he that denieth that Jesus is the Christ? He is antichrist, that denieth the Father and the Son.
> Whosoever denieth the Son, the same hath not the Father: *(but) he that acknowledgeth the Son hath the Father also.*
> (1 John 2:22-23 AV)

Read through the following passages, and decide for yourself who is the Rock of the Church.

And did all drink the same spiritual drink: for they drank of that spiritual Rock that followed them: and **that Rock was Christ**. (1 Corinthians 10:4 AV)

And are built upon the foundation of the apostles and prophets, **Jesus Christ himself being the chief corner** *stone*. (Ephesians 2:20 AV)

For other foundation can no man lay than that is laid, which is Jesus Christ. (1 Corinthians 3:11 AV)

My soul, wait thou only upon God; for my expectation *is* from him. **He only** *is* **my rock and my salvation**: *he is* my defence; I shall not be moved. (Psalms 62:5-6 AV)

The rock of the Catholic Church is not God. Their rock is only a man trying to take God's place.

For their rock *is* **not as our Rock**, even our enemies themselves *being* judges. For their vine *is* of the vine of Sodom, and of the fields of Gomorrah: their grapes *are* grapes of gall, their clusters *are* bitter: **Their wine** *is* **the poison of dragons, and the cruel venom of asps**. (Deuteronomy 32:31-33 AV)

And he shall say, **Where** *are* **their gods,** *their* **rock in whom they trusted**. (Deuteronomy 32:37 AV)

By claiming that Peter is the rock, the pope has denied that Jesus is the rock, which is essentially a denial that Jesus is the Christ. The pope has fulfilled the prophesy in 1 John 2:22-23, which states that the antichrist will deny that Jesus is the Christ. Who then does the pope claim is the Christ? The answer is found when we compare what the Holy Bible says about Christ with what the pope has said. What does it mean when we say that Jesus is Christ? It means that he is the one anointed "God with us." In Matthew 1:23, Jesus is identified as "Emmanuel, which being interpreted is, God with us." The pope, however, claims that he is God with us. **"[W]e hold upon this earth the place of God Almighty."** *Pope Leo XIII* (emphasis added).[580]

Jesus Christ is "an advocate with the Father" for us. 1 John 2:1. He is the "one mediator between God and men." 1 Timothy 2:5. The pope, however, claims the title of Supreme Pontiff. Pontiff means literally bridge builder; it connotes that the pontiff is one who is a bridge or intermediary between God and man.

The pope has stated: "To be subject to the Roman Pontiff is to every human creature altogether necessary for salvation." *The Bull Sanctum*, November 18, 1302. In addition, the Catholic Church teaches that Mary and the saints are advocates before the throne of God for us. "[The saints'] . . . intercession is their most exalted service to God's plan. **We can and should ask them to intercede for us and for the whole world.** *CATECHISM OF THE CATHOLIC CHURCH*, § 2683, 1994."

Jesus Christ is the "author and finisher of our faith." Hebrew 12:2. "For by grace are ye saved through faith; and that not of yourselves: *it is* the gift of God: Not of works, lest any man should boast." (Ephesians 2:8-9 AV) The pope, however, states that faith comes from man and it must be joined with works, i.e. started and finished by man, not Jesus.

The Catholic Church even teaches that works done after death by others are effective for the salvation of the deceased. "[T]he souls . . . are cleansed after death by purgatorial punishments; and so that they may be relieved from punishments of this kind, namely, the sacrifices of Masses, prayers, and almsgiving, and other works of piety, which are customarily performed by the faithful for other faithful according to the institutions of the Church." COUNCIL OF FLORENCE, 1439.[581]

Jesus Christ is the "blessed and only Potentate." 1 Timothy 6:15.

Pope Innocent II claimed ownership of the entire universe as the "TEMPORAL SOVEREIGN OF THE UNIVERSE."[582] Pope Boniface VIII pronounced: "**I have the authority of the King of kings. I am all in all and above all, so that God, Himself and I, The Vicar of God, have but one consistory, and I am able to do almost all that God can do. What therefore, *can* you make of me but God.**" *The Bull Sanctum*, November 18, 1302 (emphasis added).[583] Even today the Pope wears a triple crown because he claims to rule as king over Heaven, Hell, and Earth. Jesus Christ is the "great high priest" of God almighty. Hebrews 4:14. The pope claims to be the great high priest. As already mentioned above, the pope claims the title of Supreme Pontiff. He is the successor of the emperors of Rome who were seriatim the Supreme Pontiff (*Pontifex Maximus*),[584] which was the high priest of the pagan religions of Rome.[585]

Jesus is higher than the kings of the earth. Psalms 89:27. The pope claims, however, authority over the kings of the earth. "[T]he Roman pontiff possess **primacy over the whole world**." *The Vatican Council*, Session IV, chapter III, July 18, 1870 (emphasis added).

Jesus is "Lord of all." Acts 10:36. The pope, though, claims that all must submit to him: "The Roman Pontiff judges all man, but is judged by no one. We declare, assert, define and pronounce: to be subject to the Roman Pontiff is to every human creature altogether necessary for salvation. . . . That which was spoken of Christ . . . 'Thou hast subdued all things under His feet,' may well seem verified in me." *The Bull Sanctum*, November 18, 1302 (emphasis added).[586] The pope has claimed every attribute of Christ for himself. He has essentially denied that Jesus is the Christ and laid claim himself to being Christ. The Holy Bible identifies such a one as antichrist. 1 John 2:20-23.

The Bible says that the antichrist will deny the Son and, implicitly, deny the Father. 1 John 2:20-23. The pope makes his identity as the antichrist clear by expressly denying the Father. The pope claims the title "Holy Father." *See Catechism of the Catholic Church*, at § 10. Holy Father is a title that appears only once in all the

Holy Scriptures and is reserved for God the Father. John 17:11.

The pope considers himself the vicar of Christ. What does it mean to be a vicar? The word vicar means one who acts in place of another. We derive the English word vice from vicar. For example the Vice President acts in place of the President during those times when the President himself cannot act. The Bible talks about one who would come and deceive the world into believing that he is in place of Christ. He is identified as the **antichrist.** The pope himself is acknowledging that he is the antichrist by claiming to be the vicar of Christ. Vicar of Christ means antichrist. Noah Webster defined the prefix "anti" as a preposition meaning not only against but also in place of the noun it follows.[587] The Oxford English Dictionary[588] defines "anti" as meaning "opposite, against, in exchange, instead, representing, rivaling, simulating." Antichrist means one who is against Christ and at the same time purports to take the place of Christ. **Therefore, vicar of Christ = antichrist.**

Is there one who Jesus promised would act in his name? Yes, the Holy Ghost, not the pope of Rome!

These things have I spoken unto you, being *yet* present with you. **But the Comforter, *which is* the Holy Ghost, whom the Father will send in my name, he shall teach you all things, and bring all things to your remembrance, whatsoever I have said unto you.** (John 14:25-26 AV)

Nevertheless I tell you the truth; It is expedient for you that I go away: for **if I go not away, the Comforter will not come unto you; but if I depart, I will send him unto you.** (John 16:7 AV)

The Pope even takes the title of God the Father. For example, the *Catechism of the Catholic Church*, at § 10 refers to Pope John II as the "Holy Father, Pope John II." The pope goes by other majestic titles such as "Your Holiness." Pope John Paul II, himself, admits that such titles are inimical to the Gospel. He even cites the Bible passage that condemns such practices. He simply explains that the

Catholic traditions of men implicitly authorize this violation of God's commands.

> Have no fear when people call me the 'Vicar of Christ,' when they say to me 'Holy Father,' or 'Your Holiness,' or use titles similar to these, which seem even inimical to the Gospel. Christ declared: 'Call no one on earth your father; you have one Father in heaven. Do not be called 'Master;' you have but one master, the Messiah' (Mt 23:9-10). These expressions, nevertheless, have evolved out of a long tradition, becoming part of common usage. One must not be afraid of these words either. *Pope John Paul II.*[589]

The term "Holy Father" was used in the Holy Scripture only one time, it was used by Jesus the night before his crucifixion to refer to God the Father. Implicit in taking God's name is taking his position and authority. As Jesus said in John 14:28, God the Father is greater than Jesus. By taking the title "Holy Father," the Pope is implicitly presenting himself as greater than Jesus Christ.

> And now I am no more in the world, but these are in the world, and I come to thee. **Holy Father**, keep through thine own name those whom thou hast given me, that they may be one, as we *are*. (John 17:11 AV)

In the book of Revelation it states that the beast will blaspheme God.

> And **he opened his mouth in blasphemy against God**, to blaspheme his name, and his tabernacle, and them that dwell in heaven. And it was given unto him to make war with the saints, and to overcome them: and power was given him over all kindreds, and tongues, and nations. And all that dwell upon the earth shall worship him, whose names are not written in the book of life of the Lamb slain from the foundation of the world. Revelation 13:6-8. *See also,* Revelation 13:1, 17:3; Daniel 7:20, 25; 11:26, 37.

Protestant Christians could never submit to the antichrist and the pope would never permit anything less than blind obedience. Apparently, those who are signing as representatives of Protestants have betrayed their heritage and have entered into a compact with the antichrist. The Catholic signers have not betrayed anything, because as we have seen, the manifesto is a clever subterfuge designed to deceive unwary Christians without compromising Catholic doctrine.

The Catholic Church will never compromise on any doctrine, because that organization believes itself to be infallible. The Roman Catholic Church claims that teaching office of the Catholic Church, which is known as the Magisterium of the Church, has **sole** authority to interpret the word of God.

> The task of giving an **authentic interpretation of the Word of God**, whether in its written form or in the form of Tradition, has been **entrusted to the living, teaching office of the church alone**. Its authority in this matter is exercised in the name of Jesus Christ. This means that the task of the interpretation has been entrusted to the bishops in communion with the successor of Peter, the bishop of Rome. *CATECHISM OF THE CATHOLIC CHURCH*, § 85 (1994) (emphasis added).

Not only does the Catholic Church claim sole authority to interpret the word of God, but claims that the Pope's interpretation is **infallible**.

> [T]his See of Saint Peter remains ever **free from all blemish of error** . . it is a dogma divinely revealed: that the Roman Pontiff, when he speaks *ex cathedra*, that is, when, in discharge of the office of pastor of all Christians, by virtue of his **supreme Apostolic authority**, he defines a doctrine regarding faith or morals to be held by the universal Church, is, by the divine assistance promised to him in Blessed Peter, possessed of that **infallibility** with which the divine Redeemer willed that His Church should be endowed in defining doctrine regarding faith or morals; and that,

therefore, such definitions of the Roman Pontiff are of themselves, and not from the consent of the church, irreformable. **But if anyone** - which may God avert! - **presume to contradict this our definition, let him be anathema**. *The Vatican Council*, Session IV, chapter IV, July 18, 1870 (emphasis added).

49 Mother of Harlots and
Abominations of the Earth

The counterfeit "Christian" signatories to the ECT and *The Gift of Salvation* manifestos have entered into an agreement with the "Mother of Harlots and Abominations of the Earth." Revelation 17:5. The Holy bible depicts the church of Jesus as a chaste bride. The bride of Christ is described as new Jerusalem. Revelation 19:7-9, 21:2. When Israel was unfaithful to God, he compared Israel to a harlot. The passage at Ezekiel 16:14-40 depicts the spiritual unfaithfulness and harlotry of Israel. That passage parallels the sins of idolatry in the Catholic Church depicted in Revelatioin 17:1-7. The Vatican and Israel are spiritually one. They are bound by a hatred for Christ and Christians.

The Roman Church in particular considers Mary not only the mother of Jesus, but also the mother of the church.[590] There is a mother mentioned in the Holy Bible, who is much like the whorish women in Ezekiel; she is the Mother of Harlots and Abominations of the Earth - the Roman Catholic Church.

And there came one of the seven angels which had the seven vials, and talked with me, saying unto me, Come hither; I will shew unto thee the judgment of the **great whore** that

sitteth upon many waters: With whom the kings of the
earth have committed fornication, and the inhabitants of the
earth have been made drunk with the wine of her
fornication. So he carried me away in the spirit into the
wilderness: and I saw a woman sit upon a scarlet coloured
beast, full of names of blasphemy, having seven heads and
ten horns. And the woman was **arrayed in purple and
scarlet colour, and decked with gold and precious stones
and pearls**, having a golden cup in her hand full of
abominations and filthiness of her fornication: And upon
her forehead *was* a name written, **MYSTERY, BABYLON
THE GREAT, THE MOTHER OF HARLOTS AND
ABOMINATIONS OF THE EARTH**. And I saw the
woman drunken with the blood of the saints, and with the
blood of the martyrs of Jesus: and when I saw her, I
wondered with great admiration. And the angel said unto
me, Wherefore didst thou marvel? (Revelation 17:1-7 AV)

God reveals that Babylon the Great is "drunken with the blood of
the saints, and with the blood of the martyrs of Jesus" (Revelation
17:6) It is clear that this city is a powerful enemy of God. Many have
debated the identity of the great harlot. God, however, reveals the
mystery of the woman. First, God identifies the woman as a great
city. "And the woman which thou sawest is that great city, which
reigneth over the kings of the earth." (Revelation 17:18 AV)

God also identifies the great harlot as sitting on seven mountains.
A mountain is simply a large mass of earth that rises above the
common or adjacent land. It does not have to be of any definite
altitude. Mountain accurately describes a large hill.[591] There is only
one city that can meet the description of a city on seven mountains,
Rome. Rome is famous for the seven mountains upon which it sits.
The mountains are the Capitoline, the Quirinal, the Viminal, the
Esquiline, the Caelian, the Avenue, and the Palatine.[592] The Catholic
Encyclopedia states that **"[i]t is within Rome, called the city of
seven hills, that the entire Vatican State is now confined."**[593]

I will tell thee the mystery of the woman, and of the beast

that carrieth her, which hath the seven heads and ten horns.
The beast that thou sawest was, and is not; and shall ascend
out of the bottomless pit, and go into perdition: and they that
dwell on the earth shall wonder, whose names were not
written in the book of life from the foundation of the world,
when they behold the beast that was, and is not, and yet is.
And here *is* the mind which hath wisdom. **The seven heads
are seven mountains, on which the woman sitteth**.
(Revelation 17:7-9 AV)

So we know that the mystery harlot is a great city that sits on
seven mountains. Rome is famous for the seven mountains upon
which it sits, and the mountains are so prominent that each of them is
named.[594] The fact is indisputable, and it is confirmed by the Catholic
Encyclopedia.[595]

The glorification of the queen of heaven is in a sense a
glorification by proxy of the Roman Catholic Church. That is why the
Catholic hierarchy refers to their organization as "Mother Church."[596]
It is true that the Catholic Church is a mother, **"THE MOTHER OF
HARLOTS AND ABOMINATIONS OF THE EARTH."**
(Revelation 17:4-5 AV) That mother of harlots "saith in her heart, I
sit a **queen**." Revelation 18:7.

There is a spiritual parallel between the wicked harlot queen in
the book of Revelation and Mary the queen of heaven glorified by the
Catholic Church. The harlot of Revelation and Mary the queen of
heaven both draw men from Jesus Christ, who "is the blessed and
only Potentate, the Lord of lords and King of kings." 1 Timothy 6:15.

The passages above accurately represents the Roman Catholic
Church. She is a whore, even as is her spiritual sister in witchcraft,
Israel. God refers to the Catholic Church as the mother of harlots.
Notice in Revelation 17:4 the colors of the Catholic hierarchy (purple
and scarlet) are described as arraying the great whore. God in his
Holy word has described the Roman Catholic church not as a chaste
bride but as an imperious whore. God commands that his chosen
people come out of the church of the great whore. *See* Revelation

18:4. Just as God judged Israel for its unfaithfulness, God will also Judge the Catholic Church for its antichrist doctrines. The following passages tells the end of that great harlot, the Roman Catholic Church.

And the woman which thou sawest is that **great city**, which reigneth over the kings of the earth. And after these things I saw another angel come down from heaven, having great power; and the earth was lightened with his glory. And he cried mightily with a strong voice, saying, **Babylon the great is fallen, is fallen, and is become the habitation of devils, and the hold of every foul spirit, and a cage of every unclean and hateful bird**. For all nations have drunk of the wine of the wrath of her fornication, and the kings of the earth have committed fornication with her, and the merchants of the earth are waxed rich through the abundance of her delicacies. And I heard another voice from heaven, saying, Come out of her, my people, that ye be not partakers of her sins, and that ye receive not of her plagues. For her sins have reached unto heaven, and God hath remembered her iniquities. **Reward her even as she rewarded you, and double unto her double according to her works: in the cup which she hath filled fill to her double**. How much she hath glorified herself, and lived deliciously, so much torment and sorrow give her: for she saith in her heart, I sit a queen, and am no widow, and shall see no sorrow. Therefore shall her plagues come in one day, death, and mourning, and famine; and she shall be utterly burned with fire: for strong *is* the Lord God who judgeth her. And the kings of the earth, who have committed fornication and lived deliciously with her, shall bewail her, and lament for her, when they shall see the smoke of her burning, Standing afar off for the fear of her torment, saying, Alas, alas, that great city Babylon, that mighty city! for in one hour is thy judgment come. And the merchants of the earth shall weep and mourn over her; for no man buyeth their merchandise any more: The merchandise of gold, and silver, and precious stones, and of pearls, and fine linen, and purple, and silk, and scarlet, and all thyine wood, and all manner vessels of ivory, and all manner vessels of most precious wood, and of brass, and iron, and marble, And cinnamon, and odours, and ointments, and frankincense, and wine, and oil, and fine flour, and wheat, and beasts, and sheep, and horses, and chariots, and slaves, and souls of men. And the fruits that thy soul lusted after are departed from thee, and all things which were dainty and goodly are departed from thee, and thou shalt find them no more at all. The merchants of these things, which were made rich by her, shall stand afar off for the fear of her torment, weeping and wailing, And saying, Alas, alas, **that great city, that was clothed in fine linen, and purple, and scarlet, and decked with gold, and precious stones, and pearls! For in one hour so great riches is come to nought**. And every shipmaster, and all the company in ships, and sailors, and as many as trade by sea, stood afar off, And cried when they saw the smoke of her burning, saying, What *city is* like unto this great city! And they cast dust on their heads, and cried, weeping and wailing, saying, Alas, alas, that great city, wherein were made rich all that had ships in the sea by reason of her costliness! for in one hour is she made desolate. Rejoice over her, *thou* heaven, and *ye* holy apostles and prophets; for God hath avenged you on her. And a mighty angel took up a stone like a great millstone, and cast *it* into the sea, saying, Thus with violence shall that great city Babylon be thrown down, and shall be found no more at all. And the voice of harpers, and musicians, and of pipers, and trumpeters, shall be heard no more at all in thee; and no craftsman, of whatsoever craft *he be*, shall be found any more in thee; and the sound of a millstone shall be heard no more at all in thee; **And the light of a candle shall shine no more at all in thee; and the voice of the bridegroom and of the bride shall be heard no more at all in thee: for thy merchants were the great men of the earth; for by thy sorceries were all nations deceived**. And in her was found the blood of prophets, and of saints, and of all that were slain upon the earth. And after these things I heard a great voice of much

people in heaven, saying, Alleluia; Salvation, and glory, and
honour, and power, unto the Lord our God: For true and
righteous *are* his judgments: for he hath judged the great
whore, which did corrupt the earth with her fornication, and
hath avenged the blood of his servants at her hand. And
again they said, Alleluia. And her smoke arose up for ever
and ever. And the four and twenty elders and the four
beasts fell down and worshipped God that sat on the throne,
saying, Amen; Alleluia.   And a voice came out of the
throne, saying, Praise our God, all ye his servants, and ye
that fear him, both small and great. And I heard as it were
the voice of a great multitude, and as the voice of many
waters, and as the voice of mighty thunderings, saying,
Alleluia: for the Lord God omnipotent reigneth. (Revelation
17:18-20:6 AV)

The signatories of the ECT and *The Gift of Salvation* manifestos,
recommend that parishioners stay in the Catholic Church. God, on the
other hand, commands his elect to come out of that great harlot
church.

And I heard another voice from heaven, saying, **Come out
of her, my people, that ye be not partakers of her sins,
and that ye receive not of her plagues**. For her sins have
reached unto heaven, and God hath remembered her
iniquities. Reward her even as she rewarded you, and
double unto her double according to her works: in the cup
which she hath filled fill to her double. How much she hath
glorified herself, and lived deliciously, so much torment and
sorrow give her: for she saith in her heart, I sit a queen, and
am no widow, and shall see no sorrow. Therefore shall her
plagues come in one day, death, and mourning, and famine;
and she shall be utterly burned with fire: for strong *is* the
Lord God who judgeth her. (Revelation 18:4-8 AV)

Endnotes

1.Online Etymology Dictionary, http://www.etymonline.com/index.php?term=anti- (web address current as of December 27, 2005).

2.Noah Webster, THE AMERICAN DICTIONARY OF THE ENGLISH LANGUAGE (1828).

3.MICHAEL BUNKER, SWARMS OF LOCUSTS, *The Jesuit Attack on the Faith,* pg. 26 (2002).

4.MICHAEL BUNKER, SWARMS OF LOCUSTS, *The Jesuit Attack on the Faith,* pg. 26 (2002).

5.MICHAEL BUNKER, SWARMS OF LOCUSTS, *The Jesuit Attack on the Faith,* pg. 26 (2002).

6.MICHAEL BUNKER, SWARMS OF LOCUSTS, *The Jesuit Attack on the Faith,* pg. 30 (2002).

7.MICHAEL BUNKER, SWARMS OF LOCUSTS, *The Jesuit Attack on the Faith,* pg. 44 (2002).

8.Michael Bunker, *The Ultimate Conspiracy - Dave Hunt and the Jesuit Attempt to Hijack the Christian Faith,* http://www.swrb.com/newslett/actualNLs/dave-hunt-jes uits.htm (last visited on October 23, 2011).

9.Michael Bunker, *The Ultimate Conspiracy - Dave Hunt and the Jesuit Attempt to Hijack the Christian Faith,* http://www.swrb.com/newslett/actualNLs/dave-hunt-jes uits.htm (last visited on October 23, 2011).

10.John MacArthur's Misrepresentation of Arminianism, Countering the Rise of Calvinism,

April 1, 2011,
http://counteringcalvinism.wordpress.com/2011/04/01/jo
hn-macarthurs-misrepresentation-of-arminianism/.

11.MICHAEL BUNKER, SWARMS OF LOCUSTS,
The Jesuit Attack on the Faith, pg. 42-52 (2002).

12.MICHAEL BUNKER, SWARMS OF LOCUSTS,
The Jesuit Attack on the Faith, pg. 47 (2002).

13.Augustus Toplady, Aminianism,
http://www.apuritansmind.com/Arminianism/AugustusT
oplady%20Arminianism.htm (web address current as of
September 18, 2005).

14.Augustus Toplady, Aminianism,
http://www.apuritansmind.com/Arminianism/AugustusT
oplady%20Arminianism.htm (web address current as of
September 18, 2005).

15.Augustus Toplady, Aminianism,
http://www.apuritansmind.com/Arminianism/AugustusT
oplady%20Arminianism.htm (web address current as of
September 18, 2005).

16.Augustus Toplady, Aminianism,
http://www.apuritansmind.com/Arminianism/AugustusT
oplady%20Arminianism.htm (web address current as of
September 18, 2005).

17.Arminius, in Oper. P.115. Ludg. 1629. (See book for
Latin.).

18.Augustus Toplady, *Arminianism: The Road to
Rome!,*
http://www.swrb.com/newslett/actualNLs/RHNarmin.ht
m (last visited on October 23, 2011).

19.Dennis Bratcher, *The Five Articles of the Remonstrants (1610)*, http://www.crivoice.org/creedremonstrants.html (last visited on October 13, 2011).

20.Dennis Bratcher, *The Canons of Dordt (1618-1619)*, http://www.crivoice.org/creeddordt.html (last visited on October 13, 2011).

21.Dennis Bratcher, *"TULIP" Calvinism Compared to Wesleyan Perspectives*, http://www.crivoice.org/tulip.html (last visited on October 13, 2011).

22.Paul Enns, MOODY HANDBOOK OF THEOLOGY, Moody Bible Institute, Moody Press, at 489 (1989).

23.Paul Enns, MOODY HANDBOOK OF THEOLOGY, Moody Bible Institute, Moody Press, at 628 (1989).

24.John Calvin, *Concerning the Eternal Predestination of God*, 148 (1552), quoted at Controversial Calvinism, http://controversialcalvinism.blogspot.com/2008/09/john-calvin-on-1john-22-kendall-of.html (last visited on October 7, 2011).

25.John Calvin, *Sermon CXVI on the Book of Job* (31:29-32), quoted by Marc D. Carpenter in *Why We No Longer Call Ourselves "Reformed" or "Calvinists"*, Outside the Camp, Volume 6, Number 2 - May 2002, http://www.outsidethecamp.org/norefcal.htm (last visited on October 7, 2011).

26.John Calvin, *Commentary on Romans 5:18*, quoted by Marc D. Carpenter in *Why We No Longer Call Ourselves "Reformed" or "Calvinists"*, Outside the Camp, Volume 6, Number 2 - May 2002, http://www.outsidethecamp.org/norefcal.htm (last visited on October 7, 2011).

27.Brother Cloud, I Have a Question, Way of Life Literature, http://www.wayoflife.org/wayoflife/questions.html (last visited on November 11, 2011).

28.David Cloud, *The Calvinism Debate*, Fundamental Baptist Information Service, January 27, 2009, http://www.wayoflife.org/database/calvinismdebate.html .

29.David Cloud, *The Calvinism Debate*, Fundamental Baptist Information Service, January 27, 2009, http://www.wayoflife.org/database/calvinismdebate.html .

30.David Cloud, *The Calvinism Debate*, Fundamental Baptist Information Service, January 27, 2009, http://www.wayoflife.org/database/calvinismdebate.html .

31.Five Point Calvinism, The Position of Fundamental Baptist World-Wide Mission, http://www.biblebelievers.net/calvinism/kjcalvn1.htm (last visited on October 5, 2011).

32.Five Point Calvinism, The Position of Fundamental Baptist World-Wide Mission, http://www.biblebelievers.net/calvinism/kjcalvn1.htm (last visited on October 5, 2011).

33.Five Point Calvinism, The Position of Fundamental Baptist World-Wide Mission, http://www.biblebelievers.net/calvinism/kjcalvn1.htm (last visited on October 5, 2011).

34.Michael Bunker, *The Ultimate Conspiracy - Dave Hunt and the Jesuit Attempt to Hijack the Christian Faith*, http://www.swrb.com/newslett/actualNLs/dave-hunt-jes

uits.htm (last visited on October 4, 2011).

35.Michael Bunker, *The Ultimate Conspiracy - Dave Hunt and the Jesuit Attempt to Hijack the Christian Faith*, http://www.swrb.com/newslett/actualNLs/dave-hunt-jes uits.htm (last visited on October 4, 2011).

36.Keith Drury, *The Triumph of Arminianism (and its dangers)*, http://www.crivoice.org/arminianism.html (last visited on October 13, 2011).

37.Professor Arthur Noble, The Jesuit Oath Exposed, http://www.ianpaisley.org/article.asp?ArtKey=jesuit (web address current as of November 14, 2005).

38.Professor Arthur Noble, The Jesuit Oath Exposed, http://www.ianpaisley.org/article.asp?ArtKey=jesuit (web address current as of November 14, 2005).

39.Professor Arthur Noble, The Jesuit Oath Exposed, http://www.ianpaisley.org/article.asp?ArtKey=jesuit (web address current as of November 14, 2005).

40.COLLIER'S ENCYCLOPEDIA, vol. 13, p. 550 (1991).

41.*Id.*

42.*Id. See also,* EDMOND PARIS, THE SECRET HISTORY OF THE JESUITS, p. 39 (1975).

43.COLLIER'S ENCYCLOPEDIA, volume 13, p. 550 (1991).

44.Anglicanism, http://www.newadvent.org/cathen/01498a.htm (web address current as of September 18, 2005).

45.PAUL ENNS, THE MOODY HANDBOOK OF THEOLOGY, p. 494, 496 (1989).

46.Mark Herzer, *Arminianism Exposed*, http://www.the-highway.com/Arminianism_Exposed2.ht ml (last visited on October 25, 2011), citing K. Jones, Theology of Holiness and Love, 215.

47.Mark Herzer, *Arminianism Exposed*, http://www.the-highway.com/Arminianism_Exposed2.ht ml (last visited on October 25, 2011).

48.John Miley, *Systematic Theology*, reprint ed. (New York: Hunt & Eaton, 1893) II:246, quoted by Mark Herzer, *Arminianism Exposed*, http://www.the-highway.com/Arminianism_Exposed2.ht ml (last visited on November 2, 2011).

49.Arminius, *Complete Works of Arminius*, Vol. 2, Letter to the Reader, 'Certain Articles to be Diligently Examined and Weighed', (On Faith), quoted in John MacArthur's Misrepresentation of Arminianism, Countering the Rise of Calvinism, April 1, 2011, http://counteringcalvinism.wordpress.com/2011/04/01/jo hn-macarthurs-misrepresentation-of-arminianism/.

50.The Constitution Of The North American General Conference, Paragraph 8, Man's Choice, http://www.bible.ca/cr-wesleyan.htm#choice (web address current as of September 19, 2005).

51.Ernest Reisinger, God's Will, Man's Will, and Free Will, http://www.founders.org/FJ25/article2.html (web address current as of September 11, 2005).

52.Nick Bibile, God's Grace or the Free Will of Man, http://www.sounddoctrine.net/Nick/freewill.htm (last visited on September 15, 2011).

53.The Outreach 100, The 100 Largest and Fastest Growing Churches in America, 2008, http://www.sermoncentral.com/articleb.asp?article=Top-100-Largest-Churches.

54.Jack Graham Biography, http://www.prestonwood.org/dallas/who-we-are/meet-our-leadership/pastor/jack-graham-biography/ (last visited on October 17, 2011).

55.Tom Ascol, Jack Graham on "The Truth about Grace," Pt. 2, August 31, 2005, Founders Ministry Blog, http://www.founders.org/blog/2005/08/jack-graham-on-truth-about-grace-pt-2.html.

56.John Hendryx, *A Short Response to the Arminian Doctrine of Prevenient Grace*, http://www.monergism.com/thethreshold/articles/onsite/prevenient.html (last visited on October 19, 2011).

57.Tom Gender, *The Narrow Road: How Does God Save Sinners?*, at 109 (2010).

58.Brother Cloud, I Have a Question, Way of Life Literature, http://www.wayoflife.org/wayoflife/questions.html (last visited on November 11, 2011).

59.What Is Way of Life Literature?, http://www.wayoflife.org/wayoflife/whatiswayoflife.html (last visited on November 11, 2011).

60.What Is Way of Life Literature?, http://www.wayoflife.org/wayoflife/whatiswayoflife.html (last visited on November 11, 2011).

61.What Is Way of Life Literature?, http://www.wayoflife.org/wayoflife/whatiswayoflife.html (last visited on November 11, 2011).

62.David Cloud, *The Calvinism Debate*, Fundamental Baptist Information Service, January 27, 2009, http://www.wayoflife.org/database/calvinismdebate.html .

63.David Cloud, *The Calvinism Debate*, Fundamental Baptist Information Service, January 27, 2009, http://www.wayoflife.org/database/calvinismdebate.html .

64.John G. Mitchell, An Everlasting Love, at pp. 134-135 (1982).

65.What Is Way of Life Literature?, http://www.wayoflife.org/wayoflife/whatiswayoflife.html (last visited on November 11, 2011).

66.Dan Corner, Charles Spurgeon's *Defense of Calvinism*: Examined and Refuted With Scripture, http://www.evangelicaloutreach.org/spurgeon.htm (web address current as of September 17, 2005).

67.Dan Corner, Charles Spurgeon's *Defense of Calvinism*: Examined and Refuted With Scripture, http://www.evangelicaloutreach.org/spurgeon.htm (last visited on November 8, 2011).

68.Jack Graham Biography, http://www.prestonwood.org/dallas/who-we-are/meet-our-leadership/pastor/jack-graham-biography/ (last visited on October 17, 2011).

69.Tom Ascol, Jack Graham on "The Truth about Grace," Pt. 1, August 1, 2005, Founders Ministry Blog, http://www.founders.org/blog/2005/08/jack-graham-on-truth-about-grace-pt-1.html.

70.Tom Ascol, Jack Graham on "The Truth about Grace," Pt. 1, August 1, 2005, Founders Ministry Blog,

http://www.founders.org/blog/2005/08/jack-graham-on-t
ruth-about-grace-pt-1.html.

71.David Cloud, *The Calvinism Debate, Who is the
Enemy?*, Way of Life Literature,
http://www.wayoflife.org/fbns/calvinismdebate.html
(web page current as of January 8, 2004).

72.David Cloud, *The Calvinism Debate, Who is the
Enemy?*, Way of Life Literature,
http://www.wayoflife.org/fbns/calvinismdebate.html
(web page current as of January 8, 2004).

73.David Cloud, *The Calvinism Debate, Who is the
Enemy?*, Way of Life Literature,
http://www.wayoflife.org/fbns/calvinismdebate.html
(web page current as of January 8, 2004).

74.John Hendryx, *A Short Response to the Arminian
Doctrine of Prevenient Grace*,
http://www.monergism.com/thethreshold/articles/onsite/
prevenient.html (last visited on October 19, 2011).

75.Kevin T. Bauder, The Electrum, The Electrum, 18
February 2011,
http://centralseminary.edu/resources/nick-of-time/305-th
e-electrum.

76.Kenneth Talbot, Gary W. Crampton, D. James
Kennedy, *Calvinism, Hyper-calvinism, & Arminianism:
A Workbook*, at 38 (2007).

77.Dave Hunt, What Love is This?, at 211, quoted in
Dave Hunt A False Berean,
http://www.atruechurch.info/davehunt.html (last visited
on November 24, 2011).

78.David Bennett, Romans 8:29-30, May 30, 2011,
http://www.freewill-predestination.com/files/Romans8.p

543

df.

79.David Bennett, Romans 8:29-30, May 30, 2011,
http://www.freewill-predestination.com/files/Romans8.p
df.

80.John Wesley, On Predestination, Sermon 58,
http://new.gbgm-umc.org/umhistory/wesley/sermons/58/
(last visited on November 24, 2011).

81.John Wesley, On Predestination, Sermon 58,
http://new.gbgm-umc.org/umhistory/wesley/sermons/58/
(last visited on November 24, 2011).

82.B.J. Oropeza, Some Great Comments on Corporate
Election, Apostasy/Perseverance, and Rom 8:28-39,
http://evangelicalarminians.org/Perseverance-Oropeza-o
n-Romans-8.28-39 (last visited on November 23, 2011).

83.Andrew Telford, Subjects of Sovereignty,
Predestination (Refutation of Five Point Calvinism),
http://www.biblebelievers.net/calvinism/kjcprede.htm
(last visited on November 23, 2011).

84.Andrew Telford, Subjects of Sovereignty,
Predestination (Refutation of Five Point Calvinism),
http://www.biblebelievers.net/calvinism/kjcprede.htm
(last visited on November 23, 2011).

85.Brian Schwertley, *An Examination of the Five Points
of Calvinism - Part II: Unconditional Election*,
http://www.monergism.com/thethreshold/articles/onsite/
schwerley_election.html (last visited on October 14,
2011).

86.Brian Schwertley, *An Examination of the Five Points
of Calvinism - Part II: Unconditional Election*,
http://www.monergism.com/thethreshold/articles/onsite/

schwerley_election.html (last visited on October 14, 2011).

87.Micael Horton, Evangelical Arminians, Option or Oxymoron?, November 28, 2011, http://www.reformationonline.com/arminians.htm.

88.John Murray, The Epistle to the Romans, Vol. I, pp. 316-318, quoted by David N. Steele and Curtis C. Thomas, The Meaning of "FOREKNEW" in Romans 8:29, http://www.monergism.com/thethreshold/articles/onsite/foreknew.html (last visited on November 26, 2011).

89.Brian Schwertley, *An Examination of the Five Points of Calvinism - Part II: Unconditional Election*, http://www.monergism.com/thethreshold/articles/onsite/schwerley_election.html (last visited on October 14, 2011).

90.Society of Evangelical Arminians, http://evangelicalarminians.org/ (last visited on November 28, 2011).

91.Micael Horton, Evangelical Arminians, Option or Oxymoron?, November 28, 2011, http://www.reformationonline.com/arminians.htm.

92.Franklin Graham, *Expect Suffering, But Not Forever*, April 27, 2011, Billy Graham Evangelistic Association, http://www.billygraham.org/articlepage.asp?articleid=1162.

93.David J. Stewart, *Was Spurgeon a Calvinist?*, http://www.jesus-is-savior.com/False%20Doctrines/Calvinism/spurgeon.htm (last visited on November 8, 2011).

94. David J. Stewart, *Was Spurgeon a Calvinist?*, http://www.jesus-is-savior.com/False%20Doctrines/Cal vinism/spurgeon.htm (last visited on November 8, 2011).

95. D.A. Waite, *Calvin's Error of Limited Atonement*, http://www.biblebelievers.net/calvinism/kjcalvn4.htm#T erms_John112 (last visited on November 8, 2011).

96. D.A. Waite, *Calvin's Error of Limited Atonement*, http://www.biblebelievers.net/calvinism/kjcalvn4.htm#T erms_John112 (last visited on November 8, 2011).

97. D.A. Waite, *Calvin's Error of Limited Atonement*, http://www.biblebelievers.net/calvinism/kjcalvn4.htm#T erms_John112 (last visited on November 8, 2011).

98. COUNCIL OF TRENT, SESSION VI, DECREE ON JUSTIFICATION, Canon XVII, January 13, 1547.

99. E.g., Kevin Jackson, How Revelation 3:20 Creates a Dilemma for Calvinism, September 6, 2010, http://evangelicalarminians.org/jackson.How-Revelation -3.20-Creates-a-Dilemma-for-Calvinism.

100. Michael Boling, Calvinism vs. Arminianism, http://www.scribd.com/doc/58931314/Boling-Calvinism -vs-Arminianism (last visited on December 24, 2011).

101. What Is Way of Life Literature?, http://www.wayoflife.org/wayoflife/whatiswayoflife.ht ml (last visited on November 11, 2011).

102. David Cloud, *The Calvinism Debate*, Fundamental Baptist Information Service, January 27, 2009, http://www.wayoflife.org/database/calvinismdebate.html .

103. David Cloud, *The Calvinism Debate*, Fundamental Baptist Information Service, January 27, 2009, http://www.wayoflife.org/database/calvinismdebate.html
.

104. Jim McGuiggan, *Hebrews 6 & 10 and Falling Away*, Spending Time With Jim McGuiggan, http://www.jimmcguiggan.com/reflections3.asp?status= Hebrews&id=472 (last visited on November 12, 2011).

105. E.g., Norman Geisler, Chosen But Free, A Balanced View of God's Sovereignty and Free Will, at 102, (2010), http://books.google.com/books?id=FRuvF3DukwQC&p g=PA102&lpg=PA102&dq=Matthew+23:37+geisler&s ource=bl&ots=b-dfedKgST&sig=lk6T1P7hy_Z5qeS0A2 9g6YTMaks&hl=en&ei=CmjnTu74MYTb0QGrvJ2bCg &sa=X&oi=book_result&ct=result&resnum=1&ved=0C B8Q6AEwADgK#v=onepage&q&f=false.

106. E.g., Norman Geisler, Chosen But Free, A Balanced View of God's Sovereignty and Free Will, at 103, (2010), http://books.google.com/books?id=FRuvF3DukwQC&p g=PA102&lpg=PA102&dq=Matthew+23:37+geisler&s ource=bl&ots=b-dfedKgST&sig=lk6T1P7hy_Z5qeS0A2 9g6YTMaks&hl=en&ei=CmjnTu74MYTb0QGrvJ2bCg &sa=X&oi=book_result&ct=result&resnum=1&ved=0C B8Q6AEwADgK#v=onepage&q&f=false.

107. Chad Meister, God, Free Will, and Evil: A Response to E. Calvin Beisner, How Should Christians Approach the Problem of Evil, http://www.equip.org/articles/how-should-christians-app roach-the-problem-of-evil (last visited on December 9, 2011).

547

108.Chad Meister, God, Free Will, and Evil: A
Response to E. Calvin Beisner, How Should Christians
Approach the Problem of Evil,
http://www.equip.org/articles/how-should-christians-app
roach-the-problem-of-evil (last visited on December 9,
2011).

109.Richard P. Bucher, Calvinistic Theology,
http://www.orlutheran.com/html/calvinisttheology.html
(last visited on December 14, 2011).

110.John G. Reisinger, *There Are Only Two Religions in
the World*, http://www.the-highway.com/2religions.html
(last visited on October 24, 2011).

111.Zanchius, J., & Toplady, A. (1811). The Doctrine of
Absolute Predestination Stated and Asserted, Alexander
Pringle, Recommendatory Preface, at 1-2, 12. New
York: George Lindsay,
http://www.archive.org/stream/doctrineofabsolu00zanci
ala#page/n9/mode/2up.

112.Daniel Whedon on John 6:40,
http://arminian.com/daniel-whedon-on-john-640.html
(last visited on December 6, 2011).

113.Greg Johnson, *Can a Christian Lose His or Her
Salvation?*,
http://gregscouch.homestead.com/files/eternalsecurity.ht
m (last visited on October 30, 2011).

114.Gary A. Hand, JACOBUS ARMINIUS and
ARMINIANISM,
http://www.ondoctrine.com/10armini.htm (last visited
on October 30, 2011).

115.R.C. Sproul, *The Sufficiency of Grace* (excerpt from
R.C. Sproul's book, Willing to Believe),
http://www.monergism.com/thethreshold/articles/onsite/

willing.html (last visited on October 31, 2011).

116.Jim McGuiggan, *Hebrews 6 & 10 and Falling Away*, Spending Time With Jim McGuiggan, http://www.jimmcguiggan.com/reflections3.asp?status= Hebrews&id=472 (last visited on November 12, 2011).

117.Mark Herzer, *Arminianism Exposed*, http://www.the-highway.com/Arminianism_Exposed2.ht ml (last visited on October 25, 2011).

118.Mark Herzer, *Arminianism Exposed*, http://www.the-highway.com/Arminianism_Exposed2.ht ml (last visited on October 25, 2011).

119.Mark Herzer, *Arminianism Exposed*, http://www.the-highway.com/Arminianism_Exposed2.ht ml (last visited on October 25, 2011), quoting John Mark Hicks, "The Righteousness of Saving Faith: Arminian Versus Remonstrant Grace," Evangelical Journal 9.1 (1991) 34. John Hicks did his doctoral work on this very issue. See The Theology of Grace in the Though of Jacobus Arminius and Philip van Limborch: A Study in the Development of Seventeenth Century Dutch Arminianism (Ph.d. Dissertation, Westminster Theological Seminary, 1985).

120.Mark Herzer, *Arminianism Exposed*, http://www.the-highway.com/Arminianism_Exposed2.ht ml (last visited on October 25, 2011), quoting H. Orton Wiley, Christian Theology, II:454. The word he uses is 'sanctification' but that was not his criticism in the previous page. Wiley believes our theory of justification led to our denial of perfection: "Thus with their peculiar form of a substitutionary atonement, they held to a belief in the imputation to Him of our sins, and to us of His righteousness for our justification, and for our sanctification also, in so far as it applied to the cleansing from guilt" (II:453).

121.Mark Herzer, *Arminianism Exposed*, http://www.the-highway.com/Arminianism_Exposed2.ht ml (last visited on October 25, 2011), citing Wakefield, Christian Theology, 448.

122.John G. Reisinger, There Are Only Two Religions in the Whole World!, http://soundofgrace.com/jgr/index004.htm (web address current as of April 28, 2006).

123.MERRIAM WEBSTER'S COLLEGIATE DICTIONARY (10th ed.1999).

124.NOAH WEBSTER, AMERICAN DICTIONARY OF THE ENGLISH LANGUAGE (1st ed. 1828) republished by Foundation for American Christian Education, San Francisco, California. *See also,* THE RANDOM HOUSE DICTIONARY OF THE ENGLISH LANGUAGE, unabridged edition, 1973.

125.John Hendryx, Jesus Teaches that Regeneration Precedes Faith, http://www.monergism.com/thethreshold/articles/onsite/newbirth2.html (last visited on October 19, 2011).

126.Eric Landstrom, God, Evil, and Grace in Calvinist and Arminian Theology, December 1, 2010, http://evangelicalarminians.org/Landstrom.God-Evil-and-Grace-in-Calvinist-and-Arminian-Theology.

127.Chad Meister, God, Free Will, and Evil: A Response to E. Calvin Beisner, How Should Christians Approach the Problem of Evil, http://www.equip.org/articles/how-should-christians-approach-the-problem-of-evil (last visited on December 9, 2011).

128.William W. Birch, http://www.williamwbirch.com/p/about.html (last visited on February 16, 2012.

129.William W. Birch, If Calvinism Were True, The Arminian, November 2, 2011.

130.Roger E. Olson, Biography, http://www.patheos.com/blogs/rogereolson/biography-2/ (Last visited on February 16, 2012).

131.Roger E. Olson, Biography, http://www.patheos.com/blogs/rogereolson/biography-2/ (Last visited on February 16, 2012).

132.E. Calvin Beisner, General Objections to the Free Will Defense: A Response to Chad Meister, How Should Christians Approach the Problem of Evil, http://www.equip.org/articles/how-should-christians-app roach-the-problem-of-evil (last visited on December 9, 2011).

133.William W. Birch, If Calvinism Were True, The Arminian, November 2, 2011, http://thearminian.net/2011/11/02/if-calvinism-were-true /, quoting Roger E. Olson, Against Calvinism (Grand Rapids: Zondervan, 2011), 85.

134.E. Calvin Beisner, If God Exists, Why Is There Evil?, How Should Christians Approach the Problem of Evil, http://www.equip.org/articles/how-should-christians-app roach-the-problem-of-evil (last visited on December 9, 2011).

135.Christian Apologetics and Research Ministry, http://www.carm.org/open/God_know.htm (web address current as of April 23, 2006).

136.Clark Pinnock et al., The Openness of God, 121.

137.Richard Rice, 'Divine Foreknowledge and Free-Will Theism' in A Case for Arminianism, 134.

138.For example, Richard Rice, God's Foreknowledge and Man's Free Will (Minneapolis: Bethany House, 1980) 10. He does not only preclude absolute divine knowledge but he even precludes absolute divine decrees. Richard Rice says in another book that "God's will does not guarantee the outcome that he desires" (The Openness of God, 54-55).

139.Mark Herzer, *Arminianism Exposed*, http://www.the-highway.com/Arminianism_Exposed2.ht ml (last visited on October 25, 2011).

140.Frederick Sontag, 'Does Omnipotence Necessarily Entail Omniscience?' JETS 34 (Dec. 1991): 508. Sontag also seems to suggest that a fixed future might actually detract from God's creativity. Clark Pinnock parrots Sontag's notion of surprise and boredom: "We do not limit God by saying that he can be surprised by what his creatures do. It would be a serious limitation if God could not experience surprise and delight. The world would be a boring place without anything unexpected ever happening" (The Openness of God, 123).

141.J. Sanders, The God Who Risks: A Theology of Providence (Downers Grove, IL: IVP, 1998) 169.

142. Ibid., 172.

143.Mark Herzer, *Arminianism Exposed*, http://www.the-highway.com/Arminianism_Exposed2.ht ml (last visited on October 25, 2011), citing in an endnote to Sanders, The God Who Risks: A Theology of Providence (Downers Grove, IL: IVP, 1998) 11.

144.E.g., D.A. Waite, *Calvin's Error of Limited Atonement*, http://www.biblebelievers.net/calvinism/kjcalvn4.htm#T erms_John112 (last visited on November 8, 2011).

145.Tom Ascol, Jack Graham on "The Truth about Grace," Pt. 1, August 1, 2005, Founders Ministry Blog, http://www.founders.org/blog/2005/08/jack-graham-on-t ruth-about-grace-pt-1.html.

146.Tom Ascol, Jack Graham on "The Truth about Grace," Pt. 1, August 1, 2005, Founders Ministry Blog, http://www.founders.org/blog/2005/08/jack-graham-on-t ruth-about-grace-pt-1.html.

147.Tom Ascol, Jack Graham on "The Truth about Grace," Pt. 1, August 1, 2005, Founders Ministry Blog, http://www.founders.org/blog/2005/08/jack-graham-on-t ruth-about-grace-pt-1.html.

148.D.A. Waite, *Calvin's Error of Limited Atonement*, http://www.biblebelievers.net/calvinism/kjcalvn4.htm#T erms_John112 (last visited on November 8, 2011).

149.John Cheeseman, *Another Gospel*, http://www.the-highway.com/angospel_Cheeseman.html (last visited on October 19, 2011).

150.Jim Hendryx, The Unconditional Love of God, http://www.reformationtheology.com/2011/10/the_unco nditional_love_of_god.php (last visited on October 26, 2011).

151.E.g., D.A. Waite, *Calvin's Error of Limited Atonement*, http://www.biblebelievers.net/calvinism/kjcalvn4.htm#T erms_John112 (last visited on November 8, 2011).

152.D.A. Waite, *Calvin's Error of Limited Atonement*, http://www.biblebelievers.net/calvinism/kjcalvn4.htm#T erms_John112 (last visited on November 8, 2011).

153.D.A. Waite, *Calvin's Error of Limited Atonement*, http://www.biblebelievers.net/calvinism/kjcalvn4.htm#T erms_John112 (last visited on November 8, 2011).

154.Dave Hunt, What Love is This?, at 248, quoted in *Dave Hunt A False Berean*, http://www.atruechurch.info/davehunt.html (last visited on November 24, 2011).

155.D.A. Waite, *Calvin's Error of Limited Atonement*, http://www.biblebelievers.net/calvinism/kjcalvn4.htm#T erms_John112 (last visited on November 8, 2011).

156.Marc D. Carpenter, *Gospel Atonement*, Outside the Camp, Volume 7, Number 2 - May 2003, http://www.outsidethecamp.org/gospatone.htm.

157.Arminianism vs. Calvinism Controversy 3 of 5, http://www.abacus-news.co.uk/faith/08/arminianistcalvi nistdebate3.php (last visited on October 28, 2011).

158.D.A. Waite, *Calvin's Error of Limited Atonement*, http://www.biblebelievers.net/calvinism/kjcalvn4.htm#T erms_John112 (last visited on November 8, 2011).

159.Grider, J.K., "Arminianism" in *Evangelical Dictionary of Theology* [Grand Rapids: Baker Book House, 1984] 80), quoted by Mark Herzer, *Arminianism Exposed*, http://www.the-highway.com/Arminianism_Exposed2.ht ml (last visited on October 25, 2011).

160.Pope, A Compendium of Christian Theology (New York: Hunt & Eaton, n.d.) II:314, cited by Mark Herzer, *Arminianism Exposed*, http://www.the-highway.com/Arminianism Exposed2.ht ml (last visited on October 25, 2011).

161.Donald M. Lake, "He Died for All: The Universal Dimension of the Atonement" in *Grace Unlimited*, Clark H. Pinnock, ed. (Minneapolis: Bethany House Publishers, 1975) 47-48, quoted by Mark Herzer, *Arminianism Exposed*, http://www.the-highway.com/Arminianism Exposed2.ht ml (last visited on October 25, 2011).

162.Donald M. Lake, "He Died for All: The Universal Dimension of the Atonement" in *Grace Unlimited*, Clark H. Pinnock, ed. (Minneapolis: Bethany House Publishers, 1975) 47-48, quoted by Mark Herzer, *Arminianism Exposed*, http://www.the-highway.com/Arminianism Exposed2.ht ml (last visited on October 25, 2011).

163.Mark Herzer, *Arminianism Exposed*, http://www.the-highway.com/Arminianism Exposed2.ht ml (last visited on October 25, 2011).

164.Adam Clarke, Christian Theology (London: Thomas & Son, 1835) 156, 158, quoted by Mark Herzer, *Arminianism Exposed*, http://www.the-highway.com/Arminianism Exposed2.ht ml (last visited on November 2, 2011).

165.R. Watson, Theological Institutes, 300. This reference is also found in Berkhof's Vicarious Atonement, 135, quoted by Mark Herzer, *Arminianism Exposed*, http://www.the-highway.com/Arminianism Exposed2.ht ml (last visited on November 2, 2011).

166.A. M. Hills, Fundamental Christian Theology: A Systematic Theology (Salem, OH: Schmul Publishing

Co., 1980) II:184, quoted by Mark Herzer, *Arminianism Exposed*, http://www.the-highway.com/Arminianism_Exposed2.ht ml (last visited on November 2, 2011).

167.Pope, *A Higher Catechism of Theology*, 228, quoted by Mark Herzer, *Arminianism Exposed*, http://www.the-highway.com/Arminianism_Exposed2.ht ml (last visited on November 2, 2011).

168.Robert P. Lightner, *The Death Christ Died -A Case for Unlimited Atonement*, http://www.biblebelievers.net/calvinism/kjcalvn6.htm (last visited on November 10, 2011).

169.Samual Telloyan, *Did Christ Die For All?*, http://www.biblebelievers.net/calvinism/kjcalvn2.htm (last visited on November 10, 2011).

170.Simon Escobedo III, *2 Peter 2:1 and Universal Redemption*, http://vintage.aomin.org/2PE21.html (last visited on November 10, 2011).

171.Wayne Grudem, *Systematic Theology An Introduction to Biblical Doctrine*, (Great Britain: Inter-Varsity Press and Grand Rapids: Zondervan Publishing House, 1994), p. 600, quoted by Simon Escobedo III, *2 Peter 2:1 and Universal Redemption*, http://vintage.aomin.org/2PE21.html (last visited on November 10, 2011).

172.William W. Birch, On Faith and Repentance, November 19, 2010, citing The Arminian Confession of 1621, trans. and ed. Mark A. Ellis (Eugene, OR: Pickwick Publications, 2005), 76-78, http://thearminian.net/2010/11/19/on-faith-and-repentan ce/.

173.William W. Birch, On Faith and Repentance, November 19, 2010, citing The Arminian Confession of 1621, trans. and ed. Mark A. Ellis (Eugene, OR: Pickwick Publications, 2005), 76-78, http://thearminian.net/2010/11/19/on-faith-and-repentance/.

174.Remonstrance of 1610, Article V, http://thearminian.net/beliefs/ (last visited on November 21, 2011).

175.Micael Horton, Evangelical Arminians, Option or Oxymoron?, November 28, 2011, http://www.reformationonline.com/arminians.htm.

176.Micael Horton, Evangelical Arminians, Option or Oxymoron?, November 28, 2011, http://www.reformationonline.com/arminians.htm, quoting Dr. Clark Pinnock, A Case for Arminianism: The Grace of God and the Will of Man (Zondervan, 1989), p. 15.

177.Dan Corner, Calvinism Refuted, Refuting Calvinism from the Scriptures, http://www.evangelicaloutreach.org/calvinismrefuted.htm (last visited on November 13, 2011).

178.Dan Corner, *Backsliders*, Defense of the Christian Gospel, http://www.dancorner.org/?p=57 (last November 13, 2011).

179.CATECHISM OF THE CATHOLIC CHURCH, §§ 1030-1031 (1994).

180.Augustus Toplady, Arminianism: The Road to Rome, http://www.spurgeon.org/~phil/history/toplady.htm (last visited on December 17, 2011).

181.Doug Wilson, Wrestling With Wesley, http://www.reformed.org/webfiles/antithesis/index.html ?mainframe=/webfiles/antithesis/v2n1/ant_v2n1_Wesle y.html (last visited on December 17, 2011).

182.Doug Wilson, Wrestling With Wesley, http://www.reformed.org/webfiles/antithesis/index.html ?mainframe=/webfiles/antithesis/v2n1/ant_v2n1_Wesle y.html (last visited on December 17, 2011).

183.Doug Wilson, Wrestling With Wesley, http://www.reformed.org/webfiles/antithesis/index.html ?mainframe=/webfiles/antithesis/v2n1/ant_v2n1_Wesle y.html (last visited on December 17, 2011).

184.Doug Wilson, Wrestling With Wesley, http://www.reformed.org/webfiles/antithesis/index.html ?mainframe=/webfiles/antithesis/v2n1/ant_v2n1_Wesle y.html (last visited on December 17, 2011).

185.Zanchius, J., & Toplady, A. (1811). The Doctrine of Absolute Predestination Stated and Asserted, at 27, New York: George Lindsay, http://www.archive.org/stream/doctrineofabsolu00zanci ala#page/n9/mode/2up.

186.Doug Wilson, Wrestling With Wesley, http://www.reformed.org/webfiles/antithesis/index.html ?mainframe=/webfiles/antithesis/v2n1/ant_v2n1_Wesle y.html (last visited on December 17, 2011).

187.Augustus Toplady, A Letter To The Rev. John Wesley Relative to His Pretended Abridgment of Zanchius on Predestination, March 26, 1770, http://homepage.mac.com/shanerosenthal/reformationin k/attoptowes.htm.

188.John Wesley, The Consequence Proved, http://www.toplady.org.uk./opponent%20writings/The%

20Consequence%20Proved.htm (last visited on December 21, 2011).

189.William MacLean, John Wesley's Shameful Persecution of Toplady - Another Example of Arminian Hatred for Calvinism, http://www.sermonaudio.com/new_details3.asp?ID=133 67 (last visited on December 17, 2011).

190.Randy Alcom, Believer's Judgment of Works, February 18, 2010, http://www.epm.org/resources/2010/Feb/18/believers-ju dgment-works/.

191.Randy Alcom, Believer's Judgment of Works, February 18, 2010, http://www.epm.org/resources/2010/Feb/18/believers-ju dgment-works/.

192.John Hamel, The Judgment Seat of Christ, A Scrutinizing Investigation of Every Born Again Christian, http://www.johnhamelministries.org/judgment_seat_of_ Christ.htm (last visited on November 14, 2011).

193.Advanced Bible Studies Series volume on First Corinthians, Way of Life Literature, http://www.wayoflife.org/fbns/judgment-seat-of-christ.h tml, website last visited on September 8, 2007.

194.Kenneth Emilio, Judgment Loss for Believers?, http://www.remnantreport.com/cgi-bin/imcart/read.cgi?a rticle_id=70&sub=25 (last visited on November 17, 2011).

195.Paul Benware's Payday, Dividing All Believers Into Two Distinct Groups, http://www.middletownbiblechurch.org/doctrine/payday .htm (last visited on November 17, 2011).

196.Paul Benware's Payday, Dividing All Believers Into Two Distinct Groups, http://www.middletownbiblechurch.org/doctrine/payday .htm (last visited on November 17, 2011).

197.Paul Benware's Payday, Dividing All Believers Into Two Distinct Groups, http://www.middletownbiblechurch.org/doctrine/payday .htm (last visited on November 17, 2011).

198.Paul Benware's Payday, Dividing All Believers Into Two Distinct Groups, http://www.middletownbiblechurch.org/doctrine/payday .htm (last visited on November 17, 2011).

199.Kenneth Emilio, Judgment Loss for Believers?, http://www.remnantreport.com/cgi-bin/imcart/read.cgi?a rticle_id=70&sub=25 (last visited on November 17, 2011).

200.J. Hampton Keathley, III , Th.M., The Doctrine of Rewards: The Judgment Seat (Bema) of Christ, http://www.bible.org/page.php?page_id=407, website visited on September 8, 2007.

201.J. Hampton Keathley, III , Th.M., The Doctrine of Rewards: The Judgment Seat (Bema) of Christ, http://www.bible.org/page.php?page_id=407, website visited on September 8, 2007.

202.J. Hampton Keathley, III , Th.M., The Doctrine of Rewards: The Judgment Seat (Bema) of Christ, http://www.bible.org/page.php?page_id=407, website visited on September 8, 2007.

203.John MacArthur, *Believer's Rewards*, Grace to You, July 29, 1973, http://www.gty.org/resources/sermons/1327/Believers-R ewards.

204.CATECHISM OF THE CATHOLIC CHURCH, §§
1030-1031 (1994).

205.Robert Sumner, A Protestant Purgatory!, The
Rod--Will God Spare It?, An Extended Review of a
Book by J. D. Faust,
http://www.middletownbiblechurch.org/doctrine/faustrs.
htm (last visited on November 15, 2011).

206.Robert Sumner, A Protestant Purgatory!, The
Rod--Will God Spare It?, An Extended Review of a
Book by J. D. Faust,
http://www.middletownbiblechurch.org/doctrine/faustrs.
htm (last visited on November 15, 2011), quoting J.D.
Faust, *THE ROD: WILL GOD SPARE IT?.*

207.Dr. Douglas D. Stauffer, About the Author,
http://www.biblebelievers.com/stauffer/about_author.ht
ml (last visited on November 15, 2011).

208.Douglas D. Stauffer, Judgment Seat of Christ, Key
of Knowledge Ministries,
http://www.biblebelievers.com/stauffer/stauffer_judgme
nt-seat.html# (last visited on November 15, 2011).

209.Randy Alcom, Believer's Judgment of Works,
February 18, 2010,
http://www.epm.org/resources/2010/Feb/18/believers-ju
dgment-works/.

210.Randy Alcom, Believer's Judgment of Works,
February 18, 2010,
http://www.epm.org/resources/2010/Feb/18/believers-ju
dgment-works/.

211.Robert Sumner, A Protestant Purgatory!, The
Rod--Will God Spare It?, An Extended Review of a
Book by J. D. Faust,
http://www.middletownbiblechurch.org/doctrine/faustrs.

htm (last visited on November 15, 2011), quoting J.D. Faust, *THE ROD: WILL GOD SPARE IT?*.

212. J. Hampton Keathley, III , Th.M., The Doctrine of Rewards: The Judgment Seat (Bema) of Christ, http://www.bible.org/page.php?page_id=407, website visited on September 8, 2007.

213. J. Hampton Keathley, III , Th.M., The Doctrine of Rewards: The Judgment Seat (Bema) of Christ, http://www.bible.org/page.php?page_id=407, website visited on September 8, 2007.

214. J. Hampton Keathley, III , Th.M., The Doctrine of Rewards: The Judgment Seat (Bema) of Christ, http://www.bible.org/page.php?page_id=407, website visited on September 8, 2007.

215. J. Hampton Keathley, III , Th.M., The Doctrine of Rewards: The Judgment Seat (Bema) of Christ, http://www.bible.org/page.php?page_id=407, website visited on September 8, 2007.

216. J. Hampton Keathley, III , Th.M., The Doctrine of Rewards: The Judgment Seat (Bema) of Christ, http://www.bible.org/page.php?page_id=407, website visited on September 8, 2007.

217. H.A. Ironside, The Judgment-Seat of Christ, http://www.wholesomewords.org/etexts/ironside/care4.html (last December 26, 2011).

218. Lee Roberson, Some Golden Daybreak (1957), http://www.jesus-is-savior.com/Books,%20Tracts%20&%20Preaching/Printed%20Books/Golden/sgdb-chap_02.htm.

219. James Melton, Judgment Seat of Christ, http://www.av1611.org/jmelton/Judgment.html (last

visited on December 26, 2011).

220.Douglas Stauffer, Judgment Seat of Christ, http://www.biblebelievers.com/stauffer/stauffer_judgme nt-seat.html (last visited on December 26, 2011).

221.Douglas Stauffer, Judgment Seat of Christ, http://www.biblebelievers.com/stauffer/stauffer_judgme nt-seat.html (last visited on December 26, 2011).

222.Douglas Stauffer, Judgment Seat of Christ, http://www.biblebelievers.com/stauffer/stauffer_judgme nt-seat.html (last visited on December 26, 2011).

223.Chuck Smith, CALVINISM, ARMINIANISM & THE WORD OF GOD A CALVARY CHAPEL PERSPECTIVE, http://www.calvarychapel.com/library/smith-chuck/book s/caatwog.htm (web address current as of September 21, 2005).

224.Chuck Smith, CALVINISM, ARMINIANISM & THE WORD OF GOD A CALVARY CHAPEL PERSPECTIVE, http://www.calvarychapel.com/library/smith-chuck/book s/caatwog.htm (web address current as of September 21, 2005).

225.Chuck Smith, CALVINISM, ARMINIANISM & THE WORD OF GOD A CALVARY CHAPEL PERSPECTIVE, http://www.calvarychapel.com/library/smith-chuck/book s/caatwog.htm (web address current as of September 21, 2005).

226.Chuck Smith, Calvary Chapel Distinctives, http://www.calvarychapel.com/redbarn/ccd11.htm (web address current as of Septermber 24, 2005).

227.Brian Brodersen, Assistant Pastor, Calvary Chapel, Costa Mesa, Ephesians 4, http://www.calvarychapel.com/library/brodersen-brian/studies-books/49-EPH-2002/49-EPH-004-001-text.htm (web address current as of September 24, 2005).

228.Chuck Smith, Calvary Chapel Distinctives, http://www.calvarychapel.com/redbarn/ccd11.htm (web address current as of Septermber 24, 2005).

229.Chuck Smith, Calvary Chapel Distinctives, http://www.calvarychapel.com/redbarn/ccd11.htm (web address current as of Septermber 24, 2005).

230.Luisa Kroll, Megachurches, Megabusinesses, Forbes, September 17, 2003.

231.Luisa Kroll, Megachurches, Megabusinesses, Forbes, September 17, 2003.

232.Rick Meisel, Chuck Smith, General Teachings/Activities, *Biblical Discernment Ministries*, January 2002, http://www.rapidnet.com/~jbeard/bdm/exposes/smith/general.htm (web address current as of September 24, 2005), quoting Chuck Smith, Answers for Today, p. 157 (1993).

233.Luisa Kroll, Megachurches, Megabusinesses, Forbes, September 17, 2003.

234.Rick Meisel, Calvary Chapel Movement, Biblical Doctrine or Charismatic and Ecumenical?, *Biblical Discernment Ministries*, January 2002, http://www.rapidnet.com/~jbeard/bdm/Psychology/calvary/chapel.htm (web address current as of September 24, 2005).

235.Rick Meisel, Chuck Smith, General Teachings/Activities, *Biblical Discernment Ministries*, January 2002, http://www.rapidnet.com/~jbeard/bdm/exposes/smith/ge neral.htm (web address current as of September 24, 2005), quoting Chuck Smith, Answers for Today, p. 157 (1993).

236.Smithfield, Song that Died Away, http://www.calvarychapelmusic.org/Products/songthatdi edaway.html (web address current as of October 10, 2005).

237.Calvary Chapel Music, http://www.calvarychapelmusic.org/links.html (web address current as of October 10, 2005).

238.The Surfaris, http://www.thesurfaris.com/Home.html (web address current as of October 10, 2005).

239.Worship Life, Anchored Deep, http://www.calvarychapelmusic.org/anchoreddeep.html (web address current as of October 12. 2005).

240.DAVID NOEBEL, THE MARXIST MINSTRELS.

241.Terry Watkins, Christian Rock, Blessing or Blasphemy, http://www.av1611.org/crock.html (web address current as of October 8, 2005).

242.Michael Talks to Oprah - 10 February 1993, http://www.mjshouse.com/stories/oprah.html (web address current as of October 12, 2005).

243.Santos: Deep and Rich, http://www.calvarychapelmusic.org/deepandrich.html (web address current as of October 10, 2005).

244.Santos: Deep and Rich,
http://www.calvarychapelmusic.org/deepandrich.html
(web address current as of October 10, 2005).

245.Judas Priest,
http://www.judaspriest.com/disc/default.asp (web
address current as of October 11, 2005).

246.Terry Watkins, It's Only Rock and Roll . . . But it
Kills,
http://72.14.207.104/search?q=cache:4IOXertGmYAJ:w
ww.av1611.org/rockm.html+site:www.av1611.org+juda
s+priest&hl=en (web address current as of October 10,
2005).

247.Testimony of John Todd,
http://www.av1611.org/crock.html (web address current
as of 9-26-05).

248.John Todd: Dividing the Brethren,
http://www.holysmoke.org/jtc-cri.txt (web address
current as of October 13, 2005).

249.John Todd: Dividing the Brethren,
http://www.holysmoke.org/jtc-cri.txt (web address
current as of October 13, 2005).

250.John Todd: Dividing the Brethren,
http://www.holysmoke.org/jtc-cri.txt (web address
current as of October 13, 2005).

251.John Todd: Dividing the Brethren,
http://www.holysmoke.org/jtc-cri.txt (web address
current as of October 13, 2005).

252.David de Sabatino, History of the Jesus Movement,
http://www.ottawainnercityministries.ca/newsArticlesSt
ats/Jesus_Movement.htm (web address current as of
October 14, 2005).

253.John Todd: Dividing the Brethren, http://www.holysmoke.org/jtc-cri.txt (web address current as of October 13, 2005).

254.John Todd: Dividing the Brethren, http://www.holysmoke.org/jtc-cri.txt (web address current as of October 13, 2005).

255.John Todd: Dividing the Brethren, http://www.holysmoke.org/jtc-cri.txt (web address current as of October 13, 2005).

256.Chuck Smith, Calvary Chapel Costa Mesa, Complete History, http://calvarychapelcostamesa.org/low/aboutus/complete history.php, (web address current as of October 15, 2005).   See also Chuck Smith, The History of Calvary Chapel, Last Times, Fall 1981, http://calvarychapelcostamesa.org/high/images/historyof calvary.pdf, (web address current as of October 15, 2005).

257.John Todd: Dividing the Brethren, http://www.holysmoke.org/jtc-cri.txt (web address current as of October 13, 2005).

258.FRITZ SPRINGMEIER, BLOODLINES OF THE ILLUMINATI, p. 75 (1999).

259.Spellbound, Angel of Light, and the Broken Cross, Chick Publications, http://www.chick.com/catalog/comiclist.asp, (web address current as of September 26, 2005). *See* http://www.holysmoke.org/jtc-jtc.txt for an explanation by Jack Chick on the methods used to discredit Todd.

260.Calvary Chapel Santa Rosa, http://www.calvarychapel.com/santarosa/links.html (web address current as of October 8, 2005).

261.Terry Watkins, Christian Rock, Blessing or Blasphemy, http://www.av1611.org/crock.html (web address current as of October 8, 2005).

262.Timeline of Trends in Music (1970-1979), http://en.wikipedia.org/wiki/1970s_in_music (web address current as of October 12, 2005).

263.Love Song, http://one-way.org/lovesong/music.htm (web address current as of October 13, 2005).

264.Love Song, http://one-way.org/lovesong/ (web address current as of October 8, 2005).

265.Love Song, http://one-way.org/lovesong/chuksong.htm (web address current as of October 8, 2005).

266.Love Song, http://one-way.org/lovesong/ (web address current as of October 8, 2005).

267.Love Song, http://one-way.org/lovesong/lovesong.htm (web address current as of October 8, 2005).

268.Erick Nelson, Recollections, Love Song, June 12, 1997 http://one-way.org/lovesong/ericknel.htm (web address current as of October 15, 2005).

269.Erick Nelson, Recollections, Love Song, June 12, 1997 http://one-way.org/lovesong/ericknel.htm (web address current as of October 15, 2005).

270.Erick Nelson, Recollections, Love Song, June 12, 1997 http://one-way.org/lovesong/ericknel.htm (web address current as of October 15, 2005).

271.Terry Watkins, Christian Rock, Blessing or Blasphemy, http://www.av1611.org/crock.html (web address current as of October 8, 2005).

272.Donald Phau, THE SATANIC ROOTS OF ROCK, http://www.av1611.org/othpubls/roots.html (web address current as of October 8, 2005).

273.Donald Phau, THE SATANIC ROOTS OF ROCK, http://www.av1611.org/othpubls/roots.html (web address current as of October 8, 2005).

274.Donald Phau, THE SATANIC ROOTS OF ROCK, http://www.av1611.org/othpubls/roots.html (web address current as of October 8, 2005).

275.Temple Mount Fanatics Foment a New Thirty Years' War, *Executive Intelligence Review,* November 3, 2000, http://www.larouchepub.com/other/2000/temple_mount_2743.html (web address current as of November 11, 2005).

276.Temple Mount Fanatics Foment a New Thirty Years' War, *Executive Intelligence Review,* November 3, 2000, http://www.larouchepub.com/other/2000/temple_mount_2743.html (web address current as of November 11, 2005).

277.Temple Mount Fanatics Foment a New Thirty Years' War, *Executive Intelligence Review,* November 3, 2000, http://www.larouchepub.com/other/2000/temple_mount_2743.html (web address current as of November 11, 2005).

278.Temple Mount Fanatics Foment a New Thirty Years' War, *Executive Intelligence Review,* November 3, 2000, http://www.larouchepub.com/other/2000/temple_mount

_2743.html (web address current as of November 11, 2005).

279.Arno Weinstein, In the Shadow of Stern: The Inside Story of a LEHI Intelligence Officer, B'tzedek, http://www.btzedek.com/focus/focus01.html (web address current as of November 11, 2005).

280.Arno Weinstein, In the Shadow of Stern: The Inside Story of a LEHI Intelligence Officer, B'tzedek, http://www.btzedek.com/focus/focus01.html (web address current as of November 11, 2005).

281.Evangelical Christians and the Building of the Temple, The Hebrew University of Jerusalem, http://sicsa.huji.ac.il/20Ariel.html (web address current as of November 11, 2005).

282.Evangelical Christians and the Building of the Temple, The Hebrew University of Jerusalem, http://sicsa.huji.ac.il/20Ariel.html (web address current as of November 11, 2005).

283.Evangelical Christians and the Building of the Temple, The Hebrew University of Jerusalem, http://sicsa.huji.ac.il/20Ariel.html (web address current as of November 11, 2005).

284.COLLIER'S ENCYCLOPEDIA, volume 12, p. 516 (1991).

285.SIDNEY HUNTER, IS ALBERTO FOR REAL?, p. 21 (1991); *see also,* EDMOND PARIS, THE SECRET HISTORY OF THE JESUITS, p. 35 (1975).

286.SIDNEY HUNTER, IS ALBERTO FOR REAL?, Chick Publications, p. 21-23 (1988).

287.See Generally William Guy Carr, PAWNS IN THE GAME, pp. 11-14, 104-07.

288.Anti-Zion, Jews on the Jewish Question, http://www.diac.com/~bkennedy/az/A-E.html (current as of September 10, 2001).

289.Ivan Fraser, Protocols of the Learned Elders of Zion, Proofs of an Ancient Conspiracy, http://www.vegan.swinternet.co.uk/articles/conspiracies/protocols_proof.html (current as of September 10, 2001).

290.ERIC JON PHELPS, VATICAN ASSASSINS: "WOUNDED IN THE HOUSE OF MY FRIENDS," P. 206 (2001).

291.WILLIAM STILL, NEW WORLD ORDER, The Ancient Plan of Secret Societies, p. 79 (1990).

292.MICHAEL BUNKER, SWARMS OF LOCUSTS, *The Jesuit Attack on the Faith,* pg. 22 (2002).

293.Teresa Morris, *Freemasons Roots & Links to the Occult,* http://www.crossroad.to/articles2/006/freemasons.htm, citing John Daniel, *Scarlet and the Beast,* Vol. I., pages 330-331). See also Iniquity Unveiled, Freemasonry and Order of Illuminati, http://www.biblebelievers.org.au/masonry5.htm (web address current as of April 17, 2004); Paul A. Fisher, *Their God is the Devil,* American Research Foundation, Inc., P.O. Box 5687, Baltimore, Maryland 21210, at p. 17 (1991).

294.David Allen Rivera, The Illuminati Leadership Changes, Final Warning: A History of the New World Order, http://www.the7thfire.com/new_world_order/final_warn

ing/illuminati_leadership_changes.htm (web address current as of April 17, 2004).

295.Herbert G. Dorsey III, The Historical Influence of International Banking, http://www.illuminati-news.com/international-banking.htm (web address current as of April 17, 2004).

296.ERIC JON PHELPS, VATICAN ASSASSINS: "WOUNDED IN THE HOUSE OF MY FRIENDS," p. 180 (2001).

297.ALBERT PIKE, MORALS AND DOGMA OF THE ANCIENT AND ACCEPTED SCOTTISH RITE OF FREEMASONRY, p. 741 (1871).

298.ALBERT PIKE, MORALS AND DOGMA OF THE ANCIENT AND ACCEPTED SCOTTISH RITE OF FREEMASONRY, p. 205 (1871).

299.DES GRIFFIN, THE FOURTH REICH OF THE RICH, p. 70 (1993).

300.WILLIAM STILL, NEW WORLD ORDER, The Ancient Plan of Secret Societies, pp. 81-91 (1990).

301.DES GRIFFIN, FOURTH REICH OF THE RICH, p. 62 (1976).

302.Id.

303.Id. at p. 59-62.

304.ERIC JON PHELPS, VATICAN ASSASSINS: "WOUNDED IN THE HOUSE OF MY FRIENDS," p. 167-77 (2001).

305.See Generally William Guy Carr, PAWNS IN THE GAME, pp.104-07.

306. See Generally William Guy Carr, PAWNS IN THE GAME, pp.104-07.

307. JOHN L. BRAY, MILLENNIUM - THE BIG QUESTION, P. 59 (1984) (quoting ERNEST R. SANDEEN, THE ROOTS OF FUNDAMENTALISM, p. 37 (1970)).

308. JOHN L. BRAY, MILLENNIUM - THE BIG QUESTION, P. 59 (1984) (quoting ERNEST R. SANDEEN, THE ROOTS OF FUNDAMENTALISM, p. 37 (1970)); WILLIAM R. KIMBALL, THE RAPTURE, A Question of Timing, p. 31 (1985) (OSWALD T. ALLIS, PROPHECY AND THE CHURCH, p. 297).

309. WILLIAM R. KIMBALL, THE RAPTURE, A Question of Timing, p. 31 (1985).

310. *Id.*

311. JOHN L. BRAY, MILLENNIUM - THE BIG QUESTION, P. 59 (1984) (quoting ERNEST R. SANDEEN, THE ROOTS OF FUNDAMENTALISM, p. 37 (1970)); WILLIAM R. KIMBALL, THE RAPTURE, A Question of Timing, p. 31 (1985) (OSWALD T. ALLIS, PROPHECY AND THE CHURCH, p. 297).

312. JOHN L. BRAY, MILLENNIUM - THE BIG QUESTION, P. 59 (1984) (quoting ERNEST R. SANDEEN, THE ROOTS OF FUNDAMENTALISM, p. 37 (1970)).

313. WILLIAM R. KIMBALL, THE RAPTURE, A Question of Timing, p. 31 (1985) (quoting LEROY E. FROOM, THE PROPHETIC FAITH OF OUR FATHERS, vol. 2, p. 495).

314.WILLIAM R. KIMBALL, THE RAPTURE, A Question of Timing, p. 32 (1985).

315.*Id.*

316.*Id.*

317.JOHN L. BRAY, MILLENNIUM - THE BIG QUESTION, p. 59 (1984) (quoting ERNEST R. SANDEEN, THE ROOTS OF FUNDAMENTALISM, p. 37 (1970)).

318.JOHN L. BRAY, THE ORIGIN OF THE PRETRIBULATION RAPTURE TEACHING, p. 12-13 (1982).

319.JOHN L. BRAY, THE ORIGIN OF THE PRETRIBULATION RAPTURE TEACHING, p. 4-9 (1982).

320.JOHN L. BRAY, MILLENNIUM - THE BIG QUESTION, P. 34 (1984).

321.Ivan Fraser, Protocols of the Learned Elders of Zion, Proofs of an Ancient Conspiracy, http://www.vegan.swinternet.co.uk/articles/conspiracies/ protocols_proof.html (current as of September 10, 2001).

322.Chuck Smith, THE TRIBULATION AND THE CHURCH, http://www.calvarychapel.org/library/smith-chuck/books /ttatc.htm (web address current as of November 11, 2005).

323.C.E. Carlson, The Zionist Created Scofield "bible," http://christianparty.net/scofield.htm (website address current as of August 9, 2003).

324.C.E. Carlson, The Zionist Created Scofield "bible,"
http://christianparty.net/scofield.htm (website address
current as of August 9, 2003).

325.C.E. Carlson, The Zionist Created Scofield "bible,"
http://christianparty.net/scofield.htm (website address
current as of August 9, 2003).

326.C.E. Carlson, The Zionist Created Scofield "bible,"
http://christianparty.net/scofield.htm (website address
current as of August 9, 2003).

327.CYRUS SCOFIELD -- WHO WAS HE? Excerpt
from "The Unified Conspiracy Theory,"
http://www.sweetliberty.org/issues/hoax/scofield.htm
(website address current as of August 9, 2003).

328.CYRUS SCOFIELD -- WHO WAS HE? Excerpt
from "The Unified Conspiracy Theory,"
http://www.sweetliberty.org/issues/hoax/scofield.htm
(website address current as of August 9, 2003).

329.C.E. Carlson, The Zionist Created Scofield "bible,"
http://christianparty.net/scofield.htm (website address
current as of August 9, 2003).

330.CYRUS SCOFIELD -- WHO WAS HE? Excerpt
from "The Unified Conspiracy Theory,"
http://www.sweetliberty.org/issues/hoax/scofield.htm
(website address current as of August 9, 2003).

331.CYRUS SCOFIELD -- WHO WAS HE? Excerpt
from "The Unified Conspiracy Theory,"
http://www.sweetliberty.org/issues/hoax/scofield.htm
(website address current as of August 9, 2003).

332.CYRUS SCOFIELD -- WHO WAS HE? Excerpt
from "The Unified Conspiracy Theory,"
http://www.sweetliberty.org/issues/hoax/scofield.htm

(website address current as of August 9, 2003).
Scofield: The Christian Leader With Feet of Clay,
http://www.virginiawater.co.uk/christchurch/articles/sco
field1.html (website address current as of August 9,
2003).

333.'Largest' Christian Publisher Zondervan, is a
Division of Harper Collins, which Publishes the Satanic
Bible, http://truthinheart.com/Zondervan.htm (web
address current as of October 8, 2005).

334.'Largest' Christian Publisher Zondervan, is a
Division of Harper Collins, which Publishes the Satanic
Bible, http://truthinheart.com/Zondervan.htm (web
address current as of October 8, 2005).

335.G. A. RIPLINGER, THE LANGUAGE OF THE
KING JAMES BIBLE, p. 128 (1998).

336.*Id.*

337.*Id.*

338.*Id.*

339.G.A. RIPLINGER, BLIND GUIDES, p. 19.

340.G.A. RIPLINGER, BLIND GUIDES, p. 19.

341.Will Kinney, Calvinism and the King James Bible,
http://www.scionofzion.com/calvinism_kjb.htm (web
address current as of October 9, 2005).

342.Will Kinney, Calvinism and the King James Bible,
http://www.scionofzion.com/calvinism_kjb.htm (web
address current as of October 9, 2005).

343.LES GARETT, WHICH BIBLE CAN WE
TRUST?, p. 16 (1982); *See also,* COLLIER'S

ENCYCLOPEDIA, volume 22, p. 563.

344.*Id.*

345.DR. LAWRENCE DUNEGAN, NEW ORDER OF
BARBARIANS (1990),
http://www.thewinds.org/library/order1.html (current as
of March 24, 2002).

346.G. A. RIPLINGER, NEW AGE BIBLE
VERSIONS, p. 141-148 (1993).

347.GERARDUS D. BOUW, GEOCENTRICITY, p.
120 (1992).

348.*Id.*

349.LES GARRETT, WHICH BIBLE CAN WE
TRUST?, p. 82 (1982).

350.*Id.*

351.SAMUEL C. GIPP, AN UNDERSTANDABLE
HISTORY OF THE BIBLE, p. 70 (1987).

352.*Id.*

353.*Id.* at p. 71.

354.*Id.* at p. 70.

355.*Id.* at p. 71.

356.*Id.* at p. 70.

357.*Id.* at p. 71.

358.*Id.*

359.*Id.* at p. 72.

360.LES GARRETT, WHICH BIBLE CAN WE TRUST?, p. 151 (1982).

361.LES GARRETT, WHICH BIBLE CAN WE TRUST?, p. 151 (1982).

362.LES GARRETT, WHICH BIBLE CAN WE TRUST?, p. 151 (1982).

363.G.A. RIPLINGER, NEW AGE BIBLE VERSIONS, p. 433 (1993), quoting DEAN BURGON, THE REVISION REVISED.

364.SAMUEL C. GIPP, AN UNDERSTANDABLE HISTORY OF THE BIBLE, p. 116-130 (1987).

365.*Id.*

366.*Id.* at 126-29.

367.*Id.* at 131-68.

368.*Id.*

369.*Id.*

370.*Id.*

371.*Id.*

372.*Id.*

373.*Id.* at p. 405.

374.*Id.* at p. 400.

375.*Id.*

376.*Id.* at p. 406.

377.G.A. RIPLINGER, NEW AGE BIBLE VERSIONS, p. 435 (1993).

378.*Id.*at p. 432.

379.G. A. RIPLINGER, THE LANGUAGE OF THE KING JAMES BIBLE, p. 66 (1998).

380.*Id.* at p. 132 (quoting *Carlo Martini, In the Thick of the Ministry,* p. 42, the Liturgical Press, Collegeville, Minn., 1990).

381.Luisa Kroll, Megachurches, Megabusinesses, Forbes, September 17, 2003.

382.Luisa Kroll, Megachurches, Megabusinesses, Forbes, September 17, 2003.

383.http://www.southeastchristian.org/preach_home.cfm (web address current as of October 22, 2005).

384.Bob Russell, "All I Want For Christmas Is… Someone To Rescue Me," www.southeastchristian.org/emplibrary/preach_Christm as_RescueMe.pdf (web address current as of October 22, 2005).

385.How You Can Be Born Again!, http://www.swrc.com/faith/bornagain.htm (web address current as of October 23, 2005).

386.How You Can Be Born Again!, http://www.swrc.com/faith/bornagain.htm (web address current as of October 23, 2005).

387.Terry Watkins, *Joel Osteen True or False,* http://www.av1611.org/osteen.html (web address current as of October 15, 2005).

388.Luisa Kroll, Megachurches, Megabusinesses, Forbes, September 17, 2003.

389.Archdiocese of Galveston-Houston, Statistics, http://www.diogh.org/about_stats.htm (web address current as of October 23, 2005).

390.Charismatic Priest-musician to Build Largest Church in Brazil, *Catholic World News*, August 2, 2004, http://cwnews.com/news/viewstory.cfm?recnum=31230, (web address current as of October 23, 2005).

391.Terry Watkins, *Joel Osteen True or False*, http://www.av1611.org/osteen.html (web address current as of October 15, 2005).

392.Terry Watkins, *Joel Osteen True or False*, http://www.av1611.org/osteen.html (web address current as of October 15, 2005). See also http://64.233.161.104/search?q=cache:g9xBLFq9UvIJ:www.joelosteen.com/site/PageServer%3Fpagename%3DLarryKingLetter+site:www.joelosteen.com. The immediately preceding web address is a cached page on Google of the original letter written and posted by Osteen on his website. Osteen has removed the letter from his website, so it is necessary to access it through the cached address.

393.Terry Watkins, *Joel Osteen True or False*, http://www.av1611.org/osteen.html (web address current as of October 15, 2005).

394.http://64.233.161.104/search?q=cache:g9xBLFq9UvIJ:www.joelosteen.com/site/PageServer%3Fpagename%3DLarryKingLetter+site:www.joelosteen.com. The immediately preceding web address is a cached page on Google of the original letter written and posted by

Osteen on his website. Osteen has removed the letter from his website, so it is necessary to access it through the cached address. See also Terry Watkins, *Joel Osteen True or False*, http://www.av1611.org/osteen.html (web address current as of October 15, 2005).

395.http://64.233.161.104/search?q=cache:g9xBLFq9U vIJ:www.joelosteen.com/site/PageServer%3Fpagename %3DLarryKingLetter+site:www.joelosteen.com. The immediately preceding web address is a cached page on Google of the original letter written and posted by Osteen on his website. Osteen has removed the letter from his website, so it is necessary to access it through the cached address. See also Terry Watkins, *Joel Osteen True or False*, http://www.av1611.org/osteen.html (web address current as of October 15, 2005).

396.http://www.bookschristian.com/sys/product.php?PR ODUCT=145708 (web address current as of October 16, 2005).

397.Heterodoxy Hall of Shame, http://www.outsidethecamp.org/heterodoxy52.htm (web address current as of October 16, 2005).

398.CATECHISM OF THE ROMAN CATHOLIC CHURCH § 847 (1994).

399.CATECHISM OF THE CATHOLIC CHURCH § 846 (1994) (emphasis added).

400.CATECHISM OF THE CATHOLIC CHURCH § 839 (1994) (footnotes omitted, internal quotation marks omitted).

401.CATECHISM OF THE CATHOLIC CHURCH § 846 (1994).

402.*McCalls Magazine*, January 1978.

403.DAVID O'BEALE, IN PURSUIT OF PURITY, p. 264 (1986). David W. Cloud, Way of Life Literature, Bible Baptist Church, 1701 Harns Rd., Oak Harbor, WA 98277; http://wayoflife.org/~dcloud/fbns/falwellandrome.htm.

404.*See generally,* ERROLL HULSE, BILLY GRAHAM - THE PASTOR'S DILEMMA (1966).

405.Michael Hoffman, *Judaism Discovered*, at 785 (2008).

406.Babylonian Talmud: Tractate 'Abodah Zarah, Folio 17a.

407.Babylonian Talmud: Tractate Sanhedrin Folio 106a.

408.Babylonian Talmud: Tractate Gittin Folio 57a.

409.Michael Hoffman, *Judaism Discovered*, at 357 (2008).

410.Michael Hoffman, *Judaism Discovered*, at 529 (2008) (quoting Roman A. Foxbrunner, *Habad: The Hasidism of Shneur of Lyady*, at 108-09 (1993) (quoting Rabbi Shneur Zalman)).

411.Michael Hoffman, *Judaism Discovered*, at 534 (2008).

412.Michael Hoffman, *Judaism Discovered*, at 382 (2008).

413.Babylonian Talmud: *Tractate Sanhedrin, Folio 90a,* Sanhedrin Translated into English with Notes, Glossary and Indices Chapters I - VI by Jacob Shachter, Chapters VII - XI by H. Freedman, B.A., Ph.D., Under the Editorship of Rabbi Dr I. Epstein B.A., Ph.D., D. Lit. (1961),

available at
http://www.come-and-hear.com/sanhedrin/sanhedrin_90
.html.

414.Babylonian Talmud: *Tractate Sanhedrin, Folio 90a,*
Sanhedrin Translated into English with Notes, Glossary
and Indices Chapters I - VI by Jacob Shachter, Chapters
VII - XI
by H. Freedman, B.A., Ph.D., Under the Editorship of
Rabbi Dr I. Epstein B.A., Ph.D., D. Lit. (1961),
available at
http://www.come-and-hear.com/sanhedrin/sanhedrin_90
.html.

415.Elizabeth Dilling, *The Jewish Religion, Its Influence
Today* (1963), *at*
http://www.come-and-hear.com/dilling/chapt03.html#Th
e_18_Benedictions.

416.http://www.rapidnet.com/~jbeard/bdm/exposes/grah
am/general.htm (site active as of July 17, 2001).

417.*O Timothy,* Vol. 10, Issue 9, 1993, pp. 16-17.

418.*The Lutheran Standard,* October 10, 1961.

419.http://www.cuttingedge.org/n1082.html (site active
as of July 17, 2001).

420.DES GRIFFIN, THE FOURTH REICH OF THE
RICH, p. 70 (1993).

421.WILLIAM R. KIMBALL, THE RAPTURE, A
Question of Timing, p. 52 (1985).

422.*Christianity Today,* February 21, 1986. David W.
Cloud, Way of Life Literature, Bible Baptist Church,
1701 Harns Rd., Oak Harbor, WA 98277;
http://wayoflife.org/~dcloud/fbns/falwellandrome.htm.

423.David W. Cloud, Way of Life Literature, Bible Baptist Church, 1701 Harns Rd., Oak Harbor, WA 98277; http://wayoflife.org/~dcloud/fbns/falwellandrome.htm.

424.Luisa Kroll, Megachurches, Megabusinesses, Forbes, September 17, 2003.

425.Church of the Mighty Dollar, *Business Week*, May 23, 2005, http://www.businessweek.com/magazine/content/05_21/b3934016_mz001.htm (web address current as of October 23, 2005).

426.Church of the Mighty Dollar, *Business Week*, May 23, 2005, http://www.businessweek.com/magazine/content/05_21/b3934016_mz001.htm (web address current as of October 23, 2005).

427.Creflo Dollar, http://www.gospelgrace.com/falseprophets/creflodollar/creflodollar.htm, (web address current as of October 22, 2005), quoting Creflo Dollar, Audio-Clip, "Creflo Dollar: Christian Celebrity or Charismatic Gnostic?" #0418.

428.Creflo Dollar, http://www.gospelgrace.com/falseprophets/creflodollar/creflodollar.htm, (web address current as of October 22, 2005), quoting Creflo Dollar, Audio clip from, "The Bible answer-man," Hank Hanegraaff July 10, 2003.

429.Creflo Dollar, http://www.gospelgrace.com/falseprophets/creflodollar/creflodollar.htm, (web address current as of October 22, 2005), quoting Creflo Dollar April 16, 2002 Changing Your World, Lesea Broadcasting.

430.T.D. Jakes, http://www.myfortress.org/TDJakes.html (web address current as of October 22, 2005).

431.G. Richard Fisher, "GET READY" FOR T.D. JAKES THE VELCRO BISHOP WITH ANOTHER GOSPEL, http://www.pfo.org/jakes.html, (web address current as of October 22, 2005), quoting Ken Walker, "Thunder From Heaven," Charisma magazine, November 1996, pg. 37.

432.T.D. Jakes, http://www.myfortress.org/TDJakes.html (web address current as of October 22, 2005).

433.Bishop T.D. Jakes' Statement on the Passing of Pope John Paul II, http://www.thepottershouse.org/_downloads/pr_200504 07_01.pdf (web address current as of October 29, 2005).

434.Luisa Kroll, Megachurches, Megabusinesses, Forbes, September 17, 2003.

435.T. D. Jakes, Bill Hybels, And Willow Creek Leadership Summit 2004, http://www.myfortress.org/Jakes-WillowCreek.html (web address current as of October 22, 2005).

436.Luisa Kroll, Megachurches, Megabusinesses, Forbes, September 17, 2003.

437.Nathan Busenitz, The Gospel According to Hybels & Warren, http://www.biblebb.com/files/gathw.htm (web address current as of October 22, 2005).

438.Kenneth Copeland, http://www.gospelgrace.com/falseprophets/kencopeland/ KennethCopeland.html (web address current as of October 22, 2005), quoting Following the Faith of

Abraham, side 1.

439.Kenneth Copeland, http://www.gospelgrace.com/falseprophets/kencopeland/ KennethCopeland.html (web address current as of October 22, 2005), quoting Kenneth Copeland, "Believer's Voice of Victory", Feb. 1987, p.9.

440.Kenneth Copeland, http://www.gospelgrace.com/falseprophets/kencopeland/ KennethCopeland.html (web address current as of October 22, 2005), quoting God's Covenants With Man II 1985, audiotape #01-4404, side 1.

441.Kenneth Copeland, http://www.gospelgrace.com/falseprophets/kencopeland/ KennethCopeland.html (web address current as of October 22, 2005), quoting Kenneth Copeland, "Believer's Voice of Victory" broadcast on TBN, recorded 7/9/87.

442.Kenneth Copeland, http://www.gospelgrace.com/falseprophets/kencopeland/ KennethCopeland.html (web address current as of October 22, 2005), quoting Praise-a-Thon program on TBN [April 1988].

443.The Points and Pitfalls of Calvinism, http://bibledefended.com/Calvinism/Irresistible%20Grac e.htm (last visited on October 21, 2011).

444.Greg Warner, *Calvinist Churches Targeted by Florida Baptist Convention*, Associated Baptist Press, June 7, 2007, http://www.abpnews.com/content/view/2568/120/.

445.Clarence Walker, Introduction, *The Trail Of Blood, Following the Christians Down Through the Centuries or The History of Baptist Churches From the Time of*

Christ, Their Founder,
to the Present Day by J. M. Carroll, Fundamental
Baptist Institute.
http://www.fbinstitute.com/trail/intro.htm (last visited
on October 27, 2011).

446.Clarence Walker, Introduction, *The Trail Of Blood,*
Following the Christians Down Through the Centuries
or The History of Baptist Churches From the Time of
Christ, Their Founder,
to the Present Day by J. M. Carroll, Fundamental
Baptist Institute.
http://www.fbinstitute.com/trail/intro.htm (last visited
on October 27, 2011).

447.J. M. Carroll, *The Trail Of Blood, Following the*
Christians Down Through the Centuries or The History
of Baptist Churches From the Time of Christ, Their
Founder,
to the Present Day,
http://www.biblepreaching.com/trailofblood.html (last
visited on October 27, 2011).

448.Founders Ministry, Committed to Historic Baptist
Principles, http://www.founders.org/info/about.html
(last visited on October 27, 2011).

449.Greg Warner, *Calvinist Churches Targeted by*
Florida Baptist Convention, Associated Baptist Press,
June 7, 2007,
http://www.abpnews.com/content/view/2568/120/.

450.Greg Warner, *Calvinist Churches Targeted by*
Florida Baptist Convention, Associated Baptist Press,
June 7, 2007,
http://www.abpnews.com/content/view/2568/120/.

587

451.Four Spiritual Laws English, Campus Crusade for Christ, http://www.campuscrusade.com/fourlawseng.htm (last visited on October 21, 2011).

452.Four Spiritual Laws English, Campus Crusade for Christ, http://www.campuscrusade.com/fourlawseng.htm (last visited on October 21, 2011).

453.Four Spiritual Laws English, Campus Crusade for Christ, http://www.campuscrusade.com/fourlawseng.htm (last visited on October 21, 2011).

454.Four Spiritual Laws English, Campus Crusade for Christ, http://www.campuscrusade.com/fourlawseng.htm (last visited on October 21, 2011).

455.Four Spiritual Laws English, Campus Crusade for Christ, http://www.campuscrusade.com/fourlawseng.htm (last visited on October 21, 2011).

456.Evangelicals and Catholics Together, The Christian Mission in the Third Millennium, http://www.leaderu.com/ftissues/ft9405/articles/mission.html (web address current as of October 27, 2005).

457.Heterodoxy Hall of Shame, Outside the Camp, vol.1, number 4, November 1997, http://www.outsidethecamp.org/heterodoxy14.htm.

458.William Birch, *Calvinism and Evangelistic Method*, Society of Evangelical Arminians, http://evangelicalarminians.org/birch.Calvinism-and-Evangelistic-Method (last visited on October 27, 2011).

459.William Birch, *Calvinism and Evangelistic Method*, Society of Evangelical Arminians, April 19, 2011, http://evangelicalarminians.org/birch.Calvinism-and-Eva ngelistic-Method.

460.Evangelicals and Catholics Together, The Christian Mission in the Third Millennium, http://www.leaderu.com/ftissues/ft9405/articles/mission. html (web address current as of October 27, 2005).

461.Evangelicals and Catholics Together, The Christian Mission in the Third Millennium, http://www.leaderu.com/ftissues/ft9405/articles/mission. html (web address current as of October 27, 2005).

462.Evangelicals and Catholics Together, The Christian Mission in the Third Millennium, http://www.leaderu.com/ftissues/ft9405/articles/mission. html (web address current as of October 27, 2005).

463.Evangelicals and Catholics Together, The Christian Mission in the Third Millennium, http://www.leaderu.com/ftissues/ft9405/articles/mission. html (web address current as of October 27, 2005).

464.Evangelicals and Catholics Together, The Christian Mission in the Third Millennium, http://www.leaderu.com/ftissues/ft9405/articles/mission. html (web address current as of October 27, 2005).

465.Joe Maxwell, Evangelicals Clarify Accord with Catholics, http://www.leaderu.com/ect/ect3.html (web address current as of November 11, 2005).

466.Dr. Bill Bright, Founder and President Campus Crusade for Christ International, *Why I Decided To Become A Signatory on the Document, "Evangelicals And Catholics Together: The Christian Mission In The Third Millennium,"* http://www.leaderu.com/ect/ect1.html (web address current as of October 20, 2005).

467.Dr. Bill Bright, Founder and President Campus Crusade for Christ International, *Why I Decided To Become A Signatory on the Document, "Evangelicals And Catholics Together: The Christian Mission In The Third Millennium,"* http://www.leaderu.com/ect/ect1.html (web address current as of October 20, 2005).

468.Dr. Bill Bright, Founder and President Campus Crusade for Christ International, *Why I Decided To Become A Signatory on the Document, "Evangelicals And Catholics Together: The Christian Mission In The Third Millennium,"* http://www.leaderu.com/ect/ect1.html (web address current as of October 20, 2005).

469.Dr. Bill Bright, Founder and President Campus Crusade for Christ International, *Why I Decided To Become A Signatory on the Document, "Evangelicals And Catholics Together: The Christian Mission In The Third Millennium,"* http://www.leaderu.com/ect/ect1.html (web address current as of October 20, 2005).

470.Dr. Bill Bright, Founder and President Campus Crusade for Christ International, *Why I Decided To Become A Signatory on the Document, "Evangelicals And Catholics Together: The Christian Mission In The Third Millennium,"* http://www.leaderu.com/ect/ect1.html (web address current as of October 20, 2005).

471.THE RANDOM HOUSE DICTIONARY OF THE ENGLISH LANGUAGE, unabridged edition, 1973.

472.*Id.* at § 716b.

473.*Id.* at § 717.

474.RALPH E. WOODROW, BAYLON MYSTERY RELIGION, p. 22, 1966.

475.CATECHISM OF THE CATHOLIC CHURCH, § 2675-2679, 1994.

476.Salvation is Obtained From . . . Mary?, http://www.aloha.net/~mikesch/mary.htm (web address current as of April 3, 2005), quoting Arthur Burton Calkins, TOTUS TUUS, pp.21, 27, Academy of the Immaculate, New Bedford, Massachusetts, ISBN 0-9635345-0-5, Nihil Obstat and Imprimatur of the Catholic Church.

477.Salvation is Obtained From . . . Mary?, http://www.aloha.net/~mikesch/mary.htm (web address current as of April 3, 2005), quoting Arthur Burton Calkins, TOTUS TUUS, pp.21, 27, Academy of the Immaculate, New Bedford, Massachusetts, ISBN 0-9635345-0-5, Nihil Obstat and Imprimatur of the Catholic Church.

478.The Rosary, Roses of Prayer for The Queen of Heaven, Daniel A. Lord, S.J., Nihil Obstat Athur J. Scanlan S.T.D: Censor Liborum, Imprimatur + Francis J. Spellman, D.D. Archbishop, New York, http://www.truecatholic.org/rosary.htm (web address current as of March 20, 2005).

479.COLLIER'S ENCYCLOPEDIA, volume 20, p. 169 (1991).

480.G.A. RIPLINGER, NEW AGE BIBLE VERSIONS, p. 133 (1993).

481.*E.g., CATECHISM OF THE CATHOLIC CHURCH,*
§§ 105, 1141,1163, 1203, 1249, 1667 (1997),
http://www.scborromeo.org/index2.htm (web address
current as of March 22, 2005).

482.The Rosary, Roses of Prayer for The Queen of
Heaven, Daniel A. Lord, S.J., Nihil Obstat Athur J.
Scanlan S.T.D: Censor Liborum, Imprimatur + Francis
J. Spellman, D.D. Archbishop, New York,
http://www.truecatholic.org/rosary.htm (web address
current as of March 20, 2005).

483.Rosary Meditations,
http://www.cfalive.org/ReadRosary.htm (web address
current as of March 20, 2005).

484.Prayer to Mary, Queen of Heaven,
http://www.catholic-forum.com/saints/pray0421.htm
(web address current as of March 20, 2005).

485.J.NEUNER, S.J & J. DUPUIS, S.J., THE
CHRISTIAN FAITH IN THE DOCTRINAL
DOCUMENTS OF THE CATHOLIC CHURCH, PIUS
X, ENCYCLICAL LETTER *AD DIEM* § 712 (6th ed.
1996).

486.J.NEUNER, S.J & J. DUPUIS, S.J., THE
CHRISTIAN FAITH IN THE DOCTRINAL
DOCUMENTS OF THE CATHOLIC CHURCH, THE
SECOND VATICAL COUNCIL, DOGMATIC
CONSTITUTION *LUMEN GENTIUM,* § 716a (6th ed.
1996).

487.CATECHISM OF THE CATHOLIC CHURCH, §
2679, 1994.

488.J.NEUNER, S.J & J. DUPUIS, S.J., THE
CHRISTIAN FAITH IN THE DOCTRINAL
DOCUMENTS OF THE CATHOLIC CHURCH, THE

592

SECOND VATICAL COUNCIL, DOGMATIC
CONSTITUTION *LUMEN GENTIUM*, § 718a (6th ed.
1996).

489.*Id.* at § 718b.

490.CATECHISM OF THE CATHOLIC CHURCH, §
2677, 1994.

491.J.NEUNER, S.J & J. DUPUIS, S.J., THE
CHRISTIAN FAITH IN THE DOCTRINAL
DOCUMENTS OF THE CATHOLIC CHURCH, THE
SECOND VATICAL COUNCIL, DOGMATIC
CONSTITUTION *LUMEN GENTIUM*, § 716a (6th ed.
1996).

492.J.NEUNER, S.J & J. DUPUIS, S.J., THE
CHRISTIAN FAITH IN THE DOCTRINAL
DOCUMENTS OF THE CATHOLIC CHURCH, § 713,
PIUS XII, APOSTOLIC CONSTITUTION,
MUNIFICENTISSIMUS DEUS (6th ed. 1996).

493.J.NEUNER, S.J & J. DUPUIS, S.J., THE
CHRISTIAN FAITH IN THE DOCTRINAL
DOCUMENTS OF THE CATHOLIC CHURCH, § 716a
(6th ed. 1996).

494.Edward Hendrie, *Solving the Mystery of BABYLON
THE GREAT*, at 26-27, 209-212, 232 (2011).

495.Athol Bloomer, *The Eucharist and The Jewish
Mystical Tradition* • *Part 3*, Association of Hebrew
Catholics, *at*
http://hebrewcatholic.org/HCLives/Bloomer-Athol/euch
aristandjewi.html, (originally published in The Hebrew
Catholic #80 (Spring/Summer 2004)).

496.Daniel Chanan Matt, *Zohar, The Book of
Enlightenment*, at 132 (1983), *at*

http://books.google.com/.

497.Kabbalah, Jewish Virtual Library,
http://www.jewishvirtuallibrary.org/jsource/judaica/ejud
_0002_0011_0_10514.html (last visited on March 3,
2010).

498.Aharon Yosef, A Catholic Jew Pontificates, *Miriam
ha Kedosha the Lady Moon of Israel*, January 10, 2008,
at
http://aronbengilad.blogspot.com/2008/01/miriam-haked
osha-lady-moon-of-israel.html.

499.Michael Hoffman, *Judaism Discovered*, at 269
(2008).

500.*Id.* at § 709.

501.ORDERED BY THE COUNCIL OF TRENT,
EDITED UNDER ST. CHARLES BORROMEO,
PUBLISHED BY DECREE OF POPE ST. PIUS V,
1566, TAN Books, 1982 at p. 233.

502.PETER J. ELLIOTT, CEREMONIES OF THE
MODERN ROMAN RITE, Ignatius Press, § 663, p. 245
(1994).

503.PETER J. ELLIOTT, CEREMONIES OF THE
MODERN ROMAN RITE, Ignatius Press, p. 264
(1994).

504.Statement by Protestant Signers to ECT, January 19,
1995, http://www.leaderu.com/ect/ect2.html (web
address current as of November 11, 2005).

505.John Robbins, The Gift of Salvation Show, Healing
the Wound,
http://www.the-highway.com/robbins_show.html (web
address current as of October 27, 2005).

506.The Gift of Salvation, http://www.firstthings.com/ftissues/ft9801/articles/gift.html (web address current as of November 7, 2005).

507.John Robbins, The Gift of Salvation Show, Healing the Wound, http://www.the-highway.com/robbins_show.html (web address current as of October 27, 2005).

508.John Robbins, The Gift of Salvation Show, Healing the Wound, http://www.the-highway.com/robbins_show.html (web address current as of October 27, 2005).

509.John Robbins, The Gift of Salvation Show, Healing the Wound, http://www.the-highway.com/robbins_show.html (web address current as of October 27, 2005).

510.John Robbins, The Gift of Salvation Show, Healing the Wound, http://www.the-highway.com/robbins_show.html (web address current as of October 27, 2005).

511.Richard Bennett, The Gift of Salvation: (ECT 11) - The Lie Documented, http://www.bereanbeacon.org/articles/gift_of_salvation.htm (web address current as of November 5, 2005).

512.Richard Bennett, The Gift of Salvation: (ECT 11) - The Lie Documented, http://www.bereanbeacon.org/articles/gift_of_salvation.htm (web address current as of November 5, 2005).

513.Richard Bennett, The Gift of Salvation: (ECT 11) - The Lie Documented, http://www.bereanbeacon.org/articles/gift_of_salvation.htm (web address current as of November 5, 2005).

514.Richard Bennett, The Gift of Salvation: (ECT 11) -
The Lie Documented,
http://www.bereanbeacon.org/articles/gift_of_salvation.
htm (web address current as of November 5, 2005).

515.Richard Bennett, The Gift of Salvation: (ECT 11) -
The Lie Documented,
http://www.bereanbeacon.org/articles/gift_of_salvation.
htm (web address current as of November 5, 2005).

516.Richard Bennett, The Gift of Salvation: (ECT 11) -
The Lie Documented,
http://www.bereanbeacon.org/articles/gift_of_salvation.
htm (web address current as of November 5, 2005).

517.John Robbins, The Gift of Salvation Show, Healing
the Wound,
http://www.the-highway.com/robbins_show.html (web
address current as of October 27, 2005).

518.John Robbins, The Gift of Salvation Show, Healing
the Wound,
http://www.the-highway.com/robbins_show.html (web
address current as of October 27, 2005).

519.John Robbins, The Gift of Salvation Show, Healing
the Wound,
http://www.the-highway.com/robbins_show.html (web
address current as of October 27, 2005).

520.John W. Robbins, *Healing the Mortal Wound*, The
Trinity Foundation,
http://www.trinityfoundation.org/journal.php?id=146
(last visited on October 13, 2011).

521.The Gift of Salvation,
http://www.firstthings.com/ftissues/ft9801/articles/gift.h
tml (web address current as of November 7, 2005).

522.Edward Hendrie, *Solving the Mystery of BABYLON THE GREAT* (2011), www.mysterybabylonthegreat.net.

523.NESTA WEBSTER, SECRET SOCIETIES AND SUBVERSIVE MOVEMENTS, http://web.archive.org/web/20021005055527/http://www.plausiblefutures.com/text/SS.html (website address current as of 2-28-05) (citing Lexicon of Freemasonry, p. 323).

524.MICHAEL A. HOFFMAN, JUDAISM'S STRANGE GODS, at p. 88, (2000).

525.MICHAEL A. HOFFMAN, JUDAISM'S STRANGE GODS, at p. 88, (2000).

526.MICHAEL A. HOFFMAN, JUDAISM'S STRANGE GODS, at p. 91, (2000).

527.MICHAEL A. HOFFMAN, JUDAISM'S STRANGE GODS, at p. 92, (2000).

528.Michael L. Rodkinson: The History of the Talmud; http://www.come-and-hear.com/talmud/rodkin_ii3.html#E27 (web address current as of February 8, 2004).

529.Judaism vs. Christianity: The War The Lamb Wins, http://www.fixedearth.com/talmud.html (current as of September 11, 2001).

530.THE JEWISH ENCYCLOPEDIA, vol. V, p. 619 (1901-1906).

531.Elizabeth Dilling, THE JEWISH RELIGION: Its Influence Today, chapter IV, p. 41 (1964).

532.Judaism vs. Christianity: The War The Lamb Wins, http://www.fixedearth.com/talmud.html (current as of September 11, 2001).

533.DONN DE GRAND PRE, BARBARIANS INSIDE THE GATES, THE BLACK BOOK OF BOLSHEVISM, p. 209 (2000) (quoting BEJAMIN FREEDMAN, FACTS ARE FACTS (1954)).

534.*Israeli Youths Burn New Testaments*, USA Today, May 21, 2008, *at* http://www.usatoday.com/news/religion/2008-05-21-jew ish-new-testament_N.htm.

535.*Israeli Youths Burn New Testaments*, USA Today, May 21, 2008, *at* http://www.usatoday.com/news/religion/2008-05-21-jew ish-new-testament_N.htm.

536.John S. Torell, European-American Evangelical Association, July 1999, http://www.eaec.org/NL99jul.htm (current as of October 2, 2001).

537.John S. Torell, European-American Evangelical Association, July 1999, http://www.eaec.org/NL99jul.htm (current as of October 2, 2001).

538.John S. Torell, European-American Evangelical Association, July 1999, http://www.eaec.org/NL99jul.htm (current as of October 2, 2001).

539.Melinda Henneberger, *Vatican Says Jews' Wait for Messiah Is Validated by the Old Testament, New York Times,* January 18, 2002, http://www.hughhewitt.com/past_news_links_01.02/01. 18.02.Vatican_Says_Wait_for_Messiah.html (Current as of February 10, 2002).

540.Michael Hoffman II, Secret Societies and Psychological Warfare, at p. 75 (2001).

541.Michael Hoffman II, Secret Societies and Psychological Warfare, at p. 75 (2001).

542.CATECHISM OF THE CATHOLIC CHURCH, §§ 1579-1580 (1994).

543.*See* CATECHISM OF THE CATHOLIC CHURCH, §§ 540, 1438, 2043 (1994).

544.CATECHISM OF THE CATHOLIC CHURCH, § 1413, 1994.

545.CATECHISM OF THE CATHOLIC CHURCH, § 1374, 1994 (italics in original).

546.THE CATECHISM OF THE COUNCIL OF TRENT. ORDERED BY THE COUNCIL OF TRENT, EDITED UNDER ST. CHARLES BORROMEO, PUBLISHED BY DECREE OF POPE ST. PIUS V, 1566, TAN Books, 1982 at p. 233.

547.ORDERED BY THE COUNCIL OF TRENT, EDITED UNDER ST. CHARLES BORROMEO, PUBLISHED BY DECREE OF POPE ST. PIUS V, 1566, TAN Books, p. 258, 1982.

548.CATECHISM OF THE CATHOLIC CHURCH, § 168 (1994).

549.Dennis Costella, Baptismal Regeneration and Bible Salvation, http://www.fundamentalbiblechurch.org/Tracts/fbcbaptr.htm (web address current as of November 9, 2005).

550.COUNCIL OF TRENT, SESSION VI, DECREE ON JUSTIFICATION, Canons XXIV & XXX, January 13, 1547.

551.Dennis Costella, Baptismal Regeneration and Bible Salvation, http://www.fundamentalbiblechurch.org/Tracts/fbcbaptr. htm (web address current as of November 9, 2005).

552.*See* CHINIQUY, THE PRIEST, THE WOMAN, AND THE CONFESSIONAL, Chick Publications.

553.ORDERED BY THE COUNCIL OF TRENT, EDITED UNDER ST. CHARLES BORROMEO, PUBLISHED BY DECREE OF POPE ST. PIUS V, 1566, TAN Books, p. 331, 1982.

554.JAMES R. WHITE, THE ROMAN CATHOLIC CONTROVERSY, p. 187, 1996 (quoting *Indulgentiarum Doctrina,* January 1, 1967).

555.AVRO MANHATTAN, THE VATICAN BILLIONS, Chick Publications (1983).

556.DAVE HUNT, A WOMAN RIDES THE BEAST, p. 240 (1994).

557.*Id.* at 239.

558.*Id.*

559.*Id.* at 240.

560.AVRO MANHATTAN, THE VATICAN BILLIONS, p. 184 (1983).

561.*Id.*

562.*Id.* at p. 184.

563.*Id* at 185.

564.Jack Chick, SMOKESCREENS,
http://www.acts2.com/thebibletruth/Online%20Books/S
MOKESCREENS.pdf (web address current as of
September 23, 2003).

565.*Id.* at 187.

566.*Id.* at p. 188.

567.*Id.* at p. 188.

568.*Id.* at p. 178-179.

569.DAVE HUNT, A WOMAN RIDES THE BEAST,
p.241 (1994).

570.AVRO MANAHATTAN, THE VATICAN
BILLIONS, Chick Publications, p.41 (1983).

571.CATECHISM OF THE CATHOLIC CHURCH, §
1471-73 (1994).

572.*Id.* at § 1471.

573.AVRO MANAHATTAN, THE VATICAN
BILLIONS, Chick Publications, p.183 (1983).

574.*Id.* at p. 57-65.

575.PETER J. ELLIOTT, CEREMONIES OF THE
MODERN ROMAN RITE, Ignatius Press, § 369, p. 135
(1994).

576.RALPH E. WOODROW, BABYLON MYSTERY
RELIGION, p. 61 (1966).

577.The Gift of Salvation,
http://www.firstthings.com/ftissues/ft9801/articles/gift.h
tml (web address current as of November 7, 2005).

578.JOHN L. BRAY, THE MAN OF SIN OF II THESSALONIANS 2, p. 8 (1997) (Incidentally, Bray does not believe that the pope of Rome is the man of sin mentioned in II Thessalonians 2. He quotes from some of the traditional Protestant confessions of faith only to explain the historical Protestant view. While his survey of the historical confessions of faith is accurate, he is wrong regarding his conclusion about the pope.).

579.*Id.* at § 881-882.

580.ALBERTO RIVERA, DOUBLE CROSS, Chick publications, p. 27, 1981(quoting THE GREAT ENCYCLICAL LETTERS OF POPE LEO XIII, p. 304, Benziger Brothers (1903).

581.AVRO MANAHATTAN, THE VATICAN BILLIONS, Chick Publications, p.183 (1983).

582.AVRO MANAHATTAN, THE VATICAN BILLIONS, Chick Publications, p.41 (1983).

583.ALBERTO RIVERA, THE GODFATHERS, Chick Publications, p. 32, 1982 (quoting The Registers of Boniface VIII, The Vatican Archives, L. Fol. 387 and THE CATHOLIC ENCYCLOPEDIA, Encyclopedia Press (1913)).

584.RALPH E. WOODROW, BABYLON MYSTERY RELIGION, p. 72, 1966.

585.COLLIER'S ENCYCLOPEDIA, volume 19, p. 239 (1991).

586.ALBERTO RIVERA, THE GODFATHERS, Chick Publications, p. 32, 1982 (quoting The Registers of Boniface VIII, The Vatican Archives, L. Fol. 387 and THE CATHOLIC ENCYCLOPEDIA, Encyclopedia Press (1913)).

587.NOAH WEBSTER, AMERICAN DICTIONARY OF THE ENGLISH LANGUAGE (1st ed. 1828) republished by Foundation for American Christian Education, San Francisco, California.

588.Oxford University Press (1979).

589.*Id.* at p. 6.

590.CATECHISM OF THE CATHOLIC CHURCH, § 963 (1994).

591.NOAH WEBSTER, AMERICAN DICTIONARY OF THE ENGLISH LANGUAGE (1st ed. 1828) republished by Foundation for American Christian Education, San Francisco, California.

592.COLLIER'S ENCYCLOPEDIA, volume 20, p. 169 (1991).

593.G.A. RIPLINGER, NEW AGE BIBLE VERSIONS, p. 133 (1993).

594.COLLIER'S ENCYCLOPEDIA, volume 20, p. 169 (1991).

595.G.A. RIPLINGER, NEW AGE BIBLE VERSIONS, p. 133 (1993).

596.*E.g., CATECHISM OF THE CATHOLIC CHURCH*, §§ 105, 1141,1163, 1203, 1249, 1667 (1997), http://www.scborromeo.org/index2.htm (web address current as of March 22, 2005).

CPSIA information can be obtained at www.ICGtesting.com
Printed in the USA
LVOW01s0700020214

371926LV00003B/48/P